CORRECTIONS AND THE CRIMINAL JUSTICE SYSTEM

Laws, Policies, and Practices

THOMAS F. COURTLESS

GEORGE WASHINGTON UNIVERSITY

WEST/WADSWORTH PUBLISHING COMPANY

I(T)P® an International Thomson Publishing Company

Belmont, CA • Albany, NY • Bonn • Boston • Cincinnati • Detroit
Johannesburg • London • Los Angeles • Madrid • Melborne
Mexico City • New York • Paris • Singapore • Tokyo • Toronto • Washington

Assistant Editor	Claire Masson
Senior Editorial Assistant	Kate Barrett
Marketing Manager	Mike Dew
Production	Ruth Cottrell/Jayne Lindesmith
Copy Editor	Sheryl Rose
Designer	Diane Beasley
Print Buyer	Karen Hunt
Permissions	Peggy Meehan
Cover Designer	Sandy Drooker
Compositor	Parkwood Composition
Printer	Courier Kendallville, Inc.

Credits: see page xxi.

Printed in the United States of America
1 2 3 4 5 6 7 8 9 10

International Thomson Publishing Europe
Berkshire House 168-173
High Holborn
London, WC1V 7AA, England

Thomas Nelson Australia
102 Dodds Street
South Melbourne 3205
Victoria, Australia

Nelson Canada
1120 Birchmount Road
Scarborough, Ontario
Canada M1K 5G4

International Thomson Publishing GmbH
Königswinterer Strasse 418
53227 Bonn, Germany

International Thomson Editores
Campos Eliseos 385, Piso 7
Col. Polanco
11560 México D. F. México

International Thomson Publishing Asia
221 Henderson Road
#05-10 Henderson Building
Singapore 0315

International Thomson Publishing Japan
Hirakawacho Kyowa Building, 3F
2-2-1 Hirakawacho
Chiyoda-ku, Tokyo 102, Japan

International Thomson Publishing Southern Africa
Building 18, Constantia Park
240 Old Pretoria Road
Halfway House, 1685 South Africa

For more information, contact Wadsworth Publishing Company, 10 Davis Drive, Belmont, CA 94002, or electronically at
http://www.thomson.com/wadsworth.html

LIBRARY OF CONGRESS CATALOGING-IN-PUBLICATION DATA
Courtless, Thomas F.
    Corrections and the criminal justice system: law, policies, and practices / Thomas F. Courtless
        p. cm.
    Includes index.
    ISBN 0-314-20187-4 (soft: alk. paper)
    1. Prison administration—United States. 2. Criminal Justice, Administration of—United States. 3. Correctional
personnel—United States. I. Title.
HV9469.C69 1997
365' .973—dc20   96-26551

 This book is printed on acid-free recycled paper.

TO

JANE LLOYD COURTLESS

who let me be me, even during all this.

BRIEF CONTENTS

DETAILED CONTENTS

CRIMINAL JUSTICE, CRIMINAL SANCTIONS, AND CORRECTIONS   93

PART II

PART III   CORRECTIONS IN THE COMMUNITY   239

11   PROBATION

12   PAROLE   263

13   COMMUNITY SERVICE AND RESTITUTION   292

14   COMMUNITY-BASED CORRECTIONS   313

THE STATUS OF CORRECTIONS TODAY AND FORECASTING PART V
ITS FUTURE   385

17   CORRECTIONS TODAY AND TOMORROW   386

PREFACE

Corrections in the United States is in a state of crisis. Prison overcrowding is a major problem facing state and federal lawmakers, judges, administrators, and frontline staff of our correctional institutions and programs. There is confusion and contradiction besetting the operation of the many segments of correctional systems. Changes in sentencing laws and patterns have added to the current crisis in corrections.

Readers are encouraged to examine carefully the many strategies employed by agents of American society to "correct" offenders. Consistencies as well as inconsistencies in goals to be served by correctional sanctions will be exposed for inspection.

- **The Central Theme.** Throughout the text, the systemic nature of criminal justice is highlighted. The reader is encouraged to analyze critically corrections as an integral part of the overall system of criminal justice. Changes in goals, scope, and application of sentencing laws, for example, are shown to have significant and often unintended consequences for corrections.

  Through this text we seek to survey the corrections field, placing it squarely in the context of American criminal law and the criminal justice system. More attention will be devoted to the law of corrections than is the case with many current texts. Thus, issues such as sentencing procedures, proportionality of sentences, cruel and unusual punishments, and prisoners' rights will be highlighted. Changes over time in law as they affect corrections will be presented and analyzed.

- **Chapter Organization.** Each chapter begins with an introduction to the material to be covered. This is followed by a thorough presentation of the major topics, and evaluation of corrections' performance in relation to the objectives of various sanctions and programs, a summary of the main points presented, a list of the chapter's key concepts, and a set of discussion questions.

- **Special Features.** Each chapter contains a number of special features to illustrate significant points, and to aid the reader to critically evaluate corrections in American criminal justice. These special features include the following:

  - *On the Job.* This feature illustrates specific sanctions and correctional programs from the perspective of those actually working in the field.

  - *Focus on the Law.* These features in each chapter deal with important legal issues affecting corrections. In some of these features, appellate court decisions are presented. In others, provisions from statutes and rules of procedure are examined.

  - *Across Cultures.* In each chapter one or more "Across Cultures" features are provided so the reader can understand how correctional policy and practice in other cultures compares with the American experience. Cultures represented range from the former Soviet Union to China, Japan, New Zealand, Great Britain, the Netherlands, and Indonesia.

Chapter Seven, "The Prison as Hospital: A Case History of a Troubled Experiment," is unique in that it will use the history of one special state prison as a case study. This prison illustrates the many twists and turns in American correctional policies as those policies have been bent over time by the winds of change in laws and policies. This case study is especially significant because it illustrates how, via the enactment of an unusual sentencing statute, one state tried to incorporate rehabilitation as a major objective in its correctional system.

- **Other Pedagogical Features.** Other features that are designed to assist in the classroom are:
  - A list of *Key Terms* at the end of each chapter.
  - A set of *"Questions for Discussion"* at the end of each chapter. These may be used to stimulate classroom participation by students and to suggest essay questions for examinations.
  - A *Glossary* of important terms contained in an appendix.
  - A *"Careers in Correction"* section is provided in an appendix. This contains a brief statement of the many employment opportunities in both institutional and community-based corrections. For each state and the federal system, a listing of addresses and telephone numbers is provided so that students may make direct contact for employment requirements and openings.
  - A *Table of Cases*. This lists the major appellate court cases discussed throughout the book, with appropriate legal citations. The location of each case in the text is given for quick reference by the reader.

ACKNOWLEDGMENTS

I must especially thank a number of very helpful and professional persons at West Publishing. Joseph Terry, until recently, my editor. He encouraged me to begin the book, and for two years kept up a steady stream of supportive comments. These were particularly welcome during those episodes of discouragement when chapters seemed to be impossible to finish.

Following Joe, Sharon Adams Poore took me on as editor, and has seen me through to the end. While at times I thought her to be a particularly hard taskmaster, she, like Joe, was consistently helpful, encouraging, and good humored.

I also extend my thanks to Jayne Lindesmith, my production editor. She worked with me through all the modifications necessary to the copy edited text, and, later, galleys of the various chapters. When I felt that the project would never be completed, she always provided the right kind of lift I needed. Jayne and Sharon had the ability to make me laugh at just the right time. Then, I could get on with the work in a much better frame of mind.

Joseph Terry, Sharon Adams Poore, and Jayne Lindesmith frequently told me that I was a very easy-to-work-with author. They, without doubt, were the easiest and most helpful editors with whom to work.

Dr. Donald Atkinson of the Maryland Division of Probation and Parole and staff of the Division of Corrections were helpful in providing me listings of correctional opportunities.

I would like to express my appreciation to Elaine Douglas, Executive Aide in the Sociology Department of the George Washington University. Elaine made certain that I got out the chapter drafts on time, and was helpful with copying, and accessing the library consortium, and when I was unable to get to the library, she took time to go and check references that were not on the computer system.

This work would not have been possible without the constructive reviews of the draft chapters. The reviewers came from faculties in universities, colleges, and community colleges throughout the country. They include:

Glenn J. Abraham
The University of Dayton

Karran Baird-Olsen
Kansas State University

Robert Bing
The University of Texas at Arlington

Mary Brewster
West Chester University

Susan Brinkley
The University of Tampa

David Cary
Mary Baldwin College

Hugh Cassidy
Adelphi University

Gregory Clark
McNeese State University

B. Keith Crew
The University of Northern Iowa

Francis Crowe
Ferris State University

Robert Fitch
Penn State University

Kenneth W. Gallagher
The University of Nebraska at Omaha

Gerald R. Garrett
The University of Massachusetts at Boston

Kenneth C. Haas
The University of Delaware

William E. Harver
The University of Delaware

Philip Holley
Southwest Texas State University

Pamela Irving Jackson
Rhode Island College

Joseph Jacoby
Bowling Green State University

James Jengeleski
Shippensburg University

Jerry Jolly
Lewis-Clark State College

Gary N. Keveles
The University of Wisconsin-Superior

Harvey Kushner
Long Island University-CW Post Campus

JoAnne Lecci
Nassua Community College

Jams Marquart
Sam Houston State University

Johnette McCracken
West Liberty State College

Linda O'Daniel
The University of Texas-Pan American

E. Mario Pietrucci
Seminole Community College

Charles S. Purgavie
Ocean County College

Glenn Schleve
Eastern Wyoming College

Georgia Smith
Jacksonville State University

John R. Stratton
The University of Iowa

Zoanne Synder-Joy
Western Michigan University

Richard Tewksbury
The University of Louisville

Donald B. Walker
Kent State University

Bill Wakefield
The University of Nebraska at Omaha

Gary L. Webb
Ball State University

ABOUT THE AUTHOR

THOMAS F. COURTLESS is Professor of Law, Sociology, and Forensic Science at the George Washington University in Washington, D.C. He was awarded a Fulbright Visiting Professorship of Criminal Law and Criminology at Indonesia's Airlangga University. He served as a correctional social services officer in the State of Maryland for five years. In this capacity, he worked as a group counselor, aftercare agent, and conducted prison admissions and social history interviews of inmates and their families. Later, he was appointed Chairman of the Maryland Citizens' Advisory Board for the state's Patuxent Institution, and served on the Secretary of Public Safety and Correctional Services Prison Task Force on Patuxent Institution. He earned a bachelor's degree from the Pennsylvania State University, and master's and Ph.D. degrees in sociology from the University of Maryland. He is co-author of Criminal Law, Criminology, and Criminal Justice, *and author of* Introduction to Criminal Law: Appellate Cases and Commentaries, *as well as numerous articles in juvenile justice, corrections, and the criminal justice-mental health area.*

PHOTO CREDITS

CRIMINAL JUSTICE, CRIMINAL SANCTIONS, AND CORRECTIONS

1

CORRECTIONS AND THE CRIMINAL JUSTICE SYSTEM: AN OVERVIEW

INTRODUCTION THIS BOOK IS ABOUT the people under correctional supervision and the laws, policies, and practices of the agents, agencies, and institutions that provide that supervision. It is generally believed that the term *corrections* means prisons and the programs and activities taking place in them. However, in practice, the term is used to include a variety of court-ordered sanctions that range from probation to community facilities, and from prisons to parole. In addition, corrections has come to constitute an umbrella under which we find newer "intermediate" criminal sanctions such as home detention, community service, electronic surveillance, boot camps, and "shock" incarceration. As we proceed through the book, we will deal with each of these correctional sanctions.

We must also recognize that there is additional confusion with regard to the meaning of the term *corrections*. Its ordinary meaning is to "correct" something that is wrong. Further, it suggests that first one must determine what is wrong, and then go about the business of correcting it. Many of the correctional sanctions we will cover in this text have little or no relation to correcting wrongs. Further, the use of the term in American criminal justice historically has been limited to "correcting" offenders. Rarely is corrections applied to wrongs that might lie in the law or in society.

Almost 2.6 percent of the U.S. adult population was under some form of correctional supervision in 1993.[1] This translates to 4.9 million individuals who were under supervision by various elements of state and federal correctional systems. They included persons on probation, in jails and prisons, and on parole. For a breakdown of these correctional populations, see Table 1.1.

CRIMINAL JUSTICE AS A SYSTEM

Almost $25 billion were spent on corrections in 1990.[2] This represented just over one-third of the total of $74,249,120,000 spent on all aspects of criminal justice in America in 1990. Expenditures for corrections were the second largest, after police services.

Clearly, society is heavily committed to corrections in response to crime. Corrections is a crucial part of American criminal justice systems. In order to understand both this commitment to corrections and the role of corrections in criminal justice, we must first examine the other major elements of our system of criminal justice, the police and the courts. It is essential to examine corrections as one element of a system and understand how the laws, policies, and operations of each system's elements affects the others.

We need to come to terms with the fact that the three primary components of criminal justice—police, courts, and corrections—are clearly interrelated. The police are the entry point for the system. Police officers, exercising discretion as they perform their law enforcement role, make arrest decisions every day. A decision to arrest may mean that an offender will later become a part of the correctional population. On the other hand, a decision not to arrest keeps a suspect from further penetration into the system.

Our trial and appellate courts frequently operate both to check on police arrest and investigatory decisions, and to review the process by which defendants are found

Correctional Populations in the United States, 1993	TABLE 1.1

POPULATION	NUMBER OF OFFENDERS
Probation	2,800,000
Jail	459,804*
Prison	909,000
Parole	671,000
Under death sentences	2,716

SOURCE: *Correctional Populations in the United States,* Department of Justice, Bureau of Justice Statistics, October 1995.
*Because of the high mobility of jail inmates, this number represents the population on one day, June 30, 1993.

guilty. Once defined as criminals, most defendants will wind up under some kind of correctional supervision: probation, jail, or prison.

The correctional component of the criminal justice system receives its intake from the courts. Unlike the police and courts, corrections has little if any discretion with regard to its intake. Courts issue probation orders, and probation officers must see that the conditions imposed in these orders are followed. Should probationers fail to abide by these orders, they may again appear in court as violators for further judicial action. If a period of probation supervision fails to "correct" an offender and she or he commits a new offense, police and courts may again be involved in dealing with a new crime.

Prisons in the United States are "open admissions" institutions. That is, they almost always have to take in a person committed as a result of a sentence issued by a judge. In addition, it is difficult for a prison administrator to get rid of an unwanted prisoner or release one who has been "corrected" before his or her court-mandated sentence has expired. Recent changes in sentencing laws in many states provide for mandatory minimum prison terms, and the wardens must deal with the results. One of the many consequences of such changes in the law is the ageing of the American prison population, with the resultant increase in costs accompanying the special needs of new geriatric cell blocks.

How well American prisons and other correctional agencies work with their populations, of course, will affect both overall crime rates and the workloads of police and courts. This idea that police, courts, and corrections as well as their related elements, e.g., prosecutors, defense attorneys, presentence investigators are interrelated parts of a system, while seemingly obvious, is in reality quite new. In a revealing article, Samuel Walker points out that it was not until about 1956 that a **systems perspective** gained some recognition in American criminology and penology:

> The dominant paradigm in American criminal justice today involves a "systems" perspective, in which the administration of justice consists of a series of discretionary decisions about individual criminal cases by officials working in a set of interrelated agencies.[3]

Walker argues that until the new paradigm was recognized as accurately reflecting the reality of criminal justice, there was what he termed the **Progressive Era Paradigm** dominating evaluations of criminal justice.[4] This progressive paradigm was shaped by the efforts of many "blue ribbon" commissions that investigated failures in the administration of justice. Their conclusions were largely of the kind that urged reforms in criminal justice personnel selection and training, and demanded an end to corruption in government and law enforcement. If these corrections were made, it was assumed, justice would be administered both fairly and effectively.

But, as Walker pointed out, the progressives were "hopelessly naive" in assuming that criminal justice consisted of

> . . . a series of semiautonomous agencies where officials administered the law in an impersonal, "ministerial" fashion: that is, they did what the law required. Any exercise of discretion was an unwarranted and probably illegal departure from an official's legal mandate.[5]

The possibility that officials in justice administration might be affected by a number of extralegal factors was not acknowledged by the older paradigm. Excessively high workloads, career demands, and organizational interests and needs are understood today as vitally important factors in our analysis of justice system performance.

Throughout the remainder of this book, the reader should constantly question the systemic impact of laws, policies, and practices on the administration of criminal justice, especially the corrections element. Two examples should suffice as a start. In their zeal to combat illegal drug trafficking, state and federal legislatures have enacted draconian sentences for "possession with intent to distribute" relatively small amounts of "controlled dangerous substances." Often those sentenced are young, addicted men and women. They usually are racial and ethnic minorities coming from impoverished urban centers. The sentences are mandatory, regardless of the characteristics of the offender, bounded only by a specified measure of the illegal substance. What will these sentences mean to prison administrators and workers? Should they expend limited resources to provide substance abuse programs, or simply warehouse these prisoners?

What about the current call for "three strikes and you're out" sentences? This formula would impose life-without-parole sentences on offenders convicted three times for serious crimes. Although the expression makes a good "sound bite," there is little agreement among proponents about which serious crimes qualify for this draconian sentence. Some advocates would include convictions for any felony; others would restrict the coverage to violent felonies. What about the impact on prosecutors facing increased workloads and the sometimes conflicting use of discretion to plea bargain? Put yourself in the shoes of the prison warden receiving a rising percentage of inmates who apparently have no chance of ever being released alive.

ELEMENTS IN CRIMINAL JUSTICE SYSTEMS IN AMERICA

Police

In the United States, half a million officers in more than 15,000 public law enforcement agencies perform police duties. These officers made nearly 13 million arrests in

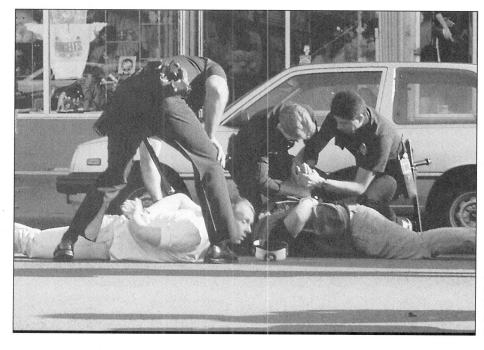

*P*olice officers rely on training and quick thinking when they are taking suspects into custody.

1990. An officer's decision to make an arrest is the first step in an often lengthy process that may eventually end with a person entering the correctional population. It may be helpful briefly to describe the arrest process. An officer's decision to make an arrest is subject to certain legal constraints. These constraints include probable cause that a person has committed a crime and, under certain circumstances, the need to apply for a warrant. For example, Tennessee law specifies that an officer may make a warrantless arrest if

- a "public offense or breach of the peace has been committed in his presence;"
- a person "has committed a felony not in his presence;"
- when the officer has "reasonable cause for believing" the person has committed a felony;
- "on a charge made, upon reasonable cause, of the commission of a felony."[5]

Even with these conditions in mind, we find that the officer's decision to arrest is a subjective one.

The **discretion** available to law enforcement officers is by no means a monopoly held by police in the United States. Barton Ingraham compared the screening of criminal complaints in France, China, the former Soviet Union, and the United States and observed that in all these countries, screening of criminal complaints is done informally and "there is very little knowledge of the way this screening activity . . . is performed or how to control it."[6]

Ingraham's observation about the nature of the decision- making process leading to these arrests tells us at least two extremely important things about policing in America: (1) Police officers and their superiors have the discretion to decide (screen in or out) what conduct and which suspects shall be introduced into the criminal justice system; and (2) these discretionary decisions are not systematically reviewed. The more than 15,000 law enforcement agencies under federal, state, county, and municipal jurisdictions employ three-quarters of a million people spending more than $28 billion every year. The unique role of policing, however, gives these organizations exceptional power to determine their own fate as well as the fate of those whom they arrest.

As stated earlier, police made nearly 13 million arrests in 1990. An officer's decision to make an arrest is the first step in the ultimate entry of many persons into the corrections systems in America. The decision and the way it is exercised on the street may well influence the later course of an offender's career in the correctional apparatus. We will now take a closer look at this decision making, keeping in mind the systemic nature of criminal justice.

Among the variables affecting an officer's arrest decision making is the pressure exerted on him or her by the public and its elected representatives. It is often believed that police organizations respond in a calculated fashion to such pressures. However, reality is much more complex. Let's look at three examples to illustrate this. The first concerns enforcement of drunk driving laws. The second deals with the police response to spouse abuse. The third covers efforts by police and prosecutors to get a handle on repeat offenders.

Mastrofski and Ritti conducted a study of drunk driving law changes in Pennsylvania.[7] These changes included greater discretion for police to stop drivers, lower thresholds to prove a driver intoxicated, and stiffer sanctions against those convicted, with the latter having the potential for increasing the number of incarcerated offenders.

These changes were a response to effective lobbying in the state and across the country by citizen groups such as MADD (Mothers Against Drunk Driving). The resulting police response, however, was unexpected: Arrest rates in the study city, "Melville," after an initial increase, fell to levels recorded prior to the new laws taking effect. Why did this happen? Mastrofski and Ritti offer several answers:

- Virtually every American police department places top priority on responding to calls for service. . . . Drunk driving offenses rarely come to the police because of a citizen's complaint. . . .[8]
- Making a DWI arrest is time-consuming . . . ; sometimes it takes four hours to process a case. An officer can commit this kind of time only if resources are adequate to handle the calls for service workload or if the department is willing to reduce the levels of response to calls for service.[9]
- ["Melville"] feels little pressure from the state to pursue DWIs. In the 1970s the department had received state funds for overtime associated with DWI enforcement, but its administrators were unable to recall any such state or federal support in the years since the 1983 law.[10]
- [The police chief stated that] "if I pull my guys off answering calls for service to do more DUI (driving under the influence), then the mayor has to answer all the citizens' complaints that we're not answering their demands for service. And then the mayor lets me know about it. I don't need that. So I keep those complaints from getting to the mayor by giving the citizens what they want."[11]

And then there are the officers' attitudes and perceptions, which play a significant role in their enforcement of the law. Many of them assign a low priority to drunk driving offenses, and believe that those in authoritative positions also share this view. Other officers, according to Mastrofski and Ritti, feel strongly that arresting these offenders is a waste of time since the courts and the corrections system will not follow up the arrests with successful actions. Instead of making arrests, police often "handle the less inebriated in alternative ways—following them home, providing . . . alternative transportation, or taking their car keys."[12]

We can see in some of these reasons why DWI and DUI arrests have not increased in spite of law changes and public pressure from citizen groups. And, of course, such offenders have not noticeably increased our prison populations in spite of the objectives of many legislators. What is required to follow up studies like those undertaken by Mastrofski and Ritti are analyses of accident data. Is the rate of accidents involving drunk drivers any different after the enactment of the new laws? This question cannot be answered simply by relating the data to police enforcement policies and practices.

What do "Melville's" judges do when DWI and DUI cases reach their courtrooms? Are some police officers correct when they state that the courts do not take effective action? Are court-ordered "correctional" programs effective? The police seem to believe they are not.

Another example illustrates both the complexity of arrest decision making and the systemic impact of these decisions. Here we look at **spouse abuse** and the police response to a crime of violence that has increasingly demanded our attention in recent years. It has been argued that all too often police have failed to respond to allegations of spouse abuse, allegations most often made by wives against their husbands. That is, police have been biased in their responses because of outdated views about women's rights in the marital relationship. Also, police have been accused of assigning a low priority to calls for intervention in spouse abuse cases. These attitudes and practices have been prevalent in the face of the undeniable violence perpetrated by abuse offenders. This should cause us to question very carefully current trends toward mandatory and lengthy prison terms handed out to other offenders for other crimes of violence.

Recently, legislative actions and police department training and regulations have been changing to reflect the need to "correct" police behavior in these cases. Such changes are thought to produce at least two system benefits. The first is to encourage police officers to recognize the seriousness of violent crimes in the domestic environment. The second is to deter both those who have been abusing their spouses and those who might at some time assault their spouses.

In a comprehensive review, Hirschel and his colleagues traced the "past, present, and future" of the law enforcement response to spouse abuse.[13] They claim that "the battle has been won" when spouse abuse is clearly seen as a felony assault. In such cases, the complaint is assigned a high priority like other felony assaults. However, at the misdemeanor level, the police seem to continue to have difficulty assigning a high priority to calls for service. "Assigning a high priority to such calls requires a major reallocation of police resources."[14] Whether police executives are willing to order such a reallocation is in doubt.

Hirschel reports that the best estimates available put the amount of violence occurring each year against women by their partners at "one in six" relationships.[15] The total number of women abused has been estimated to be somewhere between 2.1 and 8 million each year. Thus, it is clear that this is an extremely serious problem confronting the criminal justice system. Among the responses considered and adopted in many states and communities has been that of mandating the arrest of an accused spouse abuser.

Why has this step been necessary? Why have arrests of abusers not been made as a matter of course? After all, spouse abuse usually involves a violent assault on the victim. The crimes of assault, both simple and aggravated, have been listed in the criminal codes of all the states since these codes were enacted. Answers suggested for past and in many places current lack of effective police reactions to spouse abuse are:

- Violence within the family has been considered to be essentially a private matter. . . .[16]
- Female victims have been perceived as uncooperative [making] arresting and prosecuting abusers a waste of time.[17]
- Actions taken against abusers hurt their families, especially family members financially dependent on the offenders.[18]
- Intervening in family disputes was not regarded as "real police work."[19]
- Police officers responding to domestic violence calls usually are males who "typically side with offenders."[20]

In the 1960s and '70s, a shift in police behavior with regard to spouse abuse occurred with some departments moving toward a "mediation" response to domestic violence. Police officers in many communities were expected to engage in family intervention work when responding to a call involving spouse abuse. Frequently inadequately trained and prepared for this difficult counseling task, officers often failed to achieve resolution of the conflicts leading to violence. In addition, the police officer as mediator is virtually required to assume the "equal culpability between the partners" which may lead to "failure to hold the offender accountable for his actions."[21]

The current preferred response to a call for police service in a spouse abuse case is the mandatory arrest of the abuser. Statutes with mandatory arrest provisions have

FOCUS ON THE LAW

RESPONSE TO SPOUSE ABUSE CASE GETS TO THE SUPREME COURT: *THURMAN V. CITY OF TORRINGTON*

Wife and son brought civil rights action against city and police officers thereof, alleging that plaintiffs' constitutional rights were violated by the nonperformance of official duties by the officers in regard to threats and assaults by wife's estranged husband.

[On numerous occasions in 1983], the plaintiff . . . notified . . . police officers of the City . . . of repeated threats upon her life and the life of her child . . . made by her estranged husband. Attempts to file complaints . . . against her husband in response to his threats of death and maiming were ignored or rejected by the named defendants.

On or about November 5, Charles Thurman . . . using physical force took . . . Charles Thurman, Jr. from the residence. [His mother] went to . . . police headquarters to make a formal complaint. At that point, unnamed defendant police officers refused to accept the complaint, even as to trespassing.

[At this point, Thurman broke his wife's windshield with her in the car.] Following this incident, Thurman was arrested for breaking the windshield, receiving a suspended sentence and "conditionally discharged" with the stipulation that he stay away from his wife. On June 10, 1983, Thurman appeared at his wife's and demanded to speak to [her]. She called the police . . . asking that [he] be picked up for violation of his probation. After about 15 minutes, [she] went outside . . . in an effort to persuade her husband not to take or hurt

[her son]. Soon thereafter, [he] began to stab her repeatedly in the chest, neck and throat.

Approximately 25 minutes after [she had called] the police, and after the stabbing, a single officer arrived. . . . Charles Thurman was holding a bloody knife. [He] then dropped the knife and, in the presence of the officer, kicked [his wife] in the head . . . , ran into the house, returning with [his son] and dropped the child on his wounded mother. [He] then kicked [his wife] in the head a second time. He was still permitted to wander about the crowd and to threaten [his wife]. Finally, upon approaching her once again, this time while she was lying on a stretcher, he was arrested.

Police action is subject to the equal protection clause [of the Constitution], whether in the form of commission of violative acts or omission to perform required acts pursuant to the police officer's duty to protect.

If the City of Torrington wishes to discriminate against women who are the victims of domestic violence, it must articulate an important governmental interest for doing so.

A man is not allowed to physically abuse or endanger a woman merely because he is her husband. Concomitantly, a police officer may not knowingly refrain from interference in such violence, and may not "automatically" decline to make an arrest simply because the assaulter and his victim are married to each other.

SOURCE 595 F.Supp. 1521 (1984).

been enacted in at least ten states. A major stimulus to the decision to require arrests was the successful outcome for women filing lawsuits against jurisdictions where spouse abuse cases were assigned a very low priority by law enforcement agencies. One such major case was *Thurman v. City of Torrington*,[22] which became the subject of a movie drama. Because of the significance of this case, major portions of it are excerpted in the Focus on the Law feature.

In Hirschel's analysis of police responses to domestic violence referred to earlier, an examination of the **Minneapolis experiment** was carried out.[23] This study was the first in the country designed to test the deterrent impact of arrest in spouse abuse cases. The experiment specifically tested the effectiveness of three responses to abuse: (1) advising the couple—frequently with mediation; (2) separating the couple, ordering the offender to stay away for eight hours; and (3) arresting the offender, which included overnight detention in jail.

The research results showed a definite deterrent benefit for the arrest option over the other two responses. These findings were widely disseminated and were influential in changing police policies and practices in many communities. Because there also were some methodological questions about the research design (running experiments in the field frequently is much more difficult than experimenting in a laboratory), the National Institute of Justice supported a number of studies in other locales throughout the country. Preliminary results from these studies suggest that, contrary to expectations, arresting misdemeanor spouse abusers was no more effective in reducing repeat offenses than other responses that did not include arrest.[24]

Why is it that mandatory arrest of spouse abusers does not seem to be particularly successful as a deterrent? Hirschel's review of the research offers some possible answers. First, the majority of abusers are chronic offenders. They have been arrested a number of times in the past and it is not very likely that a new arrest will have much impact. Another answer offered by Hirschel is that, once arrested, an abuser is most unlikely to spend much, if any, time in jail. In one study carried out in Omaha, the average time detained was 16 hours. In Charlotte it was 9 hours, while in Milwaukee, the time spent in jail ranged from 3 to 11 hours. As Hirschel points out, "arrest with [virtually] immediate release simply may not mean much, particularly when offenders have been arrested before."[25]

Finally, and this is most important when looking at criminal justice as a system, conviction of an arrested abuser often results in ridiculously lenient punishment— when any punishment is handed down by the court. In Minneapolis, only 2 percent of convicted abusers were formally punished; in Charlotte, 1 percent spent time in jail after conviction. In Milwaukee, only 1 percent of those arrested were even convicted!

Hirschel makes the point that expecting police officers to take the lead in recognizing the seriousness of spouse abuse cases by requiring them to arrest offenders is expecting too much.

> It is a reasonably human response of police to question the efficacy of arresting spouse abusers when they already are reluctant to do so because of traditional beliefs, and they know that little will happen to such abusers as they enter the judicial system.[26]

A third example of the complexity of modifying police reaction to crime in light of that reaction's impact on criminal justice as a system has to do with the problem of repeat or career criminals. It is obvious that repeat offenders pose a particularly serious threat to the public. A number of studies have found that a relatively small percentage of offenders commit a very large number of the crimes that come to the attention of the police. Many jurisdictions have tried to work out innovative policies and procedures to deal more effectively with repeat offenders.

One such city is Phoenix, Arizona, where an experimental **repeat offender program (ROP)** was initiated in 1987. The six officers assigned to the ROP unit were able to "nominate" offenders as repeat criminals prior to an arrest. The officers worked closely with ROP attorneys from the prosecutor's office. When an ROP offender was arrested, "enhanced" activity was undertaken to develop any additional charges and to investigate as completely as possible the offender's prior record. The objectives of the ROP program were to increase the probability that those arrested would be convicted and sentenced to significant terms of imprisonment. These objectives were, in fact, realized.[27]

A policy-related ethical question is raised by repeat offender programs such as Phoenix's: The premise of these programs is that dangerous offenders can be accurately identified. Is it ethical to use past records and police intelligence data to influence prosecutorial decisions? Shouldn't a defendant be prosecuted only for the crime for which he or she is charged? Following conviction, the enhanced punishment is actually based on the conviction offense plus the offender's past record. If one accepts the view that an offender ought to receive his or her just deserts for what he or she has done, then ROP-like programs won't wash. In the next chapter we will take up the question of whether an offender should be punished more severely, not just for the offense for which he or she stands convicted at the time of sentencing, but for past offenses for which sentences have already been served.

Courts

Courts dealing with criminal charges in the United States fall into two categories: trial and appellate courts. Because there are two sets of criminal laws, one for federal crimes and one containing the criminal codes for the states, there are state and federal trial and appellate courts. The vast majority of crimes and criminal trials are covered under state laws. Recently there has been a call for expanding the federal criminal code in the wake of rising concern over violent crimes. The crime bill introduced to Congress by President Clinton and eventually enacted by Congress includes a significant expansion of the list of federal crimes, the result of which would dramatically increase the number of offenders under federal correctional supervision.

During a trial, sidebar conferences may be called so prosecuting and defense attorneys can confer with the trial judge.

In state and federal trial courts the guilt or innocence of a defendant is at issue. When a defendant pleads not guilty to a criminal charge an adversarial trial is held. That is, the defendant is presumed innocent. The prosecutor, representing the people, must attempt to prove guilt beyond a reasonable doubt. The defense must counter the prosecutor's case and try to show that there is reasonable doubt that the defendant is guilty. Such an adversarial process may take place before a jury, which is every citizen's right under the federal Constitution. A defendant may waive a jury trial and present his or her case before a judge alone.

This description of the trial process, while accurate, is a bit misleading. Adversarial trials are a most infrequent occurrence in American criminal justice. Why? Because the vast majority of defendants plead guilty, usually after they, through their attorneys, strike a **plea bargain** with the prosecutor. The bargain generally involves a reduction in the number and/or severity of the charges against the defendant. The defendant pleads guilty and, in return, receives a lesser sentence than if he or she had pleaded not guilty to the original charges and had been found guilty. Whether a defendant enters a negotiated plea of guilty or is tried and found guilty often determines the kind of correctional supervision he or she receives.

When a guilty verdict has been rendered by the trial court in a criminal case the defendant has the right of appeal to a higher court. Once the case reaches an appellate court, the judge or judges make a decision about the merits of the appeal.

Appellate courts handle only a small portion of the cases that have been heard in criminal trial courts. Most cases are settled with guilty pleas and never even reach the stage of a trial. Of those that go to trial, some are handled before a judge without a jury. Only a very few of the total number of criminal arrests and prosecutions culminate in a jury trial.

Whether the trial is before a judge alone or in front of a jury, the issues decided at the trial court level are **issues of fact.** The issues surround the question of whether the accused committed the act and if so, whether he or she was criminally responsible. The trier of fact is the jury, or in a relatively small proportion of trials, the judge when the defendant waives the right to a jury trial. The fact finder (the jury in most cases) must decide whether the evidence presented is credible to the point that the state has proved every element in a crime beyond a reasonable doubt.

The appellate courts, by contrast, deal only with **issues of law.** Appellate courts do not take up questions of fact. The appeal of a criminal case *must always go to an issue of law.* Every issue of law arises because the accused (or, more accurately, the attorney acting in the accused's behalf) or the state (that is, the prosecuting attorney acting on behalf of the state) asked the trial judge to do something the judge refused to do, or the judge acted in ways which the attorney or the prosecutor argue were not permissible by law.

For example, the attorney may ask the judge to dismiss the complaint or suppress a confession because the accused was not warned of the right to have a lawyer present before making a statement to the police. If the judge rejects the motion, the attorney may appeal. If the judge agrees with the attorney and dismisses the complaint, the prosecuting attorney may appeal.

In actual practice, appeals are usually written covering a whole host of legal issues, claiming that there were a number of "wrong decisions" or other legal errors at the trial court level.

Because it is extremely expensive to appeal a case and most criminal cases involve people with little money, most are not appealed. An important exception to this generalization, however, is made when "public interest" groups such as the National

ACROSS CULTURES

CRIMINAL TRIALS AND APPEALS IN INDONESIA

The accused came into the courtroom escorted by a National Police Service officer. He was seated in a hard chair facing the three-judge panel. While the indictment was read he remained seated, alone. This isolation at the beginning of the trial symbolizes the accuser's probable guilt and his humble status before the court. After responding to the charges, he was permitted to move to the defense table where his legal advocate was seated. Across from them was the Public Prosecutor's table, with a tall stack of documents compiled during the lengthy pretrial investigatory period.

There is no jury. Only the three judges hear the evidence and render their verdict. The Public Prosecutor recommends a sentence in the case of conviction (the usual outcome). The defense may ask for a more lenient sentence.

Both prosecutor and defense may appeal verdicts. It would violate American law to permit a prosecutor to appeal against a verdict favorable to the defense, but it frequently happens in Indonesia. Both sides have the absolute right to appeal to the next level, the High Court, and then, if desired, to the Supreme Court, which is required to consider *all* appeals. This Indonesian practice represents an effort by the authorities to encourage the public's acceptance of the fairness of the criminal justice system. It also contributes to an enormous backlog of cases. When I interviewed Supreme Court justices, I was informed that the backlog was in excess of 15,000 cases.

SOURCE: Author's visit to the Surabaya District Court, Indonesia, October 1994.

Association for the Advancement of Colored People (NAACP), the American Civil Liberties Union (ACLU), and the National Lawyers Guild become involved. These groups, on rare but significant occasions, assume the expense of appealing a case in order to try to establish a legal precedent in line with their interests in justice and equality.

Figure 1.1 presents a representation of the structure of federal and state courts in America. It provides a generalized view of the current situation. There are some exceptions and minor variations in the structure when one looks at individual states, but these do not significantly alter the general picture. The figure omits courts that do not deal with general criminal matters, for example, the U.S. Claims Court, which deals with claims lodged against the United States, and administrative agencies that deal with violations or interpretations of administrative regulations. However, Figure 1.1 should serve as a reference for the following discussion.

Figure 1.2 shows the "typical" outcome of 100 felony arrests referred by the police to their community's prosecutors. By examining it, you can see the systemic character of criminal justice from the arrest to the sentencing stages of the process.

What Figure 1.2 does not tell us, but what is important to note, is that about one-quarter of convicted felons are sentenced to probation, and another one-fifth receive "split" sentences that include some jail time followed by probation.[28] Thus, little more than half of convicted felons are sentenced to state and federal prisons.

Again looking just at those who "made it" all the way through to conviction, we can see that 54 of the arrestees carried forward for trial pleaded guilty. *Only three*

FIGURE 1.1   Federal and State Court Systems

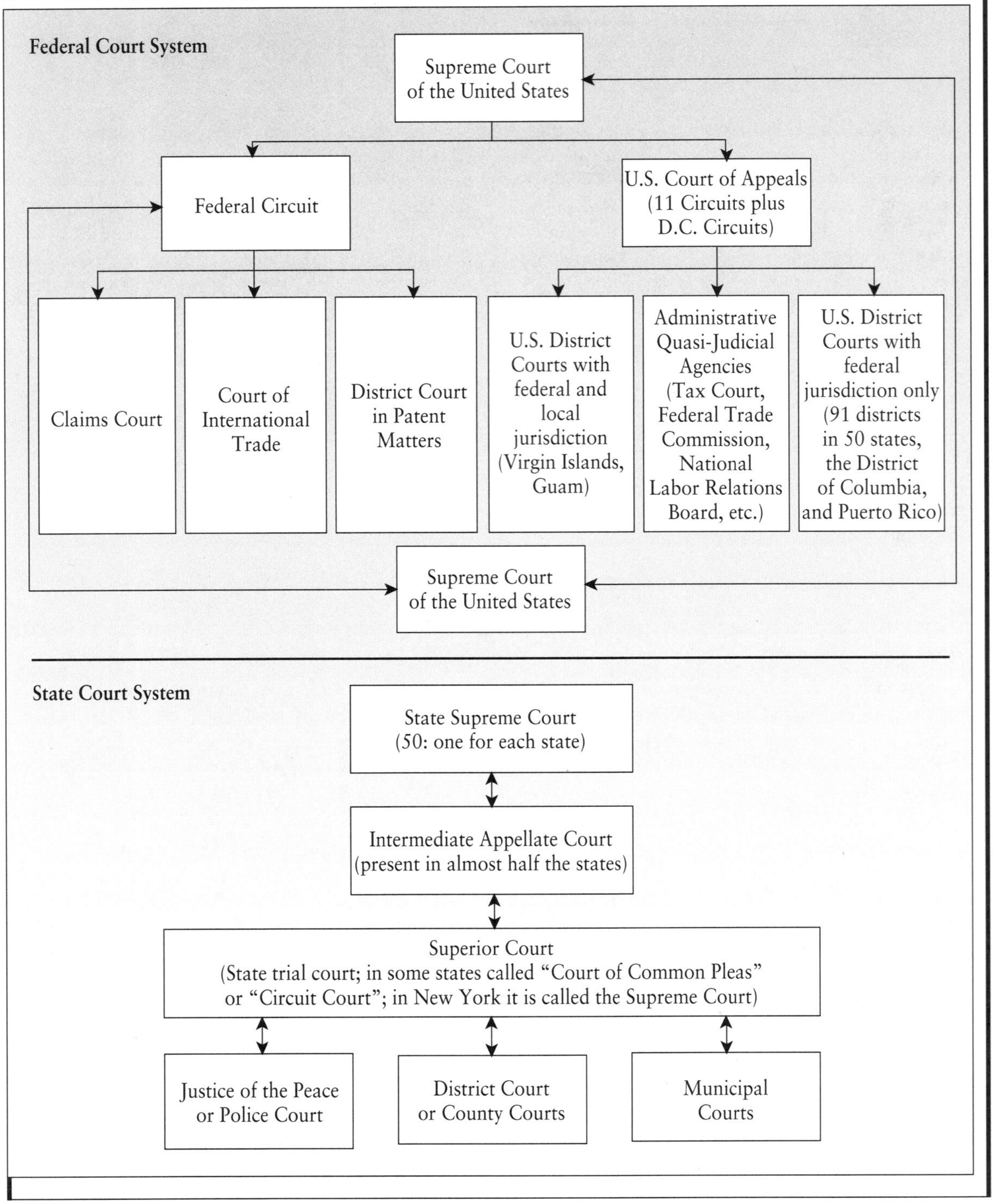

Federal Court System

```
                          Supreme Court
                        of the United States
                                │
           ┌────────────────────┴────────────────────┐
           ▼                                          ▼
     Federal Circuit                          U.S. Court of Appeals
                                                 (11 Circuits plus
                                                   D.C. Circuits)
   ┌────────┬──────────┬──────────┐     ┌──────────┬────────────┬────────────┐
   ▼        ▼          ▼          ▼     ▼          ▼            ▼
```

| Claims Court | Court of International Trade | District Court in Patent Matters | U.S. District Courts with federal and local jurisdiction (Virgin Islands, Guam) | Administrative Quasi-Judicial Agencies (Tax Court, Federal Trade Commission, National Labor Relations Board, etc.) | U.S. District Courts with federal jurisdiction only (91 districts in 50 states, the District of Columbia, and Puerto Rico) |

```
                          Supreme Court
                        of the United States
```

State Court System

```
                        State Supreme Court
                       (50: one for each state)
                                ▲
                                ▼
                    Intermediate Appellate Court
                  (present in almost half the states)
                                ▲
                                ▼
                          Superior Court
   (State trial court; in some states called "Court of Common Pleas"
     or "Circuit Court"; in New York it is called the Supreme Court)
        ▲                       ▲                       ▲
        ▼                       ▼                       ▼
```

| Justice of the Peace or Police Court | District Court or County Courts | Municipal Courts |

defendants pleaded not guilty and were involved in an adversarial proceeding, one of whom was acquitted.

What happened to the other arrestees? As shown in Figure 1.2, 18 percent of those arrested were rejected for further entry into the system following screening by prosecutors. This brings us to a consideration of the prosecutor's role in the system. Like the police, prosecuting attorneys exercise discretion when cases are brought to their attention. What charges require prosecution? What kinds of deals with defense attorneys ought to be entertained and which ones accepted? These and other questions must be answered by prosecutors every day in every jurisdiction throughout the country.

In Figure 1.2, we see that out of every 100 cases presented to the prosecutor's office, only 77 are carried forward. Five are diverted elsewhere, and 18 are rejected for prosecution. What happened to these 23 arrestees? Those who were "diverted" were referred to or placed in various settings such as drug and substance abuse treatment programs. Some were diverted to employment training centers; others were referred to other courts such as family or domestic courts.

The decisions in the 18 cases that were rejected for prosecution do not necessarily result in freedom from further action by the criminal justice system. Some of those rejected for felony prosecution are reclassified as misdemeanor cases and may later appear in the appropriate criminal court. Others may be diverted as indicated above. Finally, some of those rejected for prosecution will escape the system completely. In such cases, the prosecutor screening the charge(s) may conclude that there is insufficient evidence to produce a conviction and the matter should not be presented to the court.

Decisions to downgrade felony charges to the misdemeanor level or to reject a case outright are often tied to the police charging decision at the time of booking. That is, the police may "overcharge" a suspect in hopes that he or she will be encouraged to plea bargain. Plea bargaining, according to one recent nationwide survey, is engaged in by virtually every prosecutor.[29] Decisions to bargain and to accept offers from

Outcome of 100 Felony Cases: Nationwide Sample   **FIGURE 1.2**

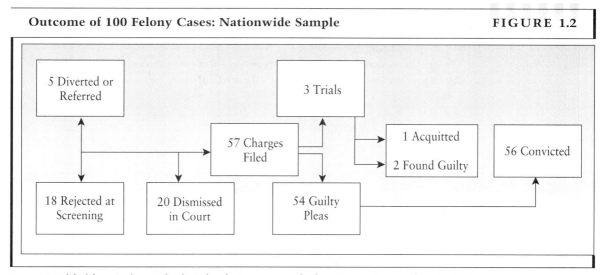

SOURCE: Modified from Barbara Boland, et al., *The Prosecution of Felony Arrests,* Bureau of Justice Statistics, 1983.

defendants are discretionary. Factors leading a prosecutor to engage in plea bargaining include:

- a defendant's prior criminal history
- a defendant's willingness to cooperate with the prosecution
- the prosecutor's workload
- the strength of the case
- evidentiary problems
- attitudes of the victim[30]

The author recently observed a number of trials and examined a sample of police and court records in his home county. That county was, and is, experiencing a rising burglary rate as it is being transformed from a rural to a suburban community. Invariably, when police arrested suspected burglars, three charges were filed: burglary, destruction of property, and larceny. The charges do make sense. A burglary was committed, usually with a "breaking in" that caused property (windows, doors) to be damaged, and something was taken from the scene (larceny).

Each of these charges, if proven, carries a specified sentence range. In sentencing those convicted on all three charges, a judge could hand down three sentences that could run consecutively, or concurrently (that is, all three start simultaneously). The state's attorney consistently bargained with defendants to obtain a guilty plea. What the prosecutor offered was quite simple: Plead guilty to one charge and the other two would be dropped. Usually, the guilty plea was to the most serious crime, burglary.

Variation on the Traditional Criminal Court Model: The Dade County Felony Drug Court.

As a response to the heavy volume of drug-related cases in Dade County (including Miami), Florida, the Eleventh Judicial District Circuit instituted a **Felony Drug Court** in 1989.[31] This innovative court-based program seeks to deliver treatment-oriented intervention programs to selected felony defendants charged with drug possession who are drug abusers. With the cooperation of the circuit court judge, selected defendants enter a highly structured and phased period of drug treatment, counseling, and vocational and educational training.

Frequently scheduled appointments and regular urine screenings are required of all defendants. Successful completion of all phases of the program usually results in the criminal charges being dropped. Preliminary evaluation results suggest that the Felony Drug Court has succeeded in producing lower incarceration rates (helping to reduce overcrowding in the state's prison system) and lower rearrest rates.[32] These results were obtained by comparing the participants with a group of similar defendants who were handled in the traditional way.

Acceptance of such new approaches in criminal justice faces an uphill struggle in this country because of conflicting perspectives as to the appropriate response to the "drug problem."

> The Eleventh Circuit's Drug Court is a hybrid combining elements of both criminal justice and drug treatment approaches. . . . Key elements include the special role for the judge and criminal court personnel, the fundamental treatment orientation, and the diversion-like framework.[33]

Whether the conflict between a more traditional punitive approach to defendants and the medical model or treatment approach can truly be melded into the court setting cannot yet be answered. We will return to this conflict in the next chapter, where we address issues such as the conflicting and sometimes competing goals of criminal sanctions.

We close this section on the courts by referring to the most publicized criminal case in recent memory: O.J. Simpson's arrest and charging for a double murder. Perhaps no other case better illustrates the need to look at criminal justice as a system, and the sometimes most serious and tragic consequences when we fail to do so. Earlier in the chapter we pointed out in some detail the hesitation of police to arrest spouse abuse suspects. And when they do, often the sentences handed out by the courts are virtually meaningless in terms of punishment or the deterrence of future assaults.

Cultural factors are said to be involved when police are reluctant to arrest the suspected offender. Probably similar factors are influential when judges sentence convicted abusers. In O.J. Simpson's case, he was arrested for the murder of his former wife and one of her friends. The charges were for murder with "special circumstances."[34] In the highly publicized aftermath of the crime, it was revealed that Simpson had been arrested before on charges of assaulting his then wife. The police report of that arrest was shown on television and reported in the major daily papers. Not only was this complaint of abuse made by Nicole Brown Simpson against her ex-husband, numerous prior 911 calls had been made with, apparently, no police response.[35]

The complaint against O.J. Simpson that did lead to a court appearance reported that:

> Nicole Simpson was suffering from a cut, swollen lip, a blackened left eye, swelling and bruises on her face and neck and a reddened imprint of a hand across her neck. O.J. Simpson tried to minimize the fight, [the prosecutor] recalled. "He tended to think that what he was doing was perfectly fine. I remember him saying, 'I don't understand what this fuss is all about.' "[36]

After Simpson pleaded guilty to a lesser charge of battery, the judge placed him on probation, ordering Simpson to complete 120 hours of community service, make a $500 contribution to a battered women's center, and undergo psychological counseling. According to the prosecutor, Simpson failed to complete his community service. The prosecutor asked the judge to sentence Simpson to jail as a probation violator. The judge refused to do so, instead ordering Simpson to complete an additional 30 days of community service.

Whether or not a more severe punishment for O.J. Simpson would have meant that Nicole Brown Simpson and the second victim, Ronald L. Goldman, would be alive today is a question we cannot answer. After all, Simpson was found not guilty. We do know that after several calls to the police for help, Nicole Brown Simpson finally did get the police to arrest her abuser. Then the judge, following a plea bargain from Simpson, handed down a very lenient sentence, refusing to enhance it even when Simpson violated the terms of his probation.

Corrections

Since corrections is the subject of this text, we will only present a few general observations here. All too often corrections is seen as somehow not part of the criminal justice system. But correctional institutions and other correctional settings receive and must deal with the populations sent them through the efforts of the police and courts. Prison and probation administrators do not have the luxury of discretion that police, prosecutors, and judges have. They cannot say, when a newly convicted and sentenced

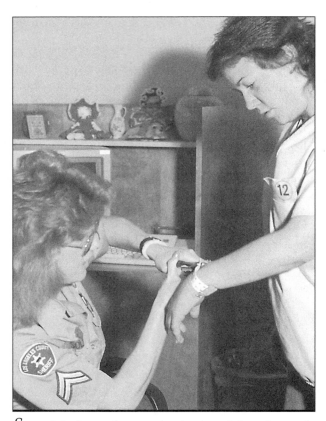

*S*ome defendants who are ordered to be jailed pending trial
must have identification bracelets attached so prisoners are
uniquely identified.

offender arrives at the prison gate or probation office, "No, you cannot come in;
you're not our type."

In the United States, offenders are imprisoned in three very general types of institutions: jails, prisons (usually called correctional institutions), and correctional boot
camps. Jails perform dual functions in our society. One function is that of detaining
persons awaiting trial or imposition of sentencing following conviction. The second
function is short-term commitment of convicted persons who have been sentenced to
jail for punishment. Today, because of serious prison crowding, many states are forced
to house inmates who should be in state prisons in jail until space for them is available.

Prisons, now housing more than one million men and women, usually contain prisoners serving sentences of one year or more. Many state and federal prisons are differentiated on the basis of level of security. That is, prisons are rated as having maximum, medium, or minimum security. Theoretically, prisoners are assigned to these
institutions after some attention is paid to their risk of escape or disruption. In a few
instances, sentencing statutes specify in which prisons persons convicted of specific
crimes are to serve their time.

We should not forget that imprisonment is by no means the only postconviction
destination for those found guilty. A major destination is probation. Although probation will be covered in Chapter 11, a brief discussion at this point may be helpful

to highlight again the systemic nature of criminal justice. In the United States, probation typically involves an order by the trial court judge. By this order a convicted offender may remain in the community, but his or her liberty is restricted by a number of conditions written into the order. In addition, a probationer is assigned a probation officer who is charged with "supervising" offenders.

The meaning of probation supervision is subject to different interpretations. To some, it means to counsel and support the probationer. To others it means to maintain some level of surveillance, in other words, to ensure that the conditions laid down in the probation order are not violated. These interpretations may be held by both probation officers and sentencing judges. As in the case with prison administrators, probation agency administrators cannot refuse to accept offenders sent by judges, no matter what the judges have in mind when ordering probation, or whether the offender is considered appropriate for supervision, or how overloaded with cases the probation officers are.

Unfortunately, judges, probation officers, and administrators do not often interact in ways that would allow them to understand one another's purposes and problems. Among the systemic consequences of this is the mediocre—at best—performance observed when probation success-failure rates are studied.

SUMMARY

CRIMINAL JUSTICE IN THE UNITED STATES must be viewed as a system consisting of three major components: police, courts, and corrections. Although this may seem obvious, this "system" often operates as though its three components are not connected in any rational way. What police do, prosecutors can undo. The courts and their judges sometimes take actions that support the other parts of the system; at other times they seem to work almost in opposition to the other components. In the case of the Dade County Felony Drug Court, judges can work constructively with other parts of the system to develop and deliver innovative programs to a specific class of offender.

The enormous amount of discretion available to police, prosecutors, and judges is exercised so freely that it is normal for the system. About the only actors who do not have much discretion are the prison administrators who must take in all those sentenced to terms of imprisonment.

Yet, as we have seen, this system of criminal justice is supported by a foundation of law. The principle of **nulla poena sine lege**—there may be no punishment unless it is specified by law—is accepted by all as fundamental. As we shall see in the next chapter, this principle, seemingly so obvious as well as simple, is in reality quite complex. Why do we sentence offenders? To cause them to suffer? To rehabilitate them? To deter them and others from committing additional crimes? Or, perhaps, simply to incapacitate those identified as criminals and thus a threat to the community?

KEY CONCEPTS

discretion
Felony Drug Court
issues of fact

issues of law
Minneapolis experiment
nulla poena sine lege

plea bargain   spouse abuse
Progressive Era Paradigm   systems perspective
repeat offender program (ROP)

QUESTIONS FOR DISCUSSION

1. What are the essential differences between the "Systems" and "Progressive Era" paradigms? Why is it that the systems paradigm is more helpful in evaluating laws, policies, and practices affecting criminal justice?
2. What are some of the significant, if unintended, consequences of the movement toward mandatory arrest of spouse abusers?
3. What are some of the impediments to effective implementation of stronger laws designed to curb drunk driving? How might these impediments be removed?
4. Critically review the practice at the police and prosecutorial stages in criminal justice of "overcharging" defendants.
5. Why is it that a tiny percentage of cases brought by police and prosecutors result in actual criminal trials? What are some of the variables that would allow you to predict which charges will actually be heard in court?

ENDNOTES

1. Tracy L. Snell, *Correctional Populations in the United States, 1993* (Department of Justice, Bureau of Justice Statistics, October 1995), p. 1.
2. U.S. Department of Justice, Office of Justice Programs, Bureau of Justice Statistics, *Justice Expenditure and Employment, 1990* (September, 1992), p. 3.
3. Samuel Walker, "Origins of the Contemporary Criminal Justice Paradigm: The American Bar Foundation Survey, 1953–1969," *Justice Quarterly* 9 (1992): 47.
4. Ibid., p. 52.
5. Irving J. Klein, *Constitutional Law for Criminal Justice Professionals,* Coral Gables Publishing Co., Miami, FLA, 1986, p. 41.
6. Barton L. Ingraham, *The Structure of Criminal Procedure* (New York: Greenwood Press, 1987), pp. 57–58.
7. Stephen D. Mastrofski and R. Richard Ritti, "You Can Lead a Horse to Water . . . : A Case Study of a Police Department's Response to Stricter Drunk-Driving Laws," *Justice Quarterly* 9 (1992): 465–491.
8. Ibid., p. 470.
9. Ibid.
10. Ibid., p. 477.
11. Ibid., p. 479.
12. Ibid., p. 484.
13. J. David Hirschel, et al., "Review Essay on the Law Enforcement Response to Spouse Abuse: Past, Present, and Future," *Justice Quarterly* 9 (1992): 247–283.
14. Ibid., p. 248.
15. Ibid., p. 254.
16. Ibid., p. 261.
17. Ibid.
18. Ibid.
19. Ibid.

20. Ibid.

21. Ibid., p. 262.

22. 595 F.Supp. 1521 (1984).

23. Lawrence W. Sherman and Richard A. Berk, *The Minneapolis Domestic Violence Experiment* (Police Foundation, 1984). Lawrence W. Sherman and Richard A. Berk, "The Specific Deterrent Effects of Arrest for Domestic Assault," *American Sociological Review* 49 (1984): 261–72.

24. Hirschel, *Law Enforcement Response to Spouse Abuse,* 271.

25. Ibid.

26. Ibid., p. 277.

27. Allan F. Abrahamse, et al., "An Experimental Evaluation of the Phoenix Repeat Offender Program," *Justice Quarterly* 8 (1991): 155.

28. United States Department of Justice, Bureau of Justice Statistics, *Report to the Nation on Crime and Justice,* 2nd ed., March 1988, p. 97.

29. John M. Dawson, et al., "Prosecutors in State Courts, 1992," *Bulletin* (Bureau of Justice Statistics, U.S. Department of Justice, December, 1993) p. 5.

30. Ibid.

31. John S. Goldkamp and Doris Weiland, *Assessing the Impact of Dade County's Felony Drug Court* (National Institute of Justice, Research in Brief, December 1993).

32. Ibid., p. 5.

33. Ibid., p. 2.

34. Under California law, murder with special circumstances can lead to the death penalty. Special circumstances can include multiple murders and particularly brutal murders.

35. Christine Spolar and William Hamilton, "As Probe Continues, O.J. Weeps at Ex-Wife's Funeral," *Washington Post,* June 17, 1994, A-1.

36. Ibid.

2

CRIMINAL SANCTIONS

INTRODUCTION WHATEVER IS DONE TO OFFENDERS under the auspices of corrections is done because legally prescribed punishment is available to the sentencing judge. Punishment is the one area of the criminal law and correctional policy and practice that has changed the most over the past quarter-century. Before examining these changes as they affect corrections, we will look at the legal basis for and the history of punishment as delivered by American criminal justice systems.

THE PRINCIPLE OF *NULLA POENA SINE LEGE*

The fundamental principle guiding the imposition of punishment in the United States is expressed by the legal statement ***nulla poena sine lege:*** No punishment unless specified by law. Punishments cannot be made up out of thin air, or set according to the uncontrolled subjective predilections of the sentencing judge. Judges cannot, in other words, set sentences because they "got up on the wrong side of the bed" that morning.

Although this much is agreed to by nearly everyone examining sentencing policy and practice, there remain many controversies and conflicts regarding criminal sanctions. For example, the Eighth Amendment of the Constitution prohibits **cruel and unusual punishments.** There is a long, complicated history of appellate cases in which various punishments, ranging from the death penalty to confiscation of property and other assets, have been questioned against the Eighth Amendment's prohibition. The Focus on the Law feature presents a brief excerpt from a U.S. Supreme Court case, *Washington v. Massey,* in which a life-without-parole sentence for a thirteen-year-old murderer was challenged and upheld by the Court in 1990.

In this excerpt, we see a couple of troubling concepts that confront those who have attempted to refine and recast sentencing law and practice in this country. The Supreme Court's requirement in this case that punishments comport with **"contemporary standards of elemental decency"** is one such concept. How does one measure just what a society considers decent? Should the results of a national public opinion poll be used? Recently, an American teenager living in Singapore, Michael Fay, was sentenced to six strokes on his bare buttocks in addition to a fine and four months' jail time. The strokes were to be administered by a "martial arts expert" using a wet rattan cane. His offense involved vandalizing several cars. While officials of the U.S. government, including the president, expressed their view that the punishment was excessive, many Americans, responding to call-in radio and TV shows, expressed their support of the actions of the Singapore authorities. Can we deduce from this that corporal punishment currently is a decent penalty at some "elemental" level?

Another difficulty in determining appropriate punishments referred to in the *Massey* case, is that of **proportionality.** This is a separate issue and should not be confused with whether a sentence is cruel. Many would agree that sentencing a shoplifter to five years for taking a can of shaving cream from a supermarket would be out of proportion to the harm he or she caused the store. A five-year prison term may not be a cruel sentence, but it may be excessive.

How does a sentencing judge, or a legislator considering the passage of a sentencing statute, decide whether a particular punishment is or is not disproportionate? This question is particularly relevant today with calls for more severe sentences, including "three strikes and you're out" formulas. We can gain some help from a 1983 Supreme Court decision in a case that involved a test of the constitutionality of a South Dakota repeat offender statute. The Focus on the Law feature gives an excerpt from the Court's decision. In it, the Court stated that the "constitutional principle of proportionality has been recognized explicitly in this Court for almost a century."

This case, *Solem v. Helm,* raises no particularly complex issues. The defendant was found guilty of a felony ("uttering a 'no account' check for $100"). Since he had three

FOCUS ON THE LAW

LIFE WITHOUT PAROLE: *WASHINGTON V. MASSEY*

Massey argues that his sentence of life imprisonment without the possibility of parole constitutes cruel and unusual punishment when applied to a 13-year-old. The test is whether in view of contemporary standards of elemental decency, the punishment is of such disproportionate character to the offense as to shock the general conscience and violate principles of fundamental fairness. . . . That test does not embody any element or consideration of the defendant's age, only a balance between the crime and the sentence imposed. Therefore, there is no cause to create a distinction between a juvenile and an adult who are sentenced to life without parole for first degree aggravated murder.

SOURCE: 803 P.2d 340 (Wash. App. 1990)

past convictions, the state repeat offender statute applied to his sentence for the fourth conviction. The language of the statute is as follows:

> When a defendant has been convicted of at least three prior convictions [sic] in addition to the principal felony, the sentence for the principal felony shall be enhanced to the sentence for a Class 1 felony.

At a superficial level, we can see that the *nulla poena sine lege* principle has been met. There is statutory language clearly providing for life imprisonment when an offender has been convicted of a felony following three previous convictions. However, the Supreme Court plainly stated that statutory language alone is not sufficient to meet the test of the Eighth Amendment.

GOALS OF PUNISHMENT

Legislating and meting out appropriate sentences are difficult, controversial, and very political activities of legislators and judges. In order to understand the sentencing process, we need to look at the goals to be served when offenders are sentenced. Setting sentencing goals is a separate issue from issues such as the cruelty or excessiveness of punishment. It has generated controversy and conflict in the United States. What is it that we wish to accomplish by sentencing Mr. Solem or Mr. Massey to life in prison? Are we interested in "correcting" them? Do we want them to suffer for the harm they caused by their criminal conduct? Is it revenge we are after? Deterrence?

As you will see in the case of imprisonment in Chapter 6, we have a history of frequently conflicting and ever-shifting objectives in mind when we sentence offenders. At certain times we incarcerated men and women in order to encourage them to become penitent, thus, the American penitentiary was born. At a later time, we sought to "reform" them through industrial and agricultural training and education—the reformatory. Still later, a major goal of imprisonment was rehabilitation, or corrections. Numerous "treatment" programs were added to the mission of the prison. Currently, it would appear that we see prison as a place simply to incapacitate

One of the duties of probation officers is to interview offenders as part of their pre- sentence investigation.

the offender. Put her or him behind walls or fences so that she or he cannot offend against us. Few, if any, resources are available to deliver programs even hinting at preparing inmates for living again in the community outside the prison.

Regardless of what the public, legislators, and judges may state are the goals of sen- tences, there is the overriding goal of punishment for criminal conduct. To make the offender suffer is a constant theme throughout our nation's history. We may hear of corrections, rehabilitation, and incapacitation, but responding punitively to the crimi- nal is never far from our consciousness as well as our policies and practices. Having recognized this, we can see that criminal sentences fall into three broad categories based on sentencing modes and the objectives sought by those imposing them. These three are punitive, incapacitating, and correctional sanctions. We now discuss each.

Punitive Sanctions

Punitive sanctions include all those that deliberately cause an offender to suffer. Pain is intended and can be of a number of different kinds. For example, the caning of Michael Fay in Singapore was a corporal punishment. Corporal punishments are no longer administered in the United States, but penalties such as flogging were routinely ordered and executed during our colonial period and for some time after our inde- pendence from Great Britain.

For many decades, corporal punishment was a commonly employed punishment meted out to prison inmates for violations of prison rules. Dorothea Dix, after visit- ing many state penitentiaries in the 1840s, reported many such floggings.[1] For years, physical punishments were routinely administered in the military services for person- nel convicted of violations under military law.

Today, it is virtually impossible to think of any court-ordered sentences that pro- vide for inflicting physical pain. It may well be that any sentence of this type would

FOCUS ON THE LAW

THE TEST FOR DISPROPORTIONATE SENTENCES: *SOLEM V. HELM*

The Eighth Amendment declares: "Excessive bail shall not be required, nor excessive fines imposed, nor cruel and unusual punishment inflicted." The final clause prohibits not only barbaric punishment, but also sentences that are disproportionate to the crime committed.

The constitutional principle of proportionality has been recognized explicitly in this Court for almost a century. . . .

[W]e hold as a matter of principle that a criminal sentence must be proportionate to the crime for which the defendant has been convicted. Reviewing courts, of course, should grant substantial deference to the broad authority that legislatures necessarily possess in determining the types and limits of punishments for crimes, as well as to the discretion that trial courts possess in sentencing. . . . But no penalty is *per se* constitutional. . . . [A] single day in prison may be unconstitutional in some circumstances.

When sentences are reviewed under the Eighth Amendment, courts should be guided by objective factors that our cases have recognized. First, we look to the gravity of the offense and harshness of the penalty. . . . Second, it may be helpful to compare the sentences imposed on other criminals in the same jurisdiction. If more serious crimes are subject to the same penalty, or to less serious penalties, that is some indication that the punishment at issue may be excessive. . . . Third, courts may find it useful to compare sentences imposed for commission of the same crime in other jurisdictions. . . . In sum, a court's proportionality analysis . . . should be guided by objective criteria, including (i) the gravity of the offense and the harshness of the penalty; (ii) the sentences imposed on other criminals in the same jurisdiction; and (iii) the sentences imposed for commission of the same crime in other jurisdictions. . . .

SOURCE: 463 U.S. 277 (1983)

be found unconstitutional under the Eighth Amendment's ban against cruel and unusual punishment. Certainly, if one were to argue for the restoration of corporal punishment, it would be challenged on the grounds that it falls below "contemporary standards of elemental decency," to borrow a phrase from the Supreme Court's decision in the *Massey* case.

When we examine capital punishment, our ambivalence with regard to deliberately causing physical pain stands out clearly. There has been a steady movement to make the death penalty more "humane" and less painful. Shifting modes of execution over time reveal that hanging, electrocution, shooting, gassing, and more recently, lethal injections have all been advocated as more humane and less painful deaths than their predecessors. One might ask why we are interested in providing relatively painless deaths for offenders who have been determined to be unfit to live. Whatever the answer to this question, capital punishment developments provide ample evidence that this society is squeamish when it comes to the outright infliction of pain onto its offender population.

Corporal punishment is, certainly, not the only way to cause an offender to suffer. It has been suggested that formally labeling a person as a convicted offender can cause social and psychological pain. An otherwise upstanding citizen who commits a crime might well feel mortified at being publicly identified (in the press and other media). She or he might then be ostracized, and continue to suffer at the hands of members of the community.

In the earliest years of this nation, some offenders were sentenced to be publicly displayed, locked in the stocks and pillories of our towns. Placards announcing their offenses were hung around their necks. Nonoffenders in the community could see them as they passed through the town squares. Examples of such punishments were described by the criminologist Edwin Sutherland in graphic terms many years ago:

> Occasionally, . . . the ears of the offender were nailed to the pillory and had to be torn loose by the efforts of the offender. The crowd often pelted the offender in the stocks and pillory with objectionable missiles. One offender who had stolen cabbages from a neighbor's garden. . . was ordered to stand in the pillory with the cabbages on his head, and in addition was banished . . . for five years.[2]

Some of these good citizens not only verbally mocked offenders, but threw objects at them. Such a punishment, clearly designed to shame the offender, is now never used. What would be the value of displaying an offender in the center (wherever that might be) of Los Angeles, or New York, or Washington, D.C.?

There is little open recognition that this kind of pain is intended as a result of a criminal conviction. One cannot find language in sentencing statutes to support inflicting such pain. But, even as an unintended consequence of the criminal process, it certainly merits our attention.

When we turn our attention to sentences that seek to cause offenders to suffer through their wallets and bank balances, we find the most commonly used punitive sanctions in the United States. From the simple parking violation fine to massive confiscations of assets in certain drug cases, the offender is made to suffer for her or his offense.

The fine as a punishment has a long history in this country, and has recently been receiving a facelift in the form of **day fines**.[3] One of the arguments against fining some offenders is that they have no way of paying, given their economic status and employment prospects. What is the point of assessing a fine of $1,000 if an offender is a minimum-wage worker? Usually, sentencing laws provide for very limited discretion in such a case. Either one pays the fine, or the statute provides for jail time. The day fine builds in flexibility so that a fine can be tailored to the ability of the offender to pay. We will discuss the day fine in some detail in a later chapter.

Forfeiture of assets in certain drug trafficking and racketeering cases is currently employed by a number of states as well as the federal government. The rationale for forfeitures is that ill-gotten gains should be forfeited to the state. One example from the drug trafficking scene should suffice. If one uses a boat for smuggling illicit drugs, the boat may be confiscated. A property purchased with funds obtained through a money laundering operation can also be forfeited.

The aims of forfeiture laws, however, are mixed. One aim is deterrence: Having one's property confiscated or threatened with confiscation is thought to operate as a strong deterrent. Another aim is quite unabashedly financial: The funds or property obtained by the state through these laws can be recycled in the war against crime. In a recent study, Miller and Selva examined twenty-eight narcotics cases in which assets seizures occurred.[4] The study was conducted from the "inside." That is, a researcher was a "confidential informant" in undercover narcotics operations in a southern state.[5]

ACROSS CULTURES

CRIMINAL SANCTIONING IN A "PRIMITIVE" SOCIETY

As reported by anthropologist I. Schapera in 1930,[1] the Hottentots, an African people, constructed a relatively simple system that dispensed speedy justice and protected defendants from unwarranted accusations. The system was employed when persons were charged with serious crimes such as murder, theft, incest, adultery, and sodomy.

Once a suspect was identified, every member of the village was empowered to effect an arrest. There was no formal law enforcement agency.

Upon apprehension, the suspect was securely detained until the tribal council was convened. When assembled, the council sat in a circle with the accused standing in the center. Accusers presented evidence, and the defendant was permitted to respond as best as he or she could. Then the councillors discussed the case among themselves. A majority vote was required for a verdict.

Should the verdict be not guilty, the exonerated party was entitled to compensation in the form of cattle from the accusers.

When the verdict was guilty, and the chief decided on the death penalty, "the sentence was immediately executed. The headman, as chief executioner, rushed towards the criminal and felled him with a heavy blow. . . ; all the other men then violently attacked him until he was beaten to death."[2]

[1] *The Khosian Peoples of South Africa* (London: Routledge, 1930), pp. 339–340.
[2] Ibid., p. 340.

One of their important findings was that asset forfeitures were frequently dysfunctional in terms of fighting any kind of effective war on drugs. Their research found that prior to forfeiture statutes, police prioritized drug cases based on the amount of drugs involved as well as the threat to the community posed by offenders. Following enactment of these laws, the amount of money that was readily available for seizure became the criterion for determining police responses to drug offenses.[6]

The dysfunctional consequences of prioritizing asset seizures could be seen by virtue of the fact that small-time dealers and their operations had the most assets (cash, for example) readily available for the taking. Larger operators posed a more difficult task for the enforcement agents. Thus, seizure efforts tended not to threaten the activities of those who threaten society the most.

We can also view sentences of imprisonment as punitive in intent. Depriving a person of her or his freedom of movement certainly can cause suffering. In the prison where the author worked, all movements of prisoners were governed by passes issued by the administration. An inmate could not leave his tier unless his pass indicated his authorized destination and the time during which he was permitted to be off the tier. Times when inmates were permitted to be in a tier day room (the recreation area) were strictly controlled, and cell doors were automatically locked at the same time each evening. Lights in all cells on a tier were switched off simultaneously, whether inmates were "ready" for darkness or not.

Contacts with family and friends on the outside are limited, and, of course, sexual interactions are generally forbidden in the American prison. The prison has become a "total institution," closed off from the world outside.

The **pains of imprisonment** have been discussed by a number of criminologists, perhaps none as thoroughly as Gresham Sykes.[7] We will pick up Sykes's analysis of these pains in a later chapter when we review the contemporary prison scene.

We should keep in mind that imprisonment is not used solely to cause suffering. For some penologists, suffering is an unfortunate by-product of confinement, a by-product that interferes with other, more important goals such as rehabilitation or "corrections."

Incapacitative Sanctions

Sentences of confinement in secure facilities certainly qualify as attempts at **incapacitation.** This category of sanctions involves the selection of sentences whose objective is to make it physically difficult, if not impossible, to commit crimes against victims in the community. Obviously, placing an offender behind a fence or wall with armed guards ordered to shoot those trying to get over the fence or wall is incapacitating.

Using a prison is not the only way to incapacitate an offender physically. Sentencing a person to "home detention" with electronic surveillance can achieve the same result without the same degree of pain as being locked in a cell. The offender is attached to the supervising agent by an electronic "umbilical cord." Should he or she stray from the court-prescribed physical limits, the agent will be alerted and law enforcement can then respond. Such sentences may also cost much less than imprisonment. In Chapter 15, we will deal with such sentences as a form of so-called "intermediate" sanctions that have recently become available to sentencing judges.

Correctional Sanctions

The third broad category of criminal sanctions consists of sentences that are intended to be correctional. Recalling the comments at the beginning of Chapter 1, correcting offenders is an ill-defined objective. Generally speaking, sentences that seek to correct are said to serve rehabilitative goals. Just what this means is open to debate. I may be injured in a motorcycle accident, losing much of the function, say, of my right arm. My physician may prescribe a course of rehabilitative therapy. The goal of this therapy is to restore as much function to my arm as possible, to return me, physically, to the state I was in prior to the accident.

In the case of a convicted offender, however, the goal as well as the treatment is not so clear. Just who is a "rehabilitated" offender? To what state do I wish to return him? Clearly, the answers to these questions will depend on the etiology involved in his criminality. A convicted child abuser may herself have been a victim of child abuse. What rehabilitative sentence will restore her to what earlier state? What about a white-collar offender convicted of insider trading in the stock market?

Perhaps an offender who is a drug addict as well as a convicted drug dealer can be rehabilitated or corrected if, as part of the sentence, he or she is required to enter a substance abuse program. We can argue that at some time in this offender's life there was no addiction. Thus, if the substance abuse treatment is successful, he or she will be returned to that state prior to the addiction. But what of the criminal offender label? Assuming the "rehabilitated" person is released from a sentence, the person will become an ex-convict, with a number of disabilities associated with that status. In the case of my motorcycle accident, if the therapy was successful, there will be no stigma attached to my becoming an ex-patient.

At a superficial level we can argue that sentences falling into any of the three categories discussed above have the goal of preventing crime or preventing an offender from committing additional offenses, in other words, preventing recidivism. But if we examine sentencing philosophies more thoroughly, we will find that this goal is but one of a number of objectives sought through the administration of justice. We will also find that deterrence is more complex than appears at first inspection. In addition, we will see that not everyone agrees on the goals of sentencing, and that some of these goals are in conflict with others. A sentencing memorandum by a federal district court judge in the case of *United States v. Bergman,* in which he gave his rationale for a prison term in a white-collar case, illustrates both the different goals sentences can seek to reach and the issues a judge has to confront when deciding on an appropriate goal in a particular case.[8]

Keep in mind when thinking about the *Bergman* case that we often assume that punishments are to be applied equally to all persons convicted of similar crimes. Yet, in this case and a multitude of sentencing decisions facing judges every day, there are factors and goals that are peculiar to individual defendants. Thus, even though there may be general agreement among those involved in enacting and applying sentencing statutes, the actual day-to-day judicial decision making is beset by uncertainty and wide variation in results.

In the *Bergman* case the defendant before the judge for sentencing was convicted after pleading guilty to two counts in an eleven-count indictment involving his defrauding the United States under the Medicaid program through the operation of nursing homes he owned. He was sixty-four years old, an ordained clergyman, and noted for his philanthropic services to the community. His attorneys argued for no prison time, and instead urged that he be allowed to do community service. Let's take a look in some detail at what was facing the trial judge.

> For purposes of the sentence now imposed, the precise details of the charges, and of the defendant's carefully phrased admission of guilt, are not matters of prime importance. Suffice it to say that the plea on Count One (carrying a maximum of five years in prison and a $10,000 fine) confesses [his] knowing and willing participation in a scheme to defraud the United States in various ways, including . . . wrongfully padded claims under the Medicaid program to [his] nursing homes. Count Three . . . carries a theoretical maximum of three years in prison and another $5,000 fine. . . .
>
> The court agrees [with defendant's attorneys] that this defendant should not be sent to prison for "rehabilitation." [N]o one should ever be sent to prison *for rehabilitation.* That is to say, nobody who would not otherwise be locked up should suffer that fate on the incongruous premise that it will be good for him or her.
>
> Equally clearly, this defendant should not be confined to incapacitate him. He is not dangerous. It is most improbable that he will commit similar, or any, offenses in the future. . . .[9]

In his memorandum, the judge went on to justify his handing down a term of imprisonment (four months). He explained his decision in terms of two "considerations":

> *First,* the aim of *general deterrence,* the effort to discourage similar wrongdoing by others through a reminder that the law's warnings are real and that the grim consequence of imprisonment is likely to follow from crimes of deception for gain like those defendant has admitted.
>
> *Second,* the related, but not identical, concern that any lesser penalty would . . . depreciate the seriousness of the defendant's crime.[10]

We now turn to a discussion of the objectives of criminal sanctions that currently are being hailed by their advocates as necessary to fight a more effective war on crime. These are deterrence, retribution (or deserts), and rehabilitation.

Deterrence

As indicated above, one can argue that any sentence imposed by a judge has an objective of deterring further crime. Deterrence effects of sentencing are of two general types: special or specific, and general. In the case of the former, the sentencer may aim at keeping an offender from committing additional crimes (either of the same kind as that for which sentence is being pronounced, or any crime). Such an expectation is grounded in the belief (assumption, actually) that people will choose to avoid pain whenever possible. If a person commits a crime and is made to suffer for so doing, he or she will not commit it again for fear of further suffering.

Even sanctions that are not primarily punitive in quality may be expected to produce a special deterrent effect. Enforced therapy can be discomforting, and usually involves loss of liberty and privacy. Measures designed to incapacitate offenders also can be painful. Thus, according to deterrence theory, these may deter the individual exposed to them.

Deterrence as a major goal of sentencing has its origins in the **classical school of criminal law** and criminology, especially through the work of Cesare Beccaria in his treatise *On Crimes and Punishments,*[11] published in 1764. Beccaria was responding to the contemporary scene, which was characterized by the chaotic administration of criminal justice. Punishments meted out for crimes were frequently out of all proportion to the gravity of the harm caused by the offender. There was a general tendency for certain offenders to receive draconian punishments while others were dealt with leniently for similar offenses. The social and economic status of defendants had more to do with the severity of sentences than their actual behavior. This was seen by Beccaria as resulting not only in an unsystematic administration of justice, but causing a loss of respect for the law itself. Thus, the law was not an effective agency of social control.

In his major contribution to the developing classical school, Beccaria laid out the essential framework of deterrence theory that has been influential in the evolution of American law and its administration for more than two centuries. Because of Beccaria's importance to modern deterrence theory, we quote him at length here.

> Prevention of crime is more important than punishment for the crime committed. Punishment is desirable only as it helps to prevent crime and does not conflict with the ends of justice.
>
> The purpose of punishment is to deter persons from the commission of crime, not to give society an opportunity for revenge. In addition, punishment must be certain and swift, with penalties determined strictly according to the social damage wrought by the crime. Therefore, celerity—the time span between crime and punishment—is a key element in deterrence.[12]

Another early advocate of deterrence as the prime goal of punishment, Jeremy Bentham, provided the etiological basis for deterrence theory in 1789. As he put it, the differential influence of pleasure and pain determined whether or not a person chose to commit a crime. To him, "pain and pleasure are the great springs of action."[13] If a person perceives the benefits associated with a criminal course of action to outweigh the possible pains of being caught and punished, crime may result.

This pleasure-pain theory of human behavior, in more or less modified form, has informed deterrence theory in the United States ever since Bentham formulated it. Certainly one can see a major flaw in its simplistic view of humans as rational decision makers basing their decisions on a pleasure-pain calculus. Beyond this simplicity are other problems. As Beccaria pointed out, "celerity" of punishment is a key ingredient in deterrence. Speedy justice is not frequently observed in this country. Delays in apprehension of suspected offenders and delays in trials and sentencing are generally extensive. In the case of the death penalty, as an extreme example, delays in the execution of sentences average more than seven years from the pronouncing of the sentence to the death of the condemned person.[14]

The probability of receiving a painful consequence for "choosing" to commit a criminal act is considerably lower than 50 percent. Police clearance rates in this country are less than 40 percent for all reported crimes.[15] As we saw in Chapter 1, little more than one-half of all persons arrested on felony charges (that is, arrested for serious crimes) are convicted. Of those convicted, about one-half are imprisoned, most of them being sentenced to terms of one year or less.

Special or specific deterrence is one of two types of deterrence expected to be achieved when enacting and imposing the provisions of sentencing statutes. The second is referred to as general deterrence. Those supporting general deterrence as a major goal of criminal sanctions hope that the threat of punishment and examples of actual sentencing practices will cause those who might contemplate committing a crime to resist the temptation. Bentham believed that "general prevention ought to be the chief end of punishment."[16] Should the law fail to punish offenders, others would be encouraged to engage in criminal conduct.

The goal of general deterrence will be affected by the problematic nature of the celerity with which punishment is handed out, and the probability of its being available as an example to the general population. Empty threats may further contribute to disrespect for the limits imposed by criminal law just as surely as the chaotic administration of criminal justice so criticized by the proponents of the classical school.

We pointed out in Chapter 1 that one must always keep in mind that actions taken in one part of a criminal justice system will have an impact on other parts. We used as one example recent changes in drunk driving laws and their enforcement. Some empirical evidence is available to test whether increases in punishments for drunk driving offenses provide specific and/or general deterrence.

Research to provide evidence about deterrence was gathered by Kingsnorth and his associates from more than 1,200 court cases in Sacramento County, California.[17] The study covered a number of years during which time the state enacted stronger penalties for DUI (driving under the influence). Kingsnorth set out to see if the law changes actually produced a specific deterrent effect. That is, did increased penalties lower the number of repeat offenses? The answer was no.

Answering this question was difficult because of a number of complicating factors and actions by police, prosecutors, and defendants. Among these are, first, plea bargaining, especially in cases in which blood-alcohol levels are at the lower end of the statutory definition for conviction. In such cases, defendants often plead guilty to reckless driving, which carries lesser penalties. Second, the reform of state DUI law emphasized increasing penalties for conviction, but there was "no commensurate emphasis on increasing the certainty of apprehension."[18]

A third intervening factor was that California law permits choices of sanctions by defendants. Such choices include reduced punitive sanctions when defendants accept "correctional" conditions such as participation in an alcohol treatment program. Reduced penalties included restricted rather than suspended licenses and little, if any, jail time.

Finally, socioeconomic class affects both plea bargaining and the perception defendants have of punishment. Thus, defendants with privately retained attorneys were much less likely to have their licenses suspended and serve jail time.

The Kingsnorth study concluded that specific deterrence was not produced as a result of major changes in California law. As he and his associates put it:

> The penalty choices offered to defendants by . . . the law may have enabled defendants of different socioeconomic backgrounds to adjust the penalty to their lives in order to minimize stigma, attachment, and/or commitment costs; thus the choices may have undermined whatever deterrent effect might otherwise have occurred as a result of increased penalties.[19]

We are not done with California's effort to deter DUI offenses. Although **specific deterrence** may not have been achieved, a significant level of **general deterrence** may well have been a consequence of the changes in state law. This possibility is suggested by data on motor vehicle accident fatalities and injuries for the period covered by the Kingsnorth study. A reduction of more than 44 percent in both alcohol-related deaths and injuries compared with far lower reductions in non-alcohol-related deaths and injuries would lend considerable support to the law's effectiveness as a general deterrent.[20] Kingsnorth cautions against interpreting these findings without taking into account other variables such as statewide declines in alcohol consumption and the aging of the driving population.

To this point we have been focusing our attention mainly on the severity of punishments as a contributor to deterrence, both specific and general. The Kingsnorth study hinted at the likelihood that there is a much more complex **sociopsychological process** involved in any sanction's deterrent impact. A person's perception of a sanction's severity, the probability of being punished, and the nonlegal costs associated with the law's enforcement play a significant role in enhancing or diminishing the deterrent impact of any punishment. The nonlegal costs of law enforcement to a person are frequently ignored when evaluating a sanction's deterrent value. Apprehension by the police and identification as a suspect can have serious negative consequences for one's position among family, friends, and community regardless of whether a criminal conviction follows.

An interesting recent study of "courtship violence" examined the social psychology of deterrence more directly.[21] Surveying single university students, Miller and Iovani "queried [them] on a variety of perceptions about formal and informal sanction risks" with regard to violence while dating.[22]

The students were asked to indicate their perception of the likelihood of police being called to respond to violence and the likelihood of being arrested. They also were questioned about their perceptions with respect to the effect on their lives of formal sanctions. Among the findings of the study that have relevance for us in looking at deterrence as a major goal of punishment are the following:

1. Society's ambivalence regarding intimate violence is not lost on the respondents in our sample, as revealed by their lack of concern in considering the risks of formal intervention by the criminal justice system.[23]
2. Respondents who believed hitting to be against the law . . . perceived a greater risk of arrest; they also believed that should they be arrested . . . it would *not* cause a major problem in their lives.[24]
3. Abusive boyfriends may think their girlfriends will not expose their violent behavior in court because of the implicit victim blaming that she might encounter.[25]
4. . . . Men who were more strongly attached to their parents and close friends were more likely to view police intervention as creating a problem in their lives.[26]

From the several studies we have examined, it is clear that producing policies and laws that seek to deter, both specifically and generally, is far easier than getting the results sought. We now turn our attention to another, albeit related, goal of criminal sentences: retribution, or as it is now fashionable to say, just deserts.

Retribution or Deserts

Closely related to the notion that punishment should be given to rational criminal actors for purposes of special and general deterrence is the belief that one should punish offenders because they "deserve" to suffer for the harm they have willingly caused their victims and the community. Justice in the form of punishment includes **retribution** as a goal. A convicted offender should be made to take his or her **just deserts**.

This approach to sentencing has the appearance of fairness as well as a certain logic. Clearly, it is grounded in the classical assumption that human actors make choices among possible behaviors. Since these choices are voluntarily made, it follows that the actor deserves what she or he receives as a consequence. Michael Moore stated a commonly expressed theoretical basis for using punishment for retributive (desert) purposes when he said that society is "justified in punishing because and only because offenders deserve it."[27] The "moral culpability" of an offender not only deserves punishment, according to Moore, it imposes a "duty" on to society to exact retribution.

Thus, *not punishing* a guilty person is a violation of society's duty to itself. Of course, carrying out this duty is a bit more complicated than arguing that there is a duty. There is, for example, the matter of **commensurate deserts**. As put by Andrew von Hirsch, offenders must "not be treated as more (or less) blameworthy than is warranted by the character of the offense."[28] Thus, while convicted offenders deserve to suffer, they must not suffer beyond what is commensurate with the degree of harm they caused.

Deciding "the degree" to which suffering is deserved has always been problematic. It depends on, among other factors, how blameworthy an offender is as well as the degree of the harm caused her or his victims. In the case of the latter, murdering someone would seem to be the highest level of harm one can cause another. Treason and wartime espionage on behalf of the nation's enemy also are offenses at the highest level of harm.

At lower degrees of crime, however, determining how much punishment is deserved is not so easy. Historically, the simplest division of crimes in terms of seriousness has been to divide them into those classed as felonies and those identified as misdemeanors. Felonies have tended to include those offenses for which punishments may range from one year of imprisonment all the way to the death penalty in those states where it is available. Misdemeanors, on the other hand, have tended to include crimes for which sentences of less than one year and/or fines are imposed.

This rudimentary classification does not reflect the real world very well. Many states have developed elaborate stratification schemes for felonies and misdemeanors, labeling them as class A, B, C, etc., or class I, II, III. The Model Penal Code includes three "degrees" of felonies that incorporate crimes from murder to "promoting prostitution."[29] These attempts by the states and the Model Penal Code seek to guide prosecutors and judges in charging defendants as well as sentencing those convicted.

Commonly committed property crimes such as burglary and theft may be difficult to calculate in terms of amount of harm caused their victims. Various attempts to produce a calculus of harm caused include simple assessments of the dollar values of property taken and/or damaged. Grand and petty theft categories represent one such attempt. A simple cutoff point is set, and those thefts involving amounts of property above the line are "grand," while those falling below are labeled "petty."

Occasionally, there have been efforts to develop more quantitative measures of the severity of offenses. One such effort was the Wolfgang-Sellin scale. To use the scale, one needed to obtain detailed information about the offense, the degree of injury suffered by the victim (from none to death), and the values of property stolen or destroyed.

The author and his colleagues employed this scale to measure the seriousness of crimes committed by a sample of offenders, half of whom were considered mentally retarded.[30] The object of the research was to explore the popular belief that retarded persons were more violent than others. The results showed that they were not. An important lesson learned from the study was that attempting to measure crime severity required such vast amounts of data (which frequently are not available) and time as to make the technique impractical.

Other ways to determine the severity of criminal offenses, and thus to assign appropriate deserts, include sampling the opinions of the public. How does the population of a city or county, or the nation, judge the seriousness of various crimes? Marvin Wolfgang and his associates were among the first criminologists to attempt this in the United States.[31] Wolfgang gave descriptions of thirty-seven offenses to survey respondents. These descriptions ranged from "A person plants a bomb in a public building. The bomb explodes and 210 people are killed," to "A person under 16 plays hooky from school."

This kind of assessment can be useful not only in providing help in determining sentencing levels, but also for other components of the criminal justice system. The police, for example, might find it useful in allocating their limited resources more cost effectively if they had a good feel for community perceptions. Although a list of offenses can never completely cover all crimes, it can be helpful in tapping into the elements to which the public reacts. Any list of offense descriptions must be carefully chosen if it is not to present a skewed distribution of crimes.

Another problem with studies such as Wolfgang's is that it would need to be updated frequently. Caution would have to be exercised to avoid skewed results that may be caused by media reports on crime, particularly unusual and widely publicized criminal investigations and trials. For example, the massive media coverage of O.J. Simpson's preliminary hearing and trial certainly could affect not only perceptions about Simpson and his guilt or innocence, but also public views about homicide and spouse abuse.

More recent surveys also use lists of offense descriptions, ranging from petty larceny to multiple murders. In one survey, Dallas, Texas, residents were asked to rate the seriousness of these offenses and then to rate the moral wrongness and degree of harm caused victims by each offense.[32] The researchers found that those answering the questions fell into two groups. One found all the offenses to be of about the same level of moral gravity; the second made distinctions based on their perceived moral wrongness of each offense.

Another survey, with college undergraduates as the respondents, found little consensus among them.[33] As the researcher concluded:

> . . . it appears that popular sentiments are far from consensual. Even when the minimum 51 percent was adopted as the standard for consensus, the vast majority of offense items failed to produce evidence of agreement within the available categories.[34]

These studies, like that of Kingsnorth, discussed earlier, suggest that simple measurements of severity as perceived by the public may not be particularly useful in aiding legislators and judges when determining punishment levels for desert purposes.

Trying to ascertain the seriousness of the harm an offender has caused is only one part of the task of calculating the just desert he or she must take or the retribution to be exacted. The other is the task of determining the degree of the offender's culpability. Just how **blameworthy** is she? Was she a co-defendant with little involvement in the planning and/or the execution of the crime? What about mitigating circumstances? Perhaps he, convicted of child abuse, was severely abused throughout his childhood. How much desert should he take as retribution?

Various attempts have been made to figure blameworthiness. One major effort is contained in state and federal sentencing guidelines.[35] We will discuss these in some detail in the following chapter. One example should suffice, and it comes from the federal guidelines.[36] These guidelines provide for adjustments to the basic sentences for crimes depending on the participation level of the defendant. That is, if the defendant was a major player in a crime, the sentence can be increased in severity, while in the case of one who played only a minor role, the sentence could be much less.

We can argue that assessing an offender's just deserts has one major advantage over other rationales for punishment: It deals fairly with the convicted person. That is, he or she gets only what is deserved. All offenders, under a deserts system, would receive only what is merited. This, it may be claimed, might lead offenders to respond to the punishment appropriately (that is, the response matches our desire to deter). The impression to be made on offenders is one of being dealt with fairly. They would see little difference in punishments among offenders committing similar crimes.

There is, however, a problem with this argument. A deserts or retributive system that claims to deal fairly with convicted persons must be able to assume that offenders are fairly situated in society. Various criminological theories challenge this assumption.[37] Expecting an offender to accept her or his sentence as just when the offender believes that social conditions such as racism, sexism, and associated difficulties in finding legitimate employment opportunities led him or her to commit crime may be expecting too much.

Rehabilitation

Although the federal judge in the Bergman case discussed earlier indicated that he would never sentence someone to prison "for rehabilitation," over the last several decades prison sentences have, in many instances, been handed down for just such a purpose. Chapter 6 presents, in a historical context, a brief discussion of the use of imprisonment to achieve rehabilitative goals. Then in Chapter 7, we examine in detail a major state initiative to bring rehabilitation front and center through a new prison designed from the ground up to deliver treatment services to a serious offender population.

At this time we can examine some of the developments leading to the belief that imprisonment can be used to deliver appropriate rehabilitative programs and services. As early as the 1870s progressive penologists were convinced that only when inmates were classified into groups in terms of their needs for services (for example, education, vocational training), and not simply in terms of degree of custody, could they be made ready for release.[38]

Some of this thinking came from first-hand observations of foreign prison systems, especially the Irish system, where elaborate classification schemes had been in place for a number of years. Many of the conclusions drawn from these observations influenced the new type of institution just opening after the Civil War: the reformatory.

More important than these observations, however, was the development of a new "scientific" or "positive" criminology, which had begun to infiltrate penology during the last quarter of the nineteenth century. Cesare Lombroso's *L'uomo Delinquente* ("Criminal Man"), published in 1875, argued that it was possible to distinguish criminals from noncriminals through physical inspection and, thereby, to understand the causes of criminal behavior.

More significant for the development of a **scientific or positive penology** were the works of later "Lombrosians" and "positivists," in particular that of Enrico Ferri, Lombroso's most influential disciple.[39] These criminologists' theories and research contributed to a growing belief that the most effective way for criminal justice systems to respond to offenders was to generate typologies based on crime causation that would have "treatment" utility.

Ferri, for example, suggested a criminal typology made up of five types, each different in terms of causation and punishment (or treatment) requirements. Going farther, Ferri sought to have criminal trials divided into two parts: the first to consider the guilt or innocence of defendants; the second to place the guilty into appropriate subgroups based on the causes of their criminal acts, followed by the necessary sentence. This innovative policy proposal was the forerunner of present-day practices such as presentence investigations and sentencing hearings.

Prison terms, however, are by no means the major way judges have to try to deliver rehabilitative services to the men and women they must sentence. Judges may order defendants to be placed on probation for specified periods of time. As we shall see in Chapter 11, probation normally is the supervised release of the offender to the community. The probation order (all official probation releases are by judicial order) contains a number of conditions, rules, and restrictions. The violation of any of these can result in the probationer's return to court and a resentencing, possibly to prison.

Most of the conditions set out in probation orders have to do with security issues. That is, probationers may not change their address or employment, leave the jurisdiction, associate with criminals, nor commit any offenses (an obvious condition!). In addition, probation orders may include a variety of "treatment" conditions. For example, a probationer may be required to attend alcohol or substance abuse counseling sessions. Others may be required to participate in mental health counseling or therapy programs.

Other sentences, especially of the so-called "intermediate" type,[40] may involve various treatment or rehabilitative components. A defendant sentenced to home detention may be required to attend school or participate in therapy programs or substance abuse sessions. In fact, someone placed on home detention may have as a condition that he or she leave home *only* to participate in rehabilitative activities.

Before leaving this chapter, we need to consider, briefly at this point, the problem of conflict in goals that results from the attempt to use the criminal sanctions described above. In later chapters this conflict will be examined in greater detail. Take a look at the objectives sought to be achieved through the imposition of sentencing: deterrence, incapacitation, retribution (deserts), and rehabilitation. Clearly, we can see that through each of these the aim is to reduce crime, that is, to lower the level of recidivism among convicted offenders, and to prevent some persons from committing crimes in the first place. So far, there would appear to be no conflict. But when we try to achieve these goals through the sanctions we have available, difficulties arise.

For now let us examine the use of incarceration and play the role of state prison administrator who must take in those ordered to serve time for their crimes. In a state, trial judges may have very different goals in mind in sentencing those convicted in their courts. A judge in a suburban county may be strongly interested in rehabilitating the persons to be sentenced. A rural judge may seek to have her sentences serve primarily retributive goals. Another judge may differentiate his sentences on the basis of certain characteristics of his convicted persons. For example, he may wish to deter white-collar crime when sentencing an embezzler, but hope for rehabilitation when a drug-addicted street criminal is sentenced.

Let us say that each of these judges sends many offenders to the state's general prison. The prison administrator must admit all these offenders. All too frequently this administrator cannot operate the variety of programs needed to meet the judges' requirements. Usually, he or she does not even know that different reasons lay behind the sentences to be served. Probably the best that can be done is to provide for the secure confinement of the prison population. At least the administrator knows that judges expect this much of the prison system.

But let's say that a prison could make a attempt to deliver rehabilitative programs to some of its population. Can we really expect to "treat" offenders in the coercive environment of the correctional institution? The author once was in the position of giving the "welcoming" interview to new inmates in a state prison that had a treatment mission. First I went over the terms of the sentence, explaining parole eligibility dates (if any) and time off for good behavior. Then I went over the "do's and don'ts" in the inmate handbook (many more don'ts than do's), the security classification (medium to maximum) system, the strict controls placed on visits from the outside, and the restricted mail privileges.

Following the presentation of these restrictions and prohibitions, I offered inmates the assurance that we wanted to help them change their situation through various counseling and education programs and activities. I must confess that I felt less than confident that inmates believed me. Or, if they did, they certainly had no intention of taking advantage of my assurances. In Chapters 6 and 7 we shall take up this problem in its historical context as well as through a case history of one state prison.

SUMMARY

In this chapter we have shown that punishment, for whatever purposes, must be grounded in law. That is, the principle *nulla poena sine lege,* no punishment without a law prescribing it may be inflicted on an offender.

Although the principle seems to be a clear requirement for those deciding sentencing policy and implementing policy in the criminal justice arena, the reality is far more complex. We saw that criminal sanctions fall into three main categories: those that inflict pain of one kind or another; those that seek to incapacitate offenders; and others that look to the rehabilitation of offenders. Selecting which of these to use is a difficult task.

The difficulty in selecting sentences is compounded by the fact that the goals of sentencers (and those who draft policies and statutes) differ widely. Deterrence, retribution, and rehabilitation compete for dominance in society's continuing "war" on crime. Unfortunately, these goals can and do conflict with one another. Corrections, the locus for our sentenced populations, is often left to sort out the mess caused by the competing and conflicting demands made by others who send them these populations.

We also found that while writing sentences into statutes may satisfy, at a superficial level, the *nulla poena sine lege* requirement, there is much more to sentencing offenders than writing statutes. Not only does the sentencer have to consider the rationale for handing down a sentence, she or he must determine "how much" to sentence. Issues such as blameworthiness and the severity of harm caused by the crime are always present. The Constitution prohibits cruel and unusual punishments, and this has been interpreted by appellate courts to mean that sentences must not be disproportionate to the crime committed. Determinations of proportionality are difficult to make, but failure to do so accurately may result in successful appeals of sentences.

Many of these issues will be developed further in the next chapter when the sentencing process is described and analyzed. The reader should keep in mind the systemic quality of criminal justice and corrections when relating these issues to the sometimes complex and not always consistent legal and administrative processes involved in the sentencing of offenders.

KEY CONCEPTS

blameworthy

classical school of criminal law

commensurate deserts

contemporary standards of elemental
    decency

cruel and unusual punishment

day fines

general deterrence

incapacitation

just deserts

nulla poena sine lege

pains of imprisonment

proportionality

punitive sanctions

retribution

scientific or positive penology

social psychology of deterrence

sociopsychological process

specific deterrence

QUESTIONS FOR DISCUSSION

1. The fundamental principle of punishment in American criminal justice is *nulla poena sine lege*. This suggests that if a punishment is provided for in a statute, it may be ordered by a judge. Why is that not quite so simple?
2. What are the major variables that need to be taken into account when determining deserts for sentencing purposes? Discuss some of the problems that arise in incorporating these variables in the overall sentence decision.
3. What are some of the issues that arise when trying to deliver rehabilitative services in a prison setting? Carefully discuss the implications each has on the corrections process.
4. What were the major contributions to criminal justice from the development of scientific or positive criminology? Discuss each of these.
5. Discuss the conflict in sentencing goals in relation to the systemic character of criminal justice.

ENDNOTES

1. Dorothea Dix, *Remarks on Prison Discipline in the United States* (Montclair, NY: Patterson Smith, 1967) (reprinted from 2nd ed., 1845).
2. Edwin H. Sutherland, *Principles of Criminology* (Chicago: J. P. Lippincott Co., 1939), p. 336.

3. Laura A. Winterfield and Sally T. Hillsman, "The Staten Island Day-Fine Project," in *Research in Brief* (National Institute of Justice, January 1993).

4. J. Mitchell Miller and Lance H. Selva, "Drug Enforcement's Double-Edged Sword: An Assessment of Asset Forfeiture Programs," *Justice Quarterly* 11 (1994): 313–335.

5. Ibid., p. 321.

6. Ibid., p. 331.

7. Gresham Sykes, *The Society of Captives: A Study of a Maximum Security Prison* (New York: Atheneum Press, 1965).

8. *United States v. Bergman*, 75, Cr. 785 (S.D.N.Y., 1976).

9. Ibid.

10. Ibid.

11. Cesare Beccaria, *On Crimes and Punishments,* trans. Henry Paolucci (Indianapolis, IN: Bobbs-Merrill, 1963).

12. Quoted in Ernst Van den Haag, "The Neoclassical Theory of Crime Control," *Criminal Justice Policy Review* 1 (1986): 1.

13. Andrew von Hirsch and Andrew Ashworth, eds., *Principled Sentencing* (Boston: Northeastern University Press, 1992), pp. 62–66.

14. *Bureau of Justice Statistics Bulletin,* "Capital Punishment, 1992," (January 1993).

15. Federal Bureau of Investigation, *Crime in the United States* (1992). A crime is considered "cleared" when a suspect is arrested and charged.

16. Jeremy Bentham, "The Principles of Penal Law," in *The Works of Jeremy Bentham,* ed. J. Browning (1838).

17. Rodney F. Kingsnorth, Lisa Alvis, and Gloria Galvia, "Specific Deterrence and the DUI Offender: The Impact of a Decade of Reform," *Justice Quarterly* 10 (1993): 265–288.

18. Ibid., p. 285.

19. Ibid., p. 286.

20. Ibid., p. 284.

21. Susan L. Miller and Leeann Iovani, "Perceived Sanctions and Courtship Violence," *Justice Quarterly* 11 (1994): 281–305.

22. Ibid., p. 288.

23. Ibid., p. 297.

24. Ibid., p. 298.

25. Ibid.

26. Ibid., p. 299.

27. Michael Moore, "The Moral Worth of Retribution," in Andrew von Hirsch, et al., eds., *Principled Sentencing* (Boston: Northeastern University Press, 1992), p. 188.

28. Andrew von Hirsch, *Doing Justice: The Choice of Punishments* (New York: Hill and Wang, 1976), p. 71.

29. The Model Penal code has been developed by the American Law Institute, a private association of attorneys, judges, and law professors. It serves as a guide for legislators and others engaged in rewriting state criminal laws. The code is revised from time to time and is published with detailed annotations to its many provisions.

30. Bertram S. Brown, David E. Silber, and Thomas F. Courtless, "Fantasy and Force: Dynamics of the Mentally Retarded Offender," *Journal of Criminal Law and Criminology* 61 (1970): 71–83.

31. Marvin Wolfgang, et al., *The National Survey of Crime Severity* (Department of Justice, Bureau of Justice Statistics, 1985).

32. Mark Warr, "What Is the Perceived Seriousness of Crimes?" *Criminology* 27 (1989): 795–821.

33. Alexis M. Durham III, "Crime Seriousness and Punitive Severity: An Assessment of Social Attitudes," *Justice Quarterly* 5 (1988): 131–153.

34. Ibid., p. 150.

35. United States Sentencing Commission, *Federal Sentencing Guidelines Manual* (St. Paul, MN: West Publishing Co., 1994).

36. Ibid.
37. "Strain" is an example of criminological theory that relates actual and perceived socioeconomic position to crime. For a general review of the area, see Joseph F. Sheley, *Criminology* (Belmont, CA: Wadsworth Publishing Co., 1991), pp. 273–292.
38. See Chapter 6, p. 126.
39. Enrico Ferri, *Criminal Sociology* (New York: D. Appleton and Co., 1896).
40. For a further discussion of intermediate sentences, see Chapter 16.

3

THE SENTENCING PROCESS

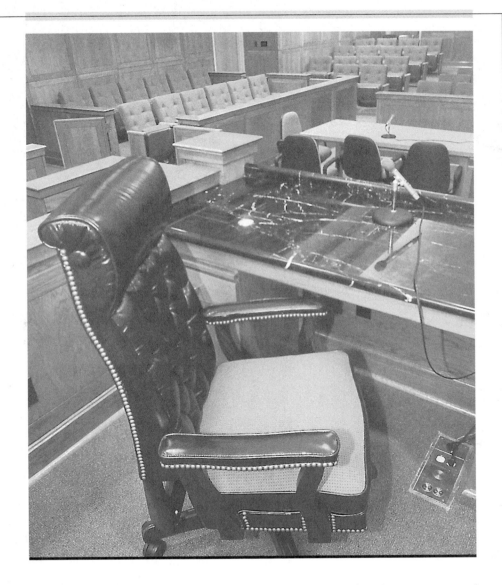

INTRODUCTION IN THIS CHAPTER WE WILL DESCRIBE the major types of sentences handed down by trial judges in both federal and state criminal courts, the legal and philosophical rationales for each, and the major criticisms voiced about them. Following this, we will discuss the process by which sentences are imposed.

There are two major types of sentences, whether they call for imprisonment or some other option selected by judges: **determinate sentences** and **indeterminate sentences.** In their simplest form, determinate sentences provide for a fixed time frame, five years, for example. An indeterminate sentence, on the other hand, lays down a range of time within which the offender is under the authority of the court or agency (the probation or prison system, for example).

We will begin with a brief discussion of the rationales for determinate and indeterminate sentences. Following this discussion we will present excerpts from a number of sentencing laws. With regard to the language of various statutes, we should recall the fundamental criminal law principle that there can be no punishment unless it is clearly provided for in law. That principle was covered in the last chapter.

Next we examine the development of sentencing guidelines, also provided for by law. These guidelines, adopted in many states as well as in federal criminal laws, while having the force of law in limiting judicial discretion, vary in terms of the latitude permitted the sentencing authority.

In the last chapter we took up the legal foundations of criminal sentencing and the many issues having to do with choosing appropriate sanctions by trial court judges. In this chapter, we shall examine in some detail the process by which sentences are decided. When reading about the process, keep in mind the issues already covered, especially those dealing with prosecutorial and judicial discretion, cruel and unusual punishments, and the goals to be sought in sentencing an offender. Remember that criminal justice is a system of interrelated elements and processes, including the sentencing component.

After setting the law foundation of the process, we will take up the presentence investigation and sentencing hearings. In the case of sentencing hearings, the special case of capital crimes will be described. Although there can be no doubt that offenders facing the death penalty are not to be considered for correctional intervention, the issues and process of death penalty hearings do help in understanding some of the problems facing the sentencing authority.

Finally, we will return to the subject of **judicial discretion.** We will see that many judges oppose limiting their discretion through the vehicle of either statutory limitations or sentencing guidelines. A number of judges view such limitations on their authority as unwise responses to public outrage about what it perceives as an "out-of-control" crime problem.

SENTENCE RATIONALES

The generally agreed upon rationale for imposing determinate sentences is derived from **classical criminal law theory.** This theory argues that punishments must fit the crimes for which they are ordered. As we saw in the last chapter, classical pioneers such as Beccaria and Bentham, and recent retributivists like von Hirsch sought to rationalize punishments by fitting them to the harm (crime) caused by offenders. In very simple terms, the classical basis for determinate sentences can be expressed by the equation: Crime A = Punishment A. Expressed this way, a judge must always sentence a convicted person in terms of the specific crime committed. That is, crime A should not be punished by sentence B, or C, or D, etc.

From our discussion in the last chapter, determining just what punishment or sentence should apply to each crime is fraught with difficulty, and may be close to impossible as a practical matter. This is especially so when one considers the deeper reasons for imposing sentences. Deterrence, specific and general, as well as retribution or deserts are hoped-for objectives when sentencing persons. Regardless of these problems and issues, using determinate sentences roughly approximates the late eighteenth-century goal of establishing a sentencing system that is logically attuned to fitting punishments to crimes.

The rationale for setting sentences of indeterminate length is very different and has its roots in **positive criminological theory.** Early positivists such as Lombroso, Ferri, Garafalo, as well as more recent ones stress the need to fit punishments (or interventions) to offenders, not to the crimes they committed. Again using a simple equation, the positivist argument is: Criminal A = Intervention A. The kind of sentence and its length must be appropriate to the offender, that is, to the offender's traits and needs; and, especially, the intervention must be appropriate to the causes of the offender's criminality.

Clearly, if we take the stand that we need to match sentences to offenders rather than to the crimes they commit, determinate sentences make no sense. In fact, determinate sentence may be counterproductive. For example, an offender whose violent crime is diagnosed as "caused" by a chemical imbalance in the brain is sentenced to five years in prison. The sentence is ordered by the judge because the statute requires it for that particular crime. At the end of the five years (or earlier if the person earns time off for good behavior) the offender will be released. But what if the chemical imbalance is not "corrected"? At the time of sentencing, argues a positivist, there is no way a judge or an agent preparing a presentence report can possibly know how long the person should remain in custody.

But, argues the classically inspired critic, indeterminate sentences are essentially unfair, providing unequal punishments for persons committing the same crimes. Further, they claim that the state of our knowledge regarding the causes of criminal behavior is so lacking as to make indeterminate sentencing irrational.

Countering these criticisms, positivists argue that simply fitting punishments to criminal acts is based on unscientific assumptions. In particular, the idea accepted by early classicists (and some recent ones), that a pleasure-pain calculus is all one needs to know about the etiology of criminal conduct, is appallingly superficial. That people freely choose behavioral options based on their perceptions of the gains and pains associated with their options, it is argued, is a poor basis for imposing sentences. That is, it is a poor basis if one really wants to change offenders into nonoffenders.

▌STATUTORY PROVISIONS

The Focus on the Law feature shows statements of purposes underlying three sentencing laws, the North Carolina and California state laws and the federal Sentencing Reform Act. In the first statement, it is clear that the legislators were more concerned with the state of prison overcrowding than with any issues having to do with classical or positivist theories of punishment. The California law clearly states that its intent is to deliver punishment proportionate to the seriousness of offenses. In the case of the federal statute, Congress set forth the complete range of goals we discussed in the last chapter: deterrence, incapacitation, "just" punishment, and rehabilitation. Just how Congress expected the federal criminal justice system to achieve these diverse goals with its reform of sentencing law is a disturbing question.

FOCUS ON
THE LAW

SELECTED STATEMENTS OF PURPOSE FROM SENTENCING STATUTES

An act to provide for structured sentencing in North Carolina consistent with the standard operating capacity of the Department of Correction and local confinement facilities and to redefine state and county responsibilities for the confinement of misdemeanants. (1993 N.C. ALS 538)

The Sentencing reform Act of 1984 (Title II of the Comprehensive Crime Control Act of 1984) provides for the development of guidelines that will further the basic purposes of criminal punishment: deterrence, incapacitation, just punishment, and rehabilitation. (United States Sentenc-

ing Commission, *Federal Sentencing Guidelines Manual,* 1993, p. 1)

. . . The Legislature finds and declares that the purpose of imprisonment for crime is punishment. This purpose is best served by terms proportionate to the seriousness of the offense with provision for uniformity in the sentences of offenders committing the same offense under similar circumstances. The Legislature further finds and declares that the elimination of disparity and the provision of uniformity can best be achieved by determinate sentences. . . . (California Penal Code § 1170)

Determinate Sentencing Statutes

Sentencing provisions that specify determinate or fixed periods of confinement often are not stated in absolute terms. For example, a statute may provide for an upper and lower limit. The sentencing judge is free to select a term within these limits. Other statutes provide for a fixed term, but then allow the judge to modify the sentence if there are **"aggravating" or "mitigating" circumstances** associated with the crime and/or the offender. In still other laws, the legislature may specify three fixed periods in ascending order from low to high. The judge may select one of these to be the sentence. Generally, the term preferred by the statute, or the **presumptive sentence,** is the middle one. The second Focus on the Law feature gives examples of each of these.

The Illinois law excerpted in the second feature represents only a small portion of the sentence provisions enacted by that state's legislature. The excerpt contains language for the crime of murder in the first degree, and for convicted murderers who are found to be "habitual criminals." But the language serves to illustrate the reach of legislatures in telling judges what terms (determinate in this case) to order.

Even though the Illinois law, and those of many other statutes, clearly seems to require judges to order specific terms of imprisonment for specific crimes, the language does not completely strip from the judge her or his authority to exercise some discretion. "If the court [the judge] finds . . . aggravating factors . . . are present," the sentence can be enhanced.

The Indiana Code gives another example of the legislature's determination to require judges to use fixed terms. In the excerpt, two levels of felonies are shown: Class A and Class B. For Class A felonies, the fixed term is 30 years; for Class B it is 10 years. But, depending on the judge's determination of the presence of aggravating or mitigating circumstances, the judge can alter the sentence substantially.

FOCUS ON
THE LAW

SELECTED STATE DETERMINATE AND INDETERMINATE STATUTES

Sentence of imprisonment for Felony. (a) Except as otherwise provided . . . , a sentence of imprisonment for a felony shall be a determinate sentence set by the court under this Section, according to the following limitations:

(1) for first degree murder, (a) term shall be not less than 20 years and not more than 60 years, or (b) if the court finds that the murder was accompanied by exceptionally brutal or heinous behavior indicative of wanton cruelty or that any of the aggravating factors listed [in another section] are present, the court may sentence the defendant to a term of natural life, or (c) if the defendant has previously been convicted of first degree murder . . . or is found guilty of murdering more than one person, the court shall sentence the defendant to a term of natural life.

(2) for a person adjudged a habitual criminal under Article 33B . . . , the sentence shall be a term of natural life. . . . (Illinois Revised Statutes Chapter 38, § 1005-8-1)

Class A Felony. A person who commits a Class A felony shall be imprisoned for a fixed term of thirty (30) years, with not more than twenty (20) years added for aggravating circumstances or not more than ten (10) years subtracted for mitigating; in addition, he may be fined not more than ten thousand dollars ($10,000).

Class B Felony. A person who commits a class B felony shall be imprisoned for a fixed term of ten (10) years, with not more than ten (10) years added for aggravating circumstances or not more than four (4) years subtracted for mitigating circumstances; in addition he may be fined not more than ten thousand dollars ($10,000). (Indiana Code §§ 35-50-2-4/5)

. . . When a judgement of imprisonment is to be imposed and the statute specifies three possible terms, the court shall order the middle term, unless there are circumstances in aggravation or mitigation of the crime. (California Penal Code § 1170(b))

The California Penal Code gives judges three possible sentences. The statute requires ("the court shall order") the judge to select the middle sentence unless "there are circumstances in aggravation or mitigation." If the judge does find these to be present, the bottom or top sentence can be selected.

In all three of these state determinate sentencing laws we see that fixed, immutable sentences are not required. Judges have opportunities to order terms of imprisonment other than the fixed terms specified in statutory language. Also, for many crimes, judges may order offenders to be released on probation, depending on a number of circumstances and factors made known to them, usually through a **presentence investigation or report.**

As we indicated earlier, more and more states are moving toward determinate sentencing as a result of increased pressure from the public to "get tough" on crime. There is a perception that a fixed or determinate sentence means that a convicted offender will end up spending time in prison and that the time will be what the statute demands. However, as we just saw, in many cases judges have the option to place an offender on probation. Prison systems operate under so-called "good time" laws and regulations, which provide for reductions in time of confinement based on an inmate's good behavior. In the system where the author worked, inmates could earn five days off their sentences for every month they were considered to be "good." Other states are more generous, giving reductions on a day-per-day basis.

Although many states and the federal government have abolished parole, some states retain it and employ determinate sentencing. In these states, the paroling authority in reality determines the actual time served by inmates. Authority to parole inmates is steadily being eroded by the states. The latest example of this is in Virginia where the newly elected governor appointed a commission to examine corrections policies and practices. The commission recommended that parole be abolished, prison sentences be increased for serious crimes, more crimes be punished by incarceration, and more prisons be built.[1]

Such proposals, of course, mean that more offenders will be sent to prisons and spend more time there. Since prisons in states like Virginia are already overcrowded, the increase in expenditures will be enormous if these changes are enacted by the legislatures.[2]

We also must reckon with the fact of **plea bargaining.** Prosecutors exercise **prosecutorial discretion** with regard to the specific charges to file against a defendant. A defendant who bargains for a reduced charge or a reduction in the number of charges will almost certainly be sentenced less severely than one who does not negotiate a plea. Thus, the sentencing process actually begins before the jury is selected and the trial begins, and this part of the process is not governed by statute.

Finally, a brief discussion of a relatively new variant on determinate sentencing: mandatory minimum sentences. As is in the case of the trend away from indeterminate sentences, the use of **mandatory sentences** reflects, at least in part, the public's concern that the crime problem has gotten out of control and that the courts are not strict enough when meting out punishments.[3]

Statutes that require judges to sentence defendants to some minimum amount of time in confinement range from those that cover the use of a firearm in the commission of a crime to others applying to repeat offenders. The most publicized of the latter class are the so-called "three strikes and you're out" (or, more accurately, "in") sentences. In Sections 902.7 and 902.8 of the Iowa criminal code are examples of mandating a minimum sentence for persons using firearms in the commission of "forcible felonies" and in the case of repeat offenders. If convicted of using a firearm in the commission of a forcible felony, "the convicted person shall serve a minimum of five years of the sentence imposed by law. A person sentenced pursuant to this section shall not be eligible for parole until the person has served the minimum sentence . . . imposed by this section."

Iowa's habitual offender section provides that a person convicted of a felony who has two prior felony convictions is a "habitual offender." "A person sentenced as a habitual offender shall not be eligible for parole until he or she has served the minimum sentence of confinement of three years."

An important U.S. Supreme Court ruling on the constitutionality of a federal criminal sentencing law illustrates the use of mandatory punishments for firearms-related crimes. It also illustrates the problems encountered when legislators try to write mandatory punishments into laws in response to strong public pressure to get tough on crime, in this case, getting tough on drug trafficking offenses by enhancing the sentence when an automatic firearm or one fitted with a silencer is "used" when committing the crime.[4] We can add that pressure from lobbying groups such as the National Rifle Association (NRA) may well be important in pressuring legislatures. The NRA has consistently argued that mandatory and severe penalties for firearms crimes is a better way to control violence than gun control legislation.

The following is a brief excerpt from the Court's opinion upholding the sentencing portion of the federal statute:

A grand jury . . . returned an indictment charging petitioner with, among other offenses, two drug trafficking crimes—conspiracy to possess cocaine with intent to distribute and attempt to possess cocaine with intent to distribute in violation of 21 U.S.C. §§ 841(a)(1), 846, and 18 U.S.C. § 2. App. 3–9. Most important here, the indictment alleged that petitioner knowingly used the MAC-10 and its silencer during and in relation to a drug trafficking crime. Under 18 U.S.C. § 924(c)(1), a defendant who so uses a firearm must be sentenced to five years' incarceration. As where, as here, the firearm is a "machinegun" or is fitted with a silencer, the sentence is 30 years. See § 924(c)(1) ("if the firearm is a machinegun, or is equipped with a firearm silencer," the sentence is 30 years"); . . . (term "machinegun" includes automatic weapons). The jury convicted petitioner on all counts.[5]

What is so interesting about the defendant's case is that he did not use the MAC-10 to threaten, shoot, or club someone. Rather, he *traded* the weapon for drugs. The Supreme Court found that the language "uses a firearm during and in relation to" a drug trafficking offense did not violate the Constitution in that the words "used a firearm" could apply to almost any use in relation to the commission of the specified crime.

Earlier we saw an example of a habitual offender sentencing clause from the Iowa criminal code. The most recent variant on such provisions is the "three strikes" formula. Advocates from President Clinton in his 1994 State of the Union address to state and local legislators and politicians have been clamoring for such laws. There is considerable confusion about the specific crimes that would make an offender eligible for a life sentence following three convictions. It is usually thought that the convictions should be for "violent" felonies. Some formulations, however, simply call for convictions for felonies of any kind.

A meeting of the National Conference of State Legislatures (NCSL) took up the three strikes issue and found many problems with it in the real world divorced from political rhetoric.[6] In an account of the meeting it was reported that the participants were concerned about the costs of "warehousing" aging inmates. State budgets are tight, and the need to create more prison space to accommodate increasing numbers of offenders serving longer sentences may strain them to the breaking point. However, the participants also made it clear that their constituents wanted them to continue to be "tough on crime."[7]

At least twelve states have enacted three strikes statutes, and Congress is considering including such a provision in a comprehensive crime control bill currently being debated. According to the report of the NCSL meeting, many legislators are urging a go-slow approach or recommending an outright abandonment of mandatory life-without-parole sentences.

It is easy to sympathize with lawmakers in this matter. Public sentiment is strongly in favor of "locking them up and throwing away the key." Unfortunately, when such measures are enacted, those who enact them are either unaware of the systemic consequences, or the consequences are unheeded.

Indeterminate Sentencing Statutes

Indeterminate sentences provide for a minimum and maximum period during which the offender is under the custody of the appropriate state agency—the state's department of corrections, for example. At some point during the time between the minimum and maximum span, the offender is eligible for a parole hearing before the state paroling authority, typically the state Parole Board. In effect, the paroling authority in such cases is the agency that actually determines the length of confinement.

Earlier we found that the rationale behind indeterminate sentencing laws was that a "positive" or scientific approach to dealing with criminals was necessary if they were to be corrected. That is, the state needed to know why offenders offend, and then to match sentences to them in such a way as to remove or ameliorate the causes of their criminality. Since such efforts may take an indefinite period of time, the length of the intervention cannot be specified in advance. Thus, at the time of sentencing, the judge cannot know how long the sentence should last.

The basic concept of an indeterminate sentence predates the onset of positive criminal law and penology by about four decades. The British penal reformer Alexander Maconochie introduced it while governor of the Norfolk Island penal colony in the 1840s.[8] He was convinced that the then current practice of setting fixed terms of servitude was not conducive to prisoner reform. Why should a prisoner change for the better if he would still have to do the time stipulated by the sentencing judge?

To change the determinate sentence to an indeterminate one, Maconochie assigned a number of "marks" to the number of years in an inmate's sentence. Sometimes referred to as the **mark system,** Maconochie's plan made the number of marks a debt the offender owed the state. Maconochie then built into his system opportunities for inmates to earn marks and pay off this debt. If paid off sooner than the length of the sentence specified, the inmate was released from confinement. In case an inmate could not earn sufficient marks for early release, he remained in custody until the fixed number of years had passed.

Maconochie's system was copied in Ireland, where it became known throughout much of the Western world as the Irish or **progressive system.**[9] Eventually the mark system was imported into the United States through the reformatory system, beginning with the Elmira, New York, state reformatory.[10]

On Norfolk Island, in Ireland, and in New York, the idea that fixed terms of imprisonment should be replaced by sentences of indeterminate length required another innovation, which today we call parole. If an inmate were to be released earlier than ordered by a judge at the time of sentencing, what was to be done with the unexpired portion of the sentence? Under Maconochie and in Ireland, the answer was the ticket of leave. The ticket of leave was a document certifying that a convict was authorized to be at liberty, or on leave from his or her sentence. Usually, an offender with a ticket was required to notify and register with the law enforcement agency in communities where he or she located after release from confinement. Failure to do so, or leaving a community without prior notification, could result in arrest and return to prison.

In the United States, the ticket of leave never really caught on. Instead, parole was introduced. In effect, parole is extended custody. That is, custody is transferred from prison to an external authority. This authority, a parole officer acting under the control of a state parole agency, is responsible for supervising paroled offenders. We shall take up parole in detail in Chapter 12.

Before moving on to some current indeterminate sentence laws, we briefly examine a flurry of indeterminate laws and correctional practices just prior to World War II and lasting until the mid-1980s. Mental health professionals and legislators banded together to bring a positive or scientific approach to what was seen as a most troubling offender: the psychopath, more specifically, the **sexual psychopath.**[11] Laws were enacted in many states to define the sexual psychopath,[12] as well as to set their sentences or periods of treatment and manner of release.

FOCUS ON
THE LAW

INDETERMINATE SENTENCES FOR
SEXUAL PSYCHOPATHS

Alabama Code, 15.438 (1955). Criminal sexual psychopaths are not to be released "until fully and permanently recovered."

California Code Annotated, § 5517 (1957). Sexual psychopath may be released when "improved to the extent that [there is] no benefit from further medical treatment and not dangerous to society."

Illinois Annotated Statutes, § 38-825a (1958). Sexually dangerous persons shall be "commit[ted] to

the Director of Public Safety who shall act as guardian and retain custody until recovered and released."

New Jersey Statutes Annotated, § 2A:164-6/8. Sex offender to be confined for a period "not to exceed period specified by law for the criminal offense." Earlier release authorized if the offender is "capable of making an acceptable social adjustment in the community."

Here we are concerned with the spate of indeterminate confinement provisions in these sexual psychopath laws. A sample of these provisions appears in the following Focus on the Law feature. When examining them, keep in mind that they are based on the positive or scientific perspective, that is, a person (a sexual psychopath) should not be sentenced to a fixed term. Such a person should not be released until "cured."

The purest example of an indeterminate sentence stipulation in the United States is to be found in the 1951 Maryland law, which was in force for more than twenty-five years.[13] This law was the latest refinement (enlargement, actually) in sexual psychopath statutes. It was specifically designed to provide confinement and treatment for a legally invented class of adult offenders, "defective delinquents."[14] The term *defective delinquent* is misleading in that all those coming under the statute were adults, and very few were "defective" (meaning, in 1951, mentally retarded). As defined in practice, those offenders who were covered by the law were formerly labeled psychopathic, including many who would have been referred to as sexual psychopaths.

The special correctional institution and treatment regimen established for these persons is the subject of Chapter 7. Here, we want only to examine the indeterminate sentence language written into the statute. Because it represented the most open-ended indeterminate law ever enacted in the United States, we quote it in detail:

> If the Court, or the jury as the case may be, shall find and determine that the said defendant is a defective delinquent, the Court shall so inform the defendant, and shall order him to be committed or returned to the Institution for confinement . . . , for an indeterminate period without either maximum or minimum limits. . . . [T]he sentence for the original criminal conviction, or any unexpired portion thereof, shall be and remain suspended. . . .[15]

This model of indeterminate sentencing is a bit unusual, although it had its roots in earlier sexual psychopathy laws in other states. It is unusual in that offenders found to be defective had already been convicted of crimes and sentenced to ordinary terms of imprisonment.[16] Usually their sentences were of a more restricted indeterminate type such as "not more than *X* years," or fixed terms. Regardless, if found to be defective, these sentences were suspended and the committed defective received a truly open-ended sentence.

This practice of restricting the use of indeterminate sentences by judges while retaining the ideal is the norm in many states. It reflects legislative (and, of course, the public's) suspicion of lenient sentencing of serious criminals should judges exercise unfettered discretion. Restrictive laws such as those we have described also reflect deep-seated suspicion of parole board decision making. Parole boards can issue rulings that result in early release of felons at the lower end of indeterminate sentences. We will discuss this issue later, in Chapter 12.

SENTENCING GUIDELINES

A more recent wave of sentencing reform has swept over a number of states and the federal government through the introduction of **sentencing guidelines.** This reform movement reflects a further erosion of support for indeterminate sentencing, a commitment to reducing judicial discretion while increasing judicial accountability for sentencing decisions, and an interest in eliminating sentence disparities in states and in the federal criminal courts. One set of guidelines, North Carolina's, reflects a more practical concern: reduction in prison overcrowding.

As a general rule, sentencing guidelines are established through legislatively mandated sentencing commissions. These commissions may be composed of judges, attorneys, criminologists, and other experts. Their recommendations can be rejected by the legislatures, and prior to the implementation of a set of guidelines, they must be acceptable to the legislature.

Minnesota was the first state to implement a sentencing guidelines system, doing so in 1980. These guidelines have been much studied, and other states have used them as models for their own efforts. Minnesota's statement of purpose for its guidelines gives us a good indication of the rationale behind this development in the law of punishment. The goals in the guidelines statement included setting "rational and consistent sentencing standards" that "will reduce sentencing disparity" and result in sentences that will be "proportional to the severity of the offense . . . and the extent of the offender's criminal history."[17]

A quick inspection of this statement cannot but leave us with the impression that it lays out a very tall order indeed. We also should note one criterion specified in the statement: the extent of an offender's prior criminal history. This criterion is common to state and federal guidelines systems. It runs counter to another popular contemporary purpose of criminal punishment: just deserts. As we pointed out in the previous chapter, a strict deserts or retributivist advocate would impose punishment (or deserved desert) only on the basis of the harm caused by the current offense of conviction, not for prior offenses for which deserts have already been received.

An elaboration on this statement of purpose enumerates several "principles" that shaped the development of the guidelines. These include: (a) sentences should be race, gender, and social status neutral; (b) sentences should be proportional in terms of offense severity and criminal histories; (c) sentences of incarceration should be limited to the most serious offenses and/or criminal histories; (d) departures from the presumptive guidelines sentences by judges should be made only when "substantial and compelling circumstances exist."[18]

By way of contrast, the federal guidelines established by the United States Sentencing Commission were shaped by the need to serve the entire range of classical and positivist principles we discussed in the previous chapter: "deterrence, incapacitation, just punishment, and rehabilitation."[19]

In a later section we will describe how state and federal sentencing guidelines are used to determine sentences. At this point, we turn briefly to a topic that concerned us in the last chapter: variations in perceived severity of crimes and how to prescribe appropriate punishments using sets of guidelines, thus reducing sentence disparity.

John H. Kramer and his associates compared sentences imposed in Minnesota, Pennsylvania, and Washington, all guidelines states.[20] What is of particular importance for our purpose is the Kramer study's relating of each state's sentencing philosophy to its prescription of ranges of punishment for various crimes.[21] Philosophically, both Minnesota and Washington adhere to a "modified just deserts" approach to punishment, that is, punishment should be proportionate to the severity of an offense. Washington, compared to Minnesota, gives more weight to prior convictions in recommending a sentence range, thus it represents a weaker just deserts approach. Pennsylvania, by contrast, retains a combination of deterrence, deserts, incapacitation, and rehabilitation, much like the federal guidelines.

The findings from the Kramer research suggest that there is considerable disagreement among the three states with respect to ranges of recommended punishments and severity of sentences for similar crimes. This conclusion supports the relevance of sentencing philosophies when seeking to reform the process through sets of guidelines. As the report concluded, "these findings show that the scope of the guidelines and the underlying philosophy of sentencing laws have important ramifications for the degree of discretion permitted by the guidelines . . . as demonstrated by the average width of the guideline ranges."[22]

A more long-term evaluation of Minnesota's guidelines experience was conducted by Stolzenberg and D'Alessio and reported in 1994.[23] They concluded that the state guidelines did reduce disparity in length of sentences to prison. Initially, prison–no prison sentences also were more equally distributed than prior to adoption of the guidelines. However, this reduced disparity in the courts decayed over time, an unexpected finding. They reported that the Minnesota Sentencing Guidelines Commission (MSGC, responsible for drafting the guidelines and periodically reviewing them) had two explanations for this return to a good deal of sentencing disparity. The first was that judges had concluded that a number of offenses simply did not warrant sentences recommended by the guidelines. "The sentencing guideline grid was constructed so that first-time violent offenders would be sentenced more severely than nonviolent repeat offenders."[24]

Feeling this way, judges departed from the guidelines mostly in response to mitigating circumstances, which Minnesota's system permits. Although departure from recommended sentences can also go in the other direction should aggravating circumstances and factors be present, Stolzenberg and D'Alessio found that this occurred much less frequently than reductions in punishment.

A second likely explanation for the return to sentence disparity was the need to "constrain the growth of Minnesota's prison population."[25] Judges, rather than add to the problems of the state prison system, were sending more and more offenders to local jails. The researchers believed that it was "plausible that judges opted to sentence increasing numbers of offenders to jails instead of prison so as to maintain prison populations within capacity constraints."[26]

Keeping in mind the systemic character of criminal justice, one may wonder how the administrators of these jails appreciate the way sentencing guidelines have affected them.

Earlier we noted the recently adopted North Carolina sentencing guidelines. Philosophical principles aside, this state's real-world problems with prison overcrowding led it, in 1993, to revise its guidelines to put a cap on prison populations. Similarly, the 1994 meeting of the National Conference of State Legislatures, referred to above, expressed concern, bordering on alarm, that recently enacted sentence reform legislation, including guidelines, was contributing to enormous increases in expenditures required to operate their criminal justice systems.

Some final comments regarding sentencing guidelines systems. Many judges, rather naturally, have complained that guidelines have hindered rather than helped them in passing fair and effective sentences. They argue that the guidelines and the factors that must be employed to utilize the guidelines often make sentence decisions for them that do not end up being fair.[27]

The most serious criticism of sentencing guidelines is that they effectively transfer discretion from the judiciary to the police and prosecutors. We saw in Chapter 1 that police discretion with regard to both arrest and charging decisions is extensively exercised in this country at all levels of law enforcement. We also saw that prosecutors have considerable control of the actual charges (as distinct from the actual criminal conduct) to be brought to the trial court.

Plea bargaining is a fact of life in American criminal justice. These bargains directly affect the eventual sentences handed down by judges. Not only do defendants who negotiate a plea receive more leniency from the court, there is evidence that others who either choose not to plea or are not given the opportunity to negotiate receive harsher penalties than they would if they had negotiated.

For unexpected matters requiring secure and private hearing a judge may call the prosecution and defense lawyers into the judge's private chambers. A possible plea agreement may be one matter that is discussed in chambers.

It is easy to understand the attraction of plea bargaining for defendants, prosecutors, and judges. From a strictly practical standpoint, the high level of guilty pleas (about 90 percent of cases) dramatically reduces the workload of already overburdened courts. Were the majority of defendants to plead not guilty and demand jury trials, criminal justice would come to a screeching halt.

Other considerations, however, are just as important, and, perhaps, more sinister than responding to crowded court dockets. Police and prosecutors may use the tactic of overcharging to encourage defendants to plead in order to achieve high levels of "successful" case closings. Plea bargains may be offered to persuade defendants to "give up" codefendants and break other cases for police and prosecutors. We only have to watch a sample of TV shows like the popular *NYPD Blue* to see how police use this powerful leverage through their interactions with prosecutorial staffs.

Of course, plea bargaining discretion by police and prosecutors has a serious impact on sentencing practice, whether or not sentencing is shaped by guidelines. Those who decry the negotiated plea when guidelines are involved argue that the exercise of discretion which produces serious unevenness in sentences simply has been shifted away from judges.[28] Further, judges may impose sentences that fall above or below a guideline range. However, at least they are required to justify their action in writing. In addition, such sentences may be appealed. In contrast, police and prosecutor discretion goes largely unreviewed.

There appears to be little that can be done satisfactorily to limit the effects of such discretion. State guidelines such as Minnesota's and others make use of "relevant" factors in a defendant's conduct to take care of possible problems caused by crimes of conviction being quite different from a defendant's actual criminal conduct. The United States Sentencing Commission's statements of policy and principles and its extensive commentaries accompanying the guidelines it developed address the issue frankly, if not with closure. The statement referred to the fact that "nearly ninety percent of all federal cases involve guilty pleas and many of these involve some form of plea agreement."[29] The Commission's report did not recommend any specific change in regard to plea bargaining, but indicated that the problem would be under continuous scrutiny.

We take up prosecutorial discretion in the next section as an integral part of the sentencing process.

THE SENTENCING PROCESS

In this section we will describe the process by which a defendant's sentence is determined. We begin with the negotiated plea or plea bargain. Then we discuss the presentence investigation, followed by the sentencing hearing. The sentencing process in capital cases will be described as a special subset of the sentencing hearing.

The Negotiated Plea

We have already seen that the common practice of negotiating guilty pleas seriously affects the ultimate sentence received by defendants. We have also seen that there are a number of important and pragmatic reasons for the practice. Before continuing to discuss the plea agreement as part of the sentencing process, we should point out two troubling aspects of the practice: Some defendants, innocent of the charges brought against them, plead guilty; and defendants who give up their due process right to a trial may effectively punish others who insist on their rights under the law.[30] These problems should always provide a background against which to judge the negotiated plea.

There are several pleas to criminal charges available to a defendant in state and federal criminal courts: not guilty, not guilty by reason of insanity (not available in all states), guilty, and *nolo contendere.* Not guilty and guilty pleas are self-explanatory. Insanity pleas in effect state that the defendant committed the criminal acts specified in the charges brought, but claim that he or she was insane at the time the acts were committed. In many jurisdictions, a person is not held responsible for criminal conduct if insane at the time of their commission.[31]

A plea of ***nolo contendere,*** or no contest, is virtually identical to a guilty plea. The main difference is that it does not admit guilt, and the plea cannot be used by a victim should a civil lawsuit be filed against the criminal defendant who pleads no contest.

To ensure that a defendant's rights are protected when and if a plea agreement is reached with the prosecutor, states and the federal government have established certain safeguards under their rules of criminal procedure. This is an essential protection since the acceptance of a guilty or *nolo contendere* plea by a judge is a conviction. The Federal Rules of Criminal Procedure (Rule 11) give us a good example of such protection. These rules provide, among other things, that a defendant be fully informed of all the implications of a guilty plea, that is, that minimum and maximum sentences will be announced, and that the defendant thereby waives her or his right to a trial. Judges are not required to accept a plea agreement. Under the federal rules, if a judge rejects the agreement the judge

> shall, on the record, inform the parties of this fact, . . . [and] afford the defendant the opportunity to . . . withdraw the plea, and advise the defendant that if the defendant persists in a guilty plea or plea of nolo contendere the disposition of the case may be less favorable to the defendant than that contemplated by the plea agreement.[32]

A plea agreement may include one or both of the following points:

1. A motion by the prosecutor to dismiss charges, if the defendant is charged with more than one crime or is charged with multiple counts of a crime.
2. A request by the prosecutor for a specific sentence for the crime or crimes to which the defendant has pleaded guilty. Frequently, this is in response to the defendant's proffer of a sentence option.

Under state and federal rules, a judge does not participate in plea negotiations and, as noted above, is not required to accept any plea agreement. The judge's role is limited to ensuring that a defendant's rights are protected and, most importantly, that a guilty or *nolo contendere* plea is entered "voluntarily." Under the federal rules, the voluntariness of a plea is determined by the judge speaking directly to the defendant and asking her or him whether the plea "is voluntary and not as a result of force or threats of force or a promise apart from a plea agreement."[33]

It should be clear that regardless of whether sentences are shaped by statutes or with the assistance of guidelines, the negotiated plea is the first and often essential step in determining any defendant's actual sentence. We now turn to what is usually the next step in determining a sentence, the presentence investigation and the resultant presentence report presented to the judge.

Presentence Investigation and Report

Following conviction in most jurisdictions, there is a period during which a presentence investigation is conducted for the court by an official, usually a probation officer. Upon completion of the report of the investigation, a sentencing hearing is held and a sentence handed down by the judge. Before describing the investigation and the sentence hearing, we should take note of the legal setting for this part of the process.

First, not every state mandates a presentence investigation and sentence hearing. Some states do, while others place these events within the discretionary power of the judge. Federal criminal law mandates a presentence report unless the judge decides it is not necessary. The federal sentencing guidelines specify that "a probation officer shall conduct a presentence investigation" and that a report of the officer's findings shall be provided to the judge prior to sentencing, "unless there is information in the record sufficient to enable the meaningful exercise of sentencing authority."[34]

Generally, defendants have certain rights during the presentence investigation and the hearing that typically follows the submission to the court of the report of the investigation.[35] They may suggest witnesses to be interviewed by the probation officer. They have the right to be represented by counsel at sentencing hearings, but not when they are interviewed by probation officers, psychologists, and psychiatrists.

It should be understood, however, that the presentence process, including the investigation and sentencing hearing, is not, legally, a truly adversarial process. That is, it is not adversarial in the sense that the pretrial and trial stages are. For example, probation officers conducting presentence investigations are considered to be officers of the court. They are not advocates for the state. Rather, they are gatherers of information for use by judges in deciding on appropriate sentences. Thus, restrictions on defendants' access to them as well as due process safeguards such as the right to cross-examine those who are interviewed by probation officers do not disturb constitutional protections.

There is, however, one exception to the principle that presentence hearings are non-adversarial. This is the sentencing stage in capital cases. Here the U.S. Supreme Court, in accepting the death penalty as nonviolative of the Eighth Amendment's cruel and unusual punishment clause, has required state and federal criminal courts to provide due process. This is accomplished by a separate sentencing phase of the criminal trial following the guilty verdict. During this phase, a sentencing hearing takes place. This hearing is virtually a full-scale adversarial trial.[36] We will return to this later.

What is contained in a presentence report? Although there is no uniformity with regard to the kinds of information contained in the report, nor even in its format, there are common elements we can derive from various state and federal presentence reports. The federal presentence report follows the requirements laid down in Rule 32(c) of the Federal Rules of Criminal Procedure. The rule states in part that the report shall contain:

- The classification of the offense and of the defendant using the Sentencing Commission categories.
- The kind of sentence and sentencing range suggested by the guidelines.
- The probation officer's explanation of any factors that indicate the appropriateness of a sentence other than that specified in the guidelines.

What this rule states is applicable to what one federal probation officer called "life after guidelines," and seems to limit the officer in the scope of her or his investigation.[37] The officer is to prepare the presentence report with the goal of "serving to

record how facts are treated by the guidelines and to aid the court in making preliminary findings of fact."[38] Life after the guidelines means that the presentence investigation no longer is "behavioral science" in character, with the flavor of a positive
approach to the sentence. Instead, the presentence investigator and the report "have
become the focus of . . . a very adversarial sentencing system."[39]

Under guidelines, the central focus of the presentence report has become the presentation of "facts, statutes, and guidelines" related to the defendant's offense behavior and prior criminal history. Offense behavior and the defendant's criminal history,
under state and federal guidelines systems, become the dominant factors in determining at least the range of the sentence to be imposed by the court. Other data collected by the probation officer are used mainly, if at all, to recommend a point within
the range that a judge might select as the actual sentence.

By contrast, before guidelines systems were established, and in states without formal
sentencing guidelines, more emphasis was given to a variety of less legalistic variables.
The presentence investigation and its culminating report to a court not operating under
a guidelines system is something of a diagnostic exercise. It conforms more to the positivist school in penology. It is more attuned to a "correctional" or treatment model of
the sentence. Typically, the report contains data on all or some of the following:

- Defendant's personal data (age, sex, race).
- Detailed description of the offenses for which defendant stands convicted.
- Prior criminal history.
- Educational background.
- Health history, including mental health. This would include any psychological, psy-
chometric, and psychiatric examination reports.
- Social data, including family history.
- Military service.
- Sentence recommendation.

The following Focus on the Law feature shows a sample presentence investigation
report submitted to a criminal court judge. This is a "composite" report, representing the common features found in state systems throughout most of the country. All
names and significant locations are fictitious. The offense and the contents of the various parts of the report are from a real case. In examining the report, ask yourself
what your recommendation would be if you were the investigating officer. Are there
sufficient data for you to make a recommendation? What additional sources would
you want to consult?

What is missing in this report, as is true of many such reports, is victim data. Historically, victims have been assigned a clearly secondary role in the drama of criminal
justice as it is played out in criminal courts. This is even reflected in the formal titles
of criminal trials. These take the form of the *People* versus Jones (or, variously, the
Commonwealth, State, the *United States*). Jones may have harmed a Mrs. Smith, but
she does not appear in the official title assigned to the trial. In fact, unless she is a wit-
ness at trial, she may not ever be seen in court.

The historical development of formal criminal law and procedures in the United
States resulted in placing victims in the background, because crimes were seen as violating the entire community, not just victims. To a large extent, this development was
a response to a perceived need to bring punishments under control. If victims or their
families were allowed to pursue their offenders and exact whatever punishment they
thought appropriate, there might be no end to punishment and the fabric of civilized
society could be jeopardized.

ON THE JOB

PRESENTENCE REPORT (COMPOSITE OF SEVERAL STATE REPORT FORMATS)

Presentence Report for the Circuit Court of Tidewater County

The People vs. Anthony Lee Perkins
Charge: Burglary
Date: August 15, 1994
Plea: Guilty
Judge: The Honorable Helen R. Lemert

Sources of Information

Anthony Lee Perkins, defendant (interview)
Assistant State's Attorney B.E. Smith (interview)
Donald F. Perkins, defendant's brother (interview)
Circuit Court (files)
State's Attorney's Office (files)
State Police Records Division (files)

Juvenile and Adult Record

No adult. Two juvenile (B&E)—one no disposition, one six months probation.

Official Version of the Crime

Defendant was charged, pleaded guilty, and was convicted of one count of burglary. Burglary took place at the private residence at 1212 Brookdale Parkway on May 3rd, 1994. Police called by occupant who heard noises at approximately 2 AM. Police arrived at scene approximately 2:30 AM and saw defendant on foot, running from scene. Upon apprehension, defendant was found to have possession of a wallet, watch, and briefcase later identified as belonging to occupants of 1212 Brookdale Parkway.

Defendant was charged with burglary, larceny, and destruction of property. Pleaded guilty to one count of burglary. Was found guilty in Circuit Court on July 21, 1994.

Defendant's Version

Defendant states that he needed money for his transportation costs to relocate in Phoenix, AZ, where a friend had offered him a job. He says he has been out of work for several months and was getting desperate. States that he is sorry for the trouble caused the victims., but "they got it all back."

Social History

Defendant was born on April 5, 1974, in Taos, NM, the only child of Henry and Eloise Perkins. Father was a noncommissioned officer in the Air Force. Mother was a housewife, accompanying her husband on his different service tours of duty.

Mother died of breast cancer when defendant was three years old. Defendant lived with father until age 17 when he left home. Between death of mother and leaving home, he and father moved four times because of father's transfers to various bases.

Defendant has completed the 11th grade. Expresses regret that he doesn't have a high school diploma.

Defendant is a 20-year-old white male, 5'8" tall, and weighs 139 pounds. He claims no illegal substance abuse and little consumption of alcohol other than beer. At the time of the offense he was living with a male friend in an efficiency apartment. He has no children or other dependents.

His assets consist of one automobile ('72 Chevy) that is "up on blocks" and a few items of clothing. His employment history is unstable. The last job was as a house painter's assistant, earning $4.50 an hour.

Recommendation

Because this is defendant's first adult offense, its nonviolent nature, and his expression of regret, it is recommended he be placed on intensive probation supervision, with special attention to additional education and vocational training to assist him to become employable.

One avenue of redress that has always been open to victims, other than whatever satisfaction they may derive from their offender's conviction and sentence, is the civil lawsuit. This avenue, however, is rarely taken and when taken, is not often successful.

Recently, however, victims' rights organizations have been formed and their pressure on state legislatures has resulted in more attention being given to the victim in the sentencing phase of criminal trials. One development tied to the new concern for victims' rights has been the use of **victim impact statements.** These are statements from victims and/or their families informing the court about the impact on them and their families of the crimes committed against them.[40]

At this time, the legal status of victim impact statements is unclear. Some critics argue that such naturally subjective reports by victims unfairly prejudice the court against defendants, and that it is difficult for defendants to counter their effect on a sentencing judge. Appellate courts have from time to time reviewed victim impact statements, mainly on the basis of defendants' claims that they violate due process and contribute to the imposition of arbitrary punishments.

The most recent court reviews of victim impact statements has been by the U.S. Supreme Court. Perhaps suggestive of the difficulty in dealing with the question as to these statements' rather newly established place in the sentencing process, two Supreme Court decisions went in completely opposite directions.[41] In the first, *Booth v. Maryland,* the Court held in 1987 that a victim impact statement in the presentence report (required by state law) resulted in the arbitrary imposition of the death penalty.

The victim impact statement in question contained vivid accounts of the good character of the victims and the emotional impact their deaths had on their children. The appeal had sought to have the sentence overturned because the defendant had no opportunity to contest these accounts, and that what should be of more weight in sentencing was his culpability, not the character of his victims and their families. The Supreme Court agreed.

Four years later, in *Payne v. Tennessee,* the Court reversed itself in another death penalty case, saying that:

> Victim impact evidence is simply another form or method of informing the sentencing authority about the specific harm caused by the crime in question, evidence of a general type long considered by sentencing authorities.[42]

This reversal of a precedent, so soon after it was set, is rather unusual for appellate courts, where the doctrine of *stare decisis* (let the prior decision stand) guides decisions. Perhaps the outrage generated by the earlier case and amplified by victims' rights groups caused the Court to reconsider the wisdom of its earlier decision. Or, possibly, it was the enormity of the crime that moved the Court to change its mind. Not to have done so would have left the victims' family and the lone survivor of a murderous assault with little "justice." Because the *Payne* decision is important for the legitimacy and value it places on victim impact statements, and as an example of the Supreme Court's changing its mind in making the "law of the land," we have reproduced an excerpt from it in the following Focus on the Law feature.

The Death Penalty and the Sentencing Process

Both *Booth* and *Payne* were capital punishment cases. This brings us to a consideration of the sentencing process in such cases. In the first place, death penalty presentence hearings are significantly more adversarial than other hearings, the result of which are sentences other than death. The Supreme Court has produced a string of capital pun-

FOCUS ON THE LAW

EXCERPTS FROM *PAYNE V. TENNESSEE*

The petitioner, Pervis Tyrone Payne, was convicted by a jury on two counts of first-degree murder and one count of assault with intent to commit murder in the first degree. He was sentenced to death for each of the murders, and to 30 years in prison for the assault.

Inside the apartment [the crime scene], the police encountered a horrifying scene. Charisse and her children were lying on the floor in the kitchen. Nicholas, despite several wounds inflicted by a butcher knife that completely penetrated through his body from front to back, was still breathing. Miraculously, he survived. . . .

During the sentencing phase of the trial, Payne presented the testimony of four witnesses: his mother and father, Bobbie Thomas, and Dr. John T. Hutson, a clinical psychologist specializing in criminal court evaluation work. Bobbie Thomas testified that she met Payne at church, during a time when she was being abused by her husband. She stated that Payne was a very caring person, and that he devoted much time and attention to her three children. . . . She said that the children had come to love him very much and would miss him, and that he "behaved just like a father that loved his kids." She asserted that he did not drink, nor did he use drugs, and that it was generally inconsistent with Payne's character to have committed these crimes.

Dr. Hutson testified that based on Payne's low score on an IQ test, Payne was "mentally handicapped."

The State presented the testimony of Charisse's mother. . . . When asked how Nicholas had been affected by the murders of his mother and sister, she responded: "He cries for his mom. He doesn't seem to understand why she doesn't come home. And he cries for his sister Lacie. He comes to me many times during the week and asks me, Grand-

mama, do you miss my Lacie. And I tell him yes. He says, I'm worried about my Lacie."

In arguing for the death penalty during closing argument, the prosecutor commented on the continuing effects of Nicholas' experience, stating:

"But we do know that Nicholas was alive. And Nicholas was in the same room. Nicholas was still conscious. His eyes were open. He responded to the paramedics. He was able to follow their directions. He was able to hold his intestines in as he was carried to the ambulance. So he knew what happened to his mother and baby sister.

"There is nothing you can do to ease the pain of any of the families involved in this case . . . , and that's a tragedy. They will have to live with it the rest of their lives. There is obviously nothing you can do for Charisse and Lacie Jo. But there is something you can do for Nicholas.

"Somewhere down the road Nicholas is going to grow up, hopefully. He's going to want to know what happened. And he is going to know what happened to his baby sister and his mother. He is going to want to know what type of justice was done. He is going to want to know what happened. With your verdict, you will provide the answer."

****

We [the Supreme Court] are now of the view that a State may properly conclude that for the jury to assess meaningfully the defendant's moral culpability and blameworthiness, it should have before it at the sentencing phase evidence of the specific harm caused by the defendant. "[T]he State has a legitimate interest in countering the mitigating evidence which the defendant is entitled to put in, by reminding the sentencer that just as the murderer should be considered as an individual, so too the victim is an individual whose death represents a unique loss to society and in particular to his family."

ishment decisions since 1972 when, in *Furman v. Georgia,* it found the death penalty as applied by Georgia to be unconstitutional.[43] This decision, although based on a number of concurring opinions by the justices and thus not providing a clear statement on the punishment, meant that states were required to revise or repeal their capital punishment statutes. About the only message to be taken from the decision was that the process whereby defendants were given the death penalty had to abide by due process safeguards. The process could not be arbitrary, random, or discriminatory.

States scrambled to respond. First, they attempted to meet the Court's objections by making capital punishment automatic for certain "capital" crimes. A later decision, *Gregg v. Georgia*, held, in effect, that such automatic or mandatory death sentences violated the Constitution.[44] In *Gregg*, the Court found that juries ought to be able to consider both mitigating and aggravating circumstances when evaluating a crime and the perpetrator. Thus was born the sentencing phase in capital offense trials. States retaining the death penalty have uniformly rewritten their statutes to provide specifications of the crimes that may carry the death penalty and the aggravating and mitigating circumstances that may be considered. All courts now have a distinct sentencing hearing at which the jury recommends the sentence. If the trial was without a jury, then the judge alone determines the sentence following the hearing.

Keep in mind that there is an important step in the capital crimes sentencing process not subject to appellate court review. That step is taken in the prosecutor's office. A prosecutor is under no obligation to charge a defendant with a capital crime. For example, the prosecutor in the O.J. Simpson double murder trial chose not to charge Simpson with murder committed "under special circumstances." In order for a convicted murderer to face the death penalty in California, the prosecution must convince a jury that one or more special circumstances (usually called aggravating circumstances in other states) accompanied the crime. These circumstances are spelled out in the statute. We can only speculate why the prosecutor chose not to try Simpson for capital murder.

For a number of reasons which we discussed earlier in this chapter, the prosecutor can exercise her or his discretion to accept a plea agreement that relieves a defendant from the possibility of the ultimate penalty.

When one factors in prosecutorial discretion, it is difficult to see how the Supreme Court's concern about the arbitrary and random application of capital punishment has been brought under control through its string of decisions since the *Furman* case.

Invoking the Sentence

Where the judge is not constrained by guidelines, the sentence is structured by relevant statutory provisions. Judges may accept the recommendation contained in a presentence report, but they are not obliged to do so. Regardless of whether the appropriate sentencing law requires a determinate, indeterminate, or mandatory sentence, judges do exercise discretion in making their choices.

Under a guidelines scheme, decision making would seem to be a far simpler matter. After all, the guidelines give judges ranges of sentences within which they are to select the punishment. Let's see how this is supposed to work. All sentencing guidelines systems essentially entail a matrix or grid within which sentence ranges are inserted in terms of the severity of the crime and the defendant's prior criminal history. Table 3.1 shows an extract from the current edition of the federal guidelines sentencing grid. It shows the sentence ranges (in months) for two offense levels (15 and

ACROSS CULTURES

THE SENTENCING PROCESS IN THE NETHERLANDS

Contrary to the trend in the United States toward statutorily mandated sentencing guidelines that limit judicial discretion, the Netherlands places sentencing squarely in the hands of prosecutors.

> In the Netherlands, there has been no real need for sentencing guidelines at the judicial level. Instead, since the prosecutors control the initiation of criminal proceedings, guidelines have been implemented at the prosecutorial level.
>
> If the prosecutor takes a case to trial, he or she makes a specific penalty recommendation to the judge. Even though they are not bound to the recommendation, judges rarely have imposed sentences harsher than the one recommended by the prosecutor.*

The initial step in the prosecutor's decision making is to categorize a new case in terms of a classification scheme (e.g., homicide, robbery). Then "salient" factors are considered such as the defendant's prior criminal record, and employment history, the victim's suffering, and the value of any property stolen or damaged. Once these have been taken into account, a "tariff" or penalty is established based on past cases with similar factors.

We can see that in the Netherlands, the sentencing factors taken into account are quite similar to those in American states where sentencing guidelines are used. The major difference is that prosecutors make the decisions, and it appears the defendant has little input into the process.

Another contrasting situation is the authority of prosecutors to resolve cases by way of issuing warnings, requiring defendants to make restitution, or perform community service.

*Marc G. Gertz and Laura B. Myers, "Prosecutorial Decision Making in the Netherlands: A Research Note," *Journal of Criminal Justice* 18 (1990): 359.

30) in relation to the criminal histories of offenders (from first offenders to those with extensive histories).

In guidelines systems, offenses typically are assigned "base levels" of severity. These can be adjusted to account for a number of variables such as the degree of the defendant's participation in the crime, the characteristics of the harm caused victims, and the nature of the victim (e.g., aged, child, handicapped). Then the defendant's past criminal history (if any) is scored and he or she is assigned a number of points. Having determined the base level for the crime, adjusted it if necessary, and scored the criminal history, the sentencing authority only has to enter the proper row and column, and *voilà*, there is the sentence range!

We saw earlier, however, that this rather straightforward exercise does not always please judges, nor does it completely eliminate their discretion. Judges can hand down sentences that fall above as well as below the calculated range. After the notorious Rodney King beating by L.A. police, two officers convicted in federal court of violating King's civil rights received sentences well below the range specified by the federal guidelines. The judge, required to make public the reasons for his decision, explained that longer sentences would make the officers subject to more violence in prison; that they had been excessively prosecuted in state and federal courts; and that their beating of King had been "provoked" by King.

On appeal, the Ninth U.S. Circuit Court of Appeals, on August 19, 1994, unanimously ordered the sentencing judge to resentence the officers.[45] The outcome points

Sentence Ranges for Two Offense Levels (Ranges given in months)   TABLE 3.1

Offense Level:	CRIMINAL HISTORY CATEGORY (CRIMINAL HISTORY POINTS)*					
	I (0 or 1)	II (2 or 3)	III (4, 5, 6)	IV (7, 8, 9)	VI (10, 11, 12)	VII (13 or more)
15	18–24	21–27	24–30	30–37	37–46	41–51
30	97–131	108–135	121–151	136–168	151–188	168–210

*Criminal history points given on basis of number of prior convictions, incarcerations, and whether defendant was on probation or parole when current offense was committed.
SOURCE: This table is a modified version of the Federal Sentencing Guidelines found in the *Guidelines Manual*, p. 320.

out that a judge's sentencing discretion under guidelines is much more constrained than it was prior to their adoption. Now, a judge must be aware that not only must a reason be given for not following guideline ranges, but the reason can be reviewed in appellate court.

We also saw that there is considerable disparity in sentencing because of prosecutorial discretion as well as disagreement about the severity levels of crimes. This discretion is not subject to effective review in court. Prosecutors may, however, have to "take the heat" from public opinion if their charging decisions generate controversy.

San Quentin's location on the water in California adds to the security level and isolation of this maximum security prison.

SUMMARY

Criminal laws in the United States make available a rather large number of differently structured sentences. Some call for determinate or fixed sentences. Others provide for indeterminate periods. Still others mandate certain minimum sentences.

Over time there has been a movement to curb sentencing disparity by enacting statutes and guidelines that reduce discretion by the sentencing authority. Whether by guideline systems or by statutes that seem to require judges to limit, or at least explain, any deviations from what legislatures want, judicial discretion has been reduced, but not eliminated.

Many argue that sentencing disparities still occur because police and prosecutors are not bound by statutory or guidelines prescriptions. Police can overcharge suspects, and prosecutors have considerable leeway in reaching plea agreements with defendants.

There still is a role for the traditional presentence investigation. However, under sentence guidelines, the function of the investigator has been restricted more to the task of assisting the sentencing authority in selecting the sentence range.

Finally, the sentencing hearing has become more adversarial, given the trend toward more severe penalties as punishment philosophy moves in the direction of retribution. In the case of capital punishment trials, the penalty phase today is more like a full-scale trial than ever before.

The various sentences described in this chapter should be examined in light of their varied impact on corrections. Increased prison populations, declining probation populations, and the steady elimination of parole throughout the nation are troubling developments for the corrections administrator and worker.

KEY CONCEPTS

aggravating or mitigating circumstances	positive criminological theory
classical criminal law theories	presentence investigation or report
determinate sentences	presumptive sentences
indeterminate sentences	progressive system
judicial discretion	prosecutorial discretion
mandatory sentences	sentencing guidelines
mark system	sexual psychopaths
nolo contendere	*stare decisis*
plea bargaining	victim impact statement

QUESTIONS FOR DISCUSSION

1. Why do you believe that indeterminate sentences have increasingly been replaced by determinate ones?
2. Do you have any suggestions for limiting the discretion prosecutors have to enter into plea agreements with defendants? What systemic consequences would your suggestions have if implemented?
3. Should the prison population explosion be taken into account when revising sentencing statutes? Fully explain your answer in terms of (a) the goals of punishment, and (b) the systemic character of criminal justice.

4. If you were a judge, what should be contained in a presentence report in (a) a guidelines jurisdiction; (b) a determinate sentence jurisdiction; and (c) indeterminate sentence jurisdiction?

5. In order to bring about "truth in sentencing," that is, a judge's sentence means just what he or she says at the time of sentencing, would you abolish parole? Fully explain your answer.

ENDNOTES

1. Peter Baker, "Allen Targets Parole," *Washington Post,* August 17, 1994, p. A-1.
2. According to a recent article, Virginia already houses 1,800 inmates in local jails in lieu of prison because of the overcrowded conditions. This is said to be in violation of state law. See Peter Baker, "Va. Housing 1,800 Inmates in Violation of State Law," *Washington Post,* August 18, 1994, p. C-1.
3. An evaluation of mandatory minimum sentences in terms of their impact on corrections as well as their deterrent effect is beyond the scope of this chapter. Those interested in pursuing this area should consult some of the studies available in the field. Two recent articles are: William D. Bales and Linda G. Gees, "Mandatory Minimum Sentencing in Florida: Past Trends and Future Implications," *Crime & Delinquency* 38 (1992): 309–329; David McDowall, Colin Liftin, and Brian Wiersema, "A Comparative Study of the Preventive Effects of Mandatory Sentencing Laws for Gun Crimes," *Journal of Criminal Law & Criminology* 83 (1992): 378–391.
4. For a more detailed presentation of this case see Thomas F. Courtless, *Introduction to the Making of Criminal Law: Cases and Commentaries* (Oklahoma City, OK: Custom Academic Publishing Company), pp. 33–42.
5. *Smith v. United States,* quoted in ibid., pp. 35–36.
6. William Claiborne, "State Legislators Rethink '3 Strikes' Laws as Costs Begin to Hit Home," *Washington Post,* August 7, 1994, p. A-18.
7. Ibid.
8. See Chapter 6, pp. 127–128.
9. See Chapter 6 for a discussion of this system.
10. See Chapter 6, p. 128.
11. Alexander D. Brooks, *Law, Psychiatry and the Mental Health System* (Boston: Little, Brown and Co., 1974), pp. 475–489.
12. In addition to the term *sexual psychopath,* many different labels were inserted into these laws. A sampling includes: criminal sexual psychopath, mentally abnormal sex offender, sexually dangerous person, and psychopathic personality.
13. Article 31B of the Maryland Annotated Code (1951).
14. Defined in § 5 as "an individual who, by the demonstration of persistent aggravated antisocial or criminal behavior, evidences a propensity toward criminal activity, and who is found to have such intellectual deficiency or emotional unbalance, or both, so to clearly demonstrate a danger to society. . . ."
15. Ibid., § 9(b).
16. In the years the author was on the staff of the institution for defective delinquents, only one referral was not sentenced to imprisonment. This inmate had been sentenced to death.
17. Sheldon Krantz and Lynn S. Branham, *The Law of Sentencing, Corrections and Prisoners' Rights,* 4th ed. (St. Paul, MN: West Publishing Co., 1991), p. 158.
18. Ibid., p. 159.
19. *Federal Sentencing Guidelines Manual,* p. 1.
20. John H. Kramer, Robin L. Lubitz, and Cynthia A. Kempinen, "Sentencing Guidelines, a Quantitative Comparison of Sentencing Policies in Minnesota, Pennsylvania, and Washington," *Justice Quarterly* 6 (1989): 565–587.

21. Ibid., pp. 569–570.

22. Ibid., p. 583.

23. Lisa Stolzenberg and Stewart J. D'Alessio, "Sentencing and Unwarranted Disparity: an Empirical Assessment of the Long-Term Impact of Sentencing Guidelines in Minnesota," *Criminology* 32 (1994): 301–310.

24. Ibid., p. 307.

25. Ibid.

26. Ibid.

27. For somewhat opposing views of two federal judges commenting on their experiences with the federal guidelines, see Andrew J. Kleinfeld, "The Sentencing Guidelines Promote Truth and Justice," and G. Thomas Eisele, "The Sentencing Guidelines System? No. Sentencing Guidelines? Yes." Both are in *Federal Probation* 55 (1991): 16–25.

28. Gerald W. Heaney, "Revise Guidelines Now," *The State of Corrections*, Proceedings of the American Correctional Association Annual Conferences (1993), pp. 112–118.

29. USSC, *Guidelines Manual*, p. 8.

30. Krantz and Branham, p. 24.

31. There is an important distinction to be made with regard to insanity *at the time* crimes are committed and sometime *after* the acts are committed. In the latter case, it may be determined that a defendant is incompetent to stand trial. In such cases, a defendant may be tried if he or she regains competence. In some situations, a person may not regain competence and may be committed to a mental health system. In a very few cases, a person found guilty may become legally insane later. In this circumstances, imposition of punishment must be suspended until sanity is restored.

32. *Federal Rules of Criminal Procedure,* Rule 11(e)(4).

33. Ibid., Rule 11(d).

34. *Federal Sentencing Guidelines Manual,* § 6A1.1, p. 367.

35. For a concise discussion of these rights, see Krantz and Branham, Chapter 3.

36. The *Payne* case described in this chapter is an example of the adversarial nature of sentencing hearings.

37. Jerry D. Denzlinger and David E. Miller, "The Federal Probation Officer: Life Before and After Guideline Sentencing," *Federal Probation* 55 (1991): 49–53.

38. Ibid., p. 50.

39. Ibid., p. 51.

40. One recent study of victims' taking advantage of the new climate showed that a very small number of victims appear and testify at sentencing hearings. See Edwin Villmoare and Virginia V. Neto, "Victim Appearances at Sentencing under California's Victim's Bill of Rights," National Institute of Justice, *Research in Brief* (August, 1987). They reported that less than 3 percent of victims testified after the law went into effect.

41. For a more detailed discussion of these cases, see Courtless, pp. 5–6, 102–117.

42. Ibid., p. 113.

43. 408 U.S. 238 (1972).

44. 428 U.S. 153 (1976).

45. Article attributed to News Services title: "Around the Nation: King Beating Officers Ordered Resentenced." *Washington Post,* August 20, 1994, p. A-2.

CAPITAL PUNISHMENT: THE ULTIMATE CORRECTION

SMYRNA, DEL., JAN. 25—Convicted murderer Billy Bailey was hanged today, dropping silently from an outdoor gallows at the state penitentiary here in the most violent legal execution Delaware has performed in half a century.

Bailey, who shotgunned an elderly farm couple to death without provocation in 1979, was already standing on the 15-foot wooden platform when witnesses entered the compound . . . at midnight. The noose swung beside him in a bitterly cold wind.

Bailey, 49, faced forward without expression, flanked by guards wearing black suits and black hoods. The guards then led the squat, 200-pound man onto the trap door, placed a strap around his ankles and pulled a black hood over his head and upper chest. The noose was fastened over the hood and tightened beneath Bailey's chin.

Several times [the warden] felt at the hood to be certain that the top of the hangman's knot lay beneath Bailey's left ear, the placement old Army regulations specify to assure the . . . rope has the best chance of bringing quick death by severing the spinal cord. Finally, the warden stepped back and pulled a gray wooden lever with both hands.

The trapdoor opened with a thump. Five feet of manila rope followed Bailey through the hole and snapped taut 10 feet above the sodden ground.

Bailey's body spun counterclockwise six times, then rotated once in the opposite direction.

Eleven minutes later, a voice behind the tarp announced that the official time of death was 12:15 A.M. A Correction Department spokeswoman later declared that the execution occurred "without complication." An independent trauma surgeon said 11 minutes was not an unusual time to wait for the pulse to stop after the spinal cord has been cut.[1]

INTRODUCTION

It may seem odd to include a chapter on capital punishment in a corrections text. A work on corrections should focus primarily on laws, policies, and practices that are designed to "correct" offenders. Capital punishment eliminates offenders convicted of capital crimes.* However, because corrections appears to be conceived as encompassing all criminal sanctions, the omission of the ultimate penalty here would shortchange those who read this text.

A general problem that arises when examining capital punishment is that no other sanction in our inventory of weapons against crime evokes as much debate, controversy, and just plain outpouring of emotion as the death penalty. It has been called barbaric, cruel and unusual, just deserts, revenge, and retribution. Disagreement about almost every aspect of capital punishment characterizes the discourse in scholarly and popular publications.

Questions continue to be asked about the purposes, effectiveness, procedures to determine who should be executed, modes of execution, and the often lengthy appellate process that accompanies death penalty sentences. So far, no answers have been completely satisfactory. Two things are clear, however: Most Americans want the death penalty for those who commit the most heinous of murders; and the United States is the only country in the Western world to have and use the ultimate penalty.

Historically, many rationales have been advanced to support and reject the death penalty. Enactment of capital punishment statutes and the successes and failures of abolitionist movements have been subject to the pushes and pulls of social, political, and economic factors. We must not ignore this fact if we are to understand the cur-

---

*Capital crimes are variously, but similarly, defined in state and federal statutes. As a general rule, murder is the only crime that may be punished by death in the United States. Capital murder, by statute, is murder accompanied by aggravated or special circumstances. These circumstances must be proved by the prosecution at the sentencing phase of a trial. Defendants have an opportunity to offer mitigating circumstances. This procedure is referred to as "guided jury discretion."

rent status of this punishment. Study of the fate of death penalty statutes in several states between 1897 and the end of the 1930s clearly demonstrates that whether or not states enact, retain, abolish, or reinstate capital punishment may have little to do with crime rates, but much to do with other factors.[2]

Among the major factors affecting abolition and then reinstatement of capital punishment was the lynching of accused and convicted offenders in some states where capital punishment had been abolished:

> Lynchings emerged as the most important common triggering event in reinstatement of the death penalty . . . . These lynchings often alerted officials that the public was unwilling to consistently support abolition. Ironically, the belief that without capital punishment lynchings inevitably would occur caused many death penalty opponents to re-think their positions. To these individuals, the death penalty became the lesser of two evils.[3]

Thus, those appalled by lynchings and those advocating reinstatement of capital punishment laws joined forces to end abolition.

Economic conditions also were found to be correlated with the fate of abolitionist movements. Death penalty sentences were reenacted during two economic recession periods: just after World War I, and during the "Great Depression" of the 1930s. Galliher, Ray, and Cook argue that we must understand the interplay between macro- and microsociological variables to make sense of the role of the death penalty in the United States. They state that "society used the death penalty not only to oppress minorities and protect the majority, but also as a repressive response to Depression-era conditions of social dislocation and economic turmoil."[4]

In this chapter we will examine the many issues and questions that arise as America expands the use of capital punishment. We will pay particular attention to the rationales that support and oppose the death penalty, the legal aspects of capital punishment, and research findings regarding its effectiveness as a sanction to control serious violent crime.

CONDEMNED PRISONERS AND EXECUTIONS

Thirty-eight states, the federal system, and the military have statutes that authorize the death penalty. At the end of 1995, there were 3,054 persons under sentence of death in state and federal prisons.[5] During that year, a total of 56 men were executed. No women were executed. If we look at the amount of time the 56 men had been confined, we find that the average was eleven years and two[6] months.

We know this about those under sentence of death:

- Fifty-five percent were located in Southern states.
- Thirty-five (1.3 percent) were women.
- Fifty-seven percent were white.
- Forty-six percent had at least a high school diploma.
- The median age at time of sentencing was 29 years.
- Seven condemned prisoners were age 17 or younger.
- Over two-thirds had prior felony convictions; 9 percent had a prior homicide conviction.

The Supreme Court decision in *Gregg v. Georgia*[7] upheld the Georgia death penalty statute, thus setting the stage for the resumption of executions that had been blocked by the Court's earlier decision in *Furman v. Georgia*.[8] Since the death penalty was reinstated following the 1976 *Gregg* decision, 226 persons have been executed. To put this figure in historical perspective, examine Figure 4.1, which shows the number of executions from 1930 to 1994. Then examine Figure 4.2, which shows the changes in the number of persons sentenced to death since 1953. You can see the effects of the *Furman* case as well as the effects of the reinstatement of capital punishment in 1973.

During the period from 1973 to 1993 the states and federal corrections system received a total of 4,984 persons with death sentences. As of the end of 1993,

- 226 were executed.
- 112 died from other causes.
- 1,785 had their sentences or convictions overturned.
- 122 had their sentences commuted (changed to life or a term of years).
- 23 were removed from death rows for other reasons.
- 2,716 were still under sentence of death.

How were the 226 men executed since 1973? One hundred and eight were electrocuted, 108 received lethal injections, 8 were gassed; one was hanged, and one died by firing squad.[9]

Data on those executed in 1993 (38 men) reveal that 18 were non-Hispanic and white; 13 were non-Hispanic and black; 4 were white and Hispanic; 2 were of "unknown Hispanic" origin.[10]

ARGUMENTS FOR AND AGAINST THE DEATH PENALTY

In this section we will present the major arguments for the use of capital punishment, the counterarguments, and some additional arguments against the death penalty.

John Kaplan reviewed the major arguments often made in favor of capital punishment.[11] These are:

- Capital punishment acts as a general deterrent.
- Capital punishment is incapacitative.
- Capital punishment is deserved retribution.
- Capital punishment is less expensive than its alternative, life imprisonment.
- It is virtually impossible to execute innocent persons.
- Death sentences are imposed on only the most brutal offenders.
- Most Americans favor the death penalty for at least some serious crimes.

We shall now examine these arguments.

Capital Punishment Is a Deterrent

The deterrence argument claims that the threat of death will deter at least some people from committing the most serious, violent crimes. This seems to be a plausible argument, for as van den Haag stated:

> There is no statistical evidence for . . . [deterrence]; I doubt that there ever can be. But experience and common sense tell us that people fear nothing more than death. It seems likely, therefore, that fear of death, or the risk of death, will deter more from crime, than fear of anything else, including imprisonment.[12]

Ernst van den Haag's belief that the deterrent impact of the death penalty can never be proven empirically fuels the controversy for those who support and reject the

Persons Executed, 1930–1994

FIGURE 4.1

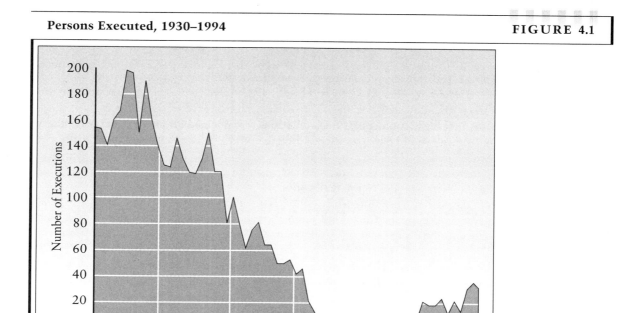

SOURCE: *Capital Punishment, 1994*, Bureau of Justice Statistics.

Persons under Sentence of Death, 1954–1994

FIGURE 4.2

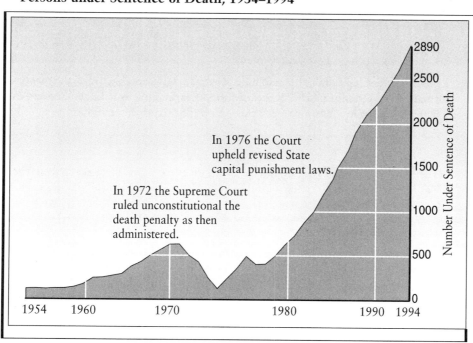

SOURCE: *Capital Punishment, 1994*, Bureau of Justice Statistics.

punishment on grounds of deterrence. Most commentators and researchers have concluded that there is little, if any, scientific basis for using capital punishment as a **general deterrence** for murder or other violent crimes. Perhaps the most publicized research that does indicate a deterrent value in the death penalty was conducted by Isaac Ehrlich using a complex econometric model.[13]

Examining data for the period from 1933 to 1965, Ehrlich claimed to have found that "an additional execution per year . . . may have resulted on the average in seven or eight fewer murders."[14] Such a finding, if replicated for contemporary conditions, obviously would have considerable impact on the debate that rages over the use of the death penalty. However, Ehrlich's work was criticized by a number of researchers.[15] The criticisms generally focus on the assumptions Ehrlich had to make to build his econometric model of the real world.

There has been some research that counters the belief that the death penalty deters. A report by Cochran, Chamlin and Seth examined the impact of Oklahoma's resumption of executions following a 25-year lapse.[16] (Note that Oklahoma's resumption of executions took place before the bombing of the federal building in Oklahoma City.) The researchers sought to assess the impact using a two-part disaggregation of murder: felony murders and murders of strangers. Two opposing hypotheses were tested. The first states that executions deter "deterrable" murders. Deterrable murders are those that are felony murders. That is, killings take place in the course of committing another crime, for example, during the course of a robbery or drug transaction. The second hypothesis states that executions brutalize by legitimizing lethal violence.

The deterrence argument was found to be difficult to support:

Because it is essentially impossible for the lay public either to know or accurately estimate the proportion of capital murders for which executions have been carried out . . . , it is unlikely that the death penalty could deter even "deterrable" potential offenders. In all likelihood, only those executions receiving significant media coverage are likely to have any deterrent potential.[17]

The researchers did find some evidence to support a **"brutalization" hypothesis.** This hypothesis is based on the following:

- Executions devalue human life and indicate that it is acceptable to kill the unworthy.
- Offenders may identify with the executioner, especially in stranger homicides in which they perceive an injury from the victim that requires retribution.

The authors utilized weekly time-series data on the two specific types of homicides. Their results were:

[There is] no clear evidence of any impact of the [recent] execution on either the total or the felony homicide series. Yet a slight brutalization effect . . . of the execution seems to be suggested by the higher spikes evident in the post-intervention portion of the stranger homicide series. . . . In addition, a comparison of the pre- and post-intervention [data] . . . shows a statistically significant increase in the level of stranger homicides.[18]

Cochran and his associates suggested that the increase in stranger homicide may be related to the resumption of capital punishment because it "weakens socially based inhibitions against the use of deadly force to settle disputes."[19] Further, they argued that:

Regardless of the functional form of the model, the analyses show that the execution . . . had no effect on either total, total felony, stranger-felony, death-eligible felony, or robbery-felony homicides.[20]

From these conclusions, one can argue logically that should the pace of executions pick up, the brutalization effect will increase. Or, it is possible that if executions become relatively commonplace, media coverage will decrease, especially sensationalist coverage, and thus there may be a reduction in brutalizing effects and possibly an increase in deterrence effects.

A much earlier study that examined the possible brutalizing consequences of capital punishment reviewed executions carried out in New York state.[21] The analytical method employed:

> is a simple one. It asks how the number of homicides in a given month is affected by the occurrences of executions throughout the proceeding year. The data are homicides and executions occurring monthly. The monthly homicide figures run from their starting point in January 1907 through January 1964, a year after the last execution. . . .[22]

The conclusions drawn by the researchers include the following:

- [S]ome of those who were stimulated to kill by the occurrence of an execution would have done so anyway, but did so *sooner* because of the execution.
- These data suggest a third additional homicide in the second month after an execution, [and] they also suggest (though less strongly) that one of the three might have occurred a month or so later. . . .
- In any case, the data definitely show an addition of at least two to the incidence of homicides, not simply a change in the timing of homicides.[23]

The authors point out that they may actually have underestimated the brutalization effect because they did not take into account homicides that occurred in the same month as an execution. Further, the study convinced them that "brutalization occurs among the pool of potential killers . . . and not the population at large." Thus, persons who are in a state of "readiness to kill, in which the potential killer has a justification, a plan, a weapon, and above all a specific victim in mind," may well be moved to act because of an execution.[24]

Another study of deterrence effects by Peterson and Bailey reviewed available data on deterrence during two historical periods: pre- and post-*Furman*.[25] They concluded that:

> [S]tudies of changes in murder rates before and after the abolition and/or reinstatement of capital punishment revealed that states which abolished the death penalty did not experience unusual increases in homicides. Rather, abolition and/or reintroduction of capital punishment was sometimes followed by an increase in murders and sometimes not.[26]

After Ehrlich's research concluded that executions would save innocent lives, a number of studies employing time-series and cross-sectional methodologies have consistently found no support for the deterrent value of the death penalty. As Peterson and Bailey state, "some analyses have discovered that the presence and/or use of the death penalty may even have a brutalizing effect thereby contributing to rather than reducing homicides."[27]

Looking at the situation after the *Furman* decision, Peterson and Bailey concluded that for the period 1973–1984, research findings "provide no indication that our national return to capital punishment since *Furman* (1972) has had even a slight downward impact on the homicide problem."[28] They go on to say that this conclusion supports the position that the "roots" of the murder problem in the United States go much deeper into the nation's political economy and its treatment of minorities, especially blacks.

It is important to recognize that the arguments for and against capital punishment as a deterrent are complicated by the need to answer two questions: What is it that capital punishment is supposed to deter? And who is to be deterred? Deterrence theory assumes that persons are rational decision makers when it comes to committing criminal acts and that they will consider the possible penalties they may suffer from acting criminally. However,

> From what we know about murder, . . . there is reason to doubt these assumptions. Most murders are acts of passion between angry or frustrated people who know one another. Indeed, many murders are the results of assaults occurring under the influence of alcohol, and many of the murderers are persons who previously and repeatedly assaulted the victim.[29]

Thus, it is argued, no threatened punishment, including death, will have much effect on these killers.

Capital Punishment Is Incapacitative

A second argument in support of capital punishment, that the death penalty is incapacitating, is, of course, an argument with which it is impossible to disagree. Death incapacitates absolutely. Of course, opponents argue, **incapacitation** can be achieved by sentencing murderers to life without parole. Some studies question the need to employ such an extreme penalty to achieve an incapacitative effect. One such study, published in 1988, tracked 17 former death-row inmates who were paroled after their sentences were commuted following the *Furman* decision.[30] Table 14.1 shows the results of the tracking. Although these findings are not based on a large sample or population, they do suggest that a large majority of murderers do not recidivate.

Capital Punishment Is Deserved Punishment

A third argument in favor of capital punishment is that it is deserved; it is retributive. Not only is it **retribution** for the suffering offenders bring to their victims,

TABLE 4.1	Postprison Outcome for Kentucky's Death Sentence–Commuted Parolees	
OUTCOME*		NUMBER
Successfully completed parole		1
On "administrative" supervision"**		11
Technical parole violator		1
Convicted of new crimes		4
Robbery		2
Burglary		1
Drug possession		1

*Outcome as of study completion.
**A symbolic form of supervision with no requirement to report to a parole officer.
SOURCE: Modified from Gennaro F. Vito and Deborah G. Wilson, "Back from the Dead: Tracking the Progress of Kentucky's Furman—Commuted Death Row Population," *Justice Quarterly*, 5 (1988): 106.

[It is retribution] for the harm they do to society by making life insecure, by threatening everyone, and by requiring protective measures. Punishment, ultimately, is a vindication of the moral and legal order of society. . . .[31]

This theme was taken up by Justice Stewart in the *Furman* case when he referred to retribution as necessary for maintaining social solidarity, a thoroughly Durkheimian idea. However, true retribution would require that the condemned offender suffer the same degree of pain inflicted on the victim. In the United States, we execute offenders as "painlessly" as possible.

Capital Punishment Is Cost-Effective

A fourth major argument for capital punishment claims that it costs less than alternatives such as life without parole. Thus, if deterrence cannot be proven and retribution does not quite fit the offender and her or his crime, then the bottom line should be considered. Certainly, imprisonment for many years must cost society more than a lethal injection, a few thousand volts of electricity, lethal gas, or a hangman's noose and scaffold. Unfortunately for those who use cost as a justification for capital punishment, the bottom line is not easy to calculate.

Consider the fact that when an execution is carried out, it has taken nearly eight years on average from the date of initial sentencing.[32] This period of confinement is very expensive because of the heightened level of security required and the labor-intensive nature of inmate supervision on death row.

The costs of death row confinement are by no means the only costs to be computed if we are to calculate the expenditures required to maintain capital punishment. Whenever a capital trial is held, there will be more lawyers active in the case, jury selection will be more time consuming and expensive, and the trial will last much longer than a noncapital felony trial. Then there is the sentencing phase, which can last days or even longer, with all the attendant costs this involves.

Once the trial and sentencing phase have ended, there is the appellate process, which can take years before closure is reached. It is this appellate process that contributes most of the time, making up the average of nearly eight years from the date of sentencing to the execution.

With regard to the effort to provide a cost accounting of the death penalty, Kaplan claims that we ask the wrong question:

> The issue is not really whether it is cheaper to process and execute a particular person than to keep him imprisoned for life. The real question is: is it cheaper to have a system of capital punishment than it is to have a system without the death penalty? We must remember that for every person who in fact is executed, there will inevitably be several who have had to go through varying steps of the capital punishment procedures at increased expense.[33]

There is one aspect of the death penalty that may well save the state some expense. Faced with the threat of execution, some defendants will bargain with the prosecutor, pleading guilty to noncapital murder. In these cases there will be no trial, no sentencing hearing, and probably no appeal.

The Majority Favors Capital Punishment

A fifth argument made in support of the death penalty is that most Americans favor it for some of the most serious crimes. Since polls indicate a large majority in favor of death, it is argued that the state is justified in using it. Recent survey data indicate that

77 percent of Americans favor the death penalty for murder.[34] A review of the literature supporting capital punishment based on its alleged popularity, however, suggests another motive for using survey data: It helps to negate the counterargument that capital punishment is cruel and unusual. Most Americans would not support a punishment that was cruel, and with a majority in favor, it cannot be considered unusual as a sanction. As the great Supreme Court Justice Oliver Wendell Holmes stated long ago, "[the] first requirement of a sound body of law is that it should correspond with the actual feelings and demands of the community, whether right or wrong."[35]

The results of many surveys of public opinion suggest that general support for the death penalty is based on a variety of rationales, including **revenge**, retribution, and deterrence. However, understanding what is meant by retribution is clouded by vague responses when people are asked to define their reasons for supporting capital punishment.[36] Even Supreme Court justices are unclear or contradictory when they review appeals. In *Furman v. Georgia,* for example, Justice Stewart held that retribution was a necessary response in order to maintain social solidarity.[37] Justice Marshall, on the other hand, felt in the same case that retribution really amounted to vengeance, which he viewed as inappropriate in civilized society.[38]

Some opinion research has found that public support for capital punishment, for whatever reason, is not as strong as commonly believed. This research has found that when offered the alternative of life without parole sentences, support for the ultimate penalty sharply declines. For example, when the Gallup Organization asked, "In your opinion, what should be the penalty for murder—the death penalty or life imprisonment with absolutely no possibility of parole?" only 50 percent gave unqualified approval of capital punishment.[39]

Innocent Persons Are Not Executed

Another argument favoring capital punishment is actually a counter to the argument of opponents that innocent persons have been executed. Since death is final, there is no recourse available should errors be made. Supporters of capital punishment point out that so many safeguards are built into the system that the chance of an innocent person being executed is exceedingly rare. Among the safeguards are the following:

- Defendants must be notified in advance that the state will seek the death penalty. The notification must include the statutorily prescribed aggravating or special circumstances required to be proved at the sentencing stage of the trial.[40]
- A separate sentencing hearing must be held at which time the defendant has an opportunity to present mitigating circumstances and counter the state's argument for death.
- The jury (unless a jury trial has been waived) must unanimously agree on a death sentence.
- Defendants sentenced to death may petition for a new trial if convincing evidence comes to light after conviction.
- Ample opportunities are available to appeal both the conviction and the sentence.[41]

A most troubling argument against capital punishment is grounded in the undeniable fact that criminal justice is a human enterprise. Therefore, mistakes are inevitable. In the case of capital punishment, mistakes leading to the execution of an innocent person cannot be remedied. This argument is difficult to support or reject empirically, although attempts have been made to do so. We shall review some of these now.

Even the most dedicated supporters of capital punishment concede that executions of innocent persons have occurred and are inevitable. However, such deaths are said to be rare and may be considered as the lesser of evils. That is, failing to carry out the death penalty will result in an increase in murder rates, thus causing the deaths of more innocent victims. The only research that sought to document that innocent defendants have been executed was the Bedau-Radelet study reported on in 1987. The authors claimed that between 1905 and 1974, 23 defendants, erroneously convicted of murder or rape, were executed, and many others would have been wrongly executed had they been sentenced to death.[42]

A critical review of the Bedau-Radelet study points out that it included "potentially" capital cases in its study population, that is, convictions for murder or rape in which the death penalty was either not sought or not imposed. The review concluded that 23 executions, even if clearly shown to have been in error, "confirms—as convincingly as possible—the view that the risk is too small to be a significant factor in the debate over the death penalty."[43]

Van den Haag, a strong supporter of capital punishment, states that the very real but very rare occurrence of erroneous executions causes great pain to the condemned, and results from unavoidable accidents in criminal procedure. Although an execution is "more harmful to the community than an accidental death, I believe that the moral and material need for justice outweighs this painful harm."[44] This argument that innocent defendants should be sacrificed in order to serve the greater needs of justice is a chilling one.

The possibility that innocent defendants may be executed is complicated by the fact that we are not considering just those who actually were innocent of any murders. Many defendants are certainly guilty of criminal homicide, but not of capital homicide. That is, they should be sentenced to a punishment other than death. Instead, because of any number of reasons, including police investigatory competence, prosecutorial discretion, faulty jury or judicial decision making, and inadequate legal counsel, some are convicted of the most serious homicides and sentenced to death.[45]

Capital Punishment Is Imposed Only on the Worst Offenders

A number of studies have found that those sentenced to death either commit the most serious murders, have extensive criminal careers, or both. One study of pre-*Furman* death sentences found that:

> The greatest single factor associated with being sentenced to death . . . was whether the murder was committed in the course of another felony. . . . These data suggest that Texas jurors, in the pre-*Furman* period, made a qualitative distinction between murder situations.[46]

Further, this research found that "[those] who received death sentences had worse criminal histories and had committed more serious homicides."[47]

Additional Arguments Against the Death Penalty

There are arguments against capital punishment that are not directly counter to the arguments in favor that we have just discussed. We take these up now. The first is that death sentences discriminate against certain classes of offenders. Recall the discussions in Chapters 2 and 3 that discretion is exercised by all the major actors in criminal justice. This normative characteristic of justice in America is particularly important to note with respect to punishment. Since capital punishment is so final a sanction, we need to examine carefully the argument that death sentences not only result from the discretionary actions of police, prosecutors, judges, and juries, but that this discretion may well be exercised in ways that discriminate against some defendants.

In a study of 1,017 homicide cases in Florida, Radelet and Pierce presented evidence that blacks have been subjected to the death penalty as a result of "extralegal" factors.[48]

> It appears that not only are prosecutors sometimes motivated to seek a death sentence for reasons that reflect the racial configuration of the crime, but that they do so in a way that greatly reduces the possibilities for discovering evidence of discrimination and arbitrariness when only later stages of the judicial process are examined.[49]

For many years, opponents of the death penalty have argued that it is applied in ways that are racially discriminatory. The discrimination is not so much in terms of the offender as it is based on the race of the victim. Some research has suggested that if one kills a white victim, the chances of receiving the death penalty are four times greater than if the victim were black. This finding together with other data were submitted to the Supreme Court in a appeal by Warren McCleskey, who was sentenced to death for the felony-murder of a white Georgia police officer.[50]

McCleskey lost his appeal, primarily because the Court found that he did not show that any discrimination was purposefully aimed at him. The case presents an especially troubling and ironic issue with regard to capital punishment: In all fairness, the **equal protection of the laws** argument raised by McCleskey and those opposed to capital punishment should be applied to black victims and potential victims as well as to defendants.[51] However, should victim disparities be eliminated, we would find the

> disturbing irony that diminishing race-of-the-victim disparities while maintaining capital punishment might actually lead to the execution of more black defendants. In Georgia, as elsewhere, most killers of blacks are other blacks.[52]

One study, which compared murderers receiving death sentences with others sentenced to prison, also concluded that the victim's rather than the offender's race was significantly related to sentence decisions. It found that the victim's race "appears to be more important than the offender's in sentencing decisions."[53]

The Death Penalty Diminishes the Dignity of the Condemned

> [The death penalty] diminishes human stature and dignity. . . . [It] eliminates the development of the individual potential of human beings. . . . [It] employs human beings as tools of impersonal bureaucracies or of power-seeking individuals.[54]

There is a direct counterargument frequently made to those who question the death penalty on the grounds that it attacks the dignity of the individual. It is that "holding people generally responsible for their actions and in some cases imposing the ancient standard of a 'life for a life' enhances human dignity."[55]

Capital Punishment Harms Secondary Victims

Some argue that when a defendant is convicted, spends many years on death row, and is executed he or she is by no means the only one who suffers. Direct victims are not the only victims. There are **secondary or collateral "victims"** who are said to suffer

*P*eople used to attend hangings as the visual and public recognition of justice being served. This is an artist's interpretation of the 1887 hanging of the Haymarket riot conspirators.

psychological pain awaiting the fate of those legally condemned.[56] These collateral victims are the families of defendants sentenced to death.

Some who contest the point of view that capital punishment harms collateral victims may actually provide support for abolishing the death penalty. Consider, for example, these comments by Friedrichs:

> It can also be suggested that the families of murderers are not uniformly innocent parties. Those murderers who become candidates for execution disproportionately have suffered various forms of family abuse. Conversely, the supportive stance of some families of murderers—"We'll stand by him regardless of what horrors he has perpetrated"—is not necessarily admirable or constructive.[57]

Perhaps a bias against capital punishment is showing, but executing persons who themselves have been victims of family abuse hardly serves to make a strong case in favor of the ultimate sanction.

CHANGING MODES OF EXECUTION

Changing methods of executions over time illustrate clearly our ambivalence about the death penalty, especially as regards its retributive and deterrent functions. Centuries-old methods that included drawing and quartering the condemned are obviously as offensive to our present notions of punishment as would be accompanying executions with torture. A historical review of modes of execution shows that we have employed hanging, shooting, electrocution, lethal gas, and lethal injection, usually with the rationale that the newer method is more humane, painless, and therefore does not violate the cruel and unusual clause in the Eighth Amendment, and thus validates our society as decent and civilized.

There may be something counterproductive involved in seeking to execute people humanely or painlessly. If deterrence is one of the objectives of capital punishment, delivering painless deaths to condemned murderers may not deter effectively. By the same token, if retribution is what is sought by executing a vicious killer, then lethal injection hardly seems to be appropriate.

Some states permit the condemned to choose from among execution modes. Why a person, considered to be so reprehensible as to be killed, should be able to choose her or his method of execution is a another illustration of our ambivalent attitudes toward not only the punishment, but also the offender.

Until about 60 years ago, executions in the United States frequently were carried out in public. Since then, executions have been increasingly out of sight of the public. This chapter opened with a description of Billy Bailey's hanging in Delaware. His execution was carried out at midnight deep within the prison compound, clearly far from public view. We learn about executions from accounts in the broadcast and print media, sometimes with sensationalist detail. Official witnesses are permitted by law to be present. These include state officials—one of whom must be a physician—and the press. Even when witnesses are present, sometimes the death chamber is concealed from view by blinds or curtains.

Recently, some relatives of the victims of murderers have argued successfully for permission to be present at executions. Televising executions has been suggested, but it is not permitted anywhere in the United States. A number of suits have been brought in state and federal courts to allow such broadcasts, but to no avail.[58] Again, we must ask why the death penalty is virtually a secret enterprise. Surely, if general deterrence is a major goal of executions, it would seem to make sense to have them clearly visible to as wide an audience as possible.

THE LEGAL DEBATE OVER CAPITAL PUNISHMENT

In this section we will focus on the major legal challenges to capital punishment. We will trace these challenges, with major emphasis on the Supreme Court decision in *Furman v. Georgia,*[59] and subsequent decisions. This is because these decisions led, in short order, to the end of what had been an informal execution moratorium, and the beginning of a successful effort to reestablish the death penalty on a legally acceptable footing.

These areas of legal challenge are as follows:

- Capital punishment is cruel and unusual punishment, prohibited by the Eighth Amendment to the Constitution.

- Capital punishment discriminates against minority defendants and discounts the lives of some victims of murder.
- Juvenile offenders should not be subjected to capital punishment.
- Persons who are insane or mentally retarded should not be sentenced to death, nor executed.

Cruel and Unusual Punishment

The argument that the death penalty is **cruel and unusual punishment** per se and thus prohibited by the Eighth Amendment to the Constitution has never been accepted by the Supreme Court. In fact, the Fifth and Fourteenth amendments' language that no state shall "deprive any person of *life,* liberty or property without due process of law"* seems to mean that capital punishment was accepted as a sanction by those who wrote the amendments. Subsequent challenges based on the Eighth Amendment's ban against "cruel and unusual punishments" have been rejected.

We may wonder why appellants have used the "cruel and unusual" argument. Apparently, it is because of the view that the Constitution is a "living" document and that "evolving standards of decency"[60] require that the standards for judging what is a cruel and unusual punishment need not be the same as those of the framers of the Bill of Rights and the Fourteenth Amendment.

There have been appeals that resulted in a capital sentence being overturned that came close to acceptance of the cruel and unusual argument. These, however, were based on a finding by the Court that death was disproportionate to the specific crime for which the defendant was convicted, or that improper procedures were employed to decide upon the sentence.

A 1947 decision of the Supreme Court in a particularly gruesome and botched execution illustrates the Court's reluctance to find the death penalty cruel and unusual punishment.[61] In this case a fifteen-year-old felony murderer, Andrew Francis, was sentenced to be electrocuted. A first attempt failed even to render the condemned unconscious, and the state governor rescheduled the execution for the next week. An appeal to the Supreme Court claimed that a second attempt to execute would violate the Eighth Amendment. The Court disagreed, holding that the failed execution was an "unforeseeable accident" and that the state did not intend to "inflict unnecessary pain" in the first attempt, nor in a second one, which succeeded in killing him.

A more recent example of the Supreme Court's evaluation of capital punishment in relation to the Eighth Amendment is *Coker v. Georgia,* decided in 1977.[62] This decision sheds light on the Court's view of cruel and unusual punishment as well as the issue of capital punishment and **proportionality.**

Early in the Court's opinion it stated that:

> It is now settled that the death penalty is not invariably cruel and unusual punishment within the meaning of the Eighth Amendment; it is not inherently barbaric or an unacceptable mode of punishment for crime; nor is it always disproportionate to the crime for which it is imposed. . . .[63]

The Court did, however, go on to state that the death penalty (as well as other sentences) may be "excessive" in some circumstances. The *Coker* case presented such a circumstance: the rape of an adult woman who "was unharmed."[64] The justices in the majority referred to an earlier decision, *Gregg v. Georgia,*[65] which presented two criteria for judging whether a punishment was a disproportionate one. The first

---

*Amendment XIV, Section 1. Emphasis added.

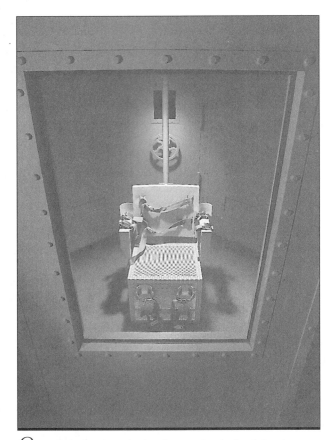

*O*ne of the legal methods of execution is death by electrocution. Here is one of the electric chairs that is still used in some prisons today.

criterion is that a sentence is excessive if "it makes no measurable contribution to acceptable goals of punishment and hence is nothing more than the purposeless and needless imposition of pain and suffering." The second criterion stated that a sentence is excessive if "it is grossly out of proportion to the severity of the crime."

To apply these criteria the Court laid out the following:

> A punishment might fail the test on either ground. . . . [J]udgment should be informed by objective factors to the maximum possible extent. To this end, attention must be given to the public attitudes concerning a particular sentence—history and precedent, legislative attitudes, and the response of juries reflected in their sentencing decisions are to be consulted.[66]

In *Gregg*, the Court determined that the death sentence did not fail the test when matched against the criteria, given that the defendant's crime was first-degree murder. But "the Court reserved the question of the constitutionality of the death penalty when imposed for other crimes. . . ."[67]

The challenge to capital punishment on the ground that it discriminates against minority-group members (both as to defendants and victims) was discussed earlier. The Court's opinion in *McCleskey v. Kemp* effectively shut out appellants from this argument unless discrimination could be shown to be directed specifically against them.

Death sentences have been challenged because of the manner in which they are determined in individual cases. Until *Furman v. Georgia* was decided by the Supreme

*S*an Quentin's death row prisoners were executed in this gas chamber until the method of death by lethal injection was prescribed by the courts.

Court in 1972, this argument had not been made successfully. In *Furman*, a badly divided Court struck down the Georgia death penalty statute mainly because the procedure used to sentence defendants to death was subject to virtually unbridled discretion. No guidance was provided to juries in the sentencing phase. This decision voided all death penalty statutes that were based on the Georgia model.

Georgia and over thirty other states hastened to draft and enact new laws that would correct the deficiency noted by the Court. The correction took the form of statutorily defined **guided jury discretion.** Juries are guided during the sentencing phase by a statute's listing of aggravating circumstances that, if proven, could justify the death penalty. Due process is available to the defendant by permitting her or him to present evidence in mitigation and to contest the state's presentation of aggravating circumstances.

In 1976, the case of *Gregg v. Georgia* tested the new guided jury discretion procedure. The Supreme Court found the procedure met constitutional requirements. The decision effectively closed the door to challenges on the grounds of arbitrariness or unfettered discretion.

Execution of Juveniles

Until recently, there has been little in the way of settled law with regard to imposing the death penalty on juveniles. In part, this is related to developments in juvenile law and notions of juvenile delinquency. For many decades after the enactment of the first juvenile court in 1899, most states used 18 as the age at which a person becomes an adult for the purpose of bringing criminal charges. Even so, all juvenile statutes provided for mechanisms for transferring juvenile defendants from juvenile to criminal courts, usually for capital crimes.[68] Lately, many states, responding to real or perceived increases in serious crimes committed by juveniles, have lowered their statutory age limits for adult status, especially when serious offenses are involved.

Regardless of the developments in juvenile law, there appears as yet to be no clear statement, other than in some state statutes, with respect to any age below which a person may not be executed.[69] The Supreme Court did rule in this area in the case of *Stanford v. Kentucky* in 1989.[70] In the decision, rejecting the argument that a death sentence for juveniles was cruel and unusual, the Court stated that executing juveniles was not "one of those modes of punishment that had been considered cruel and unusual at the time the Bill of Rights was adopted."[71] More significantly, the Court found that sentencing juveniles to death did not violate the "**evolving standards of decency** that mark the progress of a maturing society."[72]

In the text of the opinion, written by Justice Scalia, the argument was made that several states permit execution of defendants who were at least sixteen years of age at the time they committed their crimes, as was defendant Stanford. This suggests that capital punishment for offenders under 16 might be found unconstitutional. The thinking of the Court's majority seems to be that if a state legislature authorizes death for 16- and 17-year-old defendants, such sentences will pass muster provided juries are given the opportunity to take age into account as a mitigating factor during the sentencing phase.[73]

Execution of the Insane or Mentally Retarded

Finally, we come to the question of capital punishment for defendants who are insane or mentally retarded. Mental condition in relation to criminal conduct and criminal procedure is a complex legal and policy area. Issues such as the mental state of the defendant at the time of the crime, her or his mental condition at the time of trial, mental or emotional factors at the sentencing phase of the trial, and the offender's mental state or condition at the time sentence is to be executed are certainly important. We are interested here in the last of these issues: a condemned person's mental state at the time he or she is to be executed. Should a person sentenced to death be executed who becomes mentally ill or is found to be mentally retarded prior to the execution date? This is of more than passing interest. The lengthy delays, on-and-off-again execution dates, and tantalizing hopes (often fantasies) of receiving a commutation of sentence must have terrible and deleterious effects on the mind.

It is established in the law of sentencing that a sentence is not to be executed against an offender if he or she is unable to appreciate why the punishment is to be suffered. Legal insanity and mental retardation would seem to be reasons for refraining from executing a sentence. In the case of *Penry v. Lynaugh*,[74] the Supreme Court held that the mental age and IQ of a defendant should have been considered by the jury at his sentencing hearing. Such data (his IQ was measured as falling between 50 and 63; his mental age was calculated to be about 6 years) were appropriate to be offered in mitigation. However, the Court did not rule out a death sentence because of a defendant's mental retardation. In effect, the Court would not bar the execution of such a person, provided the jury at sentencing so recommended it after hearing about the defendant's mental condition and weighing it along with all other relevant factors.

Earlier, the Court was called upon to review the death sentence of a murderer who became insane while awaiting execution. In this case, *Ford v. Wainwright*,[75] the Court noted that "no State in the Union permits the execution of the insane," probably because it would be impossible to believe that retributive justice could be achieved when the condemned could not appreciate why he or she was being executed.[76] The decision by the Court returned the matter to the state because it had failed to give the defendant sufficient due process opportunities to present evidence of insanity and adequately to contest the findings of state-appointed psychiatrists, who found him to be able to appreciate the meaning of his execution.

In a 1990 case, the state of Louisiana wanted forcibly to medicate an insane offender on death row in order to make him competent to be executed. The Louisiana court stated its rationale in legally formal, if chilling language:

> The state's interest in administering psychotropic medication to [a] mentally disturbed inmate in order to render him competent to be executed outweighs inmate's right to refuse medical treatment.[77]

Eventually, this case got to the Supreme Court, which remanded it back to Louisiana for reconsideration based on the Court's ruling in another case, *Washington v. Harper*.[78] This case involved a prison inmate who was serving a sentence for robbery. He was diagnosed as a schizophrenic, and he refused to take prescribed psychotropic medication. The Supreme Court determined that the state's interest was

> an accommodation between an inmate's liberty interest in avoiding the forced [medication] . . . and the State's interests in providing appropriate medical treatment to reduce the danger an inmate suffering from a serious mental disorder represents to himself or others.[79]

The Supreme Court in the cases discussed above was mainly interested in whether states provide adequate procedural safeguards when they seek forcibly to medicate and/or execute a person who may be mentally ill. The Court really did not address the substantive issue of capital punishment and the condemned's competency to appreciate its meaning. The language quoted from the *Harper* decision to the effect that the state might forcibly medicate an inmate to protect the inmate from himself or others seems to be completely irrelevant on death row. There inmates are under the tightest security. Of course, if an insane condemned inmate poses a serious danger to himself unless medicated, might he or she not save the state the expense of an execution by what amounts to suicide?

EVALUATION OF CAPITAL PUNISHMENT

As we indicated earlier, a major argument for capital punishment is that it absolutely deters offenders from committing additional crimes, and acts as a general deterrent, saving innocent lives. Aside from a few studies such as Ehrlich's in the 1970s, there has been little research that sheds light on the question of the deterrent value of capital punishment. One interesting study, which we presented earlier, followed up prisoners whose death sentences were commuted to life imprisonment following the 1972

ACROSS
CULTURES

PREPARING FOR DEATH IN BRITAIN'S NEWGATE PRISON

The Deity presided indispensably over the condemneds' last days. In Newgate his agent was the Revd [sic] Henry Cotton. Cotton's job . . . was to insert the fear of God and damnation in his charges. The main business . . . is to break the spirits of capital convicts, so that they make no physical resistance to the hangman.

The work of the Reverend Cotton was mainly accomplished in Newgate's chapel where a pew, painted black, was reserved for all prisoners sentenced to death. It was located just below the pulpit. In the center of the aisle was placed a coffin.

Following each court session of the Old Bailey, there were "a score or so" condemned prisoners in the pew. On each Sunday prior to an execution, a sermon for the condemned was delivered. The sermon lasted about ten minutes and highlighted all the sins caused and sorrows inflicted by those awaiting execution. It usually ended by a statement that "death would come tomorrow for the benefit of society."

SOURCE: V. A. C. Gatrell, *The Hanging Tree* (New York: Oxford University Press, 1994), p. 44.

Furman v. Georgia Supreme Court decision.[80] The researchers were thus able to test, in effect, whether such an extreme penalty is necessary.

The study tracked the twenty-one inmates whose death sentences were commuted to terms of imprisonment. At the time the results were compiled, seventeen had been paroled. These results showed that the majority of the parolees did not commit new crimes once they were back on the streets. In fact, only two of these men saved from execution committed violent crimes (robbery).[81]

Another way of evaluating capital punishment is to examine whether discrimination in its application has been reduced. For many decades opposition to this sanction has centered on alleged biases against blacks and other minorities. Such bias, if proven, clearly would violate the equal protection clause of the Constitution.

Georgia, as well as other states, eventually sought to end the arbitrary and discriminatory effects of their statutes by providing for sentencing hearing phases in capital trials. These hearings are to guide juries in their sentence recommendation.[82] This procedural change was supported by the Supreme Court in its 1976 *Gregg* decision, which permitted states to continue discretionary death sentences. However, discretion was to be "guided" through evidence presented at sentencing hearings in which prosecution and defense would have an opportunity to provide the sentencing authority with aggravating and mitigating circumstances.

Keil and Vito examined black-white execution ratios in the South following this sentencing law change.[83] They reported that during the period 1900–1987, out of a total of 4,294 executions in two Southern regions, blacks accounted for just under 75 percent of those executed.[84] Looking at the situation after *Gregg*, they concluded that:

> The system established in *Gregg* [guided discretion] had the desired effect of reducing the most apparent and visible forms of discrimination in capital sentencing: it lowered the disparity in black-white executions.[85]

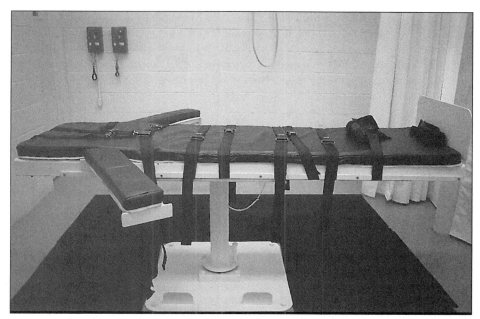

*C*ondemned prisoners are strapped to this gurney and executed by lethal injection. The two telephones are provided on the wall so a telephone line is always available in case a last minute stay of the execution would be granted.

However, discrimination did not end with the advent of guided discretion. "In fact, reducing racial bias indicated by the race of the executed has masked the nature of discrimination."[86] They found that race continued to have a profound effect on executions. The race of victims is the culprit:

> Cases with white victims, especially those with black killers, are more likely to result in a death sentence. There is evidence of discrimination against blacks at every stage of the process: (1) they are more likely to be charged with a capital offense by the prosecution, (2) they are more likely to be convicted, and (3) they are more likely to be sentenced to death.[87]

As we saw earlier, the Supreme Court in *McCleskey v. Kemp* rejected the argument that a death sentence should be overturned because of the racial discrimination alluded to above.[88] The Court held that any alleged discrimination had to be purposeful or deliberately employed against a defendant. Since the Court refuses to ban capital punishment based on clearly established empirical evidence of discrimination based on victimization, we must conclude that death sentences inadequately protect many potential victims in America. Thus, the death penalty fails to perform perhaps the major objective of any punishment: protection of the public from the most violent crime.

As far as a serving as an effective general deterrent, our review of the available research tells us that the death penalty fails to protect society:

> We simply do not know whether the threat of capital punishment exerts any overall deterrent upon the number of murders in our society. What one can say, however, is that anyone who claims to have a fixed and clear viewpoint on this issue is either disguising the real reason why he or she is for or against the death penalty, or else has simply not researched and thought about the matter carefully.[89]

A complication that confounds the deterrence argument has to do with the two mechanisms by which punishment is supposed to work to deter, but which actually may "cause" people to commit murder. The first is the simple threat: If you kill, you will be killed. The second mechanism is through the proposition that murder is so terrible an act that society uses the most terrible punishment against those who kill. Kaplan argues that, in the first instance, some people commit murder in order to be killed.[90]

In the case of the second deterrence mechanism, the deterrence threat "may be perverted . . . through the distillation of the principle that an appropriate method of settling a dispute is for one of the parties to kill the other."[91] This, of course, is a variation of the brutalization hypothesis discussed earlier.

Turning to the argument that executions will save more innocent lives than other sanctions because of the absolute incapacitative effect, Kaplan states that statistical data from empirical research show that less than 1 percent of convicted first-degree murderers kill again. In fact, released armed robbers are more dangerous than murderers because they are considerably younger than released murderers, the latter having spent far longer in prison before being released.[92]

Another argument is that death is an appropriate, deserved punishment for killing a person. In other words, capital punishment is to be used to exact retribution from the offender. However, retribution is never exacted in direct proportion to the degree of pain caused murderers' victims. We have sought, as shown in the section on modes of execution, to execute the condemned in relatively painless (at least in the physical sense) ways.

Many of the most "deserving" capital offenders have themselves been victims of child abuse or other traumatic experiences prior to committing murder. These, arguably, are not satisfactory candidates for retributive justice.

SUMMARY

Capital punishment is used in the United States, but in no other industrialized nation in the world. Its use is plagued by controversy and questions as to its constitutionality, goals, effectiveness, and morality. Yet, in spite of these controversies and questions, a substantial proportion of Americans support death as the ultimate sanction for at least some of the most violent criminals.

Studies regarding its deterrent impact on crime, especially the crime of murder, have from time to time produced data purporting to show that capital punishment saves innocent lives. However, the consensus among researchers is that execution and capital crime rates are independent variables. Some research even suggests that executions have a brutalizing effect, pushing up murder rates.

Legal challenges to the death penalty have focused on the Eighth Amendment's prohibition against cruel and unusual punishments, and on the penalty's alleged discriminatory and arbitrary application. A string of Supreme Court decisions since *Furman v. Georgia* has resulted in a uniform view that capital punishment per se does not violate the Constitution's ban on cruel and unusual punishments. Further, the Court has, in effect, provided the states with guidance to reinstate the death penalty following *Furman*. This guidance includes a requirement that state trial courts must provide a bifurcated trial in capital cases, the first trial to determine guilt or innocence, the second to determine the penalty for the guilty. At this second trial or hearing, the state and defense have an opportunity to prove aggravating and/or mitigating circumstances.

There is some evidence that capital punishment is applied in a way that discriminates against minorities, particularly against blacks. This discrimination occurs because death sentences are disproportionately imposed on those who kill whites. Thus, innocent potential victims who are black are not protected by death penalty statutes and prosecutions under them.

Finally, we note the often-used argument that capital punishment is widely supported by the public. A number of studies of public opinion about the death penalty cast doubt on the breadth and weight of support.[93] Support seems to depend on a number of variables, including the goals to be achieved (e.g., retribution, revenge, protection) and whether those surveyed about their opinions are asked to consider any alternatives (e.g., life without parole) to the death sentence.

KEY CONCEPTS

Brutalization hypothesis	Incapacitation
Cruel and unusual punishment	Proportionality
Equal protection of the laws	Retribution
Evolving standards of decency	Revenge
General deterrence	Secondary or collateral victims
Guided jury discretion	

QUESTIONS FOR DISCUSSION

1. The argument that executions may save some innocent lives may be countered by the argument that executions may have a brutalizing effect. Thus, no potential victims' lives may be saved. Do you agree or disagree? Fully explain your answer.
2. No other industrialized nation currently has the death penalty. Why do you believe this is so? What explains its retention in the United States?
3. Most students of capital punishment consider it inevitable that some "innocent" defendants will be sentenced to death and executed. However, this is a more complicated issue than would seem from a cursory examination. What are the major complicating issues and variables?
4. Discuss critically the proposition that discrimination against black victims actually saves lives. Why does the Supreme Court not take this discrimination into account?

ENDNOTES

1. *Washington Post*, January 26, 1996, p. B-1.
2. John F. Galliher, Gregory Ray, and Brent Cook, "Abolition and Reinstatement of Capital Punishment During the Progressive Era and Early 20th Century," *Journal of Criminal Law & Criminology* 83 (1992): 538–576.
3. Ibid., p. 574.
4. Ibid., p. 576.
5. Tracy L. Snell, "Capital Punishment 1995," Bureau of Justice Statistics, *Bulletin*, December 1996, p. 1.

6. Ibid.

7. 428 U.S. 153 (1976).

8. 408 U.S. 238 (1972).

9. Stephan and Brien, "Capital Punishment 1993," p. 12.

10. Ibid., p. 1.

11. John Kaplan, "The Problem of Capital Punishment," *University of Illinois Law Review* (1983): 555–557.

12. Ernest van den Haag, "Comment on John Kaplan's 'Administering Capital Punishment,'" *University of Florida Law Review* 36 (1984): 193.

13. Isaac Ehrlich, "The Deterrent Effect of Capital Punishment: A Question of Life and Death," *American Economic Review* 65 (1975): 397–417.

14. Ibid., p. 414.

15. William J. Bowers and Glenn L. Pierce, "The Illusion of Deterrence in Isaac Ehrlich's Research on Capital Punishment," *Yale Law Journal* 85 (1975): 187–208.

16. John K. Cochran, Mitchell B. Chamlin, and Mark Seth, "Deterrence or Brutalization? An Impact Assessment of Oklahoma's Return to Capital Punishment," *Criminology* 32 (1994): 107–134.

17. Cochran, et al., "Deterrence or Brutalization?" p. 121.

18. Ibid.

19. Ibid., p. 125.

20. Ibid., p. 129.

21. William J. Bowers and Glenn L. Pierce, "Deterrence or Brutalization: What Is the Effect of Executions?" *Crime & Delinquency* 26 (1980): 453–484.

22. Ibid., pp. 469–470.

23. Ibid., p. 481. Emphasis in the original.

24. Ibid., pp. 482–483.

25. Ruth D. Peterson and William C. Bailey, "Murder and Capital Punishment in the Evolving Context of the Post-*Furman* Era," *Social Forces* 66 (1988): 774–807.

26. Ibid., p. 776.

27. Ibid., p. 777.

28. Ibid., p. 800.

29. Bowers and Pierce, "Deterrence or Brutalization," p. 454.

30. Gennaro F. Vito and Deborah G. Wilson, "Back from the Dead: Tracking the Progress of Kentucky's *Furman*-Commuted Death-Row Population," *Justice Quarterly* 5 (1988): 101–111.

31. Ernest van den Haag, "The death penalty once more," *University of California Davis Law Review* 18 (1985): 970.

32. Stephan and Brien, "Capital Punishment 1993."

33. Kaplan, "Problem of Capital Punishment," p. 574.

34. Bureau of Justice Statistics, *Sourcebook of Criminal Justice Statistics—1994,* p. 181.

35. *The Common Law,* 1938 ed., p. 41.

36. Robert M. Bohm, Ronald E. Vogel, and Albert A. Maisto, "Knowledge and Death Penalty Opinion: A Panel Study," *Journal of Criminal Justice* 21 (1993): 29–45; James O. Fickenauer, "Public Support for the Death Penalty: Retribution as Just Deserts or Retribution as Revenge," *Justice Quarterly* 5 (1988): 81–100; Thomas J. Keil and Gennaro F. Vito, "Fear of Crime and Attitudes Toward Capital Punishment: A Structural Equations Model," *Justice Quarterly* 8 (1991): 447–474.

37. 408 U.S. 238, 308 (1972).

38. Ibid., p. 322.

39. *Sourcebook of Criminal Justice Statistics,* p. 181.

40. For example, the defendants in the 1995 bombing of the Oklahoma City federal building received written notice from the Justice Department that the death penalty was to be sought. This notice was sent many months before the trial began.

41. For a discussion of these safeguards, see Steven J. Markman and Paul G. Cassell, "Protecting the Innocent: A Response to the Bedau-Radelet Study," *Stanford Law Review* 41 (1988): 121–160.

42. Hugo Adam Bedau & Michael L. Radelet, "Miscarriages of Justice in Potentially Capital Cases," *Stanford Law Review* 40 (1987): 21–179.

43. Markman and Cassell, "Protecting the Innocent," ibid.

44. Van den Haag, "Death Penalty Once More," p. 195.

45. Robert Bohm, "Humanism and the Death Penalty, with Special Emphasis on the Post-*Furman* Experience," *Justice Quarterly* 6 (1989): 173–195.

46. Paige H. Ralph, Jonathan R. Sorenson, and James W. Marquart, "Comparison of Death-Sentenced and Incarcerated Murderers in Pre-*Furman* Texas," *Justice Quarterly* 9 (1992): 200.

47. Ibid., p. 207.

48. Michael L. Radelet and Glenn L. Pierce, "Race and Prosecutorial Discretion in Homicide Cases," *Law & Society Review* 19 (1985): 587–621.

49. Ibid., p. 618.

50. *McCleskey v. Kemp,* 481 U.S. 279, 107 S.Ct. 1756 (1987).

51. This issue is discussed fully in Randall L. Kennedy, "*McCleskey v. Kemp:* Race, Capital Punishment and the Supreme Court," *Harvard Law Review* 101 (1988): 1388–1443.

52. Ibid., p. 1392.

53. Ralph, Sorenson, and Marquart, "Comparison . . . ," p. 191.

54. Bohm, "Humanism and the Death Penalty," p. 177.

55. David O. Friedrichs, "Comment—Humanism and the Death Penalty: An Alternative Perspective," *Justice Quarterly* 6 (1989): 199.

56. These secondary victims are the subject of discussion in Michael L. Radiolead, ed., *Facing the Death Penalty: Essays on a Cruel and Unusual Punishment* (Temple University Press, 1989).

57. Friedrichs, "Comment," p. 204.

58. For discussions of the law and issues involved regarding televising executions see the following: John D. Bessler, "Televised Executions and the Constitution: Recognizing a First Amendment Right of Access to State Executions," *Federal Communications Law Journal* 45 (Spring 1993): 355–435; Victoria Slind-Flor, "Film at 11?" *National Law Journal* 13 (1991): 8.

59. 408 U.S. 238 (1972).

60. *Trop v. Dulles,* 356 U.S. 86 (1958). In this decision (in a case involving revocation of U.S. citizenship), the Supreme Court majority said that the Eighth Amendment "must draw its meaning from the evolving standards of decency that mark the progress of a maturing society" (p. 101).

61. *Louisiana ex rel. Francis v. Resweber,* 329 U.S. 459 (1947).

62. 433 U.S. 584, S.Ct. 2861 (1977).

63. Ibid.

64. How the Justices determined that the victim, forcibly raped, was unharmed, is a mystery.

65. 428 U.S. 153, 96 S.Ct. 2909 (1976).

66. Ibid.

67. Ibid.

68. See the case of *Washington v. Massey,* 803 P.2d 340 (1990), in which the appellate court upheld a life without parole sentence imposed on a thirteen-year-old murderer.

69. Mark S. Hamm, "Legislator Ideology and Capital Punishment: The Special Case for Indiana Juveniles," *Justice Quarterly* 6 (1989): 219–232. At the time this article was published, Indiana had the nation's lowest age for executing juveniles: 10 years.

70. 492 U.S. 361 (1989) at p. 368.

71. Ibid., p. 361.

72. Ibid., p. 369. Emphasis added. "Evolving standards of decency" as a criterion for judging a sentence was announced by the Court in *Trop v. Dulles,* 356 U.S. 86 (1985).

73. For a detailed discussion of the Court's thinking with regard to capital punishment for juveniles, see Mark C. Seis and Kenneth L. Elbe, "The Death Penalty for Juveniles: Bridging the Gap Between an Evolving Standard of Decency and Legislative Policy," *Justice Quarterly* 8 (1991): 465–487.

74. 109 S.Ct. 2934 (1989).

75. 477 U.S. 399 (1986).

76. For a discussion of these and other grounds for not executing sentence against insane or mentally retarded defendants see Sheldon Krantz and Lynn S. Branham, *The Law of Sentencing, Corrections, and Prisoners' Rights,* 4th ed. (St. Paul: West Publishing, 1991), pp. 235–237.

77. *Perry v. Louisiana,* 111 S.Ct. 449 (1990). The Court denied Perry his petition for a hearing. For a discussion of this case see Thomas F. Courtless, *Introduction to the Making of Criminal Law: Appellate Cases and Commentaries* (Oklahoma City: Custom Academic Publishing Co., 1993), pp. 66–67.

78. 110 S.Ct. 1028 (1990).

79. 494 U.S. 210 (1990) at p. 236.

80. Vito and Wilson, "Back from the Dead," pp. 101–111.

81. Ibid., p. 105. Table 14.1 is a summary of the study's reported findings.

82. We discussed this development in Chapter 3.

83. Thomas J. Keil and Gennaro F. Vito, "The Effects of the *Furman* and *Gregg* Decisions on Black-White Execution Ratios in the South," *Journal of Criminal Justice* 20 (1992): 217–226.

84. Keil and Vito chose the South for the study for two reasons: first, "the South consistently has had a greater number of blacks than whites executed . . . ; and [second,] findings regarding racial bias in capital sentencing consistently point to the South," (p. 219).

85. Ibid., p. 224.

86. Ibid.

87. Ibid., p. 224.

88. *McCleskey v. Kemp,* 481 U.S. 279, 107 S.Ct. 1756 (1987).

89. Kaplan, "Problem of Capital Punishment," p. 559.

90. ibid., p. 560.

91. Ibid., p. 561.

92. Ibid., p. 563–564.

93. See Robert M. Bohm, "Retribution and Capital Punishment: Toward a Better Understanding of Death Penalty Opinion," *Journal of Criminal Justice* 20 (1992): 227–236; James O. Fickenauer, "Public Support for the Death Penalty: Retribution as Just Deserts or Retribution for Revenge," *Justice Quarterly* 5 (1988): 81–100; Keil and Vito, "Fear of Crime and Attitudes Toward Capital Punishment," pp. 447–464.

CRIMINAL JUSTICE, CRIMINAL SANCTIONS, AND CORRECTIONS

PART

II

5

JAILS

INTRODUCTION THE JAIL IS A UNIQUE INSTITUTION in criminal justice. It is the oldest institution for incarcerating law violators . . . and performs a wide variety of functions, including housing accused offenders awaiting trial, incarcerating convicted misdemeanants, and holding convicted offenders who await sentencing and sentenced offenders who await transportation to prison.[1]

In addition to these functions, jails in many American states hold convicted and sentenced offenders until space is available in overcrowded prisons. This often results in offenders serving significant portions of their sentences in local facilities that are not equipped to deal with them.

For many accused persons the jail serves as the criminal justice entry point. Jails have been called a "dumping ground for some of society's problems. When other institutions were either not available or full, people were placed in jail because there was no other place to put them."[2] Goldfarb described them as "the ultimate ghetto."[3] Irwin referred to jail populations as "rabble."[4] The experiences of jailed inmates, particularly those who have not yet been convicted, are significant socially, psychologically, and legally. Although many are not incarcerated as punishment, the time they spend waiting for their trials can be very punishing.

In this chapter we will discuss many of the characteristics and issues related to these institutions, including bail, jail populations and programs, and alternatives to jails. We will especially look at the jail as a criminal justice system-dependent institution. We begin this discussion with bail since failure to post bail or being denied bail are the main reasons why many people are in our jails.

PRETRIAL DETENTION OR RELEASE

According to a study conducted in America's seventy-five largest counties during the month of May, 1992, 63 percent of state felony defendants were released by the courts before their trials.[5] As is to be expected, the severity of criminal charges against defendants had considerable influence on pretrial release decisions. Murder defendants were the least likely to be released (24 percent), followed by rape (48 percent), robbery (50 percent), and burglary (51 percent) defendants. Interestingly, in this time of a highly publicized and politicized war on drugs, more than two-thirds of all felony drug defendants were released prior to their trials.[6] We now take a look at the process whereby decisions are reached regarding pretrial detention.

Preliminary Hearing

Prior to a trial, there is some sort of hearing before a judge or magistrate. This is usually called the preliminary hearing. In some jurisdictions, it is called the "first appearance" or arraignment. Three important matters are taken up at this time: (1) defendants' rights; (2) whether to bind defendants over for trial; and (3) whether to grant **bail.**

Usually the first order of business is to advise a defendant of her or his rights. These include the right to an attorney (if one is not already retained or assigned through the local public defender service) and the right to a jury trial. Following this, the defendant is read the charges and asked to enter a plea to them.

Before criminal defendants are brought into a court for trial, the evidence against them must meet a minimum standard. Frequently, the required evidence need only be "sufficient." In some jurisdictions, the standard is referred to as evidence showing the "probable" guilt of the defendant. There are two ways the evidence is judged in America: through the decision of a grand jury, and by way of a preliminary hearing before a judge. In either case, the prosecutor presents some or all of the evidence against the defendant.[7] The grand jury or the judge then decides whether the evidence is sufficient to bind the defendant over for a trial. Usually, we call the decision to bind over the defendant an "indictment."

Pretrial Release Decision Making

Should the evidence be judged sufficient and the defendant be bound over, a decision must be made whether to hold him or her in custody until the trial. At this stage several options are available to the court:

ACROSS CULTURES

PRETRIAL PROCESS IN JAPAN

Japanese criminal law and procedure are in many ways very similar to those in state and federal jurisdictions in the United States. This is no accident, since the Japanese constitution was written largely under American supervision during the occupation following World War II. There are, however, a number of important differences. First, Japan is a civil law nation. "The law" is found in five codes dealing with civil, commercial, and penal law, and criminal and civil procedure. There is no "case law" based on the principle of *stare decisis* as in the United States, a common law nation. Perhaps nowhere are the differences between the situation in Japan and in the United States more striking than in the area of criminal pretrial procedure.

In Japan, an accused person has no right to bail or access to an attorney during interrogation by police or the prosecutor. Within 48 hours of arrest, the accused must be released or turned over to the prosecutor, who may detain her or him for up to 23 days prior to filing an indictment. While detained, an accused person must be warned of the right to remain silent, but in more than 85 percent of cases, confessions are obtained. Many critics of Japanese pretrial procedures question the voluntary nature of these confessions. A review of appeals covering a six-year period found that only four felony convictions were overturned because of coerced confessions.

Public prosecutors serve under the Ministry of Justice. They have the authority to conduct investigations, indict, or suggest a settlement between offenders and victims which, if accepted, can result in no indictment. Prosecutors may appeal unfavorable verdicts and sentences.

Very unlike the situation in the United States, "it should be stated . . . that there is no plea bargaining in Japan." The prosecutor can and often does ask the police for additional information prior to making a decision regarding an indictment even though "the case sent to the prosecutor may be a foot thick for an average case."* There are three reasons for the extensive investigations by both police and prosecutor:

1. Under the Japanese constitution, a conviction cannot be supported solely by a confession.
2. Prosecutors require a mass of data on the crime, offender, and victim before deciding whether to seek an indictment or call for an informal settlement.
3. Prosecutors have considerable power to obtain the sentences they recommend, and they use the data collected by police to justify their recommendations.

*A. Didrick Castberg, *Japanese Criminal Justice* (New York: Praeger, 1990), p. 58.

- Defendant released on **personal recognizance** (no bail required).
- Defendant released on the responsibility of another (family, attorney, etc.; no bail required).
- Defendant released after posting minimal bond.
- Defendant required to post high bond.
- Defendant to remain in custody; no bail.

Determining which of the five options shall apply is based on the court's review of the following information:

- Defendant's past criminal history

- Seriousness of the charges
- Defendant's ties to the community
- The likelihood of flight to avoid prosecution
- Defendant's potential threat to the community

The last of these criteria, the defendant's potential threat to the community, has always been a controversial one. How to determine the risk posed by a defendant should he or she be released prior to trial is a difficult task. Certainly, some of those released from custody commit crimes while awaiting trial, and some of these crimes are violent ones. In addition, witnesses may be at risk should a defendant remain in the community. Concern about these threats has resulted in the enactment of a number of preventive detention statutes at the state and federal level. The federal **Bail Reform Act** of 1984 authorizes pretrial detention for certain categories of offenders: those charged with capital crimes, drug-related offenses carrying heavy sentences, and recidivists.[8] The constitutionality of **preventive detention** statutes has been challenged in appellate courts, and the resulting case law has uniformly upheld them.[9]

One of the unintended consequences of the Bail Reform Act has been the increased pretrial detention of defendants charged with nonviolent crimes.[10] It is apparent that this legislation and its implementation has not substantially altered the rate at which crimes are committed nor, surprisingly, the rate of "no-shows" for trial. What it has contributed to is the crowding of our jails by widening the net and capturing a larger segment of the accused population.

There is a tendency to be reluctant to release on bail or personal recognizance those defendants who abuse drugs (especially those who test positive on drug screening tests). This reluctance on the part of judges and magistrates is grounded in a presumption that such defendants will commit offenses while in the community, and will often fail to appear for trial.[11] A study in the District of Columbia, however, throws considerable doubt on this. The study found that when defendants are released on condition that they be regularly tested for continued drug use, their rates of rearrest and failure to appear for trial are considerably lower than anticipated.

The key here is "regular" drug-use screening while awaiting disposition of the charges against defendants. Apparently, consistent follow-up discourages both continued drug use and flight to avoid prosecution. Another key element in the District of Columbia success is the study's finding that one should not lump together all defendants who test positive for any and all drugs. In particular, those offenders who were "no-shows" (failed to appear for court proceedings) "more often used heroin and cocaine, alone or especially in combination."[12]

Another approach to pretrial release decision making with respect to drug abusers is a federal program in the Eastern District of Pennsylvania.[13] Known as the Miramont program, it was based on the authority of court orders to defendants to complete satisfactorily a 28-day treatment regimen prior to being released before their trials. During a one-year period, a total of 66 defendants were ordered to enter the program. Pointing up the difficulty such programs encounter when dealing with drug offenders, follow-up research found that nearly 57 percent violated one or more conditions imposed by the court.[14] These violations included failure to appear in court, rearrests, and positive urine test results.

One may question the wisdom of continuing programs of this type, at a daily cost of $226, with such high violation levels. We should not, however, be too quick to abandoned pretrial efforts such as this one on the basis of these discouraging results. Why? Because the Miramont intake process permitted at least two different populations of defendants to enter treatment. One group consisted of defendants who were admitted within 24 hours of arrest. A second group (58 percent of the total admitted) included defendants who had violated their pretrial release conditions and who were admitted to the program following a violation hearing.[15] Three-fourths of this second group violated conditions, thus becoming "double failures." In considering whether to develop or continue such pretrial programs, jurisdictions need to be aware that mixing defendant populations as was done at Miramont will have significant consequences for "success and failure" rates.

Data from the National Pretrial Reporting Program suggest that released felony drug offenders are not rearrested in large numbers.[16] These defendants did, however, have the highest failure to appear rates of all released defendants, with 27 percent failing to show up for further court appearances.[17] From the data reported in the program, we are unable to separate released defendants who received treatment such as in Pennsylvania from those who did not.

As a final word on the use of drug testing as predictive of pretrial misconduct, we look at the results of a study of Manhattan arrestees.[18] This research pointed out that it is essential to analyze comprehensive empirical data because there are a number of controversial issues having to do with the reliability of drug tests, the constitutionality of drug testing under certain circumstances, and the unanswered question of whether drug testing has any noticeable impact on pretrial conduct and future drug addiction.[19]

Among the findings of this study were the following:

- Thirty-nine percent of released defendants failed to appear for trial.
- Most of those failing to appear had failed to appear in the past and had extensive prior criminal charges.
- Thirty-four percent of released defendants with negative drug test results failed to appear compared to 44 percent of those testing positive for drug use.

Concluding that there was no "clear evidence" that urine test results could help judges determine which defendants are at risk, the researchers stated that there is an unintended, systemic consequence of massive pretrial drug testing. That is, it is "possible . . . that a drug testing program would . . . increase pretrial detention." More pretrial conditions create "more opportunities for a defendant to be held in contempt of court, then punished with pretrial detention."[20]

We might take this opportunity to look ahead to Chapter 11 where we discuss probation violations. In particular, we note that, again contrary to expectations, drug offenders do not seem to violate their probation more frequently than offenders who do not abuse drugs. Perhaps the bias against drug users at the pretrial and sentencing stages is misplaced and might more accurately be related to political pressure to wage an aggressive war against drug offenders.

A recently published study of drug testing of arrestees in six jurisdictions noted an important methodological problem with respect to employing testing to predict pretrial misconduct.[21] The authors point out that the research literature provides "ambiguous" results from testing pretrial defendants. They say that this is a consequence of the system's "inability to separate high-rate users from low-rate users, those who are addicted and who will commit crimes to maintain their drug needs from those who may buy drugs on a casual basis with money earned legitimately."[22]

Another possible bias in pretrial release decision making that has received attention in the research literature is that of gender differences. Steury and Frank examined gender differences in a Wisconsin sample of nearly 2,000 felony defendants.[23] After examining the sample for differences in "lenient" release decisions by gender and seriousness of criminal charges, the researchers concluded that:

> . . . females are treated more leniently by the court and that this leniency may be related to the lesser seriousness of the charges against them rather than to their gender per se. We also conclude that the apparent leniency toward females does not result in a higher failure-to-appear rate for females.[24]

The final decision regarding bail is often made in an adversarial setting. That is, the prosecutor may argue against bail, while the defendant argues for release. Setting bail in the United States is limited to some extent by the Eighth Amendment to the Constitution, which states that "excessive bail shall not be required." Of course, setting criteria for determining when bail is "excessive" is quite difficult. There is the matter of a defendant's ability to post bail, especially if he or she has limited income or other assets. Usually, a defendant is required to pay a 10 percent fee for a bond to a bail bondsman. The bondsman must pay the entire amount if the defendant flees, while the defendant cannot recover the 10 percent regardless of the outcome of the trial.

Because the time between the bail decision and trial can be a lengthy one, the threat of having bail refused may, as a consequence, encourage defendants to plea bargain. Not only will this result in a lesser penalty being imposed, it will almost certainly result in a shorter period of confinement.

Jail Crowding and Pretrial Release Decisions

We need to mention at this point the systemic consequences jail overcrowding can have on police behavior, especially where courts order municipalities to reduce jail populations. One response to overcrowding is to avoid booking arrestees into jail. New York State and California have been doing this for some time. Police in New York City and state have been issuing Desk Appearance Tickets (DAT). These do not require defendants to be jailed pending further dispositions. In California, citations are issued that are similar to New York's DATs. A study in California looked in some detail at the consequences of this approach.[25] Under state law, police can issue citations as a mechanism for arresting, but not booking into jail, misdemeanant defendants.[26] Under the law, persons arrested may be given citations and then released. As a "condition" they must sign a statement agreeing to show up in court for further proceedings.

In 1988, California municipal police officers issued a total of 292,000 citations, 25 percent of the total misdemeanant arrests.[27] Interestingly, and contrary to what one might expect, the rates of citations did not differ significantly in counties under court order to reduce jail crowding compared to those not under court order. Citation rates *did* increase in both groups of counties, reflecting, according to the researcher, a perception by the police that arrestees would be released at the jail anyway, regardless of the effects of any court-ordered reduction in jail populations.

New York City was the site of a serious effort to reduce both the size of its jail populations and the length of confinement while awaiting trial. The mechanism for this effort involved the use of financial incentives to city prosecutors.[28] This program, the Speedy Disposition Program (SDP), was a response to a 1983 federal court order requiring the city to reduce its jail population. Initially, because of the court order, the city was forced to release "scores of incarcerated defendants awaiting trial in the city's back-logged courts—a serious political embarrassment to a mayor whose administration was

In the past, jails utilized a linear style of cells for inmates. Here is part of the layout of Deer Island Jail in Boston.

grounded in toughness on criminal justice matters."[29] As a more acceptable reply to the court order, the city made available $9 million as incentives to the district attorneys to encourage them to dispose of their oldest cases. In effect, prosecutors competed against one another during a two-year period. Those with the greatest success in reducing the number of old pending cases and jail cases received the lion's share of the available money.[30]

How well did SDP work? Results after two years show that jail overcrowding *increased*. From about 6,500 pretrial detainees at the beginning of SDP, the total reached 7,600 two years later.[31] There was a modest reduction in felony cases pending for over six months (336 cases during a two-year period), but with a total backlog of 14,000 cases in the city's courts, this reduction is not remarkable. Also, the population of long-term detainees actually increased by over 12 percent.[32]

The authors of an evaluation of the SDP program clearly pointed to the systemic sources of the program's failure to address the issue of jail crowding and long-term detention of criminal defendants. Court delays are beyond the capacity of prosecutors to influence, and political factors are vitally important, especially when it comes to offering plea bargains to defendants in order to clear them from the growing back-log. Simple financial incentives are insufficient to overcome these system variables.

> Our broad conclusion . . . is that financial inducement was not the only, and perhaps not even the most important, determinant of the behavior of the different [district attorneys'] offices. The organizational culture of the offices differed, as did the particular financial and political situation of each district attorney.[33]

That jail is a system-dependent institution was clearly pointed out by United States District Court Judge Vincent Broderick, formerly New York City Police Commissioner, as he criticized the "draconian" approach to crime control in both federal and state sentencing laws and practices. Judge Broderick noted that the presumption of innocence is fundamental in American criminal procedure. However, judges "must resolve the tension between" this presumption, the need to "insure the resolution of the charge by preventing flight and to protect the community."[34]

Congress enacted legislation to assist federal judges when making pretrial detention decisions by authorizing pretrial services offices and agents. Such services are designed to provide decision makers with adequate information on which to base their decisions and to supervise or monitor defendants released prior to trial. Certainly, this appears to be a logical response to the issues raised by Judge Broderick. Also, providing pretrial services to courts might be expected to lower the rate of detention. But, according to Broderick, "[I]t has not worked out that way."[35] Since 1988, federal pretrial detention has more than doubled, with the population now at 18,000 defendants.[36]

Why is this so? One reason is that a major increase in drug cases has flooded the courts. Defendants in these cases face very long sentences, thus raising fears of flight to avoid conviction, and the threat of committing more crimes if released. These fears have been exacerbated by federal guidelines that significantly lower the possibility that convicted offenders will be sentenced to probation. The single most powerful factor leading to a rise in pretrial detention "has been the flood of mandatory minimum sentences which Congress has prescribed."[37]

> Pretrial detention can create—and in many circumstances has created—crises of mammoth proportions, creating problems for every element of the criminal justice system: those charged with crime; defense counsel; pretrial services and probation officers; judges; prosecutors; marshals; and the Bureau of Prisons.[38]

JAILS

First, we need to recognize the jail as a criminal justice system–dependent institution. Changes in any component in the system will almost always affect jails. As we have seen, for example, bail reform through legislative action has seriously affected local detention facilities. Reforming bail systems has had the objective of reducing the number of court no-shows and pretrial crimes committed by persons who either made bail or were released on personal recognizance.[39] It is difficult to find convincing evidence that a large percentage of pretrial-released defendants fail to appear for trial, or that their crime rates are inordinately high. We do know from what we have noted earlier that one result of this legislation is to fill the jails with people who are not dangerous and would have shown for court, but are too poor to post bond.[40]

A recent national survey found that 27 percent of jails are overcrowded to the extent that courts have ordered them to reduce their populations.[41] A related problem is that overcrowding contributes to a number of problems and deleterious conditions. The same survey found that almost a third of jails surveyed were under court orders to correct one or more conditions the courts considered to be so injurious to the health and welfare of inmates as to warrant judicial intervention.

Statutes that require judges to impose prison sentences contribute to overcrowded state prisons. One result is that many offenders must be housed in local jails until bed space is available in state institutions. Thus, jails are crowded with inmates who never were meant to be incarcerated there.

The Traditional Jail

Jails throughout the country have certain features in common. They are overcrowded with inmate populations of widely different backgrounds, problems, and needs. Jails are locally administered and often lack adequate funding for the professional staffing and correctional and other program services that their diverse populations require. Recently, overcrowding has become more of a problem since jails must keep more offenders awaiting space at state prisons. They have responded to court orders by releasing early those over whom they have authority, resulting in criticism from the public and political leaders.

Most jails in the United States are small facilities that can hold less than fifty inmates and are located in counties or municipalities. One consequence is that jails vary markedly in terms of physical characteristics and programs. The development of widely applied minimum standards has been a slow process partly because of the preference for local control of detention centers. In 1980, the American Correctional Association (ACA) organized an accreditation body, the Commission on Accreditation for Corrections, which developed standards to certify prisons and local detention institutions.[42]

The ACA standards have resulted in some improvements in the conditions and programs of those facilities where they are used. They also are employed by those who legally challenge jail conditions. In over 150 court cases arising out of such challenges, ACA standards have been offered as supporting evidence for inmates. Frequently, the result has been either court-ordered compliance with the standards, or consent decrees under which jail administrators agree to comply.[43]

One important benefit for the jail resulting from complying with accreditation standards is lower insurance costs: "some officials have found that insurance companies provide a reduced premium for their facilities once [they are] accredited."[44] Another benefit of accreditation standards is that they can be used by administrators and others as "leverage toward new and renovated buildings."[45]

Since the 1970s, the federal government has provided local jurisdictions with technical and financial assistance to upgrade their jails. To a large extent, federal involvement in such a localized government activity has been rationalized by the need to house federal detainees in these facilities pending transfers to federal institutions. In response to this need the United States Department of Justice produced its Prison and Jail Standards. Jails failing to meet these standards may not be eligible for housing federal prisoners and, thus, are ineligible for various forms of federal assistance. The threat of loss of federal funds and technical assistance has spurred many states and localities to upgrade their detention facilities and programs to meet the federal standards.

Jail crowding, like that of prisons, is a serious problem, affecting general conditions and program availability. The population problem can be addressed in a number of ways, including using alternatives to pretrial and postconviction incarceration, which we shall discuss later in this chapter. Another approach to relieve crowding is, obviously, new jail construction. This approach is expensive, and runs into the problem of where to locate a new facility. In urban and suburban settings space is at a premium. In addition, there is often resistance to putting a jail anywhere near residential areas. "Not in my backyard" is a common response to proposals for establishing new jails and prisons.

New York City attacked this resistance as well as the limited availability of land by building an 800-bed floating detention center in 1988.[46] Floating prisons and jails are not new developments. As Cottrell and Shanahan point out, Great Britain used prison ships during the Revolutionary War period, and New York City had experience with floating jails when its Department of Corrections converted old ferry boats and barges into correctional facilities.[47]

Such jails must meet significant federal and state requirements. The United States Coast Guard, the American Bureau of Shipping, and the National Fire Protection Association each has certification standards to which floating jails must conform. In New York's case, Coast Guard standards were not available until construction had started. The result was an additional $35 million spent to achieve certification. This brought the total cost to $160,000,000.

A short-term response to jail overcrowding that has become more common in recent years is simply for one jurisdiction to contract for jail space in another, one presumably with the room to accommodate more prisoners. In Virginia, jail crowding is so serious a problem that local sheriffs have filed lawsuits against the state corrections department. The basis for their suits was a law that requires transfer of convicted felons to state prisons within 60 days of sentencing.[48] As a response, the state transferred a total of 800 inmates to Texas under a contract with that state. Other measures included adding 2,100 additional beds to the already crowded state correctional institutions.

On first impression, this seems to be a pragmatic, if not ideal solution for both jurisdictions. The crowded jail system gets relief, while the other system earns some needed hard cash. However, what of the consequences for the transferred prisoners? An obvious drawback for these inmates and their families is the virtual impossibility of maintaining contact while separated by thousands of miles. Not only will this cause personal hardship for many, it can and will negatively affect the correctional process.

The "New Generation" Jail

A different approach to "rehabilitating" the American jail began with the opening in 1975 of the federal Metropolitan Correctional Centers in Chicago, New York City, and San Diego. These detention facilities were based on what became known as the **new generation philosophy**.[49] These and other new generation jails that eventually opened in a number of states were designed to avoid some of the problems we have discussed in this chapter.[50]

New generation philosophy depends on an awareness of the interaction between the jail as a physical plant and staff-inmate organization and relationships. To appreciate what the advocates of new generation jails have in mind, we need to understand more about the layout and staffing of traditional American jails. We can generalize to the extent of saying that typical local jails are **linear jails** in design and layout, characterized by cells or living spaces arranged along straight-line corridors. Cells are

*C*urrently, the "new generation" or podular detention facility is utilized at the Santa Rita County Jail in California and other facilities. Inmates are confined to the security pods during the day and released into the common pod area or exercise court after their confinement each day.

multiple occupancy units, the interiors of which can only be seen by staff when almost directly in front of barred doors.

> The facility's design by and large determines the inmate supervision style. In the linear jail, inmate supervision is intermittent; staff must continuously patrol the corridors in order to observe inmates. Hardware such as bars, metal doors, sally ports, electronic surveillance, and eavesdropping equipment augment staff supervision and control of inmates.[51]

Historically, such architectural designs and supervision styles were related to certain perceptions of the nature of inmates and the role of the detention facility. Inmates were assumed to be potentially dangerous persons who would likely destroy institution property and try to escape. Further, through much of the jail's history in America, it was assumed that staff could not be found or trained to deliver adequate supervision of the inmate population. Thus, the architecture of jails had to compensate for deficiencies in staff control of inmate behavior.

However, linear jails and their typical staffing patterns result in inmates being largely free of any kind of **direct supervision.** Violent and nonviolent illegal activities frequently go unobserved. Inmate victimization by other inmates occurs quite often. As Hans Toch once commented, inmates threatened by their jail mates have the limited option of "flight or fight."[52] Suicide, the leading cause of death in jails, is difficult to prevent in the linear jail.

New generation jails are often referred to as "podular/direct supervision" facilities. This refers to the architecture and inmate/staff interaction. The characteristic features of these jails are:

- Inmate populations are divided into groups of 16 to 46 persons housed in pods or modules.

- Each module is staffed 24 hours a day by officers specifically trained for direct supervision work.
- Each module is self-contained with housing, visiting, and recreation areas.
- Inmate movement is generally restricted to her or his module.[53]

Even the furniture and furnishings of the new generation jail often are selected not necessarily to resist wear and tear but to "reduce inmate stress associated with crowding, excessive noise, lack of privacy, and isolation from the outside world."[54] The new generation philosophy's "primary goal is to create an incarceration environment that is safe and humane for inmates and staff alike."[55]

What has been the record of the new generation of podular jails? Limited evaluation research indicates that these institutions are at least as secure as traditional jails. This is a very important finding. After all, jails must be able to show that they can keep their inmates in. Beyond this, there is evidence that "podular/direct supervision facilities are safer and provide a more positive incarcerative and work environment for inmates and staff than do traditional jails."[56]

One of the essential ingredients of a successful new generation jail is trained staff attuned to the needs of direct supervision of inmates. Unfortunately, availability of such staff is problematic given such impediments as low salaries and the lack of other benefits. And the shortage of trained staff is not the only problem. Jail and other correctional workers are notoriously resistant to change. To change from the **intermittent supervision** in the linear jail to the direct supervision required in podular facilities may well be too difficult for many jail workers.[57]

A study of staff at six new generation jails found a high turnover rate that is troubling, since staff at these institutions were carefully selected and trained specifically for work in podular/direct supervision institutions.[58] The single most powerful variable predicting staff turnover rates was overcrowding. In the words of the researchers, "it seems clear that the first step to improving the operation of [a jail] is to *reduce the population to its approved carrying capacity.*"[59]

It may well be that the courts will provide the impetus needed to improve jail conditions. As will see in Chapter 10, courts have given up the so-called hands-off policies of the past. They have been taking a long, hard look at prisons and local detention facilities, sometimes issuing orders to state and local administrators to clean up their acts.[60]

Jail Privatization

Another approach to improving local jails is to transfer them, or some of their services, to the private sector. As will be discussed in Chapter 8, **privatization** of state prisons and correctional services is rather modestly underway in the United States. There is nothing that could be called a trend toward privatization in jail systems. Some localities have moved in this direction, and there have been calls for more privatization because "private is better."[61] Among the factors that have slowed the privatization of jails is the complex of legal issues that must be resolved by local communities. As the American Bar Association put it, communities that want to privatize their detention facilities and programs should take the time to consider carefully all the "constitutional, statutory, and contractual issues" that are involved.[62] Another major factor that must be considered is the "adversarial relationship with public correctional agencies, employee unions, professional associations, and prisoner advocate groups."[63]

There is considerable disagreement regarding whether the private sector should take over the running of entire institutions, or only some of the programs and services offered by these facilities. There is no one model of privatization that allows us to generalize about the situation at this time. Suffice it to say that in some communities jails are administered and all services are provided and delivered by private contractors. In more instances, private sector involvement is limited to delivering services such as medical care and food. Until recently, local detention facilities that have gone the privatization route mainly have been juvenile institutions and nonsecure facilities such as halfway houses.

WHO IS IN AMERICAN JAILS?

A recent census of American jails revealed the following facts about their populations:

- On June 30, 1995, there were an estimated 541,913 offenders in local jails.[64]
- In 1993, there were 13,245,000 admissions to the nation's local jails.[65]
- The number of jail inmates per 100,000 in the general adult population rose from 108 to 193 between 1985 and 1995.[66]
- The jail incarceration rate for blacks was six times that for whites.[67]
- Slightly over half the population (51 percent) consisted of adults awaiting trial. The remainder included those serving sentences and others awaiting transfer to the prison system or extradition to other jurisdictions.[68]

The degree and frequency of the guards' supervision depends on the standards of the facility and the type of prisoners imprisoned within the institution.

HIV infection was found to be an increasing problem for jails. AIDS-related deaths represented about 10 percent of all reported deaths, although the leading cause of death (36.2 percent of all deaths) remains suicide.[69]

Tables 5.1 and 5.2 show the increase in jail populations and rate of jail incarceration between 1983 and 1994. As we can see, there has been a striking increase of almost 257,000 inmates during those twelve years.

One description of jail populations claims that jail incarceration is, intended or otherwise, primarily for a "rabble" segment of the general population.[70] Other studies have found that jail populations contain a wide array of persons with serious mental health, medical, and drug and alcohol dependence problems. Such a problem-plagued population raises serious difficulties for detention facility administrators and staff. At this point, we will examine the findings of these studies in order to get a better understanding of who is in prison.

John Backstrand and his colleagues attempted to test John Irwin's "rabble" hypothesis. Irwin's contention is that those in jails are members of the underclass or the "rabble" and are often detained not because they pose a threat to the community, are serious or violent offenders, or pose a risk of failing to appear for trial, but because they are "defined as offensive persons by the police and/or other members of the community."[71]

The Backstrand research studied two jail systems, one in Portland, Oregon, the other in Washington state. Using the statutory categories delineating degrees of misdemeanors and felonies to judge the seriousness of charges (Irwin had criminology students evaluate seriousness), it was found that nearly 47 percent of those detained

Local Jail Inmates and Their Number per 100,000 U.S. Residents, Midyear, 1983–1994   **TABLE 5.1**

	NUMBER OF LOCAL JAIL INMATES			
Year	All	Per 100,000 Residents of All Ages	Adults	Per 100,000 Residents Age 18 or Older
1994	490,442	188	483,717	251
1993*	459,804	178	455,500	239
1992	444,584	174	441,781	234
1991	426,479	169	424,129	277
1990	405,320	163	403,019	218
1989	395,553	160	393,303	214
1988	343,569	141	341,893	189
1987	295,873	122	294,092	164
1986	274,444	114	272,736	154
1985	256,615	108	254,986	145
1984	234,500	99	233,018	134
1983	223,551	96	221,815	130

*Because of the high mobility of jail inmates, this number represents the population on one day.
SOURCE: *Jails and Jail Inmates, 1993–94,* Bureau of Justice Statistics, April 1995, p. 2.

TABLE 5.2	Average Daily Population and Number of Men, Women, and Juveniles in Local Jails, Midyear, 1985, 1990–95						
	1985	1990	1991	1992	1993	1994	1995
Average daily population	265,010	408,075	422,609	441,889	466,155	479,757	509,828
Number of Inmates, June 30	256,615	405,320	426,479	444,584	459,804	490,442	515,122
Adults	254,986	403,019	424,129	441,780	455,500	483,717	507,234
Male	235,909	365,821	384,628	401,106	411,500	434,838	455,098
Female	19,077	37,198	39,501	40,674	44,100	48,879	52,136
Juveniles	1,629	2,301	2,350	2,804	4,300	6,725	7,888
Held as adults	—	—	—	—	3,300	5,139	6,018
Held as juveniles	1,629	2,301	2,350	2,804	1,000	1,586	1,870

Source: *Prison and Jail Inmates, 1995,* Washington, D.C., Bureau of Justice Statistics, August 1996, p. 10.

in jails following their booking by the police were charged with felonies, with an additional 44 percent charged with the most serious misdemeanors. They also looked at the one-day populations of the sample jails and found that 82.5 percent of those either awaiting trial or convicted of crimes were charged with felonies. Thus they argue that Irwin's rabble hypothesis is exaggerated.[72]

Regardless of the fate of the "rabble" hypothesis, there is ample evidence that jails hold large numbers of mentally ill and disturbed persons, many of whom should be in other, more appropriate facilities. An editorial in the *American Journal of Public Health* quoted a number of findings from studies and reports that point out this fact, and stated:

> By default the criminal justice system has replaced the mental health system as a primary provider of care to many homeless mentally ill persons. . . . Homeless persons are not inherently more prone to criminal behavior. Rather, the homeless lifestyle itself leads to victimization and criminal involvement.[73]

The editorial went on to say that local detention facilities have become the "dumping grounds of mentally ill and retarded people in our society," and that as many as 600,000 persons in jails "are suffering from mental illness."[74] Most of them have been accused or convicted of committing relatively minor crimes that are symptomatic of their mental illnesses.

Two studies by Linda Telpin, reported on in 1990 and 1994, provide empirical support for these editorial comments. She found that the prevalence of "severe" mental disorder "is significantly higher in a typical urban jail than in the general population."[75] She also found that:

> The majority of disordered subjects were arrested for nonviolent crimes. Many of the severely ill detainees could have been diverted into the mental health system before arrest, before trial, or after release.[76]

A combination of factors contributing to the use of local jails as "dumping grounds" for the mentally ill has been identified. These factors include a decline in community mental health facilities and programs and the release of patients from mental hospitals (many of those released becoming part of the homeless population). Because of funding deficiencies and the relatively short period of jail confinement, treatment options for these persons are often nonexistent or, at best, inadequate.

A related characteristic of the American jail population is that it is more suicidal than the general population. As many as 1,000 inmates commit suicide each year and many more make one or more attempts to take their own lives. Many believe that suicide is the leading cause of death in American jails.[77]

Among suicide-risk factors that have been identified are drug and alcohol use and history of mental illness. Efforts at developing profiles that would allow authorities to predict and, possibly, prevent suicides have been unsuccessful.[78] We do know that some of the physical properties of jails and detention centers contribute to the suicide problem, including bedding (blankets and sheets that can be used in place of ropes), some furniture, and the steel bars and overhead pipes that are common in cells. Inadequate supervision of inmates also plays a role in the high rate of suicide and attempted suicide. Those who commit or attempt to commit suicide do so in the first few hours after admission, so, at the very least, detainees should be closely supervised during this early portion of their confinement.[79]

A recurring question regarding suicide in jail is whether jail personnel are legally responsible for preventing inmates from killing themselves. Although risk profiles have been found wanting, there are signs that some detainees are at risk. How should jail workers and administrators respond? A number of Supreme Court decisions tell us that unless there has been "deliberate indifference" or "gross" negligence by officials, there is no legal redress available to inmates who attempt suicide or to relatives of those who succeed in ending their lives.[80]

We must also recognize that U.S. jail populations now contain many more offenders convicted of serious crimes than in the past. A major reason for this is systemic in nature. As we pointed out in Chapter 2, there have been significant changes in sentencing laws, including increased use of mandatory sentences as well as the introduction of sentencing guidelines, over the past fifteen years. Some of these changes were enacted to produce equity in sentencing ("truth in sentencing"); another reason was to control prison population growth. However, little attention was paid until recently to the impact of these law revisions on jail populations and programs.

A 1995 article examined the impact of Minnesota's sentencing guidelines system on the state's jails.[81] With special attention to sentencing "repeat property offenders," this research found that rates of jail incarceration rose significantly after Minnesota implemented its sentencing guidelines. Judges were found to employ the mitigating factors available in the guidelines in order to avoid sentencing many offenders to state prisons, frequently sending them to local jails instead. The effects of prison crowding were found to exert more influence on sentencing decisions than the goal of sentencing equity. The study concluded that "sentencing reforms that place limits only on the growth of prison populations may result in substantial increase in jail use," and therefore, "erode policymakers' efforts to produce long-term effects" on the incarceration population.[82]

JAIL PROGRAMS

Providing programs, correctional or otherwise, to jail inmates is a hit or miss proposition in the United States. Among the problems confronting jail administrators who wish to do so are lack of funds at the local level and the relatively short time most inmates are incarcerated. Three program areas are examined here: general education, AIDS prevention, and drug and alcohol abuse counseling and education, These would seem to be obvious choices for local jails, given the nature of the needs of their populations.

General Education

Educational services are offered in only about 20 percent of American jails, although, as might be expected, a higher percentage of larger jail systems offer some educational programs.[83] However, only 9 percent of jail inmates participate in these programs. The federal government has made an effort to provide local jurisdictions with the wherewithal to offer educational services to more inmates.[84] For example, a demonstration project recently was funded in Jefferson County (Kentucky). Called Real Opportunities Behind Bars for Employment (ROBBE), the project "sought to

*P*risoners learn new skills that may help them in the business world once they are released.

sponsor the development of the skills necessary to compete in a global economy."[85] We suggest this is a tall order indeed for the local jail administrator.

The ROBBE project required the cooperation of the Jefferson County Department of Corrections and the county's Public Schools Adult Education Center. Limited to medium security inmates, the program significantly increased inmates' reading and math skills.

> The early results from the . . . program are promising. They indicate that jail inmates can profit from individualized instruction. . . . Of course, the major question here is whether this improvement translates into success on the streets.[86]

Certainly, this is the question that must be answered about any correctional program. As yet, we do not have a definitive answer to this question with regard to programs such as ROBBE.

AIDS Prevention Education

Much more narrowly focused educational programs in jails are those that address HIV infection and AIDS. Because jail populations contain significant numbers of intravenous drug users as well as sexually active inmates, it makes sense to provide at least some education toward making prisoners more prevention-conscious. One problem, common to all jail programs, is the relatively short time inmates are available. One study, funded by the National Institute on Drug Abuse, found that subjects would need to be incarcerated from two to six months if an educational program had much chance for success.[87]

Many AIDS educational programs stress the need to help people at risk become more knowledgeable about the dangers they face with either intravenous drug use, sexual activity, or both. A study of women drug users in Phoenix, Arizona, found that drug users are already fairly knowledgeable about the dangers of needle sharing.[88] Similarly, inmates were aware of the risks of HIV infection from sexual activity. However, little was learned about the actual behavior of the study subjects after they were released from custody. Whether or not their behavior in the community changed needs to be studied in follow-up research.

This question about the long-term postrelease benefits of jail programs is largely unanswered regardless of the type of program or services delivered to prisoner populations. We mentioned this earlier with regard to basic literacy and math courses. Without the ability to know whether these and other programs contribute to postrelease behavior, it is impossible to recommend any specific correctional measures for local detention facilities. This conclusion is bolstered by the general resistance of jail personnel to correctional programs as well as inherent obstacles to service delivery. As was found in the AIDS education program in Phoenix, this resistance and institutional obstacles include:

- Lack of support from jail administrators and line staff
- Stigmatization by staff of inmates who participate in classes such sex education and AIDS awareness
- Lack of adequate facilities (e.g., classrooms, audiovisual equipment)

Drug and Alcohol Abuse Education and Counseling

A nationwide survey of 1,737 jails reported on in 1992 examined a serious problem for America's jails: the sharp rise in inmates with drug abuse problems.[89]

Because only a few drug-involved felony offenders are convicted and sent to state prison, the absence of in-jail treatment programs or linkage to community agencies following release . . . means that the vast majority of serious drug abusers return to the streets without gaining additional skills to prevent drug relapse.[90]

Previous research suggested that there are very few substance abuse programs in the nation's jails. Those that were found were primarily based on the Alcoholics Anonymous model. A 1992 survey found that only 28 percent of the surveyed jails offered any drug treatment other than detoxification.[91] The probability of a jail having treatment programs varied noticeably with geographic location and jail size. Jails in the northeast reported more programs than any other region, while the larger the facility, the greater the likelihood of having drug treatment available.

What kinds of "treatment" programs were reported by the institutions? The survey found that about 20 percent claimed to have detoxification programs. These probably cannot be defined as treatment programs. In an effort to determine how many jails had "comprehensive" programs, the researchers established the following criteria: (a) group counseling, (b) drug education, (c) transition planning, and (d) referral to outside agencies for further treatment following release. Only 7 percent of the responding institutions met all these criteria.[92] Even those jails with comprehensive programs provided on average less than seven hours of inmate participation per week. Survey findings found that despite the observed "link" between drug abuse and crime, "a significant number of jails still do not have adequate drug treatment services."[93]

One example of a county jail that does deliver comprehensive services to its alcohol abusing population is located in the Virginia suburbs of Washington, D.C.[94] Based on Alcoholics Anonymous group principles, the Alexandria Detention Center operates a "total treatment environment" that includes a Sober Living Unit to treat alcoholics and serious alcohol abusers who have been sentenced to the center.

Perhaps not surprisingly, more correctional services currently are offered in facilities that have been introduced as alternatives to jails. These programs include day reporting centers, pretrial diversion, and a number of innovative nonresidential settings. We now discuss each of these.

ALTERNATIVES TO JAILS

Day Reporting Centers

A number of jurisdictions have sought to deal with issues such as overcrowding and other deleterious jail conditions in both traditional and new generation facilities, not by building new jails, floating or otherwise, but by developing alternatives to residential detention facilities. One model of an alternative to jail is the **day reporting center.** As a general rule, these centers are designed for offenders who have been convicted of misdemeanors. "Day reporting offers the punishment of confinement combined with the rehabilitative effects of allowing the offender to continue employment and receive treatment."[95]

The day reporting center concept originated in Great Britain in the 1970s and was first implemented in the United States in 1986 when the Hampden County (Massachusetts) Sheriff's Department began its early release program for convicted jail inmates. Although the original population to be served by reporting centers was limited to convicted offenders, the Hampden center and many others established since have expanded their reach to include probationers, those released from prison under supervision, and persons awaiting trial.[96]

This expansion of coverage does carry the risk of "widening the net," which is a risk shared by nearly all alternative programs, as we note in later chapters. Under the pressure of rapidly growing prison, parole, and probation populations, the day reporting center may be easy prey to those who must find some way to alleviate the pressure. One recommendation from workers in the field is that:

> Day reporting should be reserved for the offender whose behavior has not been corrected by probation and who has evidenced a need for greater structure in his or her treatment. This is a niche that day reporting will fill in a correctional continuum that endeavors to apply the proper amount of control and treatment to ensure the correction of the individual.

Should this recommendation be followed, pressure on local jails may not be relieved since the target population (probationers) is facing risk of prison confinement, not jail incarceration, if they violate the terms of their release.

Pretrial Diversion

Pretrial diversion is another alternative to detention while awaiting trial. But diversion, as understood in the correctional community, is not simply diverting a defendant away from a detention facility. Rather, it is inserting the person into a program of one kind or another related to the criminal charges or problems facing her or him. Diversion involves "the halting or suspension, before conviction, of formal criminal proceedings against a person, conditioned on some form of counter performance by the defendant."[98]

Recent pretrial diversion programs are linked to changing attitudes toward drunk driving offenders. The 1982 Alcohol Traffic Safety and National Driver Registration Act[99] offers grants to states that take steps to reduce drunk driving–related accidents. Such steps have included stiffening penalties, including more frequent use of jail terms, for law violators. Perhaps more importantly, the large number of drunk driving offenders jailed in local facilities has required these institutions to invest heavily in programs aimed at "rehabilitating" those who drink and drive. Frequently, these offenders are problem drinkers, if not alcoholics, and more than simple incarceration is required if they are to be deterred from continuing to pose a threat to themselves and others on the highways. Many drunk driving defendants will face jail terms if convicted, while others will be required to attend special classes and treatment sessions. To some in corrections, it makes sense to start the latter activities before trial is held. Historically, pretrial diversion programs for drug abuse defendants have a relatively long history, and now they are being extended to alcohol-abusing drivers.[100]

Nonresidential Programs

A variation on both the day reporting center and diversion is to blend treatment or correctional programs with diversion from prosecution. An example is the Lehigh County (Pennsylvania) Day Program initiated in 1991.[101] Women offenders accepted into the program have their needs assessed with special attention to employment, drug abuse, personal and family budgeting, and education.

Participation in the Lehigh County program can be voluntary or by court order. Some women enter it as a condition of pretrial release, others as a condition of parole or probation. Still others come to the program as a lesser or "intermediate" level of confinement. This varied population makes this program difficult if not impossible to evaluate. What can be said of its success or failure in dealing with its multifaceted population? Unfortunately, not much reliable evidence has been found to answer this question. The Lehigh County program has not been formally evaluated, and its supporters can only say that it should offer its participants "an opportunity to change their lives and become productive members of society."[102]

We need to add here that one reported advantage of the Lehigh County program is its reported lower cost than incarceration. The per diem cost for the Day Program was said to be $11.64, while in the local jail the cost was $71 per day.

SUMMARY

AMERICAN JAILS ARE OVERCROWDED with a wide variety of inmates. Some are awaiting trial because they have been denied or been unable to afford bail; others are detained because they violated the conditions of their release; still others are in jail with sentences to these facilities; some prisoners are awaiting transfer to a state or federal prison to serve their sentences; and, finally, there are inmates awaiting transfers to other jurisdictions.

Not only do jails house diverse populations, they are seriously overcrowded. Overcrowding largely can be attributed to changes in charging and sentencing practices, especially in the areas of drunk driving and drug offenses. Unless laws and attitudes are changed, it is unlikely that jail crowding can be reduced significantly. Solutions that have been suggested, and sometimes tried, include building new jails and developing alternatives to traditional pretrial detention.

The population of jails in the United States now consists of many persons with serious health problems, including mental illness, substance abuse offenders, suicidal inmates, and chronic violent offenders. Instituting correctional programs and maintaining security in jails is an extraordinary task for the jail administrator. For several years it was thought that building a "new generation" of jails would provide an answer to the question of how to deliver needed services in a secure setting. However, the architectural changes built into new generation jails frequently cannot overcome population explosions, funding shortfalls, and correctional worker antipathy to correctional programs.

KEY CONCEPTS

Bail
Bail Reform Act
Day reporting centers
Direct supervision
Intermittent supervision
Linear jails

New generation philosophy
Personal recognizance
Pretrial diversion
Preventive detention
Privatization

❙QUESTIONS FOR DISCUSSION

1. From the vantage point of a jail administrator, what are the most serious issues you confront because of the diverse population you must securely hold?
2. Fully explain the statement "Jails are criminal justice system–dependent institutions."
3. How can jail crowding be effectively remedied, given the current public preference for "getting tough" with offenders?
4. Can jail programs ever be evaluated, given the diverse populations they must accept? Fully explain your answer.
5. A number of alternatives to jail incarceration are discussed in this chapter. Which seem to offer some real hope for correcting the many problems these facilities are experiencing? Justify your answer.
6. The "new generation" jails have not met the goals set for them. Why is this so?

❙ENDNOTES

1. G. Larry Mayes and Joel A. Thompson, "Mayberry Revisited: The Characteristics and Operation of America's Small Jails," *Justice Quarterly* 5 (1988): 422.
2. J. M. Moyahan and Early K. Stewart, *The American Jail: Its Growth and Development* (Chicago: Nelson-Hall, 1980), p. 104.
3. Ronald L. Goldfarb, *Jails: The Ultimate Ghetto* (Garden City, N.Y.: Anchor/Doubleday, 1975).
4. John Irwin, *The Jail* (Berkeley, California: University of California Press, 1985).
5. Brian A. Reeves and Jacob Perez, U.S. Department of Justice, Bureau of Justice Statistics, *Pretrial Release of Felony Defendants, 1992* (November 1994), p. 1.
6. Ibid., p. 2.
7. Prosecutors are required to make evidence and lists of potential witnesses available to the defense. This is regulated under state and federal laws of "discovery." It is beyond the scope of this chapter to do more than mention this requirement. It is sufficient to note that the prosecution must present evidence at this stage that is adequate to convince a judicial officer that a defendant may have committed a crime.
8. 18 U.S.C. 3142 (1984).
9. The U.S. Supreme court held in *United States v. Salerno,* 481 U.S. 739 (1987), that the defendant's detention did not violate the Constitution since his confinement was not punishment. The preventive detention provision of the federal law was a regulatory one with "compelling" state interest.
10. Joel A. Thompson and G. Larry Mays (eds.), *American Jails: Public Policy Issues* (Chicago: Nelson-Hall Press, 1991).
11. Christy A. Visher, "Using Drug Testing to Identify High-Risk Defendants on Release: A Study in the District of Columbia," *Journal of Criminal Justice* 20 (1992): 321–333.
12. Ibid., p. 325.
13. Thomas J. Wolf, "The Miramont Evaluation: Drug Treatment as a Condition of Pretrial Release," *Federal Probation* 58 (March 1994): 36–44.
14. Ibid., p. 38.
15. Ibid., p. 37.
16. Reeves and Perez, *Pretrial Release of Felony Defendants, 1992,* p. 11.
17. Ibid., p. 10.

18. Steven Belenko, Iona Mara-Drita, and Jerome E. McElroy, "Drug Tests and the Prediction of Pretrial Misconduct: Findings and Policy Issues," *Crime & Delinquency* 38 (1992): 557–582.

19. Ibid., p. 560.

20. Ibid., p. 573.

21. William Rhodes, Raymond Hyatt, and Paul Scheiman, "Predicting Pretrial Misconduct with Drug Tests of Arrestees: Evidence from Six Sites," *Research in Brief,* National Institute of Justice (January 1996).

22. Ibid., p. 5.

23. Ellen Hochstedler Steury & Nancy Frank, "Gender Bias and Pretrial Release: More Pieces of the Puzzle," *Journal of Criminal Justice* 18 (1990): 417–432.

24. Ibid., p. 431.

25. Wayne N. Walsh, "Changes in Arrest Policies as a Result of Court Orders Against County Jails," *Justice Quarterly* 10 (1993): 89–118.

26. California Penal Code Section 853.6 authorizes police officers to issue field citations when arresting most misdemeanants. Police may also issue citations at the police station, after which defendants are released.

27. Ibid., p. 106.

28. Thomas W. Church and Milton Heuman, "The Underexamined Assumptions of the Invisible Hand: Monetary Incentives and Policy Instruments," *Journal of Policy Analysis and Management* 8 (1993): 641–657.

29. Ibid., p. 646.

30. Ibid.

31. Ibid., p. 647.

32. Ibid.

33. Ibid., pp. 653–654.

34. Vincent Broderick, "Pretrial Detention in the Criminal Justice Process," *Federal Probation* 57 (March 1993): 4–8.

35. Ibid., p. 5.

36. Ibid.

37. Ibid.

38. Ibid.

39. The recent wave of bail reform legislation stands in stark contrast to another wave in the 1960s and '70s. In this earlier time, reform was aimed at permitting more defendants to be released prior to trial. Setting relatively high bail was judged to discriminate against the poor and minorities.

40. Joel A. Thompson and G. Larry Mays, eds., *American Jails: Public Policy Issues* (Chicago: Nelson-Hall, 1991).

41. Louis W. Jankowski, "Jail Inmates, 1991," United States Department of Justice, Bureau of Justice Statistics, *Bulletin* (June 1992).

42. Participation in the accreditation program is voluntary, although there are pressures on local jurisdictions to comply.

43. W. Wayne Huggins and Charles C. Kehoe, "Accreditation Benefits Nation's Jails, Juvenile Detention Centers," *Corrections Today* 54 (May 1992): 40–42. For more on the accreditation process, see Edward F. Reynolds, "an Auditor's View of Accreditation," in the same issue at pp. 44–46.

44. Reynolds, "An Auditor's View," p. 44.

45. Ibid.

46. James H. Cottrell and John H. Shanahan, Jr., "A Jail That Floats," *Corrections Today* 54 (April 1992): 132–133.

47. Ibid., p. 132.

48. Spencer S. Hsu, "Three Sheriffs Suspend Suit in Jail Crowding," *Washington Post*, June 9, 1995, p. D-6.

49. Linda L. Zupan and Ben A. Menke, "The New Generation Jail: An Overview," in Joel A. Thompson and G. Larry Mays, eds., *American Jails: Public Policy Issues* (Chicago: Nelson-Hall, 1991), pp. 180–194.

50. According to one estimate, there were approximately 80 new generation jails in operation by the middle of 1992.

51. Ibid., p. 181.

52. Hans Toch, *Living in Prison: The Ecology of Survival,* rev. ed. (American Psychological Association, 1992).

53. Ibid., p. 188.

54. ibid.

55. Ibid., p. 190.

56. Ibid., p. 192.

57. Joel A. Thompson and G. Larry Mays, "Paying the Piper but Changing the Tune: Policy Changes and Initiatives for the American Jail," *American Jails: Public Policy Issues* (Chicago: Nelson-Hall, 1991) pp. 240–246.

58. Mary K. Stohr, Ruth L. Self, and Nicholas P. Lovrich, "Staff Turnover in New Generation Jails: An Investigation of Its Causes and Prevention," *Journal of Criminal Justice* 20 (1992): 455–478.

59. Ibid., p. 474. Emphasis in the original.

60. Ibid., p. 243.

61. Normal R. Cox, Jr. and William E. Osterhoff, "Managing the Crisis in Local Corrections: A Public-Private Partnership Approach," *American Jails: Public Policy Issues* (Chicago: Nelson-Hall, 1991) pp. 227–239.

62. Ibid., p. 233.

63. Ibid., p. 234.

64. Darrell K. Gilliard and Allen J. Beck, *Prisons and Jail Inmates, 1995,* Washington, D.C., National Institute of Justice, Bureau of Justice Statistics, August 1996, p. 11.

65. Ibid., p. 13.

66. *Prisons and Jail Inmates, 1995,* p. 10.

67. Ibid.

68. Ibid., p. 5.

69. Ibid., p. 11.

70. Irwin, *The Jail,* pp. 11–13.

71. John A. Backstrand, Don C. Gibbons, and Joseph F. Jones, "Who Is in Jail: An Examination of the Rabble Hypothesis," *Crime & Delinquency* 38 (1992): 220.

72. Ibid., p. 226.

73. *American Journal of Public Health* 80 (1990): 656. For additional reports on the jailing of mentally ill persons, see Bruce Bower, "Jails Are Last Stop for Mentally Ill," *Science News* 125 (1984): 405–406; Katherine Briar, "Jails, Neglected Asylums," *Social Casework* 64 (1993): 397–393; Doug Shenson, Nancy Dubler, and David Michaels, "Jails and Prisons: The New Asylums?" *American Journal of Public Health* 80 (1990): 655–666.

74. Ibid.

75. Linda A. Telpin, "The Prevalance of Severe Mental Disorder Among Male Urban Jail Detainees: Comparison with the Epidemiologic Catchment Area Program," *American Journal of Public Health* 80 (1990): 666.

76. Linda A. Telpin, "Psychiatric and Substance Abuse Disorders Among Male Urban Jail Detainees," *American Journal of Public Health* 84 (1994): 291.

77. Mark S. Davis and Joshua E. Muscat, "An Epidemiologic Study of Alcohol and Suicide Risk in Ohio Jails and Lockups, 1975–1984," *Journal of Criminal Justice* 21 (1993): 277.

78. Daniel B. Kennedy and Robert J. Homant, "Predicting Custodial Suicides: Problems with Profiles," *Justice Quarterly* 5 (1988): 441–456.

79. J. Michael Olivero and James B. Roberts, "Jail Suicide and Legal Redress," *Suicide and Life-Threatening Behavior* 20 (1990): 138–147.

80. For a discussion of these cases, see Olivero and Roberts, "Jail Suicide and Legal Redress," pp. 139–146.

81. Stewart J. D'Alessio and Lisa Stolzenberg, "The Impact of Sentencing Guidelines on Jail Incarceration in Minnesota," *Criminology* 33 (1995): 283–301.

82. Ibid., p. 298.

83. Richard A. Tewksbury and Genarro F. Vito, "Improving the Educational Skills of Jail Inmates: Preliminary Program Findings," *Federal Probation* 58 (June 1994): 56.

84. This was under the U.S. Department of Education's Functional Literacy for State and Local Prisoners Program, established in 1992.

85. Tewksbury and Vito, "Improving Educational Skills," pp. 56–57.

86. Ibid., p. 58.

87. Sandra Baxter, "AIDS Education in the Jail Setting," *Crime & Delinquency* 37 (1991): 48–63.

88. Ibid., pp. 58–59.

89. Roger H. Peters, Robert L. May II, and William D. Kearns, "Drug Treatment in Jails: Results of a Nationwide Survey," *Journal of Criminal Justice* 20 (1992): 283–295. Completed questionnaires were received from a total of 1,654 institutions.

90. Ibid., p. 284.

91. Ibid., p. 286.

92. Ibid.

93. Ibid., p. 293.

94. Jennifer Nichols, "Facing Society with Sobriety: Virginia Jail Helps Offenders Get Out from under the Influence," *Corrections Today* 52 (1990): 108–110.

95. David W. Diggs and Stephen L. Pieper, "Using Day Reporting Centers as an Alternative Jail," *Federal Probation* 58 (1994): 9.

96. Ibid., p. 10.

97. Ibid., p. 12.

98. B. J. George, "Screening, Diversion, and Meditation in the United States," *New York Law School Law Review* 29 (1984): 1.

99. U.S. Code, Title 23, § 402.

100. See Lea L. Fields, "Pretrial Diversion: A Solution to California's Drunk-Driving Problem," *Federal Probation* 58 (1994): 20–21.

101. Ruth T. Wernick, Angela Valasquez, and Kate Brennan, "Day Program: Lehigh County's Intermediate Alternative," *Corrections Today* 56 (December 1994): 150–153.

102. Ibid., p. 152.

INCARCERATION: A HISTORY OF THE AMERICAN PRISON

INTRODUCTION THE FIRST AMERICAN PRISON was established in 1773 in an abandoned Connecticut copper mine. It was entered through a single shaft that led to caverns lying 25 feet below the surface. A single "lodging room" measuring 16 feet square was blasted out of rock. In order to provide security, an iron door was installed to seal it from the entrance shaft. Men who were entombed there were supposed to defray at least some of the costs of their confinement by mining copper.[1] The prison's hoped-for security was quickly shattered. Its first inmate escaped within three weeks of his admission.[2]

In the sometimes confusing history of the prison in our society we will see that at various times we have incarcerated offenders in mine shafts, committed them to years of solitary confinement, forced other prisoners to spend their years of imprisonment under draconian rules of silence and hard labor, and crammed prisoners into cells as small as 3 ½ feet by 6 feet.

To understand the prison in America, we need to trace the influence of three major ideas that at various times have guided or misguided our society's use of imprisonment as a criminal sanction. These are the **penitentiary, reformatory,** and **rehabilitative ideas.** We also must take account of the fact that until nearly the end of our colonial period we had no experience with imprisonment as a punishment for serious crime. In fact, our very first prison, Newgate of Connecticut, was an abject failure in terms of achieving any of the goals established for it. We cannot look to English or European models to help us figure out how prisons came to be in this country what they are today. Incarceration as a major weapon against serious crime is essentially an American invention, and its development must be seen in that context.

Today, over a million men and women are confined in state and federal prisons in the United States.[3] Between 1985 and the end of 1995, the prison population in the United States increased by an astonishing 121.2 percent.[4] These figures do not include the 50,966 prisoners serving at least the initial portion of their sentences in local jails following their conviction because of prison overcrowding.[5] Nor do they include the more than 500,000 inmates who make up the average jail population.[6] The rate of incarceration[7] has fluctuated over the years since rates have been calculated. At times, the rate actually has declined. However, between 1980 and 1993, the last year for which complete data are available, the rate has consistently risen from 139 prisoners per 100,000 in 1980 to 351 per 100,000 at the end of 1993.[8]

The prison population explosion has become so serious a problem in this country that as of June 30, 1990, many states were under court orders to reduce overcrowding.[9] Although the judiciary infrequently intervenes in the operation of prisons, overcrowding can result in appellate court rulings that declare the overcrowding severe enough to constitute "cruel and unusual punishment" under the Eighth Amendment of the United States Constitution.[10]

We can also get a picture of the extent of America's commitment to incarceration by looking at the amount of money spent on our state and federal prisons. The most recent data on expenditures for "corrections" puts the annual bill at $24.9 billion.[11] Although this figure includes parole, probation, and jail costs as well as prison expenditures, the latter gets the lion's share of the money.

These figures on prisoners and expenditures point dramatically to our society's continuing and increasing commitment to incarceration as a means to control crime. They do not, in themselves, suggest an answer to the question of why this commitment is so strong in the face of evidence that imprisonment does not "work." That is, the high rate of incarceration appears not to influence the rate of crime, nor, perhaps more importantly, the rate with which offenders continue to commit crimes following release from prison. We shall deal with this issue in a subsequent chapter.

In this chapter we will trace the history of the prison in the United States from the first prison, Newgate of Connecticut, to the present. We will pay special attention to several specific ideas and events that have shaped this history. Along the way we will point out some of the contradictions and conflicts that have plagued the use of the prison as a major penal sanction in American criminal justice.

NEWGATE OF CONNECTICUT: THE FIRST AMERICAN PRISON

The Connecticut legislature is credited with being the first in colonial America to authorize a prison to which certain offenders would be sentenced as punishment for their crimes.[12] Prior to this action, incarceration in the colonies, as well as in most of the rest of the world, was used mainly to confine offenders for short periods of time. Those confined were either awaiting trial or the execution of punishment, which might be the death penalty or a variety of corporal punishments. Sometimes, offenders would be jailed to serve relatively short sentences for minor crimes.

In 1773, the Connecticut Assembly passed a resolution that called for "confining, securing and profitably employing such criminals as may be committed to them by any future laws of this Colony, in lieu of the infamous punishments in divers cases now appointed."[13] The legislature provided for the incarceration of five kinds of offenders: robbers, burglars, forgers, counterfeiters, and horse thieves. The language of the resolution spelled out the goals the legislators had in mind for this new sanction: reduction of "infamous punishments," secure confinement, and "profitable employment" of criminals.

With regard to the first of these goals, we note that the legislators were influenced by the work of English and European penal reformers such as Jeremy Bentham and Cesare Beccaria. These reformers were among the first of the so-called classical school of criminology. They urged a radical rethinking of the role and severity of punishment in controlling crime.[14] Excessive use of the death penalty and brutal physical punishments were denounced as being tyrannical and counterproductive in that they encouraged disrespect for the law.[15] As we shall see below, their influence eventually spread beyond Connecticut and provided a philosophical foundation for the penitentiary movement in Pennsylvania and New York.

We have already seen that the Connecticut Assembly's objective of providing humane yet secure punishment for many serious offenders was not reached since prisoners began to escape within a few weeks of their being imprisoned. The problem of providing security and humane (or, later in time, rehabilitative) confinement has dogged efforts to reform the American prison ever since Newgate was closed. For example, when the rehabilitative idea reigned briefly supreme in corrections during the late 1950s and on through the '60s, correctional staff were confronted with the dilemma of trying to treat persons who were coercively present for treatment.

Another goal assigned to **Newgate of Connecticut** was to provide the colony with cheap labor and some profit by putting the prisoners to work in the mine. This end was never realized. Since offenders had no experience mining copper (or anything else), skilled workers had to be hired to train and supervise the convicts, thus increasing the prison's operating costs. Security concerns required hiring guards, also increasing operating costs. When managed as a private mining venture, Newgate of Connecticut had failed. Taken over by the colony as a prison, it continued to fail.

Newgate of Connecticut's dismal performance contributed to its failure to exert a lasting influence on penal development in the newly independent United States. Its goals—humane punishment, secure custody, and profitable (or, at least, some return to the state from the labor of inmates) employment of offenders—continued to be pursued by penologists, however. The next significant American prison development, one that has had a lasting impact on penal policy and practice, was the penitentiary movement.

THE PENITENTIARY IDEA

In 1790, the **Walnut Street Jail** in Philadelphia, Pennsylvania, became the setting for one of the most important events in the punishment of criminals in the United States. Beyond that, it became a beacon for later prison reform in Great Britain and elsewhere. The system of incarceration instituted in one wing of the jail came to be known as the **Pennsylvania system.** It was created as a result of the efforts of a small group of reformers who sought to deliver a more humane punishment to serious criminal offenders. Many of these reformers were repelled by the then common practice of inflicting capital and severe corporal punishments for a wide range of offenses. Other reformers focused their attention on the reformatory benefits to be derived from long-term cellular confinement of "morally diseased" criminals.

The Pennsylvania system had its roots in the jail reform movement that took place in Great Britain during the period of 1750 to 1790. According to Ignatieff, the initiation of jail reform in Britain began in earnest following the so-called **Black Assize** of 1750.[16] In that year, two typhus-infected prisoners went on trial in London's Old Bailey courtroom. Fifty persons, including the judge, lawyers, and members of the jury, caught the disease and later died. Following an investigation it was determined that the source of the disease was the jail where the defendants had been held. The investigation concluded that the jail was "[an] abominable sink of Beastliness and Corruption."[17] Outraged citizens and officials lobbied for funds to rebuild that jail as well as to investigate conditions in others throughout the country. These inquiries led to significant improvements in prison conditions. More importantly, they resulted in serious thinking about the role of incarceration in the punishment of offenders.

This reexamination of the role of imprisonment in criminal justice focused on the need to provide an **intermediate punishment,**[18] intermediate, that is, between transportation and the death penalty. Transportation of offenders was a rather popular sanction in eighteenth-century Britain. It usually involved the forced exiling (transportation) of convicts to undeveloped colonial territories (the American colonies and Australia, to mention two) where they were sentenced to penal servitude. Conditions were often exceedingly harsh. These were places to which free laborers were reluctant to go. Penal laborers were exploited to develop these areas for the mother country. Also, of course, transportation provided an effective way to be rid of at least some of Britain's "criminal class," thus protecting society from them.

At the other end of the punishment continuum, capital punishment in eighteenth- and early nineteenth-century Great Britain was used for a large number of crimes. According to Blackstone, there were 160 capital crimes in England in 1760. The list of offenses carrying the death penalty increased to the almost unbelievable total of 223 by 1819. Many of these, obviously, were neither serious nor violent offenses.[19] Many reformers, including John Howard in Britain, worked to reduce the number of such crimes and urged the substitution of incarceration for the gallows.

We should point out that not all the reformers who sought to reduce the use of capital punishment were motivated by a distaste for draconian punishments. Some were prompted to recommend incarceration because of a peculiar consequence of the long list of crimes punishable by death: Many judges and juries simply were refusing to condemn criminals to death. This was especially the case when youthful offenders were to be sentenced, and when others had been convicted of crimes judged to be too minor to warrant the ultimate penalty. Sometimes, these offenders were acquitted in the face of all reliable evidence so as to save them from the death penalty.

In a recent article entitled "Let Judges Decide," U.S. District Court Judge Harold H. Greene expressed a similar concern when he addressed the practice of enacting mandatory minimum prison sentences laws. These sentences are often applied to drug offenders without regard to the severity of their involvement in drug trafficking. Judge Greene wrote:

Jurors are not stupid or uninformed, and they by and large have a profound sense of basic fairness. When they learn . . . what will happen upon conviction under the mandatory sentence regime to those who by any rational standard are not really major offenders, they will often engage in the practice of nullification: They will choose to exercise their ability to find the defendant or defendants not guilty, no matter what the evidence.[20]

The Pennsylvania System

Quakers in Pennsylvania, influenced by the work of their coreligionists in Britain, gained control over a portion of the then-new Walnut Street Jail in 1790 and instituted a radical departure from contemporary prison and jail practices.[21] Although they certainly were committed to reducing the brutality of punishments then in vogue, they had another, more significant objective in mind. The guiding principle of these reformers was the belief that solitary confinement would induce individual offenders to strive for personal reformation. Solitude would encourage the prisoner to become sincerely penitent. In the words of one observer,

> To be abstracted from a world where he has endeavoured to confound the order of society, to be buried in a solitude where he has no companion but reflection, no counsellor but thought, the offender will find the severest punishment he can receive. The sudden change of scene that he experiences, the window which admits but a few rays of light, the midnite [*sic*] silence which surround [*sic*] him, all inspire him with a degree of horror which he never felt before. The impression is greatly heightened by his being obliged to think. No intoxicating cup benumbs his senses, no tumultuous revel dissipates his mind. Left alone and feelingly alive to the strings of remorse, he resolves on his present situation and connects it with that train of events which has banished him from society and placed him there.[22]

To readers today, the regimen described above appears to constitute cruel and unusual punishment under the Eighth Amendment of our Constitution. To the reformers, solitary confinement aided only those wishing to reform and harmed only

> . . . the most wicked and incorrigible offenders. Those, long inured to vagrancy and idleness, living abroad at hazard in conditions of exposure and vicious association, or in poor houses and jails, choosing the most corrupting companionship, dread solitude as the one great evil.[23]

On the other hand, those inmates not so incorrigible were to "find alleviation of their feelings of remorse," and will "apply [themselves] to the serious work of reformation and improvement."[24]

Dorothea Dix, the noted nineteenth-century humanitarian who made these observations, visited most of the prisons in the eastern United States during the early 1840s. In a report written in 1845, she laid out what to her were the essential criteria by which the worth of the penitentiary should be judged. We quote these criteria at length to get a real feeling for the spirit of the times that led to the creation of the penitentiary form of imprisonment.

> I understand by reformation [of prisoners], not a course of correct conduct in prisons, for often the most accomplished and incorrigible offenders are the least troublesome to their officers while working out their terms of sentence. . . . Reformation is not embraced in *expressions* of regret for past misdeeds, nor in *professions* of amendment for time to come. I feel justified in reporting only those convicts reformed, who after discharge from prison, betake themselves to industrial habits, and an honest calling; who, in place of vices practise virtues; who, instead of being addicted to crime, are observed to govern their passions, and

abstain from all injury to others. And I call those convicted who unite, with rectitude of conduct in the social and civil relations, a devout and religious spirit, nourished by Christian truth.[25]

Dix continued in her report to insist that it would take years to determine whether a released inmate was reformed. It was insufficient to follow up former convicts for short periods since, for many, "temptations are, . . . often for a time resisted."[26]

In a letter to Dorothea Dix, a counterfeiter serving time in the Western State (Pennsylvania) Penitentiary described his experience. It gives us some insight into what it must have been like to serve time under the Pennsylvania regime.[27] He said that he "had not once been out of his cell" in over two years; that he was put to work making shoes; and that he was so good at the task that he had time to work out problems in geometry.

The Auburn System

A few years following the inauguration of the Pennsylvania system in Philadelphia, a competing system was introduced in New York state. This system, also using institutions called penitentiaries, was organized on the principle of silence, much like some monastic religious orders. Inmates were confined in single cells for much of the day, but had to participate in some activities with other inmates. These "congregate" activities included work, dining, and some limited recreation in the prison "yard." However, both in their cells as well as in group activities, inmates were to remain silent unless permitted to talk with an official. To reduce the possibility of communication to a minimum, some prisons hooded their inmates, while others required them

*T*his is a view of winter in Ossining, New York, at Sing Sing Penitentiary. The prison is surrounded by ice and extra guards were stationed to prevent inmates from escaping over the ice.

to bow their heads and "cast down their eyes" when in the presence of other inmates. Such practices not only restricted illicit communication, they also acted to inculcate a feeling of humility thought to be appropriate in a criminal.

This second system of confinement was known as the **Auburn system** or plan because of its introduction at the penitentiary located in Auburn, New York. During much of the nineteenth century there was a lively controversy about the effectiveness of the Pennsylvania and Auburn systems. On the one hand, construction of a Pennsylvania-style prison was expensive. Dix reported that cells in these institutions were spacious by today's standards. Many had dimensions as large as 15 feet by 8 feet. Housing hundreds of inmates in solitary confinement in cells of this size required huge institutions. The prison at Auburn, on the other hand, contained cells that were only 7½ feet by 3½ feet. Some Auburn plan penitentiaries had cells even smaller. The cells in Concord, New Hampshire, measured 6 feet, 10 inches by 3 feet, 4 inches! Thus, one could pack many more cells into a prison, reducing construction costs.

Limitation on the use of inmate labor was another cost differential of these two early systems of incarceration. Under conditions of solitary confinement, all work performed by inmates had to be done in their cells.[28] There was no possibility of taking advantage of more efficient factory modes of production that were emerging in the society outside the prison. In addition, prison administrators could not establish prison farms, so they were not able to plant and harvest crops that might more cheaply feed their populations than purchases made in the marketplace.

The Auburn system, on the other hand, permitted inmates to work with others in factory, farm, and other settings (eventually, road gangs), thus bringing significant cost benefits to the prison administration.

Although many observers, including Dorothea Dix, discounted the possible impact of long periods of solitary confinement on inmates' mental health, many others were convinced that the Pennsylvania system was too cruel to be supported. Their view contributed to the success of the Auburn system which became the dominant system by the last third of the nineteenth century.

Lest one conclude that the Auburn system of confinement was much more humane than the Pennsylvania system, we need to take a look at the punishments inflicted on men and women at the penitentiary at Sing Sing, New York, as reported in 1844. A headache for the staff in any Auburn-type prison was enforcement of the rule of silence. Apparently, inmates were constantly finding ways to communicate with each other, and the administration responded with a variety of punishments. The two most popular ones were flogging and forcibly gagging inmates, especially women, who broke the rule of silence. Here is an excerpt from the 1844 report of a New York state prison inspector, commenting on the punishments meted out that year at the Sing Sing penitentiary:

> The gag has been sometimes applied, but it has been only among the females that it has been rendered *absolutely* necessary! . . . The number of punishments inflicted in the Sing Sing prison, during three months . . . was as follows—in April, 113 flogged; in May, 94; in June, 107. . . . In the women's prison—in April, 13 punishments; May, 11; June, 7. The least number of lashes at a time with the cat, 6, the largest number at one time I did not learn. In the men's prison the form of punishment is by the lash. . . . The present inspectors . . . [have] adopted means to do away with the lash. They are now erecting an outer ward, to contain sixteen solitary cells, for the purpose of punishing the refractory. These soon will be deprivation of food, or of bed, shower-bath, solitary confinement, and confinement in a dark cell. The three former are already used, and have reduced the amount of punishments with the lash.

In the women's prison, the lash is never used. There the punishments are confinement to their own cells in the main dormitory, or in separate cells, with reduction of food, and the application of the gag.*

Although the two systems we have described differ, both were dedicated to the principle of employing a specially designed physical environment to induce change in the offender. In essence, it was hoped that confinement would encourage, perhaps require, the inmate to become penitent.

THE REFORMATORY IDEA

As we have seen, the penitentiary idea dominated thinking about the primary objective of incarceration and the structure to be employed to achieve it. This domination lasted from the beginning of the nineteenth century to the end of the Civil War. It was challenged by an idea that began in an obscure penal colony off the coast of Australia, was later modified in Ireland, and then was brought to New York state in 1876 in the form of the **Elmira Reformatory.**

The reformatory in the United States was first conceived of as an institution for reforming younger criminal offenders. Its origins can be traced to resolutions adopted in 1870 by the first congress of the National Prison Association.[29] Two of these resolutions merit repeating here. Their significance for the eventual development of reformatories and, later, the therapeutic or medical model prison cannot be overestimated. The first of these resolutions stated:

> The progressive classification of prisoners, based on study of the individual, administered on some well adjusted system, should be established in all prisons above the common jail.[30]

The second dealt with the structure of sentences:

> Preemptory sentences ought to be replaced by those of indeterminate length. Sentences limited only by satisfactory proof of reformation should be substituted for those measured by mere lapse of time.[31]

These principles marked the beginning of about a century of efforts to move the practice of penology away from the **classical school of criminology and penology** of the previous century, toward a more "positive" criminology. To proponents of the classical school, influenced by the work of Bentham, Beccaria, and others, criminals were relatively free agents, choosing to commit illegal acts in order to gain pleasure. In addition, the idea that crime and sin were roughly the same was widely held. Offenders were tempted by the prospect of gain or pleasure, and fell into sin (or crime). The views of Dorothea Dix regarding the reformation of criminals quoted earlier clearly sum up the central theme of the classical approach to the mission of incarceration.[32]

We can also summarize this classical approach with a simple equation, crime A = punishment A. Classical reformers such as Bentham and Beccaria were very much influenced by the unstable administration of criminal justice of their day. They, as well as others, observed the uneven application of punishments for offenders committing similar crimes. Frequently, they found, some offenders received exceedingly

---

*Excerpt from a Report of New York State Prison Inspector J. W. Edmonds, August 1844. From Dorothea L. Dix, *Remarks on Prisons and Prison Discipline in the United States,* 2nd ed. (Philadelphia, PA: Joseph Kite & Co., 1845), p. 58.

harsh sentences, while others were treated with great leniency. They argued that this unsystematic performance resulted in an administration of criminal justice that had no significant impact on the crime problem. They vigorously recommended a more "rational" and utilitarian approach.

The appropriate policy to pursue, they asserted, was one that fitted the punishment to the crime committed by the offender, that is, to take the harm caused by the criminal act, *A*, and assign an effective punishment, *A*, to it. The criminal code would, under this approach, include a systematic listing of crimes and matching sentences. It is based on the assumption that crimes are "caused" by persons choosing to act in criminal ways to gain some benefit or pleasure. By the same token, persons can be deterred from choosing to commit illegal acts by the imposition of or threat to impose painful sanctions. Thus, contemporary deterrence theory owes its development to classical criminology.

Today we think of two types of deterrence: special or individual, and general. In the case of the former, an offender may be deterred from committing more criminal acts because of the experience of a punitive sanction. In the second case, those of us not having committed a crime, but perhaps contemplating one, will be deterred by the examples provided by the actual punishment of others. Together with the penitentiary idea described above, this classical approach links the pains of imprisonment with a physical and psychological structure (solitary confinement, silence). Thus, the inmate can be induced to become truly penitent, *choosing* to mend her or his ways.

Beginning with the **Declaration of Principles of 1870** and the opening of the Elmira Reformatory in 1876, more positive principles crept into American penal practices. Going back to the National Prison Association's Principles, we see that the penologists who drew them up recommended the "progressive classification of prisoners, based on study of the individual." This individualized study as contemplated by the association was clearly a forerunner of the positive or scientific criminology pioneered by Cesare Lombroso in 1876. We can summarize this positive approach with a simple equation, criminal *A* = sanction *A*. This calls for fitting the sanction to the offender, a very different approach than that advocated by classically inclined penologists.

The Mark System

Before continuing our discussion of the reformatory in America, we need to look into its antecedents prior to the 1870 Declaration of Principles. In particular, two British penal reforms merit our attention: the Norfolk Island penal colony and the Irish prison system.

The Norfolk Island penal colony, located off the coast of Australia, was taken under the governorship of Alexander Maconochie in 1840. As reported by Hermann Mannheim, the colony at that time contained "over 900 doubly and trebly convicted prisoners who were regarded as the dregs of the convict system, irreconcilable and irreclaimable."[33] Maconochie was given this appointment following his penetrating critique of Britain's use of transportation (sending convicts to colonial areas to serve sentences of penal servitude). In addition to criticizing the brutal conditions then existing in the colonies, he proposed a "New System of Prison Discipline."

Maconochie's new system included an "apparatus" to implement what he considered to be the steps necessary to reform offenders. Key elements in the apparatus were later to influence both the Irish prison system and the reformatory movement in the United States. These elements consisted of the substitution of flexible or indeterminate sentences for those fixed in length, and a gradual and progressive relaxation of custody, leading to eventual freedom for the inmate.

Maconochie's new system came to be known as the **mark system** because convicts' sentences were, in effect, converted to a debt of marks owed to the Crown. Marks earned through good behavior together with marks earned through labor were applied to this debt, thus making it possible for a prisoner to be released earlier than the original sentence had provided.

The second major feature of the mark system was the gradual loosening of the rigors of confinement as the prisoner earned marks toward his release. This early attempt to soften the shock of a prisoner's reentry into the free world contributed to Maconochie's rather speedy removal as governor of Norfolk Island. Many of his opponents in the British penal system were convinced that Maconochie's convicts had too much freedom and posed a grave threat to society. After four years in office, Maconochie was relieved.

The Irish System

The mark system lived on, however, in the Irish prisons under the direction of Sir Walter Croften. By the 1870s, what Maconochie began thirty years earlier had been fully developed with a prison system made up of institutions differentiated in terms of security levels and populations in various stages of readiness for release.[34] Like Maconochie, Croften utilized marks as signposts along the road to early release.

Much more elaborate than the Norfolk Island system, Croften's system incorporated three stages of imprisonment, each of which was housed in a specialized prison. The first stage was quite punitive, based on the Pennsylvania system. Inmates were placed in solitary confinement for several months with a reduced diet. Following this they were transferred to a general prison which in many respects was Auburn-like. Upon earning sufficient marks, inmates were transferred to an "intermediate prison," which was a minimum security facility.

In the intermediate institutions, the inmates worked outside, usually in close proximity to population centers. There were no guards in the sense that we know them today. To Croften, inmates who had earned sufficient marks through labor and good behavior were to be given the opportunity to make progress toward the complete freedom they one day would enjoy for "weal or for woe" as one observer of the **Irish system** put it in 1872. The Across Cultures feature describes the three stages in the Irish system.

The Irish prisons were studied by several early American penologists, especially some from New York state.[36] They successfully urged the New York state legislature to authorize the construction of a new type of prison to be based on some of the mark and Irish system principles. The new institution opened in 1876 as the Elmira Reformatory.

The Reformatory System

The reformatory was conceived of initially as a penal institution for the younger adult offender, an offender who was not yet impervious to change. The Elmira Reformatory, for example, received offenders who were between 16 and 30 years of age. The vast majority of them were "first offenders."[37] By 1913, eighteen state reformatories were opened. According to one description of these early reformatories, the movement's ideology considered inmates to be "undeveloped" and susceptible to the discipline and the programs aimed at improving their "higher faculties."[38]

ACROSS
CULTURES

THE THREE STAGES IN THE IRISH OR PROGRESSIVE PRISON SYSTEM

First Stage

Separate imprisonment in a cellular prison at Mountjoy, for the first eight or nine months. . . .

In Ireland it is the practice to make this stage very penal, both by a very reduced dietary during the first half of the period . . . and by the absence of interesting employment during the first three months. By the time the convict is required for hard work in the second stage, the improved dietary [in the second half of the first stage] will have rendered him physically equal to perform it; and by the end of three months . . . the idler will generally have learned to associate industry with pleasure.

Second Stage

The peculiar feature of the Irish Convict System in the second stage is the institution of marks to govern the classification. This is a minute and intelligi-

ble monthly record of the convict to govern himself, and [shows him] that progress to liberty . . . can only be furthered by the cultivation and application of qualities opposed to those which led to his conviction.

Third Stage

The training is special, and the position of the convict made as natural as possible; no more restraint is exercised over him than would be necessary in any well-regulated establishment. [Two principles govern this stage]:

1st. You have to show the convict that you really trust him. . . .

2nd. You have to show to the public that the convict, who will soon be restored to liberty for weal or for woe, may upon reasonable grounds be considered as capable of being safely restored.

SOURCE: Mary Carpenter, "Reformatory Prison Discipline in the Irish Convict Prisons" (London: Longmans, Green, Reader, and Dyer, 1872), pp. 5–8.

The first warden at the Elmira Reformatory, Zebulon Brockway, focused the institution's regimen on discipline, vocational training, and education. Regular school programs were instituted, as were vocational training and religious services. These activities were backed up by a paramilitary discipline that included military formations, badges of rank, and drill. In some ways the early reformatory resembled, in its military regimen, the correctional boot camps of today, as we shall see below.[39]

A watered-down version of the Irish system's progressive stages was put in place at Elmira as well as at other early state reformatories. This consisted mainly of a classification scheme assigning inmates to various "classes" or grades based on marks or credits earned. A "first class" inmate, for example, had moved up the institutional ladder to a point where he could be considered for parole. There was no real progression through stages, as was the case in Maconochie's and Croften's systems. At some early reformatories, the classification scheme meant little more than the wearing of military-style markings on the prison uniform.

The reformatory idea and, much later, the rehabilitative idea, was given a considerable boost through dissemination of the **positive criminology and penology** of the Italian pioneers, Cesare Lombroso, Enrico Ferri, and Raffaele Garofalo. The work of these pioneers, which began to be published in 1876, claimed to have found that criminal persons had identifiable physical and psychological traits that distinguished them from their nonoffender peers. It also was "discovered" that criminals differed one from another.

If we return for a moment to the Principles of 1870, which we examined earlier, we find they fit in rather nicely with this newly emerging positive school of criminology. To a positivist, the only rational course to take once a person has been convicted of a crime is to subject her or him to individualized diagnostic study in order to determine the most appropriate (effective) sanction to order.

Before leaving the first reformatory, let's take a closer look at the program installed at Elmira. We see that it was not the institution that the Principles of 1870 nor Walter Croften of the Irish prison system had envisioned.

Elmira Reformatory's first warden, Zebulon Brockway, described his program of "reformation" in stark terms:

> . . . [T]he prisoners are constantly under pressure of intense motives that bear directly on the mind. The indeterminateness of the sentence breeds discontent, breeds purposefulness, and prompts to new exertion. Captivity, always irksome, is now increasingly so because of the uncertainty of its duration; because the duty and responsibility of shortening it and of any modifying any undesirable present condition of it devolve upon the prisoner himself, and, again, because of the active exactions of the standard and criterion to which he must attain.[40]

In addition to educational and vocational programs, Brockway installed a rigid paramilitary regime:

> A regimental military organization of the prisoners with a band of music, swords [!] officers, and dummy guns for the rank and file of prisoners. The military membership should include all the able bodied prisoners. . . . The regular army tactics, drill, and daily dress parade should be observed.[41]

Also part of Brockway's system was a program of strenuous physical exercise. "[A]ll are assigned to the gymnasium to be examined, renovated, and quickened; they are held under this physical treatment until the intended effect is accomplished."[42]

Discipline and structure are some of the methods used both in the military and in prisons. Inmates march around the prison yard.

In many respects, the reformatory regime is a forerunner of a current fashion in American corrections: the boot camp, which we will examine in a later chapter.

The reformatory movement, or rather the idea of the prison as a place for reformative intervention, had a relatively short life. By the turn of the century, the reformatory idea was clearly on the decline. In the twentieth century, reformatories became virtually indistinguishable from the penitentiaries that came before them. Barlow gives several reasons for the demise of the reformatory movement.[43] Among these are: (1) a lack of qualified staff in the important areas of education and training; (2) a continued acceptance of the value of incarceration as a punitive experience for the inmate; (3) overcrowding that impeded full implementation of inmate classification systems; (4) a continued emphasis on custody over "reformative" programs; and (5) lack of commitment to provide the resources necessary to make the ideal a reality.

As we shall see below and in the next chapter, these problem areas have plagued prison systems ever since. By the early decades of the twentieth century, the reformatory was little more than a high-security prison.

PRISONS AND THE IDEA OF REHABILITATION

We have seen that the reformatory idea was short-lived as far as the staying power of the reformatory as a really different type of penal institution. Now we turn to a development that should not follow if logic alone were our guide: the effort to graft the rehabilitative idea on to the American penitentiary and reformatory. Although there is some evidence that rehabilitation as a goal of incarceration was in view as early as 1870 in the National Prison Association's Declaration of Principles, it was not until the advent of positive criminology that penology became significantly influenced by the notion that inmates could be rehabilitated or "corrected."

Six years after the National Prison Association adopted its Principles, the Italian criminologist Cesare Lombroso published the findings from his study of criminal men.[44] This work signaled the dawn of positive or scientific criminology and penology. Prior to Lombroso's work, classical criminology, as we have seen above, dominated the world of penology.

Lombroso considered the classical perspective to be little more than unscientific musing, characterized by the use of "abstract judicial methods."[45] These methods, which consisted chiefly of equating crimes and punishments, he argued, might have the appearance of fairness. However, they failed to take into account the fact that offenders were different, and that what caused their criminality might well be beyond their ability to control through will power. Thus, in effect, punishment was inherently unfair as well as ineffective as an offender change agent. To Lombroso, what was essential to develop an effective crime control system was a careful study of individual offenders in order to identify those factors and forces that determined their criminality. Then, and only then, could society through its criminal justice system agents apply the most appropriate sanctions.

We have seen that the reformatory idea, which was the first vehicle for this positive penology, was largely abandoned after only a few decades. Those institutions built with the reformatory idea in mind became essentially no different from the penitentiaries that came before them. The rehabilitative idea would lie dormant for several more decades, being "reinvented" with a special category of offender, the "sexual psychopath."

The state of Illinois, in 1938, became the first state to enact legislation defining and providing for special sentencing of sexual psychopaths (called "sexually dangerous persons" in the statute).[46] Several other states followed suit. In one compilation, twenty-four states and the District of Columbia at one time had statutes that defined "mentally disordered" sex offenders and specified special sentences or treatment for them.[47] Except for Maryland's Patuxent Institution, which will be discussed in detail in the next chapter, almost no effort was made to build prisons from the ground up for the purpose of implementing the rehabilitative idea or model. What did happen was that many states retitled their prisons "correctional institutions" as though this relabeling would indicate that the roles of these facilities had really shifted from custody and punishment to correction or treatment.

Thomas and Hepburn commented on these changes in the American prison scene between the ascendancy of the Auburn system in the middle of the nineteenth century and the present. During the intervening years a variety of intervention strategies came to be employed, abandoned, and sometimes reintroduced in penal institutions.

> Depending on the point in prison history being considered, they [penologists] were convinced that criminals could be converted into law-abiding citizens by harsh discipline, religion, education, vocational training, psychotherapy, group counseling, behavior modification strategies, and even in some types of brain surgery.[48]

Another commentator, Bruce Jackson, succinctly stated what the rehabilitative idea was meant to be as applied to the American prison:

Military drill with the regiment passing in review at the New York State Reformatory, Elmira, New York.

Ideally, the corrections process halts the development of a criminal career and, in the process, substitutes skills and goals that permit or encourage the criminal to support himself and maintain a life style acceptable to the general population.[49]

As we shall see in the next chapter, the attempt to graft the rehabilitative idea on to an essentially custodial and punitive institution has had significant and deleterious consequences for criminal justice. As Jackson concluded:

> Far more often, the corrections process merely causes a time gap in the criminal development; in too many cases it accelerates rather than slows or ends that development.[50]

Thomas and Hepburn observed that regardless of the attempts by a variety of professionals to bring the rehabilitative idea to the reality of the American prison, one goal has dominated this institution: the "effective and efficient confinement" of inmates. To accomplish this, prison administrators are forced to stress methods that "assure the maintenance of social control" over all other activities and programs.[51] These goals rarely are compatible with treatment modalities. In fact, the emphasis on confinement and control of a captive population may virtually require that rehabilitative programs fail. As John Conrad remarked in a seminal article marking the decline in enthusiasm for the prison as a place to "rehabilitate" offenders, "We should never have promised a hospital."[52]

THE STORY OF THE AMERICAN PRISON is full of contradictions and paradoxes. Ideals advanced by humanitarian reformers clash with the brutal realities of prison conditions and repressive control strategies. Throughout the history of corrections in this country we have employed enforced solitary confinement, silence, and coerced therapies on inmates, all in the stated interest of eventually releasing these inmates into society as men and women better able to live in harmony with others than they were before imprisonment. High rates of reimprisonment suggest that we have failed.

SUMMARY

Competing and conflicting goals have afflicted the American prison scene for nearly a century. As we have seen, this was not always the case. The attempt to implement the penitentiary idea through the Pennsylvania and Auburn systems of incarceration was, if nothing else, an attempt characterized by clarity and consistency. Since the collapse of the penitentiary idea in American penology, clarity and consistency have been notable for their absence in practice. Goals in corrections now include a plethora of incompatible programs and aims that include punishment, treatment, and incapacitation.

Lejins and Courtless, in the course of developing an evaluation model for corrections, commented that:

> . . . [I]t is essential that proposed correctional measures . . . be put forth with clear-cut statements of goals, objectives and standards as well as an accurate description of practices. Without compliance with these requirements, the evaluation process would be a waste of time. . . . Unfortunately, this requirement is being addressed to a field [penology] which has been notorious for the lack of [an] analytical and scientific approach to its problems.[53]

The price we pay for such indifference has been an inability to evaluate the effectiveness of various prison programs. Yet, we have, in this country, enthusiastically endorsed and subsequently rejected program after program. Usually, this flip-flopping has not been informed by any reliable data regarding program effectiveness. Again quoting Lejins and Courtless:

[Corrections] has managed to operate . . . in the last two centuries by resorting to or having to resort to Janus-faced programs, ambiguous terminology, and inconsistencies in operational practices. . . . Moreover, corrections does not seem to have the kind of record, either in the past or at present, on which it could fall back as a justification of what it has been doing heretofore or is doing now.[54]

In Chapter 8 we will look at the American prison today. At this point we can only note that the penitentiary, reformatory, and rehabilitative ideas no longer drive prison systems. Inmates no longer are seen as penitents or patients.

The author recently participated as a member of a state prisons task force that was charged by the state's secretary for public safety with the task of formulating new goals for the system. One of the deputy commissioners was asked what programs were currently available throughout the system. His reply was that with overcrowding and severely limited budgets, there was very little in the way of correctional programming with which to engage inmates. When pressed to tell the group what the prison population was doing, he answered, "Languishing."

KEY CONCEPTS

Auburn system

Black Assize

Classical school of criminology and penology

Declaration of Principles of 1870

Elmira Reformatory

Intermediate punishments

Irish system

Mark system

Newgate of Connecticut

Penitentiary

Pennsylvania system

Positive criminology and penology

Reformatory

Rehabilitative idea

Walnut Street Jail

QUESTIONS FOR DISCUSSION

1. In what ways was the first American prison different in terms of its goals compared with the prisons developed under the Pennsylvania and Auburn plans? How was it similar?
2. Why was the penitentiary idea compatible with the classical school in criminology?
3. The mark and Irish systems of incarceration have been considered "ahead of their time." What might we learn from them that could usefully be applied to our prisons today?
4. Is there a fundamental contradiction between the primary goals of prison administrators and those of professional treatment personnel working in the prison systems? Fully justify your answer. Indicate how the administrator and treatment professional might work together effectively.
5. The "Declaration of Principles" played an important role in the development of the American reformatory, yet the reformatory movement failed to have a lasting influence on the further development of the prison. Why is this so? Do the principles have any validity today?

ENDNOTES

1. Alex M. Durham, "Newgate of Connecticut: Origins and Early Days of an Early American Prison,' *Justice Quarterly* 6 (1989): 100.
2. Ibid., p. 101.
3. *Prison and Jail Inmates,* 1995, Washington, D.C., National Institute of Justice, Bureau of Justice Statistics, August 1996, p. 2
4. Ibid.
5. Ibid., p. 5.
6. U.S. Department of Justice, Bureau of Justice Statistics, *Sourcebook of Criminal Justice Statistics—1992,* p. 590.
7. The rate of incarceration is measured in terms of the number of sentenced prisoners in state and federal prisons per 100,000 in the U.S. "resident population." See *Sourcebook of Criminal Justice Statistics—1990,* p. 604.
8. Ibid., p. 2.
9. *Sourcebook of Criminal Justice Statistics—1990,* p. 117.
10. This Amendment states that "Excessive bail shall not be required, nor excessive fines imposed, nor cruel and unusual punishments inflicted."
11. "Justice Expenditure and Employment, 1990," U.S. Department of Justice, Bureau of Justice Statistics, *Bulletin* (September 1992), p. 3.
12. Durham, "Newgate of Connecticut," pp. 89–116.
13. Ibid., p. 90.
14. For a discussion of Bentham and Beccaria's work as well as the classical school of criminology, see Joseph E. Jacoby (ed.), *Classics of Criminology,* 2nd ed. (Oak Park, Ill.: Waveland Press, 1994), pp. 75–83, 273–286.
15. In Connecticut prior to the opening of Newgate, various disfigurements (branding, cutting off an ear), whipping, and capital punishment were meted out to burglars. For a review of the contemporary criticisms of such punishments see George Ives, *A History of Penal Methods* (Montclair, N.J.: Patterson-Smith, 1970).
16. Michael Ignatieff, *A Just Measure of Pain: The Penitentiary in the Industrial Revolution 1750–1850* (New York: Pantheon Books, 1978), pp. 44–45.
17. Ibid., p. 44.
18. It is noteworthy that today, the concept of "intermediate sanctions" is again being advocated in corrections. Now, the term is used to include sentences that fall somewhere between imprisonment and ordinary probation. Two examples of such sanctions are correctional "boot camps" and home detention. These will be discussed in detail in Chapters 15 and 16, respectively.
19. Michel Foucault, "The Body of the Condemned," in W. J. Chambliss, *Criminal Law in Action* (New York: John Wiley, 1984), p. 387.
20. *Washington Post,* November 22, 1993, p. A-21.
21. For additional information on the Walnut Street Jail, see Blake McKelvey, *American Prisons* (Montclair, N.J.: Patterson Smith, 1977); Thorsten Sellin, "The Origin of the Pennsylvania System of Prison Discipline," *Prison Journal* 50 (1970): 15–17.
22. Dorothea Dix, *Remarks on Prisons and Prison Discipline* (reprint edition of original 1845 work) (Montclair, N.J.: Patterson Smith, 1967), 27.
23. Ibid., p. 23.
24. Ibid., p. 74.
25. Ibid., p. 66. Emphasis in the original.
26. Ibid.
27. Ibid.
28. Dix reported the text of a letter from an inmate at the Eastern Penitentiary in Pennsylvania that gives a good view of the work opportunity available in solitary confinement:

[My first] employment was picking wool; it was very lonely work at first I assure you. . . . [Then] I was moved to another block . . . ; and then in a few days to making pegs and then to fitting upper for the shoes, and then my keeper gave me two lasts, and showed me all about making a whole shoe, ... [I] made 32 pair of large shoes last month, and lay idle part of two days.

29. This organization, now known as the American Correctional Association, continues to hold annual "congresses."

30. American Prison Association, "Declaration of Principles," 1870.

31. Ibid.

32. Herman Mannheim, ed., *Pioneers in Criminology* (Chicago: Quadrangle Books, 1960), pp. 36–68.

33. Ibid., p. 76.

34. For a detailed description of the Irish prison system under Croften, see Mary Carpenter, *Reformatory Prison Discipline* (Montclair, N.J.: Patterson Smith, 1967).

35. Ibid., p. 11.

36. Among those influenced by Walter Croften's work in Ireland were members of the New York Prison Association who lobbied the state legislature in 1867 for a new type of prison, the reformatory.

37. The term *first offender* must be used with care when referring to persons processed through the criminal justice system. It can mean first "conviction"; it certainly does not mean first "offense" in many cases.

38. For a statement of the reformatory "system" written while the reformatory prison was in full swing, see Zebulon Brockway, "The American Reformatory Prison System," in Joseph E. Jacoby, (ed.), *Classics of Criminology*, 2nd ed. (Oak Park, Ill.: Waveland Press, 1994), pp. 387–396.

39. For a discussion of the correctional boot camp movement in contemporary corrections, see Chapter 15.

40. Zebulon R. Brockway, "The American Reformatory Prison System," in Joseph E. Jacoby, ed., *Classics of Criminology*, 2nd ed. (Oak Park, Ill.: Waveland Press, 1994), p. 393.

41. Ibid., p. 392.

42. Ibid.

43. Hugh D. Barlow, *Introduction to Criminology*, 5th ed. (Glenview, Ill.: Scott Foresman, 1990), pp. 502–503.

44. Cesare Lombroso, *L'uomo delinquente,* Milan, 1876.

45. Ibid.

46. Ill. Ann. Stat., 38-820.01.

47. Frank T. Lindman and Donald M. McIntyre (eds.), *The Mentally Disabled and the Law* (Chicago, University of Chicago Press, 1961), pp. 314–318.

48. Charles W. Thomas and John R. Hepburn, *Crime, Criminal Law, and Criminology* (Dubuque: Wm. C. Brown, 1983), p. 481.

49. Bruce Jackson, "Our Prisons Are Criminal," in Donal E. MacNamara and Edward Sagarin (eds.), *Perspectives on Correction* (New York: Thomas Y. Crowell, 1971), p. 30.

50. Ibid.

51. Thomas and Hepburn, *Crime, Criminal Law, and Criminology,* p. 481.

52. John Conrad, "We Should Never Have Promised a Hospital," *Federal Probation* 39 (1975): 1.

53. Peter P. Lejins and Thomas F. Courtless, *Justification and Evaluation of Projects in Corrections,* State of Maryland Governor's Commission on Law Enforcement and Administration of Justice (December, 1973), p. 3.

54. Ibid., p. 4.

THE PRISON AS HOSPITAL: A CASE HISTORY OF A TROUBLED EXPERIMENT

INTRODUCTION ON AN APRIL EVENING in the early 1960s, a mass escape took place from Maryland's Patuxent Institution for Defective Delinquents, the state's premier treatment prison for mentally disordered offenders. One inmate managed either to make a key or steal one from a guard. The population of two tiers of cells, a total of sixty-four men, had an opportunity to leave. About half of them did. Within forty-eight hours almost all had been recaptured with the assistance of the state police, which maintained a barracks within a quarter mile of the institution.

Following the mass escape, a flurry of disciplinary actions and prosecutions against the escapees were instituted. One of the more interesting aspects of the affair was the staff's care in inserting into the files of all inmates on the affected tiers a notation indicating whether or not they had escaped. It was considered an important indicator of an inmate's therapeutic "progress" that he had not tried to escape when offered the opportunity.

Another interesting aspect of this event was that the institution at this time did not have a perimeter wall or fence.* Once inmates got out of the main building, they were outside, with only a relatively short run to the nearby woods. This lack of security was especially surprising since the prison population was made up of offenders who were diagnosed by mental health experts as "constituting a danger to society."

The escape points out a troubling contradiction facing corrections as it has tried to implement the rehabilitative ideal in prison settings: maintaining control over inmates while at the same time offering them treatment for the underlying causes of their criminality.

As we saw in the last chapter, the rehabilitative idea was one of the three grand ideas that have shaped the American prison over the past two centuries. The idea of rehabilitation was concisely summarized by Cullen, et al.:

> . . . [T]he rehabilitative ideal, with its policies of indeterminate sentencing, discretionary deci-
> sion making, and parole, was infused into the correctional system in the beginning decades of
> the 1900s. . . . The reformers of the Progressive era, often with a faith in the power of newly
> founded social sciences to furnish the key to unlocking the mystery of crime's origins, were
> optimistic that individualized treatment could transform lawbreakers into the law abiding.[1]

As they go on to note, this ideal lasted well into the 1960s. It was reinforced by input from psychology and psychiatry during the 1930s with the work of authorities such as William Healy and his wife Augusta Bronner.[2]

> In the 1970s, however, the general hegemony of rehabilitation was shattered. . . . The Pro-
> gressive design of individualized treatment was subjected to strong attack . . . , and correc-
> tions became "anti-Progressive."[3]

A strange collection of bedfellows was at least partly responsible for the demise of the rehabilitative ideal in American corrections. Conservative critics emphasized the need to use corrections to achieve efficient and strict crime control. They believed that the discretion to deliver individualized treatment programs to offenders resulted in lenient treatment, which diluted the rigors of deserved punishment. Joining these critics were liberals who were concerned that rehabilitation advocates were trampling on offenders' due process safeguards in their zeal to apply individualized treatment with a maximum of discretion through the medium of indeterminate sentences.

In this chapter we will trace the history of one Maryland state prison, Patuxent Institution, which embodied, as no other prison in our history did, the essence of the rehabilitative idea in corrections. The example of Patuxent Institution provides two important lessons. First, many difficulties and conflicts arise when a treatment ideal is inserted into a criminal justice system that, historically, has never been particularly receptive to it. Second, the effort to stretch the principle of legality, *nulla poena sine lege,* almost beyond recognition, in order to implement the treatment ideal, cannot be maintained in the face of public and political resistance.

▌ MENTAL HEALTH AND THE LAW OF CORRECTIONS

Sexual Psychopath Laws

The first major breakthrough for the rehabilitative idea in corrections came with the enactment of **sexual psychopath** statutes beginning in the late 1930s.[4] By 1977, 28

---

*Shortly after the escape, perimeter fencing was installed. The guard towers at strategic points along the fence were fabricated by inmates working in the sheet metal shop.

FOCUS ON
THE LAW

SAMPLING OF DEFINITIONS OF SEX PSYCHOPATHS IN STATE STATUTES

Florida: Criminal sexual psychopaths: All persons suffering from a mental disorder and not insane or feeble-minded, which mental disorder has existed for a period of not less than four months immediately prior to the appointment of the psychiatrist . . . coupled with criminal propensities to the commission of sex offenses and who may be considered dangerous to others.

Michigan: Criminal sexual psychopathic person: Any person who is suffering from a mental disorder and is not feeble-minded, which mental disorder is coupled with criminal propensities to the commission of sex offenses is hereby declared to be a *criminal sexual psychopathic person.*

Nebraska: Sexual psychopath shall mean any person who, by a course of misconduct in sexual matters, has evidenced an utter lack of power to control his sexual impulses and who, as a result, is likely to attack or otherwise inflict injury, loss,

pain, or other evil on the objects of his uncontrolled and uncontrollable desires.

Pennsylvania Statute (offender not labeled): If the court is of the opinion that a person convicted of indecent assault with intent to commit sodomy, solicitation to commit sodomy or assault with intent to ravish or rape, if at large constitutes a threat of bodily harm to members of the public, or if he is an habitual offender and mentally ill, the court may sentence such person for an indeterminate period of time to a state institution.

Vermont: Psychopathic personality shall mean those persons who by a habitual course of misconduct in sexual matters have evidenced an utter lack of power to control their sexual impulse, and who, as a result, are likely to attack or otherwise inflict injury, loss, pain, or other evil on the object of their uncontrolled desire.

states had laws targeting special sex offenders and providing procedures for their trial, sentencing, and "treatment." The Focus on the Law feature provides a sampling of definitions and terms used in these state statutes.

One of the first of these laws was Chapter 369 of the laws of Minnesota, enacted in 1939. The law defined "psychopathic personality" to be one that leads a person to engage in conduct that is "irresponsible" with "respect to sexual matters and therefore [is] dangerous to other persons."[5] Such laws were adopted in response to public outrage over highly publicized heinous crimes committed by offenders who had extensive prior convictions for sex offenses.

This outrage came at a time when a number of books and articles appeared touting the efficacy of psychiatry and psychology in dealing with serious, sometimes violent criminals. These outpourings of optimism about the advantages of employing in prisons the diagnostic tools and treatment methods of the mental health professions were accompanied by penologists' pessimistic view of the ability of ordinary correctional institutions to treat these special sex offenders effectively. Sentences needed to be reexamined as well as existing programs and treatment methods.

Regarding sentences, those advocating a different approach to sexual psychopaths called for indeterminate periods of confinement in order to reduce the likelihood of dangerous persons being released before treatment could be effective. **Indeterminate sentencing** was predicated on the belief that it was possible to identify (predict) offenders who would continue to commit sex crimes in the future unless and until they were successfully treated.

Defective Delinquency Law

Maryland ventured into this ill-defined area in which penal and mental health laws were intermixed in 1951 when it enacted its **defective delinquency** law (Article 31B of the Annotated Code). Although the sexual offender statutes that preceded it in other states focused exclusively on certain impulsive and habitual sex offenders, the Maryland law extended the state's net to include a wide range of offenders and offenses. We shall discuss this aspect of the law in a later section.

The defective delinquency law was based on recommendations made to the Maryland General Assembly by a special "Committee on Medico-Legal Psychiatry."[6] The committee was charged by the state legislature to investigate the relationship among mental condition, crime, and punishment. Following this it was instructed to survey the state prison system's programs and evaluate the system's ability to provide appropriate treatment for mentally disordered offenders.

By 1950, the Research Division of the Maryland Legislative Council, armed with the committee's report, was in a position to recommend legislation that it hoped would enable the state to deal effectively with "psychopathic" offenders by remedying certain deficiencies in existing criminal law and procedure, and by authorizing a new prison dedicated to handle these "psychopaths." The target population of the legislation and the new prison were spelled out in the council's report to be "the borderline group of people not legally insane but yet medically regarded as insane."[7] The new prison's program was expected to "secure a similar justice to that received by the legally insane as well as [to provide for] protection of society."[8]

The central feature of the recommended statute and the institution to be established by it was an indeterminate sentence provision that fixed no minimum or maximum limits of confinement. In the words of the recommendation, the indeterminate sentence was designed to "protect society from that segment of the criminal population who probably will again commit crimes if released on the expiration of a fixed sentence." A "secondary" purpose was to "effectively and humanely handle them, which aids in the cure, *where possible*."[9]

In 1951 the Maryland General Assembly enacted the recommended statute (which became Article 31B of the Maryland Code). In so doing it invented an entirely new class of criminal offender, the defective delinquent; defined the characteristics of criminals this class included; specified procedures for diagnosing suspected defectives; and established other procedures for committing those found to be defective to indeterminate periods of confinement.

In contrast to earlier sexual psychopath statutes, Article 31B was written to allow the state to cast a wide net to catch a large array of offenders and offenses. The referral section of the law clearly shows this intention of the legislature as it specified who would be sent to the institution for evaluation as a possible defective delinquent:

A person convicted and sentenced in a court of this state for a crime or offense . . . , coming under one or more of the following categories:
(1) a felony.
(2) a misdemeanor punishable by imprisonment in the penitentiary.
(3) a crime of violence.
(4) a sex crime involving: (a) physical force or violence, (b) disparity of age between an adult and a minor, or (c) a sexual act of an uncontrolled and/or repetitive nature.

(5) two or more convictions for any offenses or crimes punishable by imprisonment. . . .[10]

It is clear that the provisions for sex offenders were patterned after, if not copied directly from, other states' sex psychopath laws, as the Focus on the Law feature shows.

Other significant provisions of this statute reveal its positivist heritage. In particular, we note that these provisions follow quite closely the recommendations made nearly a century earlier by one of the pioneers of **positive criminology,** Enrico Ferri.[11] Ferri recommended in 1896 that all criminal trials be bifurcated. The first trial would deal with the issue of the accused's guilt. The second trial, in the case of those found guilty, would determine after "scientific" study what punishment or treatment should be ordered by the court.

The Maryland defective delinquency statute provided for the second of these trials (called hearings) once the staff of the new prison determined to its satisfaction that an offender was defective. Only the court, following a hearing, could order an offender committed to an indeterminate period of confinement as a defective delinquent.

In order to provide at least a semblance of due process before and at the court hearing, various provisions in the statute gave inmates diagnosed as defective a number of rights should they wish to contest the diagnosis. Chief among these were the right to be represented by counsel, to an examination by a psychiatrist not in the employ of the state, and to a jury at the hearing. In the case of a legally indigent inmate, the lawyer and psychiatrist were paid for by the state.

What was the legal definition of defective delinquency that was to be adjudicated at this second hearing? This was the language of the statute:

> [A defective delinquent is one who] . . . by the demonstration of persistent aggravated antisocial or criminal behavior, evidences a propensity toward criminal activity, and who is found to have either such intellectual deficiency or emotional unbalance, or both, as to clearly demonstrate an actual danger to society so as to require such confinement and treatment, when appropriate, as may make it reasonably safe for society to terminate the confinement and treatment.[12]

MARYLAND'S PATUXENT INSTITUTION

Almost immediately following the first admissions to the new institution, appeals were filed claiming a variety of constitutional violations of inmate rights. An early appeal to the U.S. Court of Appeals for the Fourth Circuit argued that commitment constituted double jeopardy and cruel and unusual punishment. The court upheld the statute's constitutionality against the claims of six inmates on the basis that the statute was rehabilitative and not punitive in intent.[13]

A most unusual provision in this law gave Patuxent Institution unprecedented (in correctional systems) authority to decide when, if ever, to release inmates on various "outpatient" statuses such as leaves and paroles. This authority was exercised by an Institutional Board of Review made up of senior staff members and others designated by the statute.[14] In this regard, the institution was like many state and private mental hospitals.

The institution operated under the provisions of this law until 1977, when it was first subject to significant amendment. On a number of occasions reviews of the statute and the institution's implementation of it were ordered by the legislature, although there were few if any independent studies of Patuxent's performance.[15]

A careful study of the statute and recommendations the study commission made prior to its enactment shows that the legislature had assigned a dual mission to Patuxent's staff: to identify and treat, "when appropriate," defective delinquents; and to protect society from these defectives should treatment not be possible or should it prove to be ineffective. These missions did not always coexist smoothly, and later the conflict between them provided ammunition for those seeking to repeal or amend the statute.

This apparent conflict in missions is not confined to Patuxent Institution. It is all too often characteristic of corrections in America throughout the many years of attempts to combine treatment (rehabilitation) with secure confinement. In fact, many critics of the efforts to turn prisons into treatment facilities make the argument that the fact of a dual mission, or the coercive nature of confinement, doom to failure the prison as a vehicle for rehabilitation.

Another fundamental source of later trouble for Patuxent was the requirement, embedded in the statutory definition of defective delinquency, that the diagnostic and treatment staff make predictions about **future dangerousness** among the candidates for commitment. For twenty-two years the staff made such predictions about many hundreds of offenders. In 1955, when the first inmate was received for examination, there was an optimistic attitude about the accuracy of such predictions. By the time of the institution's "first crisis," described below, very few believed in such predictive accuracy.

The Patuxent Program

The Patuxent treatment regimen was organized around a clinical view of the essential qualities of the psychopathic personality. After all, the "defective delinquent" was a legal invention, not to be found in the contemporary literature on criminality. What psychologists and psychiatrists meant by the term was psychopathy. Years later, the term became sociopathy. Some clinical definitions of the psychopath will help us understand Patuxent's program. Prantky defined the psychopath as one who is a "socially dominant low anxiety individual who engages in frequent but relatively non-violent antisocial behavior."[16] In a more extensive definition, Cleckly said that the psychopath exhibits, among other characteristics, "good intelligence . . . , absence of nervousness . . . , lack of remorse . . . , [a] failure to learn by experience . . . , loss of insight . . . , and a failure to follow any life plan."[17]

We need to keep in mind the common element in these two definitions because it provided the attack point for the Patuxent treatment program. It was the psychopath's assumed lack of anxiety. Those who wrote the statute as well as those charged with implementing it understood this lack of anxiety to mean that psychopaths (defective delinquents) should not be confined in ordinary correctional facilities. In a "garden-variety" prison, routines are so fixed that there is no way to produce the kind of anxiety necessary for an inmate to want to do the hard work of changing him or herself.

In addition, the standard practice in Maryland of sentencing offenders to either fixed or narrow indeterminate sentences was thought to encourage them simply to wait out their terms. With the state's good-time law and possible parole release, inmates could look forward to a definite end to confinement. Thus, why should they get involved in personal change? The same question might well have been asked by Maconochie as he introduced the mark system over one hundred years earlier, as we saw in the last chapter.

So how did the Patuxent staff try to break into this lack of anxiety in order to induce change in its population? The measures employed can best be described, collectively, as **structured anxiety.** The essential elements in the program to build a structure of anxiety included the following:

- The indeterminate sentence. Once an offender was committed to the institution as a defective delinquent, legally there might be no end to the sentence. Clearly, this was intended to drive a "wedge" into the apathy characteristic of the psychopathic personality.
- A rewards system. Under the "graduated tier system," inmates would start at the first, basic level and earn promotions to the highest level, the fourth. At each higher level there were more privileges and less severe custody. On the highest tier, residents locked and unlocked their own cell doors at will.[18] Anxiety was structured into the system by not specifying the criteria for promotion. Usually, a prisoner's therapist would actually decide on promotions based on a subjective evaluation of the resident's progress. For "therapeutic" as well as disciplinary reasons, inmates could be demoted to lower tiers.
- Group psychotherapy. This was the treatment of choice for the vast majority of inmates, the choice being made by the clinical staff. Inmates were expected to share their thoughts and feelings with each other to obtain mutual assistance. Clearly, many were intimidated by this experience. The therapists expected a certain amount of anxiety to be helpful in the therapeutic process.

To these "therapeutic" program elements were added the usual features of American prisons of the time: academic education, arts and crafts, recreation, and vocational training.[19] The staff considered the entire program to constitute a therapeutic community or milieu.

*G*roup psychotherapy was one of the major methods used in Patuxent Institution to help with the institution's primary goal of rehabilitation.

The First Crisis

The institution enjoyed nearly fifteen years of relative freedom from external examination. This time, referred to as the "halcyon years" by the senior staff, ended after the publication of a report by psychiatrist Emory Hodges purporting to show a remarkably high **success rate** among inmates released on parole.[20] Before looking at what happened when the so-called "halcyon years" ended, we need to ask the question, "What does success mean in corrections, and how can we measure it?" Answering this question has dogged the efforts of prison reformers from Dorothea Dix, Alexander Maconochie, Walter Crofton, and Zebulon Brockway to the present. We will briefly discuss this matter here and return to it in subsequent chapters.

How to define success and evaluate correctional programs in terms of widely accepted criteria has been a major problem ever since inmates were released from the first penitentiaries. In the middle of the nineteenth century, Dorothea Dix, following her visits to penitentiaries on the East Coast, defined a successful prison program as one that produced persons who "instead of being addicted to crime are observed to govern their passions, and abstain from all injury to others."[21]

More recent definitions of success include low rates of rearrest and low rates of reincarceration.[22] The former criterion fails to take into account whether a person rearrested after leaving a correctional program has been convicted for any offense. The latter criterion does suggest that a new conviction may have been handed down. It does not tell us anything about the nature and severity of any new offense. In fact, the reincarceration may have resulted from a technical violation of parole or probation rules, not a new crime.[23]

In addition to these issues, there is the problem of deciding whether a program is successful when the recidivist commits a new offense that is less serious than the one or ones that caused her or him to be in the program in the first place. For example, how does one classify the offender who was imprisoned for armed robbery, paroled, and then commits a number of larcenies? A success or failure?

Emory Hodges's article, appearing in 1971, concluded that the Patuxent program significantly reduced recidivism, in part because of the indeterminate sentences that stimulated inmates to change. Reported parole success rates as well as rearrest data suggested that the Patuxent program was meeting its rehabilitation goal. Success was measured by examining rearrests and technical parole violations. Not long after his report was published, however, there appeared a steady stream of articles critical of the institution as well as other correctional facilities, including attacks on the core assumption that the future dangerousness of any population could be predicted with reasonable accuracy.[24]

These articles consistently reported that predicting future violent behavior was practically impossible; that the most accurate prediction was that the occurrence of future violence in any institutionalized population was zero. Patuxent Institution, along with other mental health and correctional facilities, was said to be producing an unacceptable number of **false positives** in its effort to carry out its mission under the law. The false positives fallacy in predicting future dangerous behavior arises because, in order to predict the occurrence of the behavior, a large number of erroneous predictions must be made for every accurate one. When the state proposes to confine offenders for indefinite periods on the basis of such inaccuracy, serious legal as well as moral questions must be addressed.

Mounting criticism of the defective delinquency law and the institution's program by civil libertarians and mental health professionals led directly to the demise of the original Article 31B. Among the criticisms was one that claimed the indeterminate sentence provision kept prisoners confined well beyond ordinary sentences for similar crimes. About a dozen years after the 1977 repeal, as we shall see, attacks on Patuxent Institution centered on its apparent practice of releasing violent felons to the community too quickly. Probably this conflict between the argument on the one hand that offenders were kept too long and on the other that the community was inadequately protected was inevitable given the institution's dual mission of treatment *and* incapacitation.

In 1976 the state legislature commissioned an external study by a private organization, Contract Research Corporation (CRC), to evaluate the institution's record and recommend courses of action the General Assembly might take. The final report of this study was the proverbial straw that broke the camel's back.[25] Among the study's conclusions:

- The staff could not reliably predict future dangerousness.
- Inpatient treatment modalities showed at best mixed results.
- Recidivism among Patuxent inmates was only marginally better than at other state prisons.
- Outpatient (furloughs and paroles) services were moderately successful.

The final CRC recommendation stated that:

> The study team concludes that the portions of Article 31B dealing with the indeterminate sentence and the concept of defective delinquency should be repealed, and that the present program at Patuxent Institution should be significantly modified.[26]

Before discussing the ultimate consequences of the CRC report, we need to examine carefully one of that report's most damaging conclusions: Patuxent's recidivism level was "only marginally" better than that found at other, less expensive, state facilities. It bears directly on the question of what is success and how is it to be measured. The CRC study concluded that the recidivism level of Patuxent's releasees was not sufficiently low enough to justify the high costs involved and the questionable stretching of due process guarantees that Patuxent's commitment and treatment procedures entailed.

The study was based on a superficial examination of the available data. The Patuxent committed population (that is, those judicially determined to be defective delinquents) was a highly recidivistic one, a "loaded" population deliberately selected by the institution's diagnostic staff because of its "propensity toward criminal activity." CRC selected felons confined at the Maryland Penitentiary as a comparison group, but no one can seriously defend the proposition that this group of offenders came close to matching, on significant variables, the Patuxent population. Thus, in effect, the CRC study mixed "apples with oranges." One could sensibly argue that the Patuxent staff's modest "success rate" with its failure-prone population represented a significant advance over pre-Patuxent or ordinary incarceration.

In spite of these methodological concerns, shortly after the CRC's final report was delivered, the General Assembly of Maryland repealed the original defective delinquency statute, replacing it with a new 31B, effective July 1, 1977. The new law followed the advice of CRC and mandated "significant" modifications in Patuxent's operation.[27] In examining them we should understand that the legislature intended to retain Patuxent Institution as the state's only treatment prison. In so doing, it maintained a fundamental contradiction: implementing a treatment or hospital model within the context of coercive confinement. This contradiction always is present in correctional settings, whether they be prison, parole, or probation.

A personal example may serve to illustrate this contradiction. When the author was on the Patuxent staff, one of his frequent duties was to give an orientation to inmates who had recently arrived. This was a routine orientation explaining the law, especially the provision laying out the indeterminate sentence. Then the can-do, can't-do rules were explained. There were certainly many more of the can't-do variety.

During the orientation, the contradiction between the coercive nature of confinement and the prison's mission was clear when the indeterminate sentence section of the law was read to the new inmates. The law's language, "with no minimum or maximum limits," usually brought a startled look to their faces, then expressions of disbelief. Almost in the same breath, the orientation would go on to suggest that if, eventually, they were committed as defective delinquents, the treatment program would be available to help them change and be released, possibly earlier than if they were in some other prison. After finishing one of these orientations, the expression, "you will cooperate with us, or else . . ." came to mind.

Eligible Person Statute

Now we turn to a discussion of the 1977 law. We can summarize the changes from the original statute as follows:

- Replacement of the "defective delinquent" label by the term "eligible person."
- Elimination of the indeterminate sentence clause.
- Replacement of the prediction of future dangerousness criterion for commitment by one requiring prediction of **treatability.**
- Substitution of voluntary for involuntary admission.

As the label "defective delinquent" was invented in 1951 with the passage of the original Article 31B, it was buried when the 1977 statute was enacted. This change was in response to complaints that defective delinquency as defined in 1951 was confusing and inappropriate given the state of diagnostic art in the mental health professions. In addition it was seen as a particularly disabling label. The new law referred to those committed to the institution as **eligible persons.** This term of reference not only did away with the negative connotation associated with the earlier label, it had the additional advantage of incorporating the new and primary commitment criterion: that offenders must be "eligible" for treatment.

Specifically, the new language required the diagnostic staff to determine that an offender:

> . . . is likely to respond favorably to the programs and services provided at Patuxent Institution, and can be better rehabilitated through those programs and services than by other incarceration.[28]

Additional qualifying language defining the eligible person was almost identical to that used to define the defective delinquent since it retained the terms "intellectual deficiency or emotional unbalance" found in the earlier version.[29] Thus, an eligible person was one who was intellectually deficient or emotionally unbalanced, and who would be responsive to the Patuxent Institution treatment regimen.

The Focus on the Law feature gives the legal definition of eligible person together with the definition of defective delinquency from the earlier statute.

One advantage this definition had over its predecessor was its clear implication as to the institution's single mission: rehabilitation. Incapacitation finally was eliminated as a co-equal goal.[30]

FOCUS ON
THE LAW

DEFINITIONS OF "DEFECTIVE DELINQUENT" AND "ELIGIBLE PERSON" IN MARYLAND LAWS

[A defective delinquent is one who] . . . by the demonstration of persistent aggravated antisocial or criminal behavior, evidences a propensity toward criminal activity, and who is found to have either such intellectual deficiency or emotional unbalance, or both, as to clearly demonstrate an actual danger to society so as to require such confinement and treatment, when appropriate, as may make it reasonably safe for society to terminate the confinement and treatment. (Article 31B, 1951)

****

[An eligible person is one] who (1) has been convicted of a crime and is serving a sentence of imprisonment with at least three years remaining on it, (2) has an intellectual deficiency or emotional unbalance, (3) is likely to respond favorably to the programs and services provided at Patuxent Institution, and (4) can be better rehabilitated through those programs and services than by any other incarceration. (Article 31B, 1977)

To answer those critics who had questioned confining offenders for indeterminate periods regardless of their original sentences, the new statute made it clear that no committed eligible person could be imprisoned longer than his original sentence.* Not only did this respond to certain civil libertarian concerns, it demonstrated the legislators' commitment to limiting Patuxent Institution's mission to that of treating those offenders determined to be eligible for the treatment.

As we have seen, the original Article 31B required the diagnostic staff to predict future dangerousness before recommending commitment of offenders as defective delinquents. We have also seen that this requirement was possibly the most criticized provision in the law. The replacement law abandoned this criterion and substituted a prediction that the offender would respond "favorably" to institutional treatment. Whether or not this prediction is less subject to the false positives problem associated with predictions of dangerousness or whether it might produce an excessive number of false negatives may never be known since there has been no effort to research the accuracy of these predictions.

We must keep in mind that the 1977 statute did not completely eliminate the need to predict future dangerousness. The new statute required the treatment staff to predict that inmates released on furloughs and paroles would not put society at risk. In the words of the statute:

> If the Board of Review concludes that (1) it will not impose an unreasonable risk on society and (2) it will assist in the treatment and rehabilitation of the eligible person, it shall grant a parole . . . for a period not exceeding one year.

*****

*The statutory language in Section 11(a) contains the pronoun "his" and "he": "A person confined at the Institution shall be released upon the expiration of his sentence in the same manner . . . as if he were being released from a correctional facility." Patuxent Institution began treating 21 women as "eligible persons" as of the end of fiscal year 1989.

If a person has successfully completed three years on parole without violation, and the Board of Review concludes that he is safe to be permanently released, it may . . . petition the [sentencing] court . . . to (1) suspend the person's remaining sentence and terminate parole supervision . . . or vacate the person's remaining sentence.[31]

Finally, earlier critics had argued that a mental health–oriented treatment facility could not successfully treat mentally disordered persons within the context of involuntary commitment. Simply stated, one could not coerce an offender and expect treatment to work. Thus, the 1977 law provided that any offender referred to Patuxent could request a transfer to another facility, and the request was to be honored within 90 days.[32]

One predictable consequence of this change was that those wishing to enter the institution were mainly offenders with very long sentences. After all, what had they to lose? Offenders with relatively short sentences chose to remain in other prisons. That these prisoners were the very ones that the framers of the original Article 31B had in mind in the 1950s only added to the contradictory nature of the operation.

This was not the only change making Patuxent Institution commitments voluntary. Under a provision of the new statute, the institution could, at any time, determine that an inmate was no longer treatable (or "eligible") and have him transferred to another prison in the state system within 90 days.[33] This represented a major change from the defective delinquency law. Under the terms of the original statute, the institution could only be rid of an inmate if it reexamined him and found that the diagnosis of defective delinquency was no longer accurate, and could convince a court to accept the finding. We are again reminded of the phrase, "you will cooperate, or. . . ."

For almost a dozen years, the institution operated under the terms of the 1977 statute. Some minor changes in the law were made during this period, one being to prohibit admitting offenders with more than one life sentence. Another state law required that a parole of any inmate serving a life sentence in any state prison had to be signed by the governor, thus taking away from the institution its long-held and cherished right to complete autonomy in release decision making.

The Second and Third Crises

In 1988, Patuxent was caught up in the aftermath of the criticism of presidential candidate Dukakis's alleged softness on crime. This criticism was sparked by the early furlough of a Massachusetts murderer, Willie Horton. The Bush campaign made effective use of Horton's release and subsequent violent behavior through TV ads, associating Dukakis with Horton since Governor Dukakis had signed the Massachusetts furlough law.

Later in the campaign it came to light that Maryland had a similar program and had released from Patuxent on furloughs two notorious offenders, one a triple murderer, the other a rapist who was accused of a rape while on leave from the institution.[34] Thus, the public was alerted, apparently for the first time, to the thirty-year practice of releasing some violent offenders earlier in their sentences than was possible were they in other prisons in the system. A firestorm of criticism engulfed the institution and its director, Norma Gluckstern. The institution's Board of Review suspended all leaves, including Robert Angell's, the triple murderer whose release had triggered the explosive reaction.[35] Eventually Director Gluckstern resigned, and the General Assembly, through the mechanism of emergency legislation, repealed major portions of Article 31B, replacing them in 1989 with a number of provisions that severely limited the institution's freedom of action and, in fact, fundamentally altered the institution's character as a treatment facility.

As enacted by the 1989 General Assembly, the current 31B contains a number of major changes in the way Patuxent Institution is to be administered and its authority to admit and release inmates. Among the major areas of change are the following:

- The criteria for admission
- Revamped Board of Review (parole board)
- Mandatory notice to victims of pending furloughs and paroles
- Specification of minimum periods of incarceration before leaves and paroles for certain classes of inmates
- Secretary of Public Safety and Correctional Services to approve all paroles
- Stipulation of severe penalties for furlough and parole violators

These changes took from Patuxent Institution its special, nearly unlimited power to admit, treat, and release offenders its staff believed to be treatable. No other correctional facility in the state had the statutory authority (under the two earlier versions of 31B) to control its intake as well as its release decision making. In fact, for nearly thirty years this institution was an all-encompassing correctional system, combining diagnostic, inpatient, and outpatient services under one administrative umbrella. Its **Institutional Board of Review** served the same function as a state parole board. Its inpatient professional staff also carried outpatient (furloughed and paroled offenders) caseloads. As we have seen, its diagnostic staff could and often did reject offenders for commitment as either untreatable (the 1977 statute) or because they were not "defective" (the original statute).

Clearly, the uproar in 1988 accompanying the news of the early release of very violent inmates was heard in the legislature. Not only was Patuxent shorn of its unique authority to make release decisions, but also other statutory requirements enacted in 1988 reflected the political climate within which correctional policies must be implemented for at least the foreseeable future. Among these are:

1. Offenders serving more than one life sentence and those with a single life sentence for an aggravated crime are not eligible to be referred to Patuxent Institution. Beyond this prohibition, no convicted first-degree murderer or first-degree rapist is to be found eligible for treatment unless the sentencing judge recommends admission to Patuxent for evaluation.[36]
2. The Institutional Board of Review was restructured. In doing so, the legislature removed the positions the previous statute reserved for law and sociology professors and added places for "five members of the general public . . . , one of whom is a member of a **victims' rights** organization" (boldface added).[37] In addition, the statute specifies that before any inmate can be paroled, seven of the nine members of the board must approve (other decisions require a simple majority).
3. The Board of Review is required to give ". . . written notice to the victim or, if the victim is dead, the victim's family, that it intends to grant work release or leave to the eligible person."[38]
4. Most offenders serving life sentences for violent crimes are now required to serve at least fifteen years before becoming eligible for parole, while those on life sentences whose crimes were judged to be aggravated must be incarcerated at least twenty-five years before the Board of Review can parole them.[39]
5. The 1988 statute also defines "major violations" committed by inmates on paroles, leaves, or furloughs and mandates that they will be reinstitutionalized for at least

six months if such violations should occur. Two such violations are to result in the transfer of the violator to another prison in the system. Rather harshly, one may conclude, among the "major" violations enumerated in the law is ". . . failure to return from parole, work release, or leave within 1 hour of the time due."[40]

6. Finally, the potential onus for parole decisions is given to the politically appointed Secretary of Public Safety and Correctional Services: "The Board of Review may not release an eligible person until the parole decision has been approved by the Secretary."[41]

Patuxent Institution opened its doors to diagnose and treat defective delinquents in January, 1955. Those who drafted the original Article 31B and the institution's staff were swept along in a wave of positivist enthusiasm, certain that this new law could be used effectively to deal with a most difficult and dangerous segment of the criminal population, a population for whom the traditional or "classical" criminal law and procedure had proved so inadequate both to protect society and to rehabilitate.

Patuxent Institution represented the clearest example in American correctional history of the application of positivist principles, set forth in what might be called the **Lombrosian Legacy** (boldface added).[42] The principles in this legacy have been passed on to many penologists and correctional clinicians in the century and a quarter since Cesare Lombroso reported his famous findings about the "Criminal Man."[43] They may be summarized as:

- To control crime effectively it is necessary to study the individual criminal subject in order to determine what caused the criminal behavior.
- Using "scientific" techniques, it is possible to assign criminal offenders to etiological and treatment groups.
- Criminal offenders commit crimes because of forces beyond their ability to control.
- Criminal offenders are fundamentally different from other, noncriminal persons.

As the Patuxent staff went about its business of receiving, examining, treating, releasing some and, holding others in confinement it was, in effect, adhering to most of those principles. The "scientific" techniques consisted of an array of psychiatric and psychometric examinations and tests.[44] As a result of applying these techniques, some offenders were diagnosed as defective delinquent, while others were not.

The certainty that the framers of the original legislation felt regarding the ability of modern psychology and psychiatry to carry out the tasks assigned them at Patuxent Institution was spelled out in the original recommendation for passage of the statute:

A fundamental problem, however, is whether medical science has progressed to where we can segregate such a class of defective delinquents and handle its treatment with reasonable assurance of accomplishing the purpose of the legislation. We believe that experience elsewhere has demonstrated that this is possible. Also, we have consulted a distinguished group of Maryland psychologists and psychiatrists and their composite opinion is included herein. . . .

****

. . . [I]n many ways the Maryland plan for handling this complicated problem is the best that has yet been projected. If put into effect, it will bring the State into the forefront of penological advance. . . . [T]here is a real opportunity for scientific knowledge to be advanced in a field comparable to the scourge of cancer, so far as its effect upon the welfare of society is concerned.[46]

Much of the concern expressed in the past regarding Patuxent Institution's ability to perform satisfactorily had centered on whether its staff could accurately identify those in its inmate population who were "ready" for outpatient status. Readiness was most often operationalized strictly in terms of the patient's capacity for living in the community, and the staff's ability to provide support services for as long as required to maintain the "patient" out of the institution.

The carefully structured release decision-making process together with the provision of outpatient services through the institution's own staff resources represented a remarkable departure from traditional correctional practice. As we shall see in a subsequent chapter, traditional parole decision-making and supervision has been the responsibility of agencies separated from prisons. Often this lack of integration has resulted in inappropriate release decisions and inadequate supervision. Recently, such deficiencies have resulted in successful calls for the elimination of parole in many states and in the federal system.

The result of all this careful attention to detail, however, left the institution isolated from the general public. In the current climate the public and its political leaders were bound to revolt against what was regarded as a flagrant violation of its rights and security. Patuxent Institution's decision makers failed to take into account changing societal standards with regard to the balancing of punishment and "treatment" for serious crimes, especially in terms of length of incarceration. In the United States today, imprisonment has become the punishment of choice for serious offenders. Prison populations have been setting records for the past several years. Prison sentences are often mandatory, and for longer periods than in the past.

An editorial in the *Washington Post* put the Patuxent experience in its contemporary context:

> The problem has to do with the apparent failure to give equal, or even any, consideration to another aspect of incarceration. Prisons are about more than rehabilitation. Depriving convicted felons of liberty is intended not only or even principally to retrain and counsel them, but rather to penalize them, to protect the community and to ensure that justice has been done.
>
> . . . [I]n the Angell case, the time served is inadequate to the enormity of the crimes committed. Whether he has been rehabilitated or not, a man responsible for three vicious murders should be made to pay a price. Justice requires that it be substantial. Life sentences for crimes of this kind are a humane alternative to capital punishment. If they are to continue to be accepted as such by the public, the court's judgment cannot be easily and secretly ignored.[47]

Although the editorial no doubt reflected in part the community's increasing demand for stiffer sentences, if not a "throw away the key" or "three strikes and you're out" attitude, perhaps the *Post* was more intent in fending off those calling for more death sentences in the state courts. The *Post* has maintained a longstanding opposition to capital punishment. Should Patuxent's willingness to release even multiple murderers continue, calls for more draconian measures might have included demands for increased use of the state's gas chamber or the recently available lethal injection.

We should also take into account very recent developments in the political arena. Both President Clinton in his 1994 State of the Union address and various Congressional leaders called for legislation to mandate severe penalties for serious crimes. The most popular "sound bite" is the "three strikes and you're out" sentence law, which calls for a mandatory life-without-parole sentence after a third conviction for violent felonies.

The Patuxent staff and Review Board also failed to take into account the increasing demand for the recognition of victims' interests when prison inmates are considered for release. In the case of the two prisoners released during the 1988 presidential campaign, no one in the community was consulted about these releases. The decisions were reached in the closed atmosphere of the institution and its Board of Review. Anger over the failure to take victims and the community into account was heightened when the persons to be released had spent only a relatively short period in confinement for the most heinous of crimes. In this regard, it seems that the Patuxent Board of Review had been lulled into a false sense of insulation from responsibility for the acts of some of the inmates they released.

Under the Maryland statute governing the Board of Review then in force, board members had only to find that an inmate did not pose an "unreasonable risk" to society prior to voting in favor of a furlough or parole. We know of no instance in which an eligible person (or defective delinquent under the original statute) made threats to specified persons, nor any occasion when the board had reason to fear for the safety of particular persons. Patuxent's "liability," if any, was to the general community in a time of growing concern about crime and punishment. The staff should have been sensitive to this concern and taken the initiative to inform and educate the public about its operations and the risks incurred by these operations.

As a result of this insensitivity to the public climate, Patuxent Institution paid a very high price. Its cherished autonomy has been lost and its reputation as a "cutting edge" treatment facility has been severely damaged. By prohibiting certain serious offenders from even being considered for treatment at the institution and by specifying lengthy terms of confinement before the Board of Review may release certain inmates on life sentences, the General Assembly's latest statutory revision, it can be argued, has severely diminished Patuxent's ability to treat effectively the very population it was mandated to treat since its opening in 1955: the serious, violent criminal.

Among the changes wrought by the present statute, those aimed at making the Institutional Board of Review more responsive to the community it serves are rather like closing the barn door after the horse has left. Had the board historically been structured in such a way as to give representation to "the public" and to victim's rights organizations, had notification of victims or their families been required (or made a voluntary policy of the board), perhaps the community would have been better protected, and perhaps such radical changes in the statute would not have been required.

Certainly, we can say that it was not only Patuxent Institution that was made to pay a heavy price by the actions of the Maryland General Assembly. The public may, in the long run, receive less protection from serious, "emotionally unbalanced" offenders under the provisions of the new statute than it received under earlier versions. Clearly, many very serious and violent felons will no longer receive any rehabilitative services in the state of Maryland and will most probably sit in warehouse-like overcrowded prisons, crossing off the days on their calendars until precalculated release dates are reached. Thus, short-term gains under the new law may, paradoxically, increase long-term risks to the community.

Treatment Rights and Patuxent Institution

There is one final issue to be discussed regarding the use of the prison as a treatment setting: the matter of the right of prisoners to treatment, and their right to refuse treatment. It is generally agreed that "there is no court decision which has yet held that there is a general constitutional right to rehabilitative programs in correctional institutions."[48] Many inmates have attempted unsuccessfully to secure this right by appeals to state and federal courts.

By contrast, there is a right to at least adequate medical treatment for prisoners. The first case to find such a constitutional right was *Estelle v. Gamble,* decided by the United States Supreme Court in 1976.[49]

But what about a prisoner's right to refuse rehabilitative treatment? In his review of the relevant case law, Sheldon Krantz found no definitive answer.[50] There are subsidiary questions to be answered, such as informed consent by prisoners and the obligation of institutions to protect inmates from themselves, as well as to ensure prison security.

In the history of Patuxent Institution, the right to receive or refuse treatment was and is a quite different issue than in ordinary correctional institutions. Under the first defective delinquency law, inmates were held involuntarily. As we saw, treatment was to be provided "when appropriate." Prisoners could and did refuse participation in therapy when offered to them. This happened rarely since the result of refusal meant, in all likelihood, longer confinement.

Some inmates under the defective delinquency statute did protest their involuntary commitment by refusing to submit to psychiatric and psychological examinations. Since they were sent initially for such examinations by court order, their refusal to be tested was interpreted as contempt of court. Either they relented, or they remained in the institution until their original sentences had expired. Even then, it was not certain whether or not they could be held beyond the expiration date.

Under the terms of the eligible persons statute, an inmate's admission to the institution was voluntary. Remaining there depended on her or his amenability to treatment. Should an inmate refuse treatment, transfer to an ordinary state prison was a sure thing. Thus, to receive treatment clearly would be to the inmate's advantage. Since the statute now specified that the sole mission of Patuxent was rehabilitative treatment, the institution was obliged to provide it.

PATUXENT INSTITUTION AND THE DEFECTIVE DELINQUENCY LAW were a well-intentioned effort to apply a positive penology to a difficult question: What was to be done with offenders who were not legally insane, but mentally disordered according to the opinions of experts?

Taking the lead from other states' sexual psychopath statutes, Maryland enacted a law that covered a much wider group of offenders. This law provided for a dual mission for the new prison: incapacitation and treatment within the framework of an indeterminate sentence.

Trying to carry out these two missions, the institution's staff ran up against the contradiction of coercive confinement of a population to which it was charged to deliver treatment. The involuntary nature of inmates' incarceration may have doomed the treatment mission from the start.

The most important problem faced by the staff members during its first twenty-five years was that of predicting future dangerousness in those entrusted to their care. In the face of increasing opposition from mental health professionals, the staff persisted until the statute was amended in 1977.

SUMMARY

The second version of the law was an effort to maintain the institution as a reha-bilitation facility, while removing some of the doubtful features of its predecessor. This effort did not solve the fundamental dilemma of a coercive environment onto which was grafted a medical or treatment model.

Maintaining a steady self-assurance in its ability to perform its treatment mission without outside observation, the staff was finally caught up in the public outcry against what was perceived as inadequate attention to community safety. As a result, a third version of the law was enacted, severely curtailing the institution's autonomy.

Today, perhaps no institution can survive as a full-scale rehabilitation center. Incapacitation of serious offenders for long periods without much pretense of deliv-ering correctional services seems to be the order of the day as we shall see in the next chapter.

▍KEY CONCEPTS

Defective delinquency	Positive criminology
Eligible persons	Sexual psychopath
False positives	Structured anxiety
Future dangerousness	Success rate
Indeterminate sentencing	Treatability
Institutional Board of Review	Victims' rights
Lombrosian Legacy	

▍QUESTIONS FOR DISCUSSION

1. Why can we say that the Maryland defective delinquency statute follows in the footsteps of Cesare Lombroso's work in positive criminology?
2. Does it make sense to try to predict "future dangerousness" in a criminal popula-tion, especially given the present fear that violent crime is out of control?
3. If it is very difficult, if not impossible to predict future dangerousness, what alter-natives do we have to reduce the number of repeat violent offenders?
4. Critically evaluate Maryland's move to take victims more seriously into account by placing their representatives on Patuxent Institution's Board of Review.
5. The chapter opened by stating that the Patuxent experience should have taught us two lessons. Specifically, what illustrates these lessons? In light of these lessons crit-ically comment on the likelihood of a Patuxent-like phoenix arising from the ashes of the present one.

▍ENDNOTES

1. Francis T. Cullen, et al., "The Correctional Orientation of Prison Wardens: Is the Rehabil-itative Ideal Supported?" *Criminology* 31 (1993): 70.
2. For an introduction to the work of these contributors to the psychodynamic explanation and treatment of offenders, see William Healy, *The Individual Delinquent* (Little, Brown,

1915); William Healy and Augusta Bronner, *New Light on Juvenile Delinquency and Its Treatment* (New Haven, CT: Yale University Press, 1936).

3. Cullen, et al., p. 71.

4. For a comprehensive review of the development of sex psychopath laws see Fred Cohen, *The Law of Deprivation of Liberty: A Study in Social Control* (St. Paul, MN: West Publishing, 1980), Chapter 6.

5. Frank T. Lindman and Donald M. McIntyre, Jr., *The Mentally Disabled and the Law* (Chicago: University of Chicago Press, 1961).

6. The committee was appointed on September 7, 1949, and was chaired by Jerome Robinson.

7. Research Division, Maryland Legislative Council, "An Indeterminate Sentence Law for Defective Delinquents," *Research Report No. 29,* 1 (1950).

8. Ibid.

9. Ibid., p. 1 (emphasis added).

10. Article 31B, § 6(a).

11. Enrico Ferri, *Criminal Sociology* (New York: Appleton and Co., 1986).

12. Article 31B, § 5, 1951.

13. *Tipett, et al. v. State of Maryland.*

14. 31B (1951), § 12 specified that in addition to the director and three associate directors of the institution, membership on the board would include "the professor of the University of Maryland School of Law who is a member of the [institution's] advisory board, either of the members of the Maryland bar who are members of the advisory board and a sociologist to be appointed by the board . . . from the faculty of an accredited institution of higher education in Maryland."

15. See, for example, Legislative Council of Maryland, *Report of the Commission to Study and Re-evaluate Patuxent Institution* (Annapolis, Md., 1961); Thomsen Commission, *Interim Report of the Commission to Study Changes and Basis of Selection for Patuxent Institution* (Annapolis, Md., December 17, 1964). For an early independent review see Thomas F. Courtless, *An Analysis of the Impact of Correctional Treatment on Committed Mentally Abnormal Offenders,* University of Maryland doctoral dissertation, Dissertation Abstracts, Vol. 27, No. 9-A, 3118–3119.

16. R. Prantky, "The Neurochemistry and Neuroendrocrinology of Sexual Aggression," in D. F. Farrington and J. G. Chichester, eds., *Aggression and Dangerousness* (New York: Wiley Publishing, 1985), p. 36.

17. H. Cleckley, *The Mask of Sanity* 5th ed. (St. Louis, MO: Mosby Press, 1976), pp. 337–338.

18. In broad terms, the graduated tier system follows in the footsteps of the nineteenth-century systems of Maconochie and Walter Crofton, which we discussed in the previous chapter.

19. After a mass escape, the sheet metal vocational training class fabricated a perimeter fence and guard towers in an effort to prevent future such calamities. One may wonder why the prison was built without fencing and towers when it was intended for serious offenders.

20. Emory Hodges, "Crime Prevention by the Indeterminate Sentence Law," *American Journal of Psychiatry* 128 (1971): 291.

21. Dorothea Dix, *Remarks on Prisons and Prison Discipline* (Montclair, N.J.: Patterson Smith, 1967), p. 66. Emphasis in the original.

22. For an example of a study in which all three criteria were examined, see Alan Beck and Bernard Shipley, *Recidivism of Young Parolees* (Washington, D.C.: United States Department of Justice, Bureau of Justice Statistics, 1987). Not unexpectedly, the rate of recidivism varied markedly depending on the criterion used to measure it.

23. Technical violations of parole will be discussed in Chapter 12.

24. For a sampling of these articles, see the following: Henry J. Steadman, "The Community Adjustment and Criminal Activity of the Baxtrom Patients: 1966–1970," 129 *American Journal of Psychiatry* 304, (1972); Alan A. Stone, *Mental Health and Law: A System in Transition,* National Institute of Mental Health, Center for Studies of Crime and Delinquency (1975); Ernst Wenk, et al., "Can Violence Be Predicted?" 18 *Crime and Delinquency* 393, 1972.

25. Contract Research Corporation, *The Evaluation of Patuxent Institution: Final Report,* February 25, 1977.
26. Ibid., p. 86.
27. For a thorough discussion of the many changes wrought by the 1977 version of Article 31B see Elyce Zenoff and Thomas F. Courtless, "Autopsy of an Experiment: The Patuxent Experience," *Journal of Psychiatry and Law* 531 (Winter, 1977).
28. Article 31B (1977), § 1(g). This version of the statute hereinafter cited as 31B (1977).
29. Ibid.
30. Section 2(b) of 31B(1977) states that "the purpose of the institution is to provide efficient and adequate programs and services for the treatment and rehabilitation of eligible persons.
31. 31B (1977), § 11(b.2) and (c).
32. 31B (1977), § 11(b.1).
33. 31B (1977), § 11(b)(1).
34. For a running commentary on the accounts of these furloughs, see the following articles that appeared in the *Washington Post:* November 22, 1988 (editorial); December 2, 1988, p. A-1; and December 20, 1988, p. B-1.
35. On the evening of April 9, 1990, Angell was found semiconscious in his cell, apparently after an attempt at suicide. Six if the thirty inmates whose leaves were suspended in 1989 had been restored to that status by March, 1990. Angell was not one of these. For an account of this incident, see the *Washington Post,* April 11, 1990, p. B-3.
36. Article 31B (1988), Section 1(F)(2). The 1988 version of the statute hereinafter cited as 31B (1988).
37. 31B (1988), § 6(a).
38. 31B (1988), § 10(b).
39. 31B (1988), § 11(b)(4)(5).
40. 31B (1988), § 11(A)(1).
41. 31B (1988), § 11(D).
42. For a discussion of Cesare Lombroso's influence, see Marvin Wolfgang's essay, "Cesare Lombroso," in H. Mannheim, *Pioneers in Criminology* (1960), pp. 222–225.
43. Lombroso, *L'uomo Delinquente* (1876).
44. Among the tests used were the Weschler Adult Intelligence Scale, Bender-Gestalt, Rorschach, Draw-A-Person, Porteus Maze.
45. Supra. note 6, p. 1.
46. Ibid., p. 27.
47. "Robert Angell's Furloughs," *Washington Post,* November 22, 1988, p. A-14.
48. Sheldon Krantz, *Corrections and Prisoners' Rights in a Nutshell,* 3rd ed. (St. Paul, MN: West Publishing, 1988), p. 206.
49. 429 U.S. 97.
50. Supra. note 47, pp. 218–223.

PRISONS TODAY

INTRODUCTION IN CHAPTER 6, we dealt with the history of the prison in American society. In Chapter 7, we analyzed Patuxent Institution, a unique prison that typified the attempt to graft the rehabilitative idea onto the American prison. In this chapter we will take a close look at prisons today. We will pay particular attention to their populations, programs, and the many problems confronting them. We will find that the rehabilitative ideal, so popular during the 1960s and 1970s, no longer exercises much influence. Instead, selective incapacitation of aggregates of offenders and secure confinement are now of the highest priority. We will examine some of the major issues of prison management.

An increasingly popular solution is to privatize prisons. There are a number of possible gains to be made if prisons or some of their programs are transferred to the private sector. As we will see, however, a number of disturbing questions have been raised about privatization.

Institutions and programs for female offenders will be taken up in the next chapter. The increase in the number of women convicted and sentenced to prison has brought many complex issues to the attention of corrections departments, prison administrators, and staff that until recently have not been addressed seriously.

A major difficulty facing us as we try to understand the contemporary correctional institution is that it has undergone frequent transformations as to mission and population. We saw in Chapter 6 that over a period of two centuries incarceration has been influenced by three major ideological systems: penitentiary, reformatory, and rehabilitation. Benjamin Frank, a former official in the United States Bureau of Prisons, once described the American prison as being "rediscovered with some regularity when prisoners rebel against their captivity. . . . The prison is also rediscovered when its practices and programs are in conflict with the demands of the society which it serves."[1]

As we will see in this chapter, the American prison of today is very different from the prison in the past. The changing expectations and rationales of sentencing patterns together with shifting and expanding prison populations are certainly major factors in shaping and reshaping the contemporary prison. We must remember that correctional institutions are at the low end of the system's totem pole. They cannot refuse to receive those sentenced to them. In a sense, they are "open admissions" institutions.

THE ROLE OF THE PRISON TODAY

Although many would accept the view that prisons should deprive offenders of their liberty, preferably under harsh conditions, and a few others might feel that prisons can and should rehabilitate inmates, these are by no means the only missions today's prisons are called upon to perform. In the recent past we have even asked prisons to scare youthful offenders out of crime for fear of ending up in terrible institutions where they might be assaulted, raped, or otherwise abused.[2]

Currently, there is considerable support for prison sentences as a means of **selective incapacitation** of certain groups of offenders. Some have referred to this as a "new" penology, replacing an older version that emphasized confinement and treatment of individual inmates. This **new penology** "redirects" corrections "to actuarial consideration of aggregates . . . [and] facilitates development of a vision or model . . . that embraces increased reliance on imprisonment."[3] The major concerns are surveillance and custody. No longer does penology focus attention on individuals. Rather, it focuses on the problem of "managing aggregates of dangerous groups."[4] The emphasis today is on " 'no frills, no service' custodial centers, electronic monitoring, and statistical studies to determine 'variable detention [needs] based on risk assessment.' "[5]

Whether or not there is a new penology at work today, it is fair to say that the American prison at its "best" conforms to a **confinement model** of incarceration, which has been succinctly summarized by Logan in the following statement:

> The mission of a prison is to keep prisoners—to keep them in, keep them safe, keep them in line, keep them healthy, and keep them busy—and to do it with fairness, without undue suffering and as efficiently as possible.[6]

We can ask whether this model effectively serves the society that has spawned it. We will discuss this question in the final chapter.

PRISONS AND PRISONERS

According to a compilation by the American Correctional Association, an organization that accredits prisons, there are almost 900 state and 57 federal prisons of all types.[7] A total of 780 of these institutions are for male prisoners only, 73 are designated for women only, and 38 are co-correctional. These totals do not include correctional reception and diagnostic centers, community facilities such as prerelease or community corrections centers, boot camps, other correctional camps (such as recently reinstituted "chain gangs" in states like Alabama), or local institutions such as jails, which we discussed in Chapter 5.

At the end of 1995, state and federal prisons held 1,127,132 prisoners, an all-time high.[8] Between 1985 and 1995, the U.S. prison population grew by an astonishing 841,200 inmates, an increase of 121.2 percent! Over the decde the demand for new beds reached 1,618 per week.[9] Table 8.1 shows the yearly population figures and percent increase for the period 1985 to 1995.

Prison crowding is so severe that 32,739 prisoners have to be housed in local jails until bed space is available in state prison systems.[10] Because of overcrowding, as of June 30, 1994, 30 state prison systems and the Federal Bureau of Prisons were under either court orders or consent decrees to reduce their populations or improve their conditions.

Mandatory prison sentences are handed down by the courts in increasing numbers in response to what the public and their representatives and judges see as a crime

Changes in State and Federal Prison Populations, 1985, 1990–95 TABLE 8.1

YEAR	TOTAL INMATES IN CUSTODY	NUMBER OF STATE AND FEDERAL PRISONERS ON DECEMBER 31	
		JURISDICTION	CUSTODY
1985	744,208	502,507	487,593
1990	1,148,702	773,919	743,382
1991	1,219,014	825,559	792,535
1992	1,295,150	882,500	850,566
1993	1,369,185	969,301	909,381
1994	1,478,086	1,055,073	991,612
1995	1,585,401	1,127,132	1,078,357
Percent change, 1994–95	7.3%	6.8%	8.7%
Percent change 1985–95	113.0%	124.3%	121.2%
Annual average increase, 1985–95	7.9%	8.4%	8.3%

SOURCE: *Prison and Jail Inmates, 1995,* Washington, D.C.: United States Department of Justice, Bureau of Justice Statistics, August 1996, p. 2.

ACROSS CULTURES

DEALING WITH OVERCROWDING IN NEW ZEALAND PRISONS

Prisons in New Zealand suffer less from crowding than do prisons in the United States. Why is this so? One answer is the influence of the prison guards' union. In their collective bargaining agreements, the union "has forced standardized wage increases up to 15 percent when populations exceed agreed upon levels and because they threaten to strike if populations rise above these levels." This situation has required the government to build new prisons, and to transfer men from crowded institutions to women's prisons where there are vacancies.

SOURCE: Chris W. Eskridge and Greg Newbold, "Corrections in New Zealand," *Federal Probation* 57 (September 1993): 60.

problem perilously close to being out of control. The presumed best response to this is more incarceration. "Three strikes and you're out" sentence statutes are one favored legislative response to the crime problem. These sentences will require more cell space and additional construction and staffing costs. In addition, many states have already required or are considering requiring some offenders to spend at least 85 percent of their sentences in prison.[11]

Many assume that the increase in the prison population is due to increases in violent crime. This is not the case. That is, the dramatic expansion of the prisoner population is not due to a rising rate of violent offender commitments. As a recent Bureau of Justice Statistics report stated:

> As a percentage of all State and Federal inmates, violent offenders fell from 57% in 1980 to 45% in 1993, property offenders fell from 30% to 22%, drug offenders rose from 8% to 26%, and public-order offenders rose from 5% to 7%.[12]

Looking only at the increase in the federal prison population, the rise in the percentage of drug offenders is more dramatic. In 1980, drug offenders made up about 25 percent of the federal prison population. By 1993, they made up 60 percent.[13]

One of the first things we notice when looking at the data on prison commitments is that about 30 percent of all new prison admissions is made up of offenders who have been convicted of drug-related crimes. This represents a sharp increase from as recently as 1980, when such offenders were only about 17 percent of total correctional institution admissions.[14] In 1992, of the total state and federal prison commitments, 102,000 were for drug-related offenses. This was only exceeded by admissions for property crimes, which totaled 104,300. Historically, property offenders clearly dominated U.S. prison populations. Both drug and property offenders outnumbered those committed for violent crimes. The latter offenders only accounted for 95,300 admissions in 1992.[15] The importance of rising rates of drug- related admissions is pointed out in a survey by Wexler and his colleagues in which they found that more than 75 percent of all New York city inmates reported illegal drug use.[16] Surveying other correctional systems, they found that use of cocaine and heroin was about as prevalent as in New York City.

*I*nmates get some exercise in a recreation yard in a state prison in Raleigh, North Carolina. The communal living at prisons facilitates social interaction as a positive goal but also provides opportunities for intimidation, group violence, drug transactions, and other problems.

These surprising figures can only be explained by our continuing "war on drugs." Were it not for this war, it is unlikely that U.S. prison populations would set new records each year. While such a war may capture newspaper headlines and gain votes for elected officials, it does cause serious systemic consequences throughout the criminal justice system. Police, courts, and corrections must cope with and are sometimes casualties of the war. Steven B. Duke and Albert B. Gross carefully studied the struggle against illicit drugs and pointed to numerous unintended consequences of our chosen strategies.[17] These include not only exploding prison populations and court dockets, but also increased deaths on our streets.

Another surprising change in prison admissions over the past decade is the dramatic *decrease* in the number and rates of admissions resulting from sentences for new offenses. As stated in a recent government report,

> Court commitments account for a decreasing share of all prison admissions: 69.5% in 1992, down from 82.4% in 1980. . . . As a percentage of all admissions, those returning to prison after a conditional release increased from 17.0% to 29.5%. These conditional release violators had originally left prison as parolees, and other types of release involving community supervision.[18]

Changing parole and conditional release supervision patterns and the advent of "intensive" supervision of prison releasees undoubtedly has caused much of this shift. More conditions and heightened supervision will result in more observed violations.

Between 1980 and 1992, admissions of black offenders increased by 186 percent, while white admissions grew by 143 percent. Significantly, the rate of incarceration of young (age 25–29) black males was 6,301 (per 100,000 in the U.S. population), *six times the rate for whites*.[19] At the end of 1992, the latest figures available, there was a total of 4,094 black male inmates per 100,000 blacks in the U.S. population. This compares to only 502 adult white males per 100,000 adult whites in the general population.[20] This same census found that "among U.S. adults who either graduated from

TABLE 8.2   **Number of Sentenced Prisoners under State and Federal Jurisdiction, by Sex and Race, 1980, 1985, 1990–94**

| | | NUMBER OF SENTENCED PRISONERS | | | | | |
| | | Male | | | Female | | |
YEAR	Total	All	White	Black	All	White	Black
1980	315,974	303,643	159,500	140,600	12,331	5,900	6,300
1985	480,568	459,223	242,700	210,500	21,345	10,800	10,200
1990	739,980	699,416	346,700	344,300	40,564	20,000	20,100
1991	789,610	745,808	363,600	372,200	43,802	20,900	22,200
1992	846,277	799,776	387,600	401,200	46,501	22,100	23,700
1993	932,266	878,298	418,900	445,400	53,968	25,200	27,900
1994	1,012,463	952,585	—	—	59,878	—	—
Percent change,							
1980–94	220%	214%	—	—	386%	—	—

SOURCE: *Prisoners in 1994*, Bureau of Justice Statistics, p. 3.

high school or earned a general equivalence degree (GED), almost 6% of blacks and 1% of whites were in a Federal or State prison serving a sentence of a year or more."[21]

There has also been a significant increase in the number and rates of incarceration of women offenders. In 1980, there was a total of 12,200 women in state and federal prisons; in 1992 that total had increased to 45,800.[22] As is the case with males, the racial differential in rates of incarceration was very clear: The black female rate was *seven times* higher than that for white females.[23]

Tables 8.2 through 8.5 and Figures 8.1 and 8.2 graphically illustrate these population data.

The nearly one million prisoners are confined in various levels of security ranging from maximum to minimum custody. As of June 30, 1994, 110,594 inmates were housed at the highest security level, maximum security. Another 138,380 were confined in minimum levels of security. The remaining inmates were classified as either "close" or "medium" security.[24]

Feeley and Simon, as we saw earlier, suggest that our current prison sentencing policies and practices reflect a new penology that responds to offenders as aggregates, often as an "underclass" aggregate. Sentencing serves to incapacitate this underclass, and the lack of meaningful correctional programs will do nothing to assist them to move beyond their disadvantaged position.

> [T]he underclass is understood as a permanent marginal population, without literacy, without skills, and without hope. . . . Conceived of this way, the underclass is also a dangerous class. . . . It is treated as a high-risk group that must be managed for the protection of the rest of society. Indeed, it is this managerial task that provides one of the most powerful sources for the imperative of preventive management of the new penology. The concept of "underclass" makes clear why correctional officials increasingly regard as a bad joke the claim that their goal is to reintegrate offenders back into their community.[25]

Of course, we might ask, if there is an "underclass" should it be a correctional system's job to do something about it? If so, how would a correctional institution go

Estimated Incarceration Rates of Sentenced Prisoners in State or Federal Prisons, 1980, 1985, 1990–94. TABLE 8.3

| | | NUMBER OF SENTENCED PRISONERS PER 100,000 RESIDENTS OF RELEVANT SEX AND RACIAL GROUP | | | | | |
| | | Male | | | Female | | |
YEAR	Total	All	White	Black	All	White	Black
1980	139	275	168	1,111	11	6	45
1985	202	397	246	1,559	17	10	68
1990	297	575	339	2,376	32	19	125
1992	332	643	371	2,675	36	20	142
1993	359	698	398	2,920	41	23	165
1994	387	746	—	—	45	—	—

SOURCE: *Prisoners in 1994*, Bureau of Justice Statistics, p. 8.

about dealing with the problem? If not, whose job is it? If the criminal justice system and its correctional component help perpetuate an underclass, and if society takes no remedial action, then there may be no hope for cutting significantly into crime and the enormous costs associated in fighting it.

As we have seen in previous chapters and will see in subsequent chapters, a variety of sentencing and program alternatives such as shock incarceration, intensive probation, restitution, community service, and home detention have not worked to relieve the pressure on our overburdened correctional institutions. In fact, many of these

Admissions to State Prisons, by Type of Admission, 1980–1992 TABLE 8.4

| | | PERCENT OF ALL ADMISSIONS | | |
YEAR	All	New Court Commitments	Probation/ Parole Violators	Other
1980	159,286	82.4%	17.0%	0.6%
1981	187,113	79.7	18.2	2.1
1982	203,269	81.0	18.0	1.0
1983	221,180	78.3	19.4	2.2
1984	218,280	76.5	22.7	0.8
1985	240,598	76.1%	23.4%	0.5%
1986	273,402	74.4	25.2	0.5
1987	307,519	73.4	26.2	0.4
1988	347,028	70.7	28.4	0.9
1989	423,897	70.3	28.4	1.3
1990	460,739	70.1%	29.1%	0.8%
1991	466,285	68.0	30.5	1.5
1992	480,676	69.5	29.5	0.9

SOURCE: *Prisoners in 1993*, Bureau of Justice Statistics, p. 7.

FIGURE 8.1   **Number of New Court Commitments, by Offense and Year of Admission, 1980-1992**

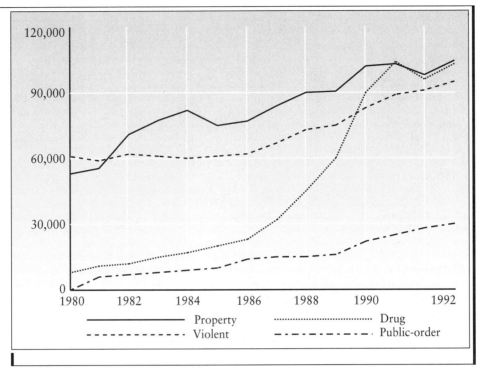

SOURCE: Bureau of Justice Statistics, *Prisoners in 1993*, p. 7.

programs produce high rates of technical and other violations of the terms of their sentences. Frequently, these violators are sent to prison. The continued pressure on these facilities will result in fewer resources being available to do more than merely incapacitate offenders. As we have seen, many states are under court orders to improve prison conditions, but the courts are generally reluctant to intervene in prison management. At times, conditions are so bad as to constitute "cruel and unusual" punishment, which is prohibited by the Eighth Amendment of the Constitution. Prisoners' rights to be protected from such punishment will be taken up in Chapter 10.

PRISON PROGRAMS

In 1967, the President's Commission on Law Enforcement and the Administration of Justice reported optimistically on the current status and future of American corrections:

> At the very least . . . [corrections] is developing the theory and practical groundwork for a new approach to rehabilitation of the most important group of offenders—those, predominantly young and lower-class, who are not committed to crime as a way of life and do not pose serious dangers to the community.[26]

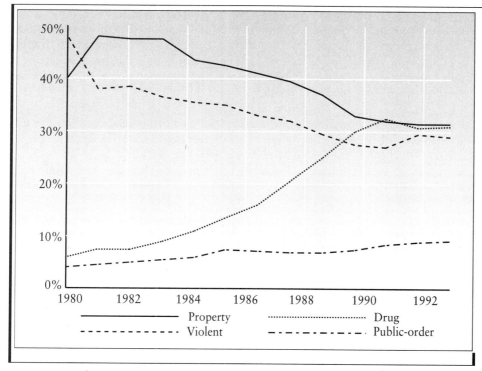

Percent of New Court Commitments, by Offense and Year of Admission, 1980-1992

FIGURE 8.2

Property — Drug ······ Violent - - - - Public-order - · - · -

SOURCE: Bureau of Justice Statistics, *Prisoners in 1993*, p. 7.

The commission suggested that there was "evidence" derived from scientific research that could guide corrections in developing effective rehabilitative program and services. It further stated that there was "widespread [public] acceptance" of rehabilitation as the major objective of incarceration.

Twenty-five years after the commission's report, as Feeley and Simon observed, a very different, new penology had evolved.[27] A penology that stresses control of aggregates of offenders. A penology in which prison administrators consider the task of reintegrating inmates into the community as a "bad joke."[28] A penology that has the support of a public no longer in favor of rehabilitative prisons. A penology that must cope with massive numbers of prisoners serving longer sentences. We turn now to a discussion of major prison treatment programs that do seek to "rehabilitate" inmates and thus stand in stark contrast to the now dominant incapacitation mission.

The Classification Process and Correctional Programs

Before we can describe correctional programs, we need to recognize that inmate participation in various programs begins with what has become known as the classification process. That is, inmates received into a prison or prison system usually are first "classified" prior to being assigned to various activities and programs. Historically, classification originated during the reformatory movement and was strongly influenced by the "Principles of 1870" as laid down by the National Prison Association.* Among the principles the association promulgated was that of "progressive classification" of individual offenders.

Today, the classification process generally involves classifying inmates into custody levels and "treatment" needs. Ideally, a newly admitted inmate is reviewed by a classification committee, assigned a custody or security status, and assigned to a minimum, medium, or maximum custody facility or section of a facility. The ideal is to apply "objective" criteria when classifying inmates for purposes of security and, when a part of the process, treatment plans.[29]

Classification may be carried out in the prison to which an offender is sentenced, in a system diagnostic and reception center (DRC), or in a special classification unit located in one of the state's institutions. In the latter two cases, offenders typically are sentenced to the department of corrections. After the classification process is completed, the offender is transferred to a particular prison. There are 40 separate DRC facilities and 71 diagnostic and reception units located in state correctional institutions.[30]

In the next section we will examine a number of treatment programs, beginning with those specifically designed for two particularly difficult inmate populations: drug and alcohol abusers and sex offenders. Following this, we will take up more general programs such as education that are provided in most prisons.

Drug and Alcohol Treatment Programs

With the significant increase in prison populations accounted for largely by the admission of more and more offenders who are substance abusers, our first inquiry into prison programming is directed at the delivery of drug and substance abuse treatment and counseling. As a preface to this section, we note that drug use *while incarcerated* is a significant problem for correctional institution administrators. Seven out of eight correctional institutions test their inmates for drug use. The results of this testing reveal the following:

- 3.6% of state and 0.4% of federal inmates tested positive for cocaine.
- 1.3% of state and 0.4% of federal inmates tested positive for heroin use.
- 2.0% of state and 0.1% of federal inmates tested positive for methamphetamines.
- 6.3% of state and 1.1% of federal inmates tested positive for marijuana use.[31]

To interdict drugs, most state and federal prisoners are "patted down" upon admission or upon return from authorized absences (e.g., work release, furloughs), and visitors' belongings are searched. In addition, in half the states, staff members were patted down when arriving for work to check for illicit drugs.

What do we know about in-prison treatment for the large number of drug-abusing inmates? The survey referred to above found the following:

- Prisons were "treating" 100,200 inmates.
- Prisons report having the capacity to treat 131,900 inmates.
- Federal inmates were using 62% of treatment capacity, state inmates 78%.

Of course, just what constitutes "treatment" is a question that is difficult to answer. The survey included detoxification, drug maintenance (using medications

---

*For a discussion of these principles, see Chapter 6.

ACROSS
CULTURES

THE JAPANESE PRISON SYSTEM

In the Japanese correctional system, a detailed classification system is employed to assign newly sentenced offenders to individualized custody and treatment classes. In the case of custody, the classes range from Class A, which includes offenders who are considered to have "less advanced criminal inclinations" to Class B consisting of those with "more advanced criminal inclinations." Other classes are assigned to mental defectives, offenders sentenced to terms of 8 years or more, persons in ill health or aged, females and youthful offenders.

> Japanese prisons, unlike those in many other nations, are not overcrowded. . . . The trend in prison admissions has been decreasing or levelling in recent years. Given the increase in the [general] population . . . , there has been virtually no increase in terms of prisoners as a percentage of population. (p. 109)

The reported level of violence in Japanese prisons is quite low in comparison with the level in the United States. For example, in 1987 there were four homicides or serious assaults, three escapes, and only eight suicides. There were no attacks on correctional officers. These numbers when related to the total of 55,000 prisoners are quite significant.

The low rate of in-prison violence is of special interest since "only hard-core criminals [Class B] and those who have committed serious crimes are sent to prison" (p. 114). Most offenders are diverted from prison into various probation or other community-based programs.

> . . . [T]he general leniency shown by both the prosecutor and the judiciary tends to ensure that only hard-core offenders and those who commit particularly heinous crimes are sent to prison in the first place. (p. 117)

SOURCE: A. Didrick Castberg, *Japanese Criminal Justice* (Praeger, 1990).

such as methadone), counseling, education, urine surveillance, and assignment of inmates to special housing units. Surveillance and segregated housing probably would not qualify as treatment. Should segregation be accompanied by counseling, we might be justified in calling it part of a treatment regimen.

What should an adequate drug treatment regimen contain? Wexler and his colleagues conducted a national survey of prison programs. They found that for "successful" treatment, there must be:

- A clear institution structure that clearly defines and stresses rules and sanctions.
- Provision of "anticrime" attitude and behavior modeling.
- Assistance for inmate problem solving that is pragmatic rather than philosophical or theoretical.
- A committed and knowledgeable staff.

In reviewing the better treatment programs, they found that they succeed when inmates in treatment are segregated from the general prison population, and have been identified as requiring treatment at the time of their initial entry into the criminal justice system. Three crucial conditions that seem to make the major difference when comparing successful and unsuccessful prison treatment programs were found: (1) amount of time in treatment; (2) release to the community and not to the general prison population when treatment is completed; and (3) supervised release with continued treatment in the community.

The first two conditions may be of particular importance:

> Time in prison seems significantly to be related to successful outcome. Cocaine and heroin abusers do best after 9–12 months of treatment followed by supervised released and continued treatment. Those who enter treatment, complete it and are returned to the general prison population often relapse.[33]

Unfortunately, all three of these conditions of successful treatment are difficult for many correctional systems to meet. The structure of prison sentences often will not allow release to the community following the recommended 9–12 months of treatment. This, of course, is related to the position of the correctional institution in the criminal justice *system*, a position that is set by law and usually not negotiable.

Second, it may not be possible to segregate inmates throughout their confinement because of space and logistical problems. Finally, many states simply do not have the resources necessary to provide the supervision and treatment required during the postprison portion of offenders' sentences.

A more general impediment to a successful drug treatment program is the shortage of qualified and committed prison staff necessary to deliver and reinforce the treatment. When qualified in-prison staff are available, they frequently suffer from burnout, are transferred to other duties, or leave the service. As Wexler commented, it may be necessary to privatize the delivery of treatment programs by contracting them out while maintaining state management of prisons.[34] We will take up privatization of corrections programs later.

The Federal Bureau of Prisons (BOP) has developed a model for delivering drug treatment in its prisons that provides a major innovative approach toward a more effective treatment delivery system while trying to solve some of the problems noted by Wexler and others.[35] Two federal laws led to the development of the bureau's approach: the Narcotic Addict Rehabilitation Act of 1966 and the Anti-Drug Abuse Act of 1988. The former "provided that the BOP [Bureau of Prisons] would treat inmates known to be addicted to narcotics whose sentences did not exceed 36 months in length and whose offense met certain specifications."[36]

The 1988 statute "created resources for in-prison drug treatment programs."[37] With these two laws as authorization, between 1990 and 1993, the bureau set up programs in all of its institutions housing more than 500 inmates, in total, 30 institutions, ranging from minimum to maximum security.

In the BOP model, there is one organizational unit responsible for all in-prison drug treatment: the Residential Drug Abuse Program (RDAP). Inmates in the program go through three stages:

1. *Orientation.* A 1–3 month period during which participant-candidates are assessed and receive drug awareness education.
2. *Treatment phase.* Lasting between five and seven months, this phase requires an inmate to "confront" her or his deficits, which were identified in the orientation phase.
3. *Transitional phase.* This one-month phase "focuses on those skills that will be necessary for the inmate to successfully transition out of the residential program."[38]
There may be counterproductive elements in the third stage, since

> the inmate may be faced with reintegration into the general [prison] population, release to the community through a halfway house or on home confinement, or direct release to the

community. It is likely that an inmate will be called upon to transition through all of the above settings.[39]

Movement from the RDAP unit to the general prison population can result in loss of positive treatment effects as noted by Wexler earlier. Direct release into the community, unless accompanied by adequate supervision under appropriate conditions, may cause reentry shocks that reduce the program's effectiveness. Those released from treatment into the general population receive only one hour of counseling per month for 12 months. Inmates released through halfway houses or placed on home confinement are required to "participate in drug treatment programming as a requirement of their community release status."[40]

A new method of providing counseling and supervision for inmates on federal conditional release, the Comprehensive Sanctions Center (CSC), began in 1992. Several centers operate in sites throughout the country. In addition, more than two dozen "Enhanced Treatment Services" are provided in federally run halfway houses. All federal drug and substance abuse releasees identified as needing treatment and assigned to these halfway houses must participate in treatment.[41] At last report, about 19 percent of all "inmates residing in the community were receiving community-based drug treatment."[42] At this time, there are insufficient data upon which to assess the Bureau of Prisons' approach.

In another treatment development, Massachusetts has taken the lead in introducing treatment for another important substance abuse area, alcohol abuse.[43] The Massachusetts initiative was designed to treat repeat drunk drivers within the context of the state's 1982 law, "An Act to Increase the Penalties for Operating a Motor Vehicle While Under the Influence of Intoxicating Liquors." This statute was passed with the primary goal of increasing the certainty of punishment for offenders through mandatory imprisonment in county facilities. This get-tough policy severely taxed the capacity of these local institutions as the mandatory admissions took effect.

In order to relieve the pressure on local facilities and to provide more effective treatment than simple confinement, the state authorized three 100-bed facilities that would "help relieve overcrowding in the county houses of correction; and . . . provide offenders . . . with the appropriate counseling and treatment services."[44] Embedded in these centers were treatment regimens that included individual and group counseling, supervised recreation, and community-based work-release. The counseling component was privatized by contracting it out to Valle Associates.[45]

The state operates these programs while stressing that the centers are "secure" facilities and that their primary mission is detention of repeat offenders. This, obviously, is in response to the legislation mentioned earlier that seeks to increase the certainty of a punitive response to repeat drunk driving. The law clearly mandates confinement, and the treatment centers' staff accommodated themselves to this mandate.

The counseling strategy adopted was organized around group counseling methods long utilized in Alcoholics Anonymous and Reality Therapy programs. The counseling was contracted out to a private agency.[46] The first of these centers, the Longwood Treatment Center, was the subject of a preliminary evaluation. The most important findings were:

- Relatively few individuals completing the . . . Program and subsequently released . . . on a parole or a discharge are rearrested and returned to prison within 1 year of release.
- [Only] 8 percent of the Longwood program completers were returned to prison within 1 year. . . . This compares to a department-wide recidivism rate of 25

percent and to a rate of 14 percent for other low security institutions similar to . . . Longwood.[47]

Unfortunately, this evaluation does not tell us what the rate of program completion was, but the report did suggest a number of areas of concern that need to be addressed should the program be expanded. These concerns have to be dealt with in all correctional institution treatment programs, not just those for alcohol or drug abusing offenders. The more important concerns were:

1. A relatively high level of security was considered necessary, given the program's primary mission of incapacitation. The Longwood custodial staff-to-inmate ratio was very high, and this staff conducted no less than 36 counts of inmates each day! These counts frequently interrupted counseling sessions, reducing their effectiveness as well as irritating both counselors and inmates. As pointed out in Chapter 7, where we dealt with the treatment model in prison, secure custody and treatment are often contradictory missions.
2. Limited aftercare resources were available to continue counseling once inmates were released to the community.
3. One-on-one counseling generally was not possible except on an infrequent basis. The reason was a very high caseload for the counseling staff. This necessitated employment of group counseling as the primary treatment modality. Staff and inmates complained that this was not adequate to deliver the most effective treatment possible.

Sex Offender Programs

For a number of years, some correctional systems have provided special treatment programs for sex offenders. As noted in Chapter 7, state sexual psychopath statutes were adopted in this country beginning in the late 1930s. These statutes contained provisions for sentences either to special facilities or for specialized treatment in existing facilities. Maryland, in its "defective delinquency" law, specifically mandated special confinement and treatment for offenders who committed certain types of sex crimes.[48]

Recently there have been a number of examples of separate treatment of sex offenders that are quite different in scope and treatment direction. One of these programs is located in Oregon in the Snake River Correctional Institution.[49] This prison, the newest in the state's system, is classed as a "megaprison." It was designed to house 3,000 inmates when completed. Currently, only 360 beds are "funded for operation."[50] Today it is unusual to find prisons that are as specialized as Snake River. Of the beds currently being occupied, 98 percent are occupied by sex offenders.

The Snake River institutional counseling program was tied to the Oregon Sex Offender Supervision Network. This network was developed by the state to provide better supervision of sex offenders living in the community. Community supervision is carried out by probation and parole officers. Since reintegration of offenders into the community after a period of confinement and treatment is crucial to the success of any treatment regime, Oregon's approach seems to be a model to be studied carefully by other states. Sooner or later offenders will reach our streets. It would be unfortunate if there were no continuing treatment to assist them in making a successful adjustment.

Other Treatment Programs and Issues

Certain correctional programs are common to most prisons. Education at all levels from basic literacy through high school (and sometimes beyond), vocational training, and group and individual counseling are found, in one form or another. A major treatment issue is how to encourage inmates to become involved in these programs. The rehabilitation model discussed in Chapters 6 and 7 suggests that participation in treatment ought to be voluntary if it is to be effective. A related issue has to do with what should happen when an inmate enrolls in and successfully completes a correctional program.

Some argue that prisons should offer only **optional treatment** programs rather like elective courses in college. If an inmate believes he or she can benefit from an activity, then he or she should "go for it." Enforced participation, the argument goes, can never be as helpful as voluntary participation. As for any compensation for successful completion of a program, one can claim that completion should be reward enough. Those taking this position do so from the perspective of the medical or sick model. As soon as we connect another reward to treatment, such as early release from a prison sentence, don't we corrupt the program?

On the other hand, if a correctional treatment is really beneficial for inmates and society (in the sense that successful treatment will result in lowered recidivism),

A cell block on New York's Sing Sing Penitentiary shows several tiers of cells. Each prisoner must decide what skills to work on to facilitate their possible return to society. These decisions are constrained by the availability of programs.

should not **mandatory treatment** be the norm? In today's climate of "just deserts" or retributive justice, this approach to correctional treatment seems to be gaining ground. The initiative for this, it is claimed, came from then Supreme Court Chief Justice Warren Burger. In an address to law students at George Washington University in 1981, Burger called for, among other "reforms," "the encouragement or requirement for all inmates to become literate and acquire a marketable skill."[51]

A task force in the Federal Bureau of Prisons was appointed and charged with the further development of the Chief Justice's suggestion. The group produced a report, the Bogan Report which called for establishing "a comprehensive ABE [Adult Basic Education] policy which will require enrollment, while simultaneously encouraging meaningful participation."[52]

The bureau's first effort at implementing the task force recommendation was to set a sixth grade level of achievement on the Standard Achievement Test (SAT). This initial policy required "any Federal prisoner, with minor exceptions, who tested below [a sixth grade level] to enroll in a literacy program for 90 days."[53]

Compulsory participation was softened somewhat by allowing an inmate to refuse to participate or to drop out of the program once enrolled. However, those inmates choosing to do so are not promoted above the entry level work grade in either prison industries or general work assignments until they complete the program. Eventually, the standard was raised to eighth grade level. In order for inmates to reach the "top inmate jobs," successful completion of the GED is required. This was formalized as of March 1, 1989.

The idea of mandatory participation in at least some prison programs is said to be acceptable given certain core values in American culture. As one corrections administrator said:

> The model of having to meet some requirement in order to get something you want is so deeply embedded in our culture that it has an almost immediate acceptance, provided, of course, that the quid pro quo is perceived to be desirable, reasonable, and fair.[54]

This administrator argues that a correctional system needs to identify those inmate desires that are in the system's power to grant, and then coordinate these with what society will tolerate with respect to correctional policy and practice. While the federal program described above is limited to educational programs, we can reasonably argue that the *quid pro quo* concept may well be extended to a variety of treatment modalities.

Treatment of inmates with emotional or mental health disorders is another area of concern to corrections today. Prisons receive inmates who are mentally disturbed or who become disturbed sometime during their confinement. Prisons, typically, are not equipped to deal effectively with these inmates. One response is to transfer disturbed inmates to a state's mental health facility and treat them until they are well enough to be returned to prison.

Another strategy is to administer psychotropic medications, especially when behavior is exhibited that is threatening to the inmate or others. This treatment can present some disturbing issues. How are inmates selected for administration of medication? Should inmates be coercively medicated, or must they give informed consent prior to medication? Sommers and Baskin examined these and other issues related to medication of prison inmates.[55] Perhaps the most troubling issue has to do with the use of psychotrophic medication to control inmates rather than to assist in their treatment. Many who have reviewed this "trend have speculated that these drugs are valued more for their ability to reduce troublesome behavior and permit coercive control than for their therapeutic functions."[56]

Sommers and Baskin examined the use of medications from two perspectives: psychiatric (based on clinical characteristics) and social control (based on social characteristics). However, they say, the dichotomy is a false one since it "ignores the point that ultimately all psychotropic medication is prescribed to achieve control of the patient."[57] In their study, based on a 1986 survey of mental disability among New York state prison inmates, they observed that females, the unmarried, inmates convicted of violent crimes, inmates with prior mental heath commitments, or inmates with histories of committing violence against self and/or others were more likely to be medicated.

Among the reasons found for the higher rate of medication of women is "role incongruence." That is, since women are not supposed to exhibit bizarre or violent behavior, they tend to be segregated in mental heath residential settings in prison, while males, exhibiting similar behavior, tend to be placed in disciplinary segregation from the general population.[58]

Before leaving this section on correctional treatment programs, we need to look at the role of prison administrators who are in a position to support or thwart rehabilitation in their prisons. Often, wardens are judged or assumed to be antitreatment and, therefore, attempts to introduce or expand treatment activities are doomed to failure.

In a nationwide survey of prison administrators, Francis Cullen and his colleagues found that these administrators are more supportive of rehabilitation than had been thought.[59] The survey found that, while the "hegemony" of correctional rehabilitation was "shattered" in the 1970s as a result of many evaluation studies showing limited or negative results with regard to recidivism, wardens are still open to the idea of rehabilitation as a major goal of their institutions:

> Their [wardens'] common sense tells them that exposing offenders to life-enhancing, skills-imparting programs is likely to keep at least some of them on the straight and narrow. And their experiences confirm that, under certain conditions, some types of programs do improve the post-release prospects of the offenders who participate in them.[60]

Wardens clearly assign the highest priority to custody and security. Rehabilitation was considered important, but secondary to custody. Wardens "ranked incapacitation as the preferred goal of punishment . . . , rehabilitation was ranked second, and retribution lagged as the least supported . . . goal."[61]

As further evidence that wardens still support rehabilitation, the survey found that they rejected the abandonment of good-time laws,[62] parole, and indeterminate sentences. These views run counter to current sentencing practices that provide for mandatory minimum prison terms, determinate sentences, and abolition of parole. The wardens also supported expansion of educational and counseling programs. They did, however, support mandatory life sentences for habitual offenders and confinement at "hard labor" sentences.

Perhaps, the authors state, the wardens' support for hard labor, education, counseling, parole, and good-time may only indicate that they want to keep inmates busy and less unruly than if these were eliminated.

PRIVATIZING PRISONS: HISTORICAL OVERVIEW

One of the more controversial developments in corrections is the **privatization** movement, that is, turning over to the private sector many of the institutions and correctional functions that traditionally have been under the complete control of government. Many advocates believe that at least some of the problems confronting corrections today can be solved by reducing the level of public involvement and introducing the profit motive as a dynamic for needed change. Although some believe this to be a new and revolutionary idea, private sector involvement in corrections has had a long and often unsavory history. For a good portion of the nineteenth century and for some decades in the early twentieth century, inmate labor was made available to private contractors. The different models of private employment of inmate laborers included:

1. *Piece-price system.* In early penitentiaries, especially those run under the Pennsylvania and Auburn systems, manufacturers supplied raw materials and inmates produced the finished product for a fixed unit price.
2. *Contract system.* Contractors bid for use of inmate workers and prison facilities.
3. *Lease system.* Prisons leased out inmates to private contractors who were responsible for their security and room and board.
4. *Public works system.* Private contractors used inmates on publicly funded projects such as highway maintenance.

In the past the most common model was to have the private employer contract for a certain number of inmates, for a certain time, at a fixed rate specified in the contract. The contractor was responsible for inmate housing, food, and custody. This model was most useful to private enterprises engaged in construction work and, less frequently, in large-scale farming.

From reports of these early privatization efforts, we find that private contractors were mainly concerned with making the most profitable arrangements possible with the state. Humane treatment of inmates entrusted to them often was a very low priority. The state, naturally, was interested in relieving itself of the costs and burdens of full-time custody of its prison population. So contracting out at least a portion of the inmate population was advantageous both to the state and private entrepreneur. We might ask whether this system benefited prisoners. As one report concluded:

> . . . private sector involvement in corrections is unrelievedly bleak, a well-documented tale of inmate abuse and political corruption. In many instances, private contractors worked inmates to death, beat or killed them for minor rule infractions, or failed to provide them with the quantity and quality of life's necessities . . . , specified in meticulously drafted contracts.[63]

PRIVATIZATION TODAY

The many negative reports on the contract-labor system, together with the rise of labor unions, resulted in a decline in such private use of inmate labor. Recently, there has been a resurgence of interest in private sector involvement in corrections. Private enterprise has similar goals as before: a ready supply of workers that will help keep labor costs low, thus maximizing profits. For the state, cost-cutting is a major goal. It is assumed by many in and out of corrections that privatizing at least some of the state's traditional correctional functions and activities will save significant sums of money.

By 1987, three states had enacted laws permitting private operation of institutions. The Corrections Corporation of America (CCA) now operates one federal halfway house, two Immigration and Naturalization Service facilities, one maximum security jail, and one minimum security state prison. Over 36 states have contracts with private organizations for one or more correctional services.[64]

Proponents argue that the private sector can:

- Reduce correctional costs by 10-25 percent.
- Make it possible to enter the free market with prison–made products.
- Bring new ideas to a system plagued by inefficiencies and old, tired ideas.
- Infuse private expertise and personnel into prisons, which "normalizes" the prison environment.
- Allow inmates to earn real-world wages, thus supporting their dependents. Training and work experience are relevant to employment outside.
- Benefit taxpayers because inmates' dependents receive support, and inmates frequently pay at least a portion of their room and board.[65]

Opponents of privatization offer the following arguments:

- Private firms have no incentive to reduce prison populations since they are often paid on a per-inmate basis.
- Issues such as quality standards, use of force, and fiscal responsibility will require a mountain of regulation.
- The state has the "moral and constitutional duty" to administer corrections as part of the criminal justice system.

Dilulio's review of the status of privatization initiatives concluded that the cost benefits of the private sector have been greatly exaggerated:

> Less than three-quarters of a penny of every dollar of total government spending goes into corrections. Even if CCA [Corrections Corporation of America] and the other firms were willing to run every single facet of America's correctional complex for free, it would not produce significant relief in public expenditures. In the context of public spending generally, correction is an unpromising place to try to save money.[66]

Cost containment is especially difficult to achieve in maximum security institutions. These facilities are labor-intensive and the most expensive to operate. According to Dilulio, private firms have shown little interest in running them, preferring minimum security institutions.

The traditional use of inmate labor, prior to privatization, has been to fill the basic jobs necessary to the "housekeeping" of a prison: kitchen work, cleaning, laundry, and some maintenance chores. In addition, most states developed special **state-use industries** that produce goods primarily for sale to state agencies and nonprofit organizations. In the prison where the author worked, the state-use industry was a mattress factory. Inmates manufactured mattresses for prisons, the state university and colleges, and the state hospital system.

A discussion of state-use industrial activity could take an entire chapter. Suffice it to say that this system evolved out of a number of actual and perceived needs of prison administrators and their superiors in state and federal government. These needs included the provision of meaningful activity to an otherwise largely unemployed and potentially troublesome population, the need to bring in some revenue to defray the cost of operating a prison system, and to deliver vocational training and work experience that might be marketable in the world outside the correctional institution.

The state-use industries approach also was a response to a spate of federal and state laws that have severely restricted prison-made goods' access to markets outside prisons. Consistent opposition to prison-made products in the free market has come from private enterprises and labor unions. We can imagine the response of private mattress manufacturers should they find inmate-made products appearing in department stores in competition with their mattresses. As we will see below, there is at least one example of prison industrial involvement in the private marketplace.

We now turn to a discussion of those models of privatization that are currently in operation, or that recently have been tried in the United States. We can identify at least six models of privatization:

1. *Inmate ownership.* A major example of this model is the Resident Operated Business Enterprises (ROBE), operated under the regulation of a state board in the Arizona Department of Corrections. At its peak it employed 103 inmates who paid rent and utilities for their 52 enterprises, consisting primarily of handicrafts/services. The program was significantly reduced in scope; because "of inmate gang activity, ROBE became too difficult to administer."[67]

2. *Cooperative, joint venture.* Another Arizona corrections program employed inmates to manufacture wooden pallets. Thirty-six inmates produced $70,000 in sales in one year. The contract terminated because the private firm refused to pay minimum wages. Three other ventures are still operating, apparently without a wage problem.

3. *Private investor.* Still another Arizona model is one in which inmates manufactured office partitions and computer tables. Fifteen inmates were employed, grossing $700,000 in sales. A private firm invested in an in-prison shop. The program was terminated because of insufficient revenues from sales.

4. *Private employment.* The Best Western Reservations Center employed women inmates to assist its reservations center to cover especially busy travel seasons. On a given day inmates were 10 percent of the company's total domestic reservations staff. Each inmate pays 30 percent of her net wages for prison room/board, plus all relevant taxes, and considerable sums for dependent support. Over 170 inmates are involved. Some were given full-time employment upon release.

   The Trans World Airline reservations center in the California Youth Authority institution in Ventura offered inmates the same pay scale as their noninmate reservations clerks. The program almost came to an end when TWA flight attendants struck the company (TWA is the only unionized company to be involved in prison programs). Strikers claimed that the inmates were strike breakers.

5. *Prison industry, free market sales.* At the Stillwater Data Processing Center in Minnesota, customized computer programming, software development, and disk duplication services were provided, employing over a 12-year period hundreds of inmates with a gross payroll of $1.5 million.

6. *Subcontracting.* There are many examples of this model. It involves a corrections department contracting for certain program services, which can be medical, counseling, education, and food services. Earlier in the chapter we saw how Minnesota contracted in the private sector for drug counseling services.

How well does privatization work in American corrections? There have been relatively few evaluations comparing private versus public institutions or correctional services.[68] Evaluating the performance of any prison or prison system is extremely difficult regardless of whether we are dealing with private or public facilities and programs. Just what is a "quality" program? What criteria should be used to make judgments? How should performance criteria be measured? These are but a few of the questions that are raised when we try to rate institutions and programs.

In a major comparison of three prisons, one of which was privately run, Charles Logan used a number of evaluation criteria tied to the confinement model of incarceration. These criteria included: (1) security; (2) safety; (3) order; (4) care; (5) activity; (6) justice; (7) living conditions; and (8) management.

Logan's research found that on almost all the criteria, the private prison performed better than the other two institutions. On only one, care, was the private institution outperformed. In addition, the private facility was shown to reduce costs significantly. Prior to transferring the inmates to the new private prison, the per diem was $80; after the transfer, the fee paid to the private contractor was $69.75 per inmate.

There is a cautionary note to be added here. That is, the private institution was evaluated after it had been in operation for only six months. It is quite possible that its quality of performance may increase or decrease after a longer time period.

PRISON MANAGEMENT PROBLEMS

Crime and Law Enforcement

Prisons are known as places where violent crimes, drug violations, illegal gambling, and illicit sexual behavior occur every day. With the rapidly expanding populations of their institutions, with more offenders serving longer sentences, our prison administrators face a tough challenge. Enforcement of criminal laws in correctional institutions is a difficult job, but a necessary one. Not only is law enforcement important for maintaining order and ensuring the safety of staff and inmates, it may be crucial to the role of a prison sentence as deterrent to crime.

It is obvious that a correctional institution in which inmate (and, sometimes, staff) crime that is not under control by the administration represents a danger to all. What may not be so obvious is that such criminal activity can undermine the twin goals of a prison sentence: delivering deserved punishment to offenders, and using pains of imprisonment as a deterrent. If we incarcerate offenders because they violate the criminal law, and then they are confined in institutions where illegal activity is not punished and frequently may even be rewarded, the deterrent impact may well be reduced to nil.

The author once had some experience in a prison where illegal gambling was rampant. Inmates could wager on almost anything imaginable. All such activity was forbidden by regulations written into handbooks distributed to all inmates when they were admitted. Undeterred by these regulations, the informal inmate social structure included a large-scale gambling organization headed by an inmate known to all as the "big con." He had under him a network of runners who took wagers from inmates and distributed any winnings. Also under the gambling "czar" were a number of enforcers who dealt with inmates who would not or could not pay their gambling debts.

The gambling currency was cigarettes, and it was not uncommon for a few inmates to owe several cartons. While the prison staff was well aware of this illegal operation, official action was taken only when an inmate was so far in debt as to fear for his safety from the enforcers. Usually, this action took the form of transferring the indebted inmate to a protective custody tier. Disciplinary action was infrequently taken against the operatives of the gambling enterprise. Why? Because it was in the interest of the staff to accommodate to the informal inmate structure since it was to the mutual benefit of inmates and staff to maintain a relatively "quiet" institution.

Cracking down on the illegal operation could result in inmates reacting violently to a shutdown of a lucrative opportunity structure.

Here we see a classic structural contradiction at work. Offenders are sentenced to prison for their crimes, and when they arrive they see that success, in terms of the inmate culture, is earned through law-violating behavior, behavior winked at by the prison staff.

A major study of law enforcement (or, rather, law underenforcement) in state prisons was conducted by Eichenthal and Jacobs and reported on in 1991.[69] The findings were based on a survey of all state directors of corrections, and another of New York district attorneys in counties where there were state prisons. The major findings they reported were:

> The small number of convictions of prison inmates for crimes committed while incarcerated contrasts strikingly with reports of the prisons as dangerous environments pervaded by violence and extortion, drugs, robbery and theft, and the destruction of public property.[70]

The researchers conclude that a variety of serious crimes committed by prisoners, including assaults, drug trafficking, and destruction of property, are not viewed as a part of the country's "crime problem." When cases are referred for prosecution, the researchers found, prosecutors had discretion to decline to proceed. In California, for example, prosecution was accepted in only 12.5 percent of such cases. This represented ". . . between one-third and one-quarter their acceptance rate for crimes committed outside prison."[71]

Why so little prosecution?

- Prison officials are reluctant to refer problems to the outside. These problems can lead to embarrassing investigations by outside agencies.
- Lack of willing and credible witnesses.
- Lack of expertise on the part of investigators (outside police and corrections department internal affairs agents).
- There is no "constituency" to demand allocation of resources to investigate and pursue prosecutions.
- There are other sanctions available that do not require prosecution in state courts: segregation of inmate violators in punishment cells and loss of good-time sentence reduction credits.

Among the recommended actions to improve prosecution rates include transferring jurisdiction from local areas to the state attorneys general and the appointment of special prosecutors. Of course, these will only be implemented if the states are really interested in cracking down on crime in their prisons. In this regard, the survey concluded that "perhaps the failure to extend the criminal law into the prison reflects a conscious or unconscious judgment that inmates assume the risk of their own victimization, or that inmate victims are not 'real victims.' "[72]

Maintaining Order and Preventing Riots

For many correctional administrators and their staffs the most important task they must face is maintaining order. This is the bedrock upon which the confinement model rests. However, this is no simple task, as we will see in this section. In fact, order in penal institutions is more problematic now than ever before. Why is this so? One answer, obviously, is that prisons are receiving record numbers of prisoners, many of whom are serious drug abusers and others who are habitual or repeat offend-

*T*he violence, disor-der, and tumult of a prison riot is shown in the aftermath of a prison riot. This cell block was under inmate control during a riot.

ers serving mandatory sentences that are longer than in the past. Frequently, wardens must cope with this influx with reduced resources because of budgetary shortfalls. These are by no means the only reasons why prisons are often disorderly, violent institutions.

A more general, and possibly more important reason is the loss of control by correctional administrators, especially at the departmental and institutional levels. Agnes Baro has looked into this loss of control and found that,

> The present analysis argues that state government lacks the capacity to administer prisons, and that this lack of capacity explains the loss of local control over prisons more fully than does overcrowding or judicial activism.[73]

Much of this loss of control has resulted, according to Baro, from court intervention on behalf of inmate litigants:

> After years of seemingly endless litigation, the battle to maintain local control over prison administration has been lost. Operating under federal court scrutiny has become a reality of modern prison administration.[74]

To "comply" with court orders, monitoring has become a fact of life for corrections systems. Some are "in-house" monitors, others are court-appointed special masters. Both types meet resistance and studied noncompliance. In-house monitors are often considered disloyal, while the activities of outside monitors are seen as meddling by persons who are inexperienced in the realities of prison management.

There are a number of areas where resistance to court orders and compliance monitors frequently occurs, but it is most noticeable with regard to the use of physical force against inmates. It is here that there are significantly different perceptions by line staff and "outsiders" of the need for physical force, especially with regard to the safety of staff and inmates.

Litigation is also fueled by the lack of meaningful inmate grievance mechanisms. The 1981 Civil Rights Act (42 U.S.C. § 1997) permits federal courts to send suits back to the states for administrative proceedings. This is based on a generally agreed-upon formula that before an inmate can access the courts, he or she must exhaust all available administrative redress procedures. But the statute also provides that a Department of Justice "certified" grievance or other administrative mechanism must be in place. Absent such a mechanism, inmate plaintiffs have only the courts available to them. Six years after the law's enactment, only two states had met the certification requirement.

In Baro's study, she found that prison overcrowding is not a major stimulus of inmate litigation. This gives rise to an important question, "Why are state governments unable to regain control over prison administration?"[75]

There are several reasons why: (a) corrections administrators lack the commitment and ability to comply with court orders; (b) state executives lack the power and interest to exert pressure to produce the reforms needed to comply; (c) state legislatures are reluctant to exercise responsibility for overseeing prisons coupled with a failure to understand that prisons are a limited resource.

In the case of legislative indifference to their oversight responsibilities we note that they have used their authority to change sentencing laws and modify or eliminate parole, thus putting more pressure on their states' correctional systems, while often refusing to appropriate the funds necessary for them to carry out their mission. In a depressing conclusion, Baro says that,

> They [legislatures] give no indication that they will exercise their overseeing responsibilities in such a way as to demand that state prisons be operated in accordance with constitutional law.[76]

Prison Riots

One clear indicator of loss of control by prison management is rioting by inmates. Perhaps this is the greatest fear of the warden. Not only do riots threaten staff and inmate safety, the political repercussions are enormous for the system as well as the warden. More than 300 riots have been recorded in the U.S. since the first one in 1774, with 90 percent occurring since 1952.

A detailed examination of one major riot, which occurred in 1986 in West Virginia, offers us insight into the causes and possible prevention of prison rioting.[77] The authors suggest that, contrary to popular perception, "prisons are controlled with the tacit consent and through the active cooperation of the inmates."[78] Thus, attempting to control a prison, using only the coercive powers of the staff, is doomed to failure. There is in this fact a "paradox. . . . Institutional control cannot rely primarily on custodial force, over time inmates have exhibited a decreased willingness to exert controls over one another."[79]

Based on a review of studies of prison riots, the authors suggest several "conceptual models" of riots:

- *Environmental.* General prison conditions are most influential in stimulating many violent outbursts.
- *Spontaneity.* A spark, perhaps an incident involving punishment of an inmate, triggers a riot.
- *Conflict.* The repressive power of the prison staff reaches a critical mass.

- *Power vacuum.* Abrupt changes in formal control because of rapid or frequent personnel turnover. No clear line of authority is evident.
- *Rising expectations.* Prison conditions have improved, leading to expectations of additional changes that are not forthcoming.

The authors point out that a more general cause can be identified when there exists significant prison administrative line-staff conflict that arises when corrections engages in "goal hopping." That is, when the corrections mission changes from custody to treatment, from controlling to changing behavior, and then returns to custody and control.[80] This can make a fertile environment for violent disturbances.

The West Virginia riot resulted from a number of events: court-ordered reforms setting up rising expectations; failure of the system to comply; frequent replacements of wardens, finally with one with whom staff and inmates had major disagreements; and seriously defective administrative decisions vis à vis custodial staffing and security arrangements on the eve of the riot. As a result, inmates apparently seemed to believe that any changes would be for the worse, thus their interest in maintaining control was eroded.

> Two factors played major roles in the riot. First, the long history of unfulfilled promises of change developed rising expectations and a strong sense of perceived deprivation among the inmates. . . . The second and final ingredient was a power vacuum which seems not to have been present until the time of the riot.[81]

Regardless of what specific factors triggered the West Virginia riot, or any prison riot, the analysis clearly shows the tightrope that correctional administrators must walk in order to maintain order in a population that is coercively under their care.

Other Order-Maintenance Problems

The emergence of gangs among prison populations is a major factor in violence and illegal inmate activity. Gang formation may have originated as a means used by some inmates to provide protection from other inmates. However, as Fong and Buentello observed:

> The emergence of prison gangs has added to the crisis already being experienced by many correctional systems. Prison gangs pursue more than self-protection; they have evolved into organized crime syndicates involved in such activities as gambling, extortion, drug-trafficking, prostitution, and contract murder.[82]

Correctional workers from wardens to custodial front-line officers need to be aware of this phenomenon, identify gangs and their members, and take effective action to counter their damaging activities. An obvious remedial action that must be taken is to end the underenforcement of criminal law that is characteristic of the prison scene.

We must take up one more area of concern with regard to the maintenance of prison order: the impact of newer life without possibility of parole (LWOP) sentences, and sentences of the "three strikes and you're out" formula, which have serious consequences for the corrections administrator and staff. Increasing numbers of offenders are admitted to prisons each year under these sentences. What are some of the consequences for correctional systems? After all, prisons cannot refuse to receive those sentenced by trial courts. A study by Sigler and Culliver looked at some of the effects already felt and those anticipated to be felt in Alabama following passage of a habitual offender statute in 1980.[83]

Looking at construction costs, it was estimated that the statute will require the state to add thousands of beds to accommodate the growth in LWOP inmates. "This projection assumes a term of incarceration of 40 years,"[84] based on the average age of 32 for those so sentenced.

> In sum, the Alabama Department of Corrections will need to build and maintain a minimum of 4,116 new beds or 10 new 400-bed institutions to accommodate these new inmates in addition to added prison construction to house any natural increase in the inmate population which can be expected as the population of the state increases.[85]

At the time Sigler and Culliver looked at the impact of the new sentencing law, LWOP prisoners were "maintaining a low profile and quiet adjustment in hope of qualifying for parole when the . . . act is overturned. . . ."[86] Apparently, these inmates believed that the act would be repealed because the state could not afford it over the long run. Corrections administrators are not so sanguine, and the optimistic inmate attitude may not last.

> All inmates indicated that at the present time they would not become involved in a riot; however, the LWOP-habitual offenders indicated they would engage in planning a riot to establish basic inmate rights or to pressure the . . . administration if conditions . . . became too unacceptable to them.[87]

It is clear that corrections systems facing an increase in lifers without hope of parole will need to be more security-conscious than they already are. More custodial staff and enhanced technology and construction attuned to the threat these inmates pose will inevitably be required. We can only offer our sympathy to the wardens in those systems where life without parole sentences are in force.

Unit Management

With all the problems confronting corrections systems discussed above, are there any effective steps that can be taken to regain control of our prisons and help fulfill their correctional mission? In the discussion above, a number of steps were suggested: more effective oversight by state legislatures, compliance with court orders, consistent and fair administration by corrections leaders and line staff, and awareness of the impact changing sentencing policies and practices have on the day-to-day operations of the prison.

However, these steps, even if taken, may be inadequate to ease the pressure on our prisons. A relatively new approach offers some hope for real improvement: the "unit management" style of prison administration. This concept first appeared in the literature in a 1973 article by Levinson and Gerad,[88] and the unit management system was introduced into Maryland's Patuxent Institution in the 1970s. Recalling the discussion of new generation jails in Chapter 5, we see that prison unit management bears a close relationship to the direct supervision style characteristic of newer "podular" jails.

Unit management includes subdividing large correctional institutions into several small "functional" units,

> operating in semi-autonomous fashion. . . . The concept is operationalized by housing about 50–100 inmates together in one physical area (preferably) and keeping them together for as long as possible. . . . The inmate groups . . . are supervised by a preferably group-specific, multidisciplinary management team.[89]

This reorganization was Massachusetts' response to an extremely violent prison environment at its Walpole State Prison (subsequently renamed the Massachusetts

Correctional Institution: Cedar Junction), reportedly one of the most violent in the nation. According to a study of the results of the unit management system, the prison still suffers from overcrowding, but "there is much less violence and fear."[90]

Introducing such a major overhaul of prison structure is, of course, no easy matter. In the Massachusetts case, violent disorder had reached the stage at which it simply could not be ignored. The state's political and corrections leadership reached a consensus on the need for radical reform. They also called in correctional consultants who carefully studied the situation and then recommended implementation of the unit management system. Also carefully attended to was convincing the prison staff that the proposed administrative changes would be in their best interest.

Super Maximum Security Prisons

Another structural response to both increased violence in prison and the influx of prisoners with long sentences is the super maximum security prison (**super-max prisons**). According to the National Institute of Justice, twenty-seven state departments of corrections operate prisons or units within their prisons that can be described as super maximum security or "maximum-maximum" facilities. Another six states are contemplating building these institutions.[91]

The first super-max institution was Alcatraz, opened as a federal prison in 1934 (in its prior life as a prison it housed military offenders) to hold the Bureau of Prison's "difficult to handle" inmates in one location. Now that Alcatraz is simply a crumbling tourist attraction, the federal government has turned to a new facility specifically designed to confine those offenders classified as requiring the highest level of security. The new institution, the Administrative Maximum Penitentiary (ADX) located in Florence, Colorado, has beds for 562 men. Over 90 percent of the inmates in this prison have been transferred from other institutions where they were considered particularly difficult to handle.

Sixty-eight cells are set aside in the "control unit," where the strictest discipline and isolation are maintained.[92]

> To be placed in this unit, inmates must appear before a due process hearing. In this unit, inmates are in their cells 23 hours a day. They eat in their cells. They are permitted to recreate seven hours per week. Each cell is 90 square feet.[93]

This regimen sounds very much like that of the Pennsylvania and Auburn systems of incarceration we discussed in Chapter 6. Those systems, abandoned over a century ago, are now resurrected in the federal and some state corrections systems.

The severity of security in the federal super-max prison's control and other units is further enhanced by physical means:

> Control unit inmates . . . are cuffed and leg shackled before they leave their cell. Three officers escort each control unit inmate. General population unit inmates are cuffed from behind for all movement and require a two-person escort.[94]

At this federal super-max institution, there is a graded system of housing and activity for the majority of inmates who have not been placed in the control unit. This system, while maintaining maximum security, does permit inmates to work, have more recreation time, and some interpersonal contact with one another.

According to one study, the super-max experience has shown that prison violence can be reduced significantly, with assaults and murders of staff and inmates declining dramatically.[95] In another study of over 1,000 inmates who experienced super-max confinement prior to the opening of the Florence federal facility, two potentially significant results were obtained: (1) "very few of these inmates suffered major mental health problems"; and (2) "half of them [from Alcatraz] never returned to prison."[96] While these results may be used to support more super-max prisons, the author of the latter study cautions that the "aging process" may have a "major share of the credit" for the apparent success of these institutions.[97]

A surge of litigation has accompanied the super-max movement. The issues of sensory deprivation and limits on inmate access to attorneys have been subject to court action, although to date, inmates have not won on these issues. In Chapter 10 we will look at prisoners' rights, including those involving super-max inmates.

We also must be aware of the serious cost penalty a super-max institution imposes on a state's correctional system. This penalty is directly related to the labor-intensive nature of the security required. Using two or three correctional officers to escort each inmate moving out of his cell is extremely, perhaps inordinately, expensive. Because of the newness of these prisons, it will be some time before we can evaluate them in terms of what society gets for its money.

INMATES WITH SPECIAL NEEDS

Recently, attention has been focused on the problems facing the prison administrator who must house increasing numbers of inmates with special needs. These inmates include those who are HIV-infected, others with physical and mental disabilities, and the elderly.

HIV-Infected Inmates

No one knows with any confidence just how many U.S. prison inmates are infected with the HIV virus. A 1993 survey conducted under the auspices of the Bureau of Justice Statistics found that 2.4 percent of federal and state prison inmates (21,538) were HIV positive. Of these, 3,765 had confirmed AIDS, and an additional 2,312 "showed lesser symptoms of infection."[98] "Confirmed AIDS cases in state and federal prisons grew . . . [by] 124%" between 1991 and 1993.[99] The number of deaths related to AIDS is climbing significantly, according to this study. In 1993, 760 inmates died from "pneumocystis carinii pneumonia, Karposi's sarcoma, or other AIDS-related diseases. . . ."[100] This number reflects a 46 percent increase over the 1991 totals.

Because HIV infection is fast becoming a major problem for corrections, we now examine the steps that are being taken to cope with it. The survey mentioned above found that in all correctional institutions in the United States, HIV testing is done on at least some inmates, and in 17 all inmates were tested. Most frequently, testing was done if an inmate showed "HIV-related symptoms, "or at the inmate's request." Twenty states tested those inmates who belonged to certain identified (not specified in the report) "high risk groups."[101] Because of the unsystematic use of screening tests, it is impossible to know whether the numbers of HIV-infected inmates reported above represent a high, middle, or low estimate of the actual infection rate in the U.S. prison population.

Taking certain precautions to limit the spread of HIV infection throughout a prison population would seem to be an obvious and high-priority step for the correctional administrator. Testing inmates, segregating those who test positive from the general prison population, and providing proper treatment for at least those who show signs of full-blown AIDS certainly qualify as precautionary measures. There are, however, a number of problems with their introduction in a correctional institution. One problem is cost. Each one of these measures will add significantly to a prison's operating costs. This is especially true with respect to testing and treatment. Given the current availability of medication, we know that the costs involved will be extremely high.

A host of legal problems confront the administrator who wishes to implement these precautions. Is segregation of HIV- positive inmates unconstitutional, in violation of the prohibition against cruel and unusual punishment? If inmates are to be subjected to mandatory blood tests, will this violate their Fourth Amendment right to be protected from unreasonable searches and seizures? If inmates are tested and found to be infected, who is authorized to have this information? In other words, does an infected inmate have a right to privacy with regard to her or his medical record?

A number of state and federal court cases have been brought by inmates in each of these legal areas. Currently, the case law seems to require corrections systems to implement measures that bear a reasonable relationship to "a legitimate penological interest."[102] A number of states have responded to inmate challenges to prison practices by enacting statutes that limit corrections' liability with regard to HIV infection. In future, such inmate-initiated litigation is unlikely to result in major changes in the way prisons currently deal with HIV and AIDS- related issues.

> Chances are that challenges using alleged violations of constitutional rights will diminish as legal questions concerning AIDS continue to be covered by state statutes. . . . These statutes are seldom declared unconstitutional by the courts, unless [they] deprive an inmate of a basic constitutional right and are not related to a legitimate penological interest. This is a heavy burden for an inmate-plaintiff to carry and does not augur well for those who believe that prisoners with AIDS deserve more rights and better protection.[103]

What we don't know from the available research is the extent to which the HIV virus is transmitted through a prison population by way of sexual contact. Transmission through sharing intravenous needles may be controlled through random searches for contraband. Attempts to segregate inmates who test positive from the general population may reduce sexual transmission. But, since testing for HIV is not done consistently on all inmates, this control mechanism is not likely to be particularly effective. Perhaps distribution of condoms would be a more effective strategy.

Disabled Inmates

Until recently, there has been relatively little attention paid to the special needs raised by disabled inmates and what corrections must do to meet them. The 1990 Americans with Disabilities Act (ADA), however, has changed the landscape.

> Programs offered to inmates must be accessible. If, for example, a hearing-impaired inmate wishes to attend Alcoholics Anonymous meetings, the corrections facility would need to make reasonable modifications that permit the inmate to participate in a meaningful way.[104]

The prison administrator, under the provisions of the law, may not confine disabled inmates separately from the general population, "unless they specifically request such an accommodation."[105]

When a correctional system provides programs in which inmate participation may lead to some benefit such as early release, they must be examined in light of their applicability to the physically or mentally disabled. Shock incarceration is one of these. Corrections officials need to evaluate such program offerings or requirements and, if necessary, provide equivalent alternative opportunities for disabled inmates.

The ADA also requires action from corrections officials with regard to the developmentally disabled as well as those disabled because of mental illness. The statute requires each facility to determine whether there are inmates who qualify as mentally or developmentally disabled.[106] If such inmates are identified, the institution's programs must be evaluated in terms of their accessibility to the disabled.

Determination of who in a prison population are "qualified" as disabled (physically, mentally, or developmentally) is a difficult task for the administrator and staff. The law provides this (not very helpful) guidance:

> A "qualified individual with a disability" means an individual who, with or without reasonable modifications to rules, policies, or practices, the removal of architectural, communication, or transportation barriers, or the provision of auxiliary aids and services, meets the essential eligibility requirements for the receipt of services . . . provided by the public entity [i.e., prison].[107]

We can expect litigation to be generated because of violations of some of the ADA's provisions should "qualified" inmates allege that they cannot access various programs. We will see in Chapter 10 that such allegations must meet the Supreme Court's test regarding possible mistreatment of prisoners, that test being that a prison's indifference to the needs of inmates must be shown to be "deliberate."[108]

Senior Citizen Inmates

Mandatory sentences, longer sentences, abolition of parole in many states, and the use of life without parole sentences have resulted in increasing numbers of seniors

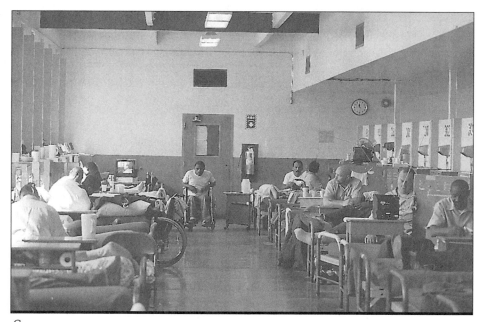

*S*tate prisons are not always equipped to house large numbers of elderly and infirm prisoners. Terminally ill, disabled, or Alzheimer's disease patients could all be stored in the same prison dormitory.

SUGGESTIONS

YOUR CONCERN IS OUR CONCERN

DESCRIBE IN DETAIL YOUR IDEA

_____

_____

_____

_____

_____

_____

_____

DESCRIBE THE BENEFITS DERIVED FROM
YOUR IDEA

_____

_____

_____

_____

_____

_____

_____

OTHER COMMENTS OR SUGGESTIONS

_____

_____

_____

_____

NAME _____

VERTIFLEX COMPANY   50001

serving time in state and federal prisons. A recent calculation found that 27,532 inmates are between 55 and 75 years of age, and 701 are over 75 years of age. It is estimated that by the year 2000, "the number of long-term prisoners over 50 will be approximately 125,000 with 40,000 to 50,000 over 65 years of age."[109]

These numbers mean that corrections systems must make a number of major and expensive adjustments:

> Issues such as providing special diets and round-the-clock nursing care, building new facilities or altering old ones, and restructuring institutional activities are becoming more frequent topics of discussion.[110]

It may be necessary to consider special geriatric units within existing prisons, and even moving some elderly and infirm inmates to hospices or secure nursing homes beyond the prison walls. These potential moves in addition to the added burden of meeting the medical and health needs of the senior prisoner will not only result in increased costs, but also will complicate already difficult management problems of institutional officials and community supervision workers such as probation and parole officers.

SUMMARY

PRISONS TODAY FACE WHAT MIGHT BE a nearly insurmountable task: somehow to meld humane, safe confinement and correctional programming within the context of ever expanding populations of drug offenders and other serious criminals who will be serving longer mandatory sentences. Prison administrators cannot avoid this task. They are at the low end of the criminal justice pecking order. What sentencing judges send them, under the authority of sentencing statutes and guidelines, they must accept.

Our prisons, never particularly safe institutions, now confront the threat of violence every day. Their wardens, as we have seen, still are supportive of rehabilitation as one of their missions. Now, however, this mission clearly is not a priority. Secure confinement is.

A number of adjustments are being tried in corrections. One is to restructure some institutions through the unit management system. Another is to identify especially troublesome inmates and place them in super-max facilities and units. While many wardens support rehabilitative programs, the actual number that are ongoing is limited by virtue of scarce resources and the priority necessarily assigned to security, custody and the maintenance of order.

This is particularly unfortunate with regard to the large number of drug and substance abuse offenders now making up such a large percentage of commitments. We have seen some progress in this regard, such as the programs initiated in the Federal Bureau of Prisons and in Massachusetts. These types of programs, however, are few and far between.

Another approach to the many problems facing corrections is to privatize entire penal institutions or at least some of their activities. We saw that some state prison systems have opted to privatize by contracting for services from organizations such as the Corrections Corporation of America. Others have turned entire institutions over to private operators. At this time, it is unclear just how successful these efforts have been. Some preliminary studies suggest that some private operators and service providers can save the state money, and others may be able to improve prison conditions. We do not yet know the effects on recidivism.

We quoted former Federal Bureau of Prisons official Benjamin Frank at the beginning of this chapter by noting that the American prison is frequently "rediscovered." An appropriate way to end the chapter is to return to Frank:

> Corrections has been caught in an inescapable dilemma. On the one hand, the major obstacle to effective correctional programs is due largely to inherited notions that equate crimes to moral and psychological illness which demanded institutional confinement; on the other hand, the variation and rates of crime are due more to conditions that produce crime: high unemployment, irrelevant education, racism, poor education, family disintegration, and government corruption. The way out of this dilemma lies in the repudiation of the prison as useless for any purpose other than locking away persons who are too dangerous.[111]

KEY CONCEPTS

Confinement model

Mandatory treatment

New penology

Optional treatment

Privatization

Selective incapacitation

State-use industries

Super-max prisons

Unit management

QUESTIONS FOR DISCUSSION

1. What do the differential rates of incarceration for blacks and whites tell us about the criminal justice system performance?
2. Critically discuss the "confinement model" of incarceration in terms of the many problems facing corrections administrators and staff.
3. Given current sentencing policies and practices, how can the American prison deliver appropriate programs and services for drug and substance abusing offenders? Keep in mind the criteria for successful treatment programs.
4. Critically review the efforts of corrections to prevent the spread of HIV infection and AIDS in prison populations.
5. The super-max prison is becoming increasingly popular. Critically evaluate its place in contemporary penal practice.
6. Unit management is one suggested strategy to gain more effective control over prison populations. What are its promises and what are the problems facing those who want to implement it?
7. Discuss some of the unintended consequences of underenforcement of criminal law in prisons.

ENDNOTES

1. Benjamin Frank, "The American Prison: The End of an Era," *Federal Probation* 43 (1979): 3–9.
2. For descriptions and evaluation of "scared straight" programs see James O. Fickenauer, *Scared Straight and the Panacea Phenomenon* (Prentice-Hall, 1982).

3. Malcom M. Feeley and Jonathan Simon, "The New Penology: Notes on the Emerging Strategy of Corrections and Its Implications," *Criminology* 30 (1992): 449.

4. Ibid.

5. Ibid., p. 457.

6. Charles H. Logan, "Well Kept: Comparing Quality of Confinement in Private and Public Prisons," *Journal of Criminal Law & Criminology* 83 (1992): 580.

7. American Correctional Association, *1995 Directory of Juvenile and Adult Correctional Departments, Institutions, Agencies, and Paroling Authorities,* p. xxii.

8. Darrell K. Gilliard and Allen J. Beck, *Prisoners and Jail Inmates, 1995,* Washington, D.C. U.S. Department of Justice, Bureau of Justice Statistics, *Bulletin,* August 1996, p. 1.

9. Ibid., p. 2.

10. Ibid, p. 7

11. Gwyn Smith Ingley, "Fiscal and Operational Impact of Three-Strikes Legislation," *Corrections Today* 57 (August 1995): 26.

12. Gilliard and Beck, *Prisoners in 1994,* p. 10.

13. Ibid., p. 11.

14. Gilliard and Beck, *Prisoners in 1993,* National Institute of Justice, June 1994, p. 7.

15. Ibid.

16. Harry K. Wexler, Douglas S. Lipton, and Bruce D. Johnson, "A Criminal Justice System Strategy for Treating Cocaine-Heroin Abusing Offenders in Custody," in Larry J. Siegel, ed., *American Justice: Research of the National Institute of Justice* (St. Paul, MN: West Publishing Company, 1990): pp. 254–269.

17. Stephen B. Duke and Albert B. Gross, *America's Longest War: Rethinking Our Tragic Crusade Against Drugs* (New York: G. P. Putnam's Sons, 1993). For a review essay of this book, see Randy E. Barnett, "Bad Trip: Drug Prohibition and the Weakness of Public Policy," *Yale Law Journal* 103 (June 1994): 2593–2630.

18. Darrell K. Gilliard and Allen J. Beck, *Prisoners in 1993,* National Institute of Justice, June 1994, p. 7.

19. Ibid.

20. Bureau of Justice Statistics, "Correctional Populations in the United States," *Executive Summary* (April 1995): 1.

21. Ibid.

22. Gilliard and Beck, *Prisoners in 1993,* p. 8.

23. Ibid.

24. American Correctional Association, *1995 Directory of Juvenile and Adult Correctional Departments,* p. xxxii.

25. Feeley and Simon, "The New Penology," pp. 467–468.

26. *Task Force Report on Corrections,* 1967, p. 6.

27. Feeley and Simon, "The New Penology," pp. 449–474.

28. Ibid., p. 468.

29. Robert A. Buchanan, Karen L. Whitlow, and James Austin, "National Evaluation of Objective Prison Classification Systems: The Current State of the Art," *Crime & Delinquency* 32 (1996): 272–291.

30. American Correctional Association, *Directory of Juvenile and Adult Correctional Departments,* p. xxii.

31. Caroline Wolf Harlow, "Drug Enforcement and Treatment in Prisons, 1990," BJS, *Special Report* July 1992. We should note that while seven of eight surveyed institutions screened inmates for drug use, this testing is not always comprehensive. Thus, we may never know the prevalence of drug use while incarcerated.

32. Wexler, Lipton, and Johnson, "A Criminal Justice System Strategy," pp. 254–269.

33. Ibid., p. 258.

34. Ibid., p. 261.

35. Sharon D. Stewart, "Community-Based Drug Treatment in the Federal Bureau of Prisons," *Federal Probation* 58 (June 1994): 24–28.

36. Ibid., p. 24.

37. Ibid.

38. Ibid., p. 25.

39. Ibid.

40. Ibid.

41. Ibid., p. 27.

42. Ibid.

43. Daniel P. LeClaire, "The Use of Prison Confinement in the Treatment of Drunken Drivers," *Federal Probation* 52 (December 1988): 46–51.

44. Ibid., p. 47.

45. Ibid., p. 48.

46. Ibid., p. 49.

47. Ibid., pp. 49–50.

48. For a detailed discussion of the provisions of this law, see Chapter 7.

49. Thomas L. Lester, "Sex Offender Facility Committed to Change and Rehabilitation," *Corrections Today* 57 (April 1995): 168–171.

50. Ibid., p. 168.

51. Quoted in Sylvia G. McCollum, "Mandatory Programs in Prison—Let's Expand the Concept," *Federal Probation* 54 (June 1990): 33.

52. Ibid.

53. Ibid., p. 34.

54. Ibid.

55. Ira Sommers and Deborah R. Baskin, "The Prescription of Psychiatric Medications in Prison: Psychiatric versus Labeling Perspectives," *Justice Quarterly* 7 (1990): 739–755.

56. Ibid., p. 739.

57. Ibid., p. 741.

58. Ibid., p. 753.

59. Francis T. Cullen, et al., "The Correctional Orientation of Prison Wardens: Is the Rehabilitative Ideal Supported?" *Criminology* 31 (1993): 69–92.

60. Quoting John Dilulio, Jr., *No Escape: The Future of American Corrections* (New York: Basic Books, 1991), p. 107.

61. Cullen, et al., "Correctional Orientation of Prison Wardens," p. 80.

62. These are laws that provide for reductions in length of sentences based on good behavior while incarcerated. States very sharply with regard to the amount of reduction. Where the author worked, inmates received 10 days" "good time" for each month served.

63. John J. Dilulio, Jr., "Private Prisons," in Larry J. Siegel, ed., *American Justice: Research of the National Institute of Justice* (St. Paul, MN: West Publishing Company, 1990): p. 340.

64. Ibid., p. 238.

65. Barbara J. Auerbach, et al., "Work in Prisons: The Private Sector Gets Involved," in Larry S. Siegel, ed., *American Justice: Research of the National Institute of Justice*, pp. 243–253.

66. Ibid., p. 240.

67. Ibid., p. 247.

68. For a summary review of some of the few studies, see Logan, "Well Kept," pp. 577–579.

69. David R. Eichenthal and James B. Jacobs, "Enforcing the Criminal Law in State Prisons," *Justice Quarterly* 8 (1991): 283–303.

70. Ibid., p. 284.

71. Ibid., p. 287.

72. Ibid., p. 302.

73. Agnes Baro, "The Loss of Local Control over Prison Administration," *Justice Quarterly* 5 (1988): 457.

74. Ibid.

75. Ibid., p. 467.

76. Ibid., p. 470.

77. Randy Martin and Sherwood Zimmerman, "A Typology of the Causes of Prison Riots and an Analytical Extension to the 1986 West Virginia Riot," *Justice Quarterly* 7 (1990): 711–737.

78. Ibid., p. 721.

79. Ibid.

80. Ibid., p. 722.

81. Ibid., p. 732.

82. Robert S. Fong and Salvador Buentello, "The Detection of Prison Gang Formation: An Empirical Assessment," *Federal Probation* 54 (March 1991): 66.

83. Robert Sigler and Concetta Culliver, "Consequences of the Habitual Offender Act on the Costs of Operating Alabama's Prisons," *Federal Probation* 52 (June 1988): 57–64.

84. Ibid., pp. 59–60.

85. Ibid., p. 61.

86. Ibid., p. 62.

87. Ibid., p. 63.

88. Robert B. Levinson and Roy E. Gerad, "Functional Units: A Different Correctional Approach," *Federal Probation* 37 (December 1973): 8–16.

89. J. Forbes Farmer, "A Case Study in Regaining Control of a Violent State Prison," *Federal Probation* 52 (March 1988): 45.

90. Ibid., p. 46.

91. National Institute of Justice, "Topical Survey: Super-Max Facilities and Units," *Summary for Corrections Administrators* (Winter 1993).

92. John N. Vanyur, "Design Meets Mission at New Federal Max Facility," *Corrections Today* 57 (July 1995): 91.

93. Ibid.

94. Ibid., p. 93.

95. Ibid.

96. David A. Ward, "A Corrections Dilemma: How to Evaluate Super-Max Regimes," *Corrections Today* 57 (July 1995): 108.

97. Ibid.

98. Peter M. Brien and Caroline Wolf Harlow, "HIV in U.S. Prisons and Jails, 1993," Bureau of Justice Statistics, *Bulletin,* August 1995, p. 1.

99. Ibid., p. 3.

100. Ibid., p. 6.

101. Ibid., p. 5.

102. Barbara A. Belbot and Rolando V. del Carmen, "AIDS in Prison: Legal Issues," *Crime & Delinquency* 37 (1991): 138. This article reviews the available case law in a number of areas encompassing the precautionary measures discussed here.

103. Ibid., p. 151.

104. Paula N. Rubin, "Questions Most Frequently Asked about the ADA by Criminal Justice Professionals," *Journal of the National Institute of Justice* (November 1994): 41.

105. Ibid.

106. Paula N. Rubin and Susan W. McCampbell, "The Americans with Disabilities Act and Criminal Justice: Mental Disabilities and Corrections," National Institute of Justice, *Research in Action* (September 1995).

107. Ibid., p. 2.

108. Ibid., p. 4.

109. Ronald H. Aday, "Golden Years behind Bars: Special Programs and Facilities for Elderly Inmates," *Federal Probation* 58 (June 1994): 47.

110. Ibid.

111. Frank, "The American Prison," p. 8.

WOMEN IN PRISON

INTRODUCTION AS SOON AS WE WERE DROPPED OFF in the prison van, they showered and deloused us and fingerprinted us and then, before the doctors had even examined us we were each given a small yellow pill . . . just to help us stay calm while we adjusted to the place we were told. I said I didn't think I needed it and the nurse responded, now don't be a troublemaker before you even get all registered. We were all supposed to take pills every day. They were supposed to be vitamins and calcium supplements but I know I felt a lot slower when I took them and I tried to hide them and not take them because they scared me.[1]

This quote is from a woman inmate describing her admission to a midwestern state prison. It reveals a good deal about how female inmates are perceived by prison staff. They are seen as potential troublemakers, unduly anxious, and are given what appears to be tranquilizers to calm them down and thus make them more manageable.

In this chapter we will see that imprisoned women suffer certain pains not suffered by men. Separation from children and outside support from family and friends affect women particularly hard. Women seek to compensate for this by establishing "quasi-families" in prisons. These offer a measure of emotional security that otherwise would be lacking. This stands in stark contrast to the situation in many men's institutions where gang formation is common, as we saw in the last chapter.

Correctional programs in women's institutions are frequently in short supply. Those that are available are often of little help in assisting women make a successful transition to life outside. The author remembers his first visit to a women's prison, then called the Women's Reformatory, now called the Women's Correctional Institution. The "industrial" area consisted of row after row of sewing machines at which many women were employed making clothing for themselves and others in the state's correctional system. In another room, cosmetology classes were being held. Here, women were learning the skills necessary to beautify the appearance of other women. These two activities, so focused on the then-accepted gender-appropriate roles of women in the workplace, together with some basic education classes, were the only "correctional" programs available for about 250 women. This was in sharp contrast to the men's prison where the author worked for several years. That prison offered, in addition to academic and vocational classes, a variety of work-related programs and activities. There was a mattress factory and a number of shops for training and employing inmates in carpentry, sheet metal fabrication, and auto repair.

As we will see, the shortage of programs for female inmates is related to at least two factors: **gender stereotyping** and economics. Women make up only about 6 percent of the prison population nationwide. How should state and federal corrections systems deliver additional services to such a small proportion of their inmate populations? Greater expenditures on women's prisons may come at the expense of reductions in outlays for the much larger population of male inmates. **Economies of scale** often dictate the resultant shortchanging of women's programs.

This chapter discusses the controversy about the call for "equality" of women's prisons and programs with those for men, versus recognizing that the problems and needs of female inmates are significantly different from those of males. As one women's prison superintendent put it, "in America, we have gotten caught up in arguments of equality but can seldom define equality or even *equal to what*."[2]

This controversy is deeply embedded in our criminal justice system. Nagel and Johnson pointed this out in their analysis of the role gender plays in sentencing, especially under sentencing guideline systems.[3] They sought to determine whether, under sentencing guidelines that are designed mainly to reduce sentence disparities, women continue to receive "lenient" sentences. Research on sentencing practices prior to the onset of guidelines has consistently concluded that female offenders have been given "preferential" treatment by presentence report writers and sentencing judges.[4] Contrary to the views of some, the application of structured sentencing guidelines such as those in the federal system has not removed this preferential treatment of women. Nagel and Johnson concluded their analysis as follows:

> In any event, the federal sentencing guidelines have not eliminated the favorable treatment of female offenders. Special treatment, not equal treatment, persists. The extent to which this differential treatment reflects differences in male and female criminality is not clear. To the extent that these findings reflect a continuation of the pre-guideline pattern of paternalistic treatment of female offenders, however, they highlight the difficulty of full implementation of sentencing reform, as well as the complexity of the issues involved.[5]

Our primary concern in this chapter is with women in correctional institutions. We will see that the composition of women's prison populations is, to a large extent, a reflection of the sentencing process. Whether this process gives preferential treatment to women is an issue that is subject to serious differences of opinion. Obviously related to this are questions about whether women's prisons provide preferential treatment to their inmates, and whether women's penal institutions and programs are equal or should be equal to those for men.

A HISTORY OF WOMEN'S PRISONS

In many ways the history of women's prisons in America parallels that of penal institutions for men. During the early decades of the nineteenth century, penitentiaries were the fashion, as we pointed out in Chapter 6. Then came the reformatory movement, followed by a relatively brief period when many prison systems were infused with the rehabilitative spirit. To a large extent, these developments can be observed in both men's and women's institutions. However, there are a number of important differences. Partly as a result of these differences, the history of women's correctional institutions in the United States is a history of "partial justice," as was concluded by one major analysis.[6]

For example, during the time when the Pennsylvania- and Auburn-style penitentiaries were in vogue, male inmates were subjected to a consistent pattern of isolation and/or silence, and strict discipline was imposed to encourage them to become penitent.[7] During this period, this penal regimen was considered inappropriate for women, who were thought to require a more "gentle" oppression. They were typically housed in groups in large cells under lax supervision and with little useful or time-consuming employment.

A historical rendering of a nineteenth century women's prison shows female inmates assigned to hard labor on a treadmill. One inmate has collapsed, and another is removed from the treadmill due to exhaustion.

ACROSS CULTURES

STEREOTYPING FEMALE INMATES IN THE IRISH PRISON SYSTEM

The Irish or "progressive" prison system was the model used by Zebulon Brockway and others who developed the American reformatory. The Irish system was designed to structure incarceration in a way that moved prisoners along in stages, each stage involving more freedom. As inmates advanced, they also earned marks, which were applied against their sentences, providing for early release.

This system was designed primarily for male inmates. There were, however, a small number of women who were incarcerated for various offenses. Mary Carpenter was an observer of the Irish system, and wrote a book about it in which she praised its success with male inmates. Her description of female inmates and the difficulties encoun-

tered with them by prison staff led her to believe that the system would probably not be beneficial.

Here is a quote from her book, revealing the contemporary stereotype of the female offender:

All who have had any practical acquaintance with the management of convicted women, are fully aware that it is one of the most difficult problems to be satisfactorily solved.

The organization of women, both mental and physical, is much more delicate and sensitive than that of men, and also is subject to peculiar conditions; it follows from this that when morally diseased and in an abnormal state, their reformation and restoration to a healthy condition, is far more difficult than that of the other sex.

SOURCE: *Reformatory Prison Discipline as Developed by the Rt. Hon. Sir Walter Croften, in the Irish Convict Prisons* (London: Longmans, Green, Reader, and Dyer, 1972), p. 67.

Until approximately 1870, generally considered to be the year the reformatory movement began, women's prisons were built and operated as custodial institutions, most often as units in penal institutions for men. They borrowed from their male counterparts a concern for retributive punishment and security. As Nicole Hahn Rafter observed, however, prison officials did not necessarily treat their female charges the same as their male counterparts. Quite the contrary, "women in custodial institutions were treated as dregs of the state prisoner population."[8] Many years later, a survey of women's institutions by Owen and Bloom found, like Rafter before them, that female inmates are "marginalized" women. A significant proportion of the female prison population shares characteristics devalued by society.[9]

When the **reformatory movement** was initiated in 1870 following the historic Cincinnati conference of the National Prison Association,* the idea of rehabilitation was grafted onto both men's and women's custodial institutions. This meant that many women's prisons and women's units at men's prisons shed some of their fortress-like structures and were built or rebuilt along "cottage" lines. Accompanying this change were significant new sentencing statutes in a number of states that had a serious impact on female offenders, an impact that clearly reveals a pattern of discrimination and inequality based on gender stereotyping.

---

*For a discussion of this conference and its influence in the reformatory movement, see Chapter 6, pp. 126–127.

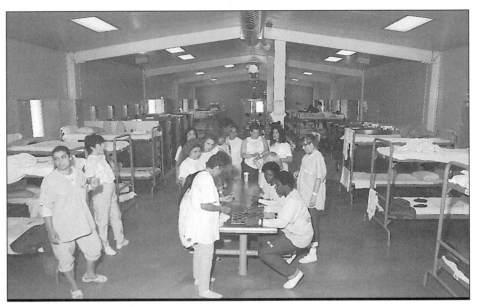

*D*ormitory housing for female inmates is one feature of this non-cottage style state prison. The interaction allowed between inmates seems to help the inmates in a positive manner.

> Legislation establishing women's reformatories enabled them to incarcerate women for pettier offenses than those of which men could be held . . . and these laws greatly extended the terms that women were required to spend behind bars.[10]

Indeterminate sentences were designed to promote successful rehabilitation of offenders, both male and female, by not releasing them until they were rehabilitated. It appears from studies by Rafter and others, however, that such sentences allowed for longer confinement of women for minor crimes. The commitment of these prisons to a strict "moral training" for their populations of "fallen women" meant that, in fact, they were at least as oppressive as their custodial antecedents.

One of the major innovations in prison design during much of the reformatory period was the **cottage plan** physical plant that characterized many of the new prisons for women. The New York Reformatory for Women at Albion was a fair representative of the cottage plan:

> [The] idea of family life, each cottage with its own kitchen, its pleasant dining-room adjoining, which matrons and girls used in common, and the living or sitting room in the second story, where the family assemble for diversion.[11]

Another innovation was a change in laws and regulations that permitted female inmates to keep their babies with them for short periods of time, rather than giving them up to family members or for adoption. Certainly, this change was expected to contribute to the family atmosphere in the cottage-style institution and to encourage women to continue or resume their gender-specific responsibilities.

By 1935, a total of seventeen women's reformatories had been built. Conflict between treatment (moral training) and control was evident from the beginning of the movement. This conflict was probably inevitable because the character of the population changed significantly from 1870 to 1935. During the early years, women admitted to reformatories were primarily younger sex offenders (prostitutes), especially those suffering venereal disease. These inmates were subjected to a rigorous moral training to lift them up from their "fallen" status.

Over time, more serious offenders were committed, leading to a return to custodial care. Security became the prime goal of prison staff. Eventually, women's reformatories became overcrowded, cursed by poor management and low-quality staff. In a number of reformatories riots broke out, the most serious occurring in 1920 at the New York Bedford Reformatory.

Accompanying demographic shifts in prisoner populations was the decline of the progressive movement following World War I and the Great Depression that began in 1929. Support for rehabilitation eroded steadily toward the end of the reformatory period. This erosion affected both men's and women's prisons.

▌WOMEN'S PRISONS AND WOMEN PRISONERS TODAY

Inmate Demographics

The numbers of women prisoners has increased steadily from 1980–1994. Just between 1993–94, the female prison population jumped by 10.6 percent.[12] For the period 1980–1994, the number of female prisoners increased at a faster pace than men, averaging 12 percent per year compared to 8.5 percent for men. Compared to the male rate of imprisonment, 746 per 100,000, the female rate was a relatively tiny 45 per 100,000.[13]

Between 1980 and 1993, there was a major difference in rates of imprisonment of black compared to white women, which mirrored differences in incarceration rates for men. By the end of 1993, the white female incarceration rate was 23 per 100,000 white women. For blacks, the rate was 165 per 100,00 black women.[14] At year's end 1995, the 65,544 women confined in state and federal prisons accounted for just over 6 percent of all inmates in the United States.[15] Not included here is the population of women in state, local, and federal detention or jail facilities.

Tracey Snell found that much of the increase in women prisoners can be accounted for by commitments of offenders convicted on drug charges. In 1986, female prisoners with drug charges made up only 12 percent of correctional institution totals, while by 1991 they made up 33 percent of the total institutionalized population.[16] Tables 9.1, 9.2, and 9.3 and Figure 9.1 show some of these population changes.

A review of several national surveys and a detailed survey of California's women's correctional institutions led Owen and Bloom to the same conclusions Snell reached: The sharp increase in the number of female prisoners cannot be accounted for by an increase in the rate of serious or violent crime committed by women.[17] In fact, they found that commitments of women for violent crimes actually decreased while those of drug offenders increased. "Nearly one in three female inmates was serving a sentence for drug offenses in 1991, compared to one in eight in 1986."[18]

Chesney-Lind and Pollock also found that women's prisons are not holding the violent, serious offenders that popular opinion assumes they are. As they observed:

> Profiles of women in prison fail to confirm the appearance of a new, serious woman offender; indeed, as women's prison populations soar, the evidence seems to suggest a *decline* in the proportion of women in prison for violent crime.[19]

Chesney-Lind and Pollock suggest a number of explanations for both the increase in women's incarceration rates and the decrease in the proportion of serious offend-

TABLE 9.1   **Estimated Rates of Incarceration for Males and Females by Race, 1980, 1985, 1990–1994**

Year	Total	MALE			FEMALE		
		All	White	Black	All	White	Black
1980	139	275	168	1,111	11	6	45
1985	202	397	246	1,559	17	10	68
1990	297	575	339	2,376	32	19	125
1992	332	643	371	2,675	36	20	142
1993	359	698	398	2,920	41	23	165
1994	387	746	—	—	45	—	—

SOURCE: *Prisoners in 1994*, Bureau of Justice Statistics, p. 8.

ers being sentenced to prison. First, they say that mandatory sentences, especially for drug offenses, account for much of the change in penal populations. A second explanation focuses on recent sentencing reforms such as sentencing guidelines and uniform determinate sentencing statutes. These seek to achieve racially and ethnically neutral sentences as well as a higher probability of incarceration sentences. One result, probably unanticipated, is that more women have been incarcerated.

A third explanation offered by Chesney-Lind and Pollock and others[20] is that a general "get tough on crime" stance has taken hold in America and that female offenders have been caught in the ever-widening incarceration net. Thus, the criminal justice system is much more likely to be tougher on all offenders at all stages in the criminal justice process. Being tougher translates into more prison sentences for all.

So, if women offenders do not constitute a threat to society, why are so many being sentenced to prison? Many women are incarcerated because the "legal response to

TABLE 9.2   **Number of Sentenced Prisoners in State and Federal Prisons, by Sex and Race, 1980, 1985, 1990–1994**

Year	Total	MALE			FEMALE		
		All	White	Black	All	White	Black
1980	315,974	303,643	159,500	140,600	12,331	5,900	6,300
1985	480,568	459,223	242,700	210,500	21,345	10,800	10,200
1990	739,980	699,416	346,700	344,300	40,564	20,000	20,100
1991	789,610	745,808	363,600	372,200	43,802	20,900	22,200
1992	846,277	799,776	387,600	401,200	46,501	22,100	23,700
1993	932,266	878,298	418,900	445,400	53,968	25,200	27,900
1994	1,012,463	952,585	—	—	59,878	—	—
Percent change, 1980–94	220%	214%	—	—	386%	—	—

SOURCE: *Prisoners in 1994*, Bureau of Justice Statistics, p.8.

HAPTER 9 *Women in Prison* 199

9 *Women in Prison* 199

CHAPTER 9 *Women in Prison*   199
9
1

Characteristics of State Prison Inmates, by Sex, 1991 and 1986   TABLE 9.3

Characteristic	PERCENT OF FEMALE INMATES		PERCENT OF MALE INMATES	
	1991	1986	1991	1986
RACE/HISPANIC ORIGIN				
White non-Hispanic	36.2%	39.7%	35.4%	39.5%
Black non-Hispanic	46.0	46.0	45.5	45.2
Hispanic	14.2	11.7	16.8	12.7
Other	3.6	2.5	2.3	2.5
AGE				
17 or younger	.1%	.2%	.7%	.5%
18–24	16.3	22.3	21.6	26.9
25–34	50.4	50.5	45.5	45.5
35–44	25.5	19.6	22.6	19.4
45–54	6.1	5.5	6.6	5.2
55 or older	1.7	1.8	3.2	2.5
Median age	31 years	29 years	30 years	29 years
MARITAL STATUS				
Married	17.3%	20.1%	18.1%	20.4%
Widowed	5.9	6.7	1.6	1.6
Divorced	19.1	20.5	18.4	18.0
Separated	12.5	11.0	5.9	5.8
Never married	45.1	41.7	55.9	54.3
EDUCATION				
8th grade or less	16.0%	16.5%	19.6%	20.9%
Some high school	45.8	49.7	46.2	50.6
High school graduate	22.7	19.1	21.9	17.7
Some college or more	15.5	14.8	12.3	10.8
PRE-ARREST EMPLOYMENT				
Employed	46.7%	47.1%	68.5%	70.1%
Full time	35.7	37.1	56.5	58.4
Part time	11.0	10.0	12.0	11.7
Unemployed	53.3%	52.9%	31.5%	30.0%
Looking	19.2	22.0	16.2	17.8
Not looking	34.1	30.9	15.3	12.2
Number of inmates	38,796	19,812	672,847	430,604

SOURCE: Bureau of Justice Statistics, "Special Report," *Women in Prison*, 1991.

drug-related behavior has become increasingly punitive, resulting in a flood of less serious offenders into the state and federal prison systems."[21] Thus, admissions to women's prisons are affected by sentencing policies and practices quite similar to those we found in the previous chapter affecting commitments to men's institutions. So a rather sinister kind of equality seems to be at work.

Beyond these cold statistics, what else can we say about the women in our correctional institutions? Significantly, a very large proportion of female inmates are moth-

FIGURE 9.1   **Increases in the Number of Inmates in State and Federal Prisons by Race and Sex, 1980–1993**

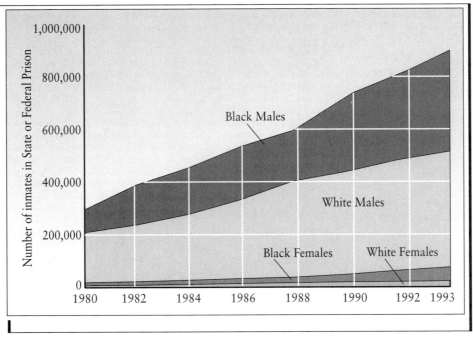

SOURCE: *Prisoners in 1994,* Bureau of Justice Statistics, p. 9.

ers and single heads of households. According to one survey, there may be as many as 80,000 mothers in local, state, and federal jails and prisons, and their dependents may total 150,000.[22] In one Illinois women's prison, 82 percent of the prisoners were single heads of households.[23]

Female prisoners have been described as:

> . . . marginalized women. A significant proportion of the female prison population shares characteristics devalued by society such as minority status, little education or work experience, and significant histories of personal and substance abuse.

> ✴✴✴✴

> Both our data and the research literature on imprisoned women stress the prominent role played by substance abuse, physical and sexual abuse, and poverty and underemployment. . . . Our survey data also support the contention that a significant proportion of female offenders are not dangerous, are not career criminals, and thus do not represent a serious threat to the community.[24]

The Environment of Women's Prisons

We have seen how the population of women's prisons is in some ways similar to, but in other ways different from the population of institutions for men. We now look at the physical and social environment of women's prisons.

We have already seen that there has been a trend away from building women's prison structures on male prison models. This has most often taken the form of the

ACROSS CULTURES

WOMEN IN SOVIET PRISONS

Helene Celmina was a prisoner in the former Soviet Union and wrote an account of her experience. She spent four years in prison for the offense of "reading foreign magazines." Her description of the intake process gives us a striking picture of life in a prison under the Soviet regime.

The prison admissions process was uniform throughout the prison system. Immediately following their entrance into a prison, inmates were placed in a closet or "box," a small space in which they were locked for up to several hours while awaiting processing. As in American prisons, new inmates are searched carefully. In the case of Soviet women prisoners, all metal objects were confiscated, and if rings could not be removed easily, they were filed through and discarded. If a woman had been convicted of theft, a gynecologist conducted an internal search.

While men had their hair shaved upon admissions, women received haircuts if their hair was considered too long. All women, however, had their pubic hair removed.

The next step was to send women to a "preliminary investigation" ward holding up to 60 inmates until the charges against them were "investigated" prior to trial. Ms. Celmina reported that the investigation was essentially irrelevant since "according to Soviet law, prisoners are guilty from the time of arrest." In this ward, the only approved social activity was to play dominoes. Inmates were permitted one book from the library every ten days.

Inmates were permitted to sew their worn garments, being issued black or white thread and two needles, which had to be turned in each evening. The only work assignment was "gluing gray paper bags which are used by stores for potato packing." For every 200 completed bags, inmates were "rewarded" by receiving a package of *mahorka*, ground stems of tobacco leaves. To roll a cigarette required newspaper, which was in short supply. "The prisoner must butter up the guards and plead for a sheet of old newspaper in order to enjoy a smoke."

SOURCE: *Women in Soviet Prisons* (New York: Paragon House Publishing, 1985).

cottage plan, which, it is thought, contributes to a more "normal" environment than the fortress-like institutions of the past. Another model, employed in local as well as state detention facilities, is the **new generation jail** for women. We discussed the new generation philosophy in Chapter 5, but it is important to take up the subject here because it illustrates an attempt in many jurisdictions to "solve" some of the problems associated with the confinement of women.

Contrary to expectations, women experience incarceration in new generation jails very differently, and much less positively, than men. In a study of a new generation jail serving Sonoma County, California, Jackson and Stearns found sharp and unexpected differences in the experiences of men and women inmates.[25] These differences, which led to policy changes, illuminate some of the problems encountered when attempting to "improve" programs for female prisoners.

As so often happens in corrections, the move in Sonoma County toward a new generation jail resulted from a civil rights lawsuit that was decided in 1982.[26] The jail system that was successfully attacked in court consisted of essentially linear-style facilities with limited supervision of inmates. It was described as having a "climate of fear, an absence of privacy."[27] One facility was further described as extremely noisy, crowded, with many blind spots that impaired security.

ON THE JOB

THE SONOMA COUNTY (CALIFORNIA) "NEW GENERATION" DETENTION FACILITY

[The facility is] a state of the art, podular style, direct supervision facility. . . . It embodies two cornerstones of the new generation philosophy. The first is a unique architectural design. The podular architecture incorporates five two-tiered, 50-bed living facilities . . . shaped in a semicircle facing an officer station that is not separated by bars, glass, or other barriers. Each . . . "pod" also contains a medical unit, an indoor recreation area, showers for individual use, carpeted floors, television in key locations . . . , and a recreation area that is exposed to light. . . . Noncontact visitation booths are also attached to each module.

The second dimension of the new generation philosophy is a direct supervision style of managing inmates. [It] incorporates extensive training in interpersonal communication and eschews reliance on brute force or steel bars to enforce compliance with rules. Module officers are trained to manage inmate issues proactively.

SOURCE: Patrick G. Jackson and Cindy A. Stearns, "Gender Issues in the New Generation Jail," *The Prison Journal* 75 (1995): 206.

By 1991, the new generation institution was ready for transfer of inmates from the older jails. The On the Job feature gives a detailed description of the layout of the institution.

From this description, we might expect that the new Sonoma County facility was just the right response to the problems of incarcerating offenders humanely and successfully in terms of future recidivism levels. We might also expect that incarcerating men and women "equally" by giving them access to a "state of the art" facility would produce positive benefits for all. Our expectations, however, are not confirmed by the results of Jackson and Stearns's study. The men were much more positive in their attitudes and perceptions than were the women. In fact, "increased dissatisfaction among female inmates" was clearly revealed in interviews conducted by the researchers.[28]

Why is this so? Jackson and Stearns suggest that new generation institutions with their direct supervision style and podular physical structure aim, intentionally, to reduce inmate peer group formation and the development of strong inmate interpersonal attachments. Certainly, if our goal is to strengthen official control of an inmate population and reduce opportunities for informal inmate social control, a new generation facility is just the ticket to accomplish it. However,

> studies of females in confinement, mostly prisons, suggest a desire to develop closer, more cooperative, and more family-like relationships with a small number of other inmates as a temporary means of supplanting their connectedness in society with family and friends. . . . [T]he direct supervision experience may be perceived as an intrusion on female inmate interpersonal relationships, which may assume a differential importance in institutional life than it does among males.[29]

What we see at work here is a problem that has dogged corrections for many generations: basing incarceration policies and practices for women on models used with male prisoners. Although the podular or new generation institution may successfully deal with the development of prison gangs and informal control structures among male prisoners, it may have a devastating effect on women.

In addition, the Sonoma County authorities imposed a number of rule changes that had a differential impact on women and their self-concepts. Once they were transferred to the new jail there was "no more makeup, no jewelry, no contact visits, no curling irons or hair dryers, . . . and there were fewer clothes permitted."[30] As Jackson and Stearns note:

> The management of appearance is central to the experience of being a woman in American society. It is a key component in the "accomplishment of gender" or **"doing gender. . . ."** Thus lack of access to the tools, means, and methods of appearance transformation may well be a significant deprivation for women in the new jail.[31] (boldface added)

We can only wonder what Sonoma County officials were thinking of when they implemented these rules in their new "state of the art" institution. Perhaps it was an attempt to respond in a strictly legalistic manner to the court challenge to the older jail system. As Jackson and Stearns point out, however, "it is clear that the new generation jail provides a near equal experience for male and female inmates. However, it is not clear that equality always ensures justice."[32] In any event, by 1994, all the female inmates at the new facility were transferred back to the older facility. This was said to be based on costs, since the very small number of confined women made podular, direct supervision incarceration prohibitively expensive. We may wonder whether the problems discussed above had something to do with the reversal.

FEMALE INMATE NEEDS AND PRISON PROGRAMS

It is not possible to study prison programs effectively unless we carefully examine the needs and problems of the women who enter our correctional institutions. All too often we evaluate the prison experience of women in terms of what we think we know about prisons for men. So much more has been written about the far larger number of these institutions for male offenders that it may be unrealistic to expect there to be a significant body of research and other literature on women's prisons. It may be unrealistic, but it is certainly indicative of a gender bias that our knowledge of inmates' imprisonment experiences is based largely on the experiences of men. Women in prison manifest a number of problems in common with men (e.g., drug dependence, lack of marketable job skills, health problems), but they have certain special needs. With regard to health, women often need special services such as gynecological examinations and prenatal and postpartum care. With respect to vocational training and placement, the training available in correctional institutions typically "does not necessarily assist women offenders in obtaining meaningful and financially rewarding work."[33]

Of course, we must also consider the fact that prisons for women offenders do not operate solely, nor even in large measure, to meet the needs of their inmates. Given the present climate in criminal justice, these institutions, like their counterparts for males, must serve punitive, retributive, and incapacitative goals.

Many imprisoned women are mothers or mothers-to-be, and the legal and practical restrictions imposed on them as they try to maintain relationships with their children significantly affect their physical and emotional well-being. As reported in one study of women who recently had been paroled from prison, the impact of loss of attachment to their children was quite traumatic. One inmate was quoted as saying,

In some institutions there are resources to help female prisoners increase their reading, math, and writing skills.

I looked at the judge and he looked at me. He didn't care that I was getting what seemed like a death sentence. Three hundred miles away and no one to leave my kids with. Why couldn't he have let me go to a program in town?[34]

At the present time there are more than 80,000 mothers in our jails and prisons, so the concern expressed by this inmate is one that must be felt by a very large number of women. Typically, mothers are not permitted to keep their children with them throughout their sentences. A number of corrections systems are reluctant to allow minor children to visit their mothers. Clearly, one program area that must be addressed by corrections concerns the needs of incarcerated mothers and their children. As we will show, services and programs for inmate-mothers constitute the majority of the special and innovative features of women's prisons today.

Mothers frequently lose custody of their children once convicted and imprisoned. Sometimes, custody is awarded informally or formally to family members. This arrangement may be less traumatic for the inmate-mother, unless she objects to the particular relative. At other times, custody is taken by the state through agencies such as Department of Social Services or Child Protective Services. Family or Domestic Relations courts frequently step in to decide custody issues. In cases where the state intervenes, children of incarcerated mothers may be placed with foster parents in individual or group home settings. The future custody of these children is problematic and may be a source of additional anxiety for inmate-mothers.

One program designed to assist inmate-mothers with their child custody problems is the Child Custody Advocacy Services Project (CHICAS). It was initiated in 1990 in California and subsequently expanded to serve clients throughout the country.[35] The project has two goals: to help imprisoned mothers retain custody of their children, and to regain custody ("reunification") if it was lost following conviction and incarceration.

Denise Johnston reported on the results of service delivery to 660 clients, three-fourths of whom were inmate-mothers, between 1990 and the end of 1994. Over 80 percent of these offenders were sentenced for drug offenses, reflecting the results of

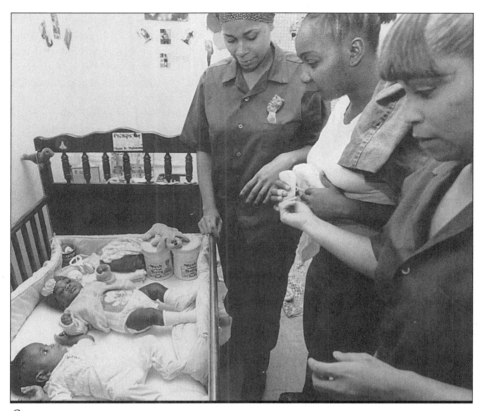

*S*ome of the incarcerated women have children before they are imprisoned. There are opportunities for the children to visit their parents if they are brought by relatives or friends of the
prisoners.

the "war on drugs." The most common problem reported by these clients was a lack
of adequate reunification services by various social service agencies, including the
courts in those cases where legal custody orders were in force. Typically,

> these women . . . had difficulties in communicating with their social workers, received no
> social services support for parent-child communication or visitation, received no referrals or
> assistance with placements in correctional or reentry programs, and/or perceived their
> social workers as hostile or opposed to reunification.[36]

When attempting to solve visitation problems, incarcerated mothers ran into considerable resistance from foster parents, and even relatives who were caring for their
children. As Johnston found in reviewing the 660 CHICAS clients, agencies such as
state Child Protective Services frequently supported foster parents and mothers' relatives who did not want to let the children in their care visit their mothers in prison.

Mothers who applied to CHICAS for service were all self-referred or referred by
friends, relatives, attorneys, judges, and prison counselors. The most frequent services
requested are enhanced visitation and reunification support. In the latter area, somewhat over one-half the mothers were reunited with their children following release
from prison.[37] Significantly, because of the large percentage of inmate-mothers who
were drug offenders, the success of reunification efforts was markedly higher for
women who left prison and entered community-based drug treatment facilities.

Results obtained after reviewing the CHICAS project led the researcher to conclude that there needs to be a major restructuring of sentences in the case of offenders who are both parents and drug dependent. For them it was recommended that their sentences provide for "residential, community-based drug treatment as an alternative to or component of sentences to incarceration."[38] But might not such sentences result in "unequal" or "preferential" treatment of offender-mothers?

Serious efforts are being made to treat inmate mothers more effectively in some prison systems. One such effort can be found at the Bedford Hills Correctional Facility in New York state. This prison is the state's maximum security institution for women, and it houses 720 inmates even though its original design called for a population of 400.[39] This, of course, is another reflection of changing sentencing policies and practices, primarily resulting from a "get tough" view, especially regarding drug offenders.

The Bedford Hills program includes:

> a vast network of support for the women and their children. There is a nursery program for women and their babies . . . with a prenatal education component. There is a program in which children are transported unescorted to visit their mothers.[40]

In addition to these program features, Bedford Hills has opportunities for children to spend a summer week with their mothers, and they can spend weekends throughout the year with them.

With regard to the special problem of mothers in prison who are drug dependent, the superintendent of Bedford Hills minces no words in her condemnation of current sentencing practices:

> We need to be more honest with ourselves that the vast majority of women receiving prison sentences are not the business operatives of the drug networks. We need to stop deluding ourselves that we are putting pushers in prison. The glass ceiling appears to operate for women whether we are talking about legitimate or illegitimate business.[41]

While recognizing that women may sell drugs in relatively small quantities to support their dependence on them, and may be employed as "mules" for men who control drug trafficking, they are simply "very small cogs in a very large system."[42] At Bedford Hills, the average minimum sentence being served is over eight years, and "more startlingly, is the reality that close to 200 women are serving sentences in excess of 10-year minimums and that close to 100 women will be imprisoned for at least 10 years of their lives."[43]

California has taken a different approach to meet the special needs of prisoners who are mothers.[44] Inmates with children under six years of age may be paroled to community halfway houses. Some women who give birth to children while incarcerated may also be paroled to these facilities. Still other states have initiated programs making it easier for children to visit and have contact visits with their prisoner-mothers. These programs generally are not available to prisoner-fathers, but they do represent a belief in some states that women who are mothers need to be treated differently than their male counterparts.

In addition to the programs described above, a number of visitors' services have been established to ease the difficulty facing family members wishing to visit their imprisoned relatives. In 1983, a California statute was enacted requiring the prison system to provide visitor centers, operated by private contractors, at each of its adult institutions.[45]

The centers provide a wide range of services to visitors, including:

- assistance getting to prison from the nearest public transportation
- child care for visitors' children
- emergency clothing, especially in relation to inclement weather
- thorough information regarding visiting rules and regulations
- referrals to appropriate agencies for social and other services
- a shelter for visitors waiting for entry to the prison

It says much about California, as well as many other states, that most of these services were not available in the past. In fact, before 1972, "visitation services for persons who visited California state prisons did not exist. This meant that rain or shine, visitors would wait outside in anticipation of prison clearance to visit."[46] With the visitor centers in operation, visits to female inmates increased dramatically. More than 80 percent of the visitors visited at least once a month.

A former staff member at Dwight Correctional Center, the only female prison in Illinois, reported that 82 percent of that institution's population were "single heads of households."[47] In that prison, some inmates were able to work in prison industries, earning money to send to relatives who were caring for their children. However, visits from children were constrained by a number of factors which bear listing here because of the centrality of maintaining family contacts. The more significant of these factors are:

- Spouses and ex-spouses who have custody of children frequently are reluctant to bring them to prison.
- Foster parents sometimes feel that if children visit their incarcerated mothers, their efforts to teach them appropriate values may be subverted.
- Because the only women's prison is located far away from major population centers, visits on any but an occasional basis may constitute a hardship.
- Because of security concerns, there are times when visitors are not permitted in the institution even though they have come great distances.

An innovative approach with respect to inmate-mothers and their contacts with their children is the National Institute of Justice–sponsored Girl Scouts Beyond Bars (GSBB) programs currently operating in at least 11 jurisdictions.[48] Among the innovative features of these programs is their focus on the effects on children of having mothers in prison. One account of the GSBB program at Maryland Correctional Institution for Women suggested that children of incarcerated mothers suffer from anxiety, depression, and aggression. They show a decrease in school performance and a significant rise in teen pregnancies.[49]

GSBB programs typically involve Girl Scout daughters visiting their mothers in prison on a regular basis. During these twice-a-month visits they work together with their mothers on Girl Scout projects and engage in more general interactions. The frequency and regularity of visits by these girls are much greater than for other inmate-mothers whose daughters are not in the GSBB program. Costs of the program (primarily for transportation) are borne partly by the appropriate Girl Scouts councils and charitable organizations, with the National Institute of Justice providing funding for start-up and demonstration projects.

The Pennsylvania Department of Corrections has for some years been providing a comprehensive set of services at its two women's prisons. These services include children's visiting centers, spousal group sessions, parenting classes, and transportation assistance for children visiting their mothers.[50] At least twenty-two somewhat similar programs currently are offered at women's correctional institutions throughout the country.[51]

As a final look at institutional programs that seek to maintain and strengthen inmate-mother–children relationships, we come to the "Motheread" program at North Carolina Correctional Institution for Women, which began in 1990.[52] This program does not involve services designed to expand prison visits by children, nor does it include services related to custody issues. Instead, Motheread aims to improve mother-child relationships and inmate educational levels through the following activity:

> The inmates improve their literacy skills when they make book audio tapes that they send home to their children. In addition, inmates develop their writing skills by composing their own stories and letters to send home to their children.[53]

An evaluation study of the first two years of the Motheread program found that it was helpful in increasing literacy skills and improved parenting attitudes and emotional health. There was "statistically significant improvement in the women's parenting attitudes over the course of Motheread, with women becoming more emphatic with and responsive to their children's needs."[54]

Staff-Inmate Relationships

Unfortunately, correctional officers and other prison staff members often perceive the problems of female inmates in ways that hinder successful interactions with them and may well impede the successful outcome of the incarceration experience. Joycelyn Pollock's study of guards at women's and men's prisons points this out clearly.[55] Her interviews with both male and female correctional officers revealed that they considered women to be more "emotional," "temperamental," "moody," and "manipulative" than men. But then, corrections has a long history of viewing women stereotypically, resulting in poor staff-inmate interactions. As Pollock reports, a nineteenth-century prison matron commented:

> It is a harder task to manage female prisoners. . . . They are more impulsive, more individual, more unreasonable and excitable than men; will not act in concert, and cannot be disciplined in masses. Each wants personal and peculiar treatment; . . . matrons having this to deal with [individuals] and having to adapt themselves to each individual case, instead of simply obeying certain fixed laws and making others obey them, as in the prison for males.[56]

What the matron reveals, of course, is that women could not at that time (1862) be coerced into the paramilitary regimen that soon was to be made popular by Warden Zebulon Brockway at the New York Elmira Reformatory.[57] It also points out, as Pollock, Rafter, and others have found, that historically we have tried to pattern prisons for women, as well as their programs, after male models. If staff at women's correctional facilities cannot shuck off such attitudes about the women they must guard and counsel, it seems that program improvements, whatever their intent, may be doomed to failure.

Correctional Treatment Programs

With the large numbers of women entering prisons for drug offenses, we would expect that treatment programs for them would be a high priority for correctional authorities. However, Prendergast and his colleagues, after surveying corrections facilities (both in the community and in prison) around the country, found a number of important "performance gaps." Among these were:

*T*his industrial training shop for female inmates is not a common sight in female prisons. This one is located at the Connecticut state prison at Niantic.

- An insufficient number of openings for treatment, especially for women with children or those who are pregnant, mentally ill, homeless, or have a history of violence.[58]
- A distinct lack of the kinds of case management that provides for adequate integrating of mental health, corrections, and drug treatment agencies so that drug treatment will be delivered successfully.[59]
- A lack of adequate transitional services that provide for women inmates to make the transition from institution to community. This deficiency is exacerbated by the fact that many women do not participate in drug treatment programs while incarcerated (either because they are not available, or because they choose not to participate), yet such treatment is a condition of parole or conditional release.[60]
- While there seems to be a trend toward "gender sensitive" treatment programs, there still are many programs that are "male oriented" in their approach to treatment.[61]

The researchers concluded that to deliver successful drug treatment programs to female offenders, a "systems" approach is essential. Women offenders manifest multiple problems that require the services of many different agencies. Corrections "needs to move toward a more system-oriented approach . . . that emphasizes linkages and coordination among programs and agencies, joint planning, shared resource allocation, and continuity for clients."[62] Unfortunately, corrections in much of the United States is characterized by disorganization and is not well received by other agencies such as those in the mental health and social services areas.

As a number of commentators have pointed out, historically women's prison programs have largely been based on what is considered to be the "proper" role of women in society and the workforce. As a counter to this, women's prisons are becoming more like men's institutions. The latter is at least partly the result of an

*G*roup counseling is an important component in female prisons. The opportunity to share experiences and collectively work out problems is a powerful experience.

equalization movement. But if women's institutions are becoming harder to distinguish from those housing men, what is happening to their programs?

Surveys have found that there have been major changes in program offerings for female inmates.[63] Many prisons have added vocational programs and educational opportunities ranging from basic literacy classes all the way to college courses. Most women who participate in these programs choose those providing basic education and that teach clerical skills. This appears to mean that to some extent, stereotyping still affects program participation. Whether this results from the women themselves accepting stereotypical role definitions, or from the direct or indirect influence of prison staff, is not clear. Perhaps it is both.

Co-Correctional Prisons

In an effort to provide a more "normal" prison environment as well as more "equality" in prison programs, confining men and women in the same correctional institution has been gaining favor. This is not to be confused with the earlier practice of establishing female wings or adjuncts in existing men's prisons. In the past, it was simply a matter of economies of scale that made such prisons attractive. The newer **co-correctional institutions** have developed in very different ways, the most notable of which is to permit the mixing of men and women in various program activities such as education, training, work, and counseling.

There are a number of reported advantages and disadvantages that have been noted in co-correctional prisons. Some of the advantages are:

- Program participation levels increase for both men and women.
- Inmate self-concepts improve.
- The social skills of both men and women improve.
- Homosexual activity, especially among men, decreases.

Among the disadvantages are the following:

- Correctional officers' workloads increase because of the necessity to keep inmates separated except when participating in authorized programs.
- Inmates' movements are severely restricted, especially in the case of female prisoners, because of the concern about possible pregnancies. Thus, some women may lack some of the freedom they experience in single-sex institutions.[64]

On balance, as concluded by Pollock,

> we may hypothesize that there is a moderation in the extreme behavior differences of men and women in co-correctional facilities, that co-correctional facilities decrease the amount of homosexuality and assaultiveness among both men and women, and that there is less of a tendency to supervise the sexes differently in the same facility than when they are housed in separate facilities.[65]

THE QUESTION OF EQUALITY OF CORRECTIONAL PROGRAMS

The Debate over Equalization

We now turn to the question that has confronted us throughout the chapter: Is it possible, or even appropriate, to build correctional programs for women that are "equal" to those available to men? The issue is stated clearly by Chesney-Lind and Pollock:

> There is a continuing debate on whether equality under the law is necessarily good for women. On the one hand, some feminist scholars argue that the only way to eliminate the discriminatory treatment and oppression that women have experienced in the past is to push for continued equalization under the law.[66]

The opposing side in this debate,

> holds that women are not the same as men. Proponents of this view believe that because equality is measured against a male standard, women will always lose. Therefore, the position calls for recognizing differential needs—following a type of **"separate but equal"** argument.[67] (boldface added)

Those who call for full equalization counter the separate but equal argument by claiming that if it should be adopted, it will mean that women will always be subjected to different definitions and treatment modalities, and thereby "run the risk of perpetuating the stereotype of women as 'different from' and 'less than' male."[68]

The effort to equalize women's corrections programs has, in large measure, resulted from litigation by inmates and their advocates. As we have indicated in this and earlier chapters, many of the changes in the situation of women, from sentencing to incarceration, have been driven by the appellate process. We will first examine a few appellate cases that have dealt with sentences received by women, and then move on to cases that focused on prison conditions and programs.

Sentence Equalization

Women offenders who are mothers or mothers-to-be have different problems and needs compared to male offenders. Does this mean that pregnant women ought to be sentenced differently? The First Circuit Court of Appeals answered this question in the negative.[69] The court held that a defendant's pregnancy was not an appropriate factor to be used by a trial court judge to depart from the federal sentencing guideline range. The guidelines do provide for a reduction in sentences should a defendant's physical condition be deemed "extraordinary." The appellate court found that pregnancy is "neither atypical nor unusual."[70]

What about women convicted of crime who are single heads of households? As we saw earlier, a very large number of inmates in women's prisons fall into this category. Should they receive different sentences from men convicted of the same or similar crimes? In *United States v. Brand*, this issue was raised.[71] The Fourth Circuit Court of Appeals found that a defendant's status as a single parent was "unfortunate," but not "out of the ordinary."[72] Thus, a defendant's parental status is not grounds for departing (downward) from a sentencing guideline.

There is case law that favors women offenders who are subjected to abuse, coercion, and domination by males, and where their criminal acts can be shown to be rationally related to such abuse, coercion, and domination. One such case, *United States v. Johnson*, resulted in the sentences of several women being vacated with the trial court instructed to reconsider in light of the fact that they were involved in drug trafficking masterminded by a violently abusive male "drug lord."[73]

Equality in Correctional Conditions and Programs

In the Federal District Court for the Eastern District of Michigan, suit was brought on behalf of women prisoners claiming that lack of a variety of programs such as those available for male prisoners constituted illegal discrimination.[74] The court distinguished between discrimination in treatment that is based on race from discrimination based on sex. In the case of the former, the court held, the treatment differences must be subjected to "strict scrutiny." The discrimination can be justified if it is the *sole* means to achieve an important government objective.

In the case of differential treatment based on sex, as in the case of *Glover v. Johnson*, strict scrutiny is not required. Instead, an "intermediate standard of review" is to be applied. Under this standard, treating men and women differently can be justified if there is a major governmental interest involved and the differential treatment is "rationally" related to it. The *Glover* court determined that there was no rational basis for providing Michigan women inmates far fewer programs than men received, especially vocational programs. It ordered the state to add programs in its women's prisons so that the menu of offerings approximated what were available to male prisoners.

In another court case, *Todaro v. Ward*, the Federal District Court for the Southern District of New York found the state deficient in its provision of medical and health care services to its female prisoners.[75]

While not strictly focusing on equalization, a suit filed by the ACLU on behalf of inmates at Hawaii Women's Prison resulted in significant gains in female prisoners' rights.[76] The suit contested prison conditions and overcrowding. A consent decree was handed down under which the state's Department of Public Safety agreed to improve and expand a number of services, programs, and conditions at the Women's Prison. These included greater access to health services, increases in education classes, and the addition of more beds to relieve severe overcrowding. The latter was the most significant change agreed to by the state under the terms of the consent decree. It clearly overshadowed programmatic reforms, and as Chesney-Lind and Pollock observed,

[with] the emphasis on parity, and with a male model of imprisonment, women are clearly shortchanged. New prison beds take the place of alternatives to prison; designs stress security over women's needs.[77]

A GOOD WAY TO BEGIN A SUMMARY of this chapter is to agree with Nicole Hahn Rafter that "problems specific to women in prison have remained fairly consistent from the establishment of the first penitentiaries into the present."[78] We also agree with the following observations Rafter made, based on her and our review of women's prisons:

- Women continue to be slighted by a correctional bureaucracy that is overwhelmingly male and predominantly occupied by the larger male population.
- When held in the same institution with men, women are still vulnerable to sexual exploitation by male staff.
- Female prisoners discover that medical services are geared toward men, and they seldom have adequate access to [obstetricians and gynecologists].
- Women . . . have fewer programs than men, and they encounter gender stereotyping in programs and staff attitudes.
- Women are more isolated than men from their families, legal aid, and community resources.

Laws, policies, and programs designed to deal with these and other problems of incarcerating a steadily increasing population of women have revealed significant disagreements. On the one hand are those who advocate making women's prisons somehow "equal" to those for men. On the other hand are many who argue that women are different, as are their needs and problems before, during, and after incarceration. Corrections, if it is to deliver justice, must recognize these needs and problems. To do so, however, means that facilities and programs will not be equal to those for men. Not to recognize the different needs and situations of women, it is argued, results in "partial justice."

The superintendent of New York state's Bedford Hills maximum security prison for women commented,

> . . . [To] make women "equal," many jurisdictions have gone on building programs to make women's prisons like or equal to men's prisons. Prison security classifications systems are designed to make prisoners who present substantially different risks to society and to the prison managers. It is almost unknown to create classification systems for women that would factor in their own particular realities and characteristics. Rather, to be "equal," we simply use instruments designed to assess the dangerousness of men and overbuild or oversecure for women at significant cost but little real gain in increased safety.[79]

The superintendent's observation that in order to respond "equally" to men and women, we have tended to utilize strategies that, historically, have been employed with male inmates brings us to a dilemma for corrections. By attempting to deliver **equal justice** to women, we ignore their special needs and problems; thus, the justice we try to dispense falls far short of being equal. Instead it has become a **partial justice.**

Because of the centrality of issues related to motherhood and the maintenance of family ties while imprisoned, a number of observers have strongly suggested that prison programming must address the special needs and problems of women inmates. George Kiser made the case for taking a number of steps in this direction:

Some institutions have already moved in this direction by such innovations as allowing family members to visit overnight, permitting an unrestricted number of visits by close family members, and allowing infants to live at the prison with their mothers.[80]

KEY CONCEPTS

Co-correctional institution	Gender stereotyping
Cottage plan	New generation jail
Doing gender	Partial justice
Economies of scale	Reformatory movement
Equal justice	Separate but equal

QUESTIONS FOR DISCUSSION

1. Critically evaluate the statement that equal correctional settings for women results not in equal justice but "partial" justice.
2. Because such a large proportion of women admitted to prison are drug offenders, what provisions should be made for their effective treatment?
3. Prisoners who are mothers suffer greatly because of their enforced separation from their children. Argue that correctional systems that prohibit or severely limit inmate-mothers from being with their children are engaged in cruel and unusual punishment.
4. What do the negative results of confining women in new generation jails teach us about the incarceration of women?
5. What are the major arguments for and against "equalization" of correctional institutions and programs for women?
6. Because of "economies of scale," it is argued, prison facilities and programs for women offenders will always be deficient. Is this a correct assessment? If so, how might these deficiencies be remedied?
7. Critically evaluate the statement that establishing co-correctional institutions is an effective way to deal with the problem of partial justice for female prisoners.

ENDNOTES

1. Statement by a Midwestern prison inmate, "Mandi," in Beverly Brown Shulke, *Women and Criminal Recidivism: A Study of Social Constraints.* Unpublished doctoral dissertation, George Washington University, May 1993, pp. 138–139.
2. Elaine Lord, "A Prison Superintendent's Perspective on Women in Prison," *Prison Journal* 75 (1995): 266.
3. Ilene H. Nagel and Barry L. Johnson, "The Role of Gender in a Structured Sentencing System: Equal Treatment, Policy Choices, and the Sentencing of Female Offenders in the United States under Sentencing Guidelines," *Journal of Criminal Law & Criminology* 85 (1994): 181–221.
4. Ibid., pp. 183–190.

5. Ibid., p. 221.

6. Nicole Hahn Rafter, *Partial Justice: Women in State Prisons, 1800–1935* (Boston, MA: Northeastern University Press, 1985).

7. Much of this review of the early history of women's prisons is taken from Rafter, *Partial Justice,* pp. xxxiii–xxxiv, 3–99.

8. Rafter, *Partial Justice,* p. 21.

9. Barbara Owen and Barbara Bloom, "Profiling women Prisoners: Findings from National Surveys and a California Sample," *Prison Journal* 75 (June 1995): 181–182.

10. Ibid., p. 23.

11. Ibid., p. 35.

12. Allen J. Beck and Darrell K. Gilliard, *Prisoners in 1994,* Bureau of Justice Statistics, Bulletin, August 1995, p. 5.

13. Ibid.

14. Ibid., p. 8.

15. *Prison and Jail Inmates, 1995,* Washington, D.C., National Institute of Justice, Bureau of Statistics, August 1996, p. 5.

16. Tracey Snell, "Women in Prison," National Institute of Justice, *Special Report,* March 1994.

17. Owen and Bloom, "Profiling Women Prisoners," pp. 165–185.

18. Ibid., p. 168.

19. Meda Chesney-Lind and Joycelyn M. Pollock, "Women's Prisons: Equality with a Vengeance," in Alida M. Merlo and Joycelyn M. Pollock, eds., *Women, Law, and Social Control* (Allyn and Bacon, 1995), p. 159 (emphasis in the original).

20. Patrick A. Langan, "America's Soaring Prison Population," *Science* 251 (March 29, 1991), p. 1569.

21. Ibid., p. 181.

22. Denise Johnston, "Child Custody Issues of Women Prisoners: A Preliminary Report from the CHICAS Project," *Prison Journal* 75 (1995): 222.

23. George C. Kiser, "Female Inmates and Their Families," *Federal Probation* 55 (September 1991): 58.

24. Owen and Bloom, "Profiling Women Prisoners," pp. 181–182.

25. Patrick G. Jackson and Cindy A. Stearns, "Gender Issues in the New Generation Jail," *Prison Journal* 75 (1995): 203–221.

26. *Cherco v. County of Sonoma.*

27. Jackson and Stearns, "Gender Issues," p. 206.

28. Ibid., pp. 211–212.

29. Ibid., p. 215.

30. Ibid., p. 217.

31. Ibid.

32. Ibid., p. 219.

33. Michael L. Prendergast, Jean Wellisch, and Gregory P. Falkin, "Assessment of and Services for Substance-Abusing Women Offenders in Community and Correctional Settings," *Prison Journal* 75 (1995): 242.

34. The words of a study interviewee in Beverly Brown Schulke, *Women and Criminal Recidivism: A Study of Social Constraints.* George Washington University doctoral dissertation, May 1993, p. 117.

35. Ibid., p. 223.

36. Ibid., p. 227.

37. Ibid., p. 233.

38. Ibid., p. 237.

39. Lord, "A Prison Superintendent's Perspective," pp. 257–269.

40. Ibid., p. 259.

41. Ibid., p. 263.

42. Ibid.

43. Ibid., p. 265.

44. Lisa G. Fuller, "Visitors to Women's Prisons in California: An Exploratory Study," *Federal Probation* 57 (December 1993): 41–47.

45. Ibid., p. 42.

46. Ibid.

47. Kiser, "Female Inmates," p. 58.

48. Marilyn C. Moses, "Keeping Incarcerated Mothers and Their Children Together: Girl Scouts Beyond Bars," National Institute of Justice, *Program Focus,* October 1995.

49. Ibid., p. 3.

50. Lance C. Couturier, "Inmates Benefit from Family Services Programs," *Corrections Today* 57 (December 1995): 102.

51. For a general description of these programs see "Programs That Work," *Corrections Today* 57 (December 1995): 118–119.

52. Sandra L. Martin and Niki U. Cotten, "Literacy Intervention for Incarcerated Women," *Corrections Today* 57 (December 1995): 120–123.

53. Ibid., pp. 120, 122.

54. Ibid., p. 123.

55. Joycelyn M. Pollock, *Sex and Supervision: Guarding Male and Female Inmates* (New York: Greenwood Press, 1986).

56. Ibid., p. 21.

57. See Chapter 6 for a discussion of Brockway's reformatory system.

58. Prendergast, et al., "Assessment and Services," p. 253.

59. Ibid.

60. Ibid.

61. Ibid.

62. Ibid., p. 254.

63. J. Crawford, *Tabulation of a Nationwide Survey of State Correctional Facilities for Adult and Juvenile Female Offenders,* American Correctional Association, 1988; T. E. Ryan, *Adult Female Offenders and Institutional Programs: A State of the Art Analysis,* National Institute of Justice, 1984.

64. Pollock, *Sex and Supervision,* p. 103.

65. Ibid., p. 109.

66. Chesney-Lind and Pollock, "Women's Prisons," p. 155.

67. Ibid., p. 156.

68. Ibid.

69. *United States v. Pozzy,* 902 F.2d 133 (1990).

70. Ibid., p. 139.

71. 907 F.2d 31 (4th Cir., 1990).

72. Ibid., p. 33.

73. 956 F.2d 894 (9th Cir., 1992). Another case, *United States v. Roe,* 976 F.2d 1216 (9th Cir. 1992), held that sentencing judges could take into account a defendant's history of childhood physical and sexual abuse in deciding upon a sentence.

74. *Glover v. Johnson,* 478 F.Supp. 1075 (E.D. Mich. 1979).

75. 432 F.Supp. 1129 (S.D.N.Y. 1977). This decision was upheld on appeal to the 2nd Circuit Court of Appeals, 565 F.2d 48 (2 Cir. 1977).

76. *Spear v. Ariyoshi,* Consent Decree, Civil No. 84-1104, U.S. District Court, District of Hawaii, June 12, 1985.

77. Chesney-Lind and Pollock, "Women's Prisons," p. 168.

78. Rafter, *Partial Justice,* p. 178.

79. Lord, "A Prison Superintendent's Perspective," pp. 266–267.

80. Kiser, "Female Inmates," p. 63.

PRISONER'S RIGHTS

INTRODUCTION COURTS HAVE BEEN BUSY handling lawsuits filed by prisoners challenging not the sentences they have been given, but the conditions of imprisonment. In 1993 these suits accounted for 23 percent of all civil filings in federal court, 50 percent in some states. In 40 states, broad orders have been issued to oversee every detail of the operation of a prison.[1]

In April, 1996, Congress enacted the Prison Litigation Reform Act, partly as a response to the explosion of suits by prisoners. The law severely limits inmate access to the courts to contest the conditions and treatment they experience in correctional institutions. It will permit states to request that court orders overseeing their prison operations resulting from inmate lawsuits be lifted after two years. If inmates want these orders reinstated, they will have to return to court.[2]

Undoubtedly, many lawsuits filed by inmates are frivolous, raising questions unrelated to serious violations of prisoners' rights.* This, to some extent, explains

---

*For example, some inmates have argued that they have been served melted ice cream and crunchy instead of smooth peanut butter, and given Converse rather than Reebok shoes. ("Prisoners and Peanut Butter," *Washington Post*, September 30, 1995, p. A32.)

the action by Congress. Prisoners do, however, have rights, and, at times, these rights have been violated by the actions or inactions of prison officials.

In this chapter we will identify inmate rights and the recourse prisoners have when they believe these rights are violated. Explosive growth in state and federal prison populations, mandatory and long-term incarceration sentences, and the increasingly heavy burden facing prison officials attempting to maintain order and deliver some correctional programming, have meant that the question of prisoners' rights has moved to the front burner.

To understand what rights prisoners have requires that we look into the development of case law over a considerable period of time. Although there are statutory and administrative laws covering the rights of prisoners (as well as the rights of prison officials), the most important statements regarding prisoners' rights have come from decisions of appellate courts on a case-by-case basis. When these decisions come from the Supreme Court, they become the "law of the land" and must be respected by state and federal correctional workers.

A nineteenth-century decision of the Virginia state Supreme Court gives us a concise view of the legal status of inmates in American prisons that has held true until relatively recently. In that decision, the court turned down an inmate's request to declare unconstitutional the treatment he received and the conditions he suffered during his confinement. In the written opinion, the court stated that:

> The Bill of Rights is a declaration of general principles to govern a society of free men, and not of convicted felons. . . . Such men have some rights it is true, such as the law in its benignity accords them, but not the rights of free men. They are slaves of the State undergoing punishment for heinous crimes committed against the laws of the land.[3]

Although this view has constitutional support,[4] it has not stopped prisoners from seeking relief for alleged rights violations by their keepers. Many legal actions have been so framed, however, that if the courts were to accept inmates' claims as valid, they would of necessity be required to intervene in the daily operation of prisons. This is a step courts have always been reluctant to take.

Whatever rights are demanded by inmates and granted by the state, paramount consideration must be given to two concepts: **prison security** and **reasonableness,** against which alleged rights and abuses are judged. That is, are the actions of officials in restricting rights reasonably related to the need for internal and external security? Related questions are whether prison conditions or the use of physical force by officials constitutes cruel and unusual punishment, and whether inmates are entitled to due process in regard to restrictions imposed as punishment for rules violations. If so, how much due process is required?

Then there is the distinction to be made between rights and privileges. In the case of the former, obviously, due process and other constitutional protections may be decisive. For denials of alleged rights that are, in fact, privileges, there is much less protection available under the law. For example, permitting conjugal visits in prison is considered a privilege to which an inmate has no right. On the other hand, sending and receiving mail, while subject to "reasonable" restrictions, is considered a right. Actions to deny this right may be successfully challenged in court.

Finally, we will take a close look at prisoners' rights in the relatively new "super-max" prisons. We discussed these institutions in a general way in Chapter 8. The super-max prison raises a number of rights issues, which we will examine.

As we begin to look at prisoners' rights it is useful to consider one important Supreme Court case because it provides a test as to whether prison officials' actions that restrict prisoners' activities or terms of confinement violate their rights. The test comes from *Turner v. Safley,*[5] decided in 1987. The framework is in the form of a set of questions:

1. Is there a logical connection between the restriction challenged and a legitimate interest the restriction is to protect?
2. Do inmates have an alternative means to exercise the right in question?
3. What is the impact of acceding to the inmate's claim of a right on prison administration, staff, and other inmates?
4. Are there any readily available alternatives that would protect the inmate's right with minimum impact of generally accepted correctional interests or objectives?
   We will return later to other aspects of this important case.

HISTORICAL REVIEW OF PRISONERS' RIGHTS

Only recently have the courts intervened to examine and sometimes order remedies for alleged violations of prisoners' rights. Courts historically have been reluctant to take steps that would put them in the business of running prisons and jails. The Supreme Court indicated this reluctance in its 1979 decision in *Bell v. Wolfish:*

> . . . [P]rison administrators should be accorded wide-ranging deference in the adoption and execution of policies and practices that in their judgment are needed to preserve internal order and discipline and to maintain institutional security.[6]

For some time now, this thinking has been changing as prisoners have increasingly sought to challenge prison conditions and officials' actions. In a review of case law, Jack Call suggested that appellate court involvement in cases alleging violations of prisoners' rights falls, historically, into three major periods: (1) hands-off period; (2) rights period; and (3) deference period.[7] We will trace the history of prisoner's rights litigation using Call's framework.

Immediately following this discussion, we will examine the situation now that prisoners' rights have been integrated into the American Correctional Association's (ACA) accreditation program. As we described in Chapter 8, the ACA has established standards for correctional institutions with respect to the rights of prisoners.* Meeting these standards is required if an institution is to be fully accredited.

The Hands-Off Period

At the beginning of the chapter we quoted from a nineteenth-century Virginia appellate court decision that declared that inmates were **slaves of the state,** to be granted only those rights and privileges the state in its mercy chose to grant them. During the **hands-off period,** which lasted until approximately 1964, state and federal courts usually considered questions of inmate rights to be the responsibility of legislatures and executive departments. Clearly, this view reflected the principle of separation of powers, a fundamental principle of governance from the foundation of the United States as an independent nation.

---

*The ACA also has standards for other elements in corrections: parole, probation, detention facilities, boot camps, to mention a few.

*O*riginally prisoner's lawsuits brought to light the harshness of prison life and inmates were represented by public interest law attorneys. In the 1960s and 1970s the courts were willing to respond to appeals by politically and economically disadvantaged groups such as prison inmates.

Another reason for the reluctance of the judiciary to intervene in the affairs of prison systems was its lack of expertise:

> Because of their lack of understanding of the operation of prisons, if courts took steps to protect prisoners' rights, they ran a great risk of interfering with the proper functioning of the institutions.[8]

During most of the hands-off period, it was an accepted principle that federal courts, including the Supreme Court, lacked jurisdiction to consider inmates' claims. The vast majority of prisoners are confined in state, not federal courts. Therefore, the federal judiciary had little if any role to play when inmates sought redress in court. The Constitution was not available as a basis for challenging state actions in most cases. This, of course, was before the "incorporation doctrine" altered the jurisprudence by incorporating much of the Bill of Rights into the Fourteenth Amendment's due process clause. After acceptance of the **incorporation doctrine,** allegations that state actions violated civil rights, such as the right not to suffer cruel and unusual punishments, could be brought to federal as well as state courts.

The Rights Period

Between 1964 and 1978, prisoners began to assert their rights more forcefully. Significantly, several concomitant developments led to a number of successful challenges against prison practices. One was the emergence of a new "public interest law" category of attorneys. These lawyers were eager to take on litigation raised by inmates. One group specifically organized to take prisoners' cases is the Prisoners Legal Services Corporation. The second development was the willingness of the courts to

FOCUS ON
THE LAW

SECTION 1983 OF THE CIVIL RIGHTS ACT OF 1871

Every person, who under color of any statute, ordinance, regulation, custom, or usage, of any State or Territory, subjects or causes to be subjected, any citizen of the United States or person within the jurisdiction thereof to the deprivation of any rights, privileges, or immunities secured by the Constitution and laws, shall be liable to the party injured in an action at law, suit in equity, or other proper proceeding for redress.

respond to appeals by politically and economically disadvantaged groups in society. One such group was prison inmates.

Another development that brought the hands-off policy to an end was the startling "discovery" that in many prisons, conditions were at least as atrocious as prisoner litigants were proclaiming in their suits. As one California appellate court said in a case brought by two women inmates, "a reading of the cases . . . presents a harsh commentary on prison life in these United States. . . . [It reveals] prison life which is harsh, brutal, filthy, unwholesome and inhumane."[9] The court referred to previous cases in which inmates were placed in solitary confinement cells "infested with bugs, worms, and vermin and when the toilet was flushed the contents ran out on the floor."[10]

During this **rights period,** a major factor was inmate use of Section 1983 of the 1871 Civil Rights Act[11] as a basis for challenging actions by state and federal prison officials. **Section 1983 suits** claim that federally protected rights have been violated by an official acting "under the color of state law."[12] Many of the suits we will discuss below were Section 1983 suits. The language of Section 1983 may be found in the accompanying Focus on the Law feature.

The surge in Section 1983 suits by inmates coincided with the civil rights movement and the initiation of "Great Society" programs sponsored by the Johnson administration. Concerns for the rights of the poor, the socially disadvantaged, and those discriminated against because of racism were reflected in a number of Supreme Court decisions (as well as the decisions of lower courts). Prison inmates clearly fit the profile of disadvantaged Americans who were intended to be the beneficiaries of changes wrought by the civil rights movement and Great Society programs.

The Deference Period

From about 1979, various appellate court decisions initiated a trend toward narrowing the interpretation of prisoners' rights. One consequence of these decisions is that it is more difficult for inmates successfully to challenge the conditions of their confinement and the actions of prison officials. During this period the courts returned to a position characteristic of much of the hands-off period: They frequently deferred to the expertise of those charged with running correctional institutions. A quote from the Supreme Court in an important decision summarizes the stance the courts would be taking during the **deference period:**

[U]nder the Constitution, the first question that must be answered is not whose plan [for operating prisons] is best, but in what branch of the Government is lodged the authority to initially devise the plan. This does not mean that constitutional rights are not to be scrupulously observed. It does mean, however, that the inquiry of federal courts into prison management must be limited to the issue of whether a particular system violates any prohibition of the Constitution. . . . The wide range of "judgment calls" that meet constitutional . . . requirements are confined to officials outside the Judicial Branch of Government.[13]

An important test of whether corrections officials violate rights such as the right to be protected from cruel and unusual punishments came during this period. It is the **deliberate indifference** test. The Supreme Court specified this standard for judging whether a punishment or official action violates the Eighth Amendment in *Estelle v. Gamble,* a 1976 case.[14] The appeal centered on the alleged denial of medical services by the Texas Department of Corrections. Because of inadequate medical care, the inmate, J. W. Gamble, said he was unfit for work assignments. He was eventually brought before the prison disciplinary committee and placed in solitary confinement. Gamble filed a complaint under Section 1983 of the Civil Rights Act of 1871. The Court took the case on appeal because "deliberate indifference to serious medical needs of prisoners constitutes 'unnecessary and wanton' infliction of pain."[15] The Supreme Court decided that, while certain alleged actions and inactions of the Texas prison medical staff may have constituted malpractice, these did not constitute cruel and unusual punishment. Should Gamble seek to pursue a malpractice suit, he was advised to file such a suit with the Texas Tort Claims Court.

With regard to general prison conditions, as opposed to specific issues such as medical treatment or use of physical force by prison officials, the Court held that inmate litigants are required to show convincing evidence that conditions in a prison or actions of its officials demonstrated that those in charge were deliberately indifferent to the effects of these conditions or actions on the prisoner population. Showing that conditions or official actions were harsh or deplorable was insufficient in most cases heard in appellate courts during this period.

The rationale for generally disregarding prison conditions as grounds for redress in the courts was that "general conditions of confinement are not part of the sentence."[16] Thus, "where general conditions of confinement are at issue, inmates must show that prison officials acted with deliberate indifference to some basic human need of inmates."[17]

During this period of judicial deference to the expertise of prison officials, we see that prisoners' rights are supported in some areas, but not in others. For example, prisoners do have right of access to the courts to press their claims. However, in the recent past, these petitioners have usually failed to obtain favorable decisions in various areas of individual rights, due process, and cruel and unusual punishments. In the following section, we will examine the results of prisoners' court challenges in these and other areas.

It is during this period that privatization of prisons and prison services began to pick up steam, as we discussed in Chapter 8. One of the important issues that must be addressed with respect to privatization is whether private contractors such as Corrections Corporation of America will be held to the same standards with regard to prisoners' rights as state agencies. There has been some concern that these private operators can and will evade compliance with constitutional and other requirements.[18] The reason for this is that "rights guaranteed by the . . . Constitution are protected only from government infringement."[19] This means that allegations that rights have been violated must show that the deprivation results from "state" action. This may not be an onerous requirement since actions by officials can be challenged successfully if one can establish that the actions are "fairly attributable to the state."[20]

According to one review of the status of prisoners' rights in private facilities and programs, there have been few court tests of private corrections' respect for prisoners' rights. In *Medina v. O'Neill*,[21] the Immigration and Naturalization Service (INS) entered into a private contract for detention of illegal immigrants. The suit against INS charged that the private operators of the detention facility maintained such poor and harmful conditions that they constituted punishment. Since the detainees had not been convicted of any crime, they argued that they were being punished without due process, a violation of the Constitution. The federal appellate court agreed, holding that the facility was required to respect the rights of its detainees since "Congress delegated its authority over immigration to the INS and because Congress authorized the INS to designate places of detention for excluded aliens, the Court concluded that both the INS and the private facilities . . . were bound by the Fifth Amendment due process standards."[22]

This ruling seems to mean that when a public entity of the state designates a private agency to carry out a mission that generally is within the public domain, the private agency must adhere to the same policies and practices with respect to prisoners' rights. In another case, the appellate court held a private facility accountable to the Constitution when confinement or treatment in such facilities is involuntary because of decisions by the state.[23]

These decisions suggest that the rights of prisoners confined in privately operated institutions will receive the same protections as those in state and federal prisons. Thus, Section 1983 suits and other avenues of access to the courts will be available to prisoners should they believe their rights have been violated. However, as one commentator noted, those who seek to advance the rights of prisoners "should be alert to the possibility that governments will deliberately use privatization . . . to evade constitutional restraints."[24]

A REVIEW OF THE CURRENT STATUS OF PRISONERS' RIGHTS

American Correctional Association Standards on Inmate Rights

Beginning in 1978, the American Correctional Association (ACA), together with the Commission on Accreditation, established a set of standards by which corrections agencies and institutions may voluntarily seek **accreditation**. There are over 400 different standards, 38 of which are mandatory.[25] Among the mandatory standards are 10 that relate to prisoners' rights. The standards begin with a statement of the operating principle: "the institution protects the safety and constitutional rights of inmates and seeks a balance between expression of individual rights and preservation of institutional order."[26] The accompanying On the Job feature lists the ACA's standards on prisoners' rights.

In addition to these rights, other standards cover areas such as mail, visitation, health services, and religious practices. Participation in the accreditation process is voluntary, and there are no direct sanctions for either failure to participate or failure to meet the ACA's standards. However, evidence that a correctional facility does not meet certain of the accreditation standards has been used by inmates and groups on their behalf to support their claims that rights have been violated.

ON THE JOB

THE AMERICAN CORRECTIONAL ASSOCIATION'S STANDARDS ON INMATE RIGHTS

The American Correctional Association's "Standards for Adult Correctional Institutions" lists the following standards on inmate rights for prisons that voluntarily submit to the accreditation process. These are among 38 "mandatory" standards in a variety of areas that must be met if an institution is to receive accreditation.

- Access to courts. Prisons must have written policy, procedure, and practice ensuring inmate access to the courts.
- *Access to counsel.* Inmates must be granted contact with attorneys and their authorized representatives.
- *Access to programs and services.* This is a set of three standards that relates to access to work assignments, equal access for male and female inmates, and "reasonable" access to and by the communications media, limited only by security needs and inmates' privacy.
- *Protection from harm.* Inmates are to be protected from "personal abuse, corporal punishment, personal injury, disease, property damage, and harassment."
- *Protection from unreasonable searches.* "Written policy, procedure, and practice govern all searches and preservation of evidence when an inmate is suspected of a new crime."
- *Freedom in personal grooming.* Inmates are to be free to make grooming choices except when a "valid interest" indicates otherwise.
- *Grievance procedures.* Inmates are to have access to an established grievance mechanism that provides for at least one appeal.

SOURCE: American Correctional Association, *Standards for Adult Correctional Institutions,* 3d ed. (Lanham, MD: January 1990).

In the following sections, we will take up many of the areas in which the ACA has set standards. Our main focus will be on the legal support, mainly through the mechanism of case law, for inmate rights.

First Amendment Rights

Mail

This area of prisoners' rights is of particular interest to the author because his first staff assignment in a state prison was that of mail censor. At that time prison censors were required to read all outgoing and incoming mail. They had authority to return outgoing letters to inmates because of rules violations, such as letters that gave detailed information about the layout of the physical plant and custodial staffing, or letters containing language that was considered obscene or pornographic. Incoming mail was rarely returned to the sender unless it contained offensive language or contraband. The possibility of mail containing contraband was especially troublesome during the Christmas season when it was easier to conceal illicit items such as drugs in Christmas cards.

Inmate mail generally is divided into two categories: special or privileged, and general. Privileged mail includes correspondence with attorneys, judges, and some public officials. It is well accepted that privileged mail usually cannot be interfered with.

*P*risoners are allowed to use law libraries set up in state prisons. There is a legal requirement to make these facilities available to prisoners.

Under some conditions, privileged mail may be opened by officials in the presence of the inmate only to check for contraband, but not to be read or censored. General mail can be opened, checked for contraband, and read for the purpose of ensuring security.

As a general rule, inmates are permitted to receive books, magazines, and other publications from outside, unless wardens determine that a publication is "detrimental to the security, good order, or discipline of the institution or might facilitate criminal activity."[27]

Right to Publish

This area has caused much controversy and litigation especially with the passage of state "Son of Sam" statutes. These laws place significant restrictions on publication of inmate memoirs and other materials related to their crimes. Many laws require that some or all royalties must be paid to victims, their families, or state victim compensation boards. There is still unsettled case law here, although the preponderance of it seems to support the principle that an inmate may not be prohibited from writing for publication, but should not profit from writing about his or her crimes. One problem with understanding just what this principle means is that case law seems to be of two minds when this issue is litigated. Of, course, when rights are in conflict, this is not unusual. For example, in *Simon & Schuster v. New York State Crime Victims Board*,[28] the Supreme Court held that New York's "Son of Sam" law was overly broad. The statute provided that proceeds from writing about one's crime must be turned over to the state's victims' compensation board. The Court's opinion stated that in order to restrict a person's free speech right, a statute must show that its "regulation is necessary to serve a compelling state interest and is narrowly drawn to achieve that end." The New York State Court of Appeals had, in an earlier case, upheld the statute. On appeal to the Supreme Court, that opinion was vacated and sent back for reconsideration in light of the *Schuster* decision.

Visitation

The right to be visited by family, friends, and attorneys is generally upheld by courts and correctional department regulations. Officials may screen potential visitors and limit both the number of approved visitors and the number of visits permitted in a certain time period (each month, for example). Where the author worked, there were restrictions placed on the number of persons on the approved list, as well as who these visitors were. An inmate's attorney did not count against the list. Departmental regulations were designed to minimize "domestic" disputes by prohibiting married inmates from having "girlfriends" on the visitors' list. Single prisoners were not permitted more than one "girlfriend." Frequently, a number of "aunts," "nieces, and "sisters" would be nominated by inmates. This required the institution's Social Services Department to verify the status of these nominees.

In some prisons such as super-max institutions, visits are more severely limited, and these restrictive policies have been upheld in the courts when challenged. **Contact visits*** can be prohibited if officials deem them to be risks to security. The majority in one Supreme Court case upheld the authority of officials to prohibit contact visits, even though it conceded that such visits could be a positive "factor contributing to the ultimate reintegration [of the prisoner] into society."[29] However, the majority concluded that "the Constitution does not require that detainees be allowed contact visits when responsible, experienced administrators have determined, in their sound discretion, that such visits will jeopardize the security of the facility."[30]

Conjugal visits are treated as privileges. Some (not many) correctional systems allow these visits on a controlled basis. Regulations provide ways for inmates to "earn" conjugal visits, much like earning good-time for good behavior. It is clear that prison administrators have to be concerned about risks to security that such physically intimate visits may pose. There are also concerns that such visits may result in pregnancies, increasing the number of dependents inmates will be unable to support while incarcerated.

Religion

There has been a considerable amount of litigation in this area. Two major issues that have arisen are the availability of religious services and special diets. What happens when an inmate is a member of a religion that is not a "mainstream" religion? In *Cruz v. Beto*, the Court held that a prisoner, a Buddhist, must be given a "reasonable opportunity of pursuing his faith comparable to the opportunity afforded fellow prisoners who adhere to conventional religious precepts."[31] Still, case law applies the "reasonableness" test to inmates' exercise of religion with regard to the special security needs of prisons. This is clear in the following case.

In the 1987 Supreme Court case of *O'Lone v. Shabazz*,[32] the issue was a corrections department regulation that prevented a Muslim inmate from returning early to the institution from a work detail in order to attend religious services held only on Fri-

---

*These are visits during which inmates and their visitors are not separated by physical barriers. In some systems, contact visits may include dining in a picnic-like setting. Conjugal visits are, of course, a type of contact visit. They are rare in American correctional practice.

*M*inisters, rabbis, priests, nuns, and religious leaders of various faiths come to the inmates and conduct religious services for individuals or groups throughout the year.

days. The inmate had a security classification that severely circumscribed his movements. He argued that the regulation violated his right to the free exercise of his religion, in violation of the free exercise clause of the First Amendment to the Constitution. The Supreme Court denied Shabazz's appeal, finding that to require the institution to bring this inmate back in order to attend services would pose a security risk. Shabazz's argument that he be allowed to remain in the prison on the day of services (Fridays) and make up his work on the next day would require the institution to devote additional resources to supervise his movements. This would impose an unreasonable burden on the prison.

Inmate Organizations

Inmates in some correctional systems have sought to organize themselves into unions, claiming the right to peaceful assembly under the First Amendment. In the case of *Jones v. N.C. Prisoners' Labor Union*,[33] inmates objected to the state's severe restrictions on the activities of their union. In addition to a First Amendment argument, they also raised a Fourteenth Amendment argument that claimed they were denied "equal protection of the laws" because other inmate organizations (such as the Jaycees and Alcoholics Anonymous) were relatively free to recruit members and engage in various activities. The Supreme Court ruled that while inmates can form organizations such as "unions," prison officials can severely restrict their activities. These restrictions may include prohibiting meetings and recruitment of members. Also, it is clear that correctional managers are under no obligation to "negotiate" with such inmate organizations. In the *Jones* case, such negotiating was specifically prohibited by a state statute. Some of the language from the Court's opinion clearly indicates the deference it gives to the expertise and needs of corrections officials to act reasonably in the interest of maintaining order:

> . . . [P]rison officials concluded that the presence, perhaps even the objectives, of a prisoners' labor union would be detrimental to order and security in the prisons. It is enough to say that they have not been shown to be conclusively wrong in this view. The interest in preserving order and authority in the prisons is self-evident. Prison life, and relations between the inmates themselves and the inmates and prison officials and staff, contain the ever-present potential for violent confrontation and conflagration. Responsible . . . officials must be permitted to take reasonable steps to forestall such a threat, and they must be permitted to act before the time when they can compile a dossier on the eve of a riot.[34]

Fourth Amendment: Searches and Seizures

The Constitution protects us against "unreasonable" searches and seizures of our persons, effects, and papers. Does an inmate have any right to protect his person and living quarters against searches and seizures by prison officials? Because of the peculiar nature of the prison setting, security needs are the dominant criteria applied when judging the reasonableness of searches and seizures. Generally, strip searches of inmates are permitted on a random or routine basis. Body cavity searches are permitted following visits from the outside. Searches of inmates' cells also are supported by law. In the words of a Supreme Court opinion:

> . . . [N]o matter how malicious, destructive or arbitrary a cell search and seizure may be, it cannot constitute an unreasonable invasion of any privacy or possessory interest that society is prepared to recognize as reasonable.[35]

Eighth Amendment: Cruel and Unusual Punishment

When, if ever, do prison conditions or acts of prison officials constitute "cruel and unusual" punishment? Given the current state of the law, inmates must show that conditions or injuries that cause suffering beyond those imposed by their sentences were the result of deliberate physical acts by officials that have no support in the prison's need to maintain security and good order. It is important to understand that "punishment" refers to the elements included in a court-imposed sentence that is a consequence of conviction for a violation of criminal law. The elements in a sentence can be challenged. For example, a sentence that calls for an excessive fine, period of confinement, or draconian restrictions and conditions of probation might be found to violate the Eighth Amendment.

Let's take a look at a specific instance of alleged violation of the Eighth Amendment prohibition against cruel and unusual punishment that was brought to the Supreme Court. The issue was not related to the sentence ordered by the trial court. Rather, it was whether the actions of prison officials at Louisiana's Angola prison against an inmate violated the Constitution. The case, *Hudson v. McMillian*,[36] was decided in 1992. The accompanying Focus on the Law feature quotes language from it.

Our reading of the account of inmate Hudson's beating might well suggest that he was subjected to punishment (for what violation of prison rules we don't know from the record) that was cruel, if not unusual. Hudson's Section 1983 suit against the officers was heard in a federal district court, which awarded him $800 in damages. However, the Fifth Circuit Court of Appeals reversed this decision because an inmate who claims officials used excessive force must prove the following before a favorable judgment may be obtained:

FOCUS ON THE LAW

PRISONERS' RIGHTS IN THE CASE OF *HUDSON V. MCMILLIAN*

At the time of the incident that is the subject of this suit, petitioner . . . Hudson was an inmate at the state penitentiary in Angola, Louisiana. Respondents Jack McMillian, Marvin Woods, and Arthur Mezo served as corrections security officers. . . . During the early morning hours of October 30, 1983, Hudson and McMillian argued. Assisted by Woods, McMillian then placed Hudson in handcuffs and shackles, took the prisoner out of his cell, and walked him toward . . . the "administrative lockdown" area. Hudson testified that, on the way there, McMillian punched [him] in the mouth, eyes, chest, and stomach while Woods held [him] in place and kicked and punched him from behind. He further testified that Mezo, the supervisor on duty, watched the beating but merely told the officers "not to have too much fun." As a result of the episode, Hudson suffered minor bruises and swelling of his face, mouth, and lip. The blows also loosened Hudson's teeth and cracked his partial dental plate, rendering it unusable for several months.

- There was a "significant injury,"
- The injury resulted "directly and only from the use of force that was clearly excessive to the need."
- The excessiveness of the force was objectively unreasonable.
- The action constituted an "unnecessary and wanton infliction of pain."[37]

Although the appellate court found that the last three of these were proved by Hudson, it still reversed the district court's award of damages because "his injuries were 'minor' and required no medical attention."[39] The case was appealed to the Supreme Court, which reiterated the general principle that the "unnecessary and wanton infliction of pain . . . constitutes cruel and unusual punishment." The Court dismissed the lower court's finding that Hudson's injuries were minor, and remarked in its decision to reverse the lower court's ruling that the correctional officers' involved beat another inmate shortly after beating Hudson. In addition, the Court found that the supervising officer "expressly condoned the use of violence in this case."[39]

In a 1991 case, *Wilson v. Seiter,* [40]inmates attacked general prison conditions as constituting cruel and unusual punishment, thus, they claimed, violating the Eighth Amendment. In this challenge, it was not the act of a particular official or group of officials as was contested in *Hudson,* but the alleged deplorable conditions. In its decision, the Court adhered to the principle that conditions in a prison (such as overcrowding and poor food and sanitary conditions) are not elements in the punishment handed down by a trial court. What inmates must prove is that prison officials acted with "deliberate indifference" to some "basic human" need by permitting the questioned conditions to persist.[41]

While the standard of "deliberate indifference" to the harm caused inmates became the measuring rod against which official action was to be judged, it was a difficult standard to evaluate. In a later case, the Court refined it by requiring that the indifference be found to constitute "recklessness" by those prison officials who should be aware of the risks to inmates of the conditions in their institutions.[42]

Medical Care

There have been a number of appellate cases in which prisoners have claimed that they were denied adequate medical care. These include *Estelle v. Gamble*,[43] and *Ruiz v. Estelle*.[44] From these and other cases, if denial of medical care is judged to constitute "deliberate indifference" to the medical needs of inmates, it is unconstitutional. Note that simple "indifference," medical malpractice, or lax care is not unconstitutional.

Fourteenth Amendment: Due Process and Disciplinary Actions

How much, if any, due process are inmates entitled to when various disciplinary actions are taken against them by officials? These actions can be, for example, transfers to other institutions, disciplinary penalties, loss of good-time,* and punitive or other segregation from the general population. Case law dictates that inmate challenges based on due process violations must be able to show that the inmate has a liberty interest protected by the Fourteenth Amendment. Even when such a showing is made, an inmate may be entitled only to a rather perfunctory due process, as in *Hewett v. Helms*,[45] (1983) in which the Supreme Court held that a prisoner placed in segregation (the "hole") was entitled only to a nonadversarial, informal disciplinary hearing.

When states make good-time credits available, courts have determined that prisoners have a liberty interest that must be protected by due process procedures when credits are to be withdrawn. A 1974 Supreme Court case, *Wolff v. McDonnell*, resulted in the requirement that inmates are entitled to a hearing, adequate notice of the reasons for denying good-time credits, an opportunity to call witnesses, present evidence, and receive a written statement following the hearing laying out the reasons for a decision to deny credits.[46]

We note that the *Wolff* decision did not give inmates an absolute right to be represented by someone (another inmate or prison staff member) when they are to be denied good-time credits. The Court did recognize that in some cases, an inmate's intelligence or level of literacy may require such assistance. In a dissent, Justice Marshall stated that there should be such a right in all cases. A number of state corrections departments have taken steps to provide some form of representation to inmates who are brought before disciplinary boards. In the example below, we examine the Texas Department of Corrections' model.

The Texas approach was triggered by the "landmark" case of *Ruiz v. Estelle*[47] which condemned extreme overcrowding and many of the policies and practices in the state's penal system. Among other responses to the court's ruling, and the ruling in the *Wolff* case, Texas introduced **substitute counsel** when disciplinary hearings were held on inmate rules violations.[48] The first such use involved custodial officers assisting inmates who were "mentally impaired, illiterate, or did not understand English, or because of the complexity of the issue, . . . inmates would not be able to collect and present evidence necessary to an adequate comprehension of the case."[49]

Although this would seem to be a significant step toward providing inmates with due process (in line with Justice Marshall's dissent in *Wolff*), there were some prob-

---

*Good-time credits are established by statutes and vary considerably from state to state. For example, Illinois provides for day-for-day credits. For each day of good behavior, a sentence is reduced by one day (Ill. Rev. Stat., § 1003-6-3). Most other states are not so generous.

lems with this model. One was that playing substitute counsel was an uncomfortable role for correctional officers. On some tiers, this problem was exacerbated because the prison administration revealed its ambivalence by making the assignment "permanent for the slow and ineffective employee."[50] Not a way to win friends and influence people to perform their duties adequately.

Other problems surfaced when it was found that substitute counsel were given no special training for their new roles, and many of them simply had neither the time nor the inclination to understand fully the charges brought against their "clients." Eventually, under pressure from inmates, a revised system was agreed to, a system that established the office of Staff Counsel, which is responsible for supervising the work of substitute counsel who no longer are correctional officers.

When inmates are charged with violations of prison rules and regulations, a set of due process steps are taken that include adequate and timely notification of the charges, assignment of a substitute counsel, investigation and documentation of the charges and possible defenses to them, and a formal hearing at which the inmate is represented by the substitute counsel. Partly as a result of these and other changes, Texas anticipates "release from monitoring and the end of 15 years of continuous judicial intervention."[51]

Due Process and Forced Treatment

As we have seen in previous chapters, prisons sometimes provide a variety of treatment services and programs, including educational and vocational classes, drug and substance abuse counseling, psychotherapy, and administration of psychotropic medications. Many inmates enter these programs voluntarily, as we saw in Chapter 8, but there is a growing sentiment among penologists that at least some of these programs should be mandatory. That is the position of the Federal Bureau of Prisons with respect to requiring a minimum SAT score of all its inmates. Do prisoners have the right to refuse? The law in this area is not particularly clear. There is one Supreme Court case in this decade that give us some insight regarding enforced treatment with psychotropic drugs. In *Washington v. Harper,*[52] the issue was tied to the Fourteenth Amendment's due process clause. The Court stated the question to be decided as "whether a judicial hearing is required before the State may treat a mentally ill prisoner with antipsychotic drugs against his will."[53]

The Court, in its decision, made it clear that this is a very important question:

> Respondent's interest in avoiding the unwarranted administration of antipsychotic drugs is not insubstantial. The forcible injection of medication into a nonconsenting person's body represents a substantial interference with that person's liberty. . . . The purpose of the drugs is to alter the chemical balance in a patient's brain, leading to changes intended to be beneficial, in his or her cognitive processes. . . . While the therapeutic benefits . . . are well documented, it is also true that the drugs can have serious, fatal, side effects.[54]

The Court reasoned that a state correctional system must strike a balance between its interest in safety and security when an inmate's mental condition poses a risk to the inmate and others, and the liberty interest of the inmate. To achieve this balance a reasonable due process procedure must be in place. *Harper* claimed that due process could only be obtained through a hearing in a court of law. The Supreme Court disagreed, finding the Washington State Policy Directive (600.30) sufficient to meet the due process test. Because it illustrates what the Supreme Court sees as sufficient due process regarding enforced treatment, and, therefore, is the law that state and federal correctional institutions must follow, we summarize below the main points in Washington's policy and procedure.

An inmate may be involuntarily medicated when:

1. A psychiatrist determines that he or she suffers from a "mental disorder."
2. The inmate is "gravely disabled" or poses a "likelihood of serious harm" to himself or others or their property.
3. If the inmate refuses the medication, he or she is entitled to a hearing before a special committee that includes a psychiatrist, psychologist, and the associate superintendent, none of whom are involved in the inmate's diagnosis or treatment.
4. The inmate has the right to attend the hearing, question witnesses, present evidence, and be assisted by a "lay advisor."
5. A majority decision of the hearing committee is required.
6. Inmates who object to a decision to medicate them may appeal to the facility's superintendent, and, failing to convince the superintendent, inmates may seek judicial intervention by way of a restraining order.
7. Once medication is begun, it may be continued only after a periodic review by a committee.

We certainly must assume that this elaborate procedure is not invoked often. We wonder whether it can be implemented in a timely fashion should an inmate be experiencing a psychotic episode.

PRISONERS' RIGHTS IN THE SUPER-MAX PRISON

The state of Maryland is facing a lawsuit by inmates in its super-max prison located in Baltimore. Among the allegations raised by the prisoners are that the institution maintains "grossly deficient" mental health services and deprives inmates of "natural" light and fresh air.[55] As we saw in Chapter 8, super-maximum prisons most often are used to house inmates identified as causing serious disciplinary and security problems in a correctional system's ordinary prisons. In the words of Maryland's director of correctional services, the super-max prison's population consists of those "who are extremely violent, have escaped from other prisons, assaulted staff or inmates, or simply caused too much trouble."[56] Currently, the population of 250 inmates includes 105 murderers and 19 rapists. Most of the others have assaulted staff and inmates in other prisons.[57]

Maryland's problem with its super-max institution surfaced when Deval L. Patrick, Assistant United States Attorney General, ordered an investigation of numerous inmate complaints. In a letter to Maryland Governor Parris Glendening, Patrick stated that the investigation uncovered:

> conditions of extreme social isolation and reduced environmental stimulation, like the conditions at Supermax, violate evolving standards of humanity, and decency which imposed on those who are at particularly high risk for suffering very serious or severe injury to their mental health.[58]

A major complaint against Maryland's policy and practice is that many of the super-max inmates are mentally disordered, not simply troublemakers. At the super-max prison, according to the investigation, mental health services are in short supply, which raises a "cruel and unusual" constitutional question.

ACROSS CULTURES

PRISONERS' RIGHTS IN THE GERMAN DEMOCRATIC REPUBLIC

In the former German Democratic Republic (GDR), all prisoners had the right to work and be compensated for their labor. Not only were they entitled to paid employment while imprisoned,

> It meant paid work with all the normal social security benefits. In terms of social insurance, prisoners were placed on an equal footing with workers outside prisons. The wages of prisoners were not the same as those of workers outside; they amounted to only 18 per cent of the take home pay a normal worker would get for performing the same task. (p. 85)

During the period leading up to the reunification of Germany, GDR inmates were concerned that some of their rights would be denied once there was a unified prison system. A "crisis" developed in the system brought on by "attempted escapes, hunger strikes, suicide threats . . . and demands for improvement in prison conditions and review of sentences" (p. 89).

Among the results of these actions by prisoners, many were granted amnesty, had their convictions overturned, and a large number released conditionally. Other rights gained as a result of prisoner actions included:

- Up to three weeks home leave per year.
- Use of personal radio and TV sets.
- End to limitations on amount of correspondence.
- Expansion of visiting privileges.
- Free street clothing at time of release.

SOURCE: Jorg Arnold, "Corrections in the German Democratic Republic," *British Journal of Criminology* 35 (Winter 1995): 85, 89.

While denying that there are many mentally disordered prisoners at the institution, the system's director claimed that there is a "fundamental misunderstanding" regarding the super-max mission. It is not a "correctional" facility in the traditional sense. Even the name of the facility, "Maryland Correctional Adjustment Center," conveys the idea that it exists to "adjust" inmates to prison life. There are no educational, vocational, or counseling programs. Once "adjusted," inmates are supposed to be returned to other institutions. Without the option of transferring troublesome inmates to the adjustment center, the ordinary prisons would be much more violent places, the director stated.

The regimen is severe. Inmates live in single cells with 65 square feet of space. The Justice Department investigation found that prisoners are taken out of these cells "only every two or three days, and were never exposed to fresh air—despite a Division of Corrections policy entitling inmates to an hour away from their cells each day."[59]

There has been little case law with respect to the rights of prisoners in a super-maximum facility. One such case, *Madrid v. Gomez*,[60] did hold that certain conditions in California's Pelican Bay institution violated the Eighth Amendment. In particular, the District Court for the Northern District of California found that housing mentally ill inmates in the institution was unconstitutional because mental health services were inadequate. This case may well be a precedent that will apply in the Maryland case, should the Department of Justice decide to proceed with a lawsuit.

SUMMARY

THE RECOGNITION THAT PRISONERS have rights has come a long way from the time when Virginia, and other states, considered them to be "slaves of the state." With the incorporation doctrine making state actions reviewable under the Bill of Rights (because they have been incorporated in the Fourteenth Amendment's due process clause), and the availability of Section 1983 of the Civil Rights Act of 1871, inmates have had much easier access to the courts to press their claims against prison officials.

However, access to the courts does not always mean that prisoners succeed in winning their cases. Case law over the past thirty-five and more years clearly suggests three distinguishable patterns with regard to appellate court decisions: a hands-off period during which the courts kept their hands largely off prison administration; a rights period in which courts seemed to get their hands full by frequently deciding against prison officials; and a deference period, a period in which the courts did not quite return to the hands-off mode of an earlier time, but deferred more often to corrections administrators than they did during the rights period.

Our review of case law showed that inmates' claims that their constitutional rights have been violated received scant attention until the Supreme Court under the leadership of Chief Justice Earl Warren took up many issues affecting individual civil rights, both in and out of prisons. Section 1983 of the Civil Rights Act of 1871 was accepted as the major vehicle for prisoners to file suit against their keepers.

More recently, prisoners have had relatively little success in convincing appellate courts that prison conditions or actions of officials constituted cruel and unusual punishment, or violations of their civil rights. A 1987 Supreme Court case, *Turner v. Safley,*[61] stated what seems to be the Court's current stance vis à vis restrictions on inmates' rights under the Constitution: "When a regulation impinges on inmates' constitutional rights, the regulation is valid if it is reasonably related to legitimate penological interests."[62] As we have seen, legitimate penological interests means that prison administrators have wide discretion to take steps to maintain good order, discipline, and security in their institutions.

Today, as we discussed in Chapter 8, imprisonment in the United States tends to conform to the confinement model. This means that the main duty of corrections officials is to provide for the secure and humane confinement of offenders. Much of the currently operable case law defers to the policies and actions of prison officials when those are reasonably related to security. Whether confinement in some prisons is inhumane is a question that frequently has come before the courts. At this time in history, prison systems have wide latitude when it comes to the general conditions in their institutions. The law appears to accept what outsiders may judge to be inhuman conditions in many prisons. This acceptance or deference is limited only by the requirement that officials not act with "deliberate indifference" to the point of recklessness with regard to the effects deplorable conditions have on inmates.

There has been some movement in the direction of support for "humane" confinement of offenders with the development of the accreditation process initiated by the American Correctional Association in 1978. Correctional systems that volunteer to participate in this process must meet certain basic standards with respect to prisoners' rights. We note, however, that as of April, 1996, only 366 correctional institutions out of a total of almost 900 have been fully accredited.[63]

The trend toward building more super-max prisons will almost certainly pose serious legal questions for corrections officials. As we saw above, conditions and deprivations in at least two states that have these prisons have led to inmate challenges, and one federal court case has been decided in their favor.

With strong public support for more mandatory and harsh prison sentences, we believe that the current stance taken by the courts and legislatures to defer to the "expert" discretion of corrections administrators will continue.

KEY CONCEPTS

Accreditation	Prison security
Contact visits	Reasonableness
Deference period	Rights period
Deliberate indifference	Section 1983 suits
Hands-off period	Slaves of the state
Incorporation doctrine	Substitute counsel

QUESTIONS FOR DISCUSSION

1. Prisons may severely restrict visits permitted inmates. Critically discuss how this policy can be reconciled with the view that maintaining contact with friends and relatives is essential to the rehabilitative process.
2. How has the Supreme Court interpreted the "deliberate indifference" standard when judging the actions of corrections officers that may violate prisoners' rights?
3. Is "legitimate penological interests" too broad a standard to use when evaluating whether a prison system violates an inmate's constitutional right? Fully justify your answer.
4. In *Harper v. Washington,* the Supreme Court accepted Washington state's procedures for involuntarily medicating a mentally disturbed inmate. Carefully consider these procedures. Are they not so difficult to implement that they jeopardize the safety of inmates and staff?
5. The super-max prison is a trendy response to difficult inmates in our overcrowded prisons. Conditions in these institutions raise a number of prisoner rights issues. Are these so important and difficult to deal with that the trend toward building more of these institutions should be stopped?

ENDNOTES

1. "Prisoners and Peanut Butter," *Washington Post,* September 30, 1995, p. A22.
2. John R. Dunne, "Unconscionable Limits on Prisoners' Lawsuits," *Washington Post,* November 8, 1995, p. A-17.
3. *Ruffin v. Commonwealth,* 62 Va. 790 (1871).
4. In *Murray v. Mississippi Department of Corrections,* the Fifth U.S. Circuit Court of Appeals held that the Thirteenth Amendment of the Constitution "specifically allows involuntary servitude as punishment after conviction of a crime." 911 F.2d 1167 (1991).
5. 482 U.S. 78 (1987).
6. 411 U.S. 520 (1979).
7. Jack E. Call, "The Supreme Court and Prisoners' Rights," *Federal Probation* 59 (March 1995): 36–46.

8. Ibid., p. 36.
9. *People v. Lovercamp,* 43 Cal.App. 3d 823 (1975).
10. Ibid.
11. 42 U.S.C. § 1983.
12. Call, "The Supreme Court and Prisoners' Rights, p. 37.
13. *Bell v. Wolfish,* 99 S.Ct. 562 (1979).
14. 97 S.Ct. 285 (1976).
15. Ibid.
16. Call, "The Supreme Court and Prisoners' Rights," p. 40.
17. Ibid.
18. Harold J. Sullivan, "Privatization of Corrections and the Constitutional Rights of Prisoners," *Federal probation* 53 (June 1989): 36–42.
19. Ibid., p. 36.
20. Ibid.
21. 589 F.Supp. 1028 (1984).
22. Sullivan, "Privatization of Corrections," p. 39.
23. *Milonas v. Williams,* 691 F.2d 931 (1982).
24. Sullivan, "Privatization of Corrections," p. 42.
25. American Correctional Association, *Standards for Adult Correctional Institutions,* 3d ed. (Lanham, MD: January 1990), p. vi.
26. Ibid., p. 87.
27. Sheldon Krantz and Lynn S. Branham, *The Law of Sentencing, Corrections and Prisoners' Rights,* 4th ed. (St. Paul, MN: West Publishing Company, 19??), p. 293.
28. 112 S.Ct. 501, 1991.
29. *Block v. Rutherford,* 104 S.Ct. 3227 (1984).
30. Ibid.
31. 405 U.S. 319, 322 (1971).
32. 107 S.Ct. 2400 (1987).
33. 97 S.Ct. 2532 (1977).
34. Ibid., 2541–42.
35. *Hudson v. Palmer,* 468 U.S. 517 (1984).
36. *Hudson v. McMillian,* 112 S.Ct. 995 (1992). For a summary and discussion of this case see Thomas Courtless, *Introduction to the Making of Criminal Law: Appellate Cases and Commentaries* (Oklahoma City, OK: Custom Academic Publishing Co., 1993), pp. 65–66, 74–80.
37. Courtless, pp. 75–76.
38. Ibid., p. 76.
39. Ibid., p. 80.
40. 111 S.Ct. 2321 (1991).
41. Call, "The Supreme Court and Prisoners' Rights," p. 40.
42. *Farmer v. Brennan,* 54 CrL 2156 (1994).
43. 429 U.S. 97 (1976).
44. 679 F.2d. 1115 (5th Cir. 1982).
45. 459 U.S. 460 (1983).
46. 94 S.Ct. 2963 (1974).
47. 503 F.Supp. 1265 (S.D. Tex. 1980).
48. Marilyn D. McShane and H. Michael Gentry, "The Use of Counsel Substitutes: Prison Discipline in Texas," *Federal Probation* 52 (September 1988): 27–31.
49. Ibid., p. 29.
50. Ibid.
51. Ibid., p. 31.
52. 110 S.Ct. 1028 (1990).
53. Quoted in Courtless, *Introduction to the Making of Criminal Law,* p. 91.
54. Ibid., p. 99.

55. Kate Shatzkin, "State May Face Prison Lawsuit," *Baltimore Sun,* May 8, 1996, p. 1A.

56. Ibid., p. 6A.

57. Charles Babington, "U.S. Alleges Rights Abuse at High-Security Prison," *Washington Post,* May 9, 1996, p. C1.

58. Ibid., p. C6.

59. Kate Shatzken, "U.S. May Sue State Over Prison," *Baltimore Sun,* May 8, 1996, p. 6A.

60. 889 F.Supp. 1146 (1995).

61. 107 S.Ct. 2254 (1987).

62. Ibid.

63. American Correctional Association, *Accredited Facilities and Programs* (Lanham, MD: American Correctional Association, April 23, 1966), p. 52.

CORRECTIONS
IN THE COMMUNITY

11

PROBATION

INTRODUCTION ACCORDING TO THE United States Bureau of Justice Statistics, 3,410,000 adult offenders are under correctional supervision in our communities.[1] Of these, approximately 2.8 million persons are on probation in the United States.[2] (The remainder are parolees.) This number represents 59 percent of all persons under correctional supervision.

Probation is a sentence imposed by criminal court judges under the authority of various sentencing statutes and guidelines. It can be defined as the court-ordered release of an offender to the community for a prescribed period of time under certain conditions imposed by the court.

We can distinguish at least four broad categories of probation currently employed in the United States: informal, formal unsupervised, formal supervised, and mixed sentence probation. We will emphasize two in this chapter: formal supervised and mixed sentence probation. These are the only ones that can be considered as delivering any correctional service.

Informal probation is the only type that does not involve a judicial order; the other three require an order from a judge specifying the terms and restrictions placed on the probationer. Informal probation, like supervised and unsupervised probation, permits an offender to remain in the community. Usually few if any conditions are placed on her or his liberty, and there is no supervision or counseling of the probationer by a probation officer. Informal probation does not entail any confinement of the offender in a jail or prison. There is no correctional service delivery to the probationer.

Formal unsupervised probation is ordered by a judge for a specified time, but without the assignment of an officer to "supervise" the offender. Conditions may be attached to the probationer's liberty. Frequently these require that the probationer not leave the jurisdiction and refrain from violating the law. Again, there is no pretense that an offender is to be corrected. The probation order may include a suggestion or recommendation that the offender seek some help from an agency in the community.

There are at least six identifiable subtypes of formal supervised probation, which order an offender to be under the supervision of a probation officer, usually for a specified period of time.[3] These six types are:

- *Straight probation*. This involves a sentence only to probation.
- *Split or mixed sentence*. This is probation following a term of incarceration.
- *Modification of sentence*. An offender may have a sentence of imprisonment modified by the sentencing judge to a term of probation.
- *Shock probation*. Probation follows a brief period of "shock" incarceration.
- *Intermittent probation*. Offenders are incarcerated on weekends or evenings, usually in a local jail or detention center.
- *Intensive supervision probation (ISP)*. The distinguishing feature is the "intensive" quality of supervision. Typically, to qualify as intensive, supervision contacts by probation officers are made one or more times a week, and testing for substance abuse is required. Some intensive supervision probation includes **electronic monitoring** and detailed curfew conditions. Any of the preceding types of probation may include intensive supervision.

With varying degrees of detail, the supervising officer is required to submit reports to the court on a regular basis. What is contained in these reports varies widely from jurisdiction to jurisdiction. At a minimum, they report on the probationer's compliance with the conditions laid down in the probation order.

The role of the probation officer and the kinds of conditions that apply to the probationer will be taken up later in the chapter. There is little consensus as to the roles probation officers are expected to play, however, or what these roles are expected to achieve. Similarly, there is little uniformity with respect to the conditions contained in probation orders. Some jurisdictions set minimal conditions; others, a large number. Some conditions are general, even vague, while still others are specific.

Mixed sentence or **split sentence** probation orders provide that an offender be sentenced to a period of confinement in a local jail or state prison, followed by a period of supervised probation. Some judges suspend the confinement portion of the sentence. In these cases, the threat of incarceration hangs over the head of the probationer should he or she violate the probation order.

Regardless of the many types of probation orders that may be issued, probation has traditionally been seen as one of a number of correctional sanctions that can be selected by trial court judges when sentencing convicted offenders.

HISTORICAL OVERVIEW

There is general agreement that probation originated in several practices, some of which go back many centuries: benefit of clergy, judicial reprieve, standing bail, recognizance, and suspended sentence.

Benefit of Clergy

Giving an offender the benefit of clergy was a practice that arose out of conflicts between church and civil authorities at least as far back as the thirteenth century in England. Members of the clergy were exempted from prosecution in secular courts. Any charges against them were heard in religious courts should church authorities choose to do so.

Gradually, the benefit was extended to anyone who could read biblical passages to the satisfaction of the court. It was common practice for the prescribed verses to be memorized with the help of coaching. When the benefit of clergy was given to non-clergy offenders, it generally exempted them from the death penalty. Benefit of clergy was used in colonial America. The author discovered such a case in late seventeenth-century Maryland. Three indentured servants were accused of murdering their master; one servant was allowed the benefit of clergy. As a condition, he was required to hang his fellows!

Certainly this early predecessor of probation is quite out of place in late twentieth-century America. Imagine, for example, permitting someone to escape prosecution and punishment for criminal activity on the basis of being literate. There is, of course, the practice of granting immunity to those who testify against co-defendants. Even if this is not a grant of immunity, some defendants who "turn state's evidence" may receive lenient sentences such as probation and suspended prison terms.

Before moving away from benefit of clergy, we should keep in mind that it was always subject to discrimination in practice. It was not only clergy-defendants who benefited, but also those who could read, usually a privileged minority.

Judicial Reprieve

Also dating back centuries in the English common law is the **judicial reprieve.** This was based on a judge's discretion to grant leniency in individual cases. Reprieve meant a suspension of punishment for a temporary period (so, for example, an offender could get her or his affairs in order), or indefinitely "upon evidence of good behavior."[4] Thus, since there was to be evidence that the reprieved person remained on good behavior, it may be said that the judicial reprieve was the true forerunner of probation. Today, reprieves are known to the general public through publicity surrounding many death penalty cases. In these cases it is usually an appellate court that grants reprieves while the condemned person pursues an often lengthy process to challenge the sentence. A reprieve vacates the execution date until a round of appeals has been completed. Upon entering a second round, another reprieve may be granted.

Standing Bail

"Standing bail" may be defined as an agreement by a private citizen to post a bond for an offender's release, accepting responsibility for the offender's behavior and his or her return to court for further proceedings. Failure to appear for trial or committing crimes while free could result in loss of the bond. As is the case with benefit of clergy, standing bail was not available to all since only those offenders who had family, friends, or others with the means to post bonds were in a position to be released. The practice is still in use in the United States, and many defendants avail themselves of it. When returned to court, some of these offenders may be able to show that they have been model citizens, and thereby convince the court to impose lenient sentences. The first American probation officer, John Augustus, frequently stood bail for defendants.

Recognizance

Recognizance is the release of a defendant on the responsibility of a judge until the defendant is "called for." The judge, in effect, assumes responsibility for the good behavior of defendants. The first judge to make use of recognizance in the United States, as far as can be determined, was Peter Oxenbridge Thatcher in Boston in 1830.[5] Judge Thatcher was influential in encouraging John Augustus in his efforts as a probation pioneer.

Suspended Sentence

Judges have always had the option to **suspend sentences** of convicted persons. All or a portion of a sentence can be suspended. In the author's home county, judges frequently suspended some portion of a sentence of imprisonment. Usually, suspensions were ordered for very long terms. For example, the order for a 25-year sentence for second-degree murder might actually read, "You are sentenced to be committed to the Division of Correctional Services for a period of 25 years, with 10 years suspended."

Implicitly, and sometimes explicitly, the offender is made to understand that the suspended sentence will be activated should her or his behavior warrant it. It is also possible for an offender to be placed on probation for some or all of a suspended sentence.

Judicial discretion can explain why a judge might order a suspended sentence. Except where mandatory sentence statutes expressly prohibit it, judges are legally able to use this option based on their own judgment, and, possibly, based on a plea agreement between the defense and prosecuting attorneys. As we said in Chapter 3, judges are generally not bound to accept plea agreements. But once they have ascertained that such pleas are "voluntary," to reject them is most unusual.

Probation

Probation as currently understood was the "invention" of Boston bootmaker John Augustus in 1841. A public-spirited private citizen, Augustus, working with Boston Municipal Court Judge Thatcher, stood bail for almost 2,000 men and women, most of whom were charged with vice and public drunkenness offenses.[6] For many of these offenders, Augustus found housing and employment. When they returned to court, they frequently were given light fines, or had charges against them dropped.

The first formal incorporation of probation into the criminal justice system occurred in 1878 when Massachusetts enacted a probation statute. It was not until 1891, however, that a statewide system of probation was adopted. With this law we see a probation service established under the jurisdiction of the courts. That is, the judiciary was granted the power to appoint probation officers.[7] As we shall see in the section below, a probation service organizationally tied to the judiciary is not the only administrative model in America.

THE ORGANIZATION OF PROBATION

There are more than 2,000 agencies currently delivering probation services in the United States.[8] These include agencies at the local, state, and federal level. When probation was first formalized by statute, the usual practice was to bring it under the control of the judiciary. Judges appointed the officers responsible for supervising offenders on probation. It seems only natural, since these officers worked to accomplish two tasks: supervising probationers and preparing the presentence reports used by judges in making their sentencing decisions.

Over the past few decades there has been a trend in the direction of removing probation from the authority of judges and investing it in state executive departments. According to a survey by the American Correctional Association, in 34 states probation services come under the executive branch of government, either at the state (the majority) or local (city, county) level. In the remaining states, it is controlled by the state or local judiciary.[9]

There has been a lively debate surrounding the placement of probation in America. Advocates for judicial and executive administration each have valid points to make. The case for judicial control of probation includes the argument that since judges sentence offenders to probation, those who deliver probation services will be more responsive to the courts than if they were separated from them administratively. Further, judges may allow their probation staffs greater latitude in carrying out their duties since they will be "tuned in" to their need for flexibility. Assigning probation to a large executive bureaucracy can stifle initiative and lead to rigid "working to the rules" job performance.

On the other hand, it is argued that by giving the judiciary administrative responsibility for probation, judges may be inclined to assign their staffs duties other than those strictly related to service delivery. After all, judges are primarily in the business of adjudicating conflicts through application of legal doctrines.[10] They often are not experienced in administering the many different kinds of services and activities falling under the probation umbrella.

In 1973, the National Advisory Commission on Criminal Justice Standards and Goals recommended that probation be located in the executive branch for a number of reasons:

- Better coordination with corrections (the prison system).
- More effective participation in the budget process.
- Better allocation of probation services than if tied to the courts.
- More appropriate priorities can be set by executive departments.[11]

Other proponents of executive branch administration of probation argue that judges are not well equipped to administer probation services. As we shall see, the many functions of a probation agency, especially its service delivery function, may seem out of place if administered by law-trained persons rather than by those trained and experienced in public administration.

The question as to the most appropriate administrative location of probation cannot be answered simply by referring to the advantages and disadvantages of the two major options. In some states, both juvenile and adult probation are administered by the judiciary. This does make some sense since, in these states, the juvenile court is a division of the general criminal court.

According to the American Correctional Association, adult and juvenile probation administration is often bifurcated, with juvenile probation services under the control of the judiciary and adult probation administered by a state executive agency.[12] In some states the executive branch is responsible for both adult and juvenile probation services, while in others juvenile probation comes under the local (municipal or county) judiciary.

The organization of probation in the United States is further complicated by the fact that when administered in the state executive branch, it can be—and often is—

combined with parole services. As we shall see in Chapter 12, there are features that probation and parole have in common: offenders are released to the community, certain rules or conditions are imposed on them that more or less limit their freedom, and failure to abide by the terms of their release can result in imprisonment. However, probationers and parolees usually differ significantly in terms of criminal history, and, of course, a parolee is released after a period of confinement, while the typical probationer has not been confined prior to being given probation.

Certainly, where probation and parole are joined in one executive department there are benefits to be derived. The most obvious is that this model permits the agency to profit from more efficient hiring and training practices. In addition such a unified organization may have the advantage of a more comprehensive approach since both probation and parole are "community-based" corrections activities.

However, because of the differences in probationers and parolees noted above, the unified agency may not always provide the best service for either the offender or the community. Offenders who remain in the community after being placed on probation require different kinds of supervision and services on the part of officers than those who are to be reintegrated after a period of incarceration. Service delivery problems may be further exacerbated when adult and juvenile offenders are included in the agency's mission.

Both executive and judicial branch locations have advantages and disadvantages. There seem to be no research data that can help us form a recommendation. From the point of view of a systems approach, which we have stressed throughout this book, there may be a slight advantage in having probation joined with parole in an executive agency. This is especially so now that intensive supervision probation (ISP) and split-sentence probation are coming on line as options for more serious offenders, many of whom spend time in confinement prior to being placed on probation. We will discuss these below.

THE PROBATION SELECTION PROCESS

Selecting offenders for probation has always been one of the most serious problems facing judges and probation officers. Among the questions that must be asked are:

- Should repeat offenders be eligible for probation?
- Should felons be placed on probation?
- Are drug offenders suitable for probation?
- Should violent offenders be considered for probation?
- Is it possible to assign risk levels to candidates for probation?

Eligibility for probation varies by states. In general, judges have virtually unlimited discretion. In some states, however, probation is limited by statute. For example, New York's "predicate felon" law prohibits probation for those with a prior felony conviction. Maine requires sentencing of those with prior larcenies to probation under its guidelines system. Deviations must be justified.[13]

The Presentence Investigation

While some states like New York and Maine have statutes that specify eligibility for probation sentences, it is common for probation to be ordered at the discretion of a judge. Sentencing usually occurs following the completion of a **presentence investigation** conducted by a probation officer. Presentence investigations and reports of these investigations frequently consume more of the probation officer's time than supervising probationers.

Historically, and ideally, a presentence investigation is very much in tune with positive criminological and penological principles. That is, the investigator should be interested in developing sentencing-relevant information that will allow the judge to fit the sentence to the offender. As we saw in earlier chapters, positive criminology, as pioneered by Lombroso and many others, has sought to operate within the terms of the equation: Criminal *A* = Intervention *A*. Thus, it is vitally important to collect data on offenders if an "intervention" is to be appropriate to them, and not simply fit a sentence to a crime.

The kinds of data that are collected for the presentence report fall into a number of general categories:

- The offense for which sentence is to be pronounced.
- Prior criminal history.
- Family background.
- Offender's personal history.

If the data collected in these areas is detailed enough, the investigator can provide the judge with a picture of the offender together with the investigator's sentencing recommendation based on that picture. For example, a convicted child abuser may be a first offender who was seriously abused as a child by her parents. In other aspects of the offender's personal history there may be data revealing a stable employment history together with no evidence of alcohol or drug abuse. Detailed information regarding the crime of conviction will provide further information as to the offender's personal culpability, and any aggravating or mitigating circumstances surrounding the offense. At the end of the officer's report to the judge, sentencing recommendations are offered. Judges generally are free to accept or reject these as they choose.

This brief discussion of the presentence investigation process is now not as accurate as it once was, especially with the advent of sentencing guidelines systems. As we saw in Chapter 3, many states and the federal government have developed sentencing procedures that use guidelines to advise (or, in some cases, instruct) judges regarding sentence ranges appropriate for certain crimes and certain offenders. Crimes are valued in a numerical system based on their severity. Usually, crimes are assigned a "base value" to which are added or subtracted aggravating or mitigating circumstances. Offender careers are calculated based on criminal history data. Offenders with significant histories will usually be sentenced to longer terms of imprisonment than others with no previous convictions even though their crimes might be at the same base level.

If sentencing is regulated by a guidelines system, what is the role of the presentence investigator? Does he or she simply collect offense and criminal history information, get out a pocket calculator and compute the sentence range? We can almost answer this question in the affirmative. Joseph Rosecrance undertook a study of the presentence investigation process in California and offers some insights about the changing role of the investigator in both guidelines and nonguidelines systems. He argues that positivism or "individualized justice" is fast becoming a myth in American justice.[14]

In examining a sample of presentence reports submitted to sentencing judges, Rosecrance found that there was a very high correlation between presentence report recommendations and the actual sentence ordered. There are a number of reasons for this finding. An important one is the influence of plea bargaining on sentencing. If prosecutor and defense agree to negotiate a plea in return for concessions such as number and level of charges to which to plead guilty, obviously the sentence will almost be a part of the bargain. Can we expect the probation officer to change this by virtue of a presentence investigation?

Another reason for the high level of agreement between presentence recommendations and actual sentences lies with the judge's expectations.

> Judges expect probation officers to submit noncontroversial reports that provide a facade of information, accompanied by bottom-line recommendations that do not deviate significantly from a consideration of offense and prior record.[15]

For their part, probation officers often consider presentence investigations to be "dirty work" and the resulting reports to be "largely superfluous." The actual investigations and the recommendations that they produce tend to follow a common pattern of distinct stages.

The first stage consists of "typing" an offender, which in reality makes sentencing recommendations a foregone conclusion. Typing is accomplished through assembling official data ("rap" or criminal history sheets and details of the current offense). Then the case is assigned to one of five categories: (1) "deal" case (a plea bargain has been struck); (2) diversion case (for minor crimes, offenders can be diverted to other agencies); (3) "joint" case (imprisonment recommendations); (4) probation with some jail time; and (5) **straight probation**. Each category is then divided into two types: "heavyweight and lightweight."[16] These classifications are closely related to a preconceived sentence recommendation. Heavyweight cases receive recommendations for severe sentences; lightweight ones will be recommended leniency.

Following this typing is the second stage, collecting extralegal information to fill out the report submitted to the judge:

> This aspect of the presentence investigation involves considerable time and effort. . . . Such information is gathered primarily to legitimate earlier probation officer typing or to satisfy judicial requirements; recommendations are seldom changed during this stage.[17]

While investigators have considerable discretion in the selection of data to collect during this second stage, the tendency is to seek only information supportive of their first-stage notions of an appropriate sentence.

In the third and final stage, the report is reviewed by prosecutors, probation supervisors, and judges. Rosecrance concludes that presentence reports continue to be prepared so that investigators can maintain their standing with the major actors in the criminal justice drama. Certainly it would take a particularly courageous investigator to recommend against the prosecutor's plea bargain, or to upset a judge or administrative superior by recommending a sentence that goes against what the investigator knows to be their sentencing biases. Even the interviews with convicted offenders may only try to convince them that their cases are receiving individual attention. Rosecrance concluded that it is "ineffective and wasteful" to require the collection of large quantities of "social data of uncertain relevance," and that doing so only serves to "perpetuate the myth of individualized justice."[18]

WHO'S ON PROBATION?

According to a recent census, 2.8 million adults are on probation.[19] Determining who these millions of offenders are is no easy task since there is limited information avail-

TABLE 11.1   **Sentences Received by Felons Convicted in 1986**

SENTENCE	PERCENT OF ALL FELONS
Probation	52
Straight	31
With jail time	15
With prison time	6
Jail term only	6
Prison term only	40

SOURCE: Patrick A. Langan and Mark A. Cunniff, Bureau of Justice Statistics, *Special Report,* February 1992, p. 3.

able to tell us much about them. Two surveys of probation populations reported on how many were sentenced to probation for various crimes and what sentences were imposed, which we can examine in Tables 11.1, 11.2, and 11.3.

Note that in a national sample of 79,000 probationers studied between 1986 and 1989, 21 percent had *not* been recommended for probation following presentence investigations.[20] More recent data, shown in Table 11.3 tell us that almost half of all felons receive probation. The figures in Tables 11.1–11.3 suggest that probation is being used for serious offenders more frequently now than in the past. We will discuss the reasons for and consequences of this later.

RULES AND CONDITIONS OF THE PROBATION ORDER

As we said above, probation is a conditional court-ordered release to the community, usually under some form of supervision. Early in the history of probation, rules and conditions written into probation orders were relatively few and simple. Probationers were required to report regularly to their supervising officers, maintain employment, remain in the jurisdiction, and, of course, refrain from violating any laws. The

TABLE 11.2   **State Probation Sentences for Felonies, Nationwide, 1986**

OFFENSE	PROBATION WITH		
	Total	No Jail	Some Jail
Murder	6	4	2
Rape	20	10	10
Robbery	20	10	10
Assault	43	26	17
Burglary	40	25	15
Larceny	50	34	16
Drug trafficking	54	34	20
Other	56	40	16

SOURCE: Modified from BJS-sponsored 1986 National Judicial Reporting Program.

Types of Offense of Those on Probation in 1992   TABLE 11.3

TYPES OF OFFENSE	NUMBER OF PROBATIONERS	PERCENT OF ALL PROBATIONERS
Felonies	1,070,602	49
Misdemeanors	703,639	32
Driving while intoxicated	394,373	18
Other	35,136	2

SOURCE: *Correctional Populations in the United States,* 1992, p. 24.

accompanying composite of a typical probation order (Figure 11.1 on p. 251) reflects these simple conditions with the addition of a few "special conditions," which we shall now discuss.

Recently, the probation situation has changed dramatically, especially as intensive supervision probation (ISP) has become popular. At the present time, a number of "new" conditions are frequently imposed: fees for supervision, court costs, restitution, community service, urine testing, substance abuse counseling, and electronic surveillance. From the study of 79,000 probationers referred to above, we find that these additional conditions are used in a substantial number of cases. Table 11.4 on p. 252 lists some of the special conditions now imposed on probationers in order of frequency of use.

In the case of intensive supervision probation, there are additional rules and conditions, which we shall take up later in the section on supervision. At this point, it is clear that intensive supervision probation requires offenders to submit to urine screening, pay supervision fees, and be available for frequent, sometimes random checks by probation officers.

Billie Erwin and Lawrence Bennett reviewed one of the most highly structured intensive supervision programs in the United States, established in Georgia in 1982.[21] The requirements imposed on probationers in the Georgia program included five one-on-one contacts with a probation officer per week, 132 hours of community service, mandatory curfew limits, mandatory employment, weekly check of police arrest records, and routine unannounced alcohol and drug use screening. These probationers had been sentenced to prison, and after screening were diverted to probation. Thus, they may be considered a high risk group requiring more restrictive conditions than other offenders.

An extreme example of how probation orders can be loaded down with restrictive conditions may be found in the Kathy Powers case.[22] Powers participated in a Boston bank robbery in 1970 with two ex-convicts, according to her as part of a "revolutionary war" against the system. During the robbery a police officer was killed by one of her co-defendants.

A fugitive for 23 years, she turned herself in, was convicted, and was sentenced on October 6, 1993, to a total sentence of 8–12 years on state criminal charges, to be followed by probation. The special conditions attached to the probation order raise a number of legal and correctional questions. The conditions include a stipulation by Superior Court Judge Robert Banks: "I prohibit you from any activity, of any nature, which can generate profit to you for the crimes you committed." Any violation of this over the next 20 years would require her to "surrender and up to life in prison."

ACROSS CULTURES

PROBATION IN JAPAN

In Japan, probation falls under the authority of the Rehabilitation Bureau of the Ministry of Justice. This bureau controls probation offices attached to each of the country's District Courts. Approximately half of all probationers are sentenced to terms of not more than three years. It is reported that over 70 percent of offenders successfully complete probation.

As is the case in the United States, probation officers must work with heavy caseloads, usually numbering over 100 probationers. However, unlike the situation in the United States, probation officers receive substantial assistance from a corps of volunteer officers.

Volunteer probation officers are citizens who volunteer for the position, meet certain minimum qualifications, and who are then appointed by the Ministry of Justice for a two-year term, with possibility of reappointment. These volunteers are paid only for expenses such as travel—they receive no salary for their work. (p. 106)

This employment of volunteer workers certainly reflects the Japanese sense of responsibility to the community. It reminds us that the first probation officers in the United States were volunteers, beginning with John Augustus in 1841. While volunteers play a role in American corrections, usually with juveniles, they are not a significant part of the supervision of probationers as is the case in Japan.

SOURCE: A. Didrick Castberg, *Japanese Criminal Justice* (New York: Praeger, 1990).

As interpreted by the Massachusetts Department of Probation, the order bars Powers or anyone "acting on her behalf" from any "profit or benefit-generating activity relating to the publication of facts or circumstances" of her 1970 acts or her life underground. The department stated that she could speak only to her therapist or lawyer about the crime and her time as a fugitive. If anyone in her family, her friends, attorney, or the therapist wrote about the events they would be assumed to be acting in collusion with her. In such event, she would be violating probation.

Her lawyer asked whether any income from Powers's accounts of her criminal activity could be donated to charity or the victim's family. The judge responded that he would demand "strict compliance" with his order. Federal District Court Judge Nathaniel Gorton, who sentenced her on federal charges, indicated he would consider reducing her sentence should she sell her story and give the proceeds to the victim's family. But the state judge, at last report, refused to budge from his position.

As we noted in Chapter 10, there is some case law that appears to make such special conditions unconstitutional. In *Simon & Schuster v. New York Crime Victims Compensation Board*, the United States Supreme Court unanimously decided that the "Son of Sam" law was void because it violated First Amendment free speech rights.[23] The "Son of Sam" law permitted the state to seize all proceeds paid to criminals for books or movies that tell their stories.

In some instances what seem to be obvious conditions on the probationers' liberty are not always written into orders of probation. Nor are all the conditions imposed actually enforced. For example, Langan and Cunniff, after examining a sample of probationers from 17 states, found that less than half of the probationers known to

Sample Probation Order   **FIGURE 11.1**

CIRCUIT COURT FOR SOUTH COUNTY

TO: <u>Helen R. Smith</u>.   Ct. Docket No. <u>96-2345</u>.

Address: 1234 Queens Blvd, Cty, 10001.

In accordance with the authority vested by the state probation statute (Chapter IV, § 3843), you are hereby placed on probation this date October 19, 1996 by the Hon. Gladys C. Bowen for a period of two (2) years. You shall fully and faithfully abide by the following conditions of your probation.

(1) You shall refrain from violation of any local, state or federal laws. You shall immediately contact your probation officer if you are arrested or questioned by a police officer.
(2) You shall associate and communicate only with law-abiding persons and maintain reasonable hours.
(3) You shall maintain regular lawful employment and support your dependents, if any, to the best of your ability. Should you become unemployed you must immediately contact your probation officer.
(4) You shall not leave the county or state without the permission of your probation officer.
(5) You shall obtain prior written permission from your probation officer if you wish to:
   (a) Purchase a motor vehicle.
   (b) Incur debts by borrowing money or making purchases on an installment plan.
   (c) Change address or employment.
   (d) Marry.
   (e) Purchase, own or carry a firearm or other weapon.
(6) You shall follow your probation officer's instructions and advice.
(7) You shall not operate a motor vehicle unless you have liability insurance which is approved by your probation officer.
(8) You shall not possess, use, sell, distribute, manufacture, or have under your control any narcotic drugs, barbiturates, marijuana, paregoric, or extracts containing them in any form or instrument for administering them except upon prescription by a licensed physician.
(9) Special conditions are as follows:
   (a) Supervision fee of $50.00 per month.
   (b) Restitution in the amount of $1,500.00
   (c) Upon direction of my probation officer I shall report for urine testing.

I understand that the court may change the conditions of my probation, reduce or extend the period of my probation, and may issue a warrant for my arrest and revoke my probation during my probation period.

I have read, or had read to me, the above conditions of my probation. I fully understand them, and I will abide by them.

(Signed): <u>Probation Officer</u>   (Date): _____

(Signed): <u>Helen R. Smith</u>   (Date): _____

South County Circuit Court/PO1

have drug problems were required either to participate in drug treatment programs or to be tested for drug use.[24]

   Supervision levels vary markedly from one jurisdiction to another. Some probationers are reported as not being actively supervised. Either they are in the final stages of their probation terms, or they are considered not to require supervision.[25] Accord-

TABLE 11.4 **Special Conditions in Orders of Probation**

CONDITION	PERCENTAGE OF ORDERS
Court costs	48
Supervision fees	32
Drug testing	31
Restitution	29
Drug treatment	23
Alcohol abuse treatment	14

Note: Percentages total more than 100% because some conditions are used in combination with others.
SOURCE: Patrick A. Langan and Mark A. Cunniff, "Recidivism of Felons on Probation," *Special Report* (Washington, DC: Bureau of Justice Statistics)

ing to Langan and Cunniff in their survey of felony probationers, there are five distinct levels of supervision:

- *Intensive.* Nine contacts per month; 10% of the cases.
- *Maximum.* Three monthly contacts; 32% of the cases.
- *Medium.* One monthly contact; 37% of the cases.
- *Minimum.* One contact every three months; 12% of the cases.
- *Administrative.* No contact required; 9% of the cases.[26]

The ankle electronic monitoring devices used to inform the law enforcement agencies of the location of prisoners confined to home detention. The offender wears the transmitter and the receiver is located in the offender's home. The receiver sends out signals looking for the transmitter. If the receiver cannot find the transmitter a report is created so the appropriate agency can track the violation of the home monitoring sentence.

When we realize that all these probationers were convicted of felonies, we might wonder why over half of them received no more than one contact with probation officers each month.

Because it often seems that probation rules and conditions are imposed with no rational purpose in mind, we need to ask whether it is possible to design probation orders that will contain rules or conditions that bear some relationship to the characteristics of probationers and their particular problems and needs. To a large extent, the answer lies in the reason why any offender is sentenced to probation. If probation is to be used in a highly punitive way, with strict controls on the liberty of offenders, rules and conditions should reflect this. After all, such restrictions seek both to punish and incapacitate offenders as severely as possible, as with incarceration. On the other hand, if probation is to be used to help offenders with serious family, employment, and substance abuse problems, then common sense tells us that the conditions in their probation orders must take these problems into account.

There is another, systemic issue involved in the matter of probation rules, especially those that severely restrict offenders. As Geerken and Hayes observed in their study of New Orleans probationers, when probation is used to serve punitive and control objectives through ever more restrictive conditions, a real consequence may be to decrease the frequency of plea bargaining.[27] This can have the effect of overloading the courts and the prison system.

TYPES OF PROBATION SUPERVISION

One of the defining features of probation is that an offender will be under the supervision of an official agent. Usually called a probation officer, the agent may be an employee of the court or the executive branch of government. Over 2.8 million persons are being supervised in the United States, 61,922 of them receiving intensive supervision, with 9,353 subjected to electronic monitoring.[28]

But what is the nature of the supervision the officer is to provide? In the past it was relatively easy to answer this question. Probation supervision could mean one of three things: surveillance to ensure compliance with court-ordered conditions, counseling to assist probationers with the problems they were thought to have, and a combination of the first two.

Surveillance is essentially a police function exercised by a probation officer. The offender has agreed to abide by certain rules imposed as a condition of freedom from confinement. The officer takes whatever steps are necessary to see that the rules are obeyed. Failure to comply, if observed by or reported to the officer, may lead to procedures to declare the offender in violation of the probation order, and a referral back to court for resentencing.

Counseling, as a function of the probation officer's role, is not quite so easy to describe. Some officers may employ one-on-one counseling. Others use group counseling techniques. This usually involves assigning probationers with similar offenses or problems to groups. Of course, such an approach requires the officer to know the probationers quite well in order to differentiate them appropriately and engage them in counseling.

Some officers may believe that counseling is the correct strategy for dealing with a probationer, but feel unqualified to deliver it. In these cases, they may refer the probationer to another agency (for example, family services agency or mental health clinic). When this occurs, the officer may simply maintain contact with the agency to get reports of progress or lack of it.

The combination approach to counseling needs little explanation. An officer may emphasize surveillance or counseling. The officer may feel that one probationer requires little counseling, while another needs more. Perhaps this is the most frequently utilized form of supervision.

With the advent of **intensive supervision probation (ISP)**, the concept as well as the styles of supervision have changed significantly. At first glance, intensive supervision seems to mean that surveillance to keep offenders from violating their conditions is the primary, if not the only role of the officer. However, upon closer inspection, we see that this is not always the case. Styles of supervision can and do vary from jurisdiction to jurisdiction. As we saw earlier, the Georgia ISP program mandates five one-on-one probationer contacts with officers per week. Perhaps during these sessions counseling service is being delivered.

We can identify at least three models of supervision under ISP programs: team model, service delivery model, and combined model.[29] In the team model, supervision of a caseload of probationers is carried out by two officers. One team member is responsible for undertaking the surveillance function. He or she is, in effect, a police officer. The second team member is a social worker. He or she performs a counseling role. One advantage of this model is that it avoids the **role conflict** that can occur when a probation officer must try to be both monitor and counselor. Of course, a disadvantage is that the team approach is labor intensive and thus costly. Also, conflicts between team officers may arise when one or the other considers a significant action with respect to a probationer. For example, the officer responsible for surveillance may observe a technical violation that he or she believes warrants revocation. The other officer may disagree.

The second ISP model, service delivery, involves the probation officer delivering counseling when he or she is competent to do so and referring probationers to other counseling agencies when that is more appropriate. This model leaves the officer with some discretion, but assigns the officer the surveillance function when referrals are made to other agencies.

The combined model, obviously, puts the officer in both surveillance and counseling roles. This has at least two disadvantages. First, to be effective, the combined model requires small caseloads. Thus, it is more costly. Second, it presents a probation officer with the potentially serious problem of role conflict: to be both police officer and counselor.

Whether we consider probation supervision in the "ordinary" or intensive supervision setting, we need to recognize that in today's criminal justice environment, control, with its emphasis on surveillance and stringent conditions, has become a more central focus. As Patricia Harris and her colleagues found following their study of 223 probation officers:

> Service delivery no longer carries with it the connotations of rehabilitation and reintegration, but now is a more rigid enterprise that is tied to the task of monitoring client risk.[30]

This observation points out the systemic character of alterations in sentencing offenders to probation as well as incarceration. The prison population explosion explored in Chapter 8 has had the effect of increasing the proportion of high-risk offenders placed on probation. This in turn has resulted in the current emphasis on controlling, or risk containment, as a function of probation supervision. Harris and associates observed that because of prison crowding, more serious offenders are sentenced to probation than ever before, and "probationers as a whole now require more control by community supervision officers than in earlier times."[31]

As we shall see below, the changing character of probation populations not only affects the working styles of probation officers, it also has a ripple effect in terms of levels of successful completion of probation. Higher-risk offenders will, in all likelihood, more frequently violate either the conditions of their probation or commit new crimes than lower-risk offenders. The degree of supervisory control required on the part of officers with such caseloads may make the discovery of violations far easier than was the case in the past. The Langan and Cunniff study referred to above found that the highest violation rates were observed among probationers who received the most intensive supervision. This finding leads us to a number of important questions about the effectiveness of probation.

PROBATION REVOCATION

What happens when an offender violates one or more conditions of her or his probation, or commits a new criminal offense while still under a probation order? Often limited, if any, action is taken. Such violations of probation conditions are referred to as **technical probation violations.** Frequently, but not always, these are reported separately from data on new criminal offenses in the research on probation, as we will see in the next section.

As is the case throughout the criminal justice system, probation officers and their supervisors exercise considerable discretion when responding to technical violators. Legally, a failure to comply with the terms of probation is a violation of a court order. Thus, the probationer is in contempt of court. Not all violations result in procedures to revoke a person's probation. In the judgment of the officer and supervisor, some technical violations are more "technical" while others are more substantive.

If the conditions of parole are violated a probationer may be called to appear before a judge for a probation revocation hearing.

Changing one's address without prior permission is a violation of most probation orders. But is it grounds for revocation and resentencing? Failing a urine test for illicit drugs is also a violation, but may be much more likely to result in revocation.

Committing new criminal acts while on probation is, of course, a very different matter. Here, we are dealing with **recidivism** and not technical violations. Frequently, the issue of the disposition of a recidivist is taken out of the hands of the probation department. The offender may be convicted of the new offense and sentenced to imprisonment. Then the probation order is terminated. Much less frequently, a convicted probationer may not be sentenced to imprisonment and is retained on probation.

When probation revocation procedures are initiated, statutes and case law have evolved to provide certain due-process safeguards for the person facing possible resentencing. A landmark Supreme Court decision in 1967 held that a probationer was entitled to be represented by an attorney prior to being removed from probation and resentenced.[32] In 1973 a decision of the Court in *Gagnon v. Scarpelli*, resulted in the development of a multistage procedure to be followed in deciding whether to revoke an offender's probation status:

1. A preliminary hearing is held to determine whether there are sufficient facts to conclude that a violation or new offense was committed. As is the case in ordinary criminal proceedings, preliminary hearings in probation matters can be waived.
2. fact-finding hearing is held on the allegations. Written notice of charges is required. Witnesses may be called and cross-examined by the probationer. Probationers have a right to an "impartial" hearing officer and right to counsel.
3. The sentencing stage. Probationers have the right to be represented by counsel. The sentencing judge can reinstate probation or resentence to imprisonment.

Other appellate court decisions have dealt with the constitutionality of the rules and conditions imposed in probation orders. We saw earlier that restrictions on the right of probationers to write, publish, and profit from stories about their crimes cannot fully be enforced. Other Supreme Court decisions have found a number of restrictions to be unreasonable as well as unconstitutional.[34] With the increasing use of intensive probation supervision and its many restrictions and resultant violations, we may expect to see more case law developments in the future.

EVALUATION OF PROBATION

Before turning our attention to evaluation of probation effectiveness, we should examine Figure 11.2, which reports the results of a Bureau of Justice Statistics study of 79,000 felons placed on probation in 1986.[35] The study tracked the probationers over a three-year period. After three years, 38 out of every 100 felons were still on probation (although 10 of these had "absconded.") Sixty-two probationers had either been arrested for a felony, had a disciplinary hearing (for violations of probation conditions), or both. The outcome of these arrests and hearings are also reported in Figure 11.2. The results of the BJS tracking study may seem to call probation into question as an effective sentence for convicted felons. With these results as background, we now look at the state of our knowledge of the efficacy of probation.

Determining the effectiveness of probation as a correctional tool is not a simple matter. Some preliminary questions need to be asked. What does *effectiveness* mean in the probation context? Does successful completion of probation by an offender

100 Felons Followed During Their First Three Years of Probation   **FIGURE 11.2**

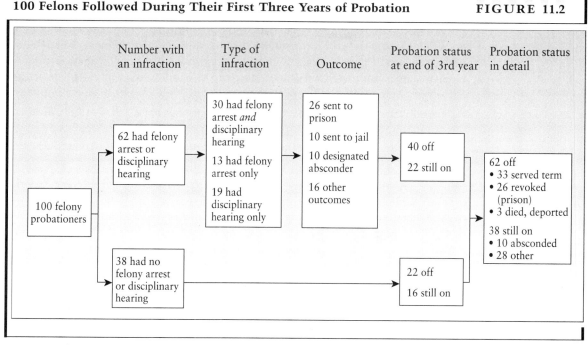

SOURCE: Patrick A. Langan and Mark A. Cunniff, "Recidivism of Felons on Probation, 1986–1989," Bureau of Justice Statistics, *Special Report*, February 1992.

mean no new criminal offenses, no "technical" violations of probation conditions, or both? Are there differences within probation populations that need to be accounted for when evaluating offender performance? What methodologies can be applied to evaluate probation?

Agreement as to what constitutes successful completion of probation is hard to come by. In the studies we will review in this section, probation success in some research is evaluated on the basis of arrest rates. That usually means that a probation population or sample is examined to determine how frequently its members are arrested while on probation.[36] In some of this research arrests for any reason are counted. Therefore, an offender arrested for a felony is marked as a probation failure as well as another who was arrested for violating one of the conditions of probation but has committed no new crimes. The latter offender is referred to as a technical violator.

Other studies report on technical violations separately. Still others apply a reconviction criterion. In these studies, failure while on probation is not counted unless the probationer was convicted on a new charge. Finally, some research employs an incarceration criterion. The probationer must be imprisoned before being counted as a failure. This last criterion has the advantage of taking into account the fact that arrests alone may not mean conviction, and that technical violations may be minor. The incarceration criterion assumes that the offender has done something significant to cause the court to hand down a sentence of imprisonment.[37] We need also to consider whether an incarceration criterion is not the most appropriate criterion if probation is used at least partly to help reduce prison populations. In a time of exploding populations, probation sentences for offenders who ordinarily might be committed to prison have become more common. Probationers who eventually are incarcerated only add to the prison crowding problem.

Perhaps the most widely circulated studies of probation outcome are those conducted by the Rand Corporation under the direction of Joan Petersilia.[38] In a nationwide study, the Petersilia team found that nearly two-thirds of probationers under intensive supervision violated one or more of the conditions of their probation, and 37 percent were rearrested for new offenses.[39] The high level of technical violations has an impact on prison crowding, as Petersilia and Turner point out:

> On any given day, about 20 percent of new [prison] admissions nationwide consist of parole and probation violators, and the resultant crowding means early release for other offenders.[40]

By way of contrast, Erwin and Bennett report that Georgia's intensive supervision program actually reduced felony admissions by 10 percent over a three-year period.[41]

John Whitehead reviewed some of the Rand studies and conducted a survey of over 2,000 felony probationers in New Jersey, following up the sample for periods of 3, 4, and 10 years.[42] He noted that the Rand research reported disappointing results, with failures approaching two-thirds (including both technical violations and new offenses). In his critique of the research, he observed that the California counties in the Rand studies were experiencing major budget constraints, and that their probation departments were significantly understaffed to the extent of probation caseloads of 375 offenders per officer. This points out a further difficulty we encounter when seeking to evaluate the effectiveness of probation (as well as other correctional programs). We need to inquire whether the resources necessary to deliver services to probationers are actually available. When such resources are in short supply it is unreasonable to expect probation to demonstrate much success with its populations. We should add to this the changing character of probation caseloads. As noted earlier, in many jurisdictions these caseloads now have much larger percentages of high-risk felony offenders than in the past. Thus, interpreting reports of "success" and "failure" on probation is a very tricky business indeed.

In the Whitehead study, recidivism levels were found to be noticeably lower than those reported in the Rand research. In particular, Whitehead found that, contrary to what has been almost conventional wisdom, probationers who were convicted of drug offenses had substantially lower failure rates than those convicted of burglary and robbery. In one of his conclusions, he stated:

> These findings provide more encouraging news for probation proponents than do the Rand study findings. . . . Especially for the drug (CDS)* offenders, probation was a reasonable option; of the three types of offenders [CDS, robbery, burglary] in the sample, the CDS offenders placed on probation in 1976–1977 had the lowest rates of recidivism.[43]

Whitehead rightly cautions those who examine his findings not to read too much into them since they were based on research on offenders placed on probation in the 1970s, and thus may not be relevant now. This is because of the current "emphasis . . . on accountability and surveillance. . . , [t]he results presented here may well mark the last hurrah for the old-fashioned officer" who delivered a service more tuned to rehabilitation and resocialization of offenders.[44]

Other research can be found to provide support for probation as an appropriate and effective correctional tool. Studies in Kentucky and Missouri found that less than

*Controlled dangerous substances.

one-quarter of felons placed on probation in the 1980s were rearrested.[45] More encouraging was the finding in the Kentucky study that only 18 percent of the sample were convicted of new offenses after three years, while in Missouri, only 12 percent were convicted after 40 months.

Another way of examining probation effectiveness in reducing recidivism is to look backward from the vantage point of convictions to determine how many persons were on probation at the time of their convictions. Geerken and Hayes did this in a study of burglary and armed robbery convictions in New Orleans between 1976 and 1986.[46] They found that only 8 percent were on probation at the time of conviction.

As can be seen from the review of studies purporting to evaluate the efficacy of probation as a correctional sanction, the results are mixed. Depending on the criteria used to measure effectiveness, we may be able to conclude that probation has been "successful." However, it may be just as accurate to conclude that probation is only moderately successful and possibly a failure. Changing probation populations, changing supervision strategies, and changing expectations all contribute to our uncertainty.

SUMMARY

PROBATION IS A WIDELY USED correctional sanction. Nearly three million men and women offenders are subjected to a variety of rules and conditions by which their freedom from incarceration is limited. Release on probation is by a judicial order. There are a number of major types of probation currently employed in the United States, including straight probation without any incarceration, mixed probation that involves some imprisonment, and intensive supervision probation that often includes punitive and incapacitative goals.

Traditionally, probation is said to promote the correction of an offender, and thus it is often viewed as serving rehabilitative goals. Recently, however, it is seen by some as more punitive and incapacitating. This is part of the general trend in this country, discussed in earlier chapters, in the direction of more severe sanctions, or getting "tough" on criminals.

As a rehabilitative or correctional measure, probation often includes some form of counseling, or at least referrals of probationers to counseling agencies. Being in the community rather than in prison tends, so it is argued, to support rehabilitative objectives since it allows, even requires, employment, schooling, and maintenance of family and community ties.

One of the key features of the major types of probation orders is supervision of offenders. Sometimes this supervision is carried out by officers of the courts. In most jurisdictions, supervision is the responsibility of an administrative agency separate from the courts.

There is a lack of uniformity with respect to the meaning of probation supervision. Some agencies and officers see the primary supervisory role as counseling to assist probationers to make a satisfactory adjustment in the community. In contrast, surveillance and control have defined the probation officer's working role in many agencies. In still other settings, counseling and surveillance are combined in a sometimes uneasy alliance. This can lead to role conflict for the probation officer.

Regardless of the meaning of supervision, a probationer's life is restricted by a number of rules and conditions. Some of these have little or no relation to the goal of "correcting" offenders. In the case of intensive supervision probation, these rules and conditions may serve strictly punitive and incapacitative goals. Thus probation may, in these instances, be a criminal justice activity that is grounded in a fundamental contradiction. In practice it includes the coercive power of the state to enforce severe limitations on liberty while maintaining the trappings of a nonpunitive rehabilitative approach. Coupled with the possibility of probation officer role conflict, probation today has become a confusing and confused criminal sanction.

With such a large proportion of the U.S. correctional population on probation, evaluating its effectiveness should be a very high priority activity. As we have seen, there are a number of serious methodological problems that must be addressed if we are ever to be able to judge probation's impact on crime in the United States. Among these are the following:

- The current selection of offenders for probation sentences has resulted in an exceedingly diverse population to be studied.
- Criteria for evaluating success vary widely and often cannot be reconciled.
- There is a clear lack of agreement as to just what we expect probation supervision to accomplish and how that supervision is to be delivered. As we have seen, variations in supervision are directly correlated with rates of probation failure and offender recidivism.

Evaluation research, not surprisingly, has produced mixed results. This leads to a number of important questions:

- Which offenders should be placed on probation?
- How long should probationers remain under supervision?
- How much of our criminal justice resources should be spent on probation services?
- How should recidivism and probation success/failure be defined, and what level of failure and recidivism can we accept?

KEY CONCEPTS

Electronic monitoring
Intensive Supervision Probation (ISP)
Judicial reprieve
Mixed sentence
Presentence investigation
Recidivism

Recognizance
Role conflict
Split sentence
Straight probation
Suspend sentences
Technical probation violations

QUESTIONS FOR DISCUSSION

1. There are many different kinds of rules and conditions imposed in probation orders. Some of these seem to have little relation to "correcting" offenders. With corrections in mind, what conditions should be imposed to maximize probation effectiveness?
2. In what ways can probation serve punitive goals? Should it?
3. Discuss the systemic consequences of the current trend toward placing more serious offenders on probation.
4. What are the pros and cons of evaluating probation using the following criteria: rearrest, reconviction, and incarceration?

5. Explain why technical violations of probation may or may not be an appropriate measure of probation effectiveness.

6. What might be done to lessen the impact of technical violations on the prison system?

ENDNOTES

1. Tracy L. Snell, "Correctional Populations in the United States, 1993," *Executive Summary* (Washington, DC: National Institute of Justice, October 1995): 1, 2.

2. Ibid., p. 1.

3. James M. Borne, "Probation," in Larry J. Siegel (ed.), *American Justice: Research of the National Institute of Justice* (St. Paul, MN: West Publishing, 1990), pp. 187–188.

4. Samuel Walker, *Popular Justice: A History of American Criminal Justice* (New York: Oxford University Press, 1980).

5. John Augustus, *A Report of the Labors of John Augustus, for the Last Ten Years, in Aid of the Unfortunate* (Boston, MA: Wright & Hasty, 1852).

6. Ibid.

7. Walker, *Popular Justice*, pp. 88–89.

8. American Correctional Association, *ACA Directory*, 1994.

9. Ibid.

10. For a summary of many of the advantages and disadvantages of various administrative models see Howard Abadinsky, *Probation and Parole: Theory and Practice* (Englewood Cliffs, NJ: Prentice-Hall, 1991), pp. 21–30.

11. National Advisory Commission on Criminal Justice Standards and Goals, *Corrections* (U.S. Government Printing Office, 1973), p. 314.

12. ACA, *ACA Directory*, 1992.

13. Patrick A. Langan and Mark A. Cunniff, "Recidivism of Felons on Probation," United States Department of Justice, Bureau of Justice Statistics, *Special Report* (February 1992), p. 3.

14. Joseph Rosecrance, "Maintaining the Myth of Individualized Justice: Probation Presentence Reports," *Justice Quarterly* 5 (1988): 235–256.

15. Ibid., p. 237.

16. Ibid., p. 243.

17. Ibid., p. 246.

18. Ibid., p. 253.

19. Snell, *Correctional Populations in the United States, 1993*, p. 1.

20. Langan and Cunniff, "Recidivism of Felons on Probation," p. 4.

21. Billie Erwin and Lawrence Bennett, "New Dimensions in Probation: Georgia's Experience with Intensive Probation Supervision (IPS)," in Larry J. Siegel (ed.), *American Justice: Research of the National Institute of Justice* (St. Paul, MN: West Publishing Company, 1990), pp. 206–212.

22. *Washington Post*, March 4, 1993.

23. "Son of Sam" laws have been enacted in a number of states in response to the activities of the notorious serial killer, "Son of Sam" Berkowitz.

24. Langan and Cunniff, "Recidivism of Felons on Probation," p. 7.

25. According to *Correctional Populations in the United States, 1992*, 238,000 offenders on probation were not actively supervised at the time of the survey.

26. Ibid.

27. Michael J. Geerken and Hennessey D. Hayes, "Probation and Parole: Public Risk and the Future of Incarceration Alternatives," *Criminology* 31 (1993): 561.

28. *Correctional Populations in the United States, 1994*; Washington, D.C., Bureau of Justice Statistics, Executive Summary, July 1996, p. 1. *Correctional Populations in the United States, 1992*, p. 32.

29. Todd R. Clear and Edward J. Latessa, "Probation Officers' Roles in Intensive Supervision: Surveillance versus Treatment," *Justice Quarterly* 10 (1993): 441–459.

30. Patricia M. Harris, Todd R. Clear, and Christopher Baird, "Have Community Supervision Officers Changed Their Attitudes Toward Their Work?" *Justice Quarterly* 6 (1989): 244.

31. Ibid.

32. *Mempa v. Rahy,* 389 U.S. 128 (1967).

33. 411 U.S. 778 (1973).

34. *Parkerson v. State,* 274 S.E.2d 799 (Ga.App. 1980). Restrictions placed on a probationer's spouse. *United States v. Smith,* 618 F.2d 280 (5th Cir. 1980). Prohibiting a probationer from making statements favorable to disobedience to any law. *United States v. Grant,* 807 F.2d. 837 (9th Cir. 1987). Failure to pay a fine held not be a failure on part of a probationer to be rehabilitated. *United States v. Turner,* 628 F.2d 461 (1980). Requirement to pay attorney's fees and travel expenses held to be an improper condition.

35. Langan and Cunniff, "Recidivism of Felons on Probation," p. 3.

36. Another question might well be asked. What about a probationer who, after "successfully" completing probation, commits a new crime?

37. Note that this criterion, which seems to be "strict" in its definition of success-failure, is subject to at least two kinds of discretion by system actors: judges who have discretion to resentence probationers, and probation officers who have discretion not to report technical violations, or to report them in ways that minimize their impact.

38. A sampling of the literature from these studies includes the following: Joan Petersilia, "Probation and Felony Offenders," *Federal Probation* 49 (1985): 4–9; Petersilia and Susan Turner, *Prison versus Probation in California: Implications for Crime and Offender Recidivism* (Santa Monica, CA: Rand Corporation, 1986); Petersilia and Turner, "Comparing Intensive and Regular Supervision for High-Risk Probationers: Early Results from an Experiment in California," *Crime and Delinquency* (1990): 87–111; Petersilia, *Intensive Supervision for High-Risk Probationers: Findings from Three California Experiments* (Rand Corporation, 1990); Petersilia, et al., "Granting Felons Probation: Public Risks and Alternatives," *Federal Probation* 49 (1985): 379–392.

39. Joan Petersilia and Susan Turner, "Evaluating Intensive Probation/Parole: Results of a Nationwide Experiment," National Institute of Justice, *Research in Brief* May 1993), p. 5.

40. Ibid., p. 9.

41. Billie S. Erwin and Lawrence A. Bennett, "New Dimensions in Probation: Georgia's Experience with Intensive Probation Supervision," in Larry J. Siegel (ed.), *American Justice: Research of the National Institute of Justice* (St. Paul, MN: West Publishing Company, 1990), p. 210.

42. John T. Whitehead, "The Effectiveness of Felony Probation: Results from an Eastern State," *Justice Quarterly* 8 (1991): 525–543.

43. Ibid., p. 539.

44. Ibid., p. 541.

45. Gennaro F. Vito, "Felony Probation and Recidivism: Replication and Response," *Federal Probation* 50 (1987): 17–25 (Kentucky data); Johnny McGaha, Michael Fichter, and Peter Hirschburg, "Felony Probation: A Re-examination of Public Risk," *American Journal of Criminal Justice* 11 (1987): 1–9 (Missouri data).

46. Geerken and Hayes, "Probation and Parole," pp. 549–564.

PAROLE

INTRODUCTION

THE JURY DELIBERATED 50 MINUTES before delivering their guilty verdict against me. With their decision 13 years ago, I was convicted of murder and sentenced to spend the rest of my life behind bars.

Since then, I have witnessed the ugliest side of what prison life can be about: the fear and mistrust, the violence and chaos, the isolation and emptiness, the hollowness of spirit that at one point brought me to contemplate suicide. But in these last few months, a setback of the worst kind has gripped me. Maryland Gov. Parris Glendening has said that, except in extraordinary circumstances, he will not consider parole for violent offenders who have received life sentences.[1]

This inmate, Larry Bratt, convicted of a double homicide in 1983, is eligible for a parole hearing in 2006 when he will be 54 years old. Under current Maryland law, paroles may not be granted to lifers unless approved by the governor. Since the governor's policy statement, 110 lifers at Bratt's prison became eligible for parole. None were paroled.

A number of questions are raised by this case. Why should a person convicted of a double murder even be considered for parole? What criteria should be used to

ACROSS CULTURES

PRISONERS TRANSPORTED TO AMERICA: AN EARLY FORM OF PAROLE

Early in the seventeenth century, Great Britain began transporting "able-bodied" convicted felons to the American colonies. This was partly in response to the colonies' labor shortage, and partly because of the pressure of increasing numbers of offenders. To transport these criminals, the Crown had to grant them reprieves or stays of execution of sentence.

At first, those to be transported were technically pardoned by the Crown, but many "somehow evaded transportation to America or had managed to return to England, through bribery or other illicit means" (p. 83). To correct this, a law was enacted in 1655 that provided that all such offenders would have their pardons revoked and they would then be subject to execution of sentence.

Arriving in America, a transported felon was sold at auction and became an indentured servant. Indentured offenders had to agree in writing to abide by certain conditions that "bear a marked similarity to conditions still imposed by parole boards throughout this country" (p. 83).

SOURCE: Alexander B. Smith and Louis Berlin, *Introduction to Probation and Parole* (St. Paul, MN: West Publishing Co., 1976).

determine who is eligible for parole release? Do prison inmates have a right to parole, or is it a privilege? What about the trend to abolish parole altogether?

What does parole mean? One definition found in standard English dictionaries is "word," as in giving one's word of honor. Its earliest usage in the history of the United States that is connected in any way to corrections is in the military. From the Revolutionary War to the Civil War, captured prisoners were frequently paroled after giving their word that they would not take any further part in the fighting. Flagrant violations of parole often resulted in denying parole to combatants subsequently captured.

However, as may be seen in the Across Cultures feature, the forerunner of modern-day parole goes back farther in our history to Great Britain's use of the transportation sanction. This practice of shipping felons to the American colonies allowed the Crown to be rid of many offenders, and assisted its labor-poor colonists to settle in to the New World. In the conditions imposed on those offenders who became indentured servants, we can see the beginnings of parole and conditional release.

In corrections, giving one's word not to violate the law is not enough to be granted parole. One must also agree to abide by a number of rules or conditions. Usually, most of these rules and conditions are similar to those imposed on offenders sentenced to probation. We must, however, distinguish between release on probation and on parole even though both permit offenders to be at liberty in the community.

In the case of probation, the offender is released pursuant to a judicial order. Violation of probation is, thus, a violation of a court order. In effect, the violator is in contempt of court. Parolees, on the other hand, are released on parole through the authority of an administrative agency, an arm of the executive branch of government. This release is an "act of grace" by the state. No inmate has a right to be released. Thus, contrary to the usual probationer, a parolee continues to serve her or his sentence of imprisonment, except that at a certain point in a sentence, it is continued in the community.

In this chapter we will trace the history of parole; examine the correctional aspects of parole; review the major controversies surrounding this correctional measure; and focus considerable attention on the recent increase in opposition to granting parole and the movement to abolish it altogether. To a large extent, this opposition is based on a desire for "truth in sentencing," that is, the sentence ordered by a trial judge should not be altered by a nonjudicial body, the parole board. Another reason for rejecting parole is that discretion as exercised by parole boards is not subject to review. It is possible for parole decisions to be perceived as unfair to offenders who are denied release, especially when the grounds for denial are neither spelled out nor reviewable. Finally, some opponents of parole believe that it results in unwarranted leniency, thus undercutting the currently popular "get tough on crime" stance.

Parole release, as we said above, is an act of grace by the state, following a hearing before an administrative board. Where parole is provided for by statute, these boards have the statutory authority to authorize or deny parole to any applicant. It is this discretion that has caused many to argue that granting and denying parole is so arbitrary as to warrant its abolition.

We also will analyze what has replaced parole in a number of states: conditional release from prison. Conditional release is not subject to the discretionary actions of parole boards. It is a mandatory release. It is similar to parole in that release is conditional. That it, a prison inmate is subject to a number of conditions and is under the supervision of an officer of the state. Violation of one or more conditions may result in reimprisonment.

According to a recent census by the Bureau of Justice Statistics, 671,000 persons were on parole at the end of 1993. This represents a 2 percent increase from the previous year. Ninety percent of these parolees were men; 51 percent were black. Of those on parole, about three-fourths were paroled by decisions of parole boards. The others were released under mandatory conditional release laws.[2] A **conditional release** is defined by the Bureau of Justice Statistics as including all those who, following release, can be reimprisoned for violating the conditions of their release.

HISTORICAL OVERVIEW

We already mentioned that parole was used over the centuries in military settings when soldiers captured by their enemies were often offered parole if they promised to go home and not take up arms again. In the correctional setting, parole as we know it today has its roots in the late eighteenth century and nineteenth century European and English practice of giving convicts **tickets of leave.** These tickets were given to offenders who were released from prison prior to the expiration of their court-imposed sentences. Since their sentences still had time remaining to be served, these offenders needed to have proof that they were lawfully at liberty. The ticket of leave provided the required documentation.

In the novel *Les Miserables,* the lead character, Jean Valjean, was being hounded by the police inspector because he had violated the terms of his ticket of leave. In Valjean's case, he was granted a ticket to be at liberty from the galleys. This element of conditional liberty characterizes parole today. Violations of the conditions laid down in a parole can result in arrest and return to confinement.

The most influential forerunners of parole in the United States were the ticket of leave practices of Alexander Maconochie and his disciple, Walter Croften. As we saw in Chapter 6, Maconochie and Croften were advocates of indeterminate sentencing,

ON THE JOB

THE PRERELEASE INTERVIEW

All inmates who were within 30 days of "maxing out" of prison were required to be interviewed by a representative of the Social Services Department. The interview was divided into three sections: financial data, postrelease data, and clothing requirements. The author conducted many interviews when he worked in a state correctional facility. What follows is an outline of the questions asked during these interviews.

I. Financial Data
   A. An inquiry into the inmate's prison account. No prisoner left the institution without a minimum balance. Should the account be below that amount, the state added funds.
   B. Potential for receipt of funds from the outside prior to release.

II. Postrelease Data
   A. Living arrangement. Does the prisoner have a place to live? Address?
   B. Does the prisoner have a responsible adult to whom he can turn after release? What relationship to prisoner?
   C. Does the prisoner have a job waiting for him? What kind of job and its location?

III. Clothing Requirements
   A. Does the prisoner have civilian clothing in storage at the institution? If no, then he was eligible to select release clothes from the prison tailor shop.
   B. If eligible for state-issue clothing, the prisoner must select either the "business suit" or the "sports ensemble."

Maconochie in the British penal colony system, Croften in the Irish prisons. They energetically argued that fixed sentences were unproductive in producing truly reformed inmates. Prisoners should be encouraged to reform by dangling the carrot of early release in front of them. However, releasing offenders prior to the end of their sentences raised a question: How can someone be outside prison while still under sentence? The answer was to grant them tickets of leave. This raised another question: How can we be certain that they will behave appropriately if we release them early? The answer, at first, was to require all "ticket" men and women to report regularly to law enforcement agencies in the communities where they lived and worked. There they would be registered and, at least theoretically, supervised by the police.

In the United States, parole originated with the ticket of leave system, which accompanied the reformatory movement. The first state reformatory, at Elmira, New York, received offenders under indeterminate sentences. The first warden at Elmira, Zebulon Brockway, imposed a strict paramilitary regimen and a scheme whereby inmates could earn marks to be used to gain early release. The reformatory's board of managers approved early release for those prisoners who had earned sufficient marks to be considered for parole.

It is interesting to note that for some time after Elmira opened in 1876, parolees were supervised by requiring them to report once every month to a designated reformatory "guardian" for a period of six months. If the board of managers agreed at the end of this period, parolees were released completely from the control of the reformatory. At any time during the six month "trial" period, the board could revoke an offender's parole.

A major argument in favor of continuing the practice of granting parole is that inmates being released to the community need considerable assistance as they reenter the free world. There needs to be some means of cushioning the shock of reentry, much as for space reentry vehicles. One of the more frustrating experiences I had when I worked in a state prison system involved interviewing inmates who were within 30 days of **maxing out**.[3] The state Division of Corrections regulations required all inmates who were to be released without parole supervision to be interviewed to prepare them for their reentry into the free world. An interview form was used for this purpose. The On the Job feature summarizes the sections of this form and the questions asked.

The frustrating part of this prerelease process was that no one, especially the interviewer, was authorized to follow up or investigate to see if all the answers were truthful. All that was required was to record the responses on the form and then submit it to the Division of Corrections. This experience illustrates clearly what parole advocates have in mind when they insist on releasing inmates under parole supervision.

THE ORGANIZATION OF THE PAROLING AUTHORITY

Most parole decisions are made by administrative boards whose members are appointed by state governors. Historically, this administrative arrangement evolved out of executive authority to pardon or otherwise exercise clemency.* This power is invested in the president of the United States in cases of federal offenders, and in state governors in the much more numerous state cases. As with parole, **executive clemency** is granted *ex gratia,* that is, it is given as an "act of grace" to which one does not have a right under law.

The actual supervision of parolees is a function that is separated from parole boards. Parole officers are employed in two main types of agencies: those that only supervise parolees, and others that combine parole and probation supervision. Maryland, like many other states, combines probation and parole supervision in one state agency, the Maryland Division of Parole and Probation, a division of the state's Department of Public Safety and Correctional Services. The parole and probation division employs over 1,000 persons and is responsible for supervising more than 90,000 probationers and parolees.[4]

We saw in the last chapter that combining parole and probation in one agency has its supporters as well as opponents. Since parole and probation supervision are carried out in the community, there is logic in locating both in the same agency. However, parolees and probationers are different offenders in terms of the law and their criminal histories.

One organizational issue that has yet to be resolved has to do with the fragmentation so common in the separation of parole releasing and revocation authority (vested in parole boards) from parole supervision, located in administrative agencies such as departments or divisions of parole (or parole and probation). One survey of parole board chairpersons found that 77 percent of them thought that,

---

*Executive clemency may include full or conditional pardons for crimes or commutation of sentences. Commutations can range from granting life or other terms to those sentenced to death, to releasing inmates after "time served" regardless of the length of an original sentence.

the merging of release, supervision, and revocation into a separate and autonomous agency would contribute to a more effective parole system. Incorporating parole supervision under the paroling authority would help ensure that such enforcement actually occurs, increase the level and frequency of communication between field services, and the board and parole accountability as a case moves from release to supervision to discharge [from parole] or revocation.[5]

THE PAROLE SELECTION PROCESS

Because granting parole is an act of grace by the executive, it is subject to a maximum amount of discretion. There are, however, some legal and administrative constraints that influence the selection of inmates for parole. What we examine now are commonly applied parole eligibility criteria. Since parole decision making is subject to considerable variation from state to state (with some states having abandoned parole altogether), it is impossible to arrive at a list of criteria that accurately portrays parole eligibility throughout the country. We can, however, note and discuss those criteria that are widely employed.

Statutory Limitations on Time of Parole Eligibility

State statutes usually specify when an offender is "eligible for a parole hearing." We often see this language in media reports: "Joseph Smith, who was convicted of armed robbery, was sentenced today to 15 years in prison. He will be eligible for parole in seven years." This can be misleading. What it does *not* mean is that Smith *will be* paroled in seven years. It simply means that, under the laws of the state, he is eligible to be heard before the state parole board in seven years.

Some state laws specify that a certain percentage of a sentence or number of years must be served in prison before an inmate is eligible for a parole hearing. Maryland, for example, requires offenders convicted of first-degree murder, rape, and a few other violent crimes to spend at least 15 years incarcerated before being considered for parole. If these crimes were committed under "aggravated circumstances," parole may not be granted for a minimum of 25 years.

These and other statutory time frames for parole hearings are usually subject to "good-time" laws and regulations. Prison sentences are generally shortened because inmates earn good time. The formula for calculating good time varies from state to state. Where I worked, inmates could earn 10 days for each month incarcerated. Other states allow "one for one" reductions, thus halving the sentence. Unfortunately, there are no readily available criteria for giving prisoners good time. In the system where I was employed, we jokingly believed that if an inmate did not destroy the institution or kill or seriously injure a staff member or other inmate, he would receive his 10 days for the month. In fact, all prisoner admissions records had the precalculated good-time date prominently displayed.

Parole Board Determination of Time of Eligibility

Where there are no statutory specifications of the amount of time to be spent in prison (either as a percentage of the sentence, or associated with the particular crime), the parole board may establish its own time frame. This gives the board maximum discretion to look into other criteria, sometimes from the moment an offender arrives at the correctional institution.

ON THE JOB

SALIENT FACTOR SCORING

Salient Factor:	Score:
Item A: Prior Convictions	
None	3
One	2
2 or 3	1
4 or more	0
Item B: Prior Commitments of more than 30 days	
None	2
1–2	1
3 or more	0
Item C: Age at time of current offense	
26 or older	2
20–25	1
19 or less	0
Item D: Recent Commitment-Free Period (3 years)	
No prior commitment of more than 30	

days or released to the community from last such commitment at least 3 years prior to the present offense 1

Otherwise 0

Item E: Probation/Parole/Confinement/Escape Status Violator (this time) Neither on probation, parole, confinement or escape status at time of current offense; nor committed as a probation, parole, confinement or escape status violator 1

Otherwise 0

SOURCE: Peter B. Hoffman, "Twenty Years of Operational Use of a Risk Prediction Instrument: The United States Parole Commission's Salient Factor Score," *Journal of Criminal Justice* 22 (1994): p. 477–494.

Institutional Record and Parole Eligibility

Regardless of the timing of parole hearings, parole boards always examine an inmate's record while incarcerated to determine whether he or she "deserves" or has "earned" a parole. Prison staff, usually the social services or classification departments, are responsible for reporting each prisoner's record while incarcerated. This record includes disciplinary, work, educational, and counseling history. In some prison systems, the record may provide a recommendation for or against parole.

Salient Factor Scores

A number of states use semiquantitative scoring instruments to assess the risk to the community posed by candidates for parole release. The most commonly used instruments are based on the one developed and employed for over 20 years by the United States Parole Commission, the **Salient Factor Score (SFS).** We will take a close look at this instrument because it will help us understand those variables many paroling authorities consider salient when inmates come before them seeking parole release.[6] Note that while federal parole has been abolished, many of the Salient Factor Score concepts and variables have been incorporated into the Federal Sentencing Guidelines. These variables have been culled from a number of recidivism prediction studies.[7]

The salient factors used to develop a score that is considered predictive of an offender's risk to the community include the following: (a) number of prior convic-

FOCUS ON THE LAW

FEDERAL STATUTORY LANGUAGE ON CONDITIONAL RELEASE FROM PRISON

The [trial] Court, in imposing a sentence to a term of imprisonment for a felony or misdemeanor, may include as a part of the sentence a requirement that the defendant be placed on a term of supervised release after imprisonment, except that the court shall include as a part of the sentence a requirement that the defendant be placed on a term of supervised release if such a term is required by statute or if the defendant has been convicted for the first time of a domestic violence crime. . . .

SOURCE: *Federal Criminal Code and Rules* (St. Paul, Minn.: West Publishing Co., 1995), p. 905.

tions; (b) number of prior commitments of more than 30 days; (c) age at current offense; (d) recent commitment-free period over the last three years; and (e) probation/parole/violator history or escape history.[8] Each of these factors is scored to arrive at a risk level. To see how the scoring is done, we have summarized the scoring sheet from the 1981 (the latest version) SFS in the second On the Job feature.

Methodologies used in sentencing and corrections to predict recidivism have long been criticized, as we pointed out in Chapter 3 and we will again discuss in Chapter 16. The salient factor scoring method has not been immune to this criticism. However, a consensus has evolved over time that predictions based on SFS-type methods are reasonably accurate. In 1986, after the Parole Commission had been using the SFS for six years, a review by a panel of the National Academy of Sciences concluded that,

> since initial implementation of federal parole guidelines, the Salient Factor Score has been revised and validated prospectively on several new samples. Two measures of predictive power . . . show that for all versions, the score and the four risk categories are at the high end of the accuracy range reported in other parole recidivism studies. In addition, these accuracy measures have been very stable over several samples.[9]

When scored on all factors, offenders are assigned to four risk categories: very good, good, fair, and poor. Based on a three-year follow-up study, results for one sample released in 1978 and a second one released in 1987 were found consistently to predict recidivism. In this study recidivism was defined as "unfavorable outcome (new criminal arrest or return to prison as parole violator)."[10]

Unfavorable outcome by risk level ranged from sixty-five percent (1978 sample), and sixty-seven percent (1987 sample) for those rated as poor risks, to only twenty-one percent (1978 sample), and sixteen percent (1987 sample) for offenders rated as very good risks, using the Salient Factor Score method.

We emphasize at this point that this research defined "unfavorable outcome" as either an arrest for any new crime (conviction not required) or return to prison for a violation of one or more parole conditions. Is this definition of recidivism really appropriate when making judgments about the success or failure of parole? We will consider this question in a later section.

CONDITIONAL RELEASE

As we indicated earlier, a number of states and the federal government have abandoned parole in favor of conditional release from confinement. While in the community, conditionally released offenders are supervised much the same as other offenders who are granted discretionary paroles. However, the mechanisms of release are quite different. As we have seen, parole boards exercise discretion to grant or deny parole to any applicant. The decision to release an offender conditionally is generally the prerogative of the sentencing judge unless a sentencing statute specifically requires or forbids such releases. Federal law specifically provides for trial judges to order conditional releases. The Focus on the Law feature describes some of the federal statutory language on conditional release from prison. It is important to recognize that the law specifies that persons convicted of domestic violence offenses are required, if their sentences include incarceration, to be released under supervision. This requirement apparently is related to a high rate of recidivism among spouse abusers, which supervised release may help to reduce. There are special conditions imposed on these offenders, which we will take up in the section on parole rules and conditions.

RULES AND CONDITIONS OF PAROLE AND CONDITIONAL RELEASE

As is the case with probation, release to the community on parole is conditioned by certain rules that parolees agree to observe on pain of return to incarceration. For much of the history of parole, these rules were virtually standardized throughout the country. They required paroles:

- To report regularly to a designated parole officer.
- To obtain permission before leaving the jurisdiction.
- To obey all laws.
- Not to purchase, own, possess, or control a firearm.
- To obey any special conditions the Parole Board may prescribe.

These conditions are spelled out in a parole agreement or contract, which is signed by the parolee and witnessed by a parole officer or other representative of the parole agency. Signing the agreement, offenders recognize that violation of any rules may result in reincarceration. The next Focus on the Law feature shows a typical set of parole rules and conditions set forth in a parole agreement.

More recently, a number of additional rules or conditions have been imposed on both parolees and those released under conditional release laws. These include requirements that parolees submit to regular or random drug testing, curfews, hours of community service, restitution, and participation in specified treatment programs (such as alcohol and drug abuse programs).

As is the case with probation, a debate arises regarding the reasons for many of the conditions and rules imposed on parolees. Some rules are designed to be punitive. That is, they serve the purpose of continuing the punishment of offenders after they leave prison. Others are clearly intended to maintain control over the parolee. Still others are intended to serve rehabilitative goals. Obviously, these different rationales may result in making supervision of parolees more difficult.

FOCUS ON THE LAW

STATEMENT OF CONDITIONS UNDER WHICH PAROLE IS GRANTED

This Certificate of Parole shall not become operative until the following Conditions are agreed to by the prisoner, and violation of any of these Conditions may result in revocation of Parole.

1. I shall report immediately to the Parole Officer under whose supervision I am paroled by personal visit.
2. I shall not change my residence or employment or leave the State without first getting the consent of my Parole Officer.
3. I shall, between the first and third day of each month, until my release from parole, make a full and truthful report to my Parole Officer in writing.
4. I shall not use narcotic drugs, or frequent places where intoxicants or drugs are sold, dispensed, or used unlawfully.
5. I shall avoid injurious habits and shall not associate with persons of bad reputations or harmful character.
6. I shall in all respect conduct myself honorably, work diligently at a lawful occupation, and support my dependents to the best of my ability.
7. I shall not violate any law.
8. I hereby waive all extradition rights and process and agree to return when the State Board of Pardons and Paroles directs at any time before my release from parole.
9. I shall promptly and truthfully answer all inquiries directed to me by the State Board of Pardons and Paroles and my Parole Officer and allow that Officer to visit me at my home, employment site or elsewhere, and carry out all instructions my Parole Officer gives.
10. If at any time it becomes necessary to communicate with my Parole Officer for any purpose and that Officer is not available, I shall contact the State Board of Pardons and Paroles.
11. I shall not marry without first seeking the advice and counsel of my Parole Officer.
12. Immediately upon release from the service of sentence in _____ and if prior to _____, I will report directly to the State Board of Pardons and Paroles, 750 Washington Avenue, Montgomery, AL 36130, either by telephone, correspondence or in person.
13. I shall pay fifteen dollars ($15.00) per month to the State Board of Pardons and Paroles as required by law.
14. I shall not own, possess or have under my control a firearm or ammunition of any kind, nor any other deadly weapon or dangerous instrument as defined by Alabama law.
15. I shall participate in alcoholic, drug treatment, or other therapeutic programs when instructed to do so by my Parole Officer.
16. I shall pay $_____ Restitution as ordered by the sentencing court or the State Board of Pardons and paroles.

I hereby certify that this statement of Conditions of Parole has been read or explained to the Parolee.

This _____ day _____ 19 __   _____

                                    Signature of Parolee

_____   _____
Member of Board or   (Give full address at
    Warden   which you can be reached)

SOURCE: Alabama Parole Board.

In a general review of parole practices, Von Hirsch and Hanrahan argue that unless parole conditions are rational and empirically sound, they will only confuse both parolee and parole officer.[11] As they see it, parole rules and conditions need to be rational, related to the task of preventing future crime. But rationality is not the only basis upon which to impose parole conditions. In addition, conditions need to be

*P*arole officers will review the rules and conditions of probation with parolees before their release from prison.

based on empirical evidence that they are necessary and effective in achieving the purposes of parole.

Federal prisoners released under conditional supervised release must meet the following requirements in addition to those we have listed above, or suffer possible reimprisonment:

- Refrain from any unlawful use of a controlled substance.
- Submit to a drug test within 15 days of release.
- Submit to at least two periodic drug tests thereafter (as determined by the court) for use of a controlled substance.[12]

We see here the clear focus on controlling drug abuse by the federal system. These conditions apparently apply to all persons conditionally released from federal confinement whether or not their offenses or prior histories included substance abuse.

Federal rules also specify the drug tests to be used and the consequences of a positive test result. Because the rules are so precisely written, we quote them below.

The results of a drug test administered in accordance with the proceeding subsection shall be subject to confirmation only if the results are positive, the defendant is subject to possible imprisonment for such failure, and either the defendant denies the accuracy of such test or there is some other reason to question the results. . . . A drug test confirmation shall be a urine drug test confirmed using gas chromatography/mass spectrometry techniques or such test as the Director of the Administrative Office of the United States Courts after consultation with the Secretary of Health and Human Services may determine to be of equivalent accuracy.[13]

Special Parole Conditions

In early 1995, a bill was introduced in the West Virginia legislature to require parolees convicted of violent and sex offenses to take out newspaper ads at their own expense one month prior to release.[14] This is one example of a trend toward setting very special and harsh conditions on certain parolees, especially sex offenders.

The parole in California of serial rapist Melvin Carter in 1994 caused an uproar throughout the state, especially in the rural, isolated community in Modoc County where he was to be released to a work camp and then paroled to the community.

The case heated up the political campaign. Governor Wilson, up for reelection partly on a tough stance against crime, was attacked for allowing the parole of the rapist, convicted on 23 counts of rape, assault, and burglary. He had been sentenced to a total of 25 years. Because of good behavior, his parole was possible after serving only 12 years.

To ease community fears and maintain his tough stance on crime, the governor imposed unusual conditions on Carter.[15] They included electronic monitoring, supervision by round-the-clock guards, frequent polygraph tests, and psychiatric evaluations.

While these examples of special parole conditions are atypical, many jurisdictions impose conditions on parolees and conditional releasees that are "special" and well beyond the commonly imposed ones. Federal conditionally released prisoners who have committed domestic violence crimes are subject to specific conditions in addition to the ordinary conditions we described earlier. These are worded as follows:

> The court shall order as an explicit condition of supervised release for a defendant convicted for the first time of a domestic violence crime . . . that the defendant attend a public, private, or private nonprofit offender rehabilitation program that has been approved by the court, in consultation with a State Coalition Against Domestic Violence or other appropriate experts. . . .[16]

SUPERVISION MODELS

Types of supervision of offenders on parole or conditional release generally are similar, if not identical, to those we discussed in the chapter on probation. Supervision can be primarily control oriented, counseling, or a combination of both. As with probation supervision, officer role conflict may be a problem as officers must integrate the needs of maintaining control (through surveillance and attention to parolees' adherence to rules and conditions) with those associated with the traditional rehabilitative role of counseling offenders in the community.

During the period when rehabilitation was considered to be a major goal in corrections, parole officers were seen as service providers,

> helping ex-prisoners reestablish a tolerable life for themselves in the community. The criterion of success would not be recidivism control, but the programs' ability to alleviate suffering and disorientation among ex-offenders.[17]

In order to operate as service providers in the rehabilitation model of supervision, parole officers generally were to do the following:

- Assure that parolees were financially secure during the first several weeks of release.
- Provide job training and/or job placement.
- Provide housing assistance to the extent of helping parolees locate adequate housing.
- Deliver on-going counseling services, or refer parolees to appropriate service providers.[18]

Every parole candidate needs to be interviewed by a parole agent prior to the parole candidate's appearance in front of the parole board.

While these activities expected of parole officers may have had (and may still have) support in the correctional setting, we may wonder whether some of them really should be carried out by a parole officer. For example, parolees should not leave prison without a modicum of financial stability. Prisons as "correctional" institutions should provide job training before inmates are released. Inmates should not be paroled without a job placement already in hand. All parolees leaving prison should have adequate housing arranged in advance. If these are not provided by the prison system, what does it tell us about that system? By assigning these tasks to the parole officer, do we not place an excessive workload on an already overloaded correctional worker? Certainly, we expect that officers will become involved in some of these tasks from time to time while their clients are on parole. But we should not expect them to have to perform them during the initial period of a parolee's release.

Some parole agencies have established supervision models for what we might call special needs parolees. For example, Maryland's Division of Parole and Probation has an Evaluation, Diagnosis, and Referral (EDR) program that targets substance abusers and operates on a regional basis to identify offenders with drug and alcohol abuse problems. The units

> conduct timely evaluation, diagnosis, and treatment referrals of parolees and probationers who have a special condition, in addition to their standard . . . conditions, relating to drug or alcohol abuse.[19]

The EDR units are staffed by teams that include not only parole and probation personnel, but personnel from the state's Addictions Services Agency, located in the Department of Mental Health and Hygiene. Teams headed by a probation or parole officer are responsible for diagnosing offenders' problems and needs and making appropriate treatment plans and, where required, referrals to other agencies.

While the Maryland approach focuses mainly on offenders entering parole or probation, it also provides assistance to a parole officer who, in the course of supervis-

ON THE JOB

PAROLE OFFICERS' PERCEPTIONS OF PERSONAL RISK

Community supervision officers have been reported to be under considerable strain as their roles have evolved away from the traditional counseling ones associated with rehabilitation and counseling offenders to assist them as they try to resume their lives in the community. To a large extent this evolution has been driven by the shift in the objectives of parole in the direction of increased emphasis on its punitive and offender control possibilities. Here a supervising parole officer briefly expresses some of the parole officers' concerns about their personal safety as they must cope with the "new" parole supervision responsibilities:

> Along with control and enforcement supervision models has come the perception by many in community supervision that both the offenders they supervise and the communities they live and work in are more violent and hostile than in earlier years. The result has been a drastic change in the orientation of supervision officers, who now want to be armed with firearms, personal defense sprays . . . , stun guns, radios, cellular phones, handcuffs, and impact weapons. (p. 31)

SOURCE: Paul W. Brown, "The Continuum of Force in Community Supervision," *Federal Probation* 58 (December 1994): 31.

ing a parolee, finds that the parolee has a substance abuse problem. The officer can refer the matter to the EDR unit for evaluation. EDR units may, following the evaluation process, recommend to the Parole Commission or the sentencing court modifications in parole or probation conditions.[20]

Because newer "indeterminate sanctions" and enhanced parole rules have resulted in the dominance of control and enforcement supervision models, there has been an increase in the potential for **role conflict.** We will examine in detail some of these newer sanctions in Chapter 16. At this point we will briefly illustrate different supervision models connected with intermediate sanctions.

New Jersey operates an innovative parole release strategy with supervision requirements significantly different from those common in the past.[21] This program involves incarcerated offenders identified as posing a "low risk" of recidivism. They are resentenced to the **Intensive Supervision Parole (ISP)** after three or four months of imprisonment.

Supervision of these persons includes 27 contacts per week on average; frequent urine tests to check for drug and alcohol abuse—13,000 tests were done in 1986 alone with 400 offenders; 16 hours of community service; a strict curfew; and full-time employment.[22] The conditions imposed on the parolees and the requirements placed on parole officers may seem draconian compared with parole as commonly supervised throughout the country. Because of the intensive supervision required and the strict surveillance necessary to ensure compliance with the rules, one-third of the subjects returned to prison within 18 months, mostly for technical violations. This result is similar to that found among probationers who are subject to intensive supervision, as we noted in Chapter 11.

One disturbing development in parole (as well as probation) supervision is a heightened sense of danger among parole officers. This has come as a result of the officers' need to supervise parolees with control and rules enforcement as primary tasks. The On the Job feature contains a description by a federal corrections administrator of parole officers' perceptions of the risks they face and their responses to them.

This development has many causes and consequences. Probably more than any other factor, release on parole or conditional release now includes many more offenders who are relatively high-risk offenders. Our review of probation in Chapter 11 found that because of prison and jail crowding, many offenders are entering probation who would not have been considered eligible in the past. The same is now true with regard to parole and conditional release.

Another factor contributing to parole officers' anxiety about their personal safety is that with increased use of parole and probation as punitive measures, offenders are more likely to perceive their supervisors as more threatening to their liberty. This factor, together with the previously discussed one, points again to the systemic nature of corrections and criminal justice.

The real world of parole supervision may be, in a number of significant ways, different from the world we have just described. If control and enforcement supervision models really characterize the parameters of the parole officer's working environment, we would expect to find that they are less rehabilitative in orientation than in the past. In a study of 108 parole and probation officers employed by the Alabama Board of Pardons and Parole, Whitehead and Lindquist found the opposite orientation to be true.[23]

These officers had caseloads of 122 offenders. Officers averaged 12 hours per week in direct contact with their clients (another 24 hours was spent each week on "paper work"). Simple math will show that the amount of time available to be spent in direct contact with 122 parolees in a week's or month's time was exceedingly small.

The research revealed that

> Alabama probation and parole officers were very pro-rehabilitation and very opposed to punishment.
>
> When one considers that these respondents were (and still are) required to carry weapons and qualify each year with those weapons and were expected to be involved in the arrest of their clients if arrest became necessary, these findings contrast markedly with the expectation held by the authors at the outset [of the study].[24]

Also contrary to expectations was the finding that there was little evidence of role conflict or **goal discordance** among the officers. A further observation is important to consider now that more punitive uses of parole and probation are popular. The more contact officers had with those in their caseloads, the less punitive they were in their attitudes and approach to supervision. As Whitehead and Lindquist point out, "a punitive, control-oriented intent stipulates greater contact and lower caseloads but these very features seem to diminish officer punitiveness."[25]

Regardless of whether a parole agency is employing a surveillance, control, or rehabilitation model, risk levels of offenders in its caseloads must always be considered. How great a risk does a parolee pose? To some extent instruments such as Salient Factor Scores can assist in predicting level of risk of recidivism or rules violations. Level of risk will, obviously, point toward, if not dictate, the supervision strategy required. However, research has found that determining risk levels and appropriate supervision is not always a matter of applying an objective methodology like calculating a salient factor score.

Edna Erez found in her study of a random sample of 613 Ohio parolees stratified by sex who were on parole between 1982 and 1986 that gender differences were extremely important in deciding on risk levels and supervision styles.[26] Erez used two instruments (one objective and the other subjective) to test for gender differences in decision making by parole officers and their supervisors. Her findings about the assessment of both risk levels and service needs were that:

> . . . the results demonstrate clearly that male parolees are viewed first and foremost as "dangerous men;" their risk score has the strongest effect on the determination of their need level. The effect of this [score] on the determination of female parolees' need level is much weaker; its importance is secondary to that of gender-based expectations. Yet because the label influences the subjective determination of women's need, the "evil women" hypothesis rather than a paternalistic thesis is supported, a finding that suggests little tolerance for women's criminality (or dangerousness).[27]

And later she says:

> Parole officers expect conformity to gender stereotypes and traditional sex roles as part of their formula for parolees' successful reintegration into society. . . . Because the female prisoner/parolee typically is a single or divorced mother, many of the women involved must perform duties traditionally expected of women (e.g., child care) as well as of men (breadwinning). . . . Gender-neutral rehabilitation is necessary for meaningful and effective reform of parolees.[28]

PAROLE REVOCATION

Revoking an offender's parole and returning the violator to prison is a process that is subject to the discretionary authority of both parole officer and judges, as well to the language of the law. For example, Federal District Court judges may

> revoke a term of supervised release, and require the defendant to serve in prison all or part of the term of supervised release authorized by statute for the offense that resulted in such term . . . without credit for time previously served on postrelease supervision, if the court . . . finds by a *preponderance of the evidence* that the defendant violated a condition of supervised release. . . .[29]

As we have seen, parole revocation takes place in a system context. A study of Texas parole revocation decision making highlighted the systemic nature of criminal justice. It argued that alterations in one part of the system "create ramifications for the operation of other segments . . . that are often . . . neither intended nor foreseen."[30] This study was conducted to examine these systemic effects, especially effects on parole board revocation decisions, of Texas legislation intended to relieve prison crowding. Enacted in 1985, the statute "was designed to expedite the swift return of 'good risk' inmates to the community by restoring good time and releasing revoked parolees in as little as three months."[31] A different style is illustrated in the Across Cultures feature.

The law was partly a response to the 1983 *Ruiz v. Estelle* appellate court decision that found numerous problems with Texas Department of Corrections management of its prisons. A Federal District Court judge issued a court order requiring the department to refuse to accept new admissions when the system reached 95 percent of its rated capacity. The new law was only one response to the order. Other responses included "front door" and "back door" actions: sharp increases in probation ("front door") and parole ("back door") caseloads in the state.

The research into the consequences of the statute, conducted by Winfree and his associates, sought to compare parole revocation procedures and decision making for

ACROSS CULTURES

DEALING WITH POSTRELEASE VIOLATORS, CHINESE STYLE

In the People's Republic of China, some persons "who have served a term of imprisonment are particularly likely to be subjected to re-education through labour after release" (p. 37). A decree issued by the National People's Congress Standing Committee states that:

> Where after release upon completion of a term of reform through labour [a criminal sanction], there are minor criminal acts not qualifying for criminal sanctions, the offender may be given the sanction of re-education through labour. (p. 37)

These "violators" are to be reeducated through labor at the place of confinement where they served their original sentences.

In a curious bit of sentence restructuring, this decree, which would seem to apply only to those who commit relatively minor violations after release from prison, can be applied to those about to be released. Amnesty International reports that "some prisoners are sentenced to re-education immediately after completing their term of imprisonment, simply because their behavior in prison was thought to be unsatisfactory" (p. 37).

In effect, this results in a form of indeterminate sentence. While the additional or "supplementary" punishment is for a determinate period as long as three years, it can be increased should the inmate's behavior not be satisfactory.

SOURCE: Amnesty International, *China, Punishment Without Crime: Administrative Detention,* Amnesty International Publications, September 1991, p. 37.

two samples of parole hearing cases: 114 cases heard prior to the law coming into effect and 94 postlaw cases.[32] Among the significant findings are the following:

- Significantly more postlaw change parolees were recommended for revocation following revocation hearings.
- Significantly more postlaw parolees were recommended for revocation for technical violations.
- Significantly more postlaw parolees were convicted for personal crimes.
- Hearing officers recommended more postlaw violators for revocation, yet the parole board's rate of revocation did not change.

We can see the systemic consequences of, first, case lawmaking (the *Ruiz* decision and subsequent court order), and second, legislative lawmaking (the good-time credit). As Winfree concluded,

> Texas's BPP [Board of Pardons and Parole] was less inclined to follow the Hearing Section's recommendation in each and every case, and particularly when the recommendation would have resulted in a commitment to the TDC.[33]

Parole Revocation Procedures

What happens when a parolee violates one or more conditions of parole? As was the case when we discussed probation violations in Chapter 11, there are at least three types of parole violators: those who commit **technical parole violations** (that is,

*P*arole violators are interviewed by police officers to determine the severity of the violation. *If the violation is a new criminal act the offender may be convicted of the new offense and sentenced to imprisonment. Then the probation order is terminated.*

violate one or more conditions); those who are arrested on criminal charges; and those convicted for new crimes while on parole. Until 1972, parole revocation decisions were made following summary procedures in most jurisdictions. Parolees accused of technical violations or even new offenses were not entitled to due process before being reincarcerated. Parole officers and their supervisors exercised their discretion in judging whether a violation warranted removing offenders from parole and returning them to prison.

In 1972, the United States Supreme Court in the case of *Morrissey v. Brewer*[34] altered the landscape by requiring certain minimum due process protections for those facing reincarceration. The Court required a preliminary hearing before a "neutral" board. The Court did not grant parolees the "full panoply of rights due a [criminal] defendant,"[35] but because the potential loss of liberty through revocation was a "grievous loss,"[36] an "orderly process" was required.[37]

It is noteworthy that the Court considered parole an extension of confinement, used so regularly that it no longer could be considered a privilege. Whether this means that a grant of parole is no longer to be considered an act of grace by the executive is unclear at this time. Certainly, parole, in the *Morrissey* decision, was not elevated to the status of a right.

In its decision, the Supreme Court laid the groundwork for a series of steps that must be taken before a parolee may be reincarcerated.[38] These are as follows:

STEP 1 Parolee to receive timely notice of the hearing, together with notice of the charges, right to appear and present evidence, and right, albeit limited, to cross-examine witnesses.

STEP 2 A preliminary hearing before a neutral body to determine whether probable cause exists that parolee has violated her or his parole. If probable cause is found, the process moves to the next step.

STEP 3 A revocation hearing to determine guilt, and if guilty, a decision as to whether the parolee is to be reincarcerated or suffer other punishment.

In step 3, the hearing to determine whether a parolee has violated parole, the standard of proof is not the "beyond reasonable doubt" required in criminal trials. Instead, a "preponderance of the evidence" standard is used, a much lighter burden for the state to carry. We may remember that the Federal Rules of Criminal Procedure explicitly requires this standard when conditionally released federal offenders are considered for revocation.

In a decision about a year later, the Court took up the question of whether parolees had a right to be represented by legal counsel at the preliminary and revocation hearings.[39] The Court took a virtual hands-off position with regard to the right to counsel. It stated that it was up to the parole agencies on a "case by case basis" to determine whether indigent parolees should have appointed counsel.* Apparently, when parolees can retain counsel at their own expense, counsel can represent them at revocation hearings.

This procedure is a sharp departure from earlier revocation processes, which frequently were quite summary in nature. I remember one case while I was a parole agent in a parole clinic in Baltimore. One parolee, in another agent's caseload, convicted of second-degree murder, was found to have violated one of the conditions of his parole. A prison guard, present for the purpose of taking him back to prison, attempted to take him in custody as he was notified of his violation. The parolee ran from the office (straight through a glass door), but was apprehended before he could reach the street. No preliminary hearing, no revocation hearing, no attorney. That same evening he was residing in a cell.

DECLINE IN THE USE OF PAROLE

> More than 85% of those released from prison receive supervision in the community. Prisoners enter parole supervision either by a discretionary decision or by fulfilling the conditions for a mandatory release.[40]

Supervised mandatory release has increased fivefold since 1977, while parole releases have declined from 72 percent to 41 percent.[41] Federal parole no longer is possible for offenders unless they committed their offenses prior to November 1987. A number of states also have abolished parole in favor of either mandatory sentences without possibility of parole, or sentences mandating conditional release from prison. Why has this happened? Part of the answer is that evaluations of parole have shown mixed, if not consistently disappointing results. We will examine the results of this research in the next section.

Another reason for the trend toward ending parole is more complex. Opposition to the discretionary authority of parole boards is at the core of the movement to abolish parole. Historically, parole board authority to grant or deny parole has not been

---

*Federal parolees are always appointed counsel if they are legally indigent.

subject to appeal. Boards were notorious for using vague selection criteria that were not explained to either offenders coming before them for consideration, nor to the general public, which frequently questioned the efficacy of releasing some offenders early in their sentences.

Vagueness of criteria together with failure to explain decisions, especially those denying parole, led prison inmates to perceive the parole system as unfair. The very positivist penology that provided the underpinning for indeterminate sentences and parole release contributed to this sense of unfair dealing. Some inmates, denied parole while others similarly situated were granted release, were demoralized, thus counteracting the correctional or rehabilitative effects incarceration was supposed to have.

We also note that,

> parole boards will never enjoy a highly popular or appealing image with the public. No matter how you look at it, the bottom line is that parole boards let convicted criminals out of jail earlier than their full term. . . .
>
> [P]arole boards will always be most visible when they're most vulnerable. The newsworthiness of any parole story is when there has been a serious failure in the system, such as a recently released inmate committing a heinous new crime.[42]

Some of the advocates of eliminating parole board discretion are supporters of the "justice model" of criminal justice. They consider unfettered parole discretionary authority to be fundamentally unjust. If it is abolished, they argue, inmates will somehow begin to feel that they were being dealt with justly. "Truth in sentencing" would be appreciated by offenders as well as the public. That is, offenders and the public will know with certainty how much time will be spent behind bars. This predictability will obtain whether sentences are served without possibility of parole or under conditional release statutes.

EVALUATION OF PAROLE

According to the United States Bureau of Justice Statistics, "more than half of all exits from parole were categorized as successful. Most of the remainder were returned to incarceration, but only a tenth of the parolees were returned . . . with a new sentence."[43] Another report from the Bureau of Justice Statistics stated that there were 155,874 "parole violators" in state prison populations in 1991.[44] Eighty percent of these violators were convicted of new crimes committed while on parole.[45] Of the remainder, 43 percent had been arrested (but not convicted) on criminal charges.

Looking only at violators considered to be technical violators (that is, not convicted of new offenses), the report listed the major reasons for their return to prison. We summarize them in Table 12.1.

An important finding that should affect parole supervision practices as well as helping to evaluate parole comes from this Bureau of Justice Statistics study: The average amount of time a parole violator spends on parole before committing a new offense or violating one or more rules is 13 months; half of the violators had been on parole less than eight months.[46] The report made the dramatic statement that, during the average of 13 months parole violators were in the community, they committed (using a "conservative" estimate) 46,000 violent crimes, 45,000 property crimes, 24,000 drug offenses, and 9,000 other crimes.[47] Clearly, these findings tell us that supervision during the first weeks and months of a parolee's life on the street must be

Major Reasons for Return to State Prisons for Technical Violators		TABLE 12.1
REASON	PERCENTAGE OF VIOLATORS	
Arrest on new charge	43.0	
Failure to report or absconded	34.2	
Left the jurisdiction without permission	14.1	
Positive drug test	10.2	
Failure to report for drug test or treatment	4.4	

SOURCE: Robyn L. Cohen, "Probation and Parole Violators in State Prisons, 1991," Bureau of Justice Statistics, Special Report, August 1995, p. 3.

intensive. Of course, the more intensive an officer's supervision, the more offenses and technical violations he or she may discover.

Do these and other discouraging figures mean that parole is unsuccessful as a correctional measure? Evaluating parole outcome, like evaluating other components of corrections, is a difficult task. What do the two concepts *success* and *failure* mean? How can we operationalize them in order to reach generalizations about parole as a correctional measure? Two examples from my experience supervising parolees may illustrate one aspect of the evaluation problem. The first involved a sixty-four-year-old white pedophile, released on parole after spending over nine years in prison, the last several years in a "treatment" facility where he was enrolled in group psychotherapy. The second example was the case of a twenty-three-year-old black burglar, paroled following three years in the same treatment facility.

The first parolee, we'll call him Fred, had received about four years of therapy when he was released from prison. His wife of many years was waiting for him and had maintained a home in the community where they had lived together for almost twenty years (when Fred wasn't in prison). He and his wife developed an elaborate "cover story" to explain his absences: Fred suffered from a chronic lung ailment and was required to spend time in an Arizona sanitarium. When he arrived home the last time, under my supervision, his wife put on a welcome home party, and all the relatives, neighbors, and family friends were there. All had a good time. No one at the party knew Fred was a parolee, let alone a pedophile.*

Fred's supervision required that I meet with him and his wife weekly for the first several months of his parole. The plan was to reduce gradually the level of supervision. Should all go well, contacts would be limited to once or twice a year, thus becoming symbolic supervision. At one of the early contact visits, Fred told me that he had figured out how to avoid being sexually excited by young children. Since this was potentially quite significant for evaluating the success of his treatment, I listened carefully. The secret was, Fred said, that the many beautiful flowering plants around his house were very attractive to children. Therefore, he was going to tear them all out. When this was done, children would stay away and Fred wouldn't "get those thoughts" again. Now, does this mean that years of therapy were successful? One of

---

*Wouldn't it be a valuable contribution to the correctional process if offenders approved for parole because they were rehabilitated could have welcome home parties for the "right" reason?

the principles of psychotherapy is that if it is successful, it helps patients gain insight into the underlying processes related to their illnesses. Could it be that the attractive plants really were the underlying cause of Fred's problems?

One of the conditions of Fred's parole, as well as all others released from that prison, was that he could be returned to prison if the staff felt it was necessary for "therapeutic" reasons. Parolees returned for these reasons were termed therapeutic violators. In Fred's case, the staff concluded that at his advanced age he did not pose a risk to the community. He remained on parole for several more years.

The second parolee, let's call him Jim, was a young man convicted of burglary who had a rather long history of property crimes, but no history of violence. He came from a poor inner-city neighborhood. His father had abandoned the family when Jim was very young. After three years in therapy Jim was paroled to his former home. As with the case with Fred, Jim's parole supervision plan called for an initial period of weekly contacts, followed by a gradual "weaning" until his supervision was more symbolic than real.

At a contact visit approximately three months into his parole, Jim came in with a young woman and introduced her as his wife. Among the conditions of Jim's parole (as well as all other parolees) was one that prohibited marriage unless "prior written permission of your parole officer" was obtained. I had never laid eyes on this young woman before that night. Jim was in violation of the parole conditions that he had signed and promised to obey. What should I do about this? As a technical violator, was Jim to be counted as a parole failure?

In discussing the situation with Jim and his wife, I learned that they were expecting a baby. Jim was vehement in his insistence that no child of his was going to be born out of wedlock. After talking with them, and with myself, I decided that Jim's actions, technically in violation of his parole, were actually evidence of a much more mature person than when he first arrived in prison. Therefore, I reported the violation to my supervisor as positively as I could and recommended that no action be taken against Jim. My recommendation was accepted, and Jim eventually "successfully" completed his parole.

Evaluation Criteria

The most difficult problem to solve when trying to evaluate parole is that of selecting appropriate criteria for judging success and failure. Often, we think of evaluation criteria in terms of parole's effect on recidivism. While this may seem at first glance to be the most appropriate criterion, it is also one that is subject to a variety of operational definitions. As Harry Allen and his colleagues observed, while "most [researchers] agree that recidivism should be a primary performance measure, there is no agreement on its definition nor the indicators to be used for its measurement."[48]

Geerken and Hayes, studying New Orleans offenders on probation and parole, commented that the "failure rate is quite sensitive to [the] failure criterion."[49] Reviewing a number of evaluation studies, they found that failure rates when measured by rearrest ranged from 25 to 46 percent. It is virtually impossible to generalize from these reported rates because of another impediment to evaluation research: "comparisons of reported parole effectiveness are also suspect because offenders, follow-up periods, jurisdictions, failure criteria, and sentencing policies vary markedly across studies."[50]

Geerken and Hayes did, however, reach one conclusion after their review of the research literature:

[I]f the criterion for failure is rearrest, a significant proportion of offenders placed on probation or parole will recidivate before their term expires. Including results obtained from our own data, from one-third to two-thirds of all probationers were rearrested, and from one-quarter to one-half of all parolees were rearrested.[51]

An important question these findings raise is: Would a reduction in or outright abolition of the use of probation and parole significantly affect crime rates? Those who propose eliminating or severely restricting the use of parole argue that high "recidivism" rates call for such action. However, do rearrests mean new crimes have been committed? If so, are the crimes serious ones? Do rearrests result in reconvictions? Aren't offenders on parole much more likely to be rearrested than others?

Results of Parole Evaluation Studies

Geerken and Hayes conducted original research in New Orleans that sought to answer another important question: How many persons arrested for certain serious crimes were on probation and parole at the time of their arrest? Specifically, they focused on arrests for burglary, the most frequent serious property offense, and armed robbery, the most frequent violent crime. Should the percentage of these crimes committed by probationers and parolees be high, there certainly would be an argument for judging probation and parole to be unsuccessful. There also would be a strong argument for the claim that these alternatives to imprisonment do not protect the public, that is, they fail to provide for incapacitation.

What did the study find? Approximately 8 percent of adults arrested for burglary and armed robbery were on probation at the time of their arrests. Between 1 and 2 percent of those arrested for these crimes were on parole at the time of their arrests. One conclusion Geerken and Hayes reached was that the findings

suggest that even the complete elimination of probation and parole would have a very negligible effect of the burglary and armed robbery rates since more than 90 percent of all burglaries and armed robberies were committed by persons *not* on probation or parole at the time of their arrest.[52]

We must point out here that there are data suggesting that the rate of new offenses committed by offenders on probation and parole is higher than that found by Geerken and Hayes. Robyn L. Cohen reported that "thirty-five percent of State prison inmates in 1991 were convicted of a new offense that they had committed while on probation or parole."[53] At this point we may well ask whether eliminating parole or severely restricting eligibility to offenders judged to be good risks would not be in order. Such policies, however, are known to have unintended as well as intended consequences.

One possible unintended consequence of denying parole or imposing more severe restrictions on eligibility might be to reduce the number of plea bargains defendants strike with prosecutors. Thus, more contested trials would jam up the system, with the likely result of even more prison crowding.

On the other hand, there are some, like Geerken and Hayes, who argue that research does not show parole to be a failure. Do they conclude that parole or probation can or should be expanded in the United States? Not so, argue the researchers:

The criminal justice system is intended by judges, prosecutors, and law enforcement officers to be selective, that is, to keep the most dangerous and active offenders behind bars. To some extent, the system succeeds, although how well it succeeds is a matter of much debate.[54]

We need to add that our analysis of prisons admissions for both men's and women's prisons, which we reviewed in Chapters 8 and 9, suggest clearly that our prison population increases are not the result of incarcerating more serious and dangerous offenders. A large proportion of admissions each year consists of parole and conditional release violators.

In this connection we refer to a recent study of Texas parolee performance.[55] The authors of this research caution that when attempting to measure the effectiveness of parole, the total correctional context must be taken into account. This is especially important when, as was the case in Texas, rapid and significant reform of the prison system was mandated following the federal appellate court decision in *Ruiz v. Estelle*.[56] This decision found much about Texas's correctional situation to be unconstitutional, particularly the overcrowded condition of the prison.

> One important consequence of the increasing reliance on parole release for managing prison populations is the increase in the parole population. . . . In Texas, as elsewhere, some of the important consequences of this increasing reliance on parole release include a significant decline in the proportion of sentence served and a substantial increase in the relative size of the parole population. As more and more inmates were released, the pool of eligible parolees became more hard core.[57]

This "hard core" population will undoubtedly be a high-risk population. We would expect to find that these parolees more frequently become rule or technical violators and are more frequently arrested, convicted, and reincarcerated.

The Texas research examined "trends in reincarceration" in four successive release groups of property offenders.[58] These groups were followed for a period of 36 months. Again pointing out the significance of the correctional context and the systemic nature of criminal justice, the researchers wanted to determine whether the "rapid change" in the operation of Texas's criminal justice system that occurred in the 1980s "affected recidivism patterns of successive yearly cohorts of property offenders. . . ."[59]

This research illustrates the complexity of the task of evaluating parole (or any correctional measure). For instance, if recidivism rates are found to be higher for parolees released earlier in their sentences than once considered normal, what can we infer from this? There are a number of possibilities:

- The shortened prison term may not have acted as a deterrent.
- A shortened period of incarceration might mean that prison treatment programs have not had sufficient time to be effective.
- Because of early release on parole to comply with court-mandated population reduction orders, many high-risk inmates are being released who would in the past still be incarcerated.

The study examined some of these issues with reference to the state's Prison Management Act (PMA) of 1987. This statute, a response to the *Ruiz* decision, mandated that once a prison's population reaches 95 percent of capacity, an "overcrowding emergency" is declared. This, in turn, requires the governor to order the warden to award extra "good time" to all "eligible" inmates. Noneligible inmates include those convicted of certain sex crimes, crimes of violence, crimes against children, and, of course, given the war against drugs, drug offenses.

The results, following parolees released early and those released "normally," suggest that the early releasees failed more often and sooner than their counterparts. The first nine months after release was a time during which technical violations of parole conditions were most frequent, and returning violators to prison was a common response. As the researchers pointed out, parole officers were "caught in a double bind."[60] If they revoked violators' paroles, they would be contributing to prison crowding. If they looked the other way and did not revoke violators, they could be accused of failing to carry out a major objective of their role: protecting the public.

Although the research provided some "indirect" support for the hypothesis that early release results in a reduced deterrent impact, it is quite possible that an alternative explanation is at least as plausible:

> [O]ne such alternative to the hypothesis is what might be termed reduced resources. That is, a sudden, unexpected release for those in the PMA [Prison Management Act] cohort may have meant fewer prior arrangements for life on the outside and thus reduced support resources. Reduced resources may have meant fewer alternatives to a return to criminal activities.[61]

Those released suddenly were also those who were at heightened risk of failure as measured by their Salient Factor Scores, which were calculated for use by the state parole board. Scores were determined by examining the number of prior convictions, prior incarcerations, age at first conviction, commitment offense, record of prior parole or probation revocation, drug and/or alcohol dependence, and employment record.[62]

Other research provides a more promising outlook for parole. A study of New Jersey's intensive supervision parole program (ISP) found a number of positive results. In this project, offenders who completed their terms of imprisonment without supervised release were compared to those released under supervision after three to four months of imprisonment.[63] As a consequence of the shortened term of incarceration for the ISP offenders, there was reported a savings of $7,000 per ISP subject. About 25 percent of the ISP releasees had new arrests vs 35 percent of the comparison group after two years.[64] These positive findings need to be examined in light of the high rate of reincarceration among the ISP offenders for technical violations because of the severity of the conditions placed on their freedom and the intensity of the supervision they received.

The research we have reviewed so far does not allow us to conclude that parole is a success or a failure as a correctional measure. The findings are a mixed bag. Before we can come to any generalizations about parole performance we must see its performance in the context of other criminal justice system variables. Edward E. Rhine and his colleagues urge those who want either to abolish or expand parole to be aware of parole's location within a system. They state that three systemic issues that must be addressed:

1. The ever-growing threat to the integrity of parole decision making posed by prison crowding.
2. The next wave of sentencing reform.
3. An increasingly vocal and organized public that opposes parole, but under certain circumstances is supportive of rehabilitative intervention.[65]

With regard to the first of these issues, the dynamic of prison crowding, strongly related to sentencing policies and practices, means that where parole is not abolished outright, it will be under tremendous pressure to accept inmates for community supervision who would in the past never be considered for release, or their release would have been postponed. An influx of high-risk parolees will obviously result in higher levels of recidivism and technical violations. This, in turn, may well increase the public's unwillingness to support parole, reducing even further support for rehabilitation.

Some light is shed on this issue by a report of a study of five years of violation rate data for offenders released from federal prisons either on parole (for those committing offenses prior to November of 1987 when parole was abolished) or on conditional release.[66] The study, conducted by Michael Bork, found an "explosive growth" in the population released from prison under supervision. In fact, Bork reported, "supervised release has now become more prevalent than probation. . . ."[67] Those offenders conditionally released from federal prisons were found to have a revocation rate of 39 percent in 1994, "the highest rate among all forms of supervision," with technical violations leading all other reasons for revocation.[68] While drug offenders constitute the largest offender group under supervision, their violation rate has not increased over the five years of the study (about 27 percent). Bork comments on the effects of the federal sentencing guidelines on probation and parole:

> Probation officers supervise many more individuals than in the past as well as prepare more detailed reports. In addition to the lengthy presentence reports . . . the number of other reports (i.e., violation reports and supervision reports) written by [them] continues to increase as their caseload increases.[69]

The remaining issues posed by Edward Rhine, the next round of sentence reforms and public opinion regarding parole, cannot easily be examined. We know that the two are closely related. The trend toward more punitive sentences that prohibit parole release is, of course, tied to public attitudes about the crime problem and corrections' responses to it. It may well be that parole will be used much less frequently in future than is the case now.

SUMMARY

HAROLD TRESTER SUCCINCTLY SUMMARIZED the situation parole finds itself in today:

> Parole is the end link in the criminal justice chain. Because of its position, it not only represents the ultimate end in the continuum of attempted change, but it is extremely vulnerable by virtue of its placement.[70]

Trester's analogy of parole as the final link in a chain, points to a continuing theme throughout this text: Criminal justice must be seen and evaluated as a system with many interrelated elements. In this chapter the significant system elements include legislatures, prosecutors, judges, prisons, parole boards, parole agencies, and parole officers.

Just to look at the relationship between prison and parole should be sufficient to convince us of the need to be aware of the systemic consequences, intended and otherwise, of the actions at various "links" in the chain. Inmates poorly prepared for the street by prison programs will surely make poor parole risks. Their violation rates will be unacceptably high. Should we blame the final link in the chain and call for the abolition of parole? The fact that parole and conditional release are virtually divorced from correctional institutions and their programs makes it almost certain that there will be little, if any, coordinated effort to deliver effective parole services.

Parole and conditional release rules and conditions now seem most often to serve punitive and control goals. No longer are parole officers primarily focused on rehabilitative goals. In the past, parole was conceptualized as a continuation of the correctional activities carried out in correctional institutions. Unfortunately, our crowded prisons, as we saw in Chapter 8, have few resources available for rehabilitation. Rather than using parole and conditional release as correctional strategies, we now are using them as ways to reduce prison crowding. Thus, more "high-risk" inmates are being released with predictable results.

What we are seeing with regard to parole is a fundamental structural contradiction. As sentencing reforms in the shape of determinate sentences, sentences without possibility of parole, and more mandatory prison terms come into play, prison crowding becomes more and more explosive. This in turn results in pressure to release inmates on parole or conditional release who would not ordinarily be released prior to the expiration of their sentences, or whose release would be delayed. Thus a more punitive response to offenders may well have the unintended consequence of producing more crime in the form of parole violations and new criminal acts, thereby adding to the prison population.

KEY CONCEPTS

Conditional release	Role conflict
Executive clemency	Salient Factor Score (SFS)
Goal discordance	Technical parole violations
Intensive Supervision Parole (ISP)	Tickets of leave
Maxing out	

QUESTIONS FOR DISCUSSION

1. The study of Texas parole revocation decisions by Winfree and his associates focused on the systemic nature of corrections. What can we learn from this study about the effects of case and statutory law changes that are designed to "improve" corrections?
2. Many research studies of parole employ measures such as rearrest for any crime or violation of parole rules and conditions to assess the recidivism of offenders while on the street. Critically comment on the appropriateness of these criteria.
3. Critically discuss the trend toward abolition of parole. Pay particular attention to the systemic consequences, intended and otherwise, of this trend.
4. Consider the use of conditions imposed on parolees and conditional releasees for (a) punitive and control purposes and (b) rehabilitative or correctional purposes. What conditions should be imposed for each of these sets of purposes?
5. Critically evaluate the following statement: Elimination of parole and substitution of conditional release from prison will result in positive changes in offenders' perceptions of the criminal justice system.

ENDNOTES

1. Larry Bratt, "Giving Me a Second Chance," *Washington Post*, May 19, 1996, p. C-1.
2. Tracy L. Snell, *Correctional Populations in the United States, 1993*, United States Department of Justice, Bureau of Justice Statistics, "Executive Summary," October 1995, p. 2.
3. Inmates were said to "max out" of their sentences when they had to be released because the statutory period of their sentences less any earned "good time" had been reached.

 4. Donald Atkinson, "Progressive Probation and parole System Plays Important Role," *Corrections Today* 51 (February 1989): 78.
 5. Edward E. Rhine, et al., "Parole: Issues and Prospects for the 1990s," *Corrections Today* 51 (December 1989): 146.
 6. Peter B. Hoffman, "Twenty Years of Operational Use of a Risk Prediction Instrument: The United States Parole Commission's Salient Factor Score," *Journal of Criminal Justice* 22 (1994): 477–494. This article begins with a concise history of parole recidivism prediction efforts going back to the 1920s.
 7. For an example of such research see Christy A. Vishner, Pamela K. Lattimore, and Richard L. Linster, "Predicting Recidivism of Serious Youthful Offenders Using Survival Models," *Criminology* 29 (1991): 329–366. This study examined California Youth Authority parolees.
 8. Hoffman, "Twenty Years . . . ," p. 490. This article provides a considerable list of references which may be consulted to learn more about the development of the salient factors.
 9. A. Blumstein, et al. (eds.), *Criminal Careers and Career Criminals,* Vol. 1, National Academy Press. Cited in Hoffman, "Twenty Years . . . ," p. 480.
10. Hoffman, "Twenty Years . . . ," p. 485.
11. Andrew von Hirsch and Kathleen J. Hanrahan, *Abolish Parole?* (Washington, D.C.: National Institute of Law Enforcement, Law Enforcement Assistance Administration, September 1978), p. 21.
12. *Federal Rules of Criminal Procedure,* Title 18, § 3853 (d).
13. Ibid.
14. *USA Today,* 26 January 95, p. 7A.
15. "Protests over Serial Rapist's Parole Subside," *New York Times,* March 20, 1994, 1, 23:1.
16. *Federal Rules of Criminal Procedure,* Title 18, § 3583 (d).
17. Von Hirsch and Hanrahan, *Abolish Parole?* p. 26.
18. Ibid.
19. Atkinson, "Progressive Probation . . . ," pp. 78–79.
20. Ibid., p. 79.
21. Frank S. Pearson and Daniel B. Bibel, "New Jersey's Intensive Supervision Program: What Is It Like? How Is It Working?" *Federal Probation* 50 (1986): p. 25–31; Voncile B. Gwody, "Intermediate Sanctions," *Research in Brief* (Washington, D.C.: National Institute of Justice, 1993): p. 2; Alice Glasel, "Intensive Supervision: Working for New Jersey," *Corrections Today* 49 (1987): p. 88–90.
22. Glasel, "Intensive Supervision," p. 88.
23. John T. Whitehead and Charles A. Lindquist, "Determinants of Probation and Parole Officer Professional Orientation," *Journal of Criminal Justice* 20 (1992): 13–24.
24. Ibid., p. 18.
25. Ibid., p. 22.
26. Edna Erez, "Dangerous Men, Evil Women: Gender and Parole Decision-Making," *Justice Quarterly* 9 (1992): 105–126.
27. Ibid., p. 121.
28. Ibid., p. 124.
29. *Federal Rules of Criminal Procedure,* Title 18, § 3583 (e)(3). Emphasis added.
30. L. Thomas Winfree, Jr., Christine S. Sellers, Veronica Smith Ballard, and Roy R. Roberg, "Responding to a Legislated Change in Correctional Practices: A Quasi-Experimental Study of Revocation Hearings and Parole Board Actions," *Journal of Criminal Justice* 18 (1990): 195–196.
31. Ibid., p. 197.
32. For a discussion of the methodology see Ibid., p. 199.
33. Ibid., p. 209.
34. 408 U.S. 471 (1972).
35. Ibid., p. 480.
36. Ibid., p. 482.
37. Ibid.

38. For a more detailed analysis of *Morrissey* and other relevant appellate court cases see Paul W. Brown, "*Morrissey* Revisited: The Probation and Parole Officer as Hearing Officer," *Federal Probation* 53 (June 1989): 13–17.

39. *Gagnon v. Scarpelli,* 411 U.S. 778 (1973).

40. Louis Jankowski, "Probation and Parole 1990," Bureau of Justice Statistics, *Bulletin,* November 1991.

41. Ibid., pp. 5–6.

42. John J. Curran, Jr., "A Priority for Parole: Agencies Must Reach Out to the Media and the Community," *Corrections Today* 51 (February 1989): 30.

43. Snell, "Correctional Populations in the United States, 1993," p. 2.

44. Robyn L. Cohen, "Probation and Parole Violators in State Prison, 1991," Bureau of Justice Statistics, *Special Report,* August 1995, p. 2.

45. Ibid.

46. Ibid., pp. 7, 10.

47. Ibid., p. 10.

48. Harry E. Allen, et al., "Probation and Parole Effectiveness," in Harry E. Allen, et al. (eds.), *Probation and Parole in America* (New York: Free Press, 1985), p. 249.

49. Michael R. Geerken and Hennesey D. Hayes, "Probation and Parole: Public Risk and the Future of Incarceration Alternatives," *Criminology* 31 (1993): 553.

50. Ibid.

51. Ibid.

52. Ibid., p. 557.

53. Cohen, "Probation and Parole Violators in State Prisons, 1991," p. 1.

54. Geerken and Hayes, "Probation and Parole," p. 561.

55. Hee-Jong Joo, Sheldon Okland-Olson, and William R. Kelley, "Recidivism among Paroled Property Offenders Released during a Period of Prison Reform," *Criminology* 33 (1995): 389–410.

56. 503 F. Supp. 1265 (1980).

57. Hee-Jong Joo, et al., "Recidivism . . . ," p. 391.

58. Ibid., pp. 393–94. The release groups were for the years 1984, 1985, 1986, and 1987.

59. Ibid., p. 396.

60. Ibid., p. 403.

61. Ibid., p. 407.

62. Ibid., p. 391.

63. Gwody, "Intermediate Sanctions," p. 4.

64. Ibid.

65. Rhine, et al., "Parole: Issues and Prospects for the 1990s," p. 78.

66. Michael V. Bork, "Five-Year Review of United States Probation Data, 1990–1994," *Federal Probation* 59 (December 1995): 27–33.

67. Ibid., p. 32.

68. Ibid., p. 33.

69. Ibid.

70. Harold B. Trester, *Supervision of the Offender* (Upper Saddle River, N.J.: Prentice-Hall, 1981), p. 319.

13 COMMUNITY SERVICE AND RESTITUTION

INTRODUCTION IN APRIL 1995, "serial tree-killer" Peter Dworan pleaded guilty to cutting down three trees in Brooklyn, New York, in violation of an environmental protection ordinance. His reason for destroying the trees, "to the great chagrin of his neighbors, was for that most precious of real estate commodities: a water view."[1] Although neighbors claimed he cut down forty trees, his plea agreement limited his culpability to three. His sentence was a complex one: 275 hours of community service and a $3,000 fine.

Dworan's attorney commented that the suggestion that his client's community service be performed in the Parks Department might not be appropriate if "he's going to be made the butt of jokes and constantly harassed" by his neighbors.[2]

In another case, this one in DuPage County, Illinois, Richard Nieves pleaded guilty to making a false report that he witnessed the kidnapping of a small child.[3] After reporting the supposed abduction, Nieves went to the police station, viewed a videotape showing a missing child, and identified that child as resembling the one he saw "kidnapped."

The DuPage police claimed that they spent over $22,000 on their investigation, and that the hopes of the parents of the missing child were raised and then dashed when it turned out that Nieves's report was a hoax. The sentence Nieves received was a combination of two years' probation, 500 hours of community service, and a $500 fine. He was ordered to pay $150 in court costs.

These two examples of community service orders as an element in sentences suggest some important issues that we will deal with in this chapter: the appropriate number of hours of service to be required of an offender, what kind of service offenders should perform, and how service orders can be integrated with other elements in a sentence.

Gordon Bazemore and Dennis Maloney surveyed community service practices throughout the country. They found that community service as a criminal sanction has

> for over two decades . . . been a visible feature of the probation landscape. . . . [V]irtually all probation and community corrections departments have had some experience with community service sanctions. . . . For a growing number of communities . . . work service requirements have become a standard part of court orders, in some cases required by policy or statute.[4]

The community service sanction requires an offender to perform a specified number of hours of unpaid "service" to the community. It is a form of restitution, often referred to as creative restitution. Traditionally, the restitution sanction required an offender to make restitution payments directly to a victim. Community service is restitution to the community. Because of this, we include both restitution and community service orders in this chapter.

Sentences that include a number of hours of community service and/or dollar amounts of restitution are appealing to legislators, judges, corrections policymakers, and the public. The chief appeal of community service sentences is that they are often premised on the idea that offenders owe a debt to their community. We frequently hear the expression that an offender should "pay his or her debt to society." As criminal law developed along with the development of nation states and then the common law, criminal acts began to be visualized as acts that harmed not just a particular victim or group of victims, but also the sovereign or the community. Thus, trials became settings for the state to prosecute defendants and punish the guilty.

In the United States, criminal trials are entitled "The People vs. Smith," or "The State (or the United States) vs. Smith." Some critics have bemoaned what they consider to be the clearly secondary role to which this practice has relegated victims. Victim rights advocates argue that victims have been lost in the criminal justice system. Criminologists have also criticized the fact that criminal justice has so removed the victim from center stage that offenders no longer are made to feel that they have actually harmed a real person. Such an acknowledgement of a victim by an offender may be necessary if corrections is to be achieved.

A number of measures to redress the imbalance are in effect today, including victim compensation boards to provide some (usually monetary) compensation to crime victims. Victim rights organizations in many states have a voice in sentencing and parole release decisions.[5] Some convicted offenders have been ordered to pay restitution to their victims as either a sole sanction or as part of a sentence of incarceration or probation. As we will see, both community service sentences and court orders requiring offenders to make restitution have similar objectives.

If crime harms all of us, not only individual victims, how can the offender be made to compensate us? Community service sentences represent one way by which to accomplish this. We will show that community service may be ordered in many forms and can be a component of a variety of sentences, including those of probation, incarceration, and parole. We will examine the history and underlying principles of this relatively new form of penal sanction. We also will consider the idea that community service orders are a form of "creative restitution."

HISTORY OF COMMUNITY SERVICE AND RESTITUTION SANCTIONS

It is not possible to be absolutely certain, but it appears that community service orders began to be issued in 1966 in Alameda County, California.[6] There, the original focus was to provide alternative sentences for poor women who were traffic law violators. Their lives would have been seriously disrupted by going to jail and/or by having to pay a fine. This practice was then extended to include drunk driving offenders.

This innovation in penal sanctioning was heralded by many as offering courts and communities real advantages over preexisting sentences such as fines and jail terms for misdemeanant offenders. After reviewing the Alameda County experience, McDonald concluded that it:

> established the basic framework for the developments that followed. Its two basic features—service to the community rather than to victims, and the provision for unpaid labor outside custodial settings—have come to define community service as a distinct penal sanction available to the courts.[7]

Using restitution as a penal and correctional sanction has a much longer history than community service orders. We can find evidence of this in the work of Albert Eglash and Stephen Schafer.[8] Eglash, a psychologist, argued in the 1950s for restitution as a therapeutic strategy.[9] Schafer, over a span of years between 1960 and the mid-1970s, wrote extensively on using restitution to bring victims back onto center stage, and to require offenders to face up to the fact that they had harmed real persons.[10]

One of the less frequently discussed restitution sanctions is the **personal service order.** That is, an offender is required to perform a specified number of hours of service to a victim. This form of restitution might well be employed in cases where offenders are unable to make cash payments, or where cash payment levels are clearly inadequate to compensate victims. In a rather surprising development, the Minnesota Restitution Center Program found that when victims participated in mediation sessions with their offenders, they frequently requested that any personal service be donated to the community.[11]

The idea that restitution can be blended with attempts to reconcile victims to their offenders through mediation was first operationalized formally in Minnesota's program, beginning in 1972.[12] This program initially was a component of parole from the state prison. Those offenders who were assigned to the center had served an average of four months in prison. Before offenders were placed in the program, many of their victims went to the state prison and met with them. At these meetings offenders and victims proceeded to "negotiate restitution agreements." Victims were "fully aware that this would result in the offenders' early release from prison."[13]

The United States Sentencing Reform Act of 1984 (Title II of the Comprehensive Crime Control Act of 1984) provides that "community service may be ordered as a condition of probation."[14] This is apparently the first instance in which a federal criminal sentencing provision was written specifically to authorize the use of work orders as a condition of probation for federal offenders.

Federal sentencing guidelines provide that whenever a defendant's sentence includes both a fine and restitution, "the court shall order that any money paid by the defendant shall first be applied to satisfy the order of restitution."[15] Further, "with the consent of the victim . . . , the court may order a defendant to perform services for the benefit of the victim in lieu of monetary restitution. . . ."[16]

D. C. McDonald has noted that community service mixes two "ancient" traditions in criminal justice: forcing offenders to make reparation for their crimes, and using work as a punishment.[17] According to Bazemore and Maloney, community service has undergone two different and often contradictory "conceptual innovations."[18] The first, early in the history of community service sentences, viewed these sentences as serving rehabilitative goals. Offenders were required to be involved significantly in the work they were to perform, which was to "repair" at least some of the damage they did to their communities.

The second conceptual innovation viewed community service as a substitute for direct restitution to actual victims. Service became **symbolic restitution.** This was, according to Bazemore and Maloney, a particularly "unfortunate" development that led to a "wholesale substitution of work hours for direct restitution to victims. . . ."[19]

Not all states have provisions permitting offenders to be subjected to service orders. In some jurisdictions, community service is an integral part of diversion programs. That is, defendants can be assigned a number of hours of unpaid labor in the community, the successful completion of which may result in dismissal of criminal charges. Failure to complete the service order can result in prosecution.

There is, however, a potential constitutional problem with community service in conjunction with diversion. The problem is with the language in the **Thirteenth Amendment** to the Constitution, which states in part:

> . . . neither slavery nor involuntary servitude except as punishment for a crime whereof the party shall have been duly convicted shall exist in the United States. . . .

A constitutional challenge could be made to a community service order requiring unpaid labor that does not result from a conviction. New York State dealt with this potential problem when it amended its penal code in 1978, specifically authorizing community service orders either as a condition of probation or as an element in a conditional discharge from prosecution.[20]

A defense against the charge that community service amounts to **involuntary servitude** can be made by the fact that in most communities service terms are often prearranged, and include the number of hours of service after a defendant reaches a plea agreement with the prosecutor and judge. Service, in effect, is "voluntary" service. However, should a defendant refuse to perform the required hours, the alternative probably is prosecution and jail time. We are reminded here of prison mental health treatment programs such as those implemented in Maryland's Patuxent Institution, dealt with in Chapter 7. There, inmates were offered places in therapy groups which they were "free" to reject. The paroling authority, of course, was made aware that an inmate had refused to enter psychotherapy. The resulting effect on the parole decision can easily be imagined.

SELECTION OF WORK SETTINGS AND OFFENDERS

Before offenders can be recommended for a community service sentence, appropriate placements must be located. Most community service hours are spent in nonprofit or governmental settings. It is vital that settings be selected carefully since a number of problems can arise when seeking to place offenders. Placements that appear promising on paper may be inappropriate because they have little or no experience with "volunteers." Others may be hostile to or take advantage of offenders. Issues such as racial, gender, or age discrimination may surface. Later, we will take up other issues relating to site selection.

When possible placements are examined for their suitability for community service, the investigating person, usually a probation officer, needs to do the following:

- Clarify the expectations, requirements, and responsibilities of the agency, the court, and the offender.
- Identify the volunteer needs of the agency.
- Assess the agency's capability to supervise offenders.
- Identify any potential problems that may arise.[21]

When an inventory of suitable placements is developed, the next step is to work toward individualized placements that match an agency's needs, an offender's interests and skills, and the requirements of the court. If the community service order will be used primarily as a punitive sanction, certain work settings will not be appropriate. If, on the other hand, a service order is directed at restorative or rehabilitative goals, different placements will be required. "The court's sentencing objective should be the first consideration in the placement decision."[22]

As stated by a supervising United States probation officer: "When probation officers devise a community service order, they must consider traditional objectives, community acceptance, and offender characteristics."[23]

*I*ndividual placements for servers of community service sentences are based on matching the participating agency's needs, an offender's interest and skills, and the requirements of the court. These offenders are protecting and maintaining trees in a public park.

A serious problem with community service sentences is the tendency to select "white-collar" or middle-class offenders in disproportionate numbers. Lower-class offenders with little or no employment experience or job skills and those convicted of "street crimes" are much less likely to receive sentences that include community service orders. For example, a study of community service probationers in the Northern District of Illinois found that the majority of these offenders were identified as middle-class and well educated.[24] More significant was the finding that the two most common offenses committed by those sentenced to community service were "fraud and income tax violation."[25]

As might be expected, most of these federal probationers were first-time offenders, and nearly 80 percent pleaded guilty. What we see here is that, at least in this district, selection of convicted offenders was limited to a low-risk population and was biased against lower status offenders convicted of street crimes.

Another major problem with selecting both placements and offenders for community service orders lies in the fact that all correctional sanctions are affected by more general trends in criminal justice philosophies and operations. That is, community service is just as system-dependent as other sanctions discussed in earlier chapters. As one federal probation officer put it:

> Even though community service seems to be working in the Northern District of Georgia and elsewhere, it is in jeopardy. Community service and other smart sentences have been adversely affected by the "get tough on crime" legislation of the past decade. Federal sentencing guidelines [and those of many states] have severely limited judges' options to impose alternative sentences.[26]

Usually, a probation officer recommends community service to the judge as a part of the presentence investigation report. Of course, as we have seen with regard to the vast majority of criminal prosecutions, plea bargaining is a fact of life. Plea agreements will often include community service and/or restitution orders. Probation officers are unlikely to recommend against such sanctions in their reports to judges. Thus, many offenders are, in effect, "automatically" selected for service or restitution orders, with little regard for their appropriateness.

The Vera Institute of Justice's community service project sought to persuade judges and prosecutors in three New York boroughs (Brooklyn, the Bronx, and Manhattan) to sentence certain misdemeanant offenders to community service in lieu of jail terms. Because of the limited scope of this project, selection of defendants for the new sanction was, theoretically, simpler than in other jurisdictions where the use of community service orders was much broader, that is, where service orders were made part of probation or parole conditions, where there was no possible incarceration of offenders, or as part of an agreement to divert defendants from prosecution.

In the New York City program, Vera Institute staff members screened cases for eligibility and worked with prosecutors and judges to sentence misdemeanants to community service as the sole punishment. Significantly, where judges were clearly the leading actors in the decision-making process, those considered eligible for community service were so sentenced more often. In the boroughs where prosecutors took a leading role, many fewer defendants were placed under service orders. These prosecutors were found to be more interested in punitive sanctions, that is, they wanted more defendants sentenced to jail.[27] Apparently they were more tuned in to the "get tough" stance pointed out earlier than were the judges. Of course, we recognize that prosecutors are elected officials whereas judges tend to be appointed for life.

VARIETIES OF COMMUNITY SERVICE TERMS AND GOALS

"Community service work orders are penal sanctions requiring offenders to complete a specified number of hours of unpaid work in nonprofit or governmental agencies."[28] This much is agreed to by those in the field. However, within the parameters of this definition, a wide range of service orders are currently imposed on offenders. These orders represent a "practice in search of a theory."[29] This is so because there is no consistent set of objectives or goals associated with community service orders. Whether court-ordered service hours are intended to be rehabilitative, punitive, restorative, or some other objective is a question that cannot be answered at this time.

Given this state of practice and theory, it is no wonder that there is much variation from court to court. Hudson and Galaway, after surveying fourteen different community service programs in the United States, found two general types to be prevalent: combined and sole sanction programs. We can add at least two more general types: integrated community corrections programs, and probation and parole violator programs. We now examine each of these types.

Combined Sanctions Programs

These programs are mainly employed with felony offenders. They combine community service with other sanctions such as fines, restitution, probation, and even jail sentences. In a bulletin issued in January 1995, the Bureau of Justice Statistics reported that in state courts, combination sentences that included either restitution or community service orders were handed down in 23 percent of cases.[30]

A more detailed breakdown for the 75 largest counties in the United States shows that of all convicted felons sentenced to probation, 22 percent were ordered to make restitution payments and 14 percent were required to perform community service.[31] The same report indicated that restitution was required in 17 percent of violent felonies and community service in 14 percent of nonviolent cases. Fewer drug offenders (again all felons), 10 percent, were ordered to pay restitution. This is not surprising since there is not likely to be an identifiable victim. Drug offenders were, however, ordered to perform community service at the same rate as other felons, 14 percent.

Figure 13.1 on p. 300 shows a community service order form used in the state of Maryland. These orders are a part of probation sentences. The offender is on notice that failure to "participate as directed" will lead to a court appearance as a probation violator. To defray the costs of the community service program, defendants are required, in most cases, to pay a $50 fee.

Integrated Community Corrections Programs

Some states have enacted legislation establishing community-based programs that include community corrections facilities and intensive community supervision of probationers and parolees. A number of these programs incorporate restitution and community service sanctions. Since 1990 the U.S. Department of Justice's Bureau of Justice Assistance has provided states and local communities with financial assistance to establish comprehensive community-based programs, which include restitution and community service as integral parts.[32]

ACROSS CULTURES

COMMUNITY SERVICE AS A PENALTY IN NEW ZEALAND

New Zealand, like the United States, has been facing increases in its prison populations. It also has seen more dramatic increases in the number of offenders sentenced to various community corrections programs. One of these programs, Periodic Detention, is a variation on community service orders.

In New Zealand, Periodic Detention offenders make up over one-third of all persons on community sentences (p. 60). Originally designed in 1963 for juvenile delinquents, the program quickly spread to adult corrections. At first, Periodic

Detention included weekend lock-up, but this has been discontinued because of the costs involved.

Currently, a Periodic Detention sentence,

allows a . . . detainee to be kept in custody . . . for up to 9 hours on any one day and for up to 15 hours per week, for up to 12 months. In practice, the bulk of periodic detainees report to a PD work center each Saturday. Accompanied by a PD warden, they go out in gangs of about 10 to work, unpaid, on community projects such as cutting scrub, picking up trash, and cleaning government buildings. (p. 60)

SOURCE: Chris W. Eskridge and Greg Newbold, "Corrections in New Zealand," *Federal Probation* 57 (September 1993): 60.

An example of this rather new development is Vermont's "Continuum of Intermediate Sanctions," which consists of two "tracks," one of which is designed for substance-abusing felons who ordinarily would be imprisoned. The second, the "Court and Reparative Track," is intended to be available for misdemeanants, and requires offenders to make reparation to victims and the community.[33]

Probation and Parole Violator Programs

A new development on the correctional scene is one that seeks to cope with the serious problem of what to do with probationers and parolees who violate the conditions of their release. In South Carolina, violators are ranked in terms of the severity of their violative behavior, with sanctions graded accordingly.[34] Among the sanction options available to the system is one that would add or increase, as a condition of probation or parole, the number of community service hours of labor to be performed. In some cases, a hearing officer has the option of requiring a technical violator to perform up to 300 hours of service to the community and/or make restitution payments if the violation caused personal and/or property harm to a victim.[35]

Sole Sanction Programs

These community service programs and restitution orders usually involve misdemeanants. Community service hours and/or restitution are the only sanctions imposed. Violation of the terms of court-imposed orders most often result in resentencing to jail or prison, depending on the level of seriousness of the offense of conviction.

FIGURE 13.1   Sample Community Service Order Form

DISTRICT COURT OF MARYLAND FOR CALVERT COUNTY

200 Duke Street

Prince Frederick, Maryland 20678

MEMORANDUM

TO: 1. Director, Community Services

             2. Defendant

FROM: County Clerk, Calvert County

RE: _____ CASE NO:_____

1. The Defendant has been assigned _____ eight-hour days in the Calvert County Community Service Program. The community service fee of $50 is to be paid unless specifically waived by the sentencing judge.

2. The Defendant has volunteered to make a donation of _____ to _____
_____

                                                            _____
                                                                         JUDGE

NOTICE TO DEFENDANT

1. IT IS YOUR RESPONSIBILITY to take this form to the District Court's Clerk's Office located on this floor to the right of the Courtroom as you exit.

2. IT IS YOUR RESPONSIBILITY then to report for and complete the work assigned by the Coordinator and directed by the Job/Activity Supervisor.

NOTE: YOU ARE A VOLUNTEER AND WILL NOT BE FORCED TO WORK, BUT YOUR FAILURE TO PARTICIPATE AS DIRECTED WILL RESULT IN A COURT APPEARANCE FOR FAILURE TO ABIDE BY A CONDITION OF YOUR PROBATION.

SOURCE: Clerk's Office, District Court for Calvert County.

Hudson and Galaway found additional variations. Some programs operate at the pretrial stage. Thus, they may be considered to be diversionary in nature. Others were strictly postadjudication. In some of the fourteen programs they reviewed, community service or restitution orders were made part of the conditions of probation; others used a community service order as a condition of parole release from prison or jail.

Community service orders vary sharply with regard to the number of hours required. Of course, this may be explained by the practice of making the number of hours required to be performed bear some relationship to the severity of the offender's crime. Probation officers in their recommendations and judges in their sentence decisions sometimes employ different standards in making their determinations. In some jurisdictions, sentencing guidelines shape the determination.

*S*ome offenders have been sentenced to community service removing graffiti from public property. This is an example of typical unskilled work available for community service orders.

If community service is ordered instead of a fine prescribed by statute, the hours required usually are related to the value of the fine. The value of the hours of unpaid labor generally is set at the minimum wage rate.[36] If the order to perform community service is imposed as an alternative to jail time, then the number of hours is related to the length of the sentence. Typically, 6–8 hours of work is equated to each day in jail. When community service is ordered for an offender who has damaged or destroyed property, the value of the property is taken into account in assigning the hours of service required. Usually, the minimum wage rate applies.

Other Types of Community Service Orders

We might expect that community service orders in the federal system would be much more consistent in type and terms of service. Such is not the case. In one federal district, for example, community service orders were frequently combined with probation, fines, restitution orders, and some incarceration time.[37] There was a wide range of hours of service, with the average being 300.

The state of Texas virtually institutionalized community service and restitution by establishing the Texas Restitution Center Program in 1983.[38] Expanded to a total of seventeen centers, the program has bed space for 700 offenders. The stimulus for this program was a court order following a federal appellate court decision in *Ruiz v. Estelle*[39] regarding prison crowding and other harmful conditions.

> Texas was faced with a crowded prison system, and a federal court order to reduce crowding. . . . The courts divert nonviolent felony offenders to the centers, where they repay victims and the community while continuing to work and pay taxes.[40]

Offenders work at their regular jobs in the community during normal working hours, returning to the **restitution centers** after work. Their wages are used to pay for their room and board, probation supervision fees, court costs, and restitution. After working at their regular jobs and on weekends they are required to perform community service. Over 3,000 offenders were sentenced to the centers during a five-year period. They performed an average of 96,000 hours of service in each of these years.

Other Issues

Before moving on, we need to look at the reality of community sanction orders, and not just what practitioners and theorists believe they accomplish or should accomplish. In a revealing statement, Bazemore and Maloney claim that the actual service performed by offenders bears little relationship to many of the goals established for it.[41] The picture they paint is not a pretty one:

> [W]hat offenders actually *do* to meet community service requirements . . . often represents the lowest common denominator of statutory mandate, policy requirements, or judicial demands. Picking up paper in parks or around office buildings is the most typical assignment when a service worker is referred to an agency; photocopying and filing tasks seem to be the preference when workers are detailed to assist inside the office. More humiliating tasks such as cleaning toilets or digging holes have characterized programs with a more explicitly punitive focus.[42]

Bazemore and Maloney argue for a **balanced justice** approach when service sanctions are designed and imposed; that is, a system that clearly "gives priority to two primary objectives: to repay or restore the community and to enhance offender competency and increase the potential for [her or his] reintegration into the community."[43] By offender competency, they mean that offenders ought to be placed in work settings that will increase their work and social skills so that they will better fit into the community when their sentences have expired. Cleaning toilets, picking up trash, and photocopying will not accomplish this.

Why is it that community service work orders are not consistent with a balanced approach to justice? According to McDonald and others, it is because community service from its inception as an innovative sanction focused on offender needs, and this premise rather quickly became a "liability."[44] Many in and out of criminal justice saw it as a mistake to promote programs that were supposed to be "good" for offenders. A "second wave of community service sanctions has begun. These are now looked upon as a good way to punish. That makes [them] ideologically attractive to many people."[45]

▐ RESTITUTION

Investment banker Gerard B. Finneran pleaded guilty to a misdemeanor and was sentenced to up to six months in jail, a $5,000 fine, and restitution in the amount of $50,000.[46] Finneran's offense: defecating on a food-service cart and threatening to harm a flight attendant while flying to New York on a commercial airline. His reason for his actions: "I was angry." We might want to ask a couple of questions about Mr. Finneran's sentence, especially about the restitution order. Why is restitution a part of his sentence? In what sense does his offense suggest that he should make restitution to his victim? Finally, how was the $50,000 amount determined? We will examine these and other issues related to the use of restitution orders.

We noted in a previous section that community service is a form of restitution. That is, the offender gives something of value (usually her or his labor) to the community in order to repay it for the harm the criminal conduct caused. The harm can be conceived of as a general loss of security, costs incurred for police protection, increased insurance premiums, and the burdens of maintaining a correctional system. In this section, we will deal with more specific restitution programs and orders that require offenders to repay victims for the injuries to their persons and/or property.

Variations in Restitution Sanctions and Goals

As is the case with community service sentences, restitution orders come in a variety of types and sentences. Some are diversionary in purpose; that is, an offender may make restitution prior to prosecution. If adequate restitution is made, prosecution and trial may be waived. The offender has no record of conviction.

More common is restitution as a condition of probation. Less frequently used are sentences that combine restitution with a term of incarceration. Texas, as discussed earlier, has developed restitution centers where some offenders are sentenced. During their terms they are required to work and make restitution payments.

Goals of Restitution Sanctions

At least seven goals are sought through imposition of restitution orders. The first is, of course, to assist in restoring to victims what they lost as a result of being victimized. A second goal is offender accountability. Through sentences that include restitution to victims, it is expected that offenders will be forced to accept responsibility for the harm they caused them. A third goal is rehabilitative or correctional. It is tied to the second goal, accountability. If an offender accepts her or his personal responsibility, this may well prove to be rehabilitative. It may also help reconcile victim and offender better than other sanctions such as incarceration, fines, and probation without restitution.

A fourth goal of restitution is to reduce prison and jail crowding. When restitution is ordered either as diversion from prosecution or as an alternative to imprisonment, it will keep offenders so sentenced out of confinement. If, however, restitution is used in a way that simply widens the net of control by targeting offenders not bound for jail or prison, then there will be little or no impact on crowding.

As a method to reduce the costs of corrections, a fifth goal sought through restitution orders, many jurisdictions see restitution as a cost-effective alternative to other sentences such as imprisonment and even probation. Not only can offenders be diverted from costly incarceration and some forms of probation supervision, but also, by contributing funds to their victims, they aid the community that otherwise might be required to assist victims through direct compensation or welfare payments. As one expert on restitution put it:

> The promise of restitution as a lower-cost penalty, as a synthetic penalty, and as a penalty which addresses victim interest will be achieved as restitution is used to reduce reliance on prisons and jails which do nothing for victims, burden taxpayers, and return offenders to society less competent to live law-abiding lives and probably more dangerous than when they were admitted.[47]

A sixth restitution goal is to deliver a more punitive response to some offenders. Thus, for example, probation can be enhanced by adding a restitution condition, as

A youthful offender is performing community service by speaking to high school students about drunk driving. He was convicted for drunk driving and this is one way of making restitution for his offense.

can a jail sentence. To maximize the punitive effect, the level of restitution can be adjusted upward, within limits, until it hurts.

A seventh, more nontraditional goal of restitution can be identified when it is incorporated into victim-offender reconciliation programs. There has been some indication that the practice of ordering restitution may be headed in the direction of "restorative justice in which the purpose . . . is to bring about peace among participants and restoration of losses."[48]

Richard Lawrence observed that restitution, when a part of these reconciliation programs, goes well beyond simply making payments to victims and/or as a way to divert offenders from confinement.[49]

> Victim-Offender Reconciliation Programs (VORP) . . . emerged from restitution and both reflect traditional justice principles that when a person wrongs another, he or she has a responsibility to make amends to the victim and society. VORP extends this principle by actually bringing the victim and the offender together in a face-to-face meeting.[50]

The goals of victim-offender restoration programs are:

1. "Humanizing" criminal justice through face-to-face mediation.
2. Emphasizing offenders' personal responsibility and accountability.
3. Providing meaningful restitution to victims.
4. Educating the public about criminal justice and the goals of penal sanctions.
5. Providing an alternative to costly prison sentences.

In an article describing the Dakota County, Minnesota, "restorative justice" program, Umbreit and Carey provide a detailed account of these goals, the necessary planning involved, and the components required of a strategy to integrate restitution in a metropolitan area's criminal justice system.[51] Clearly focusing on restoring victims to a more central position in the criminal justice process, they say:

> Severely punishing offenders is less important than providing opportunities to empower victims in their search for closure through gaining a better understanding of what happened and being able to move on with their lives, to impress upon offenders the real human impact of their behavior, and to promote restitution to victims.[52]

A major problem when attempting to deliver restorative justice is that it is a "new way of thinking" that is not "driven by offender concerns only."[53] That is, if we are to reach a point at which victims and offenders are reconciled, it is necessary to understand that simply handing down sentences to punish offenders will not get the job done. Whether "offender-driven" sanctions are based on retributive, deterrence, or rehabilitative rationales, they are inadequate to the greater task of assisting victims to "move on with their lives."

Unfortunately for those advocating this transformation, a major impediment is the tendency of many in legislatures, the judiciary, and corrections to resist new ways of thinking about crime and responses to criminals. Such new thinking that is required if we are to develop truly innovative restitution sanctions is hard to come by in a field characterized by both inertia and a inclination to go with the flow of popular, often media-driven calls for more draconian sentences.

Another impediment to developing a restorative system of sanctions has to do with the systemic nature of criminal justice. Umbreit and Carey point out that it is not easy to convince prosecutors, judges, and other major players in the system to rethink the role of sentences and support this innovative approach to restitution. Because restorative programs frequently involve **mediation** efforts that bring together victim and victimizer, it is crucial that victims be brought fully into the decision-making process, a process that may make them feel anxious. If prosecutors, judges, and others formally involved in the sentencing process are uneasy about innovative sanctions, victim anxiety will only increase.

Pure and Punitive Restitution

When we look at the varied goals sought through restitution, we can cull out two very broad categories of sanctions: pure and punitive restitution. **Pure restitution** would require offenders to accept responsibility for their crimes and to repair the damage they caused victims and society. This category does not seek to punish an offender. It is purely restorative (as far as is possible). Justice is achieved, not by punishing criminals, but by restoring victim and community. Barnett and Hagel were early advocates of pure restitution in a 1977 article.[54] Although others have argued for a transformation of sentences to remove their punitive elements, we find it difficult to find pure restitution in the real world of criminal justice. As we have said repeatedly, the dominant theme today is one that demands stiffer sanctions that will cause offenders to suffer as they deserve.

Punitive restitution incorporates the restorative idea into sentences that aim to cause offenders some amount of suffering. This can be accomplished in a number of ways: (a) deliberately making the amount of restitution such as to cause the offender some financial pain clearly beyond what might be required in order to achieve proportionality with regard to victims' losses; (b) requiring burdensome community service; and (c) attaching restitution orders to more ordinary punitive sentences such as imprisonment and intensive parole or probation supervision.[55]

One far-ranging proposal by Abel and Marsh argues for a radical restructuring of sentencing law and policy to make restitution the primary sanction for criminal behavior. They set out a carefully organized rationale for using restitution orders. As they put it:

> Those of us who believe in restitution . . . [believe] that the only really ethical, nondiscriminatory, and practical plan is to set the criminal to work repairing the damage, the courts to work assessing that damage, and the penal system to work administering the process while reintegrating the criminal and society (if possible).[57]

They even call upon support from the early positivist criminologist Raffaele Garofalo, who, more than seventy-five years ago, called for a form of restitution as the best sanction to achieve deterrence:

> If offenders were persuaded that . . . they could in no wise [sic] evade the obligation to repair the damage of which they have been the cause, the ensuing discouragement to the criminal world . . . would be far greater than that produced by temporary curtailment of liberty.[58]

Abel and Marsh further urge that "prisons should be a place from which restitution can be made, . . . and that the length of incarceration sentences be determined in large measure on the basis of the amount of restitution to be made."[59] They do not, however, specify in any detail how work in the prison setting can be made commensurate in value with work outside. Thus, how restitution amounts can reasonably be earned through prison labor is a question that would need to be addressed through statutory and policy innovations.

▌EVALUATION OF COMMUNITY SERVICE AND RESTITUTION

When it comes to evaluating community service and restitution orders, we must take into account the many and varied objectives set out for them. Evaluation criteria will be different if the objectives are pure or punitive, for example. Perhaps a major goal is to deliver a cost-effective sentence. Or it may be to provide a more effective deterrent. Evaluation strategies will be different if the goal is to reduce jail or prison populations. If the goal of a sanction is to restore victims to center stage in the criminal justice drama, a different set of evaluation strategies will be required from those commonly used to measure other objectives.

Bazemore and Maloney, in a 1994 article, give probably the best summary of the nearly impossible task of evaluating the community service sanction:

> . . . a major problem with community service today is that it is ordered and implemented in a vacuum with reference neither to sentencing objectives nor to a theory of intervention with offenders. In the absence of a guiding conceptual framework for intervention and lacking value-based guidelines and performance objectives derived from a clear mission, it is impossible to gauge success or failure of these sanctions or determine the quality of the service experience.[60]

Evaluating Compliance Levels

In some instances, it appears that evaluation research focuses simply on determining whether offenders fully comply with the terms of a sentence. One evaluation of community service orders in the federal criminal justice system followed 54 offenders who performed 40 hours of work per week over a period of at least six months.[61] The study found that all offenders completed the required service, and all but one successfully completed probation. The one failure was eventually imprisoned. Thus, simply in terms of performing all the hours required in community service orders, success can be claimed. However, we should be interested in more than this if we are to make any judgments regarding the efficacy of this sanction.

Evaluating Recidivism Levels

The Vera Institute analyzed the performance of its major community service project in three New York boroughs: the Bronx, Brooklyn, and Manhattan.[62] Each offender-participant in the project was required to perform seventy hours of community service in supervised work crews. Significantly, these crews were supervised by Vera Institute staffers, not probation officers nor representatives of the placement agencies. These crews had performed a total of 142,900 hours of service by the time the project was evaluated.

The evaluation research design was organized to ascertain whether recidivism differed for participants who would have been sentenced to jail compared to other offenders who were not candidates for detention. Remember that the primary goal of the project was a limited one: to place on service orders those who otherwise would have gone to jail. An evaluation study concluded that there would have been approximately 15 percent fewer arrests had project participants been jailed instead of being ordered to perform community service.[63] The findings indicated that approximately the same percentage (40–50 percent) in each group violated their terms within six months. This, of course, provides ammunition for those who argue that these sanctions fail to deliver sufficient incapacitation to protect the public. The study, however, did find that those who were arrested were arrested for nonviolent property crimes.

The Texas Restitution Centers program discussed in a previous section reported favorable results during the first five years of operation:

> From 1983 to 1988, more than 3,000 offenders who would have been sentenced to Texas prisons were diverted to the restitution centers. . . . [An] average of 60.5 percent of the residents were successfully discharged or successfully participating in the centers. The average percentage of residents discharged for technical or rule violations . . . was 11.7 percent. Only 1.9 percent . . . were discharged for a new offense. . . .[64]

Some have accepted the proposition that community service is an important and valuable additional sentencing option, and that offenders on these sentences who recidivate commit nonviolent offenses. But they argue that there is a need to restore a measure of incapacitation to this sanction. One of their suggestions is that existing prison and jail work-release programs be modified to provide for implementation of community service orders. That is, offenders would be sentenced to jail or prison but permitted to be in the community to work off their hours, much like the Texas Restitution Centers program. Once these hours have been fulfilled, they would be released from confinement. Of course, such a modification would increase institutional populations and the costs of running community service programs. Evaluating the cost savings, if any, of community service and restitution is our next topic.

Evaluation Based on Costs

More impressive in a time of tight budgets is the conclusion that for the Texas program the taxes collected from offenders' wages and the value of their community service hours made the program quite successful. Community service hours, valued at the minimum hourly rate, were estimated to have saved the community "over $1.6 million."[65]

The Vera Institute community service project did find that there were some cost savings associated with placing defendants under service orders rather than jailing them. But the savings were not spectacular. It was calculated that for each offender participating in the program, the cost ranged from $916 to $1,077.[66] This community service lasted for approximately 180 days for each participant. The major reason for this heavy cost factor was the employment of special staff to place and supervise offenders. This could be reduced in future, of course, should staff already in place at the work sites do the supervising. A trade-off in this case might be a loss in quality of supervision and a decline in effectiveness.

We also must consider the value to the community of the unpaid labor. In the New York City case, it is estimated the value of this labor amounted to over $200,000 per year.[67]

One of the complicating factors we need to consider when evaluating restitution and community service sentences in terms of their cost relative to other sanctions is the **net widening** effect reported in many studies. An early evaluation of one restitution program, the Indiana Prisoner and Community Together (PACT) project, found that many offenders who probably would not have been incarcerated were placed on more severe probation sentences because of the added burdens of restitution and community service that were made conditions of their release.[68] Thus, there was an increase in the likelihood of violations and, eventually, incarceration. Any cost-benefit was lost, or at least significantly reduced.

Evaluating the Goal of Reconciliation

Finally, we must ask how the objective of **reconciliation restitution,** as described by Galaway and Hudson, can be evaluated.[69] If there is a tendency, as they suggest, for restitution orders to result in victims becoming reconciled to their victimizers, evaluation research needs to be carefully constructed to tap into victims' perceptions and attitudes. What do we know about these perceptions and attitudes? Very little.

SUMMARY   IT IS DIFFICULT TO UNDERSTAND and evaluate the place of community service and restitution sentences in contemporary American criminal justice and corrections. This is because they are expected to play so many different and sometimes conflicting roles. To some, community service work orders are meant to be punitive; they are to punish offenders. To others, community service is expected to serve restitutive ends; the hours an offender is ordered to work are to "pay back" the community for the harm caused it. Conceptualizing community as victim fits in well with this view. It also fits in well with the general development of criminal law over more than two centuries, a development that gradually moved the actual victim of crime into the background.

Some critics of community service sanctions say that they are too frequently used to the detriment of victims. They urge more use of direct restitution to crime victims. At least, unpaid work ought to be of a "personal service" nature. That is, the labor of offenders should be for the benefit of their victims.

A recent innovation in restitution that is meant to bring victims back into a leading role in criminal justice is reconciliation restitution. In some communities, restitution is employed not only to "restore" victims, but to reconcile them and their victimizers. Such efforts often include mediation, confronting offenders with their victims.

Finally, community service is said to lead to the rehabilitation of offenders. By requiring them to relate a sanction to the harm they caused, make use of their skills and talents, and keep them in the community, this view argues that rehabilitation is better served than a sentence of imprisonment or straight probation.

Implementation of innovative penal sanctions, for whatever goals are intended, is subject to discretion on the part of the many actors. In addition, as McDonald observed after studying New York City's use of community service orders,

> Initiatives to change the way courts sentence criminals usually come from the world beyond the courthouse steps. They result from the actions of legislators, mayors, governors, presidents, journalists, editorialists, and private public-interest organizations such as the Vera Institute of Justice. Coming as they do from outside, these attempts to reform the courts are not usually greeted with enthusiasm all around, for they generally aim to disturb the way courthouse regulars do their work.[70]

Much the same can be said for orders requiring offenders to make restitution to their victims. However, correctional, rehabilitative, and punitive objectives are not nearly as often expressed as the goals of holding offenders accountable and restoring victims as close to their status prior to being victimized as possible.

Selecting persons to be subjected either to community service or restitution orders is often fraught with difficulty as well as social class bias. Obviously, some defendants are not in a position to make restitution payments that would be meaningful either to themselves (that is, hold them accountable for the harm they caused) or to their victims. Here, we often find that restitution as a sanction is disproportionately allocated to middle-class or affluent offenders. Attempts to determine the amount of restitution to be ordered are complicated by differences in ability to pay by otherwise eligible defendants. Should the amount be carefully computed to match or approximate the victim's loss, the offender may be unable to conform to the order. Calculating the restitution amount with the offender's ability to pay will almost certainly result in many victims feeling cheated.

Ordering community service to be performed requires a careful matching of an offender's work or other skills to available community placements. Here too, there is a complication. If community service is primarily punitive, the work to be performed will or should be different than if the aim is more restorative or restitutive.

As a substitute or alternative to incarceration, especially with regard to jail incarceration, restitution and/or community service appear from the available evidence to be successful in helping reduce jail and prison crowding. In terms of producing real cost benefits for communities, community service also seems to be successful. As far as the ability of these sanctions to reduce recidivism is concerned, the jury is still out.

Finally, we find that innovative and traditional uses of community service and restitution are not in favor in the current political atmosphere. Why? Because these sanctions have the appearance of being lenient. Responding to offenders with tough, punitive measures is a popular stance among those in a position to influence correctional policy and practice.

▌KEY CONCEPTS

Balanced justice	Pure restitution
Involuntary servitude	Reconciliation restitution
Mediation	Restitution centers
Net widening	Symbolic restitution
Personal service order	Thirteenth Amendment
Punitive restitution	

▌QUESTIONS FOR DISCUSSION

1. Can punitive restitution achieve "correctional" or rehabilitative goals? Fully justify your answer.
2. In the Vera Institute community service project, some of the New York boroughs were resistant to the idea of diverting defendants from incarceration. What was the source of this resistance? What impact did it have on the evaluation of the project? What does this resistance say about the widespread use of community service orders?
3. Some have suggested jailing defendants who committed certain crimes, but releasing them during the day to perform community service tasks. Critically comment on the value of this suggestion.
4. Many critics argue that we have used and misused community service to the detriment of direct restitution to victims. Is this a valid argument? If so, why the misuse?
5. What suggestions can you make to reduce the tendency for community service and restitution sentences to be handed out to middle-class or white-collar offenders?

▌ENDNOTES

1. Michael Cooper, "Neighborhood Report: Brownstone Brooklyn: A Serial Tree-Killer Confesses," *New York Times,* April 23, 1995, City Section, p. 10.
2. Ibid.
3. Andrew Martin, "Abduction Hoax Gets Probation," *Chicago Tribune,* August 26, 1994, Section 2, p. 2.
4. Gordon Bazemore and Dennis Maloney, "Rehabilitating Community Service: Toward Restorative Service Sanctions in a Balanced Justice System," *Federal Probation* 58 (March 1994): 24.
5. For example, the Maryland "Eligible Persons" statute, Article 31-B of the Maryland code, sets the operating parameters of the state's only treatment prison. It provides two ways for victims to participate in parole release decisions: (1) through a vote on the institution's review board, which authorizes paroles; and (2) by requiring victims or their families to be notified in advance that an inmate is being considered for release.
6. Joe Hudson and Burt Galaway, "Community Service: Toward Program Definition," *Federal Probation* 54 (June 1990): 3.
7. Douglas Corry McDonald, *Punishment Without Walls: Community Service Sentences in New York City* (New Brunswick, NJ: Rutgers University Press, 1986), pp. 8–9.

8. A review of the history of restitution and community service and the work of Eglash and Shafer can be found in Burt Galaway, "Restitution as Innovation or Unfilled Promise?" *Federal Probation* 52 (September 1988): 3–14.

9. For examples of Eglash's work see the following: "Creative Restitution—A Broader Meaning for an Old Term," *Journal of Criminal Law, Criminology and Police Science* 48 (1958): 612–622; "Creative Restitution: Some Suggestions for Prison Rehabilitation Programs," *American Journal of Corrections* 20 (1958): 20–34; "Creative Restitution: Its Roots in Psychiatry," *British Journal of Delinquency* 10 (1959): 114–119.

10. For a sampling of Schafer's contribution to empowering victims in the criminal justice process, see the following: *The Victim and His Criminal* (New York: Random House, 1968); "Victim Compensation and Responsibility," *Southern California Law Review* 43 (1970): 55–67.

11. Galaway, "Restitution as Innovation or Unfilled Promise?" pp. 4–5.

12. For a discussion of the Minnesota program, see Joe Hudson and Burt Galaway, "Undoing the Wrong: The Minnesota Restitution Center," *Social Work* 19 (1974): 313–318.

13. Galaway, "Restitution as innovation or unfilled promise?" p. 10.

14. United States Sentencing Guidelines Commission, *Federal Sentencing Guidelines Manual* (St. Paul, Minn.: West Publishing Co., 1994–95), § 5F1.3, p. 293. The "Commentary" accompanying this section states that "community service should not be imposed in excess of 400 hours. Longer terms . . . impose heavy administrative burdens relating to the selection of suitable placements and the monitoring of attendance."

15. Ibid., p. 285.

16. Ibid.

17. D. C. McDonald, *Restitution and Community Service* (Washington, D.C.: National Institute of Justice, 1989), p. 8.

18. Bazemore and Maloney, "Rehabilitating Community Service," pp. 25–26.

19. Ibid., p. 25.

20. New York Penal Code, § 65.10. For a discussion of the involuntary servitude problem and New York's solution see McDonald, *Punishment Without Walls*, pp. 42–45.

21. For a discussion of these and other concerns, see Probation Division, Administrative Office of the United States Courts, "Implementing Community Service: The Referral Process," *Federal Probation* 53 (March 1989): 4.

22. Ibid., p. 6.

23. Richard C. Maher, "Community Service: A Good Idea That Works," *Federal Probation* 58 (June 1994): 20.

24. G. Frederick Allen and Harvey Treger, "Community Service Orders in Federal Probation: Perceptions of Probationers and Host Agencies," *Federal Probation* 54 (September 1990): 8–14.

25. Ibid., p. 10.

26. Maher, "Community Service," p. 23.

27. McDonald, *Punishment Without Walls*, p. 79.

28. Hudson and Galaway, "Community Service: Toward Program Definition," p. 3.

29. Bazemore and Maloney, "Rehabilitating Community Service," p. 24.

30. Patrick A. Langan and Helen A. Graziadei, "Felony Sentences in State Courts, 1992," *Bulletin of the Bureau of Justice Statistics* (Washington, D.C.: United States Department of Justice, January 1995), p. 11.

31. Pheny Z. Smith, *Felony Defendants in Large Urban Counties, 1990* (Washington, D.C.: Bureau of Justice Statistics, May 1993), p. 18.

32. For a discussion of the Bureau of Justice Assistance (BJA) activities in this area and the response of local communities and states see James Austin, "Correctional Options, an Overview," *Corrections Today* 57 (February 1995): (unpaginated insert). The BJA's efforts were authorized by the Crime Control Act of 1990.

33. Ibid.

34. Faye S. Taxman, "Intermediate Sanctions: Dealing with Technical Violators," *Corrections Today* 57 (February 1995): 46, 50–57.

35. Ibid., p. 55.

36. Hudson and Galaway, "Community Service: Toward Program Definition," p. 6.

37. Allen & Treger, "Community Service Orders in Federal Probation," p. 10.

38. Richard Lawrence, "Restitution Programs Pay Back the Victim and Society," *Corrections Today* 52 (February 1990): 96–98.

39. 503 F.Supp. 1265 (S.D.Tex. 1980).

40. Lawrence, "Restitution Programs," p. 98.

41. Bazemore and Maloney, "Rehabilitating Community Service," pp. 24–35.

42. Ibid., p. 27.

43. Ibid.

44. McDonald, *Restitution and Community Service,* p. 9.

45. Ibid., p. 25.

46. "Banker Admits Guilt," *New York Times,* February 13, 1996, Section B, p. 4.

47. Galaway, "Restitution as Innovation or Unfilled Promise?" p. 12.

48. Burt Galaway and Joe Hudson, eds., *Criminal Justice, Restitution, and Reconciliation* (Monsey, NY: Criminal Justice Press, 1990), p. 1.

49. Richard Lawrence, "Reexamining Community Corrections Models," *Crime & Delinquency* 37 (1991): 449–464.

50. Ibid., p. 461, citing Robert Coates in Galaway and Hudson, *Criminal Justice, Restitution, and Reconciliation,* p. 126.

51. Mark S. Umbreit and Mark Carey, "Restorative Justice: Implications for Organizational Change," *Federal Probation* 59 (March 1995): 47–54.

52. Ibid., p. 47.

53. Ibid., p. 48.

54. Randy Barnett and John Hagel, "Restitution: A New Paradigm of Criminal Justice," *Ethics* 87 (1977): 279–301.

55. For a discussion of pure and punitive restitution see Joe Hudson and Burt Galaway, eds., *Victims, Offenders, and Alternative Sanctions* (Lexington, Mass.: Lexington Books, 1980). Especially valuable are two essays: "Restitution, Punishment and Debts to Society," by Richard Dagger; and "Toward the Definition of the Reparative Aim," by Sveinn Thorvaldson.

56. Charles F. Abel and Frank H. Marsh, *Punishment and Restitution: A Restitutionary Approach to Crime and the Criminal* (Westport, CT: Greenwood Press, 1984).

57. Ibid., p. 6.

58. Raffaele Garofalo, *Criminology* (Boston: Little, Brown & Co., 1914), p. 419. Quoted in Abel & Marsh, *Punishment and Restitution,* p. 18.

59. Abel and Marsh, *Punishment and Restitution,* p. 8.

60. Bazemore and Maloney, "Rehabilitating Community Service," pp. 24–25.

61. Maher, "Community Service," p. 23.

62. McDonald, *Punishment Without Walls.*

63. Ibid., p. 187.

64. Lawrence, "Restitution Programs," p. 98.

65. Ibid.

66. McDonald, *Punishment Without Walls,* pp. 195–196.

67. Ibid., p. 191.

68. Mark Umbreit, "Community Service Sentencing: Jail Alternative or Added Sanction," *Federal Probation* 45 (1981): pp. 3–14.

69. Galaway and Hudson, *Criminal Justice, Restitution, and Reconciliation.*

70. McDonald, *Punishment Without Walls,* p. 137.

COMMUNITY-BASED CORRECTIONS

INTRODUCTION THE DIRECTOR OF TALBOT HOUSE, a community-based correctional facility in Cincinnati, Ohio, described the agency's effort to expand its program offerings by instituting a work-release center for prison inmates. Here, inmates would live while employed in the community instead of remaining in jail or prison. This type of community-based facility would seem to be a natural step to take given the severe overcrowding of jails and prisons. And indeed, many communities have such centers.

The agency, however, found it extremely difficult to locate an appropriate, affordable building for the program. Opposition from the community was fierce, but, finally, an old warehouse was located in a nonresidential area. Construction began, and then,

> An uproar followed, including a flurry of phone calls from city police, building officials, and safety officials. Two of the nine city council members became personally involved.[1]

> Mass picketing of the building by protesters brought out the media. Finally, after several weeks of conflict, Talbot House negotiated with neighborhood leaders and agreed to a settlement that included exclusion of murderers and sexual offenders from the program; . . . and a 1–15 ratio of staff to residents on overnight shifts.[2]

In this chapter we will discuss certain relatively new correctional programs that deal with offenders in the community rather than in institutional settings. We will examine some of the difficulties corrections faces, like those encountered by Talbot House, when seeking to locate programs in the community.

Both community corrections and intermediate sanctions, which we will take up in Chapter 16, are similar in some respects because they involve dealing with offenders in the community. There are, however, major differences in underlying philosophies and goals. Typically, community-based corrections is more rehabilitative in philosophy, goals, and methods when compared to intermediate sanctions, which seeks retributive and incapacitative goals. We will see, however, that even this distinction has become blurred as community corrections has taken on a more punitive coloration in recent years. We include in this chapter only programs that are community-based and seek to provide services other than or in addition to those that aim to punish and/or control offenders. Our main focus will be on facilities and programs that developed more recently than "ordinary" community-based correctional activities like probation and parole.

HISTORICAL OVERVIEW

Looking back at the history of community-based corrections, we can identify a "golden age" period stretching from the late 1950s into the early 1970s. During this period, many innovative programs were established along with great optimism as to their value for correcting offenders. A **decarceration** movement was underway during this period. That is, imprisonment was to be deemphasized as a response to crime. Prisons would remain to be populated only by the most violent or career-oriented offenders. This movement to deinstitutionalize was influenced by many studies of the invidious effects of incarceration in large-scale total institutions. Early research into the "prison community" by Donald Clemmer, director of the District of Columbia Department of Corrections, pointed out the negative aspects of what he called "prisonization."[3]

As Peter Jones observed,

The watershed in the development of community corrections came around 1965. Prior to this time, community-based programs were not generally considered suitable alternatives to imprisonment. . . . During this time it was felt that rehabilitation could successfully be accomplished through incarceration. By the late 1960s, this belief was changing because prison reform efforts were felt to have largely failed. The National Advisory Commission of Criminal Justice Standards and Goals recommended a 10-year moratorium on prison construction and much greater emphasis on the development of community correctional programs.[4]

Gresham Sykes, in his classic examination of a large state penitentiary, described the "pains of imprisonment."[5] His work and that of Clemmer and others helped direct the attention of penologists to the development of alternatives to incarceration. Also of importance in this development was the example of the community mental health movement. Exposés of scandalous deficiencies in the care of mental patients in state hospitals led to legislation establishing community mental health centers and the consequent depopulation of large state hospitals. Many in corrections expected the same to occur with regard to prisons.

As community-based corrections picked up steam during this period, a wide variety of programs and facilities were established, including halfway houses for many different types of offenders and prerelease centers for those returning to the community following a term of imprisonment. One observer of community corrections' history, Richard Lawrence, identified three "primary" models of community-based programs during this period: diversion, advocacy, and reintegration.[6] Although they do not dominate the field today, examples of each can be found.

The **diversion model** consists of programs that divert offenders from significant penetration into the criminal justice system. To some extent based on **labeling theory** and the desire to avoid the stigmatizing effects of the formal system, diversion programs often are quite informal, even when offenders are assigned to them through judicial actions.

The **advocacy model** stresses the need to do more than either divert offenders from criminal justice system labeling or place them in traditional community-based programs. Supporters of advocacy programs "asserted that it was not enough to simply sentence offenders to traditional probation and rely on existing programs and resources. . . . More community programs must be made available. . . . Offenders also need advocates. . . ."[7]

The third model identified by Lawrence is the **reintegration model.** These programs aim to "help offenders establish a legitimate role in the community."[8] They have included a variety of facilities and activities such as halfway houses, prerelease centers, group homes, and work-release programs. Many of these programs seek to provide education and vocational training and job placement assistance.

As we discuss examples of community-based programs and facilities, we will find some that fit each of these three models. Recently, however, a director of a halfway house observed that "new community residential facilities for correctional clients have become increasingly difficult to develop in recent years. . . . [T]here is no doubt that these programs are misunderstood by the general public, which sees them as undesirable."[9]

Why does the public see community-based facilities as undesirable? "There are many reasons for this, including corrections' lack of credibility relative to other industries and the almost innate fear prospective neighbors have about our clients."[10] In the

ON THE JOB

A PAROLE HALFWAY HOUSE, BUT "NOT IN MY BACKYARD"

In the 1960s, Maryland's Patuxent Institution sought to provide a transitional residence in Baltimore for its parolees. As discussed in Chapter 7, the institution was in the unique position of having its own paroling authority as well as responsibility for supervising those granted parole. Transitional or halfway houses were springing up in other states, so it was not an unusual step for the Maryland institution to take.

The staff wanted the Baltimore halfway house population to include both parolees and others who were placed on weekend furloughs and work-release. Following many months of searching for a suitable building, and after meeting community resistance, a location was found and a rental agreement reached. After a relatively brief period, the staff had to close the facility. Why? The only available location was in a rundown, crime-ridden section of the city. It seemed that no one wanted these offenders in their backyards. Parolees returning to the house after work at night were in serious danger of being victimized! Eventually, a new prerelease facility had to be constructed on the grounds of the prison. Inmates approved for parole, work-release, and furloughs who had no homes outside the institution were transferred to this facility prior to release.

SOURCE: Author's personal experience.

accompanying On the Job feature we see one example of this resistance to community-based programs in Maryland at a time when establishing halfway houses was a new and promising development in corrections.

Richard Lawrence's review of the history of community corrections places the demise of diversion, advocacy, and reintegration programs in the context of the rise in support for the "justice" or "just deserts" model of corrections. Criminal sentences now are more clearly designed to serve retributive and incapacitative goals. Given this, community-based corrections virtually has had to redesign itself in order to bring offender control to the forefront. One commentator put the development into this perspective:

> [Community supervision personnel] have become the avowed enemies of their charges, operating . . . to incarcerate and, as . . . urine takers, money collectors, compliance monitors, electronic surveillance gadget readers, and law enforcers.[11]

With this brief historical context in mind, we now examine some of the programs that we categorize as community-based corrections.

COMMUNITY-BASED CORRECTIONS FACILITIES AND PROGRAMS

Community-based corrections is a catch-all term. Harold Trester maintained that the term commonly is used to include regional correctional institutions, halfway houses, work-release programs, and prerelease centers.[12] We can add to his list the more "traditional" corrections activities that are carried out in the community: probation and parole. As we have seen, in the 1960s there was a definite move to supplant incarceration with community-based programs for all but the most recalcitrant and violent offenders. Instead, as we saw in earlier chapters, incarceration has become the sanction of choice for a wide range of criminals. Every year, prison and jail populations set new records.

At a time of large increases in both the absolute number of admissions to prison and rates of incarceration, it may seem strange that community-based corrections is sparking renewed interest around the country. It comes as no surprise to many observers, however, that the demand for ever more severe punitive sanctions (as manifested in mandatory prison sentences) has opened a "window of opportunity" for community corrections:

> In [most] states, politicians and [leaders in criminal justice systems] have institutionalized incapacitation as the sole, legitimate goal of corrections. . . . These same officials recognize that a total commitment to the incarceration of all adult felons represents a costly enterprise that cannot be sustained in practice. Ironically, [this] is providing a strategic opening for community corrections and other alternatives to incarceration. . . . Practicing old strategies under new labels and/or devising new ways of releasing some felons to the streets remain crucial work tasks for correctional systems.[13]

Pay particular attention to the language, "practicing old strategies under new labels." As we examine a number of community corrections programs as well as intermediate sanctions in the next two chapters, we will indeed see that many of them have been around for a long time. Their labels, however, look refreshingly new.

Recently, we have seen a tendency to think of community- based corrections as an alternative to imprisonment, probation, and parole. We will find, however, that these

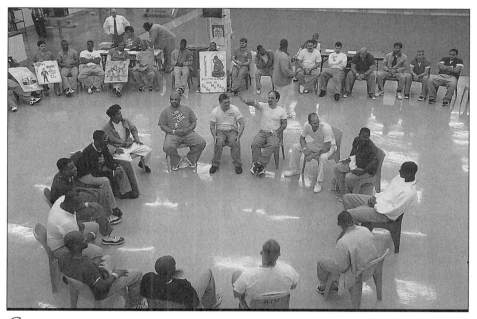

*C*ommunity-based facilities have group counseling sessions available for substance abuse offenders. Having the support of other people facing the same issues can be helpful in dealing with substance abuse.

"alternatives" often include some form of detention as well as probation and parole. We also should note as Charles Fields did that community-based corrections is not a rarely used sanction: "It is and has been for years the mainstay of corrections."[14]

Although it may be accurate to say that community-based corrections has been around for a long time, there has been a rekindling of interest in the idea.

> This renewed interest has led many jurisdictions to experiment with a range of seemingly innovative community treatment programs. Although the practice of processing and supervising offenders in the community is not new, recent applications in this area utilize a number of novel approaches that have only recently gained widespread acceptance.[15]

Of special concern to us in this chapter is the tendency for community-based corrections to be viewed as an alternative form of punishment. This is a tendency that has shifted many programs away from the original intent of those who led the fight for community corrections. That intent was clearly reintegrative through the application of rehabilitative measures. This shift has had the unintended consequences of "increased numbers of absconders and revocations coupled with growing noncompliance with conditions of probation."[16]

This trend is related to a complex set of criminal justice variables that includes public opinions regarding punishment and rehabilitation, sentencing policies and practices, severely overcrowded prison populations, and public and official perceptions about the value of "traditional" community-based programs, such as probation and parole. We now turn to a discussion of major types of community corrections facilities and programs.

Residential Alternatives to Incarceration: Halfway Houses

Community-based programs and facilities come in a variety of types and purposes. One type includes those facilities that operate as residential alternatives to incarceration in jails and prisons. They sometimes are referred to as halfway houses or community correctional centers. Others are designed as transition facilities where offenders live following release from prison. These are frequently called prerelease centers, and probably have the clearest mission of all community-based corrections programs:

> The basic philosophy of community corrections facilities is that eligible inmates begin the transition to community living in a partially controlled environment. This setting provides increasing amounts of freedom for inmates who otherwise would have made the abrupt shift from prison to community without the controls of a community corrections center.[17]

Another, very different community-based facility is the "return-to-custody" center. This is a relatively new correctional facility. Its development has been spurred by the large increase in the number of probation, parole, and intensive supervision violators. As we pointed out in Chapter 8, a high percentage of prison admissions is accounted for by those offenders who have violated the terms of their release to the community. Partly to alleviate prison crowding, some states have developed centers apart from their prisons to house these persons who must be returned to custody.

In the case of each of these major types of community-based corrections facilities, public and privately operated examples can be found. Privatization has probably made more headway in this area than in any other in corrections.

Residents and staff share in food preparation and meals at halfway house correctional facilities.

Comprehensive Community-Based Correctional Centers

Among the broad range of residential facilities or halfway houses are those that seek to deliver a comprehensive array of services to their offender clients. The accompanying Focus on the Law feature shows how one county in Iowa, working under a resolution of its governing board, set about reorganizing its community-based correctional services into one comprehensive agency. The next On the Job feature describes the day-to-day operation of this agency.

Another example of a comprehensive center, Talbot House (see the brief description at the beginning of the chapter), is run by a private agency in Cincinnati, Ohio. In operation for over 30 years, its mission is to deliver "substance abuse, mental health, and criminal justice services."[18] The agency has twelve programs: five community residential centers for correctional clients; two programs for individuals convicted of drunk driving; two other substance abuse programs; a crisis counseling and suicide prevention center; a victims-of-crime assistance program; and an employment placement project.[19] Although this center is a good example of efforts to deliver wide-ranging services

FOCUS ON
THE LAW

COMPREHENSIVE CORRECTIONS PROGRAM
IN POLK COUNTY, IOWA

Polk County, Iowa, provides an example of what a local jurisdiction can accomplish when it confronts two commonly experienced criminal justice system problems: overcrowded jails and state prisons, and a fragmented corrections system in which often contradictory and conflicting programs were operating.

A resolution of the Polk County Board of Supervisors created the Department of Court Services on January 1, 1971 (p. vii). This decision effectively organized into one agency all community-based programs that previously had been scattered among a number of administrative agencies.

The new Department of Court Services included pretrial services, supervised pretrial release programs, and the county probation unit. Eventually, the county expanded its reach into the entire Fifth Judicial District. This expansion was supported by the state's Crime Commission.

For a brief period, the Men's Residential Facility was the only alternative to jail or prison incarceration provided in the district. Then a Women's Residential Facility was authorized.

SOURCE: Fifth Judicial District Department of Court Services, *A Handbook on Community Corrections in Des Moines* (Washington, D.C.: National Institute of Law Enforcement and Criminal Justice, 1978).

---

in the community, it also illustrates the resistance put up by communities that do not want offenders in their "backyards."

Work-Release Centers

Because Talbot House's work-release center finally was able to open, we use it here as an example of this type of community-based correctional facility. The physical plant has baths, bedrooms, lounges, recreation and reception areas, and a monitoring office. Thus, it is a complete residential facility.

We saw above that certain offenders are not eligible for placement in the facility. Those who are accepted into the program fall into two groups: state prison inmates placed on work-release, and offenders sentenced directly to the program by a sentencing judge. Thus, this is a diversion population.

There is a potentially serious problem when mixing two very different offender populations in a single physical plant and program. Former prison inmates are probably more serious offenders than those whom judges divert from prison. Talbot House is proceeding to establish a separate facility for the diversion group. If, however, the difficulty encountered in opening the work-release center is any guide, the task of putting still another facility in the community will be a daunting one.

We saw in Chapter 13 that some states have established residential centers apart from their prisons that house work-release inmates who are under restitution and community service orders. For example, Texas has been operating seventeen "restitution centers." During a five-year period, over 3,000 offenders have been sentenced to these centers. The wages they earn while under sentence are used to pay restitution, support dependents, and pay supervision costs. In addition to working, residents of the restitution centers are required to perform community service.

ON THE JOB

COMMUNITY CORRECTIONS AT THE FT. DES MOINES MEN'S RESIDENTIAL FACILITY

The Ft. Des Moines Men's Residential Facility was set up in a refurbished U.S. Army barracks in Des Moines, Iowa. The facility

> functions primarily . . . as (1) a non-secure institution operating as an alternative institution for confinement, relieving the overcrowded county jail and state prisons; (2) a correctional facility providing rehabilitation programs to criminal offenders in Polk County; (3) as a work and educational release center. . . . (p. 45)

The facility's intake consists of male felons sentenced by the court. During the first week an offender is at the center, he completes an employment application and meets with a counselor and caseworker. By the end of the first three weeks, offenders have been seen by a psychiatric consultant and a vocational rehabilitation counselor.

Treatment services beyond job placement are initially provided through individual counseling. After a successful period, offenders are transferred to "triad" teams of three "clients" under the supervision of a staff counselor. The teams meet weekly to deal with problems each member may encounter. "The negative behavior of one client may result in the forfeiture of privileges by the other two members . . ." (p. 50).

> Probably as important to the prospects for rehabilitation as any program is the general atmosphere of the institution. Clients wear "street" clothes. . . . The relationship between staff and clients is quite informal, with everyone on a first-name basis. . . . The dehumanization process usually associated with correctional institutions is minimized. (p. 52)

SOURCE: Fifth Judicial District Department of Court Services, *A Handbook on Community Corrections in Des Moines* (Washington, D.C.: U.S. Department of Justice, National Institution of Law Enforcement and Criminal Justice, 1978).

Return-to-Custody Community-Based Centers

Another model of community-based corrections is designed for offenders who are returned to custody because of one or more violations of their community-release conditions. One example, in Coalinga, California, opened in response to a state statute (Senate Bill 1591) authorizing local governments to construct "small, local custody centers for parole violators and other minimum security state inmates. . . ."[20]

Reintegration Programs

The last of the major community-based models we want to describe aims to assist offenders to make the transition from prison to the community. This has led to a number of different programs and facilities. We usually think of a halfway house or prerelease center as a place where counseling and educational services are delivered with the chief aim of assisting offenders making the return to the street from prison. However, at other halfway centers the objective is reintegration through employment strategies.

It is obvious that offenders, whether reentering the community from prison, on regular probation, or in a diversion program, will have a difficult time adjusting if they are unemployed or underemployed. An Illinois initiative provides an example of

ACROSS CULTURES

COMMUNITY-BASED CORRECTIONS IN GREAT BRITAIN

Specialist hostels cater to a specific type of person. They limit their clientele to, for example, drug users; people with alcohol problems; mothers, babies, and pregnant women; people with psychiatric problems; people who are HIV positive. . . . (p. 51)

One such facility, Crowley House in Birmingham, operates as a probation hostel. Its resident population consists of up to 13 adult women and their children. The period of residence is usually one year. The "treatment" regimen is group-based, as can be seen in the following statement by Pat Carlen, who researched community-based programs in Great Britain:

> All rules here are directed at creating a reasonable environment. We have House Meetings at least once a week and any resident can call a House Meeting at any time. There is peer group control and more often than not we have to prevent them from imposing too many rules. (p. 53)

Each resident is assigned a caseworker, and counseling is available on an "open door" basis.

Another type of community-based program is the day center for women on probation. This program is also based on peer group involvement. One example of this, reported by Carlen is the Staffordshire Women's Group B, where group meetings are held once each week. The program milieu is structured to induce participation by an offender's entire family and to provide as "normal" an environment as possible:

> The pre-school children come with Mum and we run a volunteer creche in the school holidays. The group is open to offenders, wives of male offenders. (p. 82)

In addition to participation in group meetings, probationers and their families attend group outings, engage in handicraft activities, and raise money for continued support of the program.

SOURCE: Pat Carlen, *Alternatives to Women's Imprisonment* (Philadelphia, Pa.: Open University Press, 1990).

a community-based strategy for offenders with employment problems.[21] This program established "vocational networks" to provide a range of vocational services to offenders, who included probationers, parolees, local jail inmates, and some who were diverted from imprisonment.

The networks were responsible for vocational training, education, and job placement services for their offender clients. Because local community acceptance was predicted to be a problem, the program provided a number of incentives, among which were the following:

- Tax incentives for employers who hire program participants.
- Participant screening to assess offender risk levels, needs, and skills; thus saving employers considerable time and money.
- Reimbursing employers for training costs.

A number of potential and actual benefits are said to accrue to the state, which could make similar programs more palatable:

- Reducing prison populations by keeping offenders in the community and gainfully employed.
- Reducing the crime rate (unverified).

▬ Saving tax dollars for new prison construction and expanding the state's tax base through full employment of many offenders who otherwise would be unemployed or underemployed.

Innovative community-based programs such as this Illinois project seem to be a positive step toward reintegrating offenders into the community through enhancing their participation in the labor force. However, note some of the difficulties such efforts entail. First, there is the need to coordinate the activities of a number of state and local agencies. These include various criminal justice system agencies and vocational and education departments. Then, there is the problem of selling the concept to the public and to private sector employers. As we have discussed earlier, there is considerable resistance on the part of the public toward keeping offenders in the community.

In T. G. Tomlinson's description of the Illinois project, he notes particularly troublesome problems that arose because of the requirement to integrate the many bureaucracies involved in operating the vocational networks:

> The "red tape" problem comes from the innumerable forms that must be filled out for every agency. This process is an obstacle to even the most knowledgeable volunteer and can . . . intimidate an offender. Bureaucratic record keeping also poses problems because of attempts to keep data private. For instance, under new rules, the DOC [Department of Corrections] will no longer provide project personnel with records of released inmates. This means the service providers are working "blind" when trying to plan for the parolee.[22]

While, as we have seen, the project has built-in incentives for potential employers, "the lack of support from the businesses has been the greatest problem facing the networks. Businesses supply the jobs for the clients; they must be won over."[23]

COMPREHENSIVE COMMUNITY CORRECTIONS STATUTES

In response to a request from Attorney General Reno, the American Society of Criminology formed several task forces to study a number of criminal justice problem areas. One of these, chaired by Joan Petersilia, reported on community-based corrections under the title, "A Crime Control Rationale for Investing in Community Corrections."[24] This task force's charge was related to the increase in the number of high-risk offenders placed on parole and probation, and, consequently, the sharp increase in rates of violations of community supervision conditions, which in turn leads to increased public concern about safety.

In a preamble to the task force report, Petersilia argued that ordinary probation and parole, the traditional community-based correction strategies, are unsatisfactory because "probationers represent a serious continued risk to public safety," and

> by not focusing on providing probationers with an appropriate level and type of supervision, crime in the community will not be abated. Current policy simply waits until their criminality escalates to a point where incarceration, which has been proven to be costly and ineffective in reducing crime, [becomes necessary].[25]

Petersilia's report recommended that community-based corrections be grounded in "surveillance plus treatment." This is especially required for drug offenders, although not, apparently, for those convicted of drug trafficking. The report goes on to claim (to some extent, to be sure, on Petersilia's previous research, which we reported in the chapter on probation), that:

Program models now exist that are effective in reducing recidivism rates, and the public supports rehabilitation over incarceration for such offenders [i.e., drug offenders, excluding traffickers]. The cost-benefit tradeoff between prison and community corrections is among the highest for this population.[26]

The report then states that the public will support probation and parole if they are maintained under intensive supervision conditions because these have shown to reduce recidivism in some instances by as much as 20–30 percent.[27] Whether or not we can agree with the task force report as regards the reduction of recidivism is a question we will take up in the section on evaluation of community corrections.

Recently adopted **comprehensive community corrections statutes** in a number of states and in the federal system seem to offer opportunities to achieve what Petersilia and others have recommended, that is, sanctions that combine surveillance with treatment. These statutes have led to the establishment of comprehensive community corrections systems that include facilities and special programs.

The North Carolina Community Penalties Act

We begin our discussion of community-based correctional systems with the 1983 North Carolina Community Penalties Act.[28] This statute authorized a number of locally based programs for "prison-bound misdemeanants and non-violent, prison-bound felony offenders. . . ."[29] These programs, originally operating in five locales, were introduced into twelve communities. They were clearly designed to provide alternatives to incarceration. Selection of offenders was a major problem for the Community Penalties program. As we have noted before and will again later, there is a tendency for community-based and intermediate sanctions programs to select only the "best" or low-risk offenders, or to widen the net of control by selecting those who should remain in more traditional programs.

The North Carolina Community Penalties program used a Client-Specific Planning model (CSP) that was developed by the National Center on Institutions and Alternatives. This model is based on the belief that,

> each offender is an individual whose background and personal circumstances must be taken into account in designing a sentencing alternative. The programs begin with the idea that the source of the criminal action lies in personal and social problems of the offender which can best be addressed through community resources.[30]

Before we get the idea that this North Carolina initiative is some kind of liberal "coddling" of criminals, we see that those who developed the program specifics were aware that they had to "address the need to satisfy the court's interest in incorporating punitive sanctions in a sentence."[31] We now look at the components of the program.

Like diversion programs, this one usually involves other elements in the criminal justice system. Prosecutors and probation and parole agencies are especially important to the success of alternative sanctions. Sentence "packages" must be presented to judges, who must accept them. However, prior to this, prosecutors must agree to the package, which has been developed by both the CSP staff and the community supervision agents in the affected jurisdictions.

Marc Mauer sought to answer the question, "Are these programs working?"[32] In his examination of North Carolina's approach, he was interested primarily in how well the initiative was accepted by the courts. After all, innovations are of little value if sentencing judges fail to implement them in their sentencing orders. Mauer found that most of the state's Community Penalties programs have an 85 percent acceptance rate in the courts.[33] Similarly, prosecutors involved in these programs have shown a relatively high level of support. Unfortunately, Mauer was unable to examine whether the Community Penalties Act had any impact on recidivism.

Federal Comprehensive Sanctions Centers (CSC)

Another example of building community corrections options in a system is the **comprehensive sanctions centers** model utilized in the federal system. This model illustrates both the comprehensive systems approach and the difficulty encountered when trying to separate community-based programs from intermediate sanctions. Two federal probation officers, describing one such federal comprehensive sanctions center, state that its mission was twofold: retaining the community basis for treatment, and delivering a more restrictive sanction than regular probation and parole. In other words, providing "surveillance plus treatment."[34]

The CSC program integrated several components. There was an "intensive" halfway house program that included rehabilitative services and varying levels of supervision. A program review team developed a program plan for each offender. Several groups of offenders were included, thus involving more of the criminal sanctioning system:

- Newly sentenced offenders received directly from the courts.
- Offenders who violated the conditions of their release (e.g., probation, conditional releasees).
- Inmates released from federal prison who were making the transition to the street.

From this description we can see that the CSC model includes three quite different subsets: diversion from imprisonment, return-to-custody, and transitional services. Offenders selected for the center spent an average of 139 days in the program. The range of participation was from 60 to 270 days. Curiously, not all offenders who completed the program were subject to continued supervision.[35] Reminiscent of the Irish or progressive system of incarceration we discussed in Chapter 6, the center's regimen was divided into graduated levels of restrictiveness:

> For example, for "drug use" violators, level one was used to restrict the offender completely for up to 30 days while the offender was being assessed. Eventually, the offender graduated to less restrictive levels of supervision as program requirements were met.[36]

Other Comprehensive Community-Based Corrections Systems

Michael Musheno and his colleagues studied a number of comprehensive programs in three states: Oregon, Colorado, and Connecticut.[37] All three states' programs target a similar population: nonviolent felony offenders. There are other similarities and some differences that need to be discussed.

In Oregon, the state allocates funds to county departments of community corrections through the state Department of Corrections. Probation and parole officers are certified by the state and county and are responsible for the bulk of the field work. This includes both presentence investigations and community supervision of offenders.

In Colorado, the various judicial districts form advisory boards that locate and fund private agencies willing to deliver services. District court judges have the authority to sentence nonviolent offenders to community corrections within their districts instead of to prison. Probation and parole officers may serve on the local advisory boards, but service delivery personnel from private agencies often are the actual supervisors of offenders, unlike the Oregon model. Musheno found that the use of local advisory boards resulted in the highest level of community acceptance compared to the other two programs. It also seems to have resulted in political support. Community acceptance is crucial to the success of community-based programs, as we saw earlier. Disengagement from the state bureaucracy and giving the local judiciary major control of the program was of assistance in depoliticizing the whole effort.

In Connecticut, the purpose of community corrections differs from Oregon and Colorado in that Connecticut uses it for "transitional" services for nonviolent offenders and their families. That is, offenders are selected from the pool of those who are moving from prison to the community. Thus, there is a very different population as well as different objectives, which makes comparison with other programs difficult.

Recent Control-Oriented Community-Based Systems

In the 1980s, a new wave of statewide community "corrections" programs emerged. These goals are not primarily rehabilitative in nature; rather, they are related to just deserts or retribution. The Kansas experience illustrates this new wave. It also illustrates the net-widening potential so common to community programs designed to divert offenders from prison. Judges in Kansas are responsible for placing offenders directly into community-based programs, rather than sentencing them to prison. As Peter Jones pointed out, judges' decision making is difficult to modify, and there can be many occasions when offenders are sentenced to community-based programs who otherwise would be on more traditional sentences.[38] Another related issue is that sometimes offenders are retained in community programs for much longer periods of time than if they had been incarcerated or sentenced to probation. Thus, the time of control is extended.[39]

The Kansas program is based on the state's 1978 Community Corrections Act (KCCA). This statute and the programs authorized by it were modeled after the 1966 California probation subsidy program and the 1973 Minnesota Community Corrections Act. Both of these models provided funds (subsidies) to counties that reduced their rates of commitment to their states' prison system. Increased use of probation was the primary means used in these states to achieve reductions in prison admissions.

The Kansas use of its KCCA is primarily to provide intermediate (between probation and incarceration) sanctions. Participating Kansas counties receive subsidies for eligible offenders sentenced to community sanctions. Those eligible include nonviolent felons with no more than one prior felony conviction. Among the programs or sanctions available either as sole sanctions or in combination are the following:

- Work release
- Restitution
- Community service
- Employment and educational services
- Substance abuse programs
- Social-psychological diagnostic services and referrals

All program participants were subjected to intensive supervision styles by community supervision officers. After examining the Kansas experience, Jones addressed the following two questions, questions that might well be addressed to all similar community-based correctional programs. First, is comprehensive community-based corrections a real alternative to imprisonment? Second, do comprehensive community corrections statutes end up widening the net of social control? Jones concluded that in the two largest counties, community programs "did have a significant impact on prison admissions of program eligible offenders. . . . Under some circumstances, programs designed as alternatives to custody can achieve their goal."[40] In some counties, there was evidence of net-widening.

The Kansas Community Corrections Act may be achieving the goal of diverting at least some offenders from incarceration, but how do community-based programs do in terms of affecting recidivism? Before proceeding, we note that the target population of the Kansas CCA was a prison-bound felony population. Felonies considered appropriate for community sanctions were Class D and, the least serious and nonviolent felonies. Burglary, theft, and bad checks (over $50) are the most common felonies in this class. Thus, Kansas was not dealing with very serious felons who posed a threat to the personal safety of the citizens.

As Jones points out, the Kansas CCA does not lay out very clear goals, thus it is difficult to evaluate its performance in the field. The statute begins with this statement:

> For the purpose of more effectively protecting society and promoting efficiency and economy in the delivery of correctional services, the secretary of corrections is authorized to make grants to counties for the development, implementation, operation, and improvement of community correctional services. . . .[41]

Interviews with those involved in starting up the KCCA programs as well as those continuing to work in the various programs did reveal a consensus regarding a number of goals to be sought by community-based programming:

- Reduce prison admissions.
- Reduce the costs of correctional services mainly by reducing the need for new prison construction.
- "Deal more appropriately with certain felony offenders," by way of sanctions intermediate between probation and incarceration.[42]

Although many officials and workers associated with the Kansas CCA expressed concern about the "public safety" risks of keeping prison-bound offenders in the community, there never was any explicitly stated expectation as to what level of risk was acceptable. As we have repeatedly said, correctional program evaluation is an extremely difficult task under the most favorable of conditions. Not having clearly stated goals and evaluation criteria for programs makes a difficult task even more problematic. We will see what Jones and others found in their evaluation studies in the following section.

EVALUATION OF COMMUNITY CORRECTIONS

Evaluating any correctional program is an extraordinarily difficult task. Writing in *Federal Probation*, Jackson, de Keijser, and Michon urge the use of a meta-analytical approach when reviewing evaluation research.[43] **Meta-analysis** can be defined as a technique that "combine[s] the results of all the available studies of the same question."[44] The advantage of using this approach is that one can pull together a number of studies with small numbers of subjects or cases, thus producing a large sample. General conclusions can be drawn with much more confidence. Of course, the meta-analytical method has its limitations: the combined studies may be so different in methodology and measurement of important variables that joining them together will be of little value; and the errors in these separate studies will not be eliminated simply by combining the studies.

Janet Jackson and her associates point out five major problems, which we need to be aware of when we want to judge the success of programs in the community corrections area when using meta-analysis or other methods. First, if we wish to evaluate the performance of a community-based sanction against incarceration, we must be certain that the former truly is an alternative for imprisonment. Net-widening, which is a distinct possibility, may well mean that a particular sanction really targets non-prison-bound populations.

A second problem arises when we want to determine whether certain sanctions are "relatively more effective" than others. To do this we must consider whether the goals of the sanctions are the same. Comparing sanctions with different underlying philosophies and objectives makes little sense. Yet some studies have, in fact, done this.

Another serious problem is the finding that some community-based programs seem to work relatively well with *certain treatments, in certain settings, with certain offenders.*[45] Before reaching any conclusions about program effectiveness, we must know how these treatments, settings, and offenders differ.

The conceptualization and measurement of recidivism is problematic in much evaluation research, as we have noted in previous chapters. In reviewing the literature we must be aware of the "huge diversity in the way the principal dependent variable, recidivism, was measured."[46] To date there seems to be no agreement on a solution to this problem.

Finally, the time frames used in various studies are variable. To be able to assess the results of this research we need to be clear about how long offenders on community sanctions have been at risk compared to those on other, more traditional sanctions. Then, we must be certain as to the length of the follow-up period for each offender group studied.

These and other problems associated with evaluation research in the area of community-based corrections do not permit us to feel confident about making any general conclusions regarding their effectiveness. With this in mind, we now take a look at a sampling of studies purporting to evaluate the performance of community-based corrections sanctions. We will organize this review with reference to three major goals set forth for community-based corrections: alleviating prison crowding, saving costs, and reducing recidivism.

Alleviating Prison Crowding

There is some support for the conclusion that community-based programs whose major objective is to reduce prison admissions have been successful, but at the cost of some net-widening.[47] There are, however, notable exceptions. Changes in mandatory sentencing laws in some states have resulted in increases in prison admissions while at the same time, the number of offenders in community-based programs also increased.[48] We again see the systemic consequences of altering one component of the criminal justice system.

Cost Benefits

One goal of community corrections is to save taxpayers a significant amount of money by retaining offenders in the community instead of incarcerating them. Some studies suggest that savings are obtained when prison-bound offenders are diverted to community programs. In Oregon, for example, it was estimated that some of the counties participating in community-based programs were saving about $3 million year (comparing the cost of incarcerating offenders for one year).[49] However, in a number of counties such programs involved intensive, long-term supervision, which adds to the cost. "In these counties, community corrections contributes to greater control over more offenders [the net-widening effect], not to fiscal savings."[50]

Recidivism

Bearing in mind the problems associated with defining the dependent variable, recidivism, we find support for the conclusion that some community-based sanctions do relatively well compared to incarceration. However, the most general statement we can make after reviewing the research literature is that community-based sanctions do neither better nor worse than the incarceration or probation and parole alternatives. This may be discouraging, but we can put a positive spin on this conclusion. While doing neither better nor worse than other sanctions, community corrections does, in some cases, reduce prison crowding, lessen the need for costly prison construction, and, in general, demand fewer tax dollars. Now let's look at some research that specifically addresses the issue of recidivism.

An evaluation of the Kansas Community Corrections Act defined recidivism as "any arrest or conviction [for offenders in the community] after the date of sentence. For prisoners, only those arrests or convictions occurring after the date of release . . . were counted."[51] Following offenders for about three and a half years, the study found that had the offenders given community sanctions been incarcerated, there would have been "an 11.7% reduction in offending."[52] However, the study went on to show that community-based recidivists did not commit serious crimes against persons. "Those defendants who did reoffend tend to commit relatively minor public-order and property crimes."[53] Perhaps surprisingly, in the Kansas evaluation, ordinary probationers were found "consistently" to have lower recidivism rates when compared to those in community- based programs.

> One conclusion these findings generated was: If crime control and minimization of public risk are the parameters within which the success of a community-based program is to be measured, then these data do not bode well for community corrections.[54]

An evaluation of one Federal Comprehensive Sanctions Center found that a little over 78 percent of the participants actually completed the program designed for them by the center's diagnostic team, and that of these offenders, only 56 percent were judged to have a "positive" prognosis upon leaving the center.[55] When recidivism was measured, the evaluation study determined that one-quarter of those released recidivated, most committing technical violations, usually involving illegal drug use.[56] Of significance was the finding that 43 percent of the violators were given a poor prognosis upon leaving the center.

A number of critics of community-based corrections programs have argued that it is expecting too much of these programs to judge them on their success in reducing recidivism unless there is considerably more involvement in and by the community. All too often, community-based corrections focuses exclusively on offenders. As James Byrne pointed out, "*offender-based* community control strategies are incomplete, since they take a 'closed system' view of correctional interventions: *change the offender and not the community*."[57]

Richard Lawrence concluded his critique of contemporary community-based corrections, especially as it competes with more punitive intermediate sanctions, with the observation that it must "include the community as well as the offender as targets of change. . . . Until community corrections professions and policymakers approach the crime problem in this broader perspective, our crime control efforts will . . . inevitably fail."[58]

Since most community-based correctional measures do not make any serious attempt either to change the communities out of which offenders come and into which they surely will return, or the perceptions and attitudes of the public, there really is little chance that they will fulfill the expectations many have for them. We can say, with some degree of confidence, that community-based corrections affects recidivism, variously defined, about as well or poorly, depending on one's perspective, as regular or traditional measures such as probation and parole.

Much has been expected from community corrections, and, as we have seen, some programs have delivered positive results. However, it has not been able to withstand the pressure for harsher sanctions and offender control strategies that has been building for almost two decades. This is especially true with respect to intermediate sanctions, the subject of Chapter 16. With these sanctions, there is still a trace of community-based treatment programming. A number of these in-community sanctions such as home detention and intensive supervision probation and parole include "treatment" services. These are, however, clearly overshadowed by the requirements of control and punishment.

Finally, community-based corrections has been offender-based. There has been little interest in and even less action to correct the offender's community or involve the community more directly in programs carried out in its name and in its backyard. Expecting correctional programs to be successful within this limited context may be expecting too much.

SUMMARY   COMMUNITY-BASED CORRECTIONS has been around for a long time. Probation, parole, restitution, and community service all represent measures and sanctions that keep or return offenders to the community. However, newer programs carrying the label of community-based corrections have come to the forefront in recent decades. Some of these newer programs amount to little more than "practicing old strategies under new labels," but others are innovative strategies.

We can subdivide the development of "newer" community-based correctional strategies into two distinct periods in terms of the reasons why these strategies gained acceptance. In both periods, what was happening with respect to incarceration provided the driving force for innovation. The first period, beginning in the late 1950s, saw American prisons as largely unnecessary and sometimes counterproductive as regards crime control. Prison populations were to be thinned out and most offenders sentenced to various community-based facilities and programs.

The second period, from the 1980s on, saw a renewed interest in placing more offenders in the community. This time, the driving force was the prison population explosion that is overtaxing our penal institutions and the resources we can assign to them. Court orders to reduce populations and actions taken to lower the costs involved in incarcerating ever increasing numbers of offenders have forced us to seek other solutions than imprisonment.

During the first period of community-based correctional activity, rehabilitation of offenders to assist in their reintegration into the community was clearly the major objective. The second period, on the other hand, is a period in which punitive and control objectives are dominant. This, of course, is directly related to society's ever increasing demand for harsher penalties for crime. At the same time, rates of incarceration simply cannot increase without restraint. Thus, we see a renewed interest and commitment to community-based programs. This time, however, the need to build into them more punitive and restrictive elements has overshadowed the rehabilitative ideal that once was so characteristic of community-based corrections.

This reorientation of community-based corrections continues the bias toward offender-centered programs that is characteristic of the history of sanctions that are located "in the community." Instead of an earlier rehabilitative or reintegrative focus, the current wave of community-based sanctions is offender-control-oriented. Almost no attention is given to programs that seek to address problems associated with the community into which the offender will be placed.

KEY CONCEPTS

Advocacy model
Comprehensive community
    corrections statutes
Comprehensive sanctions centers
Decarceration

Diversion model
Labeling theory
Meta-analysis
Reintegration model

QUESTIONS FOR DISCUSSION

1. What is the most appropriate criterion for defining (a) recidivism, and (b) program success for community-based correctional programs?
2. Critically comment on the view that unless community-based corrections more directly involves the community in its programs, it will surely fail to achieve any of its stated objectives.
3. Is it possible for community-based corrections to thrive in current an environment that stresses just deserts and offender control strategies? Fully explain your answer.
4. How did labeling theory influence the development of community-based corrections?
5. The advocacy model of community-based corrections is out of place today. Why is this so? Is there any chance of resurrecting it?

ENDNOTES

1. Neil F. Tilow, "Community Facilities: Overcoming Obstacles and Opposition," *Corrections Today* 51 (April 1989): 90.
2. Ibid.

3. Donald Clemmer, *The Prison Community* (Boston: the Christopher Publishing House, 1940).

4. Peter R. Jones, "Community Corrections in Kansas: Extending Community-Based Corrections or Widening the Net?" *Journal of Research in Crime and Delinquency* 27 (1990): 79.

5. Gresham Sykes, *Society of Captives: A Study of a Maximum Security Prison* (New York: Atheneum, 1968).

6. Richard Lawrence, "Reexamining Community Corrections Models," *Crime & Delinquency* 37 (1991): 449–464.

7. Ibid., p. 451.

8. Ibid., p. 452.

9. Tilow, "Community Facilities," p. 88.

10. Ibid.

11. Ibid., p. 455, quoting M. Kay Harris, "Observations of a 'Friend of the Court' on the Future of Probation and Parole," *Federal Probation* 51 (1987): 21.

12. Harold B. Trester, *Supervision of the Offender* (Englewood Cliffs, N.J.: Prentice-Hall, 1981), p. 300.

13. Michael C. Musheno, et al., "Community Corrections as an Organizational Innovation: What Works and Why," *Journal of Research in Crime and Delinquency* 26 (1989): 136.

14. Charles B. Fields, ed., *Innovative Trends and Specialized Strategies in Community-Based Corrections* (New York: Garland Publishing, 1994), p. vii.

15. Ibid., p. xi.

16. Ibid., pp. xiii–xiv.

17. Thomas G. Eynon, "Building Community Support," *Corrections Today* 51 (April 1989): 148.

18. Tilow, "Community Facilities," p. 88.

19. Ibid.

20. Povl Boesen, "California Law Encourages Community Corrections," *Corrections Today* 51 (April 1989): 38.

21. Thomas C. Tomlinson, "Reintegrating the Criminal Offender Through Community-Based Vocational Networks," in Charles B. Fields, ed., *Innovative Trends and Specialized Strategies in Community-Based Corrections* (New York: Garland Publishing, 1994), pp. 205–241.

22. Ibid., p. 237.

23. Ibid.

24. Joan Petersilia, "A Crime Control Rationale for Investing in Community Corrections," *Spectrum* 68 (Summer 1995): pp. 16–27.

25. Ibid., p. 14.

26. Ibid., p. 15.

27. Ibid.

28. North Carolina General Statutes, § 143B-500 (1983).

29. Marc Mauer, "The North Carolina Community Penalties Act: A Serious Approach to Diverting Offenders from Prison," *Federal Probation* 50 (March 1988): 12.

30. Ibid.

31. Ibid.

32. Ibid., pp. 14–17.

33. Ibid., p. 14.

34. Joseph C. Callahan and Keith A. Koenning, "The Comprehensive Sanctions Center in the Northern District of Ohio," *Federal Probation* 59 (September 1995): 52.

35. Ibid., p. 53.

36. Ibid., p. 57.

37. Musheno, et al., "Community Corrections as an Organizational innovation," pp. 136–167.

38. Jones, "Community Corrections in Kansas," pp. 79–101.

39. Ibid., p. 82.

40. Ibid., p. 97.

41. Peter R. Jones, "The Risk of Recidivism: Evaluating the Public-Safety Implications of a Community Corrections Program," *Journal of Criminal Justice* 19 (1991): 51.

42. Ibid.
43. Janet L. Jackson, Jan W. de Keijser, and John A. Michon, "A Critical Look at Research on Alternatives to Custody," *Federal Probation* 59 (September 1995): 43–51.
44. Paul C. Stern and Linda Kalof, *Evaluating Social Science Research,* 2nd ed. (New York: Oxford University Press, 1996): 252.
45. Jackson, et al., "A Critical Look at Research on Alternatives to Custody," pp. 43–51.
46. Ibid., p. 47.
47. See, for example, Jones, "Community Corrections in Kansas."
48. Musheno, et al., "Community Corrections as an Organizational Innovation," pp. 152–153.
49. Ibid., pp. 155–156.
50. Ibid., p. 156.
51. Jones, "The Risk of Recidivism," p. 53.
52. Ibid., p. 54.
53. Ibid.
54. Ibid., pp. 56, 59.
55. Callahan and Koenning, "The Comprehensive Sanctions Center," p. 53.
56. Ibid., p. 56.
57. James Byrne, "Reintegrating the Concept of *Community* into Community-Based Corrections," *Crime and Delinquency* 35 (1989): 487. Emphasis in the original.
58. Lawrence, "Reexamining Community Corrections Models," p. 462.

INTERMEDIATE SANCTIONS

15 CORRECTIONAL BOOT CAMPS

INTRODUCTION THE CORRECTIONAL BOOT CAMP, or shock incarceration, is one of the newest correctional measures, the first camp opening in Georgia in 1983.[1] Its supporters claim that it lowers costs and recidivism, contributes to rehabilitation, and reduces prison crowding. Its critics argue that it produces no long-range benefits, and widens the net by drawing in populations that never would have been incarcerated. Critics also claim the assumption that a harsh military experience will result in rehabilitated offenders is based on faulty logic.

Shock incarceration programs include the following elements:

- A regimen with strict rules and discipline.
- A boot-camp, military atmosphere.
- Mandatory inmate participation in military drills, physical exercise, and hard manual labor.
- Segregation of shock inmates from the general jail or prison population.[2]

Although these elements that characterize shock incarceration might seem to be unique to the United States, it is noteworthy that methods of delivering a shock to offenders elsewhere can be quite similar. We see in the Across Cultures feature, that

ACROSS
CULTURES

DELIVERING A SHOCK TO YOUTHFUL OFFENDERS IN GREAT BRITAIN

Great Britain, beginning in the 1960s, established a number of "detention centres" for youthful offenders as an alternative to incarceration and probation. These offenders are between 14 and 21 years of age.

> A youth sentenced to a detention center is subject to a short-term, strenuous military-style regime . . . . [The] young offender sentenced to a detention center serves a 3-month term and is subjected to a high-impact treatment program." (p. 55)

The regime at these detention centers includes military drill, a rigorous physical exercise program, and very hard labor. Unlike boot camps in the United States, British detention centers are subdivided into "junior" and "senior" centers on the basis of the age of their residents. Those up to 17 years of age are sentenced to junior centers. Offenders between 17 and 21 years of age spend their three months in senior centers.

SOURCE: Wayne P. Jackson, "Treatment of the Offenders in the United Kingdom," *Federal Probation* 35 (June 1971): 50–57.

Great Britain has been employing military-style "detention centres" to shock youthful offenders for some time.

Shock incarceration is touted as a "new" correctional endeavor, but we must remember that Zebulon Brockway, first warden of the Elmira Reformatory, had already instituted a military-style regime in corrections over one hundred years ago. Here is what he said then about his reformatory system:

> A regimental military organization of the prisoners with a band of music, swords [!] for the officers, and dummy guns for the rank and file of prisoners. The military membership should include all the able bodied prisoners. . . . The regular army tactics, drill, and daily dress parade should be observed.[3]

Unlike contemporary shock incarceration programs, Brockway's introduction of a military atmosphere into the American reformatory prison was done as much to aid in the management of the prison as it was to reform inmates. Because of changes in statutes limiting sale of the products of inmates' labor, Brockway and his successors had to find ways to occupy the prisoners' time. Idle hands and minds were (and still are) presumed to become involved in criminal behavior.

The military-style reformatory benefited, like today's boot camp, from the public's attitude toward what were thought to be the virtues of military training. Following the Civil War, the public had a strong appreciation of the military which carried over into criminal justice, especially with regard to imprisonment. It was assumed that since vast numbers of citizen-soldiers adapted themselves to the rigors of military discipline, "so could the criminal."[3]

The Elmira Reformatory regimen was meant to reform offenders by:

> the heroic crushing out of conceited individualism, and the subjection of their mental growth to the opposite conditions of compulsion, classification, and collective training.[6]

Today we refer, in softer language, to a boot camp's fostering of a spirit of discipline and *esprit de corps* among its inmates. Following World War I, public respect for soldiering and war-making skills waned. As it waned, so did the military organization and regimen of the American prison. Shock incarceration today owes its considerable appeal not to the presumed virtues of military training, but to its well-advertised harshness. Thus it is seen as a potentially effective punishment as we will see below.

Most shock incarceration programs are designed for a youthful, male, nonviolent, first-offender population. Some programs are open to women, but the number of beds for them is severely limited. It is likely that correctional officials, and the public, consider the deliberately harsh regimen in a boot camp to be inappropriate for women.

There are two primary goals of shock incarceration: relieving prison crowding and reducing recidivism. A third goal, not often stressed, is to provide another means of punishment. While boot camps seek to reach these goals without long-term confinement of their populations, they have a reputation, earned or not, for being "tough" on offenders. Thus, if some might argue that sentences to shock programs are lenient because they are relatively short in duration, others believe that an offender in a boot camp receives the "benefits" of a harsh regimen.

In this chapter we will examine in some detail the goals of shock incarceration programs, their characteristics and those of their populations, and the means they employ to reach their goals. Finally, we will try to determine what these programs have accomplished since the first one opened.

THE GOALS OF SHOCK INCARCERATION

One of the frequently stated goals of boot camps is to help a correctional system reduce **prison crowding.** This, of course, requires that sentence laws be modified so offenders can be sentenced to shock programs instead of prison. Another modification permits prison inmates to be released from prison to a boot camp. In either case, shock incarceration is supposed to have the effect of reducing the number of inmates in correctional institutions. Later, we will see if this goal is being achieved.

A second goal of boot camp sentences is to reduce **recidivism,** which, of course, is usually claimed as a goal of most sentences. It is expected that boot camp inmates will be shocked out of future criminality. In the section on evaluation we will see what research can tell us about how successful shock programs have been in achieving this objective.

The shock administered in a boot camp is anticipated to act as a specific deterrent to future criminality. In the words of MacKenzie and Souryal:

> Rooted in military basic training, these core components include military drill and ceremony, physical training, strict discipline, and physical labor. Is there any value to this regimented military routine in and of itself? Clearly, it is these elements of the program in addition to incarceration itself that are expected to serve as deterrents.[7]

Shock, however, is not the only road to this goal. Many boot camps include rehabilitation as an integral component of their programs. Rehabilitative programs may include drug and substance abuse counseling, employment assistance, education, and vocational training. Because most boot campers stay in the camps for relatively short periods, there are limited opportunities for these activities to be as effective as they might be in other correctional settings. Hence, it appears that shock incarceration

*T*he basic methods used by the boot camps are physical labor, strict discipline, physical training, and military drills and ceremony. This squad is on parade in the boot camp grounds.

relies most heavily on the shock of military discipline to produce a reduction in recidivism. The On the Job feature shows the daily schedule for boot campers in several New York state shock programs. These programs do provide for counseling as well as shock in the daily routine.

The Alabama Department of Corrections put forward a broad statement of the goals it has in mind for its shock incarceration:

> [B]oot camp will provide not only judicial control, rehabilitation, discipline, and a lower recidivism rate, but promises to "reorganize thought processes."[8]

A program that seeks to lower recidivism levels, rehabilitate, and reorganize offender thought processes carries a heavy load.

There are fundamental questions to be asked about shock incarceration and the methods employed to achieve its objectives. Is there any correctional value in the highly regimented military routine in and of itself? A second question addresses the attempt to integrate rehabilitation and a harsh, shocking military-style experience. A third question asks whether a regimen originally designed to train young men for military combat roles is appropriate when dealing with offenders who will never enter the military and are expected to leave boot camps and lead peaceful civilian lives.

We encourage readers to look for answers to these questions. At this point, we can say that among the expectations many hold for boot camps is that

> . . . the experience of leading a structured, day-to-day routine may have some beneficial by-products. Political support for these programs seems, in part, to be based on the idea that the regimented lifestyle and discipline of the boot camp will be transferred to life on the outside.[9]

In a report prepared for the National Institute of Justice, James Austin and his associates summarized the expectations many hold for shock incarceration:[10]

ON THE JOB

DAILY SCHEDULE FOR OFFENDERS IN NEW YORK
SHOCK INCARCERATION FACILITIES

A.M.

5:30	Wake up and standing count
5:45–6:30	Calisthenics and drill
6:30–7:00	Run
7:00–8:00	Mandatory breakfast/cleanup
8:15	Standing count and company formation
8:30–11:55	Work/school schedules

P.M.

12:00–12:30	Mandatory lunch and standing count
12:30–3:30	Afternoon work/school schedule
3:30–4:00	Shower
4:00–4:45	Network community meeting
4:45–5:45	Mandatory dinner, prepare for evening
6:00–9:00	School, group counseling, drug counseling, prerelease counseling, decision-making classes
8:00	Count while in programs
9:15–9:30	Squad bay, prepare for bed
9:30	Standing count, lights out

SOURCE: Cherie L. Clark, David W. Aziz, and Doris L. Mackenzie, *Shock Incarceration in New York: Focus on Treatment* (Washington D.C.: National Institute of Justice, August 1994).

1. Many youthful first offenders will respond positively to a short intense shock, followed by intensive supervision probation.
2. Instilling military-style discipline will build inmate self-discipline and physical conditioning, these being missing in their lives prior to conviction.
3. With drug counseling, educational, and vocational training, these offenders will develop positive and law-abiding values.
4. Costs will be less than with ordinary incarceration. One might well ask whether, if the criminal justice system were to provide the drug counseling, education, and vocational training expected to be delivered under shock conditions, would boot camps be necessary? Why couldn't probation sentences, for example, deliver these treatment services?

One of the major criticisms of shock incarceration is that it is oriented too far in the direction of military training. One critic claims that "a boot camp . . . can only produce soldiers without a company to join"[11] once they are released.

CHARACTERISTICS OF BOOT CAMPS AND THEIR INMATES

There is some disagreement as to just what constitutes a **boot camp** or shock incarceration program. In a recent nationwide survey, Blair Bourque listed the characteristics of boot camps in both state and federal systems. We show this list in Table 15.1.

Characteristics of Boot Programs   TABLE 15.1

	FEDERAL AND STATE[1] (n = 35)	LOCAL (n = 8)	JUVENILE (n = 9)
YEAR OPENED			
Prior to 1988	7	0	0
1988–1990	13	2	0
1991–1993	14	6	6
1994	1	0	3
CAPACITY[2]			
Male	8,678	806	455
Female	626	102	0
TOTAL CAPACITY	9,304	908	455
MINIMUM LENGTH OF RESIDENTIAL BOOT CAMP			
< 3 months	2	4	1
3 months	15	2	2
4 months	9	0	5
6 months	9	2	1

[1] There were 32 states known to operate boot camps at the time of the study. Since both Georgia and Oklahoma operate two different types of boot camps, they are treated separately in the table.

[2] When a program did not break out male and female capacity, it was counted as being male. Therefore, the female capacities may be undercounted.

SOURCE: Blair B. Bourque, Mei Han, and Sarah M. Hill, "A National Survey of Aftercare: Provisions for Boot Camp Graduates," *Research in Brief* (Washington, D.C.: National Institute of Justice), p. 3.

One of the leading authorities on shock incarceration, Doris MacKenzie, assembled a set of common features of boot camps based on an examination of several studies of programs throughout the country.

Programs were considered to be shock incarceration only if they:

1. were considered an alternative to a longer term in prison;
2. had a boot camp atmosphere, with strict rules and discipline;
3. required offenders to participate in military drills and physical training; and
4. separated offenders in the program from other prison inmates.[12]

Even with MacKenzie's synthesis, we still see an enormous range of styles and programs. As she pointed out, boot camps offer varying degrees of military discipline, physical exercise, work, and counseling. There is no uniformity in program content.

In addition to the common features described by MacKenzie and others, boot camp programs generally are divided into a number of graduated stages. Usually, the first stage is one in which campers are subjected to "confrontation" tactics by staff and are required to participate in military drill, strenuous physical exercises, and hard labor. A second stage often provides counseling and preparation for release. Where

At any time for whatever reason boot camp inmates may be asked to do physical exercises under the watchful eyes of their drill instructors.

shock programs have integrated intensive aftercare or parole supervision with a harsh in-camp program, the supervised release portion of a camper's experience becomes a final stage. In some ways, these stages in shock incarceration are reminiscent of the progressive or Irish reformatory systems, discussed in Chapter 6.

With regard to the degree of military training and discipline, empirical methodologies have been developed just to measure the amount of military atmosphere in a boot camp.[13] The military atmosphere variable is particularly important when it comes to evaluating boot camps' effectiveness in reaching their objectives.

Currently, there are boot camps in thirty-two states. Three camps are operated by the federal government. Table 15.2 shows the eligibility criteria in general use to select boot campers.

As we can see from this table most states severely limit offender participation in their shock incarceration facilities. The vast majority of participants are male, youthful first offenders. Interestingly, some programs are available for violent offenders. This may well cause a problem when trying to evaluate shock incarceration since outcome may be influenced by an inmate population that is not homogeneous. We will take up this issue later when we discuss research designed to evaluate the performance of boot camps and their inmates.

At lease four models of shock incarceration facilities are currently in operation:

1. *Prison boot camps.* These camps are set up to deal with offenders sentenced to and incarcerated in prisons. Sometimes the camp is located outside the perimeter of the prison. Other camps are located within the institution, but are physically separated from ordinary prison units. Selection of inmates for shock incarceration is made by the state or local corrections department. Usually, inmates volunteer for the shock placement.

Eligibility Criteria for Boot Camps · TABLE 15.2

ELIGIBILITY REQUIREMENTS	FEDERAL AND STATE (N = 35)	LOCAL (N = 8)	JUVENILE (N = 9)
MAXIMUM AGE			NA[1]
25 or under	7	3	
26–30	8	1	
31–35	7	0	
36–40	3	0	
No limit	10[2]	4	
Maximum sentence			NA[1]
Between 1 and 4 years	9	1	
Between 5 and 10 years	15	1	
Other[3]	11	6	
Requirement that enrollment be voluntary[4]	27	6	3
Exclude those with			
Prior incarceration	23	1	0
Violent crimes	33	6	3

[1] For juvenile programs the maximum age is the age of juvenile court jurisdiction, typically age 17. Minimum ages for these programs are 14 for six programs, 12 for one, 13 for one, and 16 for one. Sentence requirements do no apply.

[2] Includes the federal program, which does not exclude older offenders but does give priority to offenders under age 36, and the Michigan program, which only accepts *probationers* under age 26 but accepts *inmates* of any age.

[3] Includes programs with sentences greater than 10 years and those with no maximums.

[4] Does not include two programs (Arizona and Hidalgo County, Texas) that do not have voluntary requirements but most of the participants do volunteer.

SOURCE: Bourque, et al., "A National Survey of Aftercare: Provisions for Boot Camp Graduates," p. 4.

2. *Special prison shock incarceration.* These programs are designed for disruptive inmates. The shock, it is hoped, will correct the inmate, producing a more compliant prisoner.

3. *Probation boot camps.* Probationers are sentenced to a portion of the probation term to be served in a boot camp.

4. *Probation detention camps.* Probation violators are assigned to a boot camp because of one or more violations of the terms of their probation.

Although most of the attention given shock incarceration has been paid to activities at the state level, many local jurisdictions have entered the field by establishing jail boot camps, as shown in Table 15.2. A major survey conducted in 1992 (200 respondents) found that all the jail camps were run by local sheriffs or correctional departments.[14] The characteristics of these camps were quite similar to those of state-level programs. For example,

The average length of stay of campers was 2–4 months.

- All jurisdictions indicated that the ideal program coupled a military-like regimen with counseling, drug programs, employment assistance, education, and vocational programs.
- Campers were usually younger than other jail inmates (age 25 and younger; many were first offenders with no history of violence or drug abuse, but the survey found no consistency.
- Only four out of the 200 programs responding had camps for women.

The selection process fell into three types: (1) The sentencing court recommends an offender for shock incarceration, and the local staff screens candidates and recommends a sentence to the court. (2) Judges directly sentence to a camp. (3) Jail staff directly admit offenders to a boot camp program without a judicial order. Upon completion or failure to complete a program, offenders typically are referred to court for disposition (discharge, probation, resentence).

The Los Angeles jail program (Regimented Inmate Diversion program, or RID), now discontinued, was found by the survey to have a comprehensive program, unlike other local and state programs. The major features of the RID program were:

1. 90 days' shock incarceration, followed by 90 days' "intensive aftercare supervision."
2. Mandatory participation in education, vocational, and drug counseling programs.
3. Participants were mainly youthful minority males with little formal education and "fairly substantial prior criminal and drug involvements."[15]

One of the many different models of shock incarceration is specifically designed, not for the first offender, nor the youthful nonviolent offender, but for the prison's problem or disruptive inmate:

*T*his drill sergeant demonstrates an example of the commonly employed "in your face" confrontation tactic at a shock incarceration facility.

Valdosta (GA) is not a typical correctional facility. From its Intensive Therapeutic Program (ITP) to its mental health program to the general population dormitories, the same theme resounds: discipline, self-pride, uniformity. This is the code of ethics for the entire institution.[16]

The ITP is a 30-day boot-camp program for "hardened" offenders, begun in 1990. Different from other boot camps, it was conceived as a method to reduce the rate and severity of disciplinary infractions in the Valdosta Correctional Institution.

Selection of inmates for this program is via the institution's classification committee. Those selected are "the most troubled inmates, the ones the committee thinks would benefit most from the self-control and discipline ITP teaches."[17]

> During the first few days the inmate is in the program, administrative and security staff strongly reinforce the program's standards and rules, sometimes speaking roughly to the inmate. The purpose of this confrontational treatment is to break down the inmate's defenses to pave the way for rebuilding the person's ego in positive ways.[18]

Here we have, through the method of "rebuilding the person's ego," an echo from the past: Zebulon Brockway's attempt to "crush the conceited individualism" in his reformatory's population.[*]

Participants are involved in a daily routine that includes educational and vocational classes, military drill, drug and other counseling. In order to maximize the military atmosphere of the program, the ITP warden has sent some camp officers to the Marine Corps training center in Virginia. The program also runs classes in "positive mental attitude" and hygiene.

After one year, the program was expanded to include mentally ill inmates who were not on medication and had not been hospitalized in the past year. Even though there is only impressionistic data available for any conclusions regarding ITP's effectiveness, its supporters report that it is "undoubtedly meeting its mission. . . . It will have a positive impact on disruptive inmates. It is also having a positive impact on the institutional environment. . . ."[19] The report also concluded that inmate attacks on staff and other prisoners have decreased, as have inmate grievances.

Shaw and MacKenzie report on a Louisiana shock program that is organized, as many boot camp programs are, in two stages. The first stage is a strict military environment located in a medium security prison, lasting between 90 and 180 days. During this stage, inmates are involved in a program that includes military discipline, ceremonial rituals, and physical training. The expectation is that "this training will instill discipline in offenders' lives and encourage them to take responsibility for their actions."

The second stage is a period of intensive parole supervision. Parolees must meet all the conditions of regular parole, plus:

1. Multiple unscheduled weekly contacts with parole officers.
2. Random drug use screening (at parolees' expense).
3. A severe curfew, requiring parolees to be home by 8 P.M.
4. Completion of at least 100 hours of community service.[21]

This Louisiana program is an example of one model of shock incarceration that incorporates intensive community supervision of offenders once they have experienced the shock of a boot camp atmosphere. Programs of this type have tried to answer a frequent critical question raised about the worth of shock in reducing recidivism: What

---

[*]See the discussion of Brockway's reformatory discipline at p. 337 above.

happens after the shock has been administered? In the next section on evaluation of boot camps, we will discuss how this question has been answered.

One final shock program example we include here is New York State's program,[22] operating four camps with a total inmate capacity of 1,570 offenders. Unlike many other programs, it includes one for women (with bed space for 180 offenders). New York's shock incarceration is guided by two statutorily defined goals:

1. To treat and release State prisoners earlier than their court-mandated minimum [sentences] without endangering public safety;
2. To reduce the need for prison bedspace.[23]

Like other boot camps we have discussed, the New York program is a two-stage operation. Each stage lasts six months. The first stage is an "intensive" period of incarceration. This is followed by "intensive community supervision."[24] In this regard, the New York program provides for a considerably longer experience than most other shock programs.

Each camper works a total of 650 hours of "hard work" before leaving the first stage.[25] Boot camp inmates perform many hours of community service for "cash-strapped" communities in locales that surround the camps. In 1993, the campers performed a total of 1.3 million hours of community service.[26] Not only does this represent a type of offender restitution,[27] it also results in significant cost savings for the affected communities.

Like some other shock incarceration settings, the treatment for drug and alcohol abusers in New York camps is based on the twelve-step principles of Alcoholics Anonymous and Narcotics Anonymous. As the daily schedule in Table 15.1 indicates, considerable portions of each day are spent in treatment and educational activities. These treatment efforts continue in the second stage of intensive supervision in the community.

EVALUATION OF SHOCK INCARCERATION PERFORMANCE

We have pointed out repeatedly in earlier chapters that evaluating correctional strategies is a complicated business. We need to ask a number of questions and not simply inquire, "Is this program effective?" Because the boot camp movement appears to be so popular with the American public and political leaders, and because so much is expected of shock incarceration, we will take a good look at the research literature.

According to Feeley and Simon, the current enthusiasm for boot camps is another example of an aggregate approach, lumping all campers together as needing a strong dose of discipline.[28] Thus, boot camp populations often are heterogeneous collections of offenders which makes evaluation research difficult. Feeley and Simon conclude that even though rehabilitative programming frequently is reported to be part of many boot camp regimens, these programs seem not to be particularly intensive. It would be impossible to do so given the short time that boot campers are under shock incarceration. In many instances, the lack of treatment while incarcerated is to some extent made up after offenders are released and are required to be under intensive community supervision. This, however, is not always the case.

It is difficult for many to believe that shock incarceration has any long-lasting positive results. Whether results are measured in terms of recidivism or attitudinal or psychological change, shock incarceration seems to be of little correctional value, especially in the longterm. However, let's see what the research literature can tell us.

*B*oot camp inmates spend a portion of each day on marching and tasks that the drill sergeants initiate. Note the lists of shock incarceration goals in both English and Spanish.

In this section we will evaluate whether shock incarceration (a) lowers recidivism rates; (b) reduces prison populations; (c) costs less than other sanctions, especially ordinary incarceration; and (d) produces other benefits that may relate to the postrelease behavior of boot campers.

Shock Incarceration and Recidivism

At the outset, we must recognize that there is relatively little reported research that will allow us to make any but the most tentative observations about recidivism rates of those who complete boot camp programs. In addition to this precautionary note, we need to be aware that shock incarceration is so new in the corrections field that our tentative conclusions are not very helpful in judging whether shock incarceration has any long-lasting affect on recidivism. Finally, as we indicated in earlier chapters, recidivism is subject to a number of different definitions and evaluation criteria.

A study of recidivism of offenders who went through a Louisiana shock incarceration program revealed mixed results.[29] The Louisiana program, called IMPACT (Intensive Motivational Program of Alternative Correctional Treatment), is located in a larger prison, but segregated from the general population. The Louisiana evaluation sought to determine whether the IMPACT experience affected technical violations occurring during the aftercare supervisory period, and the extent to which the program altered recidivism.

Specifically, the research tried to answer two questions: How well did "drug-involved" offenders do in the shock program? How well did shock graduates do in the community compared with other offenders who were on regular parole and probation? As we have said in numerous earlier chapters, measuring the success of any correctional activity is a complicated matter involving a number of possible evaluation criteria. In the Louisiana study, the criteria used were positive drug tests, drug-related arrests, any arrests, reincarceration, and revocation from probation or parole.

This study examined shock offenders' performance during a community supervision period and compared it to the performance of probationers and parolees who did not have a shock incarceration experience. The probationers had not served any time in prison. The parolees in the comparison group had been incarcerated in an ordinary prison setting.

IMPACT is a two-stage program: incarceration in a boot camp "prison" with hard labor, military drill, and physical conditioning, followed by **intensive aftercare supervision** in the community. Findings included the following:

- Arrest and revocation for technical violation for shock subjects were higher than for the other two groups.
- Arrests for new crimes and convictions were higher for the subjects not in the shock program.
- Shock graduates and dropouts were not significantly different in their failure rates.

There is some difficulty in interpreting these results. Boot camp graduates were released from incarceration under intensive supervision by parole officers, while the control groups were not. Using shock to reduce overcrowded prisons is not achieved when revocations for technical violations increase. "The net effect is that the same proportion of shock offenders as of probationers are returned to prison."[30] This, in turn, leads to a question as to what intensive supervision conditions ought to be and what their violation means.

The researchers state that "this research raises questions about why special conditions of parole are set and how the system should respond."[31] We noted in the chapters on probation and parole that establishing strict rules and conditions for aftercare will almost certainly lead to increased rates of violations. Furthermore, we must inquire whether these rules and conditions are meaningfully related to the corrections process.

According to MacKenzie, "Boot camp recidivism rates are approximately the same as those of comparison groups who serve a longer period of time in a traditional prison or who serve time on probation."[32] She points out that reintegrating shock graduates into the community "may present such overwhelming difficulties . . . that positive changes during incarceration cannot be sustained."[33]

We must carefully consider this statement. Confining inmates in a severe military environment for several months and then releasing them into their precamp communities, which are usually the very antithesis of military communities, could pose insurmountable adjustment difficulties. Thus, many advocates of shock incarceration insist on intensive aftercare supervision. However, intensive supervision uncovers violations at a greater rate than ordinary supervision. Intensive supervision, however, is not always provided, as we can see in Table 15.3, which summarizes the results of a national survey of camps. The table shows the aftercare conditions established when the programs were opened. In Table 15.4 we find a summary of aftercare supervision requirements implemented after programs had been in operation. Some programs, as we can see, did move in the direction of more intensive and "special" aftercare supervision.

There is a very important question with respect to evaluations of boot camp performance that has not yet been answered. Does the "boot camp atmosphere enhance the effect of treatment or [would] an intensive treatment program alone . . . have the same effect?"[34]

Supervision Initially Required by Boot Camp Programs			TABLE 15.3
	FEDERAL/STATE PROGRAMS (n = 35)	LOCAL PROGRAMS (n = 8)[1]	JUVENILE PROGRAMS (n = 9)
Release all or majority of graduates to intensive supervision or day treatment	AZ[2], CA, GA—1, GA—P, IL, KS, LA, MD, MA, MI, NM, NH, NY, OH, OK—RID, PA, WI, FEDERAL	NY—Nassau County NY—Riker's Island TX—Travis TX—Harris	CA—LEAD FL—Leon County FL—Manatee County FL—Martin County FL—Pinellas NY—South Kortwright OH—Cuyahoga County
	18	4	7
Release graduates to highest supervision level available in graduate's county	KY, OR		
	2	0	0
Release graduates to both intensive and standard supervision	CO, ID, MS, MT, NC, OK—SIP, TN, VA	MI—Pontiac TX—Hidalgo	
	8	2	0
Release majority of graduates to standard supervision	AL, AR, FL, NV, SC, TX, WY	TX—Brazos	AL—Mobile CO—Golden
	7	1	2

[1] There is no community supervision required for those released from the Santa Clara, California, program.
[2] Applies to county probationers only. Shock releasees are usually placed in standard supervision.
SOURCE: Bourque, et al., "A National Survey of Aftercare: Provisions for Boot Camp Graduates," p. 11.

At this point, no state has reported a statistically significant difference in recidivism when boot camp graduates' performance is compared to that of similar offenders serving different types of sentences.[35]

A recent study reported by MacKenzie and her colleagues examined recidivism rates in eight boot camp states.[36] Using arrests and revocations to compare boot camp graduates to camp dropouts, parolees, and probationers, they found no consistent pattern in outcome. Variations in "failure" rates seemed to depend on the availability of treatment services within boot camp–structured programs. The military components in shock incarceration alone had no recidivism-reducing value: "We conclude that these components in and of themselves do not reduce recidivism of participating offenders."[37]

More significantly, Georgia, the state that exhibited the poorest failure rate among boot campers, was a state whose boot camp program "stands out as the one program that has little treatment in the daily schedule of activities."[38]

An analysis of reported studies of recidivism by Mark Osler led him to offer some pessimistic conclusions:

Some of the earliest statistics on recidivism have hardly been clothed in success and have led to serious questioning of the very idea of boot camp. The oldest program in the country, in

TABLE 15.4   Special Boot Camp Aftercare Programs and Requirements

	FEDERAL/STATE PROGRAMS (n = 35)[1]	LOCAL PROGRAMS (n = 8)	JUVENILE PROGRAMS (n = 9)	TOTALS
No special requirements or programming for boot camp graduates specified	AL, AR, CO, FL,[2] GA—I,[3] ID, MS, NV, NC, OK—SIP, SC, TX, WI, WY	CA—Santa Clara MI—Pontiac TX—Brazos County	CO—Golden	
	14	3	1	18
Aftercare regimen specified, but no separate program for boot camp graduates	CA, GA—P, IL, KS, KY, LA, MA, MT, OK—RID,[3] OR, PA, TN, VA, FEDERAL	NY—Nassau NY—Riker's Island	GA—Lead FL—Manatee County FL—Martin County FL—Pinellas County FL—Leon County	
	14	2	5	21
Aftercare program designed and operated exclusively for boot camp graduates	AZ—Maricopa County MD—Baltimore MI MN—St. Paul NH NY—New York City OH	TX—Travis TX—Hidalgo TX—Harris County	AL—Mobile OH—Cuyahoga County NY—South Kortwright	
	7	3	3	13

[1] Georgia and Oklahoma operate two different types of programs: George Inmate (GA—I) and George Probation (GA—P); and Oklahoma Regimented Inmate Discipline (OK—RID) and Oklahoma Shock Incarceration (OK—SIP).
[2] Beginning July 1995, boot camp graduates will be required to spend 4–6 months in community residential centers before they are released to the community.
[3] For inmates on community custody only; inmates with delayed incarceration sentences are resentenced at the conclusion of boot camp.
SOURCE: Bourque, et al., "A National Survey of Aftercare: Provisions for Boot Camp Graduates," p. 5.

Oklahoma,* has been disappointing in terms of return rates: A Department of Corrections analysis of similar convicts sentenced to boot camp and traditional incarceration showed that after 29 months nearly half of the boot camp graduates had returned to prison. In contrast, only 28 percent of the traditionally incarcerated control group had been recommitted . . . .[39]

Osler's review of the research literature also found that Georgia's boot camp program, one of the most frequently applauded shock programs, had similarly disappointing results. After a three-year follow-up study, Osler determined that there was "little difference in recidivism rates between those . . . sent to boot camp and those who had received traditional incarceration."[40] As we saw above, more recent research has confirmed Osler's conclusion. Furthermore, the Georgia research found that teenage boot campers had a worse record of recidivism than that observed for similar offenders receiving more traditional sentences.

---

*In agreement with most sources, we have accepted Georgia as the state with the first boot camp.

Another review of evaluation research findings arrived at comparable disappointing results.[41] Pointing out that the etiology of criminal behavior includes social and economic conditions that boot camps are unlikely to influence, the review concluded that "frightening or 'discipline drilling' people who have resorted to crime will not have a long-term deterrent effect if these people cannot get satisfaction through legitimate alternatives in society."[42]

Somewhat more encouraging results were found when Burns and Vito examined the Alabama boot camp program.[43] The Alabama program is sightly different from some of those reviewed by other researchers. It is organized as a three-phase program, each phase lasting 30 days. In the first phase, called confrontation, campers are confronted by their drill instructors and other staff with the realities of their criminality and their personal responsibility for it. Phase two incorporates a **twelve-step program** based on Alcoholics Anonymous and Narcotics Anonymous principles. The third 30-day phase is a prerelease period during which the inmate is supposed to work through the problems to be encountered as he is returned to the community.

After one year of operation, the conclusion reached regarding recidivism was that the program did not produce significantly better results than other programs, but "it can save money and reduce prison crowding."[44] Thus, the researchers argue that it should be continued. This conclusion, that shock incarceration does not perform any better than other sanctions in reducing recidivism, but should be continued (and expanded) because of its other benefits, is a recurring theme in the literature on shock incarceration.

From the studies we have examined, it is quite clear that if shock incarceration is to be effective in reducing recidivism, graduates of boot camps must be followed up closely with aftercare counseling. A recent national survey of the performance of boot camp graduates concluded that "[recidivism rates have not declined . . . partly as a result of inadequate aftercare."[45] The inadequacy of aftercare services was particularly noticeable with respect to substance abusers. Here the researchers found that "few [shock facilities] had developed formal links to the community. Many released offenders to traditional probation or parole supervision."[46] Often, this traditional supervision was not equipped to deal with these offenders.

Shock Incarceration and Prison Crowding

As we noted at the beginning of the chapter, one of the major goals of shock incarceration is to provide an alternative to imprisonment that will substantially reduce prison crowding. This goal can be achieved if offenders who otherwise would be inmates in correctional institutions are, instead, boot campers. Further, if offenders assigned to shock incarceration complete boot camps satisfactorily and are not subsequently incarcerated, then the shock experience will have the desired effect on prison crowding.

On the other hand, if offenders are sentenced to shock programs who would not under ordinary circumstances be incarcerated, the impact on prison crowding would be minimal, if any at all. This possibility is a very real one because of the tendency to be **widening the net** whenever a new correctional strategy comes on line. Further, if offenders drop out of shock programs and end up in prison, then they will contribute to the crowding problem. Thus, we need to examine carefully **graduation rates** of boot campers before arriving at any conclusions. Finally, should shock incarceration graduates violate their aftercare conditions in large numbers and end up in prison, the crowding of these institutions will be exacerbated.

The net widening effect was investigated by Burns and Vito in their study of Alabama's boot camp program. Comparing three groups of offenders, boot campers, probationers, and an incarcerated group, they concluded that there was no net widening:

> Persons sentenced to shock incarceration . . . were young, first-time offenders with no prior drug history or personally identified drug problem. The boot campers fit the description of the target population set by the statute. They were first-time nonviolent offenders . . . . Therefore, if the boot camp program had not been in operation, they would have been sent to prison.[48]

Burns and Vito also reported that the 720 total boot camp beds made available by the program permitted the state prison system to admit this number of inmates housed in local jails until cell space was opened for them, thus reducing crowding at the local level.

Looking at the fact that not all boot campers complete (graduate) shock incarceration and thus are transferred to prison, the study found that a 25 percent "washout" rate was not excessive. That is, boot camp failures would not contribute to the prison population explosion.[49]

A 1989 survey of published boot camp data, however, casts some doubt on Burns and Vito's conclusions.[50] According to this survey, "about half the inmates selected for these programs complete them. Their return rates to prison are not better than the national average for most programs over a three-year followup period."

More to the point is the net widening the survey found in the Florida shock incarceration program: "Very few of the boot camp offenders in Florida have been tried on probation, and of those who have been, far fewer have violated community control . . . ."[51] The state targeted for the shock experience those offenders at the low end of the risk scale: youthful, nonviolent offenders who had never been incarcerated. Prior to the introduction of the boot camp sanction, these offenders almost certainly would have been placed on probation, thus not adding to the prison population.[52]

Doris MacKenzie also warns that at least some state and local criminal justice officials see shock incarceration as a "promising approach for controlling offenders who would otherwise be sentenced to probation."[53] If she is correct, and the literature suggests she is, then there may be no noticeable reduction in prison populations to be achieved through the boot camp movement.

Finally, let us look at the New York state shock incarceration program. In the literature this program is generally reviewed favorably for its incorporation of meaningful treatment modalities and for the relatively lengthy period campers are involved. We have already seen that a good portion of the New York program involves heavy doses of military drill, physical conditioning, and hard work. The treatment elements of the program include drug and alcohol abuse counseling and academic education classes (at least 12 hours each week). These treatment elements take up 41 percent of the total program offered the campers.

The aftercare element is particularly intensive. The parole caseload is 38 shock graduates in each caseload, managed by two probation officers. In addition, boot camp graduates have "priority access to community services . . . , and increased employment opportunities, relapse prevention counseling."[54]

As of September 1993, 8,842 graduated from shock incarceration facilities (5,331 failed to graduate).[55] How well did these graduates do? In the report released by the National Institute of Justice, we find the following results:

- 45 percent of the graduates increased their reading scores, many increasing these scores by two or more grade levels.

61 percent increased their math scores, half of whom went up by at least two levels.

Based on follow-up research at 12,- 24- and 36-month intervals following graduation, campers showed the following return-to-prison rates when compared with groups of regular parolees and shock participants who did not graduate:

At 12- and 24-month intervals, shock graduates had "significantly lower return rates" than offenders in the other groups.[56]

After 36 months, the rate of return-to-prison was lower for the shock graduates, but the "differences are only significant between the program graduates" and those parolees who had been considered for boot camps but did not enter them.[57]

The authors of the report caution us not to read too much into the findings because the research methodology could not fully differentiate the effects of preexisting differences among the subjects, and because "the research does not untangle the effects of the military atmosphere, the rehabilitation aspects of the program, and the intensive supervision. Any or all of these components . . . could affect the return-to-prison rates."[58] Considerably more research on the New York program and others throughout the country is needed to "untangle" the complex of variables that may influence the outcome of shock incarceration for its graduates.

Cost-Effective Alternative to Ordinary Incarceration

We would expect to be able to measure the **cost effectiveness** of shock incarceration without too much difficulty. Such is not the case, however. Clearly, it is possible to calculate the daily, monthly, and annual costs per inmate in a boot camp. We know that these costs will be greater for more intensive and multifaceted shock programs. Delivering only military discipline, physical exercise, and hard work will cost less than adding drug counseling, educational, and vocational elements to the boot camp. However, we also need to compare shock costs with the costs of other correctional measures.

This comparison cannot be made simply on the basis of per-inmate costs for shock incarcerees versus the costs of ordinary imprisonment. We have to compute such related cost factors as length of confinement and the costs of aftercare supervision. We know from our previous discussion that aftercare, when provided, is frequently much more intensive for boot camp graduates than it is for regular parolees and probationers. Boot camp dropout rates also must be added into the cost picture if we are to arrive at a meaningful comparison. The net-widening problem also contributes to increases in expenses for offenders who should not be in boot camps. Now we look at what has been learned about the costs of shock incarceration as compared with other correctional sentences.

A majority of reports that have examined shock incarceration for its cost benefits suggest that it can make a significant savings over ordinary incarceration. An evaluation of the New York shock program described earlier in this chapter concluded that it had "saved $305 million in custody, care, and capital construction costs."[59] The authors of the study point out that these savings are not quite as significant as they seem because the added costs of aftercare supervision, which is very intense, are not included in the Department of Correctional Services estimate.

The Alabama boot camp program was also reported to show a substantial savings over ordinary imprisonment.[60] A major reason given for the savings was that boot camp significantly reduces the time offenders are in confinement. While the per diem cost of shock incarceration might not be much different than that for inmates in the ordinary Alabama correctional facility, the reduced time in confinement makes the difference. As was the case with the New York program, one must also calculate the additional costs, if any, of aftercare supervision for boot camp graduates.

Dale Sechrest's review of several studies of shock incarceration programs concluded that "NIJ [National Institute of Justice] figures . . . simply do not support the notion that it costs less to operate these shock incarceration programs. Costs are at least the same."[61] Among the reasons Sechrest gives for this conclusion is that a number of shock facilities provide intense educational and counseling programs, while many prisons do not. In addition, a number of evaluations of boot camps make the point that offenders selected for them could well have been placed on ordinary probation, saving considerable sums of money.

Another major review of the literature on boot camps concluded that shock incarceration can and does make real savings.[62] The costs of operating a boot camp, this review found, are generally higher than prison operating costs. However, when sentence length comparisons are made, the usually shorter time a boot camper is in camp results in significant savings.

MacKenzie's survey also concluded that, as a general finding, boot camps appear to provide some savings in expenditures over ordinary incarceration.[63] Again, as noted above, we must be careful in making such statements to consider all the costs involved in providing shock programs, not just those associated with the day-to-day operating costs.

Another cost variable that is infrequently taken into account is that associated with pretrial detention of offenders who are candidates for jail boot camps. Austin's nationwide survey of jail shock incarceration found that the costs of boot camps will be more than ordinary confinement because of the added time offenders spend in detention while the selection precess weeds out those unsuitable for shock sentences.[64]

A recent examination of shock incarceration in terms of its cost savings (with regard both to reducing prison populations and the short-term period spent in boot camps) by Bourque, Han, and Hill concluded that "these programs can reduce prison overcrowding and costs because offenders spend less time [in them] than they would have served in prison."[65] Their conclusions about shock incarceration's impact on recidivism, however, were not so sanguine as we saw earlier.

Changes in Offender Attitudes and Behavior

Many critics of shock incarceration doubt that it can really effect changes in offender behavior and their attitudes toward society and toward those in authority. Some research has tried to get at what we might call the rehabilitative value of shock programs by examining certain behavioral and attitudinal dimensions that are assumed to be related to recidivism. In effect, this research examines what might be termed an "indirect check" on recidivism. That is, if a program produces positive changes in attitudes, we might conclude that it will also affect recidivism.

In a 1993 study of the Harris County, Texas, boot camp program, the investigators looked specifically for attitudinal changes in 389 camp participants.[66] This program, known by its acronym CRIPP (Courts Regimented Intensive Probation Program), is a 90-day shock incarceration experience for young felony offenders sentenced to probation. Included in CRIPP, in addition to the typical military atmosphere, are vocational services, physical conditioning, and social skills development counseling.

Following release, graduates are required to undergo a 90- day period of graduated supervision by probation officers. That is, at three-month intervals, supervisory contacts are reduced from daily to weekly.

The study questioned campers in several attitude areas, including attitudes toward camp staff, alcohol and drug counseling, AIDS education and counseling, the camp as a setting for punishment and rehabilitation, family and friends, and, finally, attitudes about their ability to cope with their problems.[67]

Using a before-and-after research design, the researchers concluded that "our findings do reveal a positive attitudinal change among a population of boot camp participants completing the . . . CRIPP program," and that this change "may potentially shape the likelihood of future criminality."[68]

The authors of this research report clearly state that they did not set out to measure recidivism. We may suggest that they set out to assess indirectly CRIPP's impact on recidivism, with the assumption that changes in the measured areas will be correlated with future criminality.

They also point out that, absent intensive, "quality" aftercare in the community, "boot camp participation alone will likely fail—as have similar correctional treatment programs—as a solution to reforming offenders."[69]

An often cited review of boot camp performance in rehabilitating offenders by Morash and Rucker casts doubt on the possibility that shock incarceration can produce the kinds of attitudinal changes described above:

> [T]he boot camp model is unlikely to provide a panacea for the needs of rehabilitation . . . [and] whether the point is to provide rehabilitation, to deter, or to divert people from prison, alternatives other than boot camps should be given careful consideration.[70]

James Shaw and Doris MacKenzie's survey of shock incarceration around the nation, which we discussed in an earlier section echoed Morash and Rucker's negative conclusion: "There is no evidence to support the notion that boot camp in and of itself is adequate as a treatment modality."[71] They stress that it is unrealistic to expect significant, positive, long-range change in boot camp graduates' behavior, given the paucity of treatment programs in these facilities and the brief period of the campers' exposure to them. Agreeing with the Morash and Rucker results, however, MacKenzie, in another report, did find that shock graduates were excited and supportive of boot camp, and that "to our knowledge it is very unusual for releasees from regular prison to feel their time in prison has been valuable."[72]

Because much is expected from shock incarceration sentences in the nation's war against drugs, we conclude this section with a strong warning from Shaw and MacKenzie following their examination of the results of a Louisiana boot camp program:

> . . . [T]here may be a tendency for policymakers to view boot camp as a treatment, that is it may be seen as a program capable of instilling within drug offenders the discipline or whatever else they are presumed to lack that "caused" them to become involved with drugs. Such a notion simply is not supported by this research.[73]

A recent published research study reported discouraging boot camp results, especially for those programs that rely almost exclusively on military discipline to "treat" offenders.[74] The report questioned whether military discipline had any correctional value at all in the eight states studied. The authors called for future research to investigate to what extent "programs similar to the boot camps but without the basic training model would reduce recidivism more or less than the boot camps."[75] Their final discussion of their results asks the question, "Does the military atmosphere add any-thing above and beyond a short-term, quality prison treatment program?" Given the state of our knowledge of shock incarceration, we cannot answer this question.

SUMMARY

TOO MUCH IS EXPECTED of shock incarceration. Its goals include general and specific **deterrence**, rehabilitation, relief from the prison crowding crisis, significant reduc-tions in correctional expenditures, and deserved punishment of offenders. The last two goals, lowered costs and deserved punishment, seem to be highly attractive incen-tives to those who support the expanded use of the boot camp as an alternative to imprisonment, while still dealing harshly with offenders.

Boot camp models vary in a number of ways. Some are intended to provide a first taste of incarceration for younger offenders. Others are designed to handle proba-tioners, while still others are populated by disruptive prison inmates. Regardless of what kind of population a camp contains, all camps share a military-style atmosphere that includes rigorous physical conditioning, discipline, and hard labor. Many, but not all, shock incarceration facilities provide some counseling, educational, and voca-tional programming. Because all shock incarceration sentences provide for short-term periods of camp exposure, there is some question as to the effectiveness of these "treatment" components.

Most authorities agree that if shock incarceration is to be effective in reaching most of the goals set for it, much attention needs to be paid to what happens to boot campers after they have been shocked. That is, aftercare (call it parole or probation) must be as intense as the camp experience. Unfortunately, not all programs provide for intensive aftercare supervision. When this is provided, costs and violation rates increase.

Evaluations of shock incarceration have reported mixed results. It appears that boot camps can reduce the costs of corrections, primarily because the period of con-finement is quite short compared with ordinary prison sentences. To some extent the cost savings are diminished because of the tendency to widen the net by placing in shock incarceration offenders who in all probability are not candidates for imprison-ment. This tendency also means that significant prison population reductions are not realized.

There is little empirical support for shock incarceration as a rehabilitative agent or deterrent. Most evaluation research seems to show that recidivism is either unaffected by boot camp programs or is about the same as ordinary probation, parole, and imprisonment. Such disappointing results appear to many to mean that we need to devote more attention to other correctional strategies such as probation and parole in order to achieve the objectives set out for shock incarceration.

MacKenzie and her colleagues' final observation from their study of shock incar-ceration's performance in treating drug abusers best sums up the extremely difficult task shock programs face in turning around these offenders. While their comments were focused only on drug offenders and abusers, they are relevant to our interest in "changing" all offenders:

A final alternative explanation [for the disappointing results] may be that although com-munity treatment and/or aftercare are important for reintegration into the community, suc-cessful reintegration may be possible only for offenders who have made a significant change in their behavior before returning to the community.... [Other research] found that drug offenders, or abusers, were unlikely to change their consumption behaviors simply by going to prison. Given offenders' lack of change, ... increasing supervision and requiring drug tests can be expected to result in very high recidivism rates. Thus, while increasing treatment and consequently supervision levels may be seen as an integral part of utilizing community resources, one likely outcome will be increased recidivism rates.[76]

KEY CONCEPTS

boot camp
cost effectiveness
deterrence
graduation rates
intensive aftercare supervision

prison crowding
recidivism
shock incarceration
twelve-step program
widening the net

QUESTIONS FOR DISCUSSION

1. Looking at the results of a number of studies of shock incarceration that cast some doubt on its deterrent value, should legislators and policymakers spend more energy and resources on parole and probation instead of opening more boot camps?
2. Is there a contradiction between the method of harsh military-style discipline so characteristic of boot camps and the goal of producing law-abiding camp graduates? Fully explain your answer.
3. Discuss some of the key questions to be asked and methodological issues to be addressed in evaluating boot camp programs.
4. What are the major issues involved in providing an effective "aftershock" component in shock incarceration?

ENDNOTES

1. Doris Layton MacKenzie and Claire Souryal, *Multisite Evaluation of Shock Incarceration* (Washington, D.C.: U.S. Department of Justice, Office of Justice Programs, November 1994), p. 1.
2. Ibid., p. 5.
3. Zebulon R. Brockway, "The American Reformatory Prison System," in Joseph E. Jacoby, ed., *Classics of Criminology* (Chicago: Waveland Press, 2nd ed., 1994), p. 393.
4. Beverly A. Smith, "Military training at New York's Elmira Reformatory, 1888–1920," *Federal Probation* 52 (March 1988): 33–40.
5. MacKenzie and Souryal, *Multisite Evaluation of Shock Incarceration* p. 12.
6. Ibid., p. 35.
7. Ibid., p. 12.
8. Mark W. Osler, "Shock Incarceration: Hard Realities and Real Possibilities," *Federal Probation* 54 (March 1991): 34.
9. Ibid., p. 36.

10. James Austin, Michael Jones, and Melissa Bolyard, "The Growing Use of Jail Boot Camps: The Current State of the Art," *Research in Brief* (Washington, D.C.: National Institute of Justice, October 1993).

11. Malcolm M. Feeley and Jonathan Simon, "The New Penology: Notes on the Emerging Strategy of Corrections and Its Implications," *Criminology* 30 (1992): 464.

12. Doris L. MacKenzie, "Boot Camp Prisons: Components, Evaluations, and Empirical Issues," *Federal Probation* 54 (September 1990): 44–45.

13. John P. Keenan, R. Barry Ruback, and Judith G. Hadely, "Measuring the Military Atmosphere of Boot Camps," *Federal Probation* 58 (March 1994): 67–71.

14. Austin, et al., "The Growing Use of Jail Boot Camps."

15. Ibid., p. 5.

16. Richard Lewis, "Boot Camp Program Promotes Discipline, Improves Self-Esteem," *Corrections Today* 56 (August 1994): 30.

17. Ibid., p. 132.

18. Ibid.

19. Ibid.

20. James W. Shaw and Doris L. MacKenzie, "The One-Year Community Supervision Performance of Drug Offenders and Louisiana DOC-Identified Substance Abusers Graduating from Shock Incarceration," *Journal of Criminal Justice* 20 (1992): 503.

21. Ibid.

22. Cherie L. Clark, David W. Aziz, and Doris L. MacKenzie, *Shock Incarceration in New York: Focus on Treatment* (Washington, D.C.: National Institute of Justice, August 1994).

23. Ibid., p. 2.

24. Ibid., p. 3.

25. Ibid., p. 5.

26. Ibid.

27. Community service as restitution was taken up in Chapter 13.

28. Feeley and Simon, "The New Penology," p. 464.

29. Doris L. MacKenzie and James W. Shaw, "The Impact of Shock Incarceration on Technical Violations and New Criminal Activities," *Justice Quarterly* 10 (1993): 463–487.

30. Ibid., p. 485.

31. Ibid.

32. Doris MacKenzie, "Boot Camps Grow in Number and Scope," *National Institute of Justice Reports* (Washington, D.C.: National Institute of Justice, November/December 1990), p. 7.

33. Ibid., p. 8.

34. Ibid.

35. Doris L. MacKenzie and Claire Souryal, "Rehabilitation, Recidivism Reduction Outrank Punishment as Main Goals," *Corrections Today* 54 (October 1991): 92.

36. Doris MacKenzie, Robert Brame, David McDowell, and Claire Souryal, "Boot Camp Prisons and Recidivism in Eight States," *Criminology* 33 (1995): 327–357.

37. Ibid., p. 351.

38. Ibid., p. 352.

39. Osler, "Shock incarceration," p. 38.

40. Ibid.

41. Dale K. Sechrest, "Prison 'Boot Camps' Do Not Measure Up," *Federal Probation* 53 (September 1989): 15–20.

42. Ibid., pp. 19–20.

43. Jerald C. Burns and Gennaro F. Vito, "An Impact Analysis of the Alabama Boot Camp Program," *Federal Probation* 59 (March 1995): 63–67.

44. Ibid., p. 65.

45. Blair B. Bourque, Mei Han, and Sarah M. Hill, "A National Survey of Aftercare Provisions for Boot Camp Graduates," *Research in Brief* (Washington, D.C.: National Institute of Justice, May 1996), p. 1.

46. Ibid.

47. Ibid., pp. 64–65.

48. Ibid.

49. Ibid., p. 65.

50. Sechrest, "Prison 'Boot Camps' Do Not Measure Up."

51. Ibid., p. 16.

52. Ibid., pp. 17–18.

53. Doris L. MacKenzie, "'Boot Camp' Programs Grow in Number and Scope," *National Institute of Justice Reports* (Washington, D.C.: National Institute of Justice, November/December 1990), p. 6.

54. Clark, Ariz, and MacKenzie, *Shock Incarceration in New York*, pp. 6–7.

55. Ibid., p. 8.

56. Ibid., p. 10.

57. Ibid.

58. Ibid.

59. Ibid., p. 2.

60. Burns and Vito, "An Impact Analysis of the Alabama Boot Camp Program," p. 65.

61. Sechrest, "Prison Boot Camps Do Not Measure Up," p. 18.

62. Osler, "Shock Incarceration."

63. MacKenzie, "Boot Camp Prisons," pp. 49–50.

64. Austin, et al., "The Growing Use of Jail Boot Camps."

65. Bourque, Han, and Hill, "A National Survey of Aftercare Provisions for Boot Camp Graduates," p. 7.

66. Velmer S. Burton, Jr., et al., "A Study of Attitudinal Change Among Boot Camp Participants," *Federal Probation* 57 (September 1993): 46–52.

67. Ibid., p. 47.

68. Ibid., p. 51.

69. Ibid.

70. Merry Morash and Lila Rucker, "A Critical Look at the Idea of Boot Camp as a Correctional Reform," *Crime & Delinquency* 36 (1990): 218–219.

71. Shaw and MacKenzie, "The One-Year Community Supervision Performance . . .," p. 513.

72. MacKenzie, "Boot Camp Prisons," p. 51.

73. Ibid., pp. 51–52.

74. MacKenzie, et al., "Boot Camp Prisons and Recidivism in Eight States."

75. Ibid., p. 354.

76. Ibid., p. 515.

16

INTERMEDIATE SANCTIONS

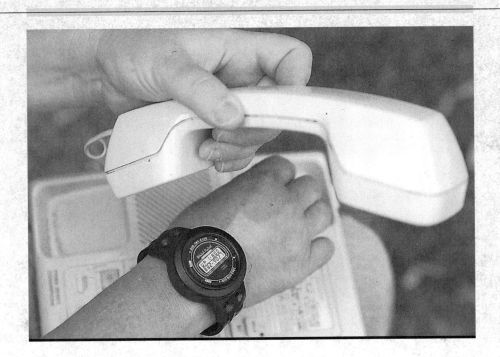

INTRODUCTION IN 1988, IN ADDISON COUNTY, Vermont, the Honorable Frances McCaffrey stunned an already cynical public when he [sic] imposed an innovative but controversial sentencing sanction on a convicted cocaine peddler who stood before him for punishment. The defendant, at 26, had been a student at Middlebury College, and was known on campus as the "pharmacist" in view of his drug dispensing capabilities. What made [him] unique was that [he] was the son of the 1984 Democratic Vice Presidential candidate, Geraldine Ferraro. . . . With his defense lawyers at his side, [he] was sentenced to serve 4 months of a one-to-five year suspended prison term under house arrest rather than behind bars.[1]

Home detention, also referred to as house arrest, is a relatively new criminal sanction that is considered to be intermediate between incarceration and various forms of conditional freedom such as probation. In the case of Ferraro's son, the sanction was perceived as a lenient one, handed down because of the status of the offender. As we will see throughout this chapter, as intermediate sanctions have evolved they have become more punitive and control oriented. They tend not to be lenient sanctions.

A 1990 book on the topic of intermediate sanctions by Norval Morris and Michael Tonry, entitled *Between Prison and Probation: Intermediate Punishments in a Rational Sentencing System*,[2] is aimed at building a rational sentencing system that makes major use of newer punishments. The title is a bit misleading. Intermediate sanctions should not be considered as simply falling somewhere between imprisonment and probation. The intermediate sanctions that we shall examine in this chapter are forms of probation, parole, diversion, and even incarceration. It would be more descriptive of this class of sanctions to characterize them as "enhanced."

In the introduction to their book, Morris and Tonry lay out the case for intermediate sanctions:

> At present, too many criminals are in prison and too few are the subjects of enforced controls in the community. We are both too lenient and too severe; too lenient with many on probation who should be subject to tighter controls in the community, and too severe with many in prison and jail who would present no serious threat if they were under control in the community.[3]

Later, in suggesting that there must be an array of sanctions that fall somewhere between probation and parole, they argue that these sanctions can and should be punitive as well as serving other goals. In their words, offenders should not be "spared punitive responses. . . . Large measures of coercion, and enforced diminution of freedom [are] entirely properly regarded as punishment."[4]

To Morris and Tonry, intermediate sanctions include intensive probation, fines, community service orders, "and a wide variety of treatments and controls to give bite and reality to intermediate punishments."[5] We saw in the last chapter that a number of community-based sanctions that retain some rehabilitative elements are, effectively, intermediate between incarceration and ordinary probation.

Sometimes intermediate sanctions are incorporated into a full-scale sentencing system. Such a system was endorsed by Michael Castle when, as governor of Delaware, he spelled out the reasons for and results of his state's sentencing commission reforms.[6] Addressing a National Institute of Justice conference on intermediate sanctions, Castle said,

> Any governor, mayor, or county executive can tell you that these remain politically and publicly sensitive issues. People expect government to protect them. They do not want government proposing programs that put unrehabilitated criminals back into their communities. The pressure they can bring to bear against these programs is difficult to overcome.
>
> * * * * *
>
> The average person in Delaware annually pays $1,000 in State personal income tax. It would take the total State tax collected from 15 Delaware residents to pay for just 1 prisoner for only 1 year. Tell people that and you not only get their attention and anger, but you get their interest in perhaps doing things differently.[7]

What has Delaware done to develop alternative sanctions? First, a set of prioritized objectives was promulgated: (a) remove violent offenders from the community; (b) restore victims to their precrime status; and (c) rehabilitate offenders.

The state established (by statute) the Sentencing Accountability Commission (SENTAC), which had a mandate to study intermediate sanctions. SENTAC produced a continuum of five levels of increasingly restrictive sanctions, which are shown in the Focus on the Law feature.

After two years, according to Governor Castle, the growth rate of the prison population "appears to be slowing, even though we are subject to the same crime trends as our neighbors."[8]

We now turn to a description of some of the more common intermediate sanctions that are popular with the public, legislators, and criminal justice system leaders,

FOCUS ON
THE LAW

DELAWARE'S COMPREHENSIVE SENTENCING SYSTEM.

Delaware has developed a sentencing system that gives judges a set of graduated responses to adult offenders. These responses are arranged in five levels of severity:

Level I: Lowest level (symbolic supervision).

Level II: Normal supervision 0–1 hour daily; weekly to monthly contacts.

Level III: Intensive supervision 1–8 hrs daily; employment and curfew checks; required treatment programs.

Level IV: Quasi-incarceration; supervision 9–24 hours daily in halfway houses; electronic monitored house arrest; residential drug treatment.

Level V: Full incarceration for the most serious offenders.

SOURCE: Michael N. Castle, "Alternative Sentencing: Selling It to the Public," National Institute of Justice, *Research in Brief* (Washington, D.C.: National Institute of Justice, September 1991), p. 4.

beginning with home detention coupled with electronic monitoring. Following this, we will examine intensive supervision sanctions and various monetary penalties.

HOME DETENTION

Home detention, sometimes referred to as house arrest or home confinement, is actually a range of increasingly restrictive sanctions, from the imposition of an evening curfew to home confinement during an offender's nonworking hours. Supervision to ensure compliance also ranges from personal contacts with a community supervision officer to 24-hour electronic surveillance coupled with personal contacts. In the next sections we will look at a number of examples of home detention, with particular emphasis on target populations, the restrictions placed on offenders, and supervision strategies.

Home Detention with Electronic Surveillance

Home detention is an "intermediate" sanction in that it provides more supervision and punishment than regular probation and less punishment than incarceration. It is expected to serve at least three purposes: incapacitation, punishment, and rehabilitation (by allowing offenders to remain in the community). Because today's climate supports increasingly harsh sentences that serve both punitive and incapacitative objectives, the use of home detention with or without electronic monitoring is something of a risk for those who endorse this seemingly "lenient" sanction, as pointed out in an article by James Walker.[9]

Electronic surveillance arose because intensive manual monitoring was labor intensive and increased the risk to public safety. It may be employed in a variety of community supervision settings, the most frequent being home detention. Offenders are sentenced to a strict regimen that requires them to be at their residences with limited

ACROSS CULTURES:

AN INTERMEDIATE SANCTION IN THE PEOPLE'S REPUBLIC OF CHINA.

Chinese courts have a number of sanctions available in dealing with offenders. These include "exemption from punishment," suspended sentences, "control," determinate prison terms, life imprisonment, and death. One type of "control" sentence is similar to some indeterminate sentences in the United States.

Called "Control plus putting a (hypothetical) bad element's hat on one's head" (p. 17) this sanction allows the offender to remain in the community, but under stringent conditions. These conditions usually include:

1. Supervised labor, more than the average labor required of a nonoffender.
2. Supervised evening study of appropriate Marxist texts, and participation in group reeducation meetings.
3. Mandatory "special labor projects" on holidays and after regular working hours.

According to Chinese law, periods of control are to last three years, but "may be extended when necessary." It is reported that courts have extended these control sentences to as long as five years (p. 17).

SOURCE: Hungdah Chiu, "Criminal Punishment in Mainland China: A Study of Some Yunnan Province Documents," *Occasional Papers/Reprints in Contemporary Asian Studies*, No. 6 (Baltimore, MD: School of Law, University of Maryland, 1978). Capital punishment sentences in China may be suspended for two years, after which the sentence is either carried out or commuted to life or a fixed term of imprisonment.

exceptions. One way to ensure that they are at home when they are supposed to be is to monitor their whereabouts electronically. As far as can be determined, the first electronic monitoring program was in Palm Beach, Florida, in 1984.[10]

Since electronic monitoring sanctions began, there have been some major changes in offenders selected for monitoring. A survey in 1987 found that three of four subjects under electronic surveillance were probationers. Later, only one of four subjects were on probation.[11] Changes in the offenses committed by those monitored were also significant: The percentage of drug offenses rose from 13.5 percent to 22.0 percent; major traffic offenses declined from 33.4 percent to 18.9 percent; property offenses (burglary and larceny) increased from 18.2 percent to 31.7 percent. These changes in offenders and offenses show clearly that the use of electronic surveillance has responded to society's increasing commitment to the war against drugs, and that a widening net has been thrown over more serious offenders, an indication that this sanction is a more punitive intermediate sanction.

If the trend toward greater use of electronic technology continues, some estimates predict a vast army of offenders will be wearing electronic bracelets:

> The estimates range from 25,000 to 1,000,000. Those guessing at the high end may ignore monitoring's cost and labor intensity in comparison to other nonincarcerative sanctions. Although per diem equipment costs are but a small fraction of the per diem costs to incarcerate an offender, there are other costs to process the information generated by the equipment and to provide community supervision.[13]

Joan Petersilia described the expectations, advantages, and disadvantages of house arrest, or home detention, with and without electronic surveillance, in a statement prepared for the National Institute of Justice.[14] Among her main points are:

1. Costs are an advantage if electronic monitoring is not used in home detention sanctions. Equipment is expensive to purchase, operate, and maintain.
2. There are major social benefits accompanying home detention. "House arrest has none of the corrupting or stigmatizing effects associated with prison. This is a particular advantage for first offenders. . . . They will not come under the influence of career criminals or be exposed to physical or sexual assaults of prison inmates."[15]
3. Home detention has the advantage of flexibility. It can be combined with other sanctions or used alone. It can be used with offenders with special needs such as the seriously ill, disabled, and pregnant women.
4. Implementation ease and speed of response is an advantage because offenders can be removed quickly from the program if necessary.

The second point above is reminiscent of the rationale many advocates of community-based corrections used during the 1950s and 1960s. Then, prisons were considered so deleterious to their inmates that they were to be replaced, whenever possible, by community correctional centers and halfway houses. Whether we can agree with Petersilia's judgement that home detention is less stigmatizing than other sanctions, we can see that it comports well with the history of both community-based corrections and intermediate sanctions.

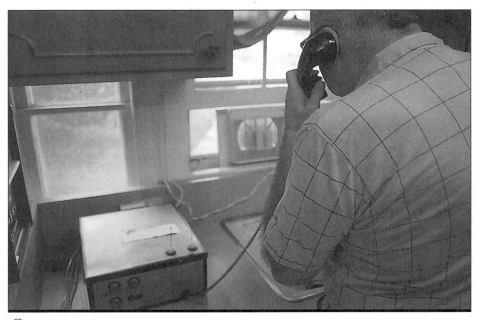

*O*ffenders' schedules of daily movements are entered into a computer and the computer will randomly call each offender. Upon receiving the call the offender must insert the home detention monitoring unit into a verifier so that the computer is informed of the offender's location. If the offender does not insert the unit into a verifier when called, a report of the missed call is issued to the appropriate agency and the violation is investigated.

There are, however, a number of disadvantages to home detention that need to be addressed:

1. Widening the net. There is a tendency to assign home detention to offenders who can do as well in other more traditional programs.
2. Narrowing the net. Critics complain that it is not sufficiently punitive. Critics such as MADD complain that it is insufficiently punitive for DWI/DUI offenders, who are frequently placed on home detention.[16]
3. Too much attention placed on surveillance. Thus, the rehabilitative ideal may be completely lost.
4. Intrusiveness of the surveillance. This may be illegal under constitutional standards with regard to searches and seizures.
5. Possible racial and social class bias. Frequently, home detention with and without electronic monitoring requires offenders to pay supervision fees and bear at least some of the costs of equipment. Thus, white collar/middle-class offenders may be selected in disproportionate numbers.

Before looking at specific applications of electronic monitoring, we will briefly examine the technology used to monitor offenders on whom the sanction has been imposed. There are a number of devices that can be used, and the technology is constantly being upgraded. Four main technologies are commonly in use at this time.

1. **Continuously signaling device.** This technology requires a transmitter, a receiver-dialer, and a computer. A miniature transmitter on a bracelet is attached to an offender, sending a continuous signal through the in-home receiver-dialer to a computer station. It will record loss of signal and recovery of signal. A computer compares data received with an offender's curfew schedule and alerts supervision officers when there are unauthorized absences. The system can store data for reporting and evaluation purposes.
2. **Programmed contact device.** A computer calls (via telephone line) an offender during monitoring hours. Calls can be either random or at specific times. There are three technologies to verify the identity of the person receiving the call: (1) voice verification technology; (2) a wrist device is programmed to transmit a special code into a touch-tone telephone; (3) a module strapped to offender's arm is inserted into a verifier box attached to the telephone. The technology exists for a fourth verification mode, visual verification via closed-circuit TV, but it is quite expensive and not in general use.
3. **Radio signaling.** An offender wears a miniature transmitter that sends a signal to a computer network, which can handle up to 25 offenders.
4. **Beepers.** A relatively simple monitoring device, which can be used to contact offenders quickly, requiring them to respond by telephone. A possible advantage, in addition to simplicity and low cost, is that carrying a beeper is less stigmatizing than wearing an electronic bracelet.

With radio signaling, an additional device may be used to provide effective monitoring when the computer center is out of range: hand-held receivers, which can be carried in the field by supervision agents. Not only can they receive signals from offenders, they can also detect tampering and low batteries.[17]

Selection of offenders for electronic surveillance coupled with home detention is subject to at least three problems. First is the tendency to select only the most **low risk offenders** available. This is only natural since a high failure rate will encourage critics to challenge this sanction as too lenient and lacking in public protection.

A second problem, mentioned earlier, is that selecting candidates for home detention under electronic surveillance may result in **socioeconomic discrimination** in favor of white-collar and affluent offenders. Typically, those selected must pay fees for the use of the equipment and the surveillance provided by a private contractor. Additionally, more affluent offenders are likely to have ties to the community not otherwise available to those of lower socioeconomic status. Thus, they are perceived as better risks.

Finally, there is the danger that this intermediate sanction will result in "widening the net" of social control. That is, as the technology becomes more accessible and affordable, many offenders who otherwise would receive ordinary parole, probation, and unsupervised release (as in release from pretrial detention) will instead be electronically monitored. This, in turn will subject a larger than necessary population to a very restrictive sanction, and probably drive up costs. Of course, this problem relates directly to a tendency to select only the "best" risks. In a later section we will look at the success/failure rates of these low-risk offenders.

Home detention, as an indeterminate sanction, usually involves additional restrictions than simply being available when an electronic device calls. Commonly an offender sentenced to home detention must also submit to urine testing, scheduled and unscheduled, and random home visits.[18] Offenders have virtually no grounds for challenging these intrusions, as a number of appellate court decisions have held.

> Intensive community correctional programs in response to prison crowding and escalating costs allow for a high risk offender to be released . . . under the most restrictive of circumstances. Many of these programs do their utmost to control clients' activities with unannounced home visits, employment visits, checks for drug use, and a close working relationship with law enforcement. Probation officers are typically granted a wide range of law enforcement powers to ensure close supervision of offenders . . . . As a special condition, many jurisdictions require that offenders submit to search at the discretion of their supervising officers.

As pointed out in Chapter 5, pretrial detention or release is subject to the Eighth Ammendment's prohibition against the imposition of "excessive" bail on defendants. Critics argue that pretrial release with electronic monitoring is in reality a punishment, not merely a method of assuring a defendant's appearance for a future trial. Defendants unable to post bond may be candidates for electronic monitoring, while the more affluent are released on bail without having to undergo surveillance and the severe restrictions associated with electronic monitoring. Further, if release under conditions of electronic monitoring is conditioned by a defendant's ability to pay for the monitoring, then it seems clearly to run afoul of the Constitution's "equal protection of the laws" requirement.

Programs Targeting Low-Risk Populations

A number of home detention sanctions focus on offender populations that are carefully selected to be at a reduced risk to the community. In other words, these programs practice **creaming**, or taking the "best" offenders from a population. A study of an electronically monitored home detention sanction in Montgomery County, Ohio, illustrates the type of intermediate sanction program that targets such a limited population: local offenders for whom the alternative sanction is confinement in jail.[20] It also illustrates some of the problems of offender selection we noted earlier. The electronic monitoring component in this program is contracted out to a private firm. To avoid as much risk as possible, the county sheriff established a "very conservative" program involving only 3 percent of the average daily jail population. The program includes the following elements:

- Only "model" prisoners are eligible.
- Prisoners must sign a contract obligating them to observe restrictive rules, including curfews and drug and alcohol testing.
- Home detainees must permit officials to enter their homes to monitor and check the equipment.
- Detainees must provide the necessary equipment.
- Detainees are responsible for the costs of monitoring by the private contractor.

This Ohio program, like so many other "innovative" correctional programs in recent years, was a response to a "large increase in the jail population over the past few years. A majority of this increase is directly related to increased drug trafficking and suppression, especially that of crack cocaine."[21] It is very important to understand the political context in which this and other home detention programs began and in which they operate. As reported by James Walker, a recent election for county prosecutor focused on the incumbent's alleged softness on drug crime. After the election,

> the police began a vigorous campaign against drugs. Possession of even trace amounts of cocaine was prosecuted as a felony. An extra grand jury was empaneled, and the court system was flooded with indictments. The presiding judge . . . dismissed the second grand jury just to slow the flood of cases.[22]

An inmate sued the overloaded jail. A federal district court judge ordered the sheriff to reduce the jail population. Some of the reduction was accomplished by either releasing some inmates or contracting (at a significant increase in cost) for their housing at other facilities. Finally, new jail construction was necessary. The county, as have many local, state, and federal jurisdictions, was faced with a difficult decision:

> Given these circumstances, it is easy to see that the county is at a crossroads. In one direction is the judicious use of a new technology [electronic monitoring] to delay or eliminate the need for expensive new construction or unpalatable release. In the other direction lies the unprincipled and random use of the program leading to unacceptable political costs for the actors involved.

In the federal system, electronic monitoring with home confinement is receiving considerable attention. In the Southern District of Mississippi, for example, the United States Probation Office has used this sanction with several different offender groups: pretrial defendants, supervision violators, and prerelease prison inmates.[24] Supervision violators were further subdivided into two categories: substance abusers and "irresponsible" offenders.[25] Selection of offenders was constrained by risk level:

> Initially, our selection criteria restricted participation in home confinement to a very select group of offenders (i.e., those with no violent, mental illness, or severe substance abuse history)[26].

As more experience was gained (and, as reported, some high- risk offenders slipped through and did well), eligibility for the program was expanded to include those who were considered poor risks. It is easy to understand the tendency to take the "cream of the crop" into various intermediate sanctions. New sanctions of this type encounter resistance from elements in the community. If only low-risk offenders participate, the chances are greater that there will be fewer cases of serious violations that harm or threaten the public. Then, assuming success with these offenders, it may be possible to expand the offender base to include persons who present a greater risk, thus reducing prison crowding and the negative effects of incarceration.

The Mississippi approach included the use of ankle bracelets, detailed daily activity schedules, and frequent contacts with supervision officers. In the words of United States probation officer Darren Gowen,

> . . . we quickly observed the incredible deterrent effect of the electronic ankle bracelet and the required adherence to a daily schedule. . . . An approved daily activity schedule, which is used to allow the offender certain times of the day to be "in range" and "out of range" from the residence, is a product of an offender actually planning his or her life ahead of time.[27]

The threat of speedy revocation and resentencing has been very effective, according to Gowen, and he gave the following description of the feedback available through use of electronic technology:

> Thanks to electronic technology, the officer receives daily, from the monitoring contractor, a facsimile consisting of reports, which summarize, among other things, offender departures from, and arrivals to, the residence. This high-precision information changes the communicable environment between officer and offender. For instance, should an offender arrive home 10–20 minutes late, the officer can confront the offender . . . , usually within 24 hours. Such feedback on seemingly small violations helps to deter more serious ones.[28]

Frequency of supervision contacts is an average of two per week, one contact at the officer's office, and "officers make at least one surprise personal visit, at home or elsewhere each week."[29] At the office visits, urine samples are taken and the electronic bracelet is checked. Contacts with employers and "collateral" others are made once each month.

Officer Gowen reports that of the initial 49 offenders on home detention, only four have failed. Two failed because of unauthorized absences from their residences; a third was revoked because of failure to pay the required utility bill and for being unemployed; and the fourth offender failed a test for cocaine use.

Another low-risk population targeted in the federal system consisted of inmates being conditionally released from federal prisons. The **Community Control Project** was established for this population, which was defined as

> selected low-need offenders . . . released directly into the community up to 180 days before the original release date. During this early release period, offenders have a curfew monitored by electronic surveillance.[30]

This approach to supervising inmates making the transition to the community is quite different from the methods we discussed in the last chapter. In these other programs, the transition is structured by releasing offenders to prerelease centers and halfway houses.

The Community Control Project probably involves lower costs than those incurred operating and maintaining prerelease facilities. Reported cost estimates for the project claim a savings of about $18 per day over halfway house costs. But this benefit comes at the expense of providing less structure and transitional services than provided in transitional centers.

Offender selection for this project was assisted by use of the United States Parole Commission's **Salient Factor Score** technique.* The majority of those included in the

---

*For a description of this instrument to predict risk levels, see Chapter 12.

program were rated as "very good" risks, although some offenders were selected who were judged to be "poor" risks.[31]

Supervision during an offender's assignment to the program is intensive. Upon release from prison, an offender must immediately report to a supervision officer and is restricted to home "except for necessary activities and curfew leave. . . . Curfew leave away from home is for constructive leisure time to be spent on weekends with family or other individuals approved in advance by the . . . officer."[32]

Curfew leaves are not permitted during the first two weeks after release. Following this, leaves may be granted according to a progressive schedule: four hours per week in weeks 3–6; six hours in weeks 6–10; and ten hours per week thereafter.[33]

Electronic monitoring is via a district computer. The intensity and comprehensiveness of the monitoring is illustrated by the following description:

> Information concerning all the parolee's entries and exits from the home, all tamper signals, all power and telephone outages is available through the district office terminal. If there is a loss of power or telephone service, monitoring staff will contact the probation officer within 15 minutes. In case of a power outage, the transmitter has a backup battery . . . that works for 24 hours to record activity. When power is restored, the computer provides a printout of exits during the power loss.[34]

In this program there are several types of "incidents" that may warrant revocation of parole status, including unauthorized absences from the home, late entrances, missed callbacks, and tamper signals. Tamper signals are designed to alert monitors that an offender may be trying to remove the bracelet transmitter, or modify it. There are reports that many, if not most, of such signals are "false alarms," which cause concern to supervision personnel and result in offender anxiety because they are suspected of **tampering,** which can result in revocation. If the monitoring staff cannot restore contact with an offender within 30 minutes of an attempt, the probation officer is notified.

In the Community Control Project, the typical offender will spend an average of 120 days under electronic surveillance. On average, each offender will be contacted personally by a supervision officer four times each month. Should violations of the terms of release be observed, there is a range of responses, including:

- A warning letter from the United States Parole Commission.
- Loss of curfew leave for periods of one week or more.
- Issuance of an arrest warrant, usually leading to return to prison.

We need to ask whether the Community Control Project and other similar sanctions aimed at low-risk populations are an efficient use of electronic technology and what appears to be a labor-intensive period of supervision. Why wouldn't ordinary parole supervision be adequate to provide both transitional services and public safety? Wouldn't more intensive probation without the addition of electronic surveillance be as effective? Evaluation studies of these and other programs, which we will discuss in a later section, have not given us an answer to this question. The emphasis of programs like the Community Control Project is on "control," however, and not on rehabilitation or reintegration. Thus, this and similar programs conform to the current commitment to a more punitive response to offenders.

Home Detention with High-Risk Populations

An example of an electronically monitored home confinement sanction directed at a **high-risk** drug-abusing population in Oregon illustrates how far this intermediate sanction has moved away from the early emphasis on surveillance that was characteristic of electronic monitoring with low-risk populations. This Oregon program, the **Intensive Drug Program (IDP),** aimed to deliver "an outpatient program that provides intensive substance abuse treatment and intensive supervision of clients in the community."[35] It is important to understand the program's goals, client population, and methods program so that we can compare it to other indeterminate sanctions that couple home detention with electronic monitoring.

The target population consists of adult offenders whose substance abuse has led to failures in prior substance abuse programs or to probation/parole violations. The program intends to meet two basic needs of this offender group: (a) to provide them with structured living without incarceration, and (b) to treat their substance abuse problems. The general methods for

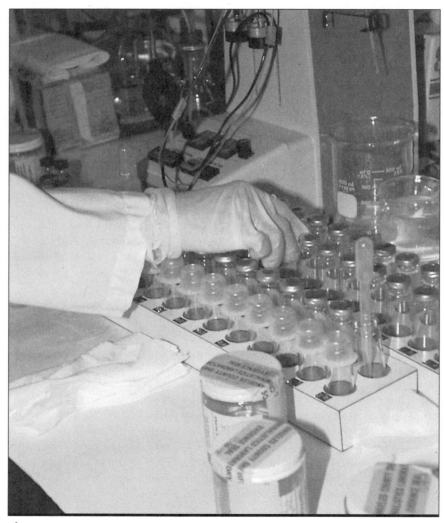

*A*s part of the sentencing for many intermediate sanctions courts will require random as well as scheduled urine testing for offenders. This is some of the equipment necessary for urine testing.

meeting these needs are around-the-clock electronic surveillance, weekly treatment meetings, and drug and alcohol testing.[36]

The target population, far from being a low-risk, net-widening one, consists of offenders who have failed in the past and usually would be considered for incarceration. The treatment regimen includes group counseling sessions, "life structuring" sessions, and participation in groups such as Narcotics Anonymous and Alcoholics Anonymous. Surveillance techniques utilize continuous signal and programmed contact methods, together with regular and random drug and alcohol testing.

It is somewhat surprising that so comprehensive a program is structured to last for a total of only twenty-eight weeks, the first fourteen of which incorporate mandatory electronic monitoring and treatment participation. In the second fourteen-week phase, participation in treatment is voluntary and supervision is more traditional, with no electronic monitoring.

Another program involving **high-risk populations** was instituted in Marion County, Indiana. As reviewed by Terry Baumer and associates, this program involved three offender groups.[37] One group consisted of adults charged with minor offenses, but not released from jail prior to their trials. The second group was made up of convicted adults for whom electronic monitoring was an alternative to imprisonment. The final offender group contained adjudicated juvenile burglars.

The Marion County program delivered an intensive supervision regimen to each group of offenders. They were frequently contacted personally in the community, and these contacts were supplemented by telephone contacts. The average time of supervision varied markedly by offender group. The post conviction group spent an average of 180 days under supervision, about the same time as most home detention programs we have reviewed. A national survey of probation officers involved in monitoring home detainees revealed that they felt that longer than six months in home confinement could lead to "cabin fever."[38] The preconviction group, however, spent less than sixty days under monitoring conditions. This is to be expected since they were to have their cases disposed of in court in three months or less. Time under supervision for the juvenile group was not reported.

When trying to evaluate the performance of each group in terms of recidivism, we have to take into account the major differences in the three groups and the differences in time each group was involved in the program. In the next section, we will examine the results of Baumer's follow-up research.

INTENSIVE SUPERVISION WITHOUT ELECTRONIC MONITORING

In a number of states and local jurisdictions, offenders are placed on intensive supervision without the aid of electronic monitoring technology or under the terms of home detention. Typically, these programs, which may include parolees as well as probationers, involve close and frequent supervision contacts, drug and alcohol abuse testing, and other restrictive conditions. One example, the Idaho Intensive Supervision Program, initiated in 1984, illustrates the common elements found in intensive supervision programs.[39] These elements include:

- Very low caseloads for supervision officers: approximately 25 offenders per officer. A typical caseload in ordinary probation and parole is 100 offenders.

▪ Twenty-four-hour supervision.
▪ Face-to-face supervision contacts for a minimum of seven times per week.
▪ Weekly supervision officer contacts with offenders' employers.
▪ A detailed twenty-four-hour schedule of offender activities and whereabouts, with unannounced supervision officer visits.

We can see from these components of the Idaho ISP that intensive supervision is a very expensive proposition compared with ordinary community supervision levels as practiced in probation and parole. This, of course, cuts into the savings hoped for when diverting offenders from prison. The anticipated savings are even less if intensive supervision is extended to offenders who would otherwise be sentenced to ordinary probation.

Beginning in the 1980s, Texas initiated a large array of community and intermediate sanctions. These included halfway houses, electronic monitoring, community service, and shock probation. Most of these initiatives were the result of successful court challenges to overcrowding and a variety of prison conditions considered to constitute cruel and unusual punishment.[40] The Texas Intensive Supervision Probation sanction (ISP) has been studied for some time.[41] As is the case in other states, the Texas ISP is designed primarily for prison-bound felony offenders whose offenses are neither serious nor violent.

Like similar programs in states with community corrections laws, which we discussed in the previous chapter, Texas provides funding to counties that develop and use intermediate sanctions. The state established a set of guidelines to determine eligibility for offender participation in ISP programs. These include:

▪ A judicial order of probation under intensive supervision.
▪ For "shock" probation, judicially ordered to a period of intensive probation following incarceration.
▪ Continued on probation by the court under intensive supervision after technically violating ordinary probation conditions.
▪ Placed on ISP if the probation department considers it needed and appropriate.[42]

The last of these guidelines, which obviously is subjective, requires documentation indicating there is either an "alcohol or drug dependency problem," or "the seriousness of the current offense" warrants intensive supervision. These guidelines are not particularly helpful in understanding who is sentenced to ISP and why. This matter of establishing guidelines is further complicated because "the sentencing of ISP offenders [is] totally within the discretion of the local judge, who may or may not observe the guidelines."[43]

In Texas, what constitutes "intensive supervision"?

For the first thirty to forty-five day period, Texas ISP clients are required to report biweekly. . . . [They] may have their reporting requirements lessened after [the initial period].[44]

Unlike some, perhaps most, ISP programs in other states, Texas does not require random drug testing. It "sometimes" requires offenders to perform community service and submit to electronic monitoring and home detention. We may ask whether the Texas intensive supervision sanction is really "intensive" and whether it truly is an intermediate sanction. Certainly, when comparing it to other programs, we may be comparing apples and oranges.

This matter of comparability is an important one. For example, an ISP program in Cleveland, Ohio, which uses essentially the same eligibility guidelines as the Texas program just described, has the following program elements:

- Weekly contacts with the community supervision officer.
- Weekly restitution and court costs payments.
- Urinalysis (scheduled and random).
- Education and employment training (as needed).[45]

New Jersey's intensive supervision program is similar in outline to those described above. However, offender supervision appears from published accounts to be more intense than the others.[46] As reported, New Jersey's intensive supervision selected low-risk inmates who were resentenced to this intermediate sanction after three to four months on incarceration. Probation officers contacted their probationers an average of twenty-seven times per week (personal and telephone contacts). All were frequently tested for illegal drug use. In one year alone, 13,000 tests were done on 400 offenders. In addition to the intensive supervision, all probationers were ordered to perform sixteen hours of community service, maintain regular employment, and observe a strict curfew.[47]

FINES AND OTHER MONETARY PENALTIES

As a sole sentence or in combination with other sanctions, fines have been available to judges throughout history. Recently, more extensive use of fines as an intermediate sanction or as an element in community-based corrections has been encouraged. Fines can have the "advantage" of causing an offender to suffer, thus, perhaps, satisfying those who insist on emphasizing the retributive, punitive objectives of criminal sentencing. On the other hand, if fines are used as sole sanctions or in conjunction with sentences that allow offenders to remain in the community, they become intermediate punishments and may contribute to rehabilitation. Offenders so fined can remain with their families, hold jobs, and continue their education.

Advocates of greater use of fines as intermediate sanctions claim a number of advantages:

- They can act as deterrents and deprive offenders of their criminally acquired assets.
- They can easily be combined with other sanctions.
- They can be adjusted to fit specific crimes.
- They are relatively inexpensive to administer.
- They produce revenue.[48]

There are some disadvantages to expanded use of fines:

- They do not incapacitate and therefore cannot be used with offenders who pose a risk to the community.
- As a general rule, fines are set by statute and are too low to produce a punitive effect.
- Fines that are sufficiently high to produce deterrence pose a difficult collection problem, and thus increase administrative costs.[49]
- The poor can't be fined, therefore they face an increased risk of imprisonment.

Ever since fines became a staple in our armory of sentences, there has been a serious drawback in their use: How to determine the appropriate amount to be levied in individual cases. Research by Hillsman and her colleagues that surveyed 126 courts found that judges felt that the affluent were not punished enough, and that imposing fines on poor offenders was essentially an empty gesture.[50] Typically, fines are assessed in amounts that correspond to the seriousness of the crime of conviction. This, at first glance, seems to be both rational and fair. All those who commit a particular crime should be fined the same. We could also determine the dollar value of a fine in terms of its deterrent impact. Obviously, we might argue, a stiffer fine deters more than one with a lesser dollar value.

Of course, such abstract reasoning is not satisfactory if we look at the real world. Clearly, some offenders are better able to handle a fine if that fine is set in relation to the severity of crimes. To offender A, a fine of $1,000 may represent a tiny fraction of her or his monthly salary. Offender B, employed at a minimum-wage job, may simply be unable to pay $1,000, even if a payment schedule were available. If, however, the two offenders were fined very differently for similar offenses, many would argue that it was unfair.

A study of financial penalties in the Los Angeles municipal courts found that using a variety of financial penalties including fines and restitution resulted in significantly lower rates of rearrest and incarceration than similar offenders who were given jail sentences.[51] This conclusion led the researchers to make a strong case for increased use of fines and other financial penalties in place of sentences that rely on a strict interpretation of the "just deserts" or retributive philosophy:

> Our purpose here is not to refute the "just deserts" model of sentencing, but only to note that, at least in the Los Angeles County municipal courts, heavy reliance on the offense as a determinate of disposition, whether mandated or not, appears to have had negative consequences.[52]

Day Fines

One quite recent move to make fines more effective and fairer is to impose **day fines**. As described by Winterfield and Hillsman,

> day fines, so called, because the amount of the fine is tied to an offender's daily earnings are common in some European and South American countries, not so in the United States, where fines have traditionally been based on the individual crime rather than on the individual offender's ability to pay.[53]

Winterfield and Hillsman examined two years of experience with one day fine system (Staten Island, New York). The system is implemented in a series of steps:

1. The sentencing judge determines how much punishment a defendant deserves. This decision can be informed by a presentence report.
2. The amount of punishment deserved is translated into punishment units, not dollar amounts.
3. The punishment units are then translated into monetary units dependent on an offender's daily earnings.

To operate a day fine system requires setting a benchmark to determine the day fine units based on seriousness of offense independent of ability to pay. These benchmarks are established by panels of judges, prosecutors, and defense attorneys. Once this is done, the monetary value of each punishment unit is determined by a percentage of the offender's daily income.

There can be, as was the case in New York, a legal impediment in putting a day fine system in place. Any new system for assessing fines must take into account statutorily mandated fines that are characteristic of most state and local jurisdictions. The statutory maximums in New York have not been changed since 1965. However, judges used the statutory limits but recorded the day fine as calculated, ignoring the legal maximums, so that eventually there would be data for the legislature to use in upgrading statutory limits.

Winterfield and Hillsman concluded that it was possible to set means-based fines "without making the process . . . too difficult or time-consuming for judges."[54] In addition to this finding, they determined that collection rates did not suffer and that the actual total amount collected increased.

Other Monetary Penalties

Currently, fines continue to be used most often as add-ons, and as imposed they tend to be below statutory limits because of the frequent imposition of other monetary "penalties." These other penalties include costs, payments to victims' compensation boards, **supervision fees,** and public defender fees. According to Hillsman,

> At least 31 states authorize the imposition of court costs: 11 states authorize surcharges on fines; 7 states permit "penalty assessments" on offenders. One Texas judge explained why he used fines infrequently: "After paying $56 court costs, $10 fee to the Crime Victim Compensation Fund, $200 public defender fee, and $100 to $500 in probation supervision fee, the defendant will be sufficiently punished."[55]

Regarding collection problems, courts in the United States are poor collection agencies, usually passing the job on to the police via warrants, to which police do not assign a high priority.

Another study of fines in municipal courts by Gordon and Glaser pointed out some serious biases with respect to offenses and offenders.[56] Studying 824 cases, they found that:

- Less than 25 of all drug offenders were fined.
- By contrast, almost two-thirds of those convicting of driving under the influence were fined.
- Fines plus restitution were imposed primarily on white, low-risk offenders.

A number of legislative actions could be taken to remedy some of these problems with fines: raising statutory ceilings, making courts more accountable via audits, lifting statutory restrictions on using fines as the sole penalty for specified crimes, and requiring judges to take offenders' economic circumstances into account when imposing fines and other monetary sanctions.

EVALUATION OF INTERMEDIATE SANCTIONS

Evaluating intermediate sanctions is difficult for a number of reasons, some of them similar to those we pointed out when evaluating the performance of community-based corrections. We need to be aware of a particularly troublesome problem: the large array of very different sanctions that fall under the intermediate umbrella, which makes it virtually impossible to reach any conclusion regarding the effectiveness of the class as a whole. When we couple this with the range of different offenders sentenced to these sanctions, comparative evaluations are nearly impossible.

We will examine a sampling of evaluation studies with reference to the commonly stated objectives of intermediate sanctions: "provide punishment in a less expensive manner while, at the same time, emphasize public protection."[57] With regard to the first of these objectives, we run up against a confounding variable when examining home detention and intensive supervision sanctions: How much of the costs of surveillance are borne by the offender? As we have seen, some programs require offenders to pay for the electronic monitoring equipment and at least a portion of the monitoring costs. Other programs do not make it a condition of release that offenders pay for one or both of these.

Evaluation of Home Detention Sanctions

In the Baumer study referred to earlier, electronic monitoring with home detention was evaluated for three different types of offenders: (1) adults criminally charged with minor offenses and unable to get pretrial release; (2) convicted offenders placed in home confinement as an alternative to incarceration; and (3) adjudicated juvenile burglars.[58]

The postconviction group were all convicted of nonviolent offenses. All subjects were on suspended sentences with monitoring as a condition of probation. In addition to electronic monitoring, all offenders were visited in the field and subjected to scheduled urine tests. The median length of home detention was 180 days. Most offenders also served a "combination" sentence with some time in jail, work release, or weekend confinement.

The pretrial group was selected on the basis of screening for criminal history, living arrangements, and length of stay in jail. They received the same monitoring as the postconviction group. However, their median time of participation was only 56 days, and if their case disposition was not reached by 90 days, they usually were released on personal recognizance (without posting bond and with no further monitoring).

The juvenile group of eligibles included those eligible for probation or suspended sentence. Those with prior convictions for serious offenses were excluded. They received the same combination of monitoring as the other two groups.

The evaluation criteria fell into two sets: (1) "indicators of compliance with home detention orders," that is, officially recorded rule violations, successful computer call records, and self-reported violations; and (2) new arrests for new offenses.

For the first group of criteria, the results were mixed: for pretrial and postconviction groups, there were similar levels of "success" in relation to rule violations and computer calls. Juveniles had the best record for rule violations and much worse for computer calls.

With respect to arrests for new offenses, the study found that between 90 and 98 percent of subjects were not arrested. With respect to absconding, pretrial subjects had the poorest record, with the others much lower. Combining all evaluation criteria, the most successful subjects were postconviction offenders. One explanation for this was the effect of "creaming," that is, actively seeking the best candidates. Presentence investigators, for example, "scout" for good candidates. This activity by investigators is extremely important to recognize when attempting to judge program effectiveness.

Incentives to comply with home detention orders varied markedly. The pretrials were unsentenced and unsure of their final disposition. Their high abscond rate may have reflected their perception that if they waited until their court dates, they could be incarcerated. The postconviction group had every incentive to comply since failure to do so could result in imprisonment. Juveniles all were adjudicated, many with suspended commitments to the state training schools, so there was a strong incentive to abide by program conditions.

There are two major implications for future sanctions of this type culled from the study:

> First, researchers and officials must realize that performance measures are composites of offenders' behavior, organizational capacity to detect behavior, and decisions about how to respond to offenders' misbehavior.[59]

Then researchers discussed a second implication that addresses the systemic consequences of these programs:

> Virtually all detention programs seek to conserve resources by not incarcerating low-risk offenders or defendants. Even so, persons on electronic monitoring face many restrictions, and the more careful attention to performance indicators indicated above may reveal violations that . . . warrant some punishment. Incarceration of rule violators may exacerbate the crowding of facilities that expanded the market for home detention in the first place.[60]

A study of a federal program, the Community Control Project, arrived at optimistic results following an informal evaluation of the performance of 457 offenders on electronically monitored home detention.[61] Defining "failure" as a "warrant issued by the United States Parole Commission for a violation of parole," 54 offenders (just over 15 percent) were counted as having failed.[62] We note that all these "failures" received Salient Factor Scores that predicted their likelihood to recidivate. Another six offenders had the conditions of their release modified because of drug involvement. No warrants were issued, and they were not reincarcerated.

From this study we can conclude that the risk predictor—the Salient Factor Score—was accurate. However, what we don't know is whether those with low risk scores would have done just as well if they had been placed on regular parole or released to a halfway house.

In another, later evaluation of the federal Community Control Project, Baer and Klein-Saffran concluded that with respect to costs, using home confinement to help offenders make the transition from prison to the community

> . . . can be provided at a much lower cost: $12 to $15 per day, compared to $30 to $35 per day for halfway houses, without jeopardizing public safety.[63]

Examining the records of 350 parolees, Baer and Klein-Saffran found that only 31 (about 9 percent) had warrants issued by the United States Parole Commission. Twenty-six of these offenders were revoked from parole status and reimprisoned. As might be expected, most (20 parolees) violated because of substance abuse. Another 10 parolees had warrants issued for absconding, tampering with the monitoring equipment, or for serious curfew violations. Significantly, only one of the 31 warrants was issued for an new offense, forgery.

A later evaluation of 357 Community Control Project parolees found that 13 percent were reimprisoned as violators. The researchers concluded that

> This does not appear to be a higher violation rate than might be expected in a halfway house but there is no conclusive evidence of this because of the lack of an adequate comparison group.[64]

Achieving significant cost reduction is, as we have said, a very important goal of home detention and other intermediate sanctions. Numerous studies lead us to conclude, as did the evaluation of the Community Control Project, that these sanctions can save money. An evaluation of electronic monitoring in one Kentucky county examined the costs of purchasing the electronic equipment and found that the county paid $300,000 for 12 monitors, which in the short term cost it more than if monitored offenders had been incarcerated in the county jail.[65] Over a longer period (monitoring offenders for one year or longer), the county saved considerable money.

One observer commented that "the costs of equipment has [sic] significantly decreased due to extensive competition among vendors."[66] Beyond this development, cost savings are achieved in many programs by charging offenders fees for equipment and supervision:

> In more than two-thirds of the jurisdictions that use electronic monitoring, costs are reduced because fees are charged to offenders capable of meeting payment schedules. The fees vary with half of the programs charging between $100 and $300 per month. A quarter of the programs charge in excess of $300. The highest fee was $450 per month for the lease of electronic equipment.[67]

We wonder who the offenders are who can pay these large sums of money for the opportunity to avoid more severe sanctions. Rather than widening the net of control, it may well be that the net is narrowed significantly.

If we look at electronic monitoring and its effects on drug abuse and recidivism, promising results can be found in an evaluation of an Oregon electronically monitored home detention sanction for drug offenders who had failed on ordinary probation. The components of this Intensive Drug Program (IDP) were described earlier in the chapter.[68] First, the study found that drug use among those sentenced to home confinement with electronic monitoring decreased from 95 percent at the beginning of their confinement to 32 percent when they completed their terms.[69] Sharp reductions were also found for alcohol use.

The researchers compared recidivism rates for IDP offenders to those observed for two other offender groups: probationers sentenced to home confinement with electronic monitoring, and work-release offenders living in a halfway house. Although, as we saw in an earlier section, IDP offenders were required to participate in counseling and drug treatment classes, neither of the comparison groups received any treatment.

When comparing overall recidivism levels for the three groups, the researchers found that the IDP group had higher rearrest rates and a higher average number of rearrests than was observed in the other groups. However, when only those offenders who completed their sentences were counted, a lower rate of recidivism was found for the IDP group. Since the effect of the IDP treatment program on drug and alcohol use and recidivism was the focus of the study, the authors felt that by comparing offenders who had completed the IDP treatment regimen to the other offenders who had completed their programs, the efficacy of treatment could be determined. In their conclusion, they stated:

> These comparisons provide evidence that the unique aspect of the IDP program—the combination of electronic surveillance with drug treatment—can lower recidivism rates.[70]

They did note, however, that the IDP group suffered from a very high drop-out rate (nearly 50 percent), and that "lowering recidivism rates for clients who complete the program deals with only a part of the problem."[71] The other part of the problem, of course, is to find ways to select offenders for this and similar programs who will be likely to complete treatment. These programs need to be careful to incorporate features that will encourage participants to stay in once selected.

Evaluation of Intensive Supervision Sanctions

In a review of a number of studies of the Intensive Supervision (ISP) programs, Clear and Braga reported the following results:

- Most ISPs did not reduce prison crowding, and in some instances actually increased institutional populations.
- Costs of ISP programs are usually more than anticipated. This is especially true when states imprison offenders who are technical violators of ISP conditions.
- ISP effect on recidivism is no better than ordinary probation.[72]

With these unhappy results in mind, Clear and Braga ask, "Why bother to establish intensive community-based sanctions?" If we focus our answer to this question on the commonly stated goals of ISP and similar sanctions—reducing prison crowding, reducing costs, and lowering recidivism—we may well not bother to continue, let alone expand them. If however, we see intermediate sanctions as serving punitive and retributive goals,

> . . . an ISP could be an effective intermediate punishment that is commensurate with the seriousness of certain acts. Indeed, there is a need in society for a penalty on the punishment continuum between traditional probation and incarceration. To refocus ISPs as a punishment for crimes of middle-range seriousness might be an important way to salvage the value of these programs.[73]

There are reports of significant cost savings using intensive supervision without either electronic supervision or home confinement. One study of intensive supervision compared ISP offenders to similar offenders who served their prison terms and were released without intensive supervision.[74] A reported savings was achieved amounting to $7,000 per ISP offender.[75]

It was further reported that with ISP fewer of the offenders were rearrested (25 percent of ISP offenders had new arrests vs 35 percent of the released inmates over a two-year follow-up period).[76] This reduction in new arrests was offset because one-third of the ISP were returned to prison within 18 months. This was said to be a consequence of the very intensive supervision that led to technical violations being observed.

As a final comment regarding the effectiveness of intensive supervision, we observe that the research findings are mixed. Certainly we cannot conclude that these sanctions significantly reduce recidivism. Many, but not all, intensive supervision programs seem to produce noticeable cost savings over incarceration and, probably, electronic surveillance sanctions. We should add here that intensive supervision is not *a* sanction, but a variety of sanctions with a variety of different offenders. Thus, generalizations about its efficacy on any criterion are impossible.

The Effectiveness of Fines and Other Monetary Penalties

As we have seen, there is considerable interest in levying fines and other monetary penalties against some offenders instead of or in addition to other sanctions. If the penalty really hurts, it can qualify as an intermediate punitive sanction. What do we know about the effectiveness of these sanctions? Again, the answer to this question, if one can be found, depends on what dependent variables we use. Recidivism, variously defined, is one way to evaluate effectiveness. Cost comparisons with other sanctions is another way.

The research conducted by Margaret Gordon and Daniel Glaser concluded that in Los Angeles municipal courts,

> Controlling for individual attributes and offense, the odds of subsequent arrest and incarceration were significantly less for those given a financial penalty than for those receiving a jail sentence.[77]

There is an argument that expanding the use of fines and other financial penalties to a wider range of offenders and offenses would result in a failure to deliver "just deserts." Gordon and Glaser counter this argument by pointing out that simply equating punishments to crimes often is counterproductive:

> . . . [T]he retributive philosophy that lies behind determinate sentencing rejects recidivism as a valid or reliable measure of the effectiveness of sentencing decisions: instead it argues in favor of the equity in meting out approximately equal punishment for the same conduct. Our purpose here is not to refute the "just deserts" model of sentencing, but only to note that, at least in the Los Angeles County municipal courts, heavy reliance on the offense as a determinate of disposition, whether mandated or not, appears consistently to have had negative consequences.[78]

Day fines are becoming increasingly popular as both a substitute for monetary penalties and as intermediate sanctions. Studying the Staten Island day fine system's first two years' experiences, Winterfield and Hillsman reported that it was able to (a) calculate fines routinely; (b) impose fines that averaged 25 percent higher than before the system was instituted; (c) impose fines that totaled 14 percent more than before; and (d) collect fines at a higher rate than before. Imposing higher fines and collecting a higher percentage of fines are important findings that counteract opponents of day fines who claim that the system will not be effective as a punishment and will not be cost-effective.

Day fines as well as more traditional fines could be more effective as intermediate punitive sanctions if their limits as defined by statutes were reexamined. As pointed out earlier, the maximum limits on fines have not been changed in many states and localities in many years. Revising these limits on the basis of a day fine scheme could result in a more appropriate and effective sanction.

SUMMARY

INTERMEDIATE SANCTIONS is a very ill-defined area in corrections. A variety of punishments and programs can be included under its umbrella. Intensive supervision probation, house detention, community-based corrections, electronic surveillance, and fines all have been referred to as intermediate. In this sense, it can be said that any sanction that falls between ordinary incarceration and probation is intermediate. This chapter included only those programs that are clearly new in this country, deal with the offender in the community, and contain a strong commitment to punishment and control.

As is the case with most correctional sanctions covered in this text, intermediate sanctions suffer from a conflicting mix of objectives. Although most, if not all, such responses to offenders emphasize retribution, just deserts, and control, many give at least lip service to rehabilitation. In addition, many intermediate sanctions are expected to deliver their response in a cost-effective way, especially in terms of reducing prison admissions. This profusion of objectives that often do not go well together was summed up by Peter Benekos in a 1990 article:

While retribution, deserts, and exclusion still reflect corrections ideology, the search for intermediate punishments is an attempt to find mid-range solutions which meet social and criminal justice needs for controlling and punishing offenders.[79]

And later, he argues that "the state of corrections is not healthy. . . ."[80] Both prison and community facilities are overextended, and policies that emphasize punishment and control have been expanded to "startling dimensions." He suggests that this development, especially with respect to intermediate sanctions, is premised on a perception among politicians and the public that we have been too soft on crime. To the contrary, our responses to offenders have been "punitive and controlling," perhaps more so than we realize.

These observations are important to bear in mind when we try to understand the place of intermediate sanctions in corrections today. These sanctions are constantly in danger of being viewed as "coddling" offenders. Studies of their effectiveness in reaching their varied and conflicting objectives provide little support for those who urge their increased use as correctional sanctions. These studies may give support for moving these sanctions ever more in the direction of punishment and control at the expense of rehabilitation and reintegration.

KEY CONCEPTS

beepers	low-risk offenders
Community Control Project	programmed contact device
continuously signaling device	radio signaling
creaming	Salient Factor Score
day fines	socioeconomic discrimination
high-risk populations	supervision fees
Intensive Drug Program (IDP)	tampering

QUESTIONS FOR DISCUSSION

1. Can you justify using electronic surveillance with offender populations who are judged to present a low risk to the community? Fully explain your answer.
2. Why is "control" such a major component in various intermediate sanctions?
3. Some intermediate sanctions programs evaluate success on the basis of offenders who complete their programs and fail to count drop-outs as "failures." Is this an appropriate way to proceed? Fully explain your answer.
4. Some have found that the use of intermediate sanctions can actually "narrow the net" of social control. How is this possible?
5. Can we separate intermediate sanctions as presented in this chapter from community-based corrections? Explain your answer.

ENDNOTES

1. Stephen J. Rackmill, "An Analysis of Home Confinement as a Sanction," *Federal Probation* 58 (March 1994): 45.

2. Norval Morris and Michael Tonry, *Between Prison and Probation: Intermediate Punishments in a Rational Sentencing System* (New York: Oxford University Press, 1990).
3. Ibid., p. 3.
4. Ibid., p. 5.
5. Ibid., p. 6.
6. Michael N. Castle, "Alternative Sentencing: Selling It to the Public," National Institute of Justice, *Research in Brief* (Washington, D.C.: National Institute of Justice, September 1991).
7. Ibid., pp. 1–2.
8. Ibid., p. 4.
9. James L. Walker, "Sharing the Credit, Sharing the Blame: Managing Political Risks in Electronically Monitored House Arrest," *Federal Probation* 54 (June 1994): 16–20.
10. Marc Renzema and David T. Skelton, "Use of Electronic Monitoring in the United States: 1989 Update," *National Institute of Justice Reports* (Washington, D.C.: National Institute of Justice, November/December 1990), p. 10.
11. Ibid.
12. Ibid., p. 11.
13. Ibid., p. 13.
14. Joan Petersilia, "House Arrest," in Larry J. Siegel (ed.), *American Justice: Research of the National Institute of Justice* (Washington D.C.: National Institute of Justice 1990), pp. 201–205.
15. Ibid., p. 202.
16. Ibid., p. 203.
17. Darren Gowen, "Electronic Monitoring in the Southern District of Mississippi," *Federal Probation* 59 (March 1995): 12.
18. Joan Petersilia, "Exploring the Option of House Arrest," *Federal Probation* 50 (June 1986).
19. Stephen J. Rackmill, "Community Corrections and the Fourth Amendment," *Federal Probation* 57 (September 1993): 40. See also Jeffrey N. Hurwitz, "House Arrest: A Critical Analysis of an Intermediate-Level Penal Sanction," *University of Pennsylvania Law Review* 135 (1987): 784–85.
20. Walker, "Sharing the Credit, Sharing the Blame."
21. Ibid., p. 17.
22. Ibid.
23. Ibid.
24. Gowen, "Electronic Monitoring in the Southern District of Mississippi," pp. 10–11.
25. Ibid., p. 10. Defined as those "who fail to report, fail to complete community service, make false statements to the probation officer. . . ."
26. Ibid., p. 10.
27. Ibid., p. 11.
28. Ibid.
29. Ibid., p. 12.
30. Benjamin F. Baer and Jody Klein-Saffran, "Home Confinement Program: Keeping Parole under Lock and Key," *Corrections Today* 52 (February 1990): 17.
31. Ibid.
32. Ibid.
33. James L. Beck, Jody Klein-Saffran, and Harold B. Wooten, "Home Confinement and the Use of Electronic Monitoring with Federal Parolees," *Federal Probation* 54 (December 1990): 267.
34. Ibid., pp. 17–18.
35. Annette Jolin and Brian Stipak, "Drug Treatment and Electronically Monitored Home Confinement: An Evaluation of a Community-Based Sentencing Option," *Crime & Delinquency* 38 (1992): 160.
36. Ibid.

37. Terry L. Baumer, Michael G. Maxfield, and Robert I. Mendelsohn, "A Comparative Analysis of Three Electronically Home Monitored Detention Programs," *Justice Quarterly* 10 (1993): 121–142.

38. Rackmill, "An Analysis of Home Confinement as a Sanction," p. 48.

39. For a detailed critical discussion f the Idaho ISP program see J. Arthur Beyer, "Assignment to Intensive Supervision: An Assessment of Offender Classification and Subjective Override in the State of Idaho," in Charles B. Fields (ed.), *Innovative Trends and Specialized Strategies in Community-Based Corrections* (New York: Garland Publishing, 194), pp. 19–39.

40. See Chapter 10 for a discussion of these and other issues of prisoners' rights.

41. For a review of the Texas ISP and some of the studies of its performance see G. Mark Jones and Terry L. Wells, "Intensive Probation in Texas," in Charles B. Fields (ed.), *Innovative Trends and Specialized Strategies in Community-Based Corrections* (New York: Garland Publishing, 1994), pp. 41–61.

42. Ibid., p. 46.

43. Ibid., p. 51.

44. Ibid.

45. Edward J. Latessa and Jill A. Gordon, "Examining the Factors Related to Success or Failure with Felony Probationers: A Study of Intensive Supervision," in Charles B. Fields, *Innovative Trends and Specialized Strategies in Community-Based Corrections* (New York: Garland Publishing, 1994), p. 68.

46. Frank S. Pearson and Daniel B. Bibel, "New Jersey's Intensive Supervision Program: What Is It Like? How Is It Working?" *Federal Probation* 50 (1986): 25–31; Voncile B. Gwody, "Intermediate Sanctions," National Institute of Justice, *Research in Brief* (Washington, D.C.: National Institute of Justice, 1993); Alice Glasel Harper, "Intensive Supervision: Working for New Jersey," *Corrections Today* 49 (1986): 88.

47. Harper, "Intensive Supervision," 88.

48. Susan T. Hillsman, et al., "Fines as Criminal Sanctions," in Larry J. Siegel (ed.), *American Justice: Research of the National Institute of Justice* (St. Paul, MN: West Publishing Company, 1989) p. 192.

49. Ibid.

50. Ibid., p. 195.

51. Margaret A. Gordon and Daniel Glaser, "The Use and Effects of Financial Penalties in Municipal Courts," *Criminology* 29 (1991): 651–676.

52. Ibid., p. 674.

53. Laura A. Winterfield and Susan T. Hillsman, "The Staten Island Day-Fine Project," National Institute of Justice, *Research in Brief* (Washington, D.C.: National Institute of Justice, January 1993), p. 1.

54. Ibid., p. 6.

55. Hillsman, "Fines as Criminal Sanctions," p. 194.

56. Gordon and Glaser, "The Use and Effects of Financial Penalties in Municipal Courts," pp. 651–676.

57. Beck, Klein-Saffran, and Wooten, "Home Confinement and the Use of Electronic Monitoring, p. 22.

58. Baumer, Maxfield, and Mendelsohn, "A Comparative Analysis of Three Electronically Home Monitored Detention Programs," pp. 121–142.

59. Ibid., p. 139.

60. Ibid., p. 140.

61. Beck, Klein-Saffran, and Wooten, "Home Confinement and the Use of Electronic Monitoring.

62. Ibid., p. 28.

63. Baer and Klein-Saffran, "Home Confinement Program," p. 17.

64. Beck, Klein-Saffran, and Wooten, "Home Confinement and the Use of Electronic Monitoring," pp. 30–31.

65. Petersilia, "Exploring the Option of House Arrest," pp. 50–59.
66. Rackmill, "An Analysis of Home Confinement as a Sanction," p. 47.
67. Ibid.
68. Jolin and Stipak, "Drug Treatment and Electronically Monitored Home Confinement," pp. 158–170.
69. Ibid., p. 162.
70. Ibid., p. 167.
71. Ibid., p. 168.
72. Todd R. Clear and Anthony A. Braga, "Intensive Supervision: Why Bother?" in Charles B. Fields (ed.), *Innovative Trends and Specialized Strategies in Community-Based Corrections* (New York: Garland Publishing, 1994), pp. 3–4.
73. Ibid., pp. 13–14.
74. Gwody, "Intermediate Sanctions."
75. Ibid., p. 4.
76. Ibid.
77. Gordon and Glaser, "The Use and Effect of Financial Penalties," p. 651.
78. Ibid., p. 674.
79. Peter J. Benekos, "Community Corrections in a Retributive Era," *Federal Probation* 54 (March 1990): 53.
80. Ibid., p. 55.

THE STATUS OF CORRECTIONS TODAY AND FORECASTING ITS FUTURE

17 CORRECTIONS TODAY AND TOMORROW

The rattle of the chain gang returned to the South today, stirring old memories, as Alabama became the first state to put shackled prisoners to work again clearing muddy ditches and cutting high weeds along the roadside.

More than 300 Alabama inmates dressed in white uniforms emblazoned with the words "CHAIN GANG" were led from prison buses along Interstate 65 . . . and ordered by shotgun-toting guards to kneel in groups of five.

Then, as caged tracking dogs howled in nearby trucks, the shackles and chains were attached to their ankles—and history repeated itself as cameras rolled from a dozen TV crews.[1]

. . . [Corrections commissioner Ron] Jones argued that the chains would reduce escape attempts, and the need to shoot inmates who try. "It's not that I'm a softy. It's expensive. You shoot somebody and you send him to the hospital and it costs $100,000 to patch him up."[2]

INTRODUCTION

NEARLY FIVE MILLION men and women in the United States are under the supervision of correctional agents. This represents 2.6 percent of the adult population of the United States. As we have seen, corrections includes an almost bewildering variety of activities: incarceration, probation, parole, house arrest or detention, electronic monitoring, day fines, and shock imprisonment or boot camp.

Throughout this book we have seen that there is considerable support for more punitive responses to offenders. This support leads to laws, policies, and practices that serve retributive and incapacitative goals. Whether these goals are sought through increased use of the death penalty, life without parole and three strikes and you're out sentences, abolition of parole, or shock incarceration, the results seem clear. Corrections has moved a considerable distance away from the rehabilitative ideal so popular only a few decades ago.

An attorney recently wrote that one result of the well- publicized war on crime has been the "emergence of a prison- industrial complex that depends on the stoking of citizen fear."[3] Some high-level corrections officials are falling into line. Here are the comments of Georgia's commissioner of corrections, Wayne Garner, upon taking office at the beginning of 1996:

> We have 60 to 65 percent of our inmate population that truly want to do better . . . but there's another 30–35 percent that ain't fit to kill, and I'm going to be there to accommodate them. . . . My goal is for the prison experience not to be a pleasant one.[4]

In addition to this tough talk, Commissioner Garner has ordered Georgia inmates to walk four miles a day to condition them physically so that health care costs can be reduced. Since many applicants for the system's correctional officer positions fail the entrance test, Commissioner Garner declared that the test will be revised to reduce the failure rate.

In their 1990 book, *Between Prison and Probation: Intermediate Punishments in a Rational Sentencing System,*[5] Norval Morris and Michael Tonry stress the difficulty facing those who want a more rational response to crime than the present simple "get tough" one. However, "the complex character of our criminal justice institutions provides bewilderingly complex problems to be solved before major new initiatives can be accomplished."[6]

In the following sections we will pull together the different criminal justice policies, sanctions, and programs that make up corrections to show what is known about the effectiveness of corrections in dealing with America's crime problem. As we proceed, we will point out that however varied, contradictory, and confusing correctional goals and activities have become, they must be seen as integral parts of the criminal justice system. What is done in one part of the system will certainly affect other parts.

In the first section we look at sentencing laws, policies, and practices. We will examine a number of specific sanctions with attention to their impact, or lack thereof, on criminal behavior and corrections. In the final section we will discuss what might be the future course of corrections. As Alabama reinvents the chain gang, for example, are we seeing a "back to the future" development?

❚ SENTENCING LAWS, POLICIES, AND PRACTICES

Some General Systemic Considerations

As we have seen, corrections must deal with legislative actions and judicial decisions. Legislatures have been moving toward statutes based on philosophies such as "truth in sentencing," "just deserts" with determinate sentences, and variations on life without parole terms of imprisonment such as "three strikes and you're out," and harsher forms of probation and parole.

The correctional administrator has little choice but to follow these laws when offenders enter the correctional domain. Prisons are "open admissions" institutions. When a convicted offender is ordered to prison for a period of time, the prison gate must be opened for her or him. Probation, parole, and other community supervision agencies also have no choice but to add to their caseloads those offenders sent them by the courts. Getting tough on crime and criminals has resulted in large increases in prison populations, electronic surveillance of probationers and parolees, boot camps, and, yes, even a return to chain gangs.

In addition to seeing their populations grow, corrections officials and workers cannot choose the type of offenders sent them. It is clear from much of the literature we have examined in previous chapters that some offenders simply are inappropriate for the sanctions they receive from the courts. Many drug offenders and others committed to prison are nonviolent persons who pose little risk to the community, yet the prison must confine them. Probation and parole caseloads are filling up with offenders who are much more serious risks to the community than ever before, but, because of overcrowded correctional institutions, community supervision agencies are required to supervise them.

Now let us turn to some specific sanctions and sentencing procedures that have major consequences for corrections and, possibly, may have an impact on crime.

The Chain Gang Sanction

With respect to the reintroduction of the chain gang into American corrections, Marylee Reynolds argues that this back-to-the-future sanction is a response to a change in public opinion: "The public is fed up with crime and criminals and seeks vengeance. Public sentiment is that prisons are not harsh enough and America coddles its inmates."[7]

Although it appears that Alabama (and other states considering a return to chain gangs) is using the chain gang to respond more harshly to offenders, punishment is not the only goal being sought. Cost-effectiveness and deterrence are companion goals, as announced by Governor James and Prison Commissioner Jones. "When inmates are chained together they require fewer guards, and when children see these gangs from the roadside, they will think twice about committing crimes."[8] As Marylee Reynolds observed, there is a presumed additional benefit: "It is also likely that the sight of inmates working on a chain gang is appealing to the public."[9]

There also is the claim that working on a chain gang is reformative. That is, "work itself is said to have a therapeutic value. . . . If inmates are not able to occupy their time in productive ways . . . ,"[10] they may resort to aggressive reactions to idleness and frustration. The "productive" use of their time involves "toiling in the hot sun, serving sentences as long as 90 days and working 12 hours per day."[11]

Clearly, we see in the chain gang a multiplicity of objectives that, it is claimed, are reached through the relatively simple device of chaining inmates together and putting them to work in the hot sun. Unfortunately for corrections, and for a rational approach to crime, multiple, conflicting, and contradictory philosophies characterize many of the sanctions it is required to implement.

We do not see the return of the chain gang as heralding a significant development for corrections' future. It does, however, illustrate the "get tough" philosophy that has been prevalent during the 1980s and '90s. Therefore, it may portend a future that will continue to require corrections to deliver more punitive measures to offender populations.

*C*hain gangs have each inmate joined to the others by ankle restraints. These inmates are digging this closely to each other out of necessity, not by choice.

Now we take a look at a number of sentencing reforms that may well carry over into the next century.

Sentencing Guidelines

A major reform in sentencing, as we pointed out in Chapters 2 and 3, is the development of sentencing guidelines in the federal and many state criminal justice systems. Guidelines have been adopted to reach a number of objectives. Among these objectives are "truth in sentencing," limitations on sentence disparities, just deserts or retribution, and rehabilitation. Guidelines are also said to have contributed to the increase in correctional populations because their application makes it more difficult to sentence offenders to community-based sanctions.

In a major study of sentencing guidelines in Pennsylvania, John Kramer and Jeffery Ulmer found evidence that guidelines do not always work in ways expected by legislators when they enact them.[12] They examined departures from Pennsylvania's sentencing guidelines during the period 1985 to 1991 to determine whether "extra-legal" factors were being used by trial judges when departing downward in their sentences. Their research included interviews with judges, prosecutors, and probation officers. They found disturbing evidence that judges take into account factors that are "associated with gender, race, and conviction by trial."[13] These factors are not among those that are intended to be used when guidelines schemes were enacted. Guidelines are supposed to be "neutral" with regard to variables such as sex, race, and socioeconomic status.

When judges depart from the guidelines, the resulting sentences tend to favor women (especially those who have dependent children), whites (those who are employed), and those who plea bargain and express "remorse." It is particularly disturbing to learn that "going to trial," that is, pleading not guilty, "carries a greater penalty in terms of dispositional departure decisions. . . ."[14]

A study of Minnesota's use of its sentencing guidelines revealed that they were linked to the state's prison population level.[15] This research by Lisa Stolzenberg and Stewart D'Alessio found that,

> Linking determinate sentencing reform to prison populations can have unintended consequences. Specifically, determinate sentencing reforms that place limits only on the growth of prison populations may result in substantial increases in jail use. . . .[16]

This is not only a potential result. Other research confirms the practice of "mitigated departures [from the guidelines]" that produces increases in local jail populations.

> The only plausible explanation for this . . . is that the organizational imperative to maintain Minnesota's prison population within acceptable limits motivated judges to circumvent the guidelines by shifting the burden of incarceration from the state to the local level.[17]

Another study, focusing on the first three years of experience with the Minnesota guidelines system, found that the legislative response to the increasing pressures on its prisons was to (a) allow good-time reductions for mandatory minimum sentences: one day of good-time credit for every two days of good behavior; (b) change the definition of "second or subsequent offense" to mitigate the longer sentences for repeaters; and (c) make all reductions retroactive to all prisoners.

Three Strikes Laws

One much heralded and debated sentence "reform" is the so-called three strikes law. Michael Turner and his associates conducted a detailed study of the provisions of all "three strikes" laws either proposed or in force in the United States.[18] They identified a total of 77 "three strikes" proposals, thirteen of which had been signed into law by state governors by the conclusion of their review.

These statutes vary widely with respect to the crimes that make offenders eligible for long-term prison sentences. For example, "Alabama, Georgia, Louisiana, New York, and Vermont each had legislative proposals that permitted offenders convicted of their second serious or violent felony to be sentenced to life in prison."[19] Some states even count as "strikes" attempts to commit the eligible crimes. In fact, "only two crimes—murder and kidnapping—were included in every jurisdiction that enacted a three-strikes . . . policy."[20]

The Turner analysis suggests that sentencing statutes providing for life without parole terms for habitual offenders will affect the corrections subsystem in three areas: prison and community supervision populations, fiscal requirements, and constitutional concerns. In the first case, the populations of both prisons and community supervision caseloads will increase. As more offenders are committed to longer sentences in prison, there are only so many options. One is to build more cells. Another is to release some inmates early to community supervision and place in community settings offenders who otherwise would be incarcerated. With either option, populations will increase and, in the case of community supervision, these populations will contain more high-risk offenders than in the past.

The fiscal burden associated with these sentencing laws is predicted to be significant. The reasons are not simply that more prisons will be needed and their operating costs will certainly soar. More risk-prone offenders will be under community supervision, and the costs of this form of supervision and control will also rise significantly.

Finally, three strikes and similar legislation may encounter serious legal challenges in the courts. Such legislation severely limits judicial discretion, and a case can be made that these limits "interfere with [a] state constitution's separation of powers doctrine."[21] A further legal objection can be raised that three strikes laws may violate, in some instances, the Eighth Amendment protection against cruel and unusual punishments.

There are ways out of some of the problems that three strikes and other sentence reform laws pose for corrections. A recent case study of New York State's experience conducted by Pamala Griset reveals how the frequently counterproductive consequences of sentence reforms can be dealt with while maintaining political and public acceptance.[22] She first points out that New York, between 1987 and 1993, was a "politically and ideologically divided" state, a situation that might be expected to minimize any legislative and executive action to deal with a rapidly growing prison population. However, the legislature was able to take action. It "pursued an incremental policy . . . through a series of adjustments that eventually led to a new policy context."[23] This new policy context allowed corrections administrators "far-ranging discretion over the duration of thousands of inmates' terms of incarceration."[24]

How was this discretion made available? Cleverly, the legislature created new prisons in Republican districts and new early release programs (a boot camp, earned eligibility for early prison release, and an alcohol and substance abuse treatment facility) in Democratic districts. Thus, both conservative and liberal lawmakers were able to feel somewhat satisfied that their correctional philosophies were being honored. With the new early release programs in place, corrections officials were in a position to decide on the actual length many inmates spent in prison. So much for "truth in sentencing."

Between 1990 and 1993, the state's budget problems made it impossible to build any more prisons or fund additional community-based alternatives. Prison populations continued to grow. The legislative response was to expand the use of already existing work-release programs and to authorize a day reporting program.* These initiatives further increased prison officials' discretion over the duration of incarceration. In fact, the exercise of discretion to release inmates early became so rampant that prison officials "modify judges' sentences as a matter of daily routine."[25]

The effect of three strikes and other enhanced sentencing laws will almost certainly be felt in increased costs in all areas of criminal justice. Perhaps surprisingly, Gwyn Ingley says that the "costs that may be felt immediately are those incurred by courts and related prosecution and defense offices"[26] as more defendants go to trial rather than plea bargain. She paints a potentially devastating picture of the impact on California if a projected increase in felony jury trials actually occurs: "A 1 percent increase in the number of felony cases resulting in jury trial would require an additional $16 million in court resources."[27] She also reports that the state optimistically predicts a long-term savings of $29.5 billion by the year 2000 through the reduced criminal activity of those offenders who have struck out. As we will see in the following section, this prediction may be unrealistic.

Peter Benekas and Alida Merlo also point out the potential for dramatic increases in criminal trials as a result of three strikes laws. One consequence of this may be that

---

*Day reporting programs are discussed in Chapter 5.

*T*his is Rhode Island's maximum security prison. Because of increasing need for detention facilities, prisons built over thirty years ago are not always equipped to handle the increasing influx of inmates.

"getting tough may in fact result in being softer" because prosecutors may have some "wiggle" room in dismissing a defendant's prior convictions or in reclassifying crimes so that they do not meet the three strikes criteria.[28]

SENTENCE REFORMS AND CRIME RATES

We need to look at certain sentence reforms not only in terms of their impact on correctional agencies but, more importantly, at their effects on crime. Do these sentences reduce crime? To answer this question is no simple matter. A number of studies attempt to inform us about the relationship between certain sentences and criminal behavior.

Thomas Marvell and Carlisle Moody studied 10 states that enacted determinate sentence laws (DSLs) between 1976 and 1984 as "natural laboratories" to estimate the impact of DSLs on both prisons and crime.[29] Among their conclusions was that "contrary to the assumption of the crime-control interests, we found little to suggest that DSLs affect crime rates. . . ."[30]

Marvell and Moody also conducted research in a much more limited area: the relationship between enhanced sentences for gun offenses and rates of gun crimes.[31] As we saw in the chapters on sentencing, a number of states and the federal government have enacted laws that provide for enhanced penalties for crimes committed with firearms. As of 1995, forty-nine states (Mississippi being the lone exception) have enacted statutes that provide for either a mandatory minimum sentence, additional prison terms, or both when crimes are committed with firearms.

Marvell and Moody found that there was "little evidence to support the intended purposes of firearm sentencing enhancements, reducing crime rates and gun use."[32]

Surprisingly, their study also found that enhanced sentencing practices did not significantly contribute to prison overcrowding. The limited impact on prison admissions was said to related to the exercise of discretion by prosecutors and judges at the time of charging and sentencing. Also, many of these enhanced penalty statutes actually add relatively little additional penalties to those already available for gun offenses. Finally, prosecutorial and judicial discretion is almost certainly exercised in relation to the states' prison population levels at any given time.

A study in Illinois by Nola Joyce examined incarceration and crime rates between 1979 and 1989.[33] She concluded that,

> the prison population increased by 100%, whereas the crime rate increased by 12% and the state population increased by 3%. Clearly, crime rates and demographic factors were not the driving force in the recent prison population growth.[34]

The dramatic rise in prison populations was directly related to the policies and practices expressed in sentencing statutes, prosecutorial and judicial discretion that "increased a criminal's probability of going to prison and staying there for a longer time."[35]

The most significant reform in Illinois was the passage of a determinate sentencing law in 1978. Under the then-new law, the discretion previously given to the state Parole and Pardon Board to release inmates early was essentially eliminated. Determinate sentences in Illinois provided that offenders serve 50 percent of their terms before they became eligible for release.

The resulting effects of the prison population can easily be seen. In response to these effects, the state introduced a "forced release" policy, which allowed the Department of Corrections to give inmates "multiple increments of 90-day grants of meritorious good-time (MGT)."[36] During a three-year period, a total of 10,019 prisoners were released early under this scheme. This approach had to be modified because the "public outcry over 'revolving door' correctional policies led to a number of lawsuits, culminating in an Illinois Supreme Court decision limiting the amount of MGT an inmate could receive to 90 days (subsequently increased to 180 days)."[37] As a result of this, the prison population again rose, increasing by 4,000 in a two-year period. A subsequent attempt to control growth was made by allowing inmates to earn one-quarter of a day for every day spent "successfully participating" in various educational and vocational programs. Whether this will cause another outburst of negative public opinion is not reported.

Joyce claims that the increase (both before and after the MGT policy was implemented and then adjusted) was primarily a result of the war on drugs. Between 1984 and 1991 prison admissions of drug offenders shot up an astonishing 742 percent. In the last year of Joyce's analysis, 40 percent of the population growth was "attributed solely to more drug offenders coming to prison."[38]

Other attempts to limit correctional population growth included allowing selected inmates to volunteer for the state's boot camp program. Successful completion of the program can result in early release.

Even with these reductions, the prison population continues to grow. Joyce concludes that "if nothing changes, the future holds the certainty of an ever increasing prison population."[39] The only way out is to take a close look at who should be sentenced to prison, and how long they should remain there. Her final comment is that "criminal justice policy . . . must be held accountable for its effect on the allocation of human and fiscal resources. At some point we must ask whether we can afford to lock up everyone who offends us."[40]

*C*hanges in policies and practices due to public opinion demanding more severe and longer punishments for offenders have led to the examinination of sentencing statutes, prosecution of cases, and judicial decisions. The increase in the length of incarceration for all types of inmates requires that more modern, electronically-controlled, and space-efficient county detention facilities are built.

In another study of increasing rates of incarceration and their impact on crime rates, Darrell Steffensmeier and Miles Harer agree with the conclusions of those studies we discussed above. With respect to rates of incarceration and rates of violent crime, they say "it is difficult to detect any overall relationship between incarceration and violence rates or to show that incarceration is a cost-effective means of reducing crime."[41]

They claim that available data "suggests that incapacitation as a crime control strategy . . . has not only increased incarceration rates for violent offenders, as intended, but incarceration rates for property and drug offenders have increased even faster."[42] They urge policymakers to concentrate not on making incarceration more certain for the majority of offenders, but on "identifying the limited number of violent, dangerous, and persistent offenders who account for a majority of serious crime. . . ."[43] If this can be done, then incarceration will be a "needed and warranted expense."

In a major study of the relationship between property and violent crime rates and incarceration, Sheldon Ekland-Olson and his colleagues compared data from California and Texas during the 1980s.[44] During this period California engaged in a major prison construction program. The data obtained by Ekland-Olson led to the conclusion that "the almost quadrupling of prison capacity . . . seemed to make little difference when it came to curbing the rate of violent crime."[45] Texas, which responded quite differently to population pressures (and court orders), as we see below, also did not see a noticeable reduction in violent crime.

With respect to property offenses, the data revealed major differences between the two states. While California's incarceration rate increased 192 percent, property crimes declined by about 17 percent. This compares with the national incarceration rate increase of 96 percent and a 4 percent drop in property crimes.[46] The Texas incarceration rate rose by only 14 percent during the same period, but its property crimes increased by 30 percent.

Texas, in contrast to California, attempted to manage the pressures on its prison population by relying on its Board of Pardons and Parole and by a very liberal good-time credits policy. Thus, the state's response stands in sharp contrast with California's approach, which emphasized new prison construction.

What explains the significant increase in the Texas property crime rate? Would a major prison building program such as California's have been more effective than early release of large numbers of prisoners? One possible answer to these questions is that the Texas approach diluted the deterrent effect of incarceration. However, the researchers noted that there was no difference in "repetitious violent offending . . . in the case of violent crimes" between Texas and California.[47]

What does appear to be correlated with significant increases in property crimes in Texas was a depressed economy and accompanying high levels of unemployment during the period studied. "Texas was experiencing heightened unemployment rates during these years triggered by a dramatic fall in oil prices and subsequent problems associated with the failure of savings and loan institutions."[48] Thus, "incarceration rates and economic conditions as reflected in unemployment patterns seem to be the most promising factors"[49] explaining the higher rates of property offenses.

Perhaps we should have known all along that rates of crime and incarceration are independent of each other. In a survey of fifty state corrections administrators, George Cox and Susan Rhodes made an important observation about the prison population explosion that began in earnest during the 1980s:

[S]ince about 1980, the proportion of the country's population with the greatest propensity to commit crimes has been declining, and the crime rate as reported in the FBI's Uniform Crime Reporting Reports has been stable . . . , so increasing crime has not been a primary cause of recent prison population growth.[50]

Prisons and Incapacitation

As we have seen in earlier chapters, there has been a good deal of attention paid to the incapacitative value of various criminal sanctions. Many argue that those sanctions providing for very long sentences produce the strongest incapacitative effects. We have shown in our chapters on prisons and various forms of community supervision that one point of contention is whether greater use of community-based sanctions significantly reduces incapacitation, resulting in increased danger to the community. But does incarceration achieve significant incapacitative effects? The answer at first seems obvious: yes, it does. However, some research has found that the answer is not so obvious. For example, the Gottfredsons studied more than 6,000 men incarcerated in California prisons during the 1960s.[51] They note that incapacitation-based sentencing is of two general types: selective and charge-based.[52] Selective strategies "involve individualized sanctioning based on . . . individualized predictions of future offending," while charge-based sentencing applies "the same or a very similar sanction . . . to all persons convicted of common offenses."[53] The men studied over a 25-year period were a random sample of all incarcerated men.

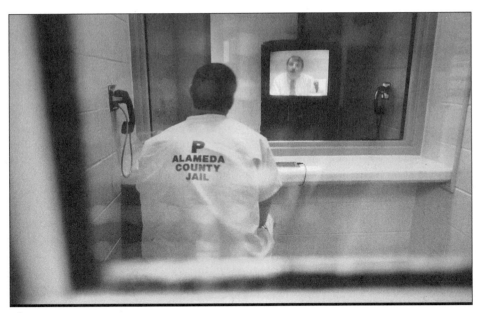

*A*n inmate is conferring with his attorney at the Alameda county jail on the video confer-encing system the jail has installed. This procedure and other "at-a-distance" contact methods are becoming common at modern facilities.

This so-called Class of 1962 "has been very active: they have been arrested well over 30,000 times since their release. . . ."[54] The Gottfredsons' concluded, regarding the hypothesized loss of incapacitative benefits resulting from the offenders' release:

> [H]ad none of these men been released . . . , more than 30,000 arrest offenses might have been prevented (if we assume, of course, that all of the arrests were legitimate, and that these offenders were the guilty parties). Almost 10,000 of these arrests were for serious offenses. The prevention (through incapacitation) of 184 homicides, 144 rapes, 2,084 assaults, 655 auto thefts, 2,756 burglaries, 2,800 thefts, and 1,193 robberies cannot be considered trivial.[55]

These numbers suggest that Californians would have been much better protected had these men never been released. But the Gottfredsons continue with their analysis and point out that "only 4,897 of these 6,310 men . . . ever were arrested after release. The 'lifetime' confinement of the other 1,413 on grounds of incapacitation must be viewed as a mistake—and a very expensive one."[56] In addition, they observe that by a ratio of three to one, the arrests that did occur were for "trivial" offenses.

They then argue that "any incapacitative approach" will depend for its success on the ability to make accurate predictions of future behavior. "In the absence of perfect prediction," it is impossible not to make two types of errors: falsely predicting future criminal behavior, and falsely predicting future law-abiding behavior. Thus, policy-makers must determine how much of the "human and monetary costs" they are willing to pay in order to maintain incapacitation as a major goal of criminal sentencing.[57]

John Irwin and James Austin add more fuel to the argument that incapacitation simply costs more than it is worth in their book about *America's Imprisonment Binge*.[58] They claim that we spend about three times as much to solve the crime problem than crime costs us—strictly in terms of dollars. The large increase in state and federal prison populations has resulted in more hostility inside prisons and less attention to programs designed to prepare inmates for eventual release. Much of the "imprisonment binge" can be laid to the public's misperceptions, fostered by the media, public officials, and criminologists:

> The public reacts to crime with fear and intensity because they have been led to believe by the media and public officials that thousands of vicious, intractable street criminals menace innocent citizens. . . .[59]

Irwin and Austin propose a solution to the problem:

> The single most direct solution that would have an immediate and dramatic impact on prison crowding and would not affect public safety is to *shorten prison terms*. This can be done swiftly and fairly through a number of existing mechanisms, such as greater use of existing good-time credit statutes and/or accelerating parole eligibility.[60]

But how will the public react to these measures?

CORRECTIONAL TREATMENT PROGRAMS

As we saw in a number of previous chapters, much of the increase in jail and prison admissions has been accounted for by drug offenders. We also have seen that many jails and prisons lack the resources and, perhaps, the will to provide specialized programs for drug and other substance abusers. To many observers, this failure cannot but contribute to high recidivism rates.

As one response to the problem posed by large numbers of drug abusers entering correctional populations, the United States has awarded a million-dollar grant to the University of Alabama for a "novel experiment" whereby everyone arrested in the city of Birmingham will be tested for drug use.[61] All those who test positive for drug abuse will be required to enter a treatment program.

Critics question whether coerced treatment will be effective. Others believe that mandatory treatment can be as effective as voluntary participation. In Chapter 7 we discussed in detail Maryland's experience with its treatment prison, Patuxent Institution. For over twenty years, mentally disordered offenders were committed indefinitely until they were "cured." Eventually, in the face of criticisms and a very modest success rate, the state's law was changed to make treatment voluntary.

On the other side of this issue is Susan Turner, a researcher at the Rand Corporation. She observed that "there isn't a whole lot of research but people who come into treatment unwillingly do seem to benefit from it. . . ."[62]

Some states, plagued by budgetary constraints, have gone in a very different direction: curtailing correctional programs. In a seemingly inexplicable decision, Maryland's Governor Parris Glendening has ordered the elimination of some of the state's prison educational programs. Of particular concern to many penologists is the fact that "Maryland would be the first to eliminate courses designed to prepare prisoners to pass high school equivalency exams and for vocational jobs such as auto repair and carpentry." The move was justified by the governor because of the state's budget shortfall. The cut in educational programming would save the state about $3.2 million and abolish forty-nine teaching positions. Perhaps correctional treatment programs are a luxury that simply cannot be afforded, especially at a time when public support for more punitive sentences is high.

An argument can be made that prisons are not the place for rehabilitative services to inmates. Charles H. Logan and Gerald Gaes have done just that.[64] They say that

*T*his is an example of the central monitoring station in an urban jail. Closed-circuit television allows the monitor to view all areas where inmates are present.

correctional institutions need to concentrate on implementing a **confinement model** and cease attempting to rehabilitate inmates. They propose a new and clearer mission statement for the American prison:

> The mission of a prison is to keep prisoners—to keep them in, keep them safe, keep them in line, keep them healthy, and keep them busy—and to do it with fairness, without undue suffering, and as efficiently as possible.[65]

Logan and Gaes state that it is not the duty of prisons to "reform, rehabilitate, or reintegrate offenders into society."[66] Although correctional institutions "*may* attempt," in their words, to accomplish these goals in addition to fulfilling the confinement mission, the responsibility for inmates' future social adjustment once out of prison lies with the inmates, not the prison.

PROBATION AND COMMUNITY-BASED CORRECTIONS

Barry Nidorf, Los Angeles County's chief probation officer, discussed the problem of maintaining a probation service at a time when incarceration is in vogue and resources are in short supply. In order to survive, his agency has

> aggressively publicized probation as a form of criminal sanction. Our decisive move away from a traditional social work emphasis and into the criminal justice arena coincided with the explosive increase in criminal violence.[67]

We might question Nidorf's statement that the "explosive" increase in violence was a major factor leading probation into the "criminal justice arena." Hasn't probation always been a part of criminal justice? The idea of a criminal justice *system* that includes probation seems to have escaped him.

Nidorf provides some astounding figures, which we must quote in detail:

- Through the aid of computers "most adult probationers are now monitored on very large 'bankloads' of 1,000 probationers."[68]
- "Selected high risk adult offenders continue to receive traditional supervision on caseloads of 200. Many high risk probationers—abusers of controlled substances, violent offenders, child molesters, and gang members—are supervised on caseloads of between 50 and 100."[69]

He does point out a significant factor with which probation and other community-based programs must deal—"a conflicted public—torn between fear of crime and fear of taxes. . . ."[70]

Commenting on probation's effect on recidivism rates, Ronald P. Corbett, Jr., points out that the public's fear of crime translates into its support for any sanction that promises to reduce recidivism.[71] However, the field of probation and related community corrections is divided on the validity of recidivism as the major criterion of success:

> Part of the reluctance to commit to recidivism as a main measure is due to the recognition that many of the forces that affect an offender's behavior—family, neighborhood, job market, availability of treatment services—are beyond the control of a probation and parole officer.[72]

This insightful statement certainly reflects a frequently cited deficiency of community-based corrections: the failure to address the community variables that have a significant impact on an offender's behavior. We noted this deficiency in Chapter 14.

Lori Scott takes a more positive view regarding the future of probation in the face of increasing calls for it to be more control and punishment oriented.[73] She finds that "criminal justice experts here and abroad predict that technology and specialization will be trends that can make community corrections safer, increasingly innovative, and cost-effective alternatives to expensive prisons."[74] Scott is referring to various technologies and methodologies that include electronic monitoring, computer tracking of offenders' work and lifestyles, and specialized probation caseloads managed by highly trained officers, assisted by specialist consultants.

SPECIAL NEEDS INMATES

Health Needs

Health needs of incarcerated offenders are predicted to be a major concern in the next century. Health problems include HIV infection and AIDS, tuberculosis, hepatitis, and mental illness. The problem of HIV infection and AIDS is especially serious for incarcerated women, who often receive the smallest piece of the resource pie. Women at high risk of infection (drug abusers and the economically disadvantaged) are concentrated in prison populations. Studies have shown that "AIDS has been identified as the eighth leading cause of death among women [in the United States] aged fifteen to forty-four."[75]

Women who are HIV positive are especially vulnerable to "opportunistic" infections such as tuberculosis and to cervical cancer.[76] The expense of medical care for an HIV-infected inmate, male or female, is very high:

ACROSS CULTURES

CRIME PREVENTION IN A COMMUNITARIAN SOCIETY: THE CASE OF THE PEOPLE'S REPUBLIC OF CHINA

As we pointed out in Chapter 14, community-based corrections has become increasingly popular because of overcrowded prison, probation, and parole populations. In the United States, many of the sanctions that fall under the community corrections umbrella emphasize punitive and control objectives and are aimed at individual offenders. Some have suggested that were the United States to adopt more communitarian strategies to deal with its crime problem, more satisfying results would be possible.

By contrast, China, a communitarian society, employs strategies designed to prevent crime and reintegrate offenders that stress the involvement of the entire community. The Chinese strategy of *bang-jiao* "is . . . a community-based remedial and preventive measure for controlling crime rather than an administrative disposition or judicial punishment" (p. 208).

Three categories of offenders are dealt with through the *bang-jiao* approach: those committing minor offenses not requiring incarceration; offenders leaving reformatories and labor camps who are at risk of recidivating; and offenders whose good behavior in labor camps results in release before their sentences have expired.

The most commonly used *bang-jiao* measure is one that involves youthful offenders' parents, neighbors, and a "member of the Neighborhood Committee." Neighborhood Committees consist of elected neighbors in the offender's community. They are paid a modest stipend by a local branch of the government.

In one large Chinese city, it has been reported that nearly 22,000 youths have been assisted through *bang-jiao*. This assistance includes helping with daily living problems, giving emotional support and love, and developing a "genuine repentance" in offenders.

SOURCE: Lening Zhang, et al., "Crime Prevention in a Communitarian Society: *Bang-Jiao* and *Tiao-Jie* in the People's Republic of China," *Justice Quarterly* 13 (1996): 199–222.

New Jersey prison authorities report that the average cost associated with caring for an infected inmate (from diagnosis to death) was $67,000, and that the average length of hospitalization was 102 days.[77]

Mark Lanier recommended that those women who develop "symptomatic AIDS"* should be released into community-based programs.[78] Since most imprisoned women are nonviolent offenders, this should not affect public safety.

With respect to HIV infection there are a number of problems facing the correctional administrator. Perhaps one of the most pressing is that of testing inmates for infection. Should this be mandatory? Who has access to the results of tests? These are important questions because the reported rate of AIDS in state and federal prisons has risen from 181 per 100,000 inmates in 1990 to 362 per 100,000 inmates in 1993.[79] As we noted in Chapter 8, a number of issues related to housing and security must be addressed by the prison administrator. Should HIV-positive inmates who show no

*This term refers to those infected with the HIV virus who show actual symptoms of AIDS such as Karposi's sarcoma, a type of cancer with highly visible skin lesions.

symptoms of AIDS be segregated? If not, how is the transmission of the virus to other inmates and staff to be prevented?

Treatment for prisoners who are HIV positive varies from state to state, and the rate of opportunistic diseases is high for prisoners whose immune systems have been devastated by the virus. Diagnosis and medical treatment are extremely costly to correctional systems already straining to operate with limited resources. One estimate claims that state correctional systems have seen their health care expenditures increase to the point that they constitute 10 percent of their total budgets.[80] A growing portion of this increase is attributed to HIV infection among prison populations.

Tuberculosis is a particularly troubling concern. "Most prison environments today are extremely conducive to TB transmission. They are vastly overcrowded . . . have poor ventilation systems, and are comprised of individuals most likely to be TB infected. . . ."[81] Some, like New York, administer mandatory TB testing upon admissions. New York's rate of active TB has increased from 15.4 per 100,000 to 105.5 per 100,000 over a ten-year period.[82]

To meet the challenges of HIV/AIDS and tuberculosis, prison administrators will need to take a number of costly steps:

- Mandatory testing of incoming inmates for TB.
- Referring TB- and HIV-infected inmates to community-based service agencies upon release.
- Improving risk-reduction education and counseling for HIV-infected inmates and evaluating their effectiveness.
- Improving the prisons physical plant in terms of ventilation and equipping staff with appropriate barrier masks and respirators whenever TB outbreaks are noted.
- Alleviating prison overcrowding, since it is a significant contributor to the spread of TB.

Substance Abusing Inmates

As increasing numbers of substance-abusing offenders enter prison, providing and delivering appropriate treatment to them has been a serious problem. Some surveys find that "the most common 'treatment' model available to inmates, experienced by at least 65% of all those in need of . . . treatment is incarceration without any specialized . . . treatment services."[83] When treatment is available, it usually is based on Alcoholics Anonymous, Narcotics Anonymous, and Cocaine Anonymous models, and a combination of drug education and counseling.

The **therapeutic community** (TC) model is one potentially promising new approach employed in some correctional systems. It relies on considerable inmate self-help together with a special relationship with the institution's staff. Frequently, a portion of staff in these programs are themselves recovering addicts.

Although there is little evidence that drug education and counseling are effective in reducing substance abuse after release or recidivism levels, there is some evidence that the TC model can produce at least a 10 percent reduction in recidivism rates.[84] One review of TC evaluation studies by Douglas Lipton concluded that the "evidence offers a window of opportunity for establishing treatment interventions that have been documented by research and supported by practice."[85]

Lipton's review of the evaluation literature included TCs in New York (Stay'n Out), the Cornerstone program in Oregon, California's Amity Prison program, and Delaware's Key-Crest program. Each of these TCs produced positive results when

ON THE JOB

WHAT IS A THERAPEUTIC COMMUNITY?

Drug abuse treatment in prison, which began more than 50 years ago, has been influenced by the development of therapeutic communities (TCs). Grounded in the self-help tradition, TCs typically house clients in residential settings that offer opportunities for intensive intervention and support that may not be available on an outpatient basis. The original TC for drug addiction was California's Synanon, which based some of its concepts on psychiatric therapeutic communities and on the fellowship concept of Alcoholics Anonymous.

TCs were originally developed to treat hard-core heroin-dependent criminals. They address not just drug use but also associated problems that reduce the drug user's capacity to function appropriately in society. For this reason, the TC has been described as "a way of defining the nature of individual drug problems as much as a therapeutic approach."

What distinguishes TCs is the "community" or group as the primary facilitator of growth and change. As applied to corrections, clients live isolated from the rest of the prison population and receive treatment to change negative patterns of behavior, thinking, and feeling that predispose them to drug use.

Participation generally lasts for an extended period. The time and the isolation are primary resources; the isolation, in particular, shields clients from competing demands of street, work, friends, and family. TCs have other features in common: use of ex-offenders and ex-addicts as staff, use of confrontation and support groups, a set of rules and sanctions to govern behavior, and promotion of prosocial attitudes. In prisons, TCs also focus on criminal behavior, sex abuse, and other issues. The drug users' transformations in conduct, attitudes, values, and emotions are monitored and mutually reinforced. It may be this multiple focus that explains why TCs are more likely to be successful in the long run than programs aimed mainly at drug abuse.

SOURCE: Douglas S. Lipton, "Prison-Based Therapeutic Communities: Their Success with Drug-Abusing Offenders," *National Institute of Justice Journal* (February 1996): 13.

recidivism was measured by rearrest rates and continued drug abuse. Lipton also looked at the cost-effectiveness of these programs and found that they were "sound investments." Specifically, he concluded that,

> It is true that programs like [New York's] Stay'n Out cost about $3,000 to $4,000 more than the standard correctional cost per inmate per year; programs like Cornerstone [in Oregon] cost a little over twice as much because they have a higher number of professional staff members and lighter caseloads. However, the savings in crime-related and drug-use-associated costs pay for the treatment in about 2 to 3 years. It is an inescapable conclusion that treatment lowers crime and health costs as well as related social and criminal justice costs.[86]

One very significant finding was that "success," whether defined in terms of recidivism (rearrest) or drug abuse, is clearly related to length of participation in a TC program. The longer the participation, the better the success rates. Simply not dropping out of a program does not predict success. The On the Job feature summarizes the essentials of a therapeutic community model.

Elderly and Mentally Ill Inmates

Inmates who are elderly or mentally ill (sometimes both) pose serious problems for corrections, especially offenders sentenced to long terms of confinement. We will take up one state's response to prisoners' access to mental health treatment services in the section below on prisoners' rights as an example of the problem and one apparently successful attempt to solve it.

The growing number of "long-term" inmates* will require prison administrators to provide a number of specialized programs and introduce modifications to their institutional routines. Among the special needs of these inmates are mental health services and services to those who may become physically disabled. Special housing units may be required to accommodate them and protect them from being victimized by the general prison population.

In addition to these in-prison needs, particular attention will have to be paid to prerelease and release programming. This may include halfway housing and nursing homes for those inmates who are elderly at time of release. Unfortunately, while

> the number and proportion of long-term inmates is growing and will continue to do so . . . [their] specialized needs will require attention from correctional systems which currently do not always effectively meet the needs of shorter-term inmates.[87]

PRISONERS' RIGHTS

Although there have been attempts to limit prisoners' access to the court to press their claims against their keepers (we discussed this in Chapter 10), lawsuits are still being filed. For example, the Justice Department is suing the Iberia parish sheriff and the warden of the Iberia Parish Criminal Justice Facility, claiming that inmates are regularly subjected to excessive force.[88] The suit has been filed under the provisions of the 1994 federal crime statute that allows the Justice Department to investigate "patterns or practices" of law enforcement misconduct. We may recall that the Justice Department has begun an investigation of the operations of Maryland's super-max prison under this same provision.** The government has alleged that "deputy sheriffs at the . . . [Iberia] jail . . . regularly bind inmates' mouths with duct tape, tie their hands and feet together in one knot and place detainees in a restraining chair for days at a time. . . ."[89]

A class action lawsuit filed on behalf of Ohio prison inmates was settled by way of a consent decree (*Dunn v. Voinovich*, CI-93-0166) on July 10, 1995.[90] The suit had alleged that Ohio's Department of Rehabilitation and Correction (DRC) "was so deficient as to violate the Eighth Amendment's proscription against cruel and unusual punishment."[91]

The consent decree was issued following a study by a team of experts which found that the DRC had too few trained staff and insufficient physical space for mentally ill offenders, and that there were "too many barriers to reaching the limited care available."[92] One important result of the consent decree process was setting a definition

---

*A long-term inmate is defined as "one who has or will be continuously confined for a period of seven years [or longer]." Wilson and Vito, p. 21.

**See Chapter 10, pp. 232–233.

of "serious mental illness" for the DRC. The language, in part, defined serious mental illness as:

> a substantial disorder of thought or mood which significantly impairs judgment, behavior, capacity to recognize reality or cope with the ordinary demands of life within the prison environment and is manifested by substantial pain or disability.[93]

The definition "does not include inmates who are substance abusers, substance dependent, including alcoholics and narcotic addicts, or persons convicted of any sex offense, who are not otherwise diagnosed as seriously mentally ill."[94]

THE FUTURE OF CORRECTIONS

When we try to predict what the future may be like for corrections, we must be extremely careful not to make the mistake of taking the present too seriously. As we saw in Chapters 6 and 7, there have been numerous twists and turns in laws, policies, and practices affecting corrections in the United States. Just looking at the history of prisons, we saw that inmates were viewed as penitents, persons who could be molded into a shape that would please us (i.e., "reformed"), patients who could be cured of their criminality, and individuals who deserved to suffer. In the next century, we may come upon still another perception of the correctional client.

We will now examine a number of areas we believe to be particularly important in the future: prison crowding, the role of the prison and intermediate sanctions in criminal justice, super-max institutions, and the prison-industrial complex.

Responding to Prison Crowding

It is vital to approach corrections systematically and with clear sets of objectives. If we fail to do this, responses to the continuing pressures on prison systems may well result in a system breakdown. Once this systemic approach has taken root, it may be possible to put together what Richard Rosenfeld and Kimberly Kempf call a **sanctions budget,** which will allow for a rational allocation of scarce resources.[95] In their words:

> As shown earlier, sound correctional policy requires rational decision making throughout integrated legislative, judicial, and executive decision stages. . . . The burden of operating within [our proposed sanctions] budget falls primarily to the judiciary through the assignment of sanctions.
>
> . . . The current crisis in corrections, and the impetus behind the search for alternatives to traditional policies and practices, are a function largely of the sheer weight of numbers.[97]

Rosenfeld and Kempf insist that sound policy and practice require that we "disentangle" the different philosophies of corrections, and understand that choices must be made with awareness of the serious "conflict between punitive and rehabilitative responses to crime."[98]

A very different approach to the problems of an ever-increasing prison population is one adopted by the Federal Bureau of Prisons (BOP).[99] Scott Higgins, chief of the Federal Bureau of Prisons Design and Construction Branch, described the bureau's response to the major increase in the federal prison population:

The high costs of new institutions have caused the BOP to asses the need for such facilities. As a result of comparing its inmate population with available bed space and reviewing additional capacity options, the BOP implemented a change in its policy on double-bunking.[100]

By double-bunking, the BOP has been able to enhance the rated capacity of its existing and proposed prisons, achieving major per-bed cost reductions. Other cost-cutting measures include creating satellite minimum security camps at some large, secure prisons where offenders classified as low risk can be housed at much less expense. Correctional "complexes consisting of more than one institution of different security levels have been feasible at a few sites across the country. . . ."[101]

Although the measures Higgins describes may, in the short term, ameliorate the conditions caused by prison population pressures and tight budgets, they do not address other crucial problems as corrections moves into the twenty-first century, problems such as determining the roles corrections, especially prisons, should be playing.

The Role of the Prison in Criminal Justice

The several missions assigned to the American prison, punishment, incapacitation, and rehabilitation, are incompatible, as we noted in Chapters 6 through 9. This was stated concisely by H. R. DeLuca and associates when they wrote that the public demands that prisons produce "a punished and rehabilitated ex-offender . . . [but] it is virtually impossible to create an environment in which punishment is inflicted while, at the same time, the social values and goals advanced by that institution are accepted and internalized by them."[102]

They offer a radical proposal for the future: The prison mission should be limited to punishment and incapacitation. If this were done and rehabilitative programs were eliminated or severely reduced, the "amount of prison time required . . . will be less than that currently being used to attempt to punish and simultaneously rehabilitate. . . ."[103] They propose that criminal sentences be divided into stages. The first stage would contain the amount of sanction calculated to punish and incapacitate (with deterrence included as an objective) through confinement. The following stages would consist of mandatory, intensive parole supervision, followed by ordinary supervision. During these stages, rehabilitative programs and services would be provided. In the Focus on the Law feature we summarize DeLuca's hypothetical sentence for a serious felony.

To ensure that the confinement period of a sentence is purely punitive, DeLuca argues that the prison should be stripped of the "amenities such as those found in today's prisons."[104] They do not "create an environment in which punishment takes place." It is not clear just what amenities are to be eliminated. We usually do not think of prisons as containing many amenities, but they probably include various educational, vocational, and counseling activities.

Others also have urged us to reconsider the roles we want our correctional institutions to play as we move into the next century. Rosenfeld and Kempf, as we saw above, suggested establishing a **sanctions budget** to better allocate scarce resources. To do this demands that we make "sound policy choices." These choices

require a recognition, indeed an elaboration, of the tensions in correctional philosophies. Correctional policy making should be embedded in an explicit conceptual framework that reflects both restrictive and expansive conceptions of correctional control.[105]

FOCUS ON
THE LAW

A PROPOSED THREE-PHASE SENTENCE TO INCLUDE
PUNISHMENT AND REHABILITATION

H. R. DeLuca and associates propose to modify sentencing statutes by dividing them into stages so that both punitive and rehabilitative objectives can be served without the conflict that exists in today's typical laws.

They suggest, as an example, that for offenders convicted of capital crimes (excluding multiple murders or rapes and organized crimes) the sentence be structured as follows:

a. Five years of confinement at hard labor.
To be followed by,

b. Fifteen years of "intensive parole supervision and rehabilitation."
To be followed by,
c. Fifteen years of "routine monitoring" by parole officers.

Thus, the total period of control for murder, for example, would be thirty-five years. No good-time credits would be awarded, nor would inmates be eligible for discretionary release by parole boards.

SOURCE: Based on H. R. DeLuca, Thomas J. Miller, and Carl F. Wiedmann, "Punishment vs. Rehabilitation: A Proposal for Revising Sentencing Practices," *Federal Probation* 55 (September 1991): 39.

The Role of Intermediate Sanctions

The search for alternatives to incarceration has led to increased use of so-called intermediate sanctions such as home detention and electronic surveillance. The presumed advantages include slowing the pace of prison admissions and cost reductions. However, these advantages may be illusory:

> Home incarceration appears to be inherently limited as a sanction alternative because it has not grown at a rate necessary to absorb more than a small fraction of the one million incarcerated. . . .[106]

Because of the special costs involved in home detention and electronic monitoring, any claimed savings are real only if we compare them to traditional incarceration. Ordinary parole and probation are much less costly.

Rosenfeld and Kempf caution against an expansion of home detention, arguing that there are constitutional questions regarding its use as a general alternative to incarceration:

> By promising to depopulate the prisons, it seems to be a restrictive correctional policy, when in fact it is maximally expansive by turning the . . . offender's (or worse yet, pretrial detainee's) home into a prison cell.[107]

The Super-Max Prison

Prison crowding and limited resources to deal with it have contributed to making prisons very uncomfortable and dangerous places. The argument is frequently made that super-maximum-security prisons are justified when inmates in standard institutions react to these conditions violently. Transferring them to a super-max facility can sig-

*T*he future of corrections requires systematic study and a clear set of objectives. The multiple ideas of American prisons to punish, incapacitate, and rehabilitate are not directed towards the same end result. Those who decide the policies for corrections must decide if they will move forward in making and enforcing policy or try to redirect the methods that have been used in the past.

nificantly improve the "quality of life and operations of other prisons in a system."[108] As we saw in Chapter 8, the United States Bureau of Prisons has concentrated its "difficult-to-manage" inmates at the Administrative Maximum Penitentiary (ADX) at Florence, Colorado. It has done so while "complying with all relevant legal guidelines."[109]

We note here that according to John Vanyur, associate warden of ADX, twenty-seven departments of corrections have super-max institutions (or super-max units in existing prisons). This suggests a trend stimulated by increasing prison populations made up of higher percentages of long-term, increasingly violent and escape-prone inmates. Thus, the twenty-first century may well see the super-max prison as a growth industry.

ADX was designed and constructed specifically for the inmate population transferred to it. It is not simply a modified standard prison. For example, "all cells have precast concrete walls, floors and ceilings. All cell furniture is made of reinforced concrete."[110] No matches or cigarette lighters are permitted, each cell having a built-in electric lighter. Plumbing fixtures are "flood-proof" and each cell has a shower so that inmate movement outside cells is reduced and privacy increased.

A key element in keeping assaults on staff to a minimum are "inmate-restraint policies" whereby inmates required to be outside their cells are cuffed and shackled. Inmates in the most controlled classification are escorted by three guards when outside the cells. The results of both design features and inmate-restraint policies have been significant, according to Warden Vanyur. In five years following the opening of ADX, there have been no staff murders, and assaults have decreased dramatically.

Because inmates spend virtually all their time in solitary confinement, there has been concern about their mental health under conditions of "sensory deprivation."

According to Warden Vanyur, ADX has sought to deal with this issue in the following way:

> Each cell has an external window that provides natural light (but does not look onto the perimeter of another cell), and [has] an internal window. . . . Each inmate controls his own lighting. Each cell has its own television set and radio.[111]

Many have criticized super-max institutions because they do not provide correctional programs. Indeed, many of these facilities are referred to as "adjustment" prisons, with their primary objective being adjusting recalcitrant inmates to prison life so that they can be returned to an ordinary institution. The ADX facility does provide educational, drug counseling, and religious programs. However, these are delivered using "distance learning methods" through television and correspondence courses. Counseling employs a one-on-one approach.

One preliminary review of federal super-max experiences found reductions in prison violence. The study, by David Ward, also found that recidivism among those confined under the most maximum control conditions was better than expected (less than half of those released from the first super-max prison, Alcatraz, returned to prison). However, it is possible, perhaps even probable, that relatively low recidivism rates can be accounted for in large measure by the age of released inmates. Those confined in and eventually released from these prisons are significantly older than other inmates.[112]

The Prison-Industrial Complex

The **prison-industrial complex** is an "iron triangle of government bureaucrats, private industry leaders and politicians who work together to expand the criminal justice system."[113] The emergence of this complex is characterized by the rapid growth of private activity in the correctional field. We described some of this activity, called privatization, in Chapters 5, 8, 14, and 16. Private contractors have been operating correctional institutions, electronically monitoring parolees and probationers, and providing educational and treatment services for some time. Whether or not these services will be expanded in the future is unclear at this time.

What corrections might be like in the twenty-first century depends on what the future holds in store for the criminal justice system. "The pendulum of U.S. correctional reform has swung back and forth . . . , reflecting the public's frustration with *both* liberal and conservative criminal justice policies."[114] At the present time, incarceration and very intensive community supervision sanctions are features of this prison-industrial complex.

The Future?

In the book *No Escape: The Future of American Corrections*,[115] John DiIulio offers four predictions about the future of corrections in America:

1. There is no escaping a much larger correctional system.
2. There is no escape from the need to provide more jail and prison space.
3. Prison and jail construction will not keep up with the demand for space. Thus, there is no escape from prison overcrowding.
4. There is no escape from the need to move seriously toward community-based programs such as home detention, electronic monitoring, community service sentences, and intensive community supervision programs.

James Byrne and Mary Brewster say that it is essential to answer a more fundamental question that puts any future into a systemic perspective: "The question is: how will [legislators and correctional administrators at the federal, state and local levels] answer basic questions about the *purpose* of corrections as they rethink their response to the various types of offenders. . . ."[116] That is, are criminal sentences to serve retributive, deterrence, rehabilitative, or control purposes, or some combination of these? What priority will be assigned to these objectives?

Over the next ten years, Byrne and Brewster wonder, will our policies and practices be more of the same, or will we move in a different direction? They say "we will need to change fundamentally the way we think about punishment, corrections, and the dynamics of community control."[117] They predict three fundamental changes in community control by the end of this century: (a) increased use of "nonsupervision sanctions—such as day fines and community service . . ."; (b) "state and local corrections [will] embrace fully the idea of unique, stand-alone intermediate sanctions" that combine punishment and treatment; and (c) "traditional probation programs [will] move out of the office and into the streets."[118] This will enable probation services to meet the needs of offenders and their victims more effectively.

Etta Morgan-Sharp and Robert Sigler make a surprising prediction: "As we enter the twenty-first century, it is probable that there will be a shift in philosophy from a preference for punishment to one of treatment . . . for offenders."[119] They claim that it will be recognized that punishment (incarceration) is too costly and does not work. "The argument will emerge that it is not enough to lock people up—something must be done to reduce the likelihood that they will continue to commit crimes."[120]

Certainly, if incarceration rates continue to rise, it will be increasingly difficult to continue to respond with more prison construction. Nola Joyce estimates that in Illinois alone "it will be necessary for the state to build 23 prisons over the next 10 years at a cost of $1.2 billion. These facilities will cost an estimated $391 million per year to operate."[121]

SUMMARY

THE FIELD OF CORRECTIONS is the final act in the drama of criminal justice. It includes a myriad of sanctions, activities, and several very different and sometimes conflicting objectives. These objectives change over time depending on public opinion, which is to a large extent informed by media reports about crime. Political leaders and criminal justice policymakers respond as best they can to the current opinion. All too often the response fails to take into account the systemic consequences. At the present time, public opinion supports a "get tough" stand against crime and criminals.

We have been particularly interested in this and earlier chapters with the failure to see corrections as part of a system that includes legislatures, prosecutors, judges, community supervision personnel, and prison administrators and their staffs. Get-tough laws usually mean that prisons become overcrowded with offenders, and too frequently it is not the most serious, violent offenders who will spend longer periods of time there than in the past. Using probation and parole and other forms of community supervision in ways that stress punishment and control almost certainly increases rates of violation. This, in turn, feeds offenders back into our prisons.

We have shown that responses to overcrowded prisons include measures that in reality violate the get-tough philosophy. Accelerated release through liberal grants of good-time credits is one such measure. A number of states have adopted legislation that requires early release when prisons reach a certain percentage of their rated

FOCUS ON
THE LAW

DOING SOFT TIME FOR THOSE WITH
THE MEANS TO PAY*

At the end of each work day . . . , Willis has driven from his job . . . and checked into one of the most exclusive rooms in Southern California.

The cost is only $55 a night, but if he fails to check in by 8PM, he will lose his spot and be forced to live in a far less comfortable place: Los Angeles County Jail.

As California, and Los Angeles in particular, experienced rapidly expanding jail populations, conditions in these facilities deteriorated, and then became more violent. Some offenders have sought through plea agreements to serve their sentences in suburban jails such as Pasadena where a new generation jail recently opened. Mose of these offend-

ers were sentenced to work-release terms, but some spend all their time in jail (in such cases, the per diem charge is $78).

The Pasadena jail supervisor was quoted as saying that the purpose of allowing some persons to serve their sentences in his institution was to "create a humane atmosphere for people to serve their time and not lose their jobs." In response to criticism that these "pay and stay" sentences discriminate against the indigent, another official claimed that some poor defendants with "good references" have been sentenced to the Pasadena jail. These offenders make up about 5 percent of the total so sentenced.

*SOURCE: Solomon Moore, "For Those With the Means to Pay, There's a Soft-cell Way to Do Time," *Los Angeles Times,* October 20, 1996, p. A14.

capacity. One recent survey of state correctional institutions found that, on average, inmates spend less than half their sentences in confinement.

In the above Focus on the Law feature, we show how far one jurisdiction in California has gone to relieve its jail population and at the same time significantly reduced the impact of incarceration as a punitive sanction. This effort, variously referred to as "pay and stay" and "soft-cell" incarceration, obviously favors those offenders who can afford the $55 to $78 per day charges in order to avoid serving their sentences in crowded and harsh facilities. Whether this development will catch on elsewhere is impossible to say at this time.

As we have observed throughout the previous chapters, corrections is system-dependent. To put it bluntly, corrections is at the mercy of legislatures, prosecutors, and the judiciary. Each of these major players in the criminal justice drama exert tremendous influence on the size and character of the correctional population in the United States. Corrections is the tail of the criminal justice dog, and the tail does not wag the dog. To the contrary, it seems that the dog spends a lot of time chasing its tail.

We see much merit in H. R. DeLuca's proposal for limiting the prison's role to that of humane and secure confinement, leaving the rehabilitation role to community-based agencies. But then we are warned by the observation of Michael Welch, who reviewed prison violence and its impact on prisoners' future outside prison.[122] Welch stated that prisons should be both civilized and civilizing. The conditions in many, if not most, prisons are distinctly uncivilized; it is unrealistic to expect that an inmate's experience will be sufficiently civilizing so that rehabilitation outside prison walls can be effective. As Welch observed:

Even for those who have not been assaulted in prison, the experience of incarceration is profound. Yet, for those who have endured violence, the effects of prison are all the more dramatic. It is no exaggeration to say that these inmates suffer a level of punishment exceeding the sentence imposed by the courts.[123]

Finally, we need to reiterate the fact that the way the nation's war on drugs has been fought has made the major contribution to the crowding of both prison and many community-based sanctions such as probation. One of the more discouraging features of corrections, especially institution-based corrections, is the inadequacy of specialized staff and treatment services for the substance-abusing offender. One small glimmer of hope in this area is the therapeutic community model, which has managed to gain a foothold in some correctional facilities.

KEY CONCEPTS

Confinement model   Sanctions budget
Prison-industrial complex   Therapeutic community (TC)

QUESTIONS FOR DISCUSSION

1. "The crisis in corrections manifested in overcrowded prisons has been caused in large measure by the war on drugs." Critically evaluate this statement. If it is accurate, what might be done to remedy the problem for corrections while still combating illegal drug use?
2. Michael Welch proposes limiting the role of the prison to humane confinement as a way to deliver deserved punishment more effectively by leaving rehabilitation to agencies outside the prison. Critically evaluate Welch's proposal.
3. Many studies of corrections' response to the pressures caused by various sentencing reforms show that these reforms are in effect negated by the exercise of discretion. Critically evaluate the effects of this discretion on the objectives of the sentence reforms.
4. Is it possible for corrections to operate successfully given the varied tasks we have assigned it? Fully explain your answer.
5. Do you believe that restricting the prison's role to deserved punishment and humane confinement will solve the problem of conflicting and contradictory goals? If this narrowing of the prison's role in criminal justice were to be put into effect, what would be the consequences for the other components of the corrections system?

ENDNOTES

1. William Booth, "The Return of the Chain Gangs," *Washington Post,* May 4, 1995, p. A-1.
2. Ibid., p. A-14.
3. Steven Donziger, "The Prison-Industrial Complex: What's Really Driving the Rush to Lock 'Em Up," *Washington Post,* March 17, 1996, p. C3.

4. "Around the Nation—Taking a Tough Stance with Georgia Inmates," *Washington Post,* January 4, 1996, p. A5.

5. Norval Morris and Michael Tonry, *Between Prison and Probation: Intermediate Punishments in a Rational Sentencing System* (New York: Oxford University Press, 1990).

6. Ibid., p. 223.

7. Marylee N. Reynolds, "Back on the Chain Gang," *Corrections Today* 58 (1996), p. 183.

8. Ibid.

9. Ibid.

10. Ibid.

11. Ibid.

12. John H. Kramer and Jeffery T. Ulmer, "Sentencing Disparity and Departures from Guidelines," *Justice Quarterly* 13 (1996): 81–106.

13. Ibid., p. 101.

14. Ibid.

15. Lisa Stolzenberg and Stewart J. D'Alessio, "The Unintended Consequences of Linking Sentencing Guidelines to Prison Populations—A Reply to Moody and Marvell," *Criminology* 34 (1996): 269–279.

16. Ibid., p. 277.

17. Ibid.

18. Michael G. Turner, et al., "'Three Strikes and You're Out' Legislation: A National Assessment," *Federal Probation* 59 (September 1995): 16–35.

19. Ibid., p. 19.

20. Ibid., p. 32.

21. Ibid., p. 34.

22. Pamala Griset, "The Politics and Economics of Increased Correctional Discretion over Time: A New York Case Study," *Justice Quarterly* 12 (1995): 307–323.

23. Ibid., pp. 319–320.

24. Ibid., p. 320.

25. Ibid.

26. Gwyn Smith Ingley, "Fiscal and Operational Impact of Three-Strikes Legislation," *Corrections Today* 57 (1995): 24.

27. Ibid.

28. Peter J. Benekas and Alida V. Merlo, "Three Strikes and You're Out!: The Political Sentencing Game," *Federal Probation* 59 (1995): 6.

29. Thomas B. Marvell and Carlisle E. Moody, "Determinate Sentencing and Abolishing Parole: The Long-Term Impacts on Prisons and Crime," *Criminology* 34 (1996): 107–128.

30. Ibid., p. 122.

31. Thomas B. Marvell and Carlisle E. Moody, "The Impact of Enhanced Prison Terms for Felonies Committed with Guns," *Criminology* 33 (1995): 247–278.

32. Ibid., p. 269.

33. Nola M. Joyce, "A View of the Future: The Effect of Policy on Prison Growth," *Crime & Delinquency* 38 (1992): 357–368.

34. Ibid.

35. Ibid.

36. Ibid., p. 361.

37. Ibid.

38. Ibid., p. 362.

39. Ibid., p. 368.

40. Ibid.

41. Darrell Steffensmeier and Miles D. Harer, "Bulging Prisons, an Aging U.S. Population, and the Nation's Crime Rate," *Federal Probation* 57 (June 1993), p. 9.

42. Ibid.

43. Ibid., p. 10.

44. Sheldon Ekland-Olson, William R. Kelly, and Michael Eisenberg, "Crime and Incarceration: Some Comparative Findings from the 1980s," *Crime & Delinquency* 38 (1992): 392–416.

45. Ibid., p. 100.
46. Ibid., p. 103.
47. Ibid., p. 409.
48. Ibid.
49. Ibid.
50. George H. Cox, Jr., and Susan L. Rhodes, "Managing Overcrowding: Corrections Administrators and the Prison Crisis," *Criminal Justice Policy Review* 4 (1990): p. 117.
51. Stephen D. Gottfredson and Don M. Gottfredson, "Behavioral Prediction and the Problem of Incapacitation," *Criminology* 32 (1994): 441–474.
52. Ibid., p. 443.
53. Ibid.
54. Ibid., p. 449.
55. Ibid., p. 468.
56. Ibid.
57. Ibid.
58. John Irwin and James Austin, *It's About Time: America's Imprisonment Binge* (Belmont, CA: Wadsworth Publishing, 1994).
59. Ibid., pp. 20–21.
60. Ibid., p. 172.
61. "Birmingham Arrestees Face Mandatory Drug Treatment: U.S. Grants $1 Million for Experiment," *Washington Post,* July 8, 1996, p. A4.
62. Ibid.
63. Jon Jeter, "Md. to Abolish Some Prison Educational Programs," *Washington Post,* February 14, 1996, p. C1.
64. Charles H. Logan and Gerald G. Gaes, "Meta-Analysis and the Rehabilitation of Punishment," *Justice Quarterly* 10 (1993): 245–263.
65. Ibid., p. 261.
66. Ibid.
67. Barry J. Nidorf, "Surviving in a 'Lock Them Up' Era," *Federal Probation* 60 (March 1996), p. 6.
68. Ibid.
69. Ibid., p. 7.
70. Ibid., p. 8.
71. Ronald P. Corbett, Jr., "When Community Corrections Means Business: Introducing 'Reinventing' Themes to Probation and Parole," *Federal Probation* 60 (March 1996): 36–42.
72. Ibid., p. 39.
73. Lori Scott, "Probation: Heading in a New Direction," in Roslyn Muraskin and Albert R. Roberts, eds., *Visions for Change: Crime and Justice in the Twenty-First Century* (Upper Saddle River, NJ: Prentice Hall, 1996), pp. 172–183.
74. Ibid., p. 173.
75. Mark M. Lanier, "Justice for Incarcerated Women with HIV in the Twenty-First Century," in Roslyn Muraskin and Albert R. Roberts, eds., *Visions for Change: Crime and Justice in the Twenty-First Century* (Upper Saddle River, NJ: Prentice Hall, 1996), p. 327.
76. Ibid., p. 329.
77. Ibid.
78. Ibid., p. 335.
79. James Tesoriero and Malcolm McCullough, "Correctional Health Care Now and into the Twenty-First Century," in Roslyn Muraskin and Albert R. Roberts, eds., *Visions for Change: Crime and Justice in the Twenty-First Century* (Upper Saddle River, NJ: Prentice Hall, 1996), p. 223.
80. Ibid., p. 225.
81 Ibid., p. 229.
82. Ibid., p. 230.
83. Ibid., p. 218.

84. Ibid., p. 220.
85. Douglas S. Lipton, "Prison-Based Therapeutic Communities: Their Success with Drug-Abusing Offenders," *National Institute of Justice Journal* (February 1996): 12.
86. Ibid., p. 17.
87. Deborah G. Wilson and Gennaro F. Vito, "Long-Term Inmates: Special Needs and Management Considerations," *Federal Probation* 52 (1988): 25.
88. "Around the Nation: Louisiana Officials Sued for Abuse of Prisoners," *Washington Post,* June 7, 1996, p. A2.
89. Ibid.
90. Fred Cohen, "Ohio's Mentally Ill Get Historic Consent Decree: Both Sides Agree," *Corrections Today* 58 (1996): 156–161.
91. Ibid., p. 156.
92. Ibid., p. 157.
93. Ibid., p. 158.
94. Ibid.
95. Richard Rosenfeld and Kimberly Kempf, "The Scope and Purposes of Corrections: Exploring Alternative Responses to Prison Crowding," *Crime & Delinquency* 37 (1991): 481–505.
96. Ibid., p. 499.
97. Ibid., p. 482.
98. Ibid.
99. Scott Higgins, "The BOP's Response to Population Growth," *Corrections Today* 58 (1996): 110–113.
100. Ibid., p. 110.
101. Ibid., p. 113.
102. H. R. DeLuca, Thomas J. Miller, and Carl F. Wiedemann, "Punishment vs. Rehabilitation: A Proposal for Revising Sentencing Practices," *Federal Probation* 55 (September 1991): 37.
103. Ibid., p. 38.
104. Ibid., p. 41.
105. Rosenfeld and Kempf, "The Scope and Purposes of Corrections," p. 483.
106. Ibid., p. 500.
107. Ibid.
108. John M. Vanyur, "In Colorado—Design Meets Mission at New Federal Max Facility," *Corrections Today* 57 (1995): 90.
109. Ibid., p. 91.
110. Ibid., p. 93.
111. Ibid., p. 94.
112. David A. Ward, "A Corrections Dilemma: How to Evaluate Super-Max Regimes," *Corrections Today* 57 (1995): 108.
113. Donziger, "The Prison-Industrial Complex," p. C3.
114. James Byrne and Mary Brewster, "Choosing the Future of American Corrections: Punishment or Reform?" *Federal Probation* 57 (December 1993): 3.
115. John DiIulio, *No Escape: The Future of American Corrections* (New York: Basic Books, 1991).
116. Byrne and Brewster, "Choosing the Future of American Corrections," p. 5.
117. Ibid., p. 8.
118. Ibid.
119. Ibid., p. 248.
120. Ibid.
121. Joyce, "A View of the Future," p. 357.
122. Michael Welch, "Prison Violence in America, Past, Present and Future," in Roslyn Muraskin and Albert R. Roberts, eds., *Visions for Change: Crime and Justice in the Twenty-First Century* (Upper Saddle River, NJ: Prentice Hall), pp. 184–198.
123. Ibid., p. 196.

GLOSSARY

12-step programs. A term for a variety of counseling programs based on Alcoholics Anonymous principles. Used mainly with alcohol and substance abuse offenders.

Accreditation. Refers to a process initiated by the American Correctional Association where correctional agencies and institutions may volunteer to meet a number of performance standards.

Advocacy model. An approach to community-based corrections that seeks to enhance offenders' access to social, economic, and mental health services in order to improve their chances for successful reintegration into the community.

Aggravating circumstances. Specified in sentencing statutes to indicate that a crime was committed under circumstances that may lead to an enhanced sentence. The circumstances must be proved to the sentencing authority, e.g., the jury, generally at the sentence phase of a trial.

Auburn System. Early 19th century penitentiary system of incarceration emphasizing silence.

Bail. The amount of bond that must be posted before a defendant may be released from custody prior to trial.

Bail Reform Act. Federal statute that sought to reform bail-setting practices so that defendants, especially those with limited resources would not be denied pretrial release.

Balanced justice. The concept that the goals of retributive and punitive sentences be balanced with some regard to rehabilitation.

Black Assize. In 1750, typhus-infected inmates spread the disease to many persons present in London's Old Bailey courtroom with fatal results. This led to the first serious investigation of the conditions in Britain's jails and prisons.

Blameworthiness. The idea that offenders should be rated in terms of how culpable they are. Blameworthiness is a variable in many guidelines systems. It is used to assist in selecting the appropriate range of sentence for a judge to order.

Brutalization hypothesis. The idea that executions "brutalize" by cheapening life and suggesting that violence is acceptable as a conflict resolution strategy.

Classical school of criminal law. Pioneered by Beccaria and Bentham in the latter 18th century, this school of thought sought to equate crimes with appropriate punishments. The underlying principle was that people are free agents.

Co-correctional institutions. Prisons housing men and women. Male and female inmates participate together in programs (e.g., education and vocational classes; counseling sessions).

Community Control Project. A transitional program developed by the Bureau of Prisons to assist inmates being released from prison. It includes electronic monitoring and graduated supervision.

Community Corrections Acts. Adopted by many states, these laws establish systems of graded sanctions with heavy emphasis on community-based programs.

Community-oriented policing. Police officers are based in decentralized "beats" and are encouraged to get to know the residents and community problems in their patrol areas of responsibility.

Comprehensive Sanctions Center. A system of mostly community-based sanctions employed by the federal system. It consists of graded sanctions that involve varying degrees of control over offenders.

Conditional release. Established by statute, inmates are released on condition much like parole release. However, there is no discretion as is the case with parole release.

Confinement model. Incarceration is to be for confinement purposes under secure and humane conditions. Any additional elements (treatment, e.g.) are optional.

Contact visits. Visits in which inmates and their approved visitors are allowed to come into physical contact. A special and very limited class of contact visits are conjugal visits.

Contemporary standards of elemental decency. Language taken from the Supreme Court case of *Furman v. Georgia* that relates the constitutionality of capital punishment to society's changing standards.

Continuously signaling devices. These are electronic devices used in electronically monitoring offenders in the community by transmitting regularly. An interruption of the signal may indicate a violation.

Cost effectiveness. A criterion sometimes used to evaluate the cost-benefit of a particular class of sanctions. Most often it is employed to evaluate the death penalty vs. life imprisonment, or an intermediate sanction against incarceration.

Cottage plan. Many women's prisons are built on this plan that emphasizes more small group living in non-fortress like buildings.

Creaming. The tendency of some operators of innovative correctional programs to take only the lowest risk offenders as their clients.

Cruel and unusual punishment. Language from a part of the Eighth Amendment of the Constitution. No punishment may be given if it is cruel or unusual. One test used to determine whether a sentence is cruel and unusual is whether it violates society's "evolving standards of decency."

Day fines. A system of imposing fines at least partly based on an offender's average daily wage. It is thought that day fines are more equitable than those rigidly defined by statute.

Day reporting centers. Used in a variety of settings, these centers are used to have offenders report at specified intervals while they are on conditional release in the community.

Decarceration. Refers to the movement in the 1960s and early 1970s to increase the use of community-based sanctions and relieve prison populations.

Declaration of Principles of 1870. A set of resolutions adopted by the National Prison Association recommending the use of indeterminate sentences and classification of inmates to achieve effective prison programming.

Defective delinquency. Originally intended to identify mentally retarded offenders, this term was used for many years in Maryland to identify psychopathic or sociopathic offenders.

Deference period. The period from about 1980 until the present during which appellate courts have tended to defer to the expertise of prison administrations when inmates have challenged the conditions of their confinement.

Deliberate indifference. A standard established by the Supreme Court to judge whether prison conditions reflect whether staff are deliberately indifferent to the harmful effects those conditions have on inmates. To succeed in challenging conditions, inmates must meet this standard.

Determinate sentences. A determinate sentence has a fixed limit which, in the case of incarceration, may be shortened if an inmate earns good-time credits. Also, in

some states, offenders serving determinate sentences may be eligible for parole.

Deterrence, general and specific. Refers to a justification of punishment on the grounds that threatened sanctions will deter the general population from committing crimes (general deterrence), and, when imposed on an individual offender they will deter her or him from continuing to offend (specific deterrence).

Different but equal. An expression denoting the problem confronting corrections as it must provide equal programs for women inmates while recognizing that women and men are different.

Direct supervision. A feature of the "new generation jail" that allows custodial officers to supervise directly relatively small numbers of inmates.

Discretion. A general term used to refer to the latitude officials (police, prosecutors, judges, and others) have to operate within the confines of laws and regulations when reaching decisions affecting defendants and offenders.

Diversion model. An approach to less serious and non-violent offenders that diverts them from prosecution and into various community-based programs.

Doing gender. This term incorporates those usually outward manifestations of gender for women's prisons. It includes dress, jewelry, and informal relationships. In some prison systems, rules and regulations may severely limit an inmate's management of appearance, which is central to the experience of being a woman in American society.

Economies of scale. Large-scale institutions tend to be more economical to operate than smaller ones. Sometimes used to justify the shortage of programs available to female inmates in the much smaller women's prisons.

Electronic monitoring. Refers to the use of a variety of electronic devices to monitor offenders in the community. Its use is growing in sanctions such as house arrest and intensive probation and parole supervision.

Eligible person. A legal term in Maryland defining certain offenders as emotionally disordered and amenable to mental health treatment in the state's treatment facility, Patuxent Institution.

Elmira Reformatory. Established in 1870, this New York state prison was the first reformatory in the United States. To some extent, it was patterned after the Irish or Progressive system of incarceration.

Equal justice. A term referring to the controversy surrounding sentencing of and prison programs for female offenders. The questions debated are: should women be subjected to absolutely equal sentences and programs as those given men? If so, is this really equal justice since women have different needs than men?

Equal protection of the laws. A constitutional right to be protected from discriminatory application of laws (especially with regard to sentencing laws). This right is provided by the 14th Amendment of the Constitution: "...nor shall any [State] deny to any person...the equal protection of the laws."

Evolving standards of decency. Language from Justice Marshall's opinion in *Furman v. Georgia*. Marshall wrote that we can understand the Eighth Amendment's cruel and unusual clause only by relating a punishment to "evolving standards of decency that mark the progress of a maturing society."

Executive clemency. The authority of state governors and the President of the United States (in cases of federal offenders) to grant convicted persons various forms of "clemency" such as pardons and commutations of sentences.

False positives. A commonly reported fault with research that purports to predict future criminality. That is, in order to predict some future crime an unacceptable number of false occurrences are predicted.

Felony Drug Court. Pioneered in Dade County, Florida, this is a hybrid court structure that deals with drug and substance abuse offenders with a combination of penal sanctions and treatment measures.

Future dangerousness. Some offenders may pose the risk of committing dangerous offenses sometime in the future. The problem for criminal justice is how, if at all, to predict those who may be dangerous. *See also* false positives.

Gender stereotyping. The tendency to classify women for purposes of sentencing and correctional programming in terms of certain alleged traits, aptitudes, and interests common to all women. Thus, prison programs for female inmates may be limited to providing training for clerical work and cosmetology.

Goal discordance. An observed tendency for multiple goals assigned to various correctional programs to work at cross-purposes.

Graduation rates. A measure sometimes used to evaluate the effectiveness of boot camps. The recidivism of those who "graduate," i.e., complete the boot camp program is measured to determine the success or failure of the experience.

Guided jury discretion. Resulting from a number of Supreme Court decisions, a death sentence can be ordered only after a separate sentencing hearing before the jury.

Habeas Corpus, writ of. Literally, "bring forth the body." If a court issues a writ, it is done to determine whether the incarceration of a person is lawful. Article I, Section 9 of the Constitution provides that "The Privilege of the Writ of Habeas Corpus shall not be suspended unless in Cases of Rebellion or Invasion the public safety may require it."

Hands-off period. Refers to the period prior to the 1960s when appellate courts were reluctant to intervene in the running of prison systems when these were challenged by inmates.

Incapacitation. A major goal of sentencing. Usually associated with terms of imprisonment, the goal is to keep offenders securely away from potential victims.

Incorporation doctrine. A constitutional law doctrine holding that most of the guarantees in the Bill of Rights limit state as well as federal governmental actions through incorporating them in the "due process" clause in the 14th Amendment.

Indeterminate sentences. Sentences that are structured with lower upper limits of time to be served (e.g., "one to five years."). Parole or conditional release may be granted at some point before the upper limit is reached.

Institutional Board of Review. Under Maryland's Defective Delinquent and Eligible Persons statutes this board was the paroling authority at Patuxent Institution.

Intensive aftercare supervision. *See* Intensive Supervision Parole.

Intensive Drug Program. Refers to any number of correctional programs in various settings in which drug and alcohol abusing offenders are placed in special treatment settings under severe supervision and treatment conditions.

Intensive Supervision Parole (ISP). A term used to cover a multitude supervision modes that involve a combination of frequent contacts with a supervision officer, electronic surveillance, drug testing, and curfews.

Intensive Supervision Probation (ISP). Similar to Intensive Supervision Parole, but restricted to offenders on probation.

Intermediate punishments. Refers to a wide range of generally restrictive sanctions that fall between incarceration and traditional community-based sanctions such as parole and probation.

Intermittent supervision. The style of supervision common to the traditional or linear jail as opposed to the direct supervision style of the "new generation" jail.

Irish System. A 19th century prison system instituted by Walter Croften incorporating progressive stages toward release on a rudimentary form of parole. An early example of indeterminate sentencing. Also called the Progressive System.

Issues of fact and issues of law. In criminal trials, juries must decide whether what they have seen and heard is factual within the context of the law of the crime being considered. At appeal, usually only issues of law and not fact are considered.

Judicial discretion. Trial judges generally can exercise discretion with respect to the sentence they hand down. That is, they have latitude to modify statutory provisions. Recently, there has been considerable movement in the direction of limiting judicial discretion in favor of uniform sentences.

Judicial reprieve. The authority available to judges to suspend the execution of a sentence for an indefinite period, usually while other judicial proceedings are contemplated or in progress.

Just deserts. A retributivist doctrine that encourages sentences that are "deserved" on the basis of the harm offenders cause and their blameworthiness. *See* retribution.

Labelling theory. A criminological perspective that stresses the socio-psychological significance of labels we assign to persons and the process whereby these labels are assigned.

Legitimate penological interests. A standard used to judge whether prison conditions and/or actions of prison officials violate the rights of inmates. If such conditions and actions are "legitimate," inmate challenges will fail.

Linear jails. Traditional jail architecture whereby jails are laid out in relatively straight lines, necessitating indirect staff supervision of inmates. *See also,* New Generation Philosophy and Jails.

Lombrosian legacy. From the work of the pioneering criminologist, Cesare Lombroso. Consists of three elements: (a) criminal etiology must be based on the study of individual offenders; (b) criminal behavior is determined by factors not within the ability of individuals to alter; (c) criminals are fundamentally different.

Low- and high-risk populations. This refers to the risk of recidivism associated with offenders placed in various programs. Many today believe that programs (e.g., parole and probation) originally designed for low-risk groups are taking on more high-risk offenders because of prison crowding.

Mandatory sentences. Sentences laid down by statute that mandate certain terms of imprisonment for certain offenses.

Mandatory treatment. A somewhat new concept that argues that some offenders (especially drug abusers) should be required to enter treatment. The Federal Bureau of Prisons has a mandatory educational program for inmates who test below certain levels upon admission to prison.

Mark System. Established by the British penologist Alexander Maconochie, this system substituted a debt of marks an offender owed for the number of years in a sentence. This system provided ways for inmates to pay off the debt early, thus becoming the first indeterminate sentence.

Maxing-out. Unconditional release from prison following the expiration of the statutorily defined maximum period of confinement.

Mediation. A process for attempting to reconcile offender and victim. Out of mediation can come agreements about compensation, restitution, and personal or community service hours.

Meta-Analysis. A method employed when attempting to collate the findings from a variety of studies in a particular area (e.g., recidivism rates for probationers) that used various methodologies.

Minneapolis experiment. A study to test the effectiveness of mandatory arrests of spouse abusers.

Miranda warnings. Resulting from the Supreme Court decision in *Miranda v. Arizona,* these warnings must be given to suspects prior to interrogation. They include the right to remain silent, have an attorney present, and that what a suspect says may be used in court.

Mitigating circumstances. These are circumstances that may be prescribed by law that defendants offer in order to gain a less severe sentence. Used especially in the sentencing phase of capital murder cases. *See also* aggravating circumstances.

Mixed sentences. A term employed to include a variety of sentence combinations. One example is a sentence to shock incarceration followed by a period of probation.

Net widening. The possibility that certain sanctions that are designed at least in part to reduce prison crowding (e.g., intensive supervision probation) may be used to control offenders who would not go to prison.

Newgate of Connecticut. The first American prison. It was established in 1773 at an abandoned copper mine in Simsbury, Connecticut.

New generation jails. These are jails whose architecture is modular or laid out in "pods" each containing small groups of inmates together with all the necessary facilities and programs. It is particularly adapted to direct supervision of inmates by staff. *See also* direct Supervision.

New generation philosophy. This philosophy theory actually is a style of jail inmate supervision that permits their direct and closer supervision by custodial staff because of the architecture of the institution.

New penology. A position in criminology arguing that sentencing laws and policies have resulted in targeting aggregates of offenders based on risk levels and seeking selective incapacitation instead of being concerned with individual-based sanctions.

Nolo Contendere. A plea of "no contest" in which a defendant acknowledges that there is sufficient evidence for a conviction. Its main utility is it cannot be used against a defendant should he or she be a defendant in a subsequent civil suit.

Nulla Poena Sine Lege. "There may be no penalty with a statutory provision for it."

Optional treatment. The idea that correctional treatment programs should be optional, much like elective courses. No offender should be required to enter any program, and further, placement in and completion of a program ought not affect release decisions.

Pains of imprisonment. A term first employed by Gresham Sykes in his study of a large state penitentiary to describe various deprivations experienced by prison inmates.

Partial justice. The view that attempting to develop correctional sanctions and programs for female offenders is not equal justice, but results in partial or incomplete justice.

Penitentiary. Originally used to define prisons in the early 19th century where inmates were secluded in order to become penitent.

Pennsylvania System. First United States system of incarceration initiated in Philadelphia, Pennsylvania. The hallmark of this system was the solitary confinement of inmates throughout their sentences.

Personal recognizance. Pre-trial release of defendants without posting a bond.

Personal service order. Like the community service order, this is a judicial order requiring an offender to perform a specified number of hours of unpaid work. Unlike the community service order, personal service orders are to be for the benefit of individuals, usually victims, and not the community at large.

Plea agreements. These are agreements reached between defense and prosecutor where defendants plead guilty, usually to a reduced charge. Also referred to as plea bargaining, defendants expect to receive reduced sentences, prosecutors avoid the necessity of trying cases, and, frequently, receive assistance from defendants in convicting co-defendants.

Plea bargaining. *See* Plea agreements.

Positive Criminology and Penology. Based largely on the Lombrosian legacy (*see* Lobrosian legacy), this is a school of thought that bases criminal sanctions on individualized study of offenders.

Positive criminological theory. Theories of crime causation that developed out of the Lombrosian legacy (*see* Lobrosian legacy).

Pre-sentence investigation. Usually required by statute, these reports of offenders' backgrounds are intended to advise a sentencing judge as to an appropriate sentence following conviction.

Presumptive sentences. Legislatively enacted minimum and maximum sentences for specified crimes. Judges are to select a sentence within these limits.

Pretrial diversion. This includes a variety of programs and activities that divert a defendant away from prosecution providing he or she meets certain conditions. Successful completion usually results in no prosecution, while unsuccessful defendants are prosecuted.

Preventive detention. Available under some state statutes and the federal system, certain defendants may be detained for specified periods because of their criminal histories, current offense, and likelihood not to appear for trial.

Prison-industrial complex. A term used to describe the contemporary prison scene that includes major prison construction and renovation projects and privatization of facilities and programs. Associated with the large increase in the use of incarceration as a sanction.

Prison security. In most states and in the federal system prisons are graded in terms of their level of security. Levels generally are graded from minimum to maximum security. Some prisons have more than one security level. Frequently, offenders are classified in terms of their security risk and assigned to an appropriate prison or section of prison.

Privatization. Private sector involvement in corrections that may take the form of contracting out the operation of entire institutions or program segments to private operators. Frequently, electronic monitoring is carried out by private contractors.

Programmed contact. In electronic monitoring, contact with offenders is programmed in relation to such parameters as curfew hours and work situations.

Progressive Era Paradigm. A reform movement in the 1930s that sought to encourage professionalism in criminal justice systems as well as promoting the individualization of sanctions.

Progressive system (of incarceration). See Irish system.

Proportionality. Punishments should be imposed in proportion to the level of harm caused by an offender.

Loosely related to the Eighth Amendment's Cruel and Unusual clause.

Prosecutorial discretion. The discretion available to prosecutors to enter into plea agreements or select possible charges for trial. Generally unrestricted by statute in most jurisdictions.

Punitive restitution. Offenders may be ordered to make restitution above and beyond that required simply to compensate or restore victims. Punishment is sought through the amount ordered to be paid.

Punitive sanctions. Any criminal sentence, the main purpose of which is to cause an offender to suffer.

Pure restitution. An ideal form of restitution whereby offenders make payments for restorative and reconciliation purposes.

Radio signaling. A technology used in electronic monitoring that involves transmitting radio signals to and from an offender.

Reasonableness. A catch-all standard for determining whether the actions of correctional (and other criminal justice actors such as police) violate such constitutional safeguards as, due process, equal protection of the laws, and prohibitions against cruel and unusual punishment.

Recidivism. Variously defined and measured, this refers to the commission of crimes in the future after an offender completes whatever sentence is ordered.

Recognizance. Release from pre-trial detention without posting a bond. *See* Personal recognizance.

Reconciliation restitution. This is court ordered restitution where a major objective is to provide an avenue whereby offender and victim may be reconciled. Often this requires that offenders and victims meet face-to-face to work out the appropriate restitution.

Reformatories. Refers to institutions established after 1870 (that being the year Elmira Reformatory opened) that were designed for younger adult offenders serving indeterminate sentences. The distinctive nature of the reformatory is largely nonexistent today.

Rehabilitative idea. One of the three major ideas that influenced the development of prisons in the United States, the other two being, the Penitentiary and the Reformatory. The rehabilitative idea stressed the function of the prison as a place in which offenders could, with appropriate programs, be rehabilitated.

Reintegration model. Frequently used to identify correctional programs in the community that are aimed primarily at softening the shock of reentry for inmates being released from prison. Halfway houses and work-release centers are examples.

Repeat Offender Program (ROP). A program initiated in Phoenix, Arizona, to focus at the charging and prose-cutorial stage certain repeat offenders in order to swiftly bring them to trial and minimize plea bargaining. A number of other communities have developed similar programs to deal with hard-core offenders.

Reprieve. Holding-off the execution of a sentence.

Restitution centers. Some states, Texas being the most prominent, have residential centers where some offenders ordered to pay restitution are housed while they are employed in the community. Frequently, these offenders are required to perform community service in addition to making restitution.

Retribution. The philosophy that holds that convicted offenders' sentences should be, at least in part, for the purpose of giving them the desert they have earned through the harm caused victims. Practically the same as the "just deserts" philosophy.

Revenge. One goal of criminal sentencing. It is often considered as inappropriate in a civilized society.

Rights period. The period from about 1960 until the late 1970s when inmate rights were frequently supported by appellate courts, leading to many court orders requiring actions by prison systems. *See also* two related periods, hands-off and deference.

Role conflict. In corrections, the potential conflict between roles of rehabilitation, control, and surveillance. The potential for role conflict is greater for supervision officers assigned to intensive supervision sanctions.

Salient Factor Scores. Initiated by the United States Parole Commission, these scores, based on a number of offense and offender characteristics, are used to predict recidivism of offenders being considered for release.

Sanctions budget. Because criminal correctional programs are a limited resource, some penologists recommend that states establish systematic planning when sentencing offenders. The hope is that resources such as prison space and community supervision caseloads can be more efficiently utilized.

Scientific or positive penology. Initiated by Cesare Lombroso, this is another term for positive penology and it bases sentences on the individual study of offenders. *See also* Lombrosian legacy.

Secondary or collateral victims. Members of the families of offenders sentenced to death are said to suffer considerable pain as they await the execution of their relatives.

Section 1983 suits. This refers to civil suits by inmates claiming violation of rights under Section 1983 of the Civil Rights Act of 1871.

Selective incapacitation. Targeting certain (selective) population for sentences that will incapacitate them. Associated with the new penology theory defined.

Sentencing guidelines. State and federal statutes established sentencing commissions to establish ranges of sentences based on the severity of crimes and offenders' criminal histories. Designed to reduce judicial discretion.

Separate but equal. In the context of women's prisons, many argue that it is possible to provide separate programs for female offenders that will be substantially equal to those provided males. Others argue that this is impossible.

Sexual psychopaths. A catch-all term used in many state statutes to refer to certain repetitive sex offenders on whom special sentences were imposed.

Slave of the state. From a Virginia Supreme Court decision, this expressed the court's opinion that a convict had no rights other than those a benevolent state gave them.

Social psychology of deterrence. When relating sentences to deterrence, one must consider a number of essentially extra-legal variables before judging their value as individual or specific deterrence. For example, how an offender perceives the social cost of being sentenced as a convicted offender.

Socioeconomic discrimination. Considerable theoretical and empirical evidence has found that some sanctions are applied to offenders based on their socioeconomic status. For example, community service orders tend to be given to white-collar or middle-class offenders.

Special boot camps. These shock incarceration programs are designed for the disruptive inmate in an ordinary prison setting.

Specific deterrence. This is deterrence as applied to an individual offender as distinct from general deterrence (*see* general deterrence).

Split sentence. *See* mixed sentence.

Spouse abuse. A general term used to cover assaultive behavior directed at one's spouse. It is a growing concern in the United States. Some argue that spouse abuse need not be confined to physically abusive behavior, and psychological assaults should be included under the spouse abuse umbrella.

Stare decisis. The legal doctrine applying to appellate cases that translates into, "let previous decisions stand." In other words, precedents ought to be consulted and applied when analogous cases are to be decided.

State-use industries. A commonly used system of restricting sales of prison-made goods to various state agencies. Some prison industries goods may be sold to non-profit organizations.

Straight probation. A probation order that is not combined with any other sanction.

Structured anxiety. The method of inducing anxiety in psychopathic or sociopathic offenders by structuring the institutional environment to maximize uncertainty regarding release dates and various rules affecting program participation. Patuxent Institution in Maryland is the prime example of this method.

Success rate. This can take many forms as correctional measures are evaluated. Rates of rearrest, reincarceration, technical violations of conditional release, and graduation from programs all have been examined in numerous studies to determine which measures are successful.

Substitute counsel. Some appellate court orders have required prison systems to provide inmates with certain due process safeguards whenever their liberty interests are threatened. These orders usually include a requirement that inmates be assisted in pressing their claims. Substitute counsel, such as developed in the Texas system, serve the role of legally assisting inmates. These substitutes are usually employees of the institution or parent system and are not attorneys.

Super-max prisons. Prisons in some states and in the federal system where a very high security is employed. Inmates in these institutions usually are transferred to them from other prisons because of serious misbehavior or escape potential.

Supervision fees. Many jurisdictions now require, as a condition of supervised release to the community, that offenders pay a fee to offset the costs of supervision. This practice is more common with intensive supervision sanctions.

Suspended sentence. Judges may suspend all or part of a sentence (usually a term of imprisonment). Frequently, offenders whose prison sentences are suspended are placed on probation. The suspended sentence may be activated should an offender violate the terms of probation.

Symbolic restitution. The idea that requiring offenders to perform community service provides a form ("symbolic") of restitution to victims without direct contact with them.

Systems paradigm. A perspective on criminal justice that sees the structures, actors and processes as part of a system. Developments in one part of the system will certainly affect the other parts.

Tampering. Since the introduction of electronic monitoring, the possibility that offenders will try to tamper with the equipment in order to defeat the surveillance. Various technologies have been developed to detect tampering, and there are reports of high rates of tampering that turn out to be false alarms.

Technical probation violations. These are violations of the terms and conditions of an offender's probation. They do not include commission of new crimes. Technical parole violations are similar.

Therapeutic community. The attempt to structure an offender's experience, usually in a residential setting, so that all aspects of the experience contribute to her or his therapeutic progress.

Thirteenth Amendment (to the United States Constitution). A portion of this amendment forbids involuntary servitude except when it is part of a sentence following conviction for a crime. Some argue that community service orders, requiring unpaid labor, may violate this amendment.

Tickets of leave. An early form of parole beginning in the mid-19th century. Inmates could earn release from their confinement and be issued tickets of leave that they showed they were lawfully at liberty even though their sentences had not expired.

Treatability. In Maryland's Patuxent Institution, an offender's must be found to be amenable to treatment before he or she can remain there. If found to be treatable, an offender is determined to be eligible for treatment. In a broader context, the success or failure of rehabilitative measures depends on the treatability of offenders. Thus, procedures for selecting subjects for treatment programs need to be carefully constructed.

Unit management. A prison management approach, breaking down large-scale institutions into smaller, hopefully more manageable, units.

Victim impact statement. This is a statement from a victim and/or a victim's family that informs the court as to the impact the crime had on them. These statements may be used at the sentencing phase of criminal trials.

Victims' rights. Until relatively recently, victims were largely held in the background throughout the criminal trial process. Now, however, victims' rights organizations and a general recognition that victims' needs must be addressed have led to a number of rights. Included are the rights to influence sentences through victim impact statements (*see* victim impact statement), and to appear before paroling authorities to testify about the possible release of their offenders.

Walnut Street Jail. In 1790, a portion of the then new Walnut Street Jail in Philadelphia, PA was converted into a state prison for confining serious offenders under the conditions of the Pennsylvania system of incarceration (*see* Pennsylvania system). Thus, it became the first penitentiary in the United States.

TABLE OF CASES

CAREERS IN CORRECTIONS

What we have covered in this text includes a very wide and rich variety of employment opportunities for those considering a career in corrections. These opportunities include such institutional settings as detention centers and prisons. Others may be found in a number of non-custodial facilities that include halfway houses, and community residential and pre-release centers. Community-based corrections offers many employment opportunities, especially in probation and parole agencies. We will now summarize some of the careers in each of these three settings.

Those wishing to obtain more specific information about job openings, qualifications, and salaries should consult the most recent edition of the American Correctional Association's Directory* of correctional agencies for addresses and telephone numbers. The directory is organized by state and federal departments, and lists all agencies delivering correctional services.

CORRECTIONAL INSTITUTIONS

Correctional Officer. These are the line officers in prison and detention facilities. These positions are usually divided into several grades depending on experience and qualifications.

Entry-level correctional officers (usually designated as Correctional Officer I) are responsible for the custody, security, and supervision of inmates. As such, they escort inmates, maintain head counts, conduct inspections of inmates and their cells, and enforce institutional rules and regulations.

Higher grades in most state and federal correctional systems include Correctional Officer II, Sergeants, Lieutenants, Captains, and Major. Each higher grade involves more supervision of personnel, and more experience, training, and education.

Correctional Case Managers. Like Correctional Officers, many correctional systems employ persons as case managers at different levels. Typically, a Correctional Case Manager at the entry level is responsible for interviewing inmates, and assembling and evaluating their relevant personal and criminal histories, and recommending (often to the prison's Classification Committee) inmates' security classification and the inmate's work, educational, and other correctional program placements.

Correctional Psychologists. Again, like Correctional Officers and Correctional Case Managers, Correctional Psychologists are divided in levels or grades depending on educational and experiential qualifications. Entry-level Correctional Psychologists typically require at least a bachelor's degree in psychology. Many require a master's degree. Some states further require a certificate that is earned through a state examination together with a master's degree.

---

*American Correctional Association, Directory of Juvenile and Adult Correctional Departments, *Institutions, Agencies and Paroling Authorities* (Laurel, MD: American Correctional Association.

Psychologists are responsible for psychometric testing of inmates, and recommending to the prison's Classification Committee specific treatment and counseling programs. Psychologists are involved in both individual and group counseling of inmates.

Correctional Social Workers. These positions may be graded into levels depending on educational and experiential qualifications. Typically, Correctional Social Workers are responsible for developing inmate social histories, and frequently, for counseling inmates. Senior grades usually require the Master's of Social Work (MSW) degree.

Correctional Recreation Officers. Historically, American corrections has placed emphasis on prison recreation programs. Consequently, many state and federal systems employ personnel trained in physical education and recreation. Correctional Recreation Officers are responsible for developing recreational programs and supervising inmate participation in them.

Fiscal Officers. Most prison systems require a variety of persons to perform functions related to the fiscal operations of their institutions. These positions include Auditors, Accountants, and Personnel Officers.

COMMUNITY SUPERVISION POSITIONS

Probation Officers. As with the other positions described previously, probation officer positions are graded into levels (two or more). The introductory level generally requires a bachelor's degree with a criminal justice-related or social science major. Advanced levels require experience and/or higher degrees.

Typically, probation officers are responsible for supervising offenders sentenced to various types of probation. Careful and accurate report writing is a very important part of the probation officer's work. These reports include those resulting from the officer's presentation investigation, and probationer progress reports. In cases where a probationer is alleged to have violated the terms of his or her probation, the officer not only will prepare recommendations for dispositions to the court, but may also be required to testify before a judge. Probation officers are responsible for making recommendations regarding modifications in probation conditions.

Parole Officers. Parole officers often are employed by combined departments of probation and parole, and persons employed in these agencies may move between parole and probation work. As one such agency stated, "the purpose of the work is to supervise, encourage, and assist convicted offenders in adopting behavior patterns acceptable to the community."

A parole officer typically will visit offenders' places of employment, interview family members, and counsel parolees. In addition, officers prepare reports on offenders' progress, and make recommendations regarding actions to be taken when parolees violate the terms of their release.

Most parole (and probation) agencies require for entry-level positions a bachelor's degree from an accredited college or university, with a minimum (often 30) credits in social, behavioral, or criminal justice-related courses.

NAME INDEX

SUBJECT INDEX